Marketing Communications

The Wiley Marketing Series

Marketing Communications

Decision-Making as a Process of Interaction Between Buyer and Seller

SECOND EDITION

Edgar Crane

John Wiley & Sons, Inc.
New York • London • Sydney • Toronto

Library of Congress Cataloging in Publication Data:

Crane, Edgar.
  Marketing communications.
    1. Marketing. 2. Advertising. I. Title.

HF5415.C694 1972   659.1′01′9   72-4505
ISBN 0-471-18401-2

Printed in the United States of America.

10 9 8 7 6 5 4 3 2 1

Contents

Contents with Research Articles

Advertisements Illustrating Insights Discussed in This Book

Chapter 0 The Textbook as a Component of Learning Situations

Communications came of age, as a discipline, when it stopped talking about what TV does to children and began asking what uses children make of TV. Marketing matured when men began looking for ways to serve people rather than to sell products. Bankers who accept the marketing concept thus ask how they can facilitate the flow of funds into and out of the household rather than seeking better ways to produce more checking accounts and auto loans. Publishers with the communications viewpoint think of their textbooks as one component in a diversity of rapidly changing learning situations.

Teachers and students will profit from the examples of publisher and banker when they join forces to create classrooms in which learning experiences occur as a replacement for the lecture halls, where teachers "give" and students "take" lectures and examinations.

This textbook has been written for such classrooms.

Conceding that my subject matter is often complex, I have called on 10 years of experience as a newspaper reporter to help in expressing this content in terms an undergraduate can understand without extensive explication by an instructor. Thus a teacher who uses the objective exams provided in the instructor's manual can use class time to extend the scope of his course and free time for students to share insights gained in applying lessons of the classroom to their lives as consumers and employees.

Marketing communications today is taught in diverse settings with varying components:

Students differ as to *goals*. Some will go on to graduate work; others will take jobs with the mass media or advertising agencies, or in research firms, retailing, or manufacturing.

Schools differ in their *mix of courses*. Most users of this book, for example, are located in either Schools of Business or Schools of Journalism. (A few are found in departments of psychology.)

Teachers differ in *background*. Some in J-schools come to teaching after experience in the media; others have almost exclusively academic experience. In business schools, quantitative types are primarily interested in models that tell how decisions ought to be made, whereas the behavioral types focus on actual rather than ideal behavior.

In the J-schools today, more and more students begin their work with a course in communications theory and method. As many as 40% of them, in some large schools, then go on to major in advertising. J-schools which use this book in the communications course are likely to supplement it with readings which emphasize application of its insights to editorial decision making.[1] Schools that use this textbook in advertising courses, on the other hand, are likely to follow it with how-to-do-it courses using a traditional, state-of-the-art textbook.[2]

Today's B-school students are likely to have been exposed to at least one course in applied psychology. This first course most often concerns human relations in management, for management pioneered the behavioral approach to decision making. Since 1965, an increasing number of B-school students also have been exposed to a course in consumer behavior, which extends insights from the highly controlled environment of superior and subordinate in the factory and firm to the more complex and less predictable relationships of buyer and seller in the marketplace. This book *can* be used as an introduction to such courses in behavioral management and consumer behavior; it is more likely to follow them in a course entitled *marketing communications* or *promotion management*.

Like these students, I represent a mixture of B- and J-school and of practitioner and academic—with my 10 years of experience on newspapers and in public relations followed by a Ph.D., 5 years of teaching in communications, and 10 years in marketing. The book itself was inspired by Stanford University's interdisciplinary program in communications, and then tested for over a decade in B-schools at the University of Notre Dame and the University of Houston.

Every textbook author, I suspect, balances uneasily between the demands of his students that his text be clear and relevant and the demands of his peers that it be precise, however complex, and that he avoid generalizing beyond the data, whatever the cost in relevance.

My first edition was written defensively, in deference to my peers. This time I have come down on the side of the students, not hesitating to speculate in the text, when this seemed necessary to integrate or apply research findings. Students should be warned of this. Teachers should expect to differ with my interpretations, and to share their differences with their students. (Indeed, the teacher will perform a great service to his students if he instills in them some degree of that basic skepticism which is his principal asset and his primary tool in teaching.) My own classes involve continual challenge to the text, from my students or from me, because of new findings published since this manuscript was written or old findings which had not come to attention or had somehow slipped from my memory.

This edition, even more than that published in 1965, has been designed to serve the wide variety of situations created by different combinations of student, teacher, and setting. This flexibility is attained by varying other ingredients in the teaching mix, as suggested in Figure 0.1, just as a staple like eggs can be variously trans-

formed into a beverage, main course, or dessert.

To illustrate this adaptability, let's look at how different teachers might use the highlights from research articles that appear in most chapters.

Teachers interested in research and students who plan to enter graduate school will probably use these highlights as an entry into the realm of research. These highlights and the additional readings suggested provide the first clue in a search of the literature. These teachers often have their students go to the original articles from which these highlights are drawn and prepare their own summaries of them. Their students often replicate these experiments, as individual, team, or class projects.

In contrast, teachers interested in advertising or selling per se, and working students already involved in real-life, day-to-day problem solving will appreciate the brevity and simplicity of the summaries. Instead of searching for more studies or seeking out more detail on the methodology employed, these teachers and students will ask how the findings can be applied to the "real world." The brevity of the highlights fits within the resources of time and effort which the application-minded have for research but extends the scope of studies to which the research-minded are exposed far beyond that afforded by a book that reprints such articles in their entirety.

This book then, is designed to fit a wide variety of learning situations. It has also been designed, we have suggested, to minimize the amount of classroom time needed for explication. This point deserves further emphasis.

Pressures to force greater productivity and more efficiency on teacher and student are intensifying each year. I noted one such source of pressure in my 1965 preface which observed that "knowledge is increasing at so rapid a pace that the businessman finds it hard to keep up. Teachers ask how they can find room for new material and

FOUR TEACHING MIXES: How *Marketing Communications* May Be Adapted to Differences in Student, Teacher and Setting

Course Title: COMMUNICATIONS THEORY

Setting: J-School
Teacher's background: Research
Students' goals: Graduate study
Students' status: Full-time

Text: MARKETING COMMUNICATIONS (Crane)
Supplementary readings: Lindgren, *Contemporary Research in Social Psychology* (New York: Wiley, 1969) or Holloway et al., *Consumer Behavior* (Boston, Houghton Mifflin, 1971)

Activity: Class replication of key experiments (See list in instructor's manual)

Course Title: PROMOTION MANAGEMENT

Setting: B-School
Teacher's background: Advertising, selling
Students' goals: Apply studies to job
Students' status: Part-time

Text: MARKETING COMMUNICATIONS (Crane)
Supplementary readings: Dunn, *Advertising* (New York: Holt, Rinehart & Winston, 1969) or Simon, *The Management of Advertising* (Englewood Cliffs: Prentice-Hall, 1971)

Activity: Students plan advertising campaign, design ads, plan media schedules, *or* use casebook such as Boyd et al., *Cases in Advertising Management* (New York: McGraw-Hill Book Co., 1964) or annual *Advertising Service for Students* (Southport, Conn.: Thomas E. Maytham)

Course Title: CONSUMER PSYCHOLOGY

Setting: Department of Psychology
Teacher's background: Academic
Students' goals: Service course for non-psychology majors

Text: MARKETING COMMUNICATIONS (Crane)
Supplementary readings: Britt, *Psychological Experiments in Consumer Behavior* (New York: Wiley, 1970) or Steiner & Fishbein, *Current Studies in Social Psychology* (New York: Holt, Rinehart and Winston, 1965)

Activity: Seminar reports on current articles in *Journal of Personality and Social Psychology* and *Journal of Applied Psychology*

Course Title: BEHAVIORAL FOUNDATIONS OF BUSINESS

Setting: B-School
Students: Introductory courses required of all business majors
Students' status: Both full-time and part-time

Texts: MARKETING COMMUNICATIONS (Crane)
MOTIVATION AND PRODUCTIVITY (Gellerman)

Activities: Team play of computer game such as MARKSIM or INTOP or discussion of casebook and preparation of original cases based on experiences as consumers and as employees

---

which of the old must give way to the new." Since 1965 this pressure, certainly, has intensified rather than abated.

Moreover, new kinds of pressure have appeared. Student picket signs have demanded "relevance," and subsequent admission of students to academic governing bodies is causing that demand to be taken seriously. Consumerism and the ecological movement which have invigorated a moribund Federal Trade Commission and won court victories are changing the very rules of the advertising and selling game. Once only the research-minded teacher found yesterday's lecture outmoded by today's discovery. Today, the application-minded instructor needs a news ticker in his office if he wants to remain relevant and accurate!

Recent changes are far-reaching and drastic in their implications. Advertisers' loss of interest in mere nosecounts and their increased concern about audience quality, which have already wiped out magazines with proud histories, today threaten *Life* and *Time*, which serve a major share of the nation's mass print audience. Cable TV's offer to viewers of a choice of 30 simultaneous programs threatens to convert TV from a mass to a selective medium just as TV, earlier, had transformed radio. National advertising, dependent on mass audiences of the mass media, may be transformed drastically.

If the more rapid rate of change and the increased volume of knowledge demand more time of both teacher and student, in class and outside, where is this time to come from?

As I said in 1965: "Is not the day past when we can afford to save students the effort of careful study of a text by using up class time in a repetition of its contents?"

Believing the answer to be affirmative, I tried then, and have tried even harder in this edition, to make such explication unnecessary. Like most teachers, however, I find myself too often enamored of the sound of my own voice; too often I have succumbed to student expectations by lecturing rather than listening. By explaining a selection, I have prevented students from developing their own learning skills. Students as well as teachers must resist such temptation.

In my experience, many students delay their study until the last minute so that they are unable to discuss it in advance of a test. Having taken the test and been graded on it, they have little motivation for a discussion afterward. Through force of habit or a hope for clues as to possible test questions, some students continue to want to be spoon-fed. Rather than accede to such demands, I now try to prepare students for a new learning experience, teaching them how to study, and giving them rapid feedback on their success.

I urge students, for example, to read the "synopsis" both before and after reading each chapter. I warn them that the book is tightly written; each sentence, rather than each paragraph, may contain an important or testable idea. I encourage students to substitute examples from their own experience for every example provided, being convinced that a concept is learned only when it can be applied.

I urge teachers to test students as soon as they have completed the first two chapters. Early testing helps familiarize them with the kind of tests that will be used, and alerts them to the need for more careful study. (Students should be warned that, to avoid a ceiling effect, the tests are designed so that the best student will score about 75 to 80% of possible.) If objective exams in the instructor's manual are used, a teacher can provide instant feedback by scoring tests before students have left the examination room, and read back the correct answers at the next session of class. Such instant feedback, of course, aids learning.

Why discuss these details here? Although most teachers are well aware of these problems, many students are not—and I hope that students, as well as teachers, will read this chapter. If students are to take on more responsibility for their own education, as both the times and the students themselves demand, they need to be prepared for the experiences they will encounter and to examine some of the assumptions of which they have been ignorant.

Many students, for example, assume that the purpose of tests is to teach; they equate tests with a programmed learning text. Class discussion, however, will soon reveal other purposes for testing, such as insuring that students have read the assignments or producing a curve which facilitates selection of able students by employers and for graduate programs. Continued discussion will suggest that these several functions are incompatible and contradictory, and that hard choices must be made. Students who have learned to repeat by rote talk of conflicting goals soon realize that they have been caught up in a situation of goal conflict, have failed to recognize it, and therefore have been unable to cope with it. They have learned through experience a lesson that no textbook can teach.

Students also need to be warned in advance of the feelings that will assail them as they move from the certainties of the secondary school, where they learned "facts" and were told what to think, to the ambiguities and contradictions of decision making in real life and in the world of research. The businessman's desire for a yes-or-no answer is familiar to any consultant, for the businessman must make yes-or-no decisions right now. The student's desire for simple and certain answers, based on habit rather than necessity, is just as strong and must be faced in any course using this book or dealing with research.

But it's obvious, says the student after working his way through some especially convoluted piece of research. *Everybody knows that.* Anticipating such a reaction, the canny teacher may well ask his students in advance to predict the outcome of a study. Does everybody know that one should *look before he leaps?* But everyone also knows that *he who hesitates is lost.* Folklore and common sense are full of such contradictions. The student must learn that

a scientist tries to specify the circumstances that make each aphorism a valid guide to behavior.

But these two experimenters disagree with one another, complains the student. *Which one are we to believe?* His hope, of course, is that the instructor, who awards his grade, will choose for him. That failing, he often tries to determine which of the contradictory sources is more authoritative in terms of discipline, institution, rank, publication, or recency. (Many students seem firmly convinced that recent is right and day before yesterday irrelevant.) Again, learning is achieved when the student begins looking at subjects and setting, at methods of gathering and analyzing data, for an explanation of the disagreements in research.

But it's irrelevant, says the student whose interest in cake mixes and detergents is affronted by a study concerning race prejudice, elections or rats in a maze. Without slighting the dangers of making marketing decisions on the basis of studies conducted in very different settings, the instructor *can* show such a student how insights and methods drawn from distant disciplines and the most unlikely of subjects have provided useful hypotheses for testing in the marketplace.

Without apology, therefore, this book tries to balance recent and practical studies, bearing directly on problems of buying and selling, with older and, perhaps, more fundamental studies. Students need to develop familiarity with both types, inventing ways to apply the fundamental findings and relating applied, finely tuned studies to larger bodies of knowledge. They should be helped to realize that tolerance for ambiguity is a symptom of the creative mind.[3] They must learn that uncertainty lies at the heart of modern business, and has been elevated to the status of a principle in modern science!

The printed pages of most textbooks do a good job of conveying cognitive content, but teachers and students are behaving and feeling as well as thinking beings. By providing cognitive content with a minimum of assistance by the instructor, this textbook can free him to do what no textbook can hope to do—to work with student feelings and to evoke participative activity from students. The first term a teacher uses this book he may well want to lecture from it, for the best way to learn a subject is to teach it. But the next term it is used, why not let students share in the learning-through-teaching experience?

We've suggested some of the *feelings* that students are likely to experience in dealing with this material and some of the ways in which teachers may help students interpret and handle them. In the instructor's manual are suggestions for classroom learning *activities*, which include use of audiovisuals to stimulate discussion or as an exercise in content analysis; case discussion of printed and production of original cases; replication of old and conduct of original experiments by individual students, teams, or entire classes.

Having dealt at length with events of the classroom, the instructional mix of which this textbook is one part, and the functions of the instructor, let us turn for a moment to the book itself.

This edition, like the first, serves as both textbook and reader. However, by making highlights of research articles briefer than those in the first edition, the author has been able to include some of the most important studies reported since 1965 and, in addition, to link related articles with a running commentary as an assistance to the reader. Completely new in this edition are the pictorial essays, which illustrate principles discussed in the text by advertisements selected from the author's collection of more than 300 possibilities.

The organization of content in this edition represents a thorough reconceptualization in which marketing communications is perceived as the convergence of nine-stage

decision processes by buyer and seller in a purchase-sale encounter. Discussion of these processes is interrupted three times. The first halt provides a closer look at the concepts of *goals* sought and achieved, as derived from meanings, attitudes and motives, and personality and role. The second halt looks at how learning and perception affect the *search for alternatives*. The third halt looks at the impact of social forces, discussed in three chapters, on the *acts of choice*. The book then concludes with a detailed examination of the six communications variables: audiences and sources, channels and media, symbols and messages.

In emphasizing communications as a convergence of two decision processes, this book draws on marketing, which emphasizes the way in which sellers *should* make their decisions, and on consumer behavior, which emphasizes how buyers in fact *do* make their decisions. (Unfortunately, at this point in history, research into how sellers actually make decisions and how consumers should make them as well as studies of the sales-purchase encounter itself, which gives meaning to both decision processes, is scanty.)

This book's nine-stage model of buyer and seller decision making is itself a simple framework. Several more elaborate models in the form of flow charts, examples of which are appended to this chapter, are available. The author feels, however, that these models, like his own, claim both too little and too much. Too little, because they fail to quantify the variables depicted and their relationships. Too much, because they suggest that the sequence of variables is both known and invariant. In my opinion, the variables shown are neither necessary nor sufficient. Any of them may be missing from a given purchase-sale; all of them together, as now measured, explain only part of the variance involved. As for sequence of flow-chart variables, cause and effect are hard to distinguish in the behavioral sciences. Reading an ad may cause an individual to buy the advertised product, but purchase of the product may also cause him to read the ad. Attitude change may precede behavioral change or follow it.

Moreover, there is a real question as to whether any single model can suffice to explain buying and selling. To speak, as some writers have done, of complete and partial decision-making processes, may have both heuristic and mnemonic values. One can, however, distinguish between true decision-making behavior, involving conscious choice among alternatives, and the much more common, much less conscious habitual acts of purchase which presumably result from repeated, rewarded decision making and substitute for conscious and deliberate choice.

An even more serious challenge to decision-making models, simple or complex, lies in the purchase and sale themselves. Face-to-face encounters between buyer and seller are rare. Negotiation and bargaining and the exchange of either information or influence tend to be limited to big-ticket items, purchased infrequently, and to first-time innovative purchases. Most purchases appear to depend on the retrieval of evaluative impressions stored in the memory. Most such storage seems to occur following exposure to messages at times when the consumer had little or no interest in buying the product advertised. Storage seems to occur, that is, in the absence of intention or reward, and so resembles incidental or latent learning. Storage may well be affected by intrinsic characteristics of the message, unrelated to product choice.

Since any purchase may be affected by an indeterminate number of messages received and stored over an indefinite period of time and by the variety of factors that affect retrieval from memory at the time of purchase, much study is needed to validate any of the existing models. This seems particularly true when a purchaser sees so little difference among brands on the market that the toss of a coin might be his

least effortful and most efficient method of choice. Far from being able to answer such questions as these, scholars have barely begun to formulate them. They are questions that the reader should keep in mind, while he uses existing models for their mnemonic value.

I began the preface to the 1965 edition with the observation: *These are exciting times.* As I look about me, six years later, I am reminded of the ancient Chinese curse: *May you live in exciting times.*

Not all students in the classroom feel the urgency and the difficulty of keeping up to date in times of rapid change. Most teachers do. And most teachers know that in a year or two these same students will feel this urgency, as they are joined on the job by new graduates whose learning makes a five-year-old degree already partly obsolescent. Teachers realize that keeping up to date is no longer just a matter of replacing last year's figures with this year's but of coping with challenges to the fundamentals themselves.

Once we talked of the *consumer franchise* that a brewer obtained by being the first to advertise that his bottles, like those in any brewery, were washed with live steam. That was before the FTC thought of asking a baker to devote 25% of his ads to apologizing for claiming that his bread, like that of most bakeries, builds bodies 12 ways.

We discuss learning that depended on animal experiments, which is now threatened by a challenge that only apes, by reason of relationship, and wolves, because of similar ecology, provide fit models for man.[4] In *Psychology Today* the public, once assured that language was the earmark of man, learns that a chimpanzee has used plastic symbols to construct a multiple-choice exam for its trainer.[5] The Hawthorne effect, bedrock of modern management, is challenged as a fraud.[6] Put on sale are feedback gadgets by which individuals can learn to control brain waves and other bodily processes we were assured were beyond man's reach.[7] Pessimists even suggest that all psychology experiments need to be reexamined for such artifacts as experimenter effect, unrepresentative volunteer subjects, and pretest sensitization.[8]

These *are* exciting times. Keeping up requires teamwork not only between instructors engaged in team teaching but between instructor and students and among students themselves. Once the excitement of the seminar was something that only graduate students enjoyed; today it has become virtually a necessity in undergraduate teaching as well.

To the extent that this excitement can be brought into a classroom it will not only improve the quality of learning but the quality of students as well.

Schools of Business have often lacked two things to attract students of the intellectual calibre needed by the modern business firm and by a society that depends on businessmen for leadership in government and in voluntary organizations. One of these was an idealism that looks beyond the interests of the individual; this has come with the increased emphasis, both in top management and in our B-schools, on social responsibility. The other was intellectual challenge—and this we now have in plenty. The question is how the challenge of rapid change and constant discovery can be met.

This book frees classroom time for the teacher who is determined to keep up and gives him some of the tools he needs. One such tool is the research highlights. Another is the list of additional research readings appended to each chapter. A third is the bibliography, which appears in an instructor's manual, that benefits from the six month's difference between deadlines for textbook and manual. In addition, I plan to issue an annual reading list. It will be available to any user of this book who addresses me in care of the publisher, and sends along his suggestions for readings, his recommendations for classroom activities, and his questions or challenges to the book itself.

I gratefully acknowledge the assistance of those individuals named in the first edition—my teachers, my colleagues, and my students. I extend thanks for help in preparing this manuscript to Betty Wolfe, Mary Venzke, and Anna Dibello of the Center for Research in Business at the University of Houston. I express appreciation to the many researchers whose work I have quoted, absolve them of any responsibility for the interpretations I have made of their work, and apologize in advance for any whose contributions have been overlooked. I dedicate this edition, as I did the first, to the four persons—Lois, Larry, Margaret Ann, and Richard—who so frequently asked, "Isn't that book done yet?" It is—and now, in your classroom and my study, must begin the work of revision.

Houston, Texas
1972

EDGAR CRANE

Notes

Chapter Zero

1. *Examples.* Journalism Monographs, published by the Association for Education in Journalism (headquarters at the University of Wisconsin) or the news research bulletins of the American Newspaper Publishers Association, 750 Third Avenue, New York 10017.
2. Such as the latest edition of C. H. Sandage and Vernon Fryburger's Advertising theory and practice, first published in 1936.
3. For a brief introduction, see pp. 226–35 of Bernard Berelson and Gary A. Steiner's "Human behavior" (New York: Harcourt, Brace & World, 1964).
4. Robert B. Lockard, "Reflections on the fall of comparative psychology . . .", American Psychologist, 27:168–79.
5. David Premack, "The education of Sarah," Psychology Today, 4:4:54–8.
6. Alex Carey, "The Hawthorne studies: a radical criticism," American Sociological Review, 32:403–16.
7. See p. 98 of Psychology Today for July 1971.
8. Robert Rosenthal and Ralph L. Rosnow, Artifact in behavioral research (New York: Academic Press, 1969).

Models of the Decision Process

Here are four flow charts, for those who find such models helpful as a memory device, of buyer or seller decision processes.

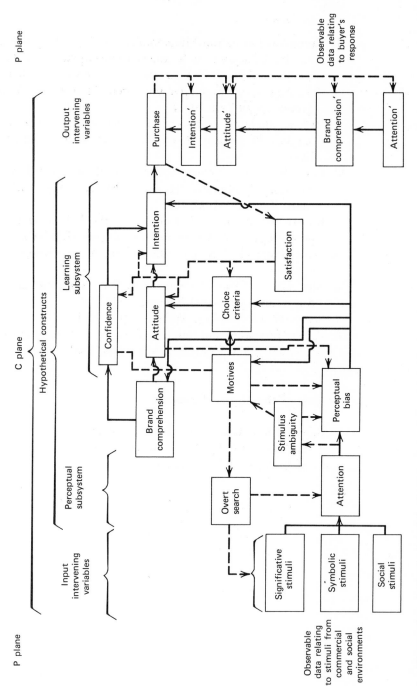

1. Howard and Sheth, Model of buyer behavior. Source: The Theory of Buyer Behavior by John A. Howard and Jagdish N. Sheth. Copyright © 1969 by John Wiley & Sons, Inc.

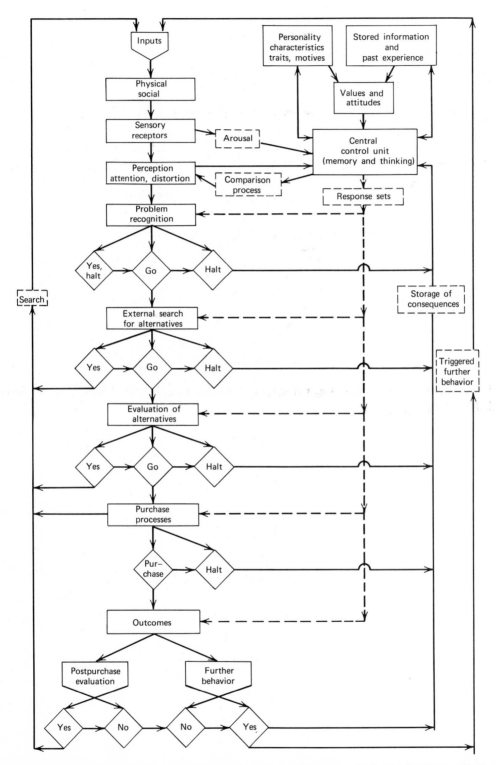

2. Engel's consumer decision-making model. Source: *Consumer Behavior* by James F. Engel, David T. Kollat, and Roger D. Blackwell. Copyright © 1968 by Holt, Rinehart and Winston, Inc.

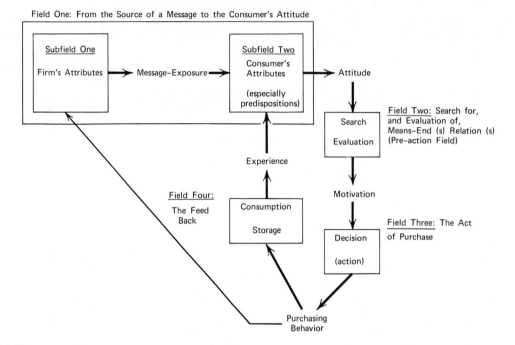

The Comprehensive Scheme: A Summary Flow Chart

Field One: From the Source of a Message to the Consumer's Attitude

3. Francesco M. Nicosia, Consumer decision processes (Englewood Cliffs, N.J.: Prentice-Hall, Inc., 1966), page 156.

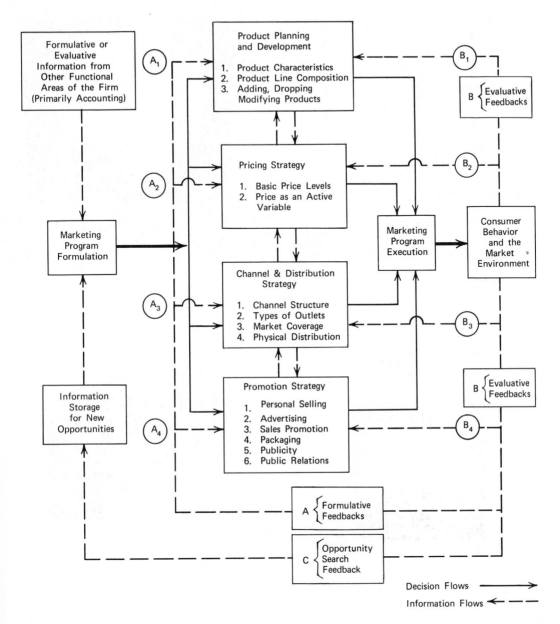

Formulative or Evaluative Information from Other Functional Areas of the Firm (Primarily Accounting)	A₁

Product Planning and Development

1. Product Characteristics
2. Product Line Composition
3. Adding, Dropping Modifying Products

B₁

B { Evaluative Feedbacks

Pricing Strategy

1. Basic Price Levels
2. Price as an Active Variable

A₂

B₂

Marketing Program Formulation

Channel & Distribution Strategy

1. Channel Structure
2. Types of Outlets
3. Market Coverage
4. Physical Distribution

A₃

Marketing Program Execution

Consumer Behavior and the Market Environment

B₃

Information Storage for New Opportunities

Promotion Strategy

1. Personal Selling
2. Advertising
3. Sales Promotion
4. Packaging
5. Publicity
6. Public Relations

A₄

B { Evaluative Feedbacks

B₄

A { Formulative Feedbacks

C { Opportunity Search Feedback

Decision Flows ⟶
Information Flows ⟵ — —

4. Richard H. Brien and James E. Stafford, "Marketing Information Systems: a New Dimension for Marketing Research," Journal of Marketing, 32:3:20.

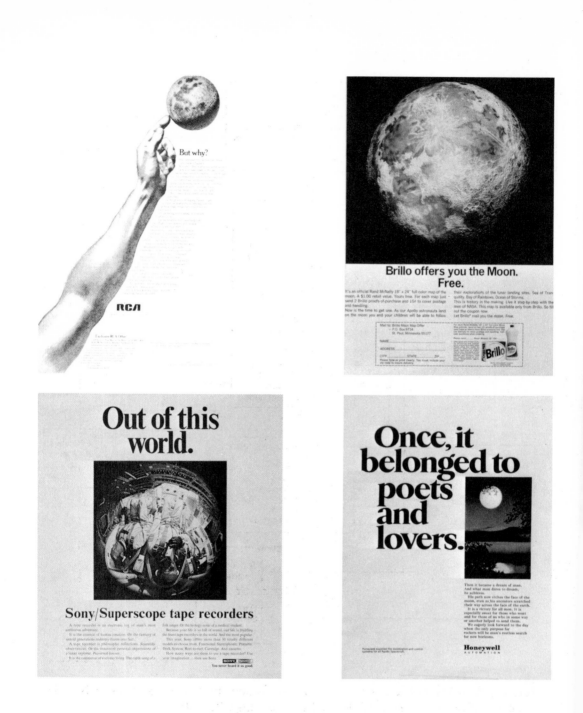

Landing on the Moon

Here are eight advertisements which used an historic event—man's landing on the moon—to attract the reader to their message. Note the variety of *goals* which sellers sought: building a corporate image, selling a product, offering a moon map for three proofs of purchase. Note the variety of *symbols* used: moon, landing craft, the faces or names of the astronauts themselves. Note variations in *message content*—ranging from philosophical speculation about poets and lovers. And note how varied the *sponsors* of the ads, ranging from TWA to Del Monte, from Brillo to the Charles River mice-breeding laboratories!

14a

Sharing the Glory

Absent from the ads on this page are the pictorial symbols one would expect— no moon, no astronauts, no landing craft. Yet each of the ads claims a share in the adventure. A trade association points to the moonship hangar, its ad one in a series citing unfamiliar uses of aluminum. Stouffer's boasts that it supplied 14 dishes that fed the astronauts during their time in quarantine after a safe landing back on earth. TWA depicts the pride and joy felt around the world, by showing nine arms throwing nine hard hats into the air, to symbolize the 3,300 employees who'd worked on the Apollo program. Even a mice-breeding laboratory gets into the act!

SPACE FOOD NOW AVAILABLE AS A HIGH-ENERGY SNACK

The Energy Snack From U.S. Aerospace Research and Pillsbury

Congratulations Neil, Buzz, and Mike. We're just glad we could help.

"A title on the door . . . rates a Bigelow on the floor"

The man who's got it made deserves every comfort he can get. That comfortable feeling you get from a plush Bigelow can make the hardest of jobs a little softer. Send for our free brochure on commercial carpets. Write to Bigelow-Sanford, Dept. B, 140 Madison Avenue, New York, N.Y. 10016. *People who know . . . buy* BIGELOW.

It's ugly, but it gets you there.

Humor and the Hard Sell

Pillsbury adopts a hard-selling newspaper format to inform the world of a moon-shot spinoff—Space Food Sticks. It cites unique product features, links them to new consumer benefits. Other advertisers on the page, bent on building corporate images, adopt a lighter note to modest humor. A popular *New Yorker* cartoonist helps Del Monte hint that it helped feed the astronauts in flight, without ever actually saying so. Bigelow adds the moon landing to its list of unusual sites in a campaign which asserts that important men deserve carpet on the floor. And Volkswagen depends on just its monogram to link two "ugly" objects, LEM and its own Bug.

Chapter 1 Synopsis

● This book is concerned with the processes by which buyer and seller make decisions to buy and sell and how their separate decision-making processes converge in the encounter between them. There are five reasons why what appears so simple as a purchase and a sale is, in fact, a most complex event:

a. This event is only one in a series of events occurring through time, each of which has both its causes and its consequences.
b. Multiple causes are operating and multiple effects are obtained at every stage in the decision process.
c. No purchase-sale can occur until two decision processes, those of buyer and of seller, converge.
d. The encounter that represents this convergence may involve face-to-face communications between buyer and seller or it may take place within the head of either.
e. The terms "buyer" and "seller" are labels for roles, often performed by groups of people, rather than for individuals. Differences must be reconciled not only between buyer and seller but within groups of sellers and of buyers.

● Theory develops, in life as in this text, in the dialogue between the "shoulds" of a *system* and the "is" of a *process*. We know a good deal about how consumers do behave and how sellers ought to; we know much less about how consumers should make decisions and how sellers actually do make them.

● Sellers seek to influence buyer behavior by four kinds of choices: product attributes, place, price, and prospects. Since buyers are influenced by their perceptions, a seller can choose to manipulate the variables of product, place, and price or the way they are perceived by his prospects. He does the latter through promotion—through sales and advertising messages.

● Messages represent one of the five variables of communications theory, the others being audiences, channels, sources, and effects. The symbols that a seller combines in his message mix are analogous to the attributes he combines in a product mix. The channels through which his messages are transmitted, personal and impersonal, are analogous to the channels through which a physical product and legal title to it are conveyed.

● The decision-making process is examined by following a single family of buyers through its 10 stages, noting the time of each, and by seeing how its decision sets off a similar decision sequence for competing sellers.

● Sellers must aggregate buyers into market segments. They can do this, at any given point in time, in terms of their stage in the decision process or their satisfaction with a set of competing brands. When satisfaction is low and repeat purchases unlikely, a seller will need to decide whether he should alter his product mix, his message mix, his media mix, or any combination of the three.

● The seller's choice of media presupposes that buyers, in their own decision processes, have already decided which sources, channels, and messages to examine, which to be informed and influenced by. Their choice will be made on the basis of cost and credibility, credibility involving perceptions of expertness and trustworthiness. Knowledge of why prospects prefer one source to another will enable a seller to predict what these choices will be.

● The messages that a seller transmits via such media contain three elements: buyer benefits, product features, and an attempt to establish a causal link between features and benefits. These three elements constitute the copy platform.

Research Articles

Market Segments.   Nations grouped into segments on basis of movie preferences (Carroll); segments vary in attributes they seek in retail stores (Berry).

Brand Preference.   Strength of preferences varies by brand and product (Pessemier); ads test strength of brand preferences as prices change (Abrams).

Price.   Perceptions of price often err (Brown); *zone of acceptance* affects response to price differences (Kamen).

Strategy.   Marketing and audience grids provide model for ad campaign plans (Colley, McCarthy); change in strategy suggested by attitude and education levels (Bauer).

Errors.   Stress increases error by message sources (Greenberg); audience tends to exaggerate rather than minimize message content (Wales).

Chapter 1 Buyer and Seller: Decision Processes and Interaction

In his office, the seller decides what features he will build into his products, what prices he will charge for them, what channels he will distribute them through, and which prospects he will seek to interest in them.

In her home, the buyer decides what stores she will visit, which friends she will query, and what advertisements she will take a second look at in deciding the products and brands she will buy. At home or in the aisles of supermarkets or department stores, she will make her final decision to buy or postpone a purchase, to spend more or less, to buy this brand or that.

Neither buyer nor seller finds making such decisions a brief, simple, or inexpensive process. Both often must weigh a large number of alternatives and, in doing so, gather and evaluate a large amount of information.

Moreover, the decision that either buyer or seller makes is meaningless in itself; overt, visible expression in a purchase-and-sale can occur only when the two decision processes converge in an exchange of information and influence and an exchange of money and goods occurs.

When such exchange occurs face to face, an observer can note how each influences the other. He can observe which appeals the salesman uses and how his prospect responds to them.

However, even in industry, where face-to-face interaction between salesman and prospect is far more common than it is in the consumer market, much of the communication that affects purchase-and-sale occurs in the head of the buyer or seller, and can be probed only by the most careful questioning by the scientist. The seller makes his decisions on the basis of responses he anticipates receiving from prospects. The housewife decides to stick with brands and retailers who have proved reliable or to try a new brand she remembers seeing advertised two weeks ago; her choices have been made before her first encounter with the seller's agent, a check-out clerk in the supermarket.

There are six reasons why understanding so simple appearing an event as a purchase-and-sale turns out to be a complex matter.

1. *The purchase-sale represents only one event in a multistage decision process occurring over time.* Although flow charts of dizzying complexity may represent this process, it is virtually impossible to say whether a given stage will occur, how long it will last, or *when* it will occur. Cause and effect relationships cannot be assumed. Reading an ad may lead to purchase of the product advertised or purchase may cause a buyer to read the ad to reassure himself that the choice he made was a wise one.

2. *At each stage of the decision-making process, multiple causes are operating.* The recognition that a problem exists which initiates the decision process may be affected by product failure, concurrent events, or messages from the seller's competitors. A man may buy new tires for his car because he is about to take a long trip, because he reads of a tire sale in his newspaper, or because a neighbor boasts of a bargain he's just taken advantage of. Rarely is any effect produced by a single cause; rarely does any cause produce a single effect.

3. *The purchase-sale occurs when two decision processes converge—the decision processes of buyer and seller.* An observer is less interested in the alternative that the buyer or seller prefers above all others than in the *set* of alternatives each will *accept.* If these two

sets overlap, the observer must determine the bargaining power of both buyer and seller if he wants to predict the outcome of the encounter between them. (If the seller was willing to accept from $1000 to $1300 for his car, and the buyer was prepared to pay between $800 and $1200, why did they finally agree on a purchase-and-sale at $1100?)

4. *The encounter between seller and buyer may take place within the head of either of them; a decision may be the delayed result of a series of personal or impersonal encounters.* Both the individual decision processes and their convergence in a sale-purchase commitment must be uncovered rather than observed. The conversation between car buyer and car seller is unlikely to reveal the limits of either participant's price range. An observer needs to question each before the encounter and, probably, after it as well. Frequently, no face-to-face encounter precedes a purchase and sale.

5. *The terms "buyer," "seller," and "observer" represent roles rather than individuals—labels for groups who perform these functions.* Husband *and* wife have to agree on make, model, color and cost of a new car; six executives of a manufacturing firm must reach consensus before a contractor can be authorized to build a new plant. The selling function requires joint efforts of a variety of persons, beginning with the manufacturer and including factory salesmen, retail sales clerks, an advertising agency, and three different advertising media. Study of decision processes may require a team of observers, including a social psychologist knowledgeable about techniques of persuasion, a cultural anthropologist who can compare the values of America in the 1970s with those of other times and places, a sociologist experienced in the effects of social class on

consumer purchases, an economist familiar with the way a wage-earner's expectations affect his desires to spend or save and a very special kind of expert to coordinate the contributions of each of the experts!

6. *Two types of group process must be studied.* One involves bargaining and conflict among peers; the other involves flows of influence and information up and down the ranks of a hierarchical organization. In each setting, the participants' goals must be determined, the extent to which these goals overlap must be determined, and estimates must be made of the ability of each participant to impose his goals on the group. (Will the comptroller, whose response to falling sales is a cost-cutting spree, be defeated by the marketing manager who feels a stepped-up sales budget is the key? Will the wife who wants a small car defer to the husband who feels his position demands a Lincoln Continental?)

These problems represent the focus of this text, which is concerned with a multistage decision process occurring within the heads of buyers and sellers. Since multiple causes operate at each stage, we are concerned with the processes by which differences are resolved within groups of buyers and within groups of sellers, as well as the resolution of differences between buyer and seller that must precede a purchase-and-sale. *Marketing communications* includes the exchange of messages between buyer and seller; the content, style, and goals of such messages; the origins of such goals in the individual; and the exchange of information and influence which reconciles divergent goals between individuals.

Nine chapters present the stages of decision making, beginning with recognition that a problem (or an opportunity) exists and ending with purchase-sale and consumption of a product. Along the way, we will take a closer look at three of the most important stages in the process, asking what the behavioral sciences have to say about *goals* (in chapters on meanings, on attitudes, and on motives-personality-role), what they have to say about *alternatives* (in chapters on learning and the senses) and what they have to say about *group processes* (in chapters on categories of people and on social class). In six final chapters dealing with the major concepts of communications—audiences, channels, media, symbols, messages, and sources—we turn to the encounter between buyer and seller.

Systems and Processes

Throughout these pages we will be engaged in a continuous dialogue between system and process. System, as we see it, attempts to *prescribe* the strategies appropriate to specified goals that must be attained by inputs of specified variables in specific amounts at the proper times. Process, as we see it, attempts to *describe* how decision makers actually deal with multiple causes and effects over time. A comparison of process and system shows that decision makers in real life often do not behave as theorists think they should.

Some system makers tend to conclude that people are no damn good—and need to be harangued or coerced into behaving properly. Some observers of real-life processes conclude that systems are a waste of time. Enlightened adherents of either school, we feel, take a third position. They compare the "shoulds" of the system maker with the actualities of real-life processes and ask whether a decision maker is, through ignorance, pursuing a strategy inappropriate to his goals, or whether his strategy suggests that his goals are other than the observer or he himself assumes.

Theory advances in this dialogue between system and process—"should" and

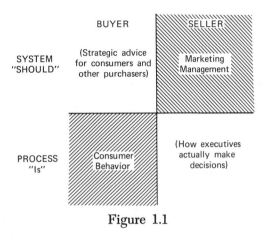

Figure 1.1

"is." Our pages echo this dialogue by contrasting the generalizations of the text with research findings, in bold type, and with examples of advertisements of selling messages in print and picture.

Textbooks in marketing management tend to prescribe how sellers should make their decisions; they represent the systems approach. Texts in consumer behavior, on the other hand, describe the steps buyers actually go through in making their decisions; they present process. (As Figure 1.1 indicates, two pieces of the puzzle are still missing: research on how business executives really make their decisions and advice as to how consumers ought to make theirs.)

The Marketing Mix

In the long run, purchase-sale can be understood only by studying the mutual exercise of influence by buyer and seller upon one another. At present, however, most of our insights reflect the viewpoint of the *seller*. Marketing theorists suggest that a seller seeks to influence buyer behavior by manipulating four variables.*

---

* Messages of salesman and advertisement are often represented as an element, called *promo-*

Product Attributes. The seller fashions a product whose form and functions, he hopes, will outperform those offered by his rivals. He attempts to find out the attributes that buyers want and a technology that will produce them.

Place. The seller offers a set of attributes, his *brand,* at places such as retail outlets that buyers find convenient. He locates factories and warehouses and selects means of transporting his products so as to minimize costs and time in transit. He seeks the cooperation of intermediaries to assist in transferring title and possession of the product to the ultimate user.

Price. The seller sets a price that buyers can afford, comparable to that of competing brands and related to his costs of production and distribution.

Prospects. The seller selects those sets of prospects—usually called *market segments* —who will respond most favorably to the combination of product features, price, and place just described. (This combination is termed his *marketing mix.*) Or, given a set of prospects, the seller selects the mix of product, price, and place that is most appealing to them.

To the seller, a *brand* consists of a set of attributes offered for sale at a specified series of prices at a specific group of locations to a specific set of prospects. The buyer, however, perceives a "brand" in terms of its potential for satisfying a set of felt needs, and tends to compare its ratio of reward and cost to the ratios of alternative brands.

The seller uses sales and advertising messages to suggest a causal link between the satisfactions desired by a given market segment and the product-price-and-place attributes of a specific seller's mix. The prospect weighs these messages against his own experience and that of his friends in deciding whether and what to buy.

Studies in consumer behavior suggest that the perceptions which determine what a prospect will buy may not reflect very accurately the cost-reward ratios of rival brands as seen by an "impartial" or "objective" observer. This means that a seller whose brand is rejected may alter his marketing mix or work on the misperceptions directly through sales and advertising messages. An automobile manufacturer may increase sales by lowering prices. Consumer research, however, may reveal that prospects believe his prices to be higher than they are, or fail to include maintenance costs or trade-in value in comparing costs. Messages that correct such misconceptions may increase sales as much as an actual cut in prices. Indeed, unless messages inform prospects of price cuts, sales cannot increase.

There are dangers in too great a dependence on messages. If the promise of a message does not test out in experience with the product, a prospect may never repeat the purchase, and his comments to friends may keep them from even trying the product. There is a great temptation to depend on messages and neglect changes in the product mix. Messages tend to be quicker in getting results, cheaper, simpler, and less likely to cause competitors to retaliate. A cut in price may force heroic cost-cutting measures; messages will not. Stubborn realities of space, time, and costs limit a seller's ability to manipulate the realities of physical distribution. Frequent or drastic changes in distribution channels upset relations with distributors. A change in product features may necessitate waiting for a technological breakthrough and often increases costs. Messages, on the other hand, may reduce the *psychological* dis-

---

tion, of the marketing mix. But promotion is both an alternative to changes in product, price, and place and a principal means by which such changes affect prospects' perceptions and behavior. We prefer to deal with them separately.

tance of an outlet whose geography remains fixed. Messages may change the way that present features are perceived by prospects without requiring any change in the features themselves.

Communications Concepts

Messages are the most visible of five concepts that the discipline of communications brings to the study of decision making by buyers and sellers. In the classic definition, communications is "the study of *what* is transmitted by *whom* over what *channels* to *whom* with what *effects*."

What. Message content may be defined as the meanings that a source wants to convey and those that the receiver perceives *or* as the attitudes that sources and receivers have toward the objects and events dealt with in the message. Successful communication requires that the attitudes and meanings of buyer and seller have an area of overlap. (A seller may be convinced that his brand is the best in the world; a buyer need only be convinced that it is the best available at the moment.)

By Whom. The sources of a message perceived by an audience affect its meaning (as measured by audience reactions) whether or not such perceptions are accurate. Source behavior, in turn, is influenced by anticipated and actual audience response.

How. The transmission of a message involves symbol systems, including words, numbers, and pictures, and the channels of transmission, either face-to-face or mediated by print and electronic channels.

Message content or the nature of one's audience may require the use of print media; this choice prevents use of the symbols of speech. Print is useless if one's prospects are illiterate and is of limited value in complex industrial sale-and-purchase encounters where the advantages of face-to-face communication are needed.

Effects. Three sets of effects must be specified: those desired by the source, those desired by the receiver, and those actually obtained. All too often, the desired effects (or goals) are assumed rather than specified, or specified for the source only. Frequently, goals are expressed in such general terms—for example, *profit* or *sales*—that they are useless either as a guide in devising messages and choosing channels or in determining whether one's communications have been successful.

Unless goals for both source and receiver are expressed in similar terms and such terms permit a comparison between aims and outcomes, it becomes impossible to say whether each participant has achieved *sufficient* success to be willing to continue the relationship or to determine which has gained the *greater* relative advantage in their encounter. (A customer will not return to a store or make a repeat purchase of a given brand if performance of either falls below his minimum expectations. He may not return if he feels the seller has obtained too great an advantage in the encounter in comparison with his own gains.)

Each of the major decisions the seller makes in choosing his marketing mix has its counterpart in decisions concerning his communications mix. His message mix, what he *says* about his brand, reflects his product mix, the attributes of form and function that he builds into his brand. These messages must be transmitted to the prospect in phase with arrival of the product itself.

Marketing communications involve an encounter between two disciplines, marketing and communications, as shown in Figure 1.2. A scientist observes the decision processes of a seller, and the discipline called *marketing* results; he observes those of the buyer, and *consumer behavior* is the

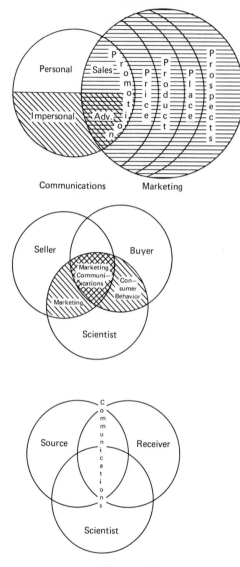

Figure 1.2

result; he observes the encounter between buyer and seller, and *marketing communications* is the result.

In communications, a scientist can observe source or receiver in isolation; sometimes he has access to only one of them. He prefers, however, to observe both sides of the exchange. He knows that receivers take account of what they assume to be the intentions of persons perceived as the

sources of a message. He infers source intentions, in turn, from his perception of the source's views concerning the identity, ability, and views of his audiences.

Decision Making: An Example

Before sellers can influence the decisions of a prospect, they must know something of the process by which such decisions are made. Such understanding is best achieved by an example.

At 7:50 P.M. on February 3, the Schumachers' TV screen goes dark. It takes the family 10 minutes to *define the problem*—to discover that the electricity hasn't failed and that the TV transmitter hasn't gone off the air. With children in the family, there must be a TV set in working order in the house: *goal-setting* takes just one minute! But for an hour and a half the family argues as to how this goal is to be attained. Is this the time to buy a new set, or is it worth repairing the old one? Finally, by 9:35, they have checked last month's bank balance and current check stubs. These *constraints* indicate that a repair job will have to do. Having rejected one choice, husband and wife then list the remaining *alternatives*. Shall they ask the repairman to make a house call or will they take the set to his shop? And which repairman? Next morning, Mrs. Schumacher begins to *gather data* from the yellow pages of her telephone directory. She turns over the results to her husband, when he comes home from work, for *analysis*. Then husband and wife *choose an alternative*. The next morning Mr. Schumacher *takes action*, hauling the set off to Joe's Repair Shop. (Joe offered the best combination of price and proximity, and a quick phone call to a neighbor indicated his reputation was good.) For a view of this process in flowchart form, see Figure 1.3.

As the dotted line at the bottom of Figure 1.3 indicates, when Mr. Schumacher

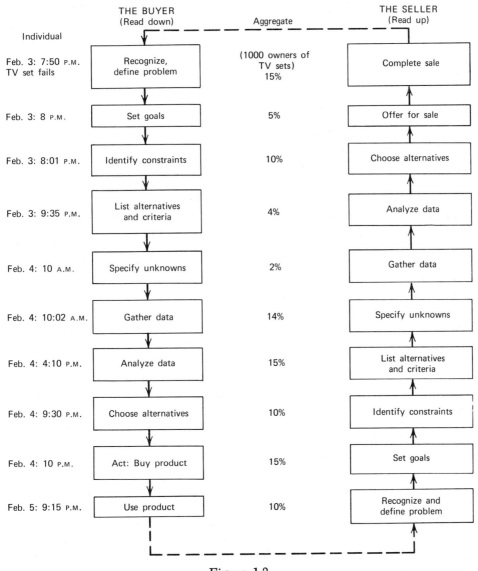

THE BUYER (Read down)		Aggregate	THE SELLER (Read up)
Individual			
Feb. 3: 7:50 P.M. TV set fails	Recognize, define problem	(1000 owners of TV sets) 15%	Complete sale
Feb. 3: 8 P.M.	Set goals	5%	Offer for sale
Feb. 3: 8:01 P.M.	Identify constraints	10%	Choose alternatives
Feb. 3: 9:35 P.M.	List alternatives and criteria	4%	Analyze data
Feb. 4: 10 A.M.	Specify unknowns	2%	Gather data
Feb. 4: 10:02 A.M.	Gather data	14%	Specify unknowns
Feb. 4: 4:10 P.M.	Analyze data	15%	List alternatives and criteria
Feb. 4: 9:30 P.M.	Choose alternatives	10%	Identify constraints
Feb. 4: 10 P.M.	Act: Buy product	15%	Set goals
Feb. 5: 9:15 P.M.	Use product	10%	Recognize and define problem

Figure 1.3

delivers his crippled TV set to Joe's shop, his act starts a problem-solving, decision-making process for the seller. (In fact, Mr. Schumacher's solution created several problems for several sellers. The repairmen whose shops he passed on the way, because their prices were too high or their reputations too low, wonder how they can meet Joe's competition. Will higher volume solve the problem and, if so, how do they get it?) But Joe has a problem: it will be at least a week before he can get to the Schumacher's set. Should he hire a part-time assistant, and take a risk on quality? Should he keep putting the Schumachers off with excuses, and risk losing not only their business but the business of friends who hear their disgruntled comments? Can he boost his business enough through advertising to hire a full-time assistant? (Follow Joe's decisions by moving upward in the flow chart on the right in Figure 1.3.)

Seller Decision Making

It may take Joe the repairman a good deal longer to go through the decision-making process the Schumachers went through, and involve more complicated data gathering and analysis; but, fortunately, most of his alternatives can be converted to dollars and cents. (The Schumachers would have found it hard to put a price on the annoyance active children can create when there's no TV set to keep them occupied.) This ability of the seller to express most of his problems in a common dollar denominator represents a significant difference between the two decision-making processes.

Perhaps Joe will decide that he can afford a full-time assistant by devising an "insurance policy" which, for a retainer paid in advance, assures patrons that their sets will be kept in order for the next year without further charge.

If Joe decides to offer such a policy, this will create a new problem-opportunity for the Schumachers: should they take out such a policy or not? Back they go through the decision process.

Joe the repairman is much less interested in the exact time that any individual act occurs than in the number of persons in each stage of the decision process at a given point in time. This is shown by the percentages in Figure 1.3 under the heading of *Aggregate*.

Market research may inform Joe that there are 1000 families in his part of town who represent good prospects for his TV repairs policy. With the data of Figure 1.3, he can then devise a communications strategy. He'll use an ad to tell the 15% who aren't convinced they have a *problem* how often TV sets run amuck and what the costs are likely to be. He may point out to the 5% still engaged in setting *goals* why it's desirable to have one's set in working order. To the 10% of consumers weighing financial constraints, Joe may suggest that easy credit terms make these constraints less onerous than they appear. By providing information as to the likelihood of different kinds of malfunctions and costs of repairing them, Joe helps prospects specify *unknowns* and provides *data* to them. Joe's door-to-door fliers, direct-mail leaflets, and radio spot announcements may *analyze the data* and simplify a prospect's *choice of alternatives;* his "limited time offer" may push them through the *action-taking* stage.

Study of prospects' *brand preferences* may tell Joe that he's losing out at the *listing alternatives* stage: his shop just isn't among those which the Schumachers consider. Or perhaps he loses out at the next-to-last stage, when the choice of a shop is made. If Joe finds he is losing out at several stages in buyer decision processes, his marketing strategy will need drastic revision. And, of course, he is not operating in a vacuum. Joe may run a lot of ads, but they won't help if people like the Schumachers don't see them or believe them. Joe's business won't improve if his competitors reach the prospects with more or better messages. If the Schumachers' set doesn't work when Joe gets through with it, the Schumachers will have to decide whether to take it somewhere else or buy a new one. If it works for a day or two and then breaks down, Joe's reputation is bound to suffer. Changes in either communications mix or marketing mix usually must be followed by changes in the other.

Prospects, as we have seen, may be assembled into aggregates in terms either of their location in the decision-making process or in terms of their "loyalty" to Joe or one of his competitors—their brand preferences.

Users, buyers, and prospective buyers of any product and brand vary in their degree of satisfaction with existing brands, as

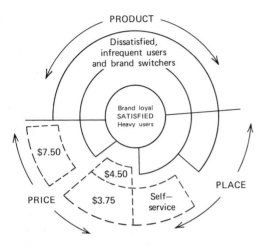

Figure 1.4 Consumer satisfaction and brand loyalty.

at a self-service outlet, foregoing the costly conveniences of sales clerk, delivery services, and 30-day credit.

Figure 1.4 pictures the present buyers of a single *brand*, differentiated in terms of their satisfaction with and loyalty to it. It is also possible to represent the entire market for a *product* by such a diagram, as in Figure 1.5, each brand getting its slice of the market, each slice being made up of loyal buyers and those who are more likely to shift around. If his slice is too thin or contains too few on-target, brand-loyal buyers, a seller would be well advised to change his marketing mix, his message mix, or both. When loyalty is low, repeat sales are unlikely, and selling costs go up.

Even the seller with a large slice and a high proportion of devoted buyers may add a new brand to his existing offering if, by doing so, he may charge a higher price or prevent a rival from moving into the market.

shown in Figure 1.4. On a target, the highly satisfied users occupying the bull's-eye are unlikely to seek an alternative brand. As one moves out from the center, he finds buyers who are less happy with existing brands, more eager to try something new, actively searching for alternatives.

By devising a *new* market mix, the seller can peel off prospects in the outer ring of such a target, and convert them into highly satisfied, loyal users of his new mix.

Two different strategies are illustrated in Figure 1.4. Some dissatisfied prospects are willing to pay $7.50, rather than the $5 they are now being charged. This may require a change in quality, involving more cost to the seller, or these prospects may interpret a minor change in design, a new brand name, or sale through a more prestigious retail outlet *as* a change in quality that justifies the higher price. Other prospects are dissatisfied because the present price is too high; some are willing to pay $4.50, others only $3.75. The former can be easily accommodated, but $3.75 will mean a loss to the seller—unless the buyer is willing, as the figure suggests, to buy

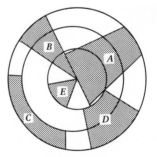

Figure 1.5 Loyalty for five brands. Brand A has a large number of loyal users in the center of this diagram of a product market. B has few loyal users, more in the outer, less-loyal circles. C, in contrast, has NO loyal users; D is slightly better off. And E has only loyal users—but not very many of them. C probably needs to improve its product. E, on the other hand, probably needs to let more people know it exists. Both B and D need to convert more occasional users in to heavy, loyal users.

Product, Message, and Media Mixes

The seller who decides his segment of the total market is unsatisfactory can change his product mix, his message mix, his media mix, or all three. Consumer studies can assist him by showing how his satisfied and dissatisfied users differ in answers to such questions as *What do you like?* and *What do you dislike?* about his and rival brands. The seller can compare these two groups on such socioeconomic attributes as age, income, social class, job, and education; on geographic location; even on personality. A survey or an analysis of sales records may reveal that truck drivers and clergymen differ in preferences as to product design or kind of stores and want a different mix of such services as credit and delivery.

Having decided on the product attributes, price, and place suited to these two market segments, the seller must now decide what media should carry his messages to them. Perhaps, as Figure 1.6 suggests, TV and newspapers can be used to reach truck drivers, but only newspapers are effective with clergymen. Copy tests indicate that both of the appeals suggested be used in advertisements aimed at clergymen but that price is not an effective appeal in ads aimed at truck drivers.

In actuality, of course, more than two media would be examined, and many more than two message elements would be tried and tested. No mass medium ever reaches every prospect whom the buyer wants to reach; every medium reaches persons whom he does not regard as prospects.* No message moves every prospect to action, although it would be difficult to prove that

any message has no effect whatsoever. Many messages fail to evoke the kind and degree of response from the number of persons which the marketer expected, however.

As the overlapping media circles indicate, TV and newspapers often duplicate coverage. This is not necessarily bad. A message may have to be repeated several times before it is stored in memory. Printing an identical ad in five consecutive issues of the newspaper need not produce identical effects each time; a man's moods change from day to day. Reading printed words is one thing; listening to spoken words is another. TV embeds an ad in entertainment, newspapers surround it with news, and men respond to the message-in-context, not the message in isolation.

A prospect's decision as to the channels and sources of information and influence he will seek out, accept, and act upon is influenced by at least three variables: the *cost* in time and effort, the extent to which he sees a given source and channel as being relevant and *expert* to his decision, and the degree to which he feels each source and channel can be *trusted*. Judgments of whether a source and channel are expert and trustworthy will be affected by two variables, the personal-impersonal dimension and whether control rests with seller or buyer.

In general, a prospect is likely to assume that channels which he, as buyer, controls are likely to cost more and to be trustworthy; he may or may not consider them to be expert. A prospect may seek out these sources or retrieve from memory messages received from them in the past. One source

---

* Given a small enough market, it is possible to reach them all by direct mail. If one defines his market as all persons entering a given store, there is a high probability that all of them will be exposed to point-of-purchase advertising. Everyone has access to the yellow pages of the telephone directory, even if he lacks a phone of

his own. Controlled-circulation publications reduce "wastage" to a minimum. There is no assurance that direct mail or publications will be read, however, even if received. The critic who redefines his market to coincide with the audience of a given medium can be frustrated by insisting that "exposure" be redefined as well.

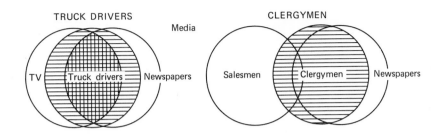

TRUCK DRIVERS   CLERGYMEN

Media

TV Truck drivers Newspapers   Salesmen Clergymen Newspapers

(Horizontal lines identify audience)

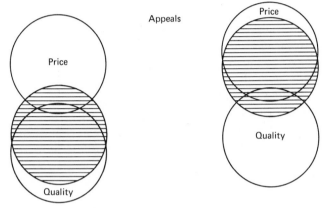

Appeals

Price

Quality

Communications mix: media and appeals

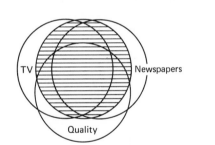

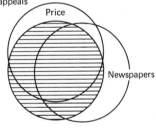

TV Newspapers   Newspapers

Quality

Figure 1.6 Most truck drivers can be reached by both TV and newspapers; only newspapers (*not* salesmen) reach clergymen. Truck drivers are indifferent, clergymen respond to price. Strategies: TV and newspapers stress quality to truck drivers; newspapers stress price to clergymen.

Nature of Influence Source:	Influence Source Controlled by:		
	SELLER	NEITHER BUYER NOR SELLER	BUYER
PERSONAL	Salesman	Stranger	Friend
IMPERSONAL	Advertisement	News story	*Consumer Reports, Changing Times*

Figure 1.7

may be influential at the stage of problem identification or goal setting; another when alternatives are being compared. (The most influential source of information, not shown in this table, is the prospect's own experience.)

Series of Channels

It is interesting to speculate as to how much effect each of the factors in Figure 1.8 would have on a receiver's decisions, given the accompanying hypothetical "credibility" ratings. Unfortunately, at this point we do not know whether such ratings should be combined by multiplying or averaging or by taking the higher or lower of the figures, or whether their sequence affects the outcome.

Other factors that affect the seller's choice of channel include:

Size of audience. Personal sources engaged in face-to-face communications can tailor their message more precisely to their audiences than can the mass media. The salesman, although more costly, is likely to be more effective.

Feedback. Salesmen are likely to be more effective because they can adapt their messages to prospects' responses.

Modality. Print has advantages for the buyer: he can read faster than he can listen, he can adjust his pace and reread at will, he can easily store print messages for future use, and he can avoid messages that don't interest him. Broadcast messages have advantages for the seller. Radio and TV can reach prospects who aren't aware that they need his product; TV can show the product in use. However, the advertiser who has a long message to transmit will prefer print. Few print vehicles turn down advertising for lack of space, but prime time on TV is sharply limited.

Audience-market overlap. The seller combines ready-made audiences offered by the media to achieve maximum congruence with his target market segments, knowing

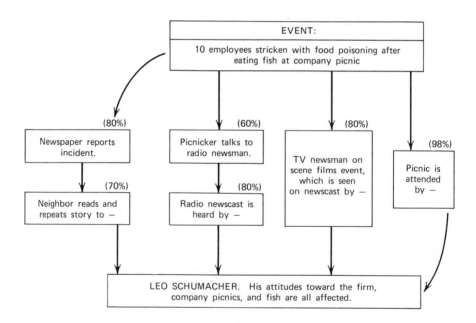

Figure 1.8 Percentages represent credibility ratings of sources.

some prospects will not be reached at all and some will be reached more than once.

Having selected media, the seller must make two decisions about messages.

Content. The information they provide about product attributes, price, and place.

Style. The symbols he selects and the skill with which they are combined.

The content of a marketing message involves three elements.

Buyer benefits. It informs or reminds the buyer of certain benefits he would like to receive, certain sensory satisfactions he would like to enjoy.

Product features. It informs or reminds the buyer of the attributes of a product and

brand, attributes that tend to distinguish this brand from others.

Causal link. It tries to establish a link between these attributes and buyer benefits by a variety of means ranging from forthright assertion to the most subtle and indirect kinds of suggestion.

These three elements are often called a *copy platform.* Expressing a good copy platform in words, pictures, numbers, and even music is difficult, but finding a good copy platform is more essential. Many colleges offer courses in symbol manipulation but few courses teach students where to look for good copy platforms or how to identify one. Many practitioners insist that the skill can't be taught, but is in a man's genes or has to be learned on the job.

The search for a copy platform may be-

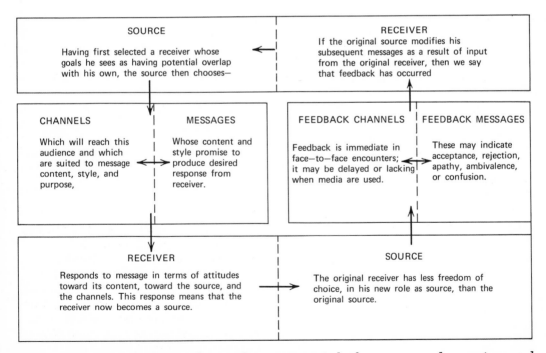

Figure 1.9 Arrows indicate that each participant is both a source and a receiver, and that choice of audience limits one's choices of message style and content and of channels. The two-headed arrows indicate that decisions concerning the message limit choices of channels, and vice versa.

gin with the *product*. Some admen visit laboratories and assembly lines, try a product out at home, compare a brand with its competitors. Having found novel or unique product attributes, they then seek buyer benefits that can be plausibly linked to them. Marketing men argue that one should first determine what a prospect wants, and then get engineers to design a product that provides these benefits. In practice, this approach presents some difficulties. Even interviewers skilled in concept testing, in getting prospects' reactions to a one-paragraph description of a product not yet designed or in production, need more to go on than the question, *What are your most pressing felt needs?*

If an advertising agency has a good consumer research department, a client may ask it to advise which of several new products has the best chance of success, or what set of product attributes is most likely to win popular favor. Other clients regard such matters as none of the agency's business.

As a message source, the seller must make three decisions. He must decide which prospects he wants as an audience, what channels to use to reach them, and what messages to transmit on those channels. The seller is also a receiver, observing prospects' behavior and listening to their responses so that he can modify elements in his marketing mix or his communications mix. Relations among the four elements of the communications model—source, message, channel, receiver—are depicted in Figure 1.9.

Thought, Talk, and Action

1. How would the decision process described in this chapter vary if it began with an automobile accident or a faulty refrigerator? By appearance of a new fashion in men's wear? In women's wear? If by an end-of-season swimwear sale? How would *place* affect decision making—suppose the auto broke down on vacation rather than at home? How would *time* affect decisions: compare a refrigerator malfunction two days *before* or two days *after* vacation.
2. Suggest copy platforms appropriate for contrasting products (cars, cake mix, cutlery) or brands (Cadillac, Volkswagen). Or find advertisements for such products and brands and analyze their different platforms.
3. Find ads that stress objective differences in products or perceptual differences in brands. Which is easier to find? Then mix them up and ask 10 people to rate each ad on a 1 to 7, believable-unbelievable scale. Which type of ads seems more believable?

Segmenting Markets on a Grand Scale

Individuals can be grouped into categories, called market segments, because they desire and will buy similar product mixes. Sometimes nations can be collected into segments, too.

More than 40% of the revenues of United States movie-makers come from foreign countries. But which films should be sent to which countries?

Box-office returns in the United States have proven to be a poor guide to overseas success even in Britain.

Researchers grouped pictures in six classes based on content and used 4000 first-year gross returns from 39 countries to rate each picture on a scale, ranging from films that grossed less than 40% of a country's average to those that doubled the average. They listed the types of movies preferred by each country and grouped countries on the basis of similar preferences:

"Nordic." Britain and the Commonwealth, Scandinavia, Germany, and Holland: push Judy Garland and mysteries; avoid Red Skelton.

"Latin." Latin America and southern Europe: semi-classical musicals.

Near East. Slapstick comedies.

Far East. Japan and the Philippines: Avoid comedy and mystery.

(Three multiethnic nations—the United States, Switzerland, and Israel—fell outside these groups.)

Box-office returns in any nation predicted returns for other nations in its class.

Source. Ronald Carroll, "Selecting motion pictures for the foreign market," *Journal of Marketing,* 17:2:162–71.

Research Involving the Five Ps

Studies involving *promotion, prospects* and *product* features are scattered through this book. Here is one example of a host of studies of *place,* defined as store image—and a series of studies on *price.*

Place

Samples of 350 charge customers for each of three department stores in Phoenix were asked three questions in a mail survey: *What do you like most,* and *what do you like least about shopping at ————? What are the major reasons why you think others shop at ————?*

The rate of return was 71%. Answers to the open-end questions were coded into 12 categories (and 44 subcategories). Three categories proved to be important: quality and assortment of merchandise, sales personnel, and store atmosphere. One store appeared to be marked by good prices and assortments. Another seemed to be high in prestige, with limited assortments and high prices. The third was handicapped by an inconvenient location.

Images varied according to customer characteristics, however. Sales clerks helped the store image with persons over 60 and those with lower incomes and less schooling. Sales clerks hurt the store image among customers with higher incomes and education.

Source. Leonard L. Berry, "The components of department store image," *Journal of Retailing,* 45:3–20.

Price

Three major constraints, aside from the law itself, limit a seller's freedom in manipulating price. One of them, *cost,* changes with technology. (A seller *may* sell a given product at a loss to help other items in his line, or cut prices below cost for a brief period of time, but ordinarily costs provide a kind of "floor" for his decision making.) The other two constraints are behavioral: the reactions of prospects and of competitors. Trying to test these factors through experiments in the marketplace is always costly and sometimes fatal. Here are two reports of experiments in a cheaper, more secure setting.

Price lists of toothpaste and cigarettes were given to 103 college students who first had indicated their favorite brands of each. They were then asked to indicate, on each of 30 shopping trips, which brand they would "buy." The price of their favorite brand was increased on 10 of these trips, to see how much "extra" they would be willing to pay before switching brands. On another 10 trials, prices of other brands were successively reduced. The third set of trials attempted to see how much their brand could rise in price before they would take a chance on a new brand. To make students take the trials seriously, three subjects picked at random were given the merchandise and change due on one of the 30 trials.

Brand preference proved stronger for cigarettes than for toothpaste; a three-cent rise in price caused 53% of toothpaste users to switch, but a five-cent change was necessary to move 58% of smokers. Within both product classes, some brands had a stronger hold on their users than others. Thus a one-cent rise cost one brand of toothpaste 25% of its buyers, but another brand only 4%. Although the leading brand (A) had 40 users to the second brand's (B) 25, it had only about half as many at the end, when students were charged a seven-cent premium for their favorite. When users of the second brand did switch, it was not to the top

of its 15 users with a one-cent increase but thereafter held the remainder.

Source. Edgar A. Pessemier, "A new way to determine buying decisions," *Journal of Marketing,* 24:2:41–6.

Pessemier's laboratory experiment was shifted to the field, by sending advertisements for 10 brands of consumer durables through the mail to matched panels of consumers.

A control group received an ad listing actual current prices; other groups had prices quoted, for the key brand, at $10, 20, 30, or 40 below existing levels—the last price representing a price cut of nearly 20%. Only the two largest price cuts caused significant brand switching in this study. Here are the differences in brand preferences shown for each condition:

Percentage Point Rise or Fall in Brand Choice
with Given Drop in Price of Test Brand

Brand	Percent Preferring at Normal Prices	Down $10	Down $20	Down $30	Down $40
Test	10	—	—	+8	+13
A	22	−1	−1	−6	− 7
B	20	+3	+3	+2	—
C	11	−1	−3	−4	− 4
Others	37	−1	−1	—	− 2

brand but to the fifth-ranking brand (E).

Two explanations were offered. One was that Brand B was new to the market. The other was that its attributes and those of E were similar, B and E being aimed at the same market segment.

As for cigarettes, the top brand (A: 19 users) held its customers despite price rises of one and two cents, but lost them thereafter; the second brand lost many

Note that the drop in price of the test brand seemed to shift users, insofar as the four groups are truly matched, from both A and C to the benefit of both the test brand and B.

Source. Jack Abrams, "A new method for testing pricing decisions," *Journal of Marketing,* 28:3:6–9.

The price that influences buyer behavior is, of course, the price that prospects perceive. If perceptions differ from objective fact, communications which correct perceptions may accomplish more than a change in price. How accurate are perceptions?

A thousand customers in five cities were asked to rank from four to seven supermarkets in their vicinity in terms of price. Actual prices were recorded twice in each store for 80 specific brands. In only one of the five cities was there a close relationship between "real" and "perceived" prices. The figures, squared correlation coefficients, indicate how much of the variation in perceptions is "explained" by genuine variations.

Havertown, Penna.	98%
Greensboro, N.C.	49
New York	6
San Francisco	0
St. Louis	0

Source. F. E. Brown, "Price image versus price reality," *Journal of Marketing Research,* 6:185–91.

Two Theories About What Happens as Prices Rise

The Weber-Fechner law, developed to explain perceptual responses to sensory input, suggests that a $5 increase in the price of a $10 item will be more visible and tend to inhibit purchases more than a $5 increase in the price of a $50 item. The zone-of-acceptance theory, developed to explain attitudinal responses to messages, suggests that each price is located in a range of fair, expected, or acceptable prices. Not until price crosses the boundary of this range will a brand be rejected as too *cheap* or too *expensive.* Thus it is possible that a $5 increase might fall within the acceptable range for a $10 pair of children's shoes but that a $5 increase would cause rejection of a record player, if $52.50 represented the top of a buyer's range. Here is support for the latter theory.

The traditional price differential per gallon between gasolines sold by 20 large firms, such as Texaco and Shell, and several hundred independent firms, is 2 cents. With regional variations, prices per gallon tend to hover around the 25- to 35-cent range. The zone-of-acceptance or "fair price" theory suggests that more users will shift to independent firms as gas prices rise beyond this range, even though the price differential remains the same.

Starting with 1400 names from Chicago and Indianapolis telephone directories, the study obtained answers from 157 users of regular grade and 62 users of premium grade gas. (Eighty-five respondents said they would stay with their preferred supplier, either independent or major brand, regardless of price.) Each respondent indicated his preference as to supplier on a seven-point scale, ranging from "definitely buy at major" to "definitely buy at independent." He provided such ratings for a series of *prices* moving in 5-cent jumps from 15¢ to 40¢, and a series of one-cent price differentials, ranging from 1¢ to 6¢.

As prices rose, independents actually needed a smaller price advantage rather than the larger one which the Weber-Fechner law would suggest. For users of regular grade, a 2¢ advantage was as effective for independent brands priced at 35¢ as a 3¢ advantage was for independents selling at 15 cents. For premium users, a 2-cent differential at a 37¢ price was as effective as a 3¢ advantage when the price was 23.5¢.

In a follow-up study, interviewers left mail-back questionnaires at households in 24 midwest cities asking respondents to indicate on a six-point scale their readiness to buy major and independent brands of regular and premium gasolines. (A typical page of the 33 which respondents checked offered these combinations: major premium 37.9¢, major-regular 35.9¢, independent premium 34.9¢, and independent regular 32.9¢.) Again, results challenged the Weber-Fechner law. As price levels rose, motorists tended to favor independent brands and regular grade at every price differential.

About a year after prices had risen by 1¢ in these 24 markets, telephone interviewers asked 1500 motorists, picked randomly from telephone directories, whether they had noticed any change. Some 7% said they didn't know, 2% said prices had dropped, 44% said they had remained the same, and 47% that they had gone up. Of the 47% who had noticed the price rise, one in seven said they had changed brands, typically to an independent.

Still unanswered is the question of how long it takes customers to adjust their zone of acceptance to a new price level. Motorists may, for a time, respond to higher prices by driving less, by forming car-pools, and by

determine the width of zones of acceptance by type of product and of purchaser and by location of product and prospect within this range, particularly in contrasting infrequent and discretionary purchases, including innovations, with recurrent purchases of necessities. As so often is true in the behavioral sciences, it is possible that the Weber-Fechner law continues to have predictive power within a certain range such as within zonal boundaries, but not outside it.

Source. Joseph M. Kamen and Robert J. Toman, "Psychophysics of prices," *Journal of Marketing Research,* 7:27–35.

Use of the Marketing Grid in Segmenting Prospects

The marketing grid helps one to visualize the process of market segmentation. Here is an example, of interest to a seller of fuel or furnaces, which begins with a three-way classification based on geography, age of installation, and type of fuel used.

Market for Heating Systems

	Existing Buildings					New Buildings			
	Oil	Gas	Electricity	Coal		Oil	Gas	Electricity	Coal
Zone I								//////	
Zone II									
Zone III									
Zone IV									
Zone V									

using public transportation as well as by buying cheaper gasoline. These new behaviors, if satisfactory, may become fixed habits, or the motorist may get used to the new, higher level of prices. Much needs to be done to

Into each cell goes the number of existing units or predictions for next year. Each of the cells can be broken down into a marketing grid of its own. The shaded portion above, for example, can be expanded thus:

Market for Electric Heating in Zone I: New Buildings

	Baseboard	Radiant	Hot-air Furnace	Hot Water	Heat Pump (Heating, Cooling)
Dwellings					
Apartment Houses					
Business Offices					
Public Buildings					

Sellers of fuel or furnaces can use such grids to find target markets and focus marketing efforts.

Source. Adapted from E. Jerome McCarthy, *Basic Marketing* (Homewood, Ill.: Richard D. Irwin, 1964).

Audience Grid Reflects Process of Persuasion

A similar grid can be used to identify the audiences for a seller's messages at any given point in time. However, since the messages are part of a *process* of persuasion, the numbers in each cell are expected to change over time, as shown on page 36.

Strategy A envisions equal effect at each stage of the process, indicating effectiveness with 50% of persons in each time-bound segment. Campaign strategy B, in contrast, ignores the hard core of prospects who don't know the product exists and focuses on prospects who know the brand, know its claims, or even accept them. Strategy B however, does not expect magazine advertising to trigger actual purchase; it may depend on another medium, such as direct mail, to do this. (Thus sales, sometimes considered the only valid measure of advertising success, obviously would not measure many of the effects which both campaigns seek.) The fourth column indicates what effects were obtained: an increase in purchases by only 5% of prospects, although this represents a 50% increase in sales.

Further study suggests that the ads must have been high in attention value, since the proportion of persons familiar with the brand's claim rose from 25% to 50%. They must have been low in credibility, however, since the proportion of prospects who *accepted* these claims did *not* increase. Furthermore, the campaign did move half of those who already preferred the brand into actually purchasing it.

By combining information from the two grids, marketing and audience, we can get results like the following hypothetical example for household oils. Research shows this competitive situation:

Use of Oils and Fats for Household Cooking

	In Salads	In Baking	In Frying
Total industry (gallons or dollars)	10,000,000	5,000,000	25,000,000
Share by Brand "A" oil	50%	50%	10%
Competing brands of oil	30	30	10
Competing products: lard, butter, oleo, etc.	20	20	80

Percent of Audience at Each Stage of Persuasion: Goals of two ad campaigns compared with before and after survey results

Letters represent stage of persuasion.
Percentages represent proportion of audience in a given stage.

- A: Don't know product
- B: Don't know brand
- C: Unaware of brand's claims
- D: Reject brand's claims
- E: Prefer Brand X
- F: Prefer our brand; haven't bought it
- G: Have bought our brand and will repeat

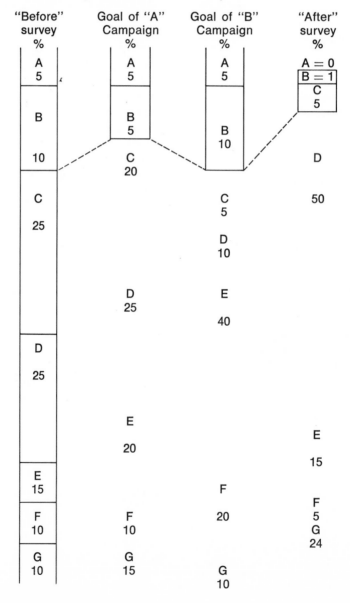

Consumer research has shown that housewives' principal demand in frying is for a substance that does not smoke, for smoke is the sign of a poor housekeeper and makes extra work for her as well. Laboratory studies have shown that Brand *A* can be heated several degrees higher than the competing fats before it begins to smoke. Consumer studies made before and after the campaign show these results:

Making Practical Use of Communications Research

The psychological laboratories in which sophomores respond to messages about social and political issues seem far removed from the world of selling and buying. The bits and pieces of knowledge that are discovered there seem remote from the decisions that a businessman must make. Here, however, is a hypothetical

Survey of Housewife Audience

	Before	After	Increase
Use some type of product for frying	25,000,000	25,000,000	
Associate Brand *A* with "no-smoke" claim	500,000	15,000,000	14,500,000
Have tried Brand *A* for frying	5,000,000	10,000,000	5,000,000
Use Brand *A* regularly for frying	2,500,000	5,000,000	2,500,000

Was the campaign a success? Not at first glance. The campaign cost $5 million which is just equal to the gross profit of two dollars each made on the additional 2,500,000 regular users. But the increase in regular users was only one of the results. Other people were moved part way toward product use; future campaigns may move them the rest of the way. The campaign also enabled the firm to add 2000 retail outlets. Some advertising was necessary to counter competitive inroads; its cost should be deducted from the 5-million-dollar figure.

example showing how two such findings *could* help the businessman. The findings: that chances of being exposed to a message and being influenced by it are affected by a prospect's education and by his attitude toward a product or brand.

(Figures in parentheses on page 38 are obtained by multiplying the two figures immediately preceding.)

We can now determine the *total effect* of the messages: 29.4% changed by one-sided and 29.7% by two-sided, or the *effect on sales:* 20.1% for one-sided and 16.5% by two-sided. But we can do something even more interesting. We can remove the actual purchasers from the population and send a second message; repeat the process and send a whole series of messages. Here is what happens with seven messages.

Source. Russell H. Colley, *Defining Advertising Goals for Measured Advertising Results* (New York: Association of National Advertisers, 1961).

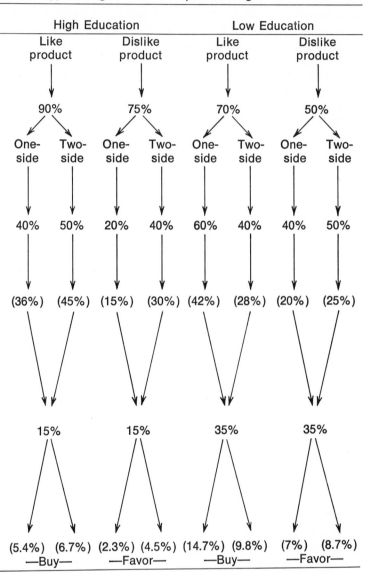

Exposed

Figures on "exposure" reflect two facts: exposure rises with education, is higher for messages one agrees with. Percentage in each group exposed:

Affected

These figures show that educated persons and those opposed to the message tend to prefer two-sided messages. Per cent in group affected:

Exposed and Affected

By multiplying the two percentages we find net effects of each message for each group:

Population

These percentages must now be applied to the actual population. (It is assumed that 30% have high education and that attitudes are equally divided pro and con the product.)

Effects of Message

Here are the actual per cents of the population favorably affected: those who liked the product buy it; those who didn't like it now do.

	High Education				Low Education			
	Like product		Dislike product		Like product		Dislike product	
	90%		75%		70%		50%	
	One-side	Two-side	One-side	Two-side	One-side	Two-side	One-side	Two-side
	40%	50%	20%	40%	60%	40%	40%	50%
	(36%)	(45%)	(15%)	(30%)	(42%)	(28%)	(20%)	(25%)
	15%		15%		35%		35%	
	(5.4%)	(6.7%)	(2.3%)	(4.5%)	(14.7%)	(9.8%)	(7%)	(8.7%)
	—Buy—		—Favor—		—Buy—		—Favor—	

Cumulative Proportion of Population Purchasing the Product

	Type of Message	
	One-sided	Two-sided
Message No.	%	%
1	20.1	16.5
2	35.8	31.8
3	48.3	45.1
4	58.1	56.2
5	66.0	65.3
6	72.4	72.7
7	77.5	78.7

These figures show that the one-sided message is best for up to six mailings; the two-sided message beyond that point. If you can *change* your message, this shows *when* the best time for that is.

Source. Raymond A. Bauer and Robert D. Buzzell, "Mating behavioral science and simulation," *Harvard Business Review*, 42: 5:116–24.

You Must Look at Both Sender and Receiver

Communications cannot be understood by looking at either sender or receiver in isolation. Who is responsible, for example, for bias in an exchange of messages?

The personal views of a reporter could influence the selections he makes from a complex event, but he is restrained by professional values which deplore such bias, as well as a possible counterbias of his audiences. What happens when, as he writes, a reporter anticipates audiences (editors, readers, news sources) whose biases are opposite to his own?

Journalism students in Wisconsin were assigned to one of three groups: a "stress" group read a report, supposedly written by the faculty, criticizing journalism students. Another group read a report praising such students; a control group received no report. Twenty-four, five-point adjective scales found that 85% of the stress group were upset, as compared with less than half of the other groups.

Each subject then wrote a news story, his efficiency being measured by time taken, words per minute, and a count of spelling, punctuation, grammatical errors, and copy changes. Messages produced by the stress group were less readable, in terms of Flesch scores. This group worked slower and made more errors. Writers under this specific stress also showed more bias in defending themselves against criticism.

Source. Bradley S. Greenberg and Percy H. Tannenbaum, "Communicator performance under cognitive stress," *Journalism Quarterly,* 39:169–78.

Bias can also originate in the receiver of a message. In an advertising course, 39 students were asked to read three pieces of copy: an ad for a sink, another ad for an Oriental airline, and a news release recommending stiffer academic standards. Then they were given 8 multiple-choice questions, each with three responses: a correct statement of fact from the copy, a statement minimizing it, and a third exaggerating it. Of the 311 scorable responses, 82% were correct. Of the 57 errors, 41 were exaggerations, 16 minimizations. Or, looking at the subjects, 9 made no errors, 4 matched every exaggeration with an error in the opposite direction, 6 tended to minimize, and 20 to exaggerate. To the extent that advertisers speak of "bigger" and "better," it would appear that they can count on the errors which readers make to be in a "favorable" direction.

Source. Max Wales, Glen Rarick and Hal Davis, "Message exaggeration by the receiver," *Journalism Quarterly,* 40:339–42.

Additional Research Readings

Market segments. Housewives' responses to 214 attitude items and 117 questions on brand and product use were factor analyzed to identify a four-segment market for drugs, and five-segment markets for food and for personal items. **Ruth Ziff, "Psychographics for market segmentation," Journal of Advertising Research, 11:1:3–9.**

Prices. When identical samples are given different prices, subjects will associate higher quality with higher price. But with prices concealed for spreads costing 13¢, 41¢, and 95¢, quality ratings reflected costs. **I. Robert Andrews and Enzo R. Valenzi, "The relationship between price and blind-rated quality for margarines and butters," Journal of Marketing Research,**

7:393–5. As prices rose, actual sales of stereos rose—and sales of toothpaste fell. **Zarrel V. Lambert, "Product perception: an important variable in price strategy," Journal of Marketing, 34:4:68–71.** When an oversupply of data makes choice difficult, buyers give up. Difficulty of choice was manipulated by asking 44 men to choose between four equally attractive or two attractive and two ugly neckties and to weigh either 15 separate attributes or a single factor of visual appeal. **Clyde Hendrick et al., "Decision time as a function of the number and complexity of equally attractive alternatives," Journal of Personality and Social Psychology, 8:313–8.**

● Depletion of inventory or appearance of a new product or brand on the market presents a problem-opportunity that initiates a decision process for the prospect if (a) he is dissatisfied with past purchases and (b) he thinks a better alternative may be available.

● Messages from a seller may evoke latent dissatisfaction, induce perceptions of real brand differences, cause premature inventory depletion through psychological obsolescence.

● Three conditions may create a problem-opportunity: entry of a new seller (brand) onto an old market, appearance of a new buyer, or simultaneous appearance of both new buyers and sellers as occurs in a major *product* innovation.

● New brands appear during the product life cycle, new buyers during the family life cycle. The regular, predictable appearance of new buyers presents the seller with multiple audiences; their position in the process of persuasion will influence seller messages.

● The degree of innovation represented by new products varies. Major innovations are hard to compare with previous products, affect the sale of many other products, and have far-reaching effects on both consumer behavior and society. Such innovations as radio and TV, being media for advertising messages, are of particular interest in marketing communications.

● The speed with which new products are accepted depends on attributes of both the product (relative advantage, degree of commitment, isolation, and ease of choice and use) and of the buyer (income, social status, youth). Word-of-mouth channels play an important role in innovation, reaching laggards and legitimizing adoption. They are important in ambiguous and risky situations.

Research Articles

Impulse Buying. Rate varies from 4 to 60% with type of store (Clover); and from 48 to 80% by type of product (Bogart).

Word-of-Mouth. May help speed purchase of a new product (Whyte) but may also slow down adoption of a new farm practice (Copp).

Demographics. Age increases purchase of some cosmetics, decreases sale of others (Woman's Day); stage of life cycle related to peak purchase rate varies by product (Katona).

Chapter 2 How Decision Making Begins: Identifying Problems and Opportunities

The problem-opportunity that triggers decision making by a buyer may originate in seller behavior, in the form of the marketing of a new product, or in buyer behavior, as when he uses up present supplies.

Neither the appearance of a new product nor the depletion of inventory by themselves need initiate buyer decision making, however, if the buyer is satisfied with his previous purchases. A consumer will "automatically" buy his preferred brand or a retailer's computer program reorder from an old supplier. In short, *dissatisfaction* with the old product must also be present if decision making is to occur. Such dissatisfaction may arise from a faulty product, from consumer boredom with the old item, or from a host of accidental factors beyond the control of any seller. It may also be deliberately created by a seller—although much more often by the claims he makes for his own brand rather than by any derogation of the buyer's present brand.

The more frequently a product is purchased, the *more* opportunities there are for brand switching, but the *less* likely that brand switching will actually occur. Decision making is too costly a process to be engaged in frequently. If milk must be purchased on every trip to the supermarket, then a preferred brand is likely to be picked after a brief period of trial and comparison; repetition will create a strong habit that resists competitors' efforts. (Home delivery, of course, establishes even stronger brand preferences by increasing the "costs" of brand switching.)

Thus, true decision making tends to occur either when strong brand preferences are lacking (which is likely when purchases are made too infrequently for habits to form) or when a buyer becomes dissatisfied with the brand he has bought in the past.

Dissatisfaction may not be perceived, even when cause for it exists; it may be induced, even when objective causes are absent. Six repair bills in one month are more likely to evoke latent dissatisfaction with a car or refrigerator than the same number of breakdowns spread over a longer period. A breakdown on the eve of a trip or a party will produce more intense dissatisfaction than if the mishap occurred in more relaxed times. Moreover, dissatisfaction by itself is not enough to evoke decision making. The buyer must also perceive that some brands are more unsatisfactory than others, that there are alternatives to choose from. In a supermarket that stocks 10,000 different items, choice appears possible—if difficult. On the other hand, suburban commuters in many major cities today have no alternative to the automobile.

Seller Messages

A seller's messages must perform two tasks. First, they must help evoke latent dissatisfaction by offering new solutions to problems a buyer may not have realized he had, such as "ho-hum breath" or "Monday morning blahs." Second, they must persuade the buyer that he does have real alternatives that are worth the effort of comparing. An actively dissatisfied consumer will seek out information about products and brands that are better than those he has been using, but no buyer can wait for this to happen. The buyer must reach prospects with a promise of better performance, extra features, lower price, or a more convenient source of supply, before their present supplies give out, for the time spent in seeking a solution may be very brief. It may, indeed, occur wholly within the head of the prospect, as he reviews messages already stored in his memory.

This means that the seller must prepare messages that grab the attention of a prospect who is, at the moment, not very much interested in the brand or product being advertised. It means he must put those messages into media that will transmit them to prospects whose interests lie elsewhere. It often means he must supplement his messages with other measures, such as samples, which get a buyer to try a new brand even though he seems satisfied with his old one. It also means he may seek to create psychological obsolescence, through annual model changes, well before inventory is really exhausted, and that he may have to overcome a Puritan-bred reluctance to throw away a still usable product by accepting it as a trade-in on a new model.

Sellers' messages are difficult to devise, since they reach an audience whose members vary remarkably in the stage of their inventories and brand satisfaction. Sometimes, however, there are exceptions. For some products, felt needs, exhausted inventories, dissatisfaction and purchase hit a large number of prospects at the same time. Hot weather will make a lot of people aware of faulty air conditioners; rainy weather will remind them of leaky roofs, and cold weather of inadequate heating facilities. Gifts must be bought at Christmas, tennis shoes when school is out, wedding gowns in June. Thus, sellers of seasonal products can predict when interest in such messages will be at its peak. (This is not to say, however, that such messages will appear only at such periods of peak interest. If advertising, backed up by lower off-season prices, can reduce peaks and valleys of the sales curve, a seller may realize considerable savings in production, inventory, and selling costs. Such messages must be carefully prepared, however, for an audience that is really not very interested.)

We have suggested that neither depletion of inventory nor appearance of a new prod-uct on the market will constitute a problem-opportunity, and so initiate a decision process, unless the buyer is dissatisfied with his previous purchase and perceives that a better brand is available. We have also suggested that messages can stimulate dissatisfaction, create premature depletion of inventory through psychological obsolescence, and persuade buyers that real differences exist among competing brands. Indeed, they must do so, often at a time when buyer interest in the product involved is at a low ebb.

These functions exist for messages in a market where buyers and sellers never change. But buyers and sellers *do* change —and when they do, messages have additional functions to perform.

A new seller may appear, either in the form of a newly organized firm or an old firm confronting a new market segment, one with which it has had no previous experience. A new buyer may appear in the form of newlyweds, a college freshman, a girl holding her first full-time job, or an heir about to buy his first share of stock. Or both buyer and seller may be new, as happens when such a radical innovation as the automobile or television comes onto the market.

New Seller, Old Buyers

Before entering an old market, a new seller can observe the behavior of his potential competition, knowing that he must break up buyers' existing brand preferences or find a group of prospects highly dissatisfied with present brands. The new seller may stress differences in form or function of his brand. He may put it on sale at a more convenient outlet or he may use hitherto-neglected media to reach prospects who are poorly informed by media that present sellers are using. He may offer permanent price concessions to bring new marginal prospects into the market or offer temporary price cuts to induce prospects who can afford present brands to give his brand a trial. (Indeed, he should decide, before entering the market, what proportion of his customers are to come from present users, and which brands are most vulnerable, and how many customers will represent first-time users.)

New sellers are likely to be attracted to an old market in which there is a wide margin between costs and revenues. Such a margin is most likely to exist during the second or growth stage of the four-stage *product life cycle*.

1. *Introduction.* By definition, competition is lacking. The product is an unsought good; the prospect must be told how and when to use it. Messages to retailers are important and so are such *sales promotion* techniques as free samples and cents-off coupons.
2. *Growth.* Profits tend to be highest at this stage. The seller may set his price high to "skim the cream" from high-income buyers, or he may set it low to discourage competitors. At this stage, rival sellers experiment with variations in price and product, and messages exploit real brand differences.
3. *Maturity.* Now brand differences disappear, as buyers indicate which prices and product features they prefer. Profit margins narrow. Messages emphasizing brand differences become more difficult to create but play a larger part in inducing purchase.
4. *Decline.* Sales themselves decline, as still newer products appear. The seller may try to start a new life cycle by changing the product or finding new uses and users for it, or he may take it off the market.

Two factors limit the usefulness of this product life-cycle concept. One is the great variability in the duration of the process: hula hoops may complete the cycle in 90 days, whereas automobiles may take 90 years—or more. The other factor is the arbitrary nature of the distinction between an old product and a new one. The record player can be regarded as a single product that suffered a temporary eclipse when radio appeared, but regained lost ground by adding high fidelity and stereophonic sound, or hi-fi and stereophonic sets may be seen as a new product.

If a new seller enters the market during the maturity stage, he may find that he has little freedom as regards price, place, and product. His success may depend on his ingenuity in devising new messages or in finding media not already exploited. For sellers as a whole, a Finnish economist[1] suggests that product quality is most important during the first stage of the cycle, and price is most important during maturity. Advertising is said to be crucial during the growth stage and again during the period of decline when messages that suggest new uses for old products are particularly effective.

New Buyers, Old Sellers

New buyers may enter the market for many reasons. If a man's income rises sharply, he may start shopping for an expensive car or a boat. A drop in income, for an individual, for a class (such as men reaching retirement age), or for society at large (as in a depression) will shift buyers from the caviar to the oatmeal market.

However, natural processes of birth, aging, and death account for the greatest influx of new buyers. For this reason, the entry of new buyers into the market is far more predictable than is the entry of new sellers. This predictability has been captured in the concept of the *family life cycle*,[2] which begins with a single individual, who marries; continues as children appear to take the family through the preschool, school, and college phases of the cycle, and ends as children leave home, returning the family to husband and wife and then, with the death of one spouse, back where it began, with a single individual.

Family needs and family resources vary at each stage of the cycle, and these variations affect buying behavior. Also affected by the cycle are the nature and locus of family decision making. As newlyweds, husband and wife make many buying decisions jointly—to express affection in joint endeavor, because each is learning the buying skills of the other, or because limited resources make each decision important. In time, however, husband and wife tend to specialize and fewer decisions are made jointly. Arrival of children not only increases the number and variety of products purchased and strains resources but also adds new members to the decision-making and decision-influencing set.

Stages of Persuasion

In communications, the continuous flow of new buyers into the market has great significance, since it means that the seller's audience will always contain persons varying widely in knowledge and preferences. Some are closer to being persuaded than others, as shown in Table 2.1, which pictures on the left the progress of a single individual through the stages of persuasion and, on the right, what a field survey of the entire market might show at a given point in time. The product involved is disposable diapers.

The process of persuasion is of great importance in marketing communications, since media must be selected and messages created with due regard for the stage in which one's audience is found. Thus, it pays to emphasize the process again, by presenting it in the form of a decision tree.

The entry of new buyers has two important implications for marketing communications. Expressed in terms of the family life cycle, it suggests that no individual, however "loyal" to a given seller, can be taken for granted; his needs and resources change and his part in decision making varies over time. Expressed in terms of stages of persuasion, it suggests that every seller must reach multiple audiences with very different kinds of messages at any given point in time.

TABLE 2.1

Individual (Time of Stage)	Stages of Persuasion	Aggregate (Proportion of Prospects, Percent)
Engaged or newlywed	Does not know product exists	10
Pregnant wife reads Spock	Knows of product; doesn't know brands	5
Expectant father reads *Parents* magazine	Aware of brand, doesn't know attributes it claims	25
Both read ad for brand	Aware of claims, but doesn't accept them	25
Parents talk to baby store salesman	Accept claims but prefer those of rival brand	15
Baby due in three months	Prefer brand but have yet to purchase it	10
Baby three weeks old	Have bought and used brand; plan to repurchase	10

TABLE 2.2 A Stages-of-Persuasion "Decision Tree"

Knows of product	Doesn't know of product
Wants product	Doesn't want product
Knows of brand	Doesn't know of brand
Knows claims of brand	Doesn't know claims of brand
Rejects claims	Accepts claims
Prefers Brand X	Prefers our brand
Hasn't bought our brand	Has bought our brand
Dissatisfied: won't buy our brand again	Satisfied: will repeat purchase
No new rival to our brand appears	New rival appears or old rival makes new claim

New Buyers and New Sellers

More complex than either of the situations just examined is the entry of new buyers *and* new sellers, as occurs with a *major product innovation*. Now there are no competitors whose behavior the seller can study and no friends whose advice the buyer can seek. Indeed, the buyer may be at a loss as to what old products to compare the new product with or what criteria to use in judging brands.

Not all innovations pose such problems, of course. One text[3] suggests that least disruption is caused by such novelties as the annual model changes in automobiles, or the addition of fluoride to toothpaste and menthol to cigarettes. Electric toothbrushes and touch-tone telephones represent somewhat greater change, but real disturbance in the market follows major inventions such as television and the computer.

Such major innovations possess four characteristics. First, they combine functions performed by products that seem to have little in common, making comparisons with existing products difficult. Second, they tend to have widespread, unforeseen effects on society in general. Third, they affect a great many other products, decreasing the sales of some and increasing the sales of others. Fourth, they affect a wide range of user behavior, often forcing a buyer to learn new skills before he can use the product, and frequently teaching him new tastes and preferences.

Radio as an Innovation

Radio represents such an innovation, one that is of peculiar interest in marketing communications. Its technological development and its first run-through of the product life cycle each took about 24 years. Invention of two tubes, the diode rectifier and triode amplifier, in 1904 and 1906, made radio feasible; military uses in World War I made it marketable. Radio's life as an advertising medium began in 1920 with the first broadcast of music and speech from a Pittsburgh station; this phase ended in 1945 when television began taking over radio's function as a mass audience medium.

Although users did not have to learn special skills to listen to radio, they found it had far-reaching, unexpected, even unsuspected effects on their behavior. Mealtimes changed to fit radio schedules; telephones went unanswered and social activity ceased during the height of Amos and Andy's popularity. For the first time, a nationwide, mass audience came into existence. To many listeners, Ma Perkins became more real than their city's mayor, a more intimate acquaintance than the neighbor three doors distant. Sharing the same experience at the same time, millions of persons began to think, feel, and even act alike. And, of course, other products felt the impact. Phonograph makers sought to increase fidelity and tried to match the continuous, effortless flow of radio sound by introducing record changers and the long-playing record. They sought new uses for phonographs, in the form of dictating machines, and new channels of distribution, such as the jukebox, for records.

Radio's own life cycle terminated abruptly, by a device that had been in the making since 1873. With the end of World War II in 1945, TV came onto the market, taking over radio's function as mass entertainer, and darkening movie houses throughout the nation. They, in turn, were forced to innovate—the movies with wide screens and drive-in theaters, radio with FM and drastic changes in programming to suit the new audiences that TV had forced radio to find.

As TV took over the mass entertainment-seeking audience, both radio and magazines began assembling specialized audiences for the seller, emphasizing *who* they reached rather than *how many*. Magazines began to pinpoint markets geographically through regional editions and to focus on special-interest groups, often based on job or leisure-time interests. Radio became a local medium, emphasizing spot announcements and station-by-station geographical coverage to match the seller's patterns of physical distribution. New kinds of programming were developed to attract lovers of popular, rhythm-and-blues, country, or classical music and persons who liked to hear themselves and others talk. With the family now clustered around TV, radio moved out of the living room to the bedroom or kitchen, car or beach. Usually listeners had only half an ear for radio, whether they were husbands driving to work, housewives at their chores, or teenagers studying math. This, in turn, affected the design of commercial messages. Lowered listener attention meant more repetition was necessary in messages; commercials had to attract and hold attention in the face of constant competition from other stimuli. With the appearance of cable TV in the 1970's, offering some 30 programs—and as many audiences—to a single community, it appeared that perhaps the role of TV, in providing a mass audience to the advertiser, was on the way out, after a quarter-century.

Short as the *product* life cycle has become—25 years for radio, 20 years for black-and-white TV—the *brand* life cycle has become even shorter. Within two years after General Electric introduced its electric toothbrush, for example, 52 competitors had entered the market.[4] This means that decisions as to media and messages can no longer wait for engineers to perfect a product; they often must be made while the product is still on the drawing boards. (In the cosmetics industry, for example, where chemistry is simple and beauty lies primarily in the eye of the beholder, messages may be prepared first and a product then tailored to fit them.) Security becomes a problem; when new products can be duplicated so speedily, test marketing becomes risky. Lacking test market feedback, sales and advertising efforts in turn become more risky. Risk, indeed, is the name of the innovation game; one study found that of every 58 new ideas, only two reach the market and only one succeeds.[5]

Diffusion of Innovations

The high rate of failure makes research of any new product more necessary; the need for speed and for security often makes field tests virtually impossible. As a result, sellers search for basic principles concerning buyer acceptance of innovations and their diffusion through the population has intensified.

Unfortunately, most studies of innovation have dealt with buyers (farmers) or products (drugs) that are not representative of the consumer market in general. The farmer is a producer and, as such, operates under different constraints, and employs different search procedures and different criteria of selection than the consumer; his decisions probably involve more time and deliberation. He differs from other producers (and resembles the consumer) mainly in being an individual rather than an organization. As for drugs, buying decisions are made when doctors write prescriptions, although it is the patient who buys and uses the product.

So long as he keeps these differences in mind, the seller may find it useful to look at a review of some 2500 studies[6] of innovation, most involving attempts to persuade farmers to adopt such new practices as contour plowing and hybrid corn. These studies have sought to explain differences in the extent and speed with which new farm practices and products spread by looking at attributes of the practice or product itself and at attributes of the adopter.

Product Attributes

Four product attributes appear to affect the rate of acceptance.

1. *Relative advantage.* The greater the superiority of a new practice over the old, the more quickly it will be adopted. This is particularly true if the advantage is easy to see, as when new and old types of corn are planted in plots side by side at a crossroads.
2. *Degree of commitment.* If a practice can be adopted piecemeal and abandoned easily if it doesn't work, farmers will be readier to try it out. If the cost is high relative to buyer income or in

terms of the number and desirability of other products that must be foregone, acceptance will be slower. Thus, farmers were slow to terrace fields in preventing erosion, because a return to the former system of plowing parallel to the boundaries of a rectangular field would have been difficult. Trial use of a new product without charge will demonstrate its value to the buyer with a minimum of risk and so speed acceptance.

3. *Isolation.* If a new practice fits into an existing process or even a system of values, it will be accepted more readily. Farmers whose reputation rested on their ability to plow a straight row were reluctant to adopt contour plowing, particularly if they had come to regard gullies as inevitable a part of nature as drought and flood. Farmers who valued self-sufficiency balked at adopting hybrid corn, since this would require them to buy new seed each year from commercial growers rather than saving the best of their own crop. (In similar fashion, many firms prefer to finance expansion out of retained profits rather than lose independence by going into the stock and bond markets for funds.) A new practice may also run into opposition because of the social system, as when a man fears what his friends will say. (At later stages, the same fears may cause him to adopt a new practice rather than appear different from his neighbors.)
4. *Ease of selection and use.* If an innovation requires the buyer to develop new skills—such as piloting an airplane, an automobile, or a pair of water skis—this may retard acceptance. (This is why some sellers offer free lessons to purchasers and lobbyists promote driver education in the schools.) A purchase that is accompanied by a large number of other buying decisions will also tend to be put off; some persons hesitate to buy a new home because it means they

must also choose, and pay for, furniture, rugs, drapes, and appliances.

Scholars suggest four degrees of complexity[7] in a new practice, with adoption slowing down as complexity rises.

1. *Changes in materials or equipment,* such as adoption of a new variety of seed, that do not require the adopter to learn new skills. These are adopted most readily.

2. *Changes in technique,* such as a new kind of crop rotation, that may require new skills but use old equipment.

3. *Changes requiring both new skills and equipment.* Contour plowing involved relocation of fences, alternation of crops, sodded waterways, and curved rather than straight plowing.

4. *Changes in the total enterprise,* such as a shift from growing crops to raising livestock.

Buyer Attributes

In looking for ways in which buyer characteristics affect adoption, one is concerned with the point in time of adoption. Adopters are commonly grouped into five classes, ranging from the innovators, who are the first to accept a new practice, to the laggards, who are the last to adopt it.

In Table 2.3, all persons who fall within one standard deviation above or below the mean time of adoption are arbitrarily assigned to the majority—early or late—the percentages being those of the normal curve. One then looks at the persons in each class to see if there is greater similarity within classes than between them. Usually there is. Innovators, for example, often have low status and little influence in their community—in part, perhaps, because they are too quick to abandon old ways and too subject to outside influences. A new practice begins to spread only after higher status adopters observe and legitimatize the innovator's experiment with it.

Early adopters are able and willing to take risks. Often they bypass a local change agent, such as the county extension worker or local dealer, and go directly to an agricultural college or the manufacturer. Late adopters, in contrast, have smaller farms and tend to be elderly; they are vulnerable to risk and so hesitate to try new ideas. Since they may distrust the county agent and tend not to belong to organizations, late adopters are more influenced by friends and relatives.

By reducing the risk associated with a new practice, three factors—youth, wealth, and prestige—tend to speed its spread. Young men tend to adopt sooner. Habits of the older farmer are fixed more firmly; he is often more interested in short-run security than in long-run profits that he won't be around to enjoy anyway. Economic security, as indicated by a high income, a large farm, and being an owner rather than a renter, encourages experimentation. High prestige protects a farmer from the risk of ridicule that might follow failure. Although

TABLE 2.3[8]

The Speed With Which a Prospect Passes Through These: *Stages of Adoption*	Determines Which Audience or Market Segment He Is Assigned to: *Class of Prospect*	And Certain Media Tend to Dominate Each Stage: *Dominant Medium*
Awareness	Innovator (2.5%)	Print: magazines, newspapers
Interest	Early adopter (13.5%)	
Evaluation	Early majority (34%)	Other farmers
Trial	Late majority (34%)	Government experts
Adoption	Laggards (16%)	

it seems plausible that years of education should show a positive correlation with speed of acceptance, this relationship disappears if age and income are held constant. (That is, the apparent effects of education are a result of the fact that better education is associated with youth and wealth; education is an intervening rather than a causal variable.)

Surveys of consumer buying made at the University of Michigan Survey Research Center[9] tend to support the farm studies. Innovations in consumer durables, such as automobiles and appliances, are adopted first by young, educated persons who expect their incomes, now in the middle range, to rise in the future.

Even the best combination of variables, however, seems to leave about 50% of the variance in adoption scores unexplained. This was the result, for example, when scholars attempted to predict rate of adoption for Kansas beef producers on the basis of age, education, group membership, gross income, "mental flexibility," and "farm professionalism." Accidental factors affect adoption rates. Use of grass silage spreads more rapidly when drought hits an area and other silage crops fail; a sick wife, or children entering a college may deny the farmer the resources needed to adopt a new practice.

Word-of-Mouth: A Key Channel

Different kinds of messages and different kinds of channels are required at each stage of the adoption process and with each type of adopter; some of these were suggested in Table 2.2. One channel appears to play a vital role in the process, however, and that is word-of-mouth.

Word-of-mouth messages have their strongest impact midway in the process, where innovations are being evaluated, and in risky situations, when the credibility of one's informant becomes crucial. The skeptical, reluctant, late adopter needs the reassurance of word-of-mouth messages from neighbors who have personal experience with the innovation before he will move.

The most effective sources of word-of-mouth messages are the influentials, men with a wide variety of contacts, who belong to and are active in many organizations, both local and nonlocal. This is true not only of farm practices, but of acceptance of new drugs by the medical profession. A check of druggists' records has revealed that the most influential sources are physicians who attend medical conventions and read research journals and pass on what they learn there to their colleagues.[10] (Physicians who seldom see a colleague are necessarily dependent upon drug salesmen for such news.)

Personal influence has most impact in uncertain and ambiguous situations (such as the first six months after a drug is introduced), when information about it is sparse, or when it is recommended for diseases whose physiology and treatment is not well understood. A colleague's recommendation is effective in high-risk situations, such as severe illnesses or in using drugs with dangerous side effects. (The manufacturer's reputation—*company image*—is also important in situations of high risk.[11])

In sum, there are four characteristics associated with a major innovation, which involves the entry of both new buyers and new sellers into a market. Some authorities would define a major innovation as one possessing these characteristics. Others prefer to define the innovation independently, and then determine the extent to which it possesses these characteristics. Whichever choice the reader prefers, the four characteristics are given below.

1. It initiates a decision-making process.
2. It affects the sales of a wide variety of

other products, often stimulating their sellers to laboratory and consumer research.

3. Its adoption is accompanied by extensive use of word-of-mouth channels.
4. The rate of adoption is affected by the extent to which a prospect's associates encourage or discourage purchase and use.

The problem-opportunity that triggers a decision process will arise when a buyer is bothered by a discrepancy between what he has and what he would like to have, and sees an alternative that will reduce this discrepancy. The seller's messages may try to influence perceptions of the actual, the ideal, and the alternative. A new buyer must be told what brands are available in the market; an old buyer must be persuaded that the offering of a new seller is superior to present brands. When both buyers and sellers are new to the market, as happens with a major product innovation, considerable interaction may be necessary for sellers to discover what buyers want, and for buyers to discover what alternatives are available and by what criteria they are to be judged. In each instance, old buyers need to be told why they should switch brands; new buyers may need to be told why they should use the product itself, as well as why they should choose a particular brand.

Thought, Talk, and Action

1. Contrast the alternatives that face a new buyer and a new seller—the decisions each must make and the kinds and sources of information used. When either buyer or seller knows his counterpart is also new, as in the instance of a product innovation, how does this affect his perception of risk? of bargaining equality?
2. What factors in product and what factors in prospect speed up and slow down the purchasing decision, at each of its stages?
3. Cable television makes possible 30 different programs in a single community. Discuss how it may affect selling, buying, and program content. Do you see any similarity to the edict that forced TV set-makers to make all sets receive UHF as well as VHF?

Notes

Chapter 2

1. Gosta Mickwitz, Marketing and competition (Helsingfors, Finland: Centraltrycheriet, 1959). Cited in Philip Kotler, Marketing management (New York: Prentice-Hall, 1967), pp. 281–3.
2. J. G. Lansing and L. Kish, "Family life cycle as an independent variable," American Sociological Review, 22:512–19.
3. James F. Engel, David T. Kollat, and Roger D. Blackwell, Consumer behavior (New York: Holt, Rinehart and Winston, 1968), p. 546.
4. Kotler (Reference No. 1), p. 315.
5. Ibid.
6. Everett Rogers, Diffusion of innovations (New York: The Free Press, 1962).

7. Herbert F. Lionberger, Adoption of new ideas and practices (Ames, Iowa: Iowa State University Press, 1960).
8. *Ibid.*, pp. 36–41.
9. Analysis of these surveys appears in George Katona, The powerful consumer (New York: McGraw-Hill Book Co., 1960).
10. Herbert Menzel and Elihu Katz, "Social relations and innovation in the medical profession: The epidemiology of a new drug," Public Opinion Quarterly, 19:337–52.
11. Donald F. Cox, Risk taking and information handling in consumer behavior (Boston: Graduate School of Business Administration, Harvard University, 1967), pp. 152–71 and 524–40.

Do People Really Ponder Their Purchases?

How often do prospects go through a real process of decision making before buying and how often is their purchase the result of an impulse? The question isn't easy to answer, as these two examples illustrate.

In the winter of 1948 a gas shortage forced retail firms in three Texas towns to close down for a day and then, a week later, for another day. Clover received sales data for retail stores for the two weeks in which stores were closed, the week between closings, and a week before and after the gas shortage.

Sales not "made up" in the week following one-day closing, he said, must represent impulse buying.

One-day closing represented a loss of 16% of the normal sales week. In 154 stores in the three towns, sales dropped 18% in the first emergency week, were about half of 1% below base during the next week, dropped 14% in the third week (which had another one-day closing), and then were 3.6% below base in the final week studied. He estimated that the range of impulse buying, as a percentage of total sales, ranged from 4% in furniture stores to 60% in variety stores. Among 19 types of retail outlet, he found four different kinds of impulse-buying situations:*

Source. Vernon T. Clover, "Relative importance of impulse buying in retail stores," *Journal of Marketing,* 15:1:66–70.

* Data reprinted from the *Journal of Marketing,* national quarterly publication of the American Marketing Association.

Change From Base Period During:

	First "Holiday" Week %	Inter- vening Week %	Second "Holiday" Week %	Final Week %	Manager's Estimate of % of Impulse Sales
Book store (strong impulse)	−32	+2	−20	+4	15
Variety store (medium impulse)	−16	+1	−16	−8	60
Grocery store (weak impulse)	−15	—	−10	−7	26
Department store (low impulse)	−25	+20	−12	+21	14

Another attempt to determine the amount of purchases made on impulse involved interviews with 10,000 women in five cities. A week after they were asked their buying intentions concerning nonfood products, they were reinterviewed to see how many intentions had been realized.

At first glance, it appeared as if they had done what they said they intended to do: 7% said they wanted a dress and, a week later, 5% had actually shopped for one; 3% said they intended to buy a dress, and a week later, 3% had actually done so. However, analysis revealed that nearly two-thirds of the dresses sold were bought by women who had *not* mentioned such intentions in the first interview. The same was true of costly items like appliances—three-fourths of these purchases had not been anticipated a week earlier.

Is a week's delay too long or too short a time for accurate anticipations? *Too long?* Grocery customers—7147 of them in 345 supermarkets—were asked what they intended to buy as they entered the store and then checked again as they left it. Here are the percentages of "unplanned" purchases:

48% detergents	80% toys
82% magazines	75% berries
74% soft goods	50% fish

Too short? Two-thirds of automobiles sold are bought by people who had indicated no such intention a year earlier.

In the study involving two interviews a week apart, many of the intentions-to-buy had actually disappeared a week later: 28% of those for washing machines, 45% of those for raincoats.

Such studies as these often leave a doubt as to whether the difference in intentions and accomplishment is the result of a "real" change in intentions or an overly casual response to the interviewer's questions. This study, however, also suggested another cause: some types of retail outlets and some individual stores were associated with a higher rate of fulfilled intentions than others. Were it possible to assign shoppers to stores at random, we could determine whether the store deserves credit or whether determined customers were more likely to choose certain types of stores.

Source. Leo Bogart, *Strategy in Advertising* (New York: Harcourt, Brace & World, Inc., 1967).

Neighbors' Purchase May Initiate the Decision Process

Keeping-up-with-the-Joneses is a familiar phenomenon in American life. A neighbor's purchase of an innovation alerts many people to a new *opportunity*, which becomes a *problem* when his children began asking, *why can't we have a widget, too?* Meanwhile, *Fortune* suggests, many sellers would do well to focus sales efforts on neighbors of early buyers.

Fortune magazine sent a research crew into Philadelphia in 1954 to count the number of air conditioning units in house windows and to question owners, asking when they bought the units, whether a friend had recommended them, what other appliances they owned, and how long they had lived on the block.

At this time, air conditioners were about to move out of the luxury class. Nationally, about 3% of all homes had them. In Philadelphia, however, of 5000 houses counted, in the first part of the study, 20% had one conditioner and 8% had two.

Young people, anticipating rising incomes, apparently were the best prospects for other appliances, too:

Appliances Owned	Air-conditioning Innovators %	U.S. Average %
Washer	84	78
Dryer	42	5
Dishwasher	11	3

Ownership was not spread evenly among even this income and age group; in one block, 6% of the homes had conditioners and in another block 35% had them. One side of the street might have six times the ownership of the other side. Air conditioners appeared to spread, like a disease, from one house to those on each side, and to those across the alley. Why? Because neighbors' children play and mothers gossip, learning about new products and brands, and developing group norms that say when a person *may* buy an air conditioner, without it being considered "putting on airs" and when he *must* buy one if he is not to be considered out of step.

Source. William H. Whyte, Jr., "The web of word of mouth," *Fortune,* 50:5, 140–3, 204–12.

On the Other Hand, Neighbors May *Delay* Response to Innovation

Sometimes, an individual hesitates to adopt an innovation he can well afford because he fears the disapproval of his neighbors, who may not be able to afford it or who may have no interest in it.

Thus, despite all of the messages that a seller may transmit via salesmen and the media to alert buyers to a new opportunity, he may find that word-of-mouth channels are frustrating his efforts.

Interviewers in Pennsylvania quizzed 175 dairy farmers about their acceptance of three innovations: control of spittle bugs, use of grass silage, and artificial drying of hay. Each farmer was given five points for each practice he had adopted, with fewer points for reporting awareness of or interest in the practice. In five cases out of six, mean scores were lowest for those who had talked to their peers:

	Cited Peers	Did Not Cite Peers
Awareness of		
Spittle bug control	2.3	3.4
Grass silage	3.2	3.7
Hay dryer	1.2	2.2
Interest in		
Spittle bug control	3.8	4.3
Grass silage	3.9	4.5
Hay dryer	3.6	3.3

Source. James H. Copp, Maurice L. Sill, and Emory J. Brown, "The function of information sources in the farm practice adoption process," *Rural Sociology,* 23:146–57.

Age Ends Some Needs, Creates Others

The makers of pablum and diapers may be hard put to forecast their market 10 years in advance, thanks to the complexities of affluence, the pill, and concern about population explosions. But once a baby is born and the aging process takes over, changes in needs become fairly predictable. At right: an example of how age affects items within the product class of cosmetics.

Source. Reprinted from *Woman's Day Reports on Toiletries,* Vol. 2 (New York: Fawcett Publications, Inc., 1963).

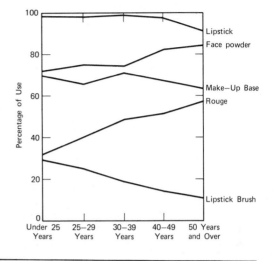

Needs Vary With the Life Cycle

With age comes marriage and with marriage children so that each stage in the family life cycle brings new needs. Needs for consumer durables often reach a peak at the very time that ability to meet them is lowest, so that the stage of household formation involves decision making of the most careful kind.

Here is a table, using data taken from the 1956 Survey of Consumer Finances, showing how life cycle affects purchase of key durable goods.

Stage in Life Cycle	Percentage of Households in This Stage	Relation Between % of Purchases and % of Population[a]				Percentages of Purchases Made on Installment Plan
		New Cars	Used Cars	Stoves	Television Sets	
Head below 45						
Unmarried	10	60	90	30	50	40
Md., no children	8	100	137	212	137	56
Md., children	35	126	140	117	134	65
Head over 45						
Md., children	12	100	116	125	100	53
Md., no children in home	21	109	47	95	85	27
Widow, widower	14	36	42	29	57	16

([a] A figure of 100% means that this group's share of purchases was equal to its proportion in the population. A figure of 60% means it bought only 60% as much as one would expect in terms of its share of the population. A figure of 126 means it bought 26% *more* than one would expect.)

Unmarried persons under 45 did *less* than their share of buying of new cars. This group accounted for 10% of the population but bought only 6% of new cars sold in 1956 (6%/10% equals 60%). Married persons with children, however, bought 26% *more* new cars than one would expect on the basis of their share of the household studied.

Source. Data from page 166 of The powerful consumer by George Katona. Copyright, 1960, McGraw-Hill Book Company. Used by permission.

Additional Research Readings

Life cycle. Reanalysis of interviews with 1000 Cleveland housewives suggests that rising incomes, education, and leisure time have swamped any differences in purchases once associated with life cycle or social class. **Stuart U. Rich and Subhash C. Jain, "Social class and life cycle as predictors of shopping behavior," Journal of Marketing Research, 5:41–9.**

Age. An individual's attitudes and behavior may relate to the aging processes, whether the year is 1812 or 1984. Or age may serve as a cue to the period in history during which he is living. The former (life-cycle) effect has been found to affect voting turnout; the latter (generation) effect influences attitudes toward foreign policy and school aid. **William R. Klecka, "The use of political generations in studying political change," Public Opinion Quarterly, 34:463–4.**

Chapter 3 Synopsis

● Goals are defined at the beginning of the decision process and frequently redefined at several subsequent stages. At the end of the process, a discrepancy between goals sought and goals attained may lead to redefining of goals sought, renewal of the decision process, or both.

● Goals are always multiple, because each individual has several goals to be satisfied in any activity and because most decisions involve more than one person. Each role and status must have its own subgoal specified in the firm's effort to reach its goals. Intermediate goals are needed to measure progress through time toward an "ultimate" goal, and to permit corrective action to be taken when necessary.

● Goals sought need to be specific, measurable, and clearly related to antecedent "causes" if they are to be used to guide the decision process and measure its efficiency and success. The goal of *profit maximization* does not appear to satisfy these conditions, either in theory or in practice. However, profit and probability do play a part in definition of a firm's goals; combined, they lead to an estimate of average anticipated value.

● The composite goals of both firm and family can be approximated if one knows the goals of individuals participating in the decision, their power to influence that decision, the probability that they will exercise such power, and the means available through which power is exerted and individual goals are reconciled.

● There are often alternative ways of measuring goals attained which are indices rather than direct measures of goals sought. Choice of a measure or index depends both on the ease of administering it and the closeness of its relationship to the "true" goal sought.

Research Articles

Field Experiment.   Advertising schedule for new product guided by market tests (Becknell).

Family Decisions.   Culture affects influence of husband and wife in family decisions (Strodtbeck); husband's influence varies with product purchased (Kenkel).

Response Differences.   Individuals differ in response to window display (Hepner); cultures differ in functions assigned to common objects (Dennis); and in meanings attached to individuals (Triandis).

Social Class.   Children's responses to prize offer vary with father's job (Douvan).

Goals Differ.   Seller and buyer disagree on desirable attributes of gift (Blum).

Chapter 3 Goals Sought and Goals Achieved

Every decision-making process begins with a purpose, some goal to be achieved. Every decision-making process ends with an effect, some goal that has been achieved.

If the two do not coincide—if goal sought and goal attained are too distant from one another—their discrepancy creates a problem which, in turn, initiates a new decision-making process. Simply put, this problem consists of the question: *Should our goal be redefined or should we keep our goal as it was set originally and seek new ways to reach it?*

The buyer's or the seller's goal may be redefined several times during the decision-making process, as suggested in Figure 3.1. A study of constraints may suggest that the goal as set is not likely to be attained. This raises the question: *Can we relax these constraints or must the goal be redefined?* None of the alternatives listed may hold much promise that the goal sought can be attained. This raises the question: *Will further search turn up feasible alternatives that improve the chance of success, or must the goal be redefined?* The cost of data gathering may be so high, the time left for a decision so brief, or the likelihood of obtaining relevant data so low that the decision maker may act without examining unknowns—and thereby change his goals, consciously or unconsciously.

A seller doubles his advertising budget and changes his advertising agency in hopes of increasing his share of the market from 10 to 15%. His share stays at 10% because his competitors tripled their effort. Or his market share rises to 15% but a fall in industry sales means this higher share actually represents fewer sales. (Perhaps next time he will express his goal more precisely: "At least 15% of total industry sales and a minimum of 100,000 items sold or dollar sales of $1,000,000.")

Goals exist in time and the goal missed this year is lost forever. (Moreover, a firm may not survive if this year's goals are not achieved.) Buyers' desires and competitors' resources may change so much that next year's goals must be drastically different from this year's.

Goal-frustrating events abound throughout the decision process. The seller who sought a 50% increase in sales (a rise in market share from 10% to 15%), looks at pretests that predict one ad campaign will be recalled by 45% and the other by 60% of their audiences and picks the latter. Unless message recall bears a high, positive relationship to purchase, the pretest data will be irrelevant to his goal. Or the ads may be very effective but lack of retail outlets or aggressive sales clerks may fail to convert eager prospects into purchasers.

The buyer faces a similar problem when he compares goals sought to goals attained. If he wanted a car that runs five years without repairs and the rear end falls out in two, does he renew his search or alter his goals? (If the only such car is a Rolls Royce, financial constraints will probably force him to alter his goals.)

Different Men, Different Goals

Up to this point we have referred to the "goal" of decision making. In buying and selling, one never deals with a "goal" but always with "goals."

A buyer wants his toothpaste to taste good—but it had better not turn his teeth black or brown. *Goals are multiple because every product has several attributes or features and every buyer seeks many benefits.*

Individual buyers differ from one another. Members of a single family differ; income, educational, and ethnic groups differ. They want different product features; a seller must develop different marketing mixes for

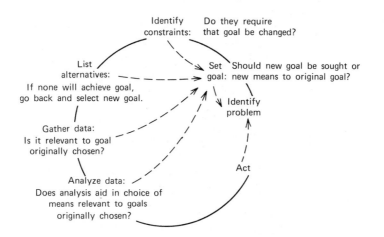

Figure 3.1 Goals may have to be redefined at each stage of the decision process.

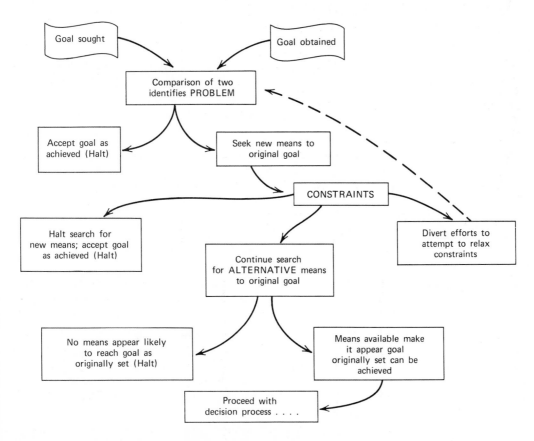

Figure 3.2 One may alter goal, seek new means, or work on constraints.

different market segments. *Goals are multiple because products must please different persons.*

Sellers, like buyers, have many goals: profit, survival of the firm, and growth are examples. Sellers differ not only in the weight given each of these goals but in their resources, market share, and aspirations. The seller who dominates the market wants to keep things as they are; the seller with a small brand share wants to change things.

Within a single firm, an employee's goals vary with his vertical and horizontal location on the organizational chart—his status and his role. (The vice-president for production may seek to cut costs by eliminating minor product variations that cause frequent retooling. The sales manager may seek to increase variations, knowing that each one will give him a firmer hold on some market segment.)

Goals within a firm also vary in *time*. The president may have a goal he wants to achieve in five years or his lifetime or that of his son and heir. The comptroller thinks in 12-month periods, and the mailroom boy lives 24 hours at a time. The advertising manager thinks in terms of deadlines: approval of TV story boards by May 1, commercials on film by mid-June, follow-up survey in the field by November 1.

Goals and Decision Making

If goals sought are to be compared with goals achieved, they must be expressed so that degree of attainment can be measured. Most firms would like to see their sales increase, but a goal must be more specific: Is the increase to be a specific market share, a specific number of items, a specific number of dollars? Must the profit from the sales increase equal out-of-pocket expenses in obtaining it? How *soon* must the break-even point be reached?

If the difference between goals sought

and attained is to guide future decision making, goals must be related to the alternatives one has to choose from. (A sales increase may vindicate one's choice of marketing mix—unless it is a result of a general rise in affluence or of a sloppy job by one's competitors. It seems appropriate to judge *media choices* in terms of numbers of prospects exposed to one's messages and to judge *messages* by the number of persons responding to them, in some fashion or another. But goals for media and messages must specify who, and in what fashion.)

To summarize, goals tend to be multiple for three reasons.

People. Several goals exist in any single individual; different sets of goals exist among different individuals, both buyers and sellers.

Organizational. Goals must be specified according to the role and status of the person who is to achieve them, and the time during which they are to be achieved.

Cause and effect. Goals must be specific and observable, so that one can say whether, when, and to what degree they have been attained. One must also be able to say by what means the goals have been attained.

Maximizing Profit as a Goal?

It would be convenient to declare, by fiat, that the fundamental goal of the seller is to maximize profit and that *all* other goals must be consistent with profit maximization. Profit maximization is a useful benchmark, since when behavior of firms and individuals is inconsistent with it, the discrepancy may raise questions that help isolate their real goals. (Occasionally, departures result from ignorance and ineptness; more often we find that the firms and individuals have very different and, in view of their circumstances, very sensible goals of their own.)

Few housewives, we suspect, push the search for alternatives to the point where they can be *sure* that they have gotten the most and best for their money. Some theorists suggest that businessmen behave in the same way: the search for alternatives halts when they find one that is "satisfactory" so that they may rush on to the next problem requiring a decision.[1] This theory—that firms *satisfice* rather than *maximize*—means that for the firm, as for the family, one must determine what goals are (and how they are arrived at) rather than being able to assume away the problem by fiat.

However, problems of goal definition are not eliminated by substituting *satisfactory* for *maximum* profits. One must specify the time span within which profits are to be achieved. (Six months is probably too short a time and 20 years too long.) The "right" time will vary with product life cycle, market share, and other factors. (Accounting practices limit choices: they categorize advertising as an *expense* to be charged off the year incurred when, in fact, we know that the effects of advertising, both positive and negative, are no respecter of fiscal years but accumulate over a considerable, if indeterminate, period.[2])

If profits are to assess the wisdom of one's decisions, other difficulties arise. Profits that arise from tax advantages reflect an industry's skill in lobbying, or result from monopolistic or fraudulent practices, and are a poor measure of management's skill in either production or marketing. Profit-sharing is too rare a phenomenon, the connection between profits and employment too remote, and forms of job security, such as unions, too obvious for stockholders' profits to have much motivational force for employees at lower levels of the organization. (Indeed, profits may not motivate managers as a group or any individual manager. A manager seeking survival and growth for his firm, rather than profit, or security for himself may avoid profitable but risky alternatives. Or he may seek an increase in power and prestige, not necessarily in his present firm or industry.)

Maximizing Sales as a Marketing Goal

Despite their difficulties, profits are often assumed to be the goal of a firm—and sales to be the goal of its marketing department, and a means to attaining the goal of the firm itself. Not all sales help the firm attain its goal: some may cost more than they're worth. Even profitable sales, however, have their shortcomings as a goal.

First, if a seller's stock of bifurcated widgets sells out by Monday noon, after he's run a four-color ad in Sunday's paper, he'd better not praise the ad, until he's sure that (1) he didn't also sell out the previous Monday, when no ad was run and (2) that the "Today" show didn't feature a pop singer using the product whose appearance set off a run on the market. (If no widgets sell on Monday, before he blames the ad he'd better check to see whether a major competitor offered the same widgets, both bifurcated and stereophonic, for $2.63 less.)

Second, if the seller designs a mix that includes just the right price, place, product features, and promotion, and sales figures prove the *combination* is a winner, sales *cannot* also measure the success of any *single element* of the mix.

(Certainly, an adequate experimental design can determine the effects of both combination and individual elements, with adjustments for a "Today" show or a competitor's sale. A seller can put his ad in half of a newspaper's *split-run*, and omit it from copies going to other readers, who provide a *control group* that measures the influence of other aspects of the environment. Split the run into enough parts, with a different ad going to each and one can eventually compare effects of alternative headlines, art, and copy.

(However, such comparisons soon become complex. If the seller wants to compare three pricing policies, two types of retail outlet, four product variations, two media schedules, and two messages, he will have 96 different combinations to be tested ($3 \times 2 \times 4 \times 2 \times 2$). If he follows a rule of thumb that each combination should be tested in three markets, he'll need 288 test markets, similar yet isolated from one another. If he follows another rule of thumb, calling for 30 subjects per combination, he'll need 2880 subjects per market.)

Even if this kind of scientific criterion for determining cause and effect can be met, there are practical arguments against using sales as a guide to day-to-day decision making. Some products, such as yachts and houses, are purchased so infrequently that one may have to wait quite awhile for results. Sales come at the end of the decision-making process and so aren't much help in guiding decisions along the way. (Before sales can indicate which of two copy platforms is superior, for example, platforms must be translated into copy, space and time bought, and the ads printed and aired.) An ad may move a prospect through one or more steps of the persuasion process but sales measure only the last step, that of actual purchase. (Sales thus ignore the things advertising is good at—creating product awareness and brand preference— and measure results that may be more affected by a retailer's prices and store layout than the seller's ads.)

In short, each element of the mix and each stage in the process of persuasion may require its own goals, to guide decision makers and measure and reward their success. Often, these goals require one to talk to prospects, and find out what they think and feel, what they have done, are doing, and plan to do.

No single goal such as sales can ever perform all the functions that goals must perform in decision making. No single goal is appropriate to all decision makers. Even if individuals, rather than groups, made

decisions and even if each individual had only a single goal, every sale-and-purchase would involve two goals: one for seller and one for buyer. (Sale-and-purchase is possible only if these goals are defined broadly enough so that they can overlap; this area of overlap represents the decision-space for the encounter. Usually this area of overlap is large enough to accommodate several different combinations of product features and consumer benefits, with seller and buyer bargaining to get the mix that each finds most advantageous.)

Because goals are always multiple, and differ for each individual and decision-making group, they must be determined, not assumed, in any decision process. To appreciate the variety of goals that guide behavior, look at the complex set of motives revealed by the behavior of Mrs. Schumacher as she pushes her grocery cart down the aisles of a supermarket.

Mrs. Schumacher checks prices carefully, for *economy* is one of her goals. She reads labels, feeling that familiar brands are more *dependable*—less risky. She pinches and prods the produce, trying to guess *flavor* from color and texture. Since she's trying to reduce, she avoids high-calorie items; but she also makes sure that the cart contains high-energy foods for Little League son and swimming-ballet daughter. Now and then she rejects a good buy in a dependable brand of a flavorful and nutritious product because she served it the day before yesterday, and Mrs. Schumacher prides herself on *variety* in her menus.

Price is also important to manufacturers and retailers when they purchase items: but so is dependability both in the product and in the time it is delivered. Brand name, style, and a wide variety of colors, sizes, or flavors are important to the retailer. Goals of retailer and manufacturer vary with the segment of the market to which they sell. The same is true of Mrs. Schumacher in the supermarket: calories dominate when she's picking food for her own lunch; economy gives way to flavor and dependability when guests join the family; her husband's subordinates and his boss will not get the same menu.

The conflict inside Mrs. Schumacher's head may be externalized over the dinner table if her husband's grimace indicates he that 500,000 persons will buy it. (Smaller markets of 200,000 and 100,000 were given equal probabilities of 30% each.) To tap these markets, two different levels of advertising and personal selling were proposed; analysis of costs and sales revenues produces these estimates of profits in Figure 3.3.

Figure 3.3   Anticipated Sales

Estimated number of buyers	100,000	200,000	500,000	
Probability that estimate is correct	30%	30%	60%	
Size of sales force	Net profits anticipated			Average payoff over time[a]
10 men	$10,000	$20,000	$30,000	$27,000
20 men	− 10,000	10,000	40,000	28,000
Size of ad budget				
$300,000	− $5,000	$10,000	$20,000	$13,500
500,000	5,000	20,000	30,000	25,500

[a] The average payoff consists of estimated anticipated profits multiplied by their probabilities under each market expectation. Thus a 10-man sales force would, on the average over a series of trials, produce $10,000 × .30 + $20,000 × .30 + $30,000 × .60 or $27,000.

thinks she has favored economy over flavor, or the baby hurls his "nutritious" spinach from high chair to floor. (Open conflict of this kind is reduced in the firm by clearer definition of role and status, and clearer delegation of decision-making duties. Conflict is more threatening to the family since it has goals other than product purchase; such goals as sex and child-rearing help hold it together.)

Goals of a Seller

In many ways, goals of the firm are simpler than those of the housewife. Profit and risk —Mrs. Schumacher's "economy" and "dependability"—are preeminent, the first being measured in dollars and the second in probabilities. An example is given below.

In his office yesterday, Mr. Schumacher, whose office door bears the title, *Vice President: Marketing*, reviewed a consumer research project on the potential of a new product. It suggested a 60% probability

Either level of sales force is preferable to either level of advertising. If, as usually is true, Schumacher plans to combine selling and advertising, he'll need more information; the effects of the two in combination might be very different from those shown above. (Advertising that paves the way for a salesman makes him vastly more effective. A sales force that gets retailers to stock an advertised brand makes effects of advertising more evident.)

History affects choice: if Schumacher's sales manager has made a series of bad decisions lately, he may not want to run even a 30% risk of losing another $10,000 for the firm. Personality has an influence: an optimistic executive may opt for the highest possible reward and hire 20 salesmen, in hopes that there really are 500,000 buyers and a $40,000 profit waiting for him; a pessimistic executive may hire only 10, on the grounds that the worst that can happen, a market of only 100,000, assures a profit of $10,000.

Goals of a Group

In both firm and family, decisions are often made by more than one person, if only because a purchase actually involves a whole series of decisions. Someone must decide that *now* is the time to buy. Someone must decide *which brand* to buy. Someone must make the actual *purchase*. And, finally, someone must *use* the brand that is bought. All four tasks may be performed by the same person, as when an adult buys cigarettes or a child buys candy. On the other hand, Mr. Schumacher may decide that he needs a new shirt, but let his wife select store and brand and make the purchase. Mrs. Schumacher may put "dog food" on the grocery list her husband takes to market on Saturday, but kids pick out the brand, their father pays for it—and the dog refuses to eat it. When several members use the same product, decisions must be made jointly. Mr. Schumacher wants a car that gets a lot of miles to the gallon; his son is more interested in miles per hour; his wife is concerned about how many hours seat covers will endure children, dogs, and pet alligators. A seller facing these different demands must determine how much influence each member has on buying decisions and whether son and mother will "gang up" against father to make style and speed decisive over performance and economy.

Three different patterns of decision making are found in American families: some decisions are habitually delegated to husband or to wife; joint decisions require discussion and agreement; other decisions are broken down into a series of smaller decisions, some delegated and others joint. Use of these patterns differs from family to family.[3] Young couples report that they make many joint decisions because they think this is how families are supposed to behave or because husband and wife have not yet learned where each is expert. In low-income families, wives decide whether money will be spent or saved, since savings usually represent delayed decisions to purchase. (In high-income families, decisions to save are essentially decisions to invest and as such are delegated to the husband. In middle-income families, save-or-spend decisions tend to be made jointly.) Personality aside, wives who work seem to have more influence than those who don't. (This may be because in a showdown, they can "resign" from the decision-making unit. It may be because their job experience gives them the skill to make and the habit of making decisions. It may be because it is, in part, their money that will be spent.)

Influence in a Firm

Decision makers in the business firm appear to possess four kinds of influence.[4] One arises from the function assigned to them —their role, as indicated by their horizontal position on the organizational chart. (Some problems are felt to fall in the sphere of the comptroller and others to be the responsibility of the vice-president for production.) The second type of power is indicated by an executive's vertical position. (His *status* or rank gives the vice-president for marketing more voice in determining policy than is possessed by the sales and advertising managers who are his immediate subordinates.) A third type of power rests in the *personality* of the individual executive. One occupant of a given role or status may be able to exert more influence than the man who preceded him in that position—or the man who will succeed him. The fourth type of power rests in an individual's ability to form *coalitions* with other members of the decision-making group.

Ultimately, a member's influence over a group rests on his ability to increase a group's chances to gain rewards and to alter the way in which rewards are divided. The man recognized as an expert has power in that sphere, because he can help the firm reach its goals. The man with whom others like to associate exercises a broader but less intense kind of influence; the rewards of "fun-to-work-with" being independent of any particular task or decision; such a man has a large number of potential coalition mates. Both types of influence are increased if they are *legitimized* formally by the firm in the role and status assigned the *expert* and the *good companion.* Power is enhanced if the man holding it feels out support and opposition prior to decision making. Skill in listening to the feelings of others and in separating what men mean from what they say and what they say from why they say it increases a man's influence. Skill in assaying the relative power held by each member of the group and in estimating his willingness to exert it is important. An ability to suggest solutions that satisfy enough needs of enough members may produce a victorious coalition.

Conflict over goals may arise in the family because interests vary with age and sex, differences that help define the family. Similar conflict "built into" the firm is symbolized by the organizational chart's differences in functions (role) and power (status). Each role and each status has built-in goals and rewards. The rewards encourage single-minded pursuit of goals that often conflict with one another. To predict how such conflicts will be resolved, one must know the importance each participant attaches to each goal, the power possessed by each and the probability he will use it, and the ability of each decision maker to increase his power through a coalition with others.

The family is a comparatively small, simple organization with strong social norms as to who should make decisions. The firm is a very complicated organization. Since even insiders often do not know exactly who makes decisions, a salesman may have a great deal of difficulty picking his targets. (Some purchasing agents are mere paper-handlers, being allowed to make only routine purchase decisions on their own. Coalitions form and reform invisibly for each decision.) Advertising is valuable in reaching such unknown, invisible, and unreachable participants in decision making.

Observing Outcomes and Causes

So far we have dealt with the problem of how goals are determined: their antecedents. Now we must look at their consequences. Goals must perform specified functions. A seller must be able to tell whether an audience has moved in a desired direction to a minimum distance within specified time limits. Often, this means using an indirect index of one's real goal. (There is no lack of possibilities: one study[5] has listed 91 different advertising objectives whereas another lists 52.[6])

It is difficult to specify the goals one seeks in such a way that they can be compared with the goals actually attained. This difficulty can be illustrated by a study in which respondents leafed through a magazine they had previously read with an interviewer who first asked, *Do you recognize this ad?* and then said: *Please rate it on a seven-point, like-dislike scale.* Even if both measures bear a high and equally strong relationship to the advertiser's true goal (whatever that may be), the existence of two different sets of results poses a problem:

	Mean Scores		
	Ad A	Ad B	Ad C
Rating on 7-point like-dislike scale	3.5	3.5	1.1
Percent of readers in survey who say they recognize ad	36%	46%	46%

Ad B appears to be preferable on both measures—but if our media schedule called for two ads, which would be our second choice?

The magazine audience, we know, was made up of at least two different kinds of people—men and women. Cross-tabulating our scores shows that sex does make a difference:

Constraints. To specify goals consistent with resources in such a way that one can say to what degree they have been achieved at some point in time, and what factors are responsible for such success or failure.

Listing alternatives. Goals must specify

	Mean Scores					
	Men			Women		
	Ad A	Ad B	Ad C	Ad A	Ad B	Ad C
Like-dislike scale	1.8	4.9	1.0	5.2	2.1	1.2
Recognition score	54%	68%	18%	18%	24%	74%

On the like-dislike scale, it now appears that ad B is preferred by men, but that women prefer ad A. Similar ads are not those with high scores, as in the first table, but those which rank low: A and C for men, B and C for women. As for recognition scores, both ads A and B score high for men; C gained high recognition in the first table because it made a strong impression on women.

Usually advertisers have more than three ads to choose from, more than two measures of their effects, and want to segment their audiences on variables like age, income, education, and occupation, none of which offers the neat, natural dichotomy of sex.

The task of selecting goals for the purchase-sale transaction can itself be viewed as a decision-making process in miniature.

Problem. To obtain a set of goals that reconcile diverse interests in a single individual and in a group for both buyer and seller, so that the two sets show overlap.

Goal. To direct the behavior of persons in different roles and statuses through time.

when the search for alternatives may cease. (The stopping point may be signaled by "optimizing" or "satisficing.")

Choice of alternative goals. There are three criteria—reconciling conflict among decision makers, directing behavior, and comparing desires with achievements.

In practice, reconciliation of opposing interest is often achieved by suboptimal choices. Optimal cause-and-effect relationships take second place to efforts, through persuasion and coalition formation, to set goals for the group consistent with goals of individual participants.

Goals, we have suggested, cannot be set by fiat but must be determined by identifying and studying actual decision makers. If this study focuses on products, we speak of meanings; if it focuses on people, we speak of attitudes. The goals expressed in meanings or attitudes originate in individual motivation and personality and organizational roles. These concepts represent the subject matter of the next three chapters.

Thought, Talk, and Action

1. Trace your career decisions, in terms of goal setting, since you entered high school. How many times have your plans changed? Why—because you learned more about yourself? about demands of the career? about probable pay? about number of openings?
2. List as many educational goals as you can think of, ranging from the general, "develop intellectually," to the specific, "pass my CPA exams." Assign weights to them. List all of the college courses you have taken; how much contribution has each made to each of these goals? List activities in this class—text, exams, lectures, etc.; how relevant is each of these to each of the goals you've listed? Compare your figures with those of others in the class.
3. Quiz friends or family on the goals of their present housing. How much do site, the building, furnishings, and neighbors contribute to each goal? How do goals differ for dormitory and apartment dwellers, for your parents' and your own actual or projected home?

Notes

Chapter 3

1. Herbert A. Simon, "Theories of decision-making in economics and behavioral science," American Economic Review, 49: 253–83.
2. Joel Dean, "Does advertising belong in the capital budget?" Journal of Marketing, 30:4:15–21.
3. Elizabeth H. Wolgast, "Do husbands or wives make the purchasing decisions?" Journal of Marketing, 23:151–8.
4. For alternative conceptualizations, see Gardner Lindzey and Elliot Aronson, editors, The handbook of social psychology, 2nd ed. (Reading, Mass.: Addison-Wesley Publishing Co., 1969), pp. 160–8.
5. Harry Deane Wolfe, James K. Brown, and G. Clark Thompson, Measuring advertising results (New York: National Industrial Conference Board, Inc., 1962).
6. Russell H. Colley, Defining advertising goals for measured advertising results (New York: Association of National Advertisers, 1961).

Goals of the Advertiser: Those Sought and Those Achieved

Du Pont faced two tough marketing problems in 1962, when its laboratories announced that a new nonstick coating for frying pans, called Teflon, was ready to be sold. First, it had to persuade cookware makers to use the material. To do that, it had to persuade retailers to stock the cookware. And to persuade retailers, it had to persuade the public to buy. That was the first difficulty. The second was that earlier that year a lower-quality version of Teflon, ineptly applied to low-quality, imported frying pans, had appeared on the market. It peeled and was easily scratched—and manufacturers, retailers, and consumers felt they'd been stung.

Obviously, Du Pont needed to show that its new version, $Teflon_2$ was different from the old, $Teflon_1$ but to do so subtly enough that retailers could still sell the

Number of Daytime Commercials Per Week

		Fall	
Winter	10	5	0
7	Detroit Springfield	Dayton	Wichita
3	Columbus	St. Louis Bangor Youngstown	(Rochester)
0	Omaha	Pittsburgh	Philadelphia Grand Rapids

old version and thus make room on their shelves for the new. Du Pont adopted a three-point strategy. It slapped a "seal of approval" on $Teflon_2$. It encouraged its use on cookware other than frying pans (where all the trouble had been). It used a new advertising appeal. ($Teflon_1$ had been promoted as a fat-free cooking device for the diet-conscious; $Teflon_2$ advertising emphasized the easy-to-clean feature.)

To test this strategy Du Pont bought a million dollars worth of TV time in 13 cities at two seasons of the year.

The problems that plague such a field experiment were not slow in appearing. A local retailer in Rochester ran a heavy advertising campaign of his own so that city had to be dropped. Shipments lagged so that retailers were frequently out of stock. Retailers refused to let researchers audit their shelves. Telephone calls to a random sample of 1000 housewives in January 1963 showed that most of those who had bought the nonstick material didn't know what it was called. (The question was revised: If housewives said the inside of their nonstick pan looked and felt different from the outside, they were scored as Teflon users.)

Advertising for Teflon might be expected to help sales of *all* cookware but such sales were *not* highest in the high-fall-and-high-winter markets nor lowest in the low-or-no fall and winter markets.

Teflon sales, however, were almost three times higher in the high-high markets; a "carryover" or "delayed

Cookware Sales Per 1000 Housewives

Winter Advertising	Fall Advertising	
	High	Low or No
High	255	282
Low or no	205	229

Teflon Cookware Sales Per 1000 Housewives

Winter Advertising	Fall Advertising	
	High	Low or No
High	70	49
Low or no	32	25

effect" was clearly shown. Another way of demonstrating the effects of advertising is to show how big Teflon's share of the cookware market was. Here are the figures: 11% in the no-ad market, 16% in the markets where ads were used only one season, either fall or winter, and 27% in the remaining, two-season ad markets.

Results were summarized in a multiple correlation of .64 (meaning 40% of Teflon cookware sales could be attributed to Du Pont advertising) and in a regression equation which used ad schedules to predict sales. [The equation: $30.76 - 1.24$ (fall ads) $+ .90$ (winter ads) $+ .57$ (winter ads $\times$ fall ads).] The study concluded with recommendations that Du Pont use 10 TV spots a week in the fall and 7 in the winter in introducing the product nationally and keep a close watch on four markets (Detroit, Springfield, Omaha, and Columbus) for signs of falling sales, since advertising might only have made consumers buy earlier than they otherwise would have, rather than buy more.

Source. James C. Becknell, Jr., and Robert W. McIsaac, "Test marketing cookware coated with 'Teflon,'" *Journal of Advertising Research*, 3:3:2–8.

Whose Goals Are Satisfied in Family Decisions?

The advertiser who knows how decision-making power is distributed in the family knows who should be the target for his messages. Stock brokers pick media aimed at husbands in upper-income families, since these husbands make investment decisions, but holiday resorts use media directed at both husband and wife since vacation sites are decided jointly.

But how does a spouse influence family decisions? An answer to this question will help design the advertising messages themselves.

In the southwestern part of the United States, a social psychologist chose 10 families of Mormons, whose religion makes the husband head of the family; 10 families of Navaho Indians, whose women are economically independent; and 10 families of Texas migrants. Each spouse was separately asked which of three families known to both was most religious, most ambitious, had the happiest children, and so on. When

husband and wife disagreed they were asked to come to a common decision. As expected, the original viewpoints of Navaho *wives* and Mormon *husbands* tended to prevail.

	Number of Disagreements	Number of Decisions "Won" by Husband
Navaho	80	34
Texans	73	39
Mormons	71	42

In a closer look at these 30 couples plus another 10 tested at Harvard, the spouse who talked most was most likely to win.

		Which Spouse Won Most?	
		Husband	Wife
Which spouse talked most?	Husband	14	5
	Wife	5	10

(Entries represent number of couples.)

Source. Fred L. Strodtbeck, "Husband-wife interaction over revealed differences," *American Sociological Review*, 16:468–73.

A similar method was used to study decision making in marketing by giving 50 college students and their wives a half-hour to decide what they would buy if they suddenly received a gift of $300.

Husbands did most of the talking, but their share varied with the kind of choice made.

	Proportion of Couples in Which Discussion Dominated by		
	Husband %	Wife %	Neither %
Total amount of talk	42	18	40
When purchase was for use by			
Husband (books, clothing)	18	24	15
Children (clothing, toys)	16	23	13
Family (car, TV)	35	30	31
Household (washer, stove)	8	8	15
Wife (clothing, jewelry)	9	11	8

Goals Sought and Goals Achieved 69

The figures suggest that when wives talked a lot, it may have been to argue the case for someone other than themselves—for husband or children. Husbands did not seem to return the favor by talking a lot to encourage purchase of things for the wife's personal use. (Maybe they didn't have to.) The column at the right also reports interesting differences among products associated with discussions in which neither husband nor wife dominated; as one might expect, these were items to be used by everyone.

Proportion of Two Types of Remarks as Related to Type of Product
(Entries Represent Percentage of Remarks)

Type of Remark	Family Use Dominance by	
	Wife	Husband
Task	35	24
Maintenance	22	35

Type of Remark	Husband's Use Dominance by	
	Wife	Husband
Task	18	19
Maintenance	21	17

Type of Remark	Household Use Dominance by	
	Wife	Husband
Task	10	10
Maintenance	6	14

	Children's Use Dominance by	
	Husband	Wife
Task	17	21
Maintenance	11	21

	Wife's Use Dominance by	
	Husband	Wife
Task	9	7
Maintenance	12	7

Contributions to a discussion may vary in type as well as amount. Generally, we distinguish two types: messages that involve decision making per se, such as offering suggestions, opinions, and information, and those designed to release tension and reward one's fellow-discussant.

The first type is called *task performance* and tends to characterize men's role in decision making; the second is called *group maintenance* and is more likely to be contributed by women.

Men and women behaved as expected in this study.

Which Talked Most	Percentage of Couples	
	Task Performance	Group Maintenance
Husband	60	20
Wife	16	72
Neither	26	8

Interesting differences showed up in each spouse's share of each type of verbal contribution, depending on which product was finally chosen; again, we would assume that these differences in talk were responsible for the choice.

Source. William F. Kenkel, "Husband-wife interaction in decision choices," *Journal of Social Psychology*, 54:255–62.

Goals of the Individual: Vive la Difference!

Ask individuals about their purchasing goals and you may get a lot of high-flown abstractions, of little use to a man who wants to design and display goods that will sell. Show them the product itself and you're likely to get responses which reveal just how divergent their goals are. Coed Henriette Fischer did just that. She stationed herself alongside a store window showing expensive women's coats and asked the women passing by, *What do you think and feel when you look at this display?* Here are the answers she got.

1. *High school senior, age 17.* Could you see me in the black one? Check those puffy sleeves. I'd look like a woman of forty: I guess my mother would like it though. I wonder why there are no cheery colors.

2. *Coed, age 18, English major.* What do I feel? I feel like a million. Just look at that one with the velvet collar . . . that's real style. Those black heels look expensive too. I like the use of the same coat on each figure. That's clever advertising. . . . I never thought beige could be so attractive when used in such quantities. That white light on their faces is good too . . . seems to be an expression of youth when there is such bright illumination.

3. *Teacher, age 45, married, 3 children.* I could walk right past and not even notice! Who wants to see six coats, all the same? What if I didn't like this one? What would make me want to go inside? Nothing.

4. *Saleswoman of department store, age 55, married.* Those sale signs got me. I love sales. What woman doesn't! It's hard to turn away at these prices. How do you think that black one would look on me? Maybe I'm too heavy. I like to see prices in the window. If I don't see them, I usually won't go in.

5. *Widow, age 57, 4 children, supported by them.* Oh, those coats are beautiful! My daughter would look stunning in that! That's what this looks like . . . a fashion show. Even the dummies look like they're modeling. I feel young looking at the pretty things and the bright coloring.

6. *College student, age 21.* It doesn't impress me. The colors are dull. The coats are very ordinary. I want style in my clothes! The coats lack personality. I'd say they were for women with average tastes and interest in clothes. I'd look to *Mademoiselle* before I'd look here for the new fashions. . . .

7. *Retired school teacher, unmarried.* The color monotone effect is easy on the eye. That I like. I guess I've seen too much Picasso lately, that's why! Do need a coat badly. Don't you think I'd look younger in that black one . . . slimmer too!

8. *Landlady, age 54, married.* They look too country clubbish for me! What would an old lady like me want with such fancy clothes anyway? Don't really think I like the coats either. It sure looks like a nice store. I've heard they look down at you if you don't look ritzy. That's not right.

9. *Librarian, age 50, married.* The window makes me feel young again. I wish there were a few hats in the window. They're my mania . . . I wouldn't go in to buy one though. Seems to be too late in the season.

Source. *Advertising*, 4th ed., by Harry Walker Hepner. Copyright, 1964, McGraw-Hill Book Company. Used by permission. (Pages 113–15)

Goals of a Culture

Three men may buy the same product to satisfy very different goals. Nowhere, perhaps, is this kind of difference in goals more clearly illustrated than in the contrast between cultures.

Societies and roles within a society differ in the attributes they use to categorize events. A physician may classify a bleeding man as a patient, and give first aid; a policeman may classify him as a victim, and start looking for the assailant. A musician in Bali will not tell a performer to hit the piano key *to the left* or *the next lower key* but the one to the *east* or *south*. (This has an advantage in communications since two persons facing one another will use the same word, not mirror opposites.)

Regardless of language, culture, or role, persons seem to use three different dimensions in evaluating their categories of objects and events. The labels for these categories necessarily reflect these dimensions of evaluation (*E:* good-bad), potency (*P:* strong-weak), and activity (*A:* fast-slow). Here, for example, are the "values" that attach to three (out of 100) such labels.

Label-Concept	Americans		
	E	P	A
Progress	High	High	High
Girl	High	LOW	LOW
Power	High	High	High

Label-Concept	Finns		
	E	P	A
Progress	High	High	LOW
Girl	High	LOW	High
Power	High	High	LOW

Label-Concept	Japanese		
	E	P	A
Progress	High	High	High
Girl	High	LOW	High
Power	LOW	LOW	High

Americans tend to see *thieves* and *criminals* as being less *successful* and more *foolish* than Italians do. Managers in Spain report that *to reprimand* is good; managers in Japan say that it is bad.

Source. Based on Harry Triandis, "Cultural influences upon cognitive processes," in Leonard Berkowitz, ed., *Advances in Experimental Social Psychology* (New York: Academic Press, 1964), Vol. 1:2–48.

Here are the answers received by a professor in Lebanon when he asked children what common objects are used for. The answers came from 900 Lebanese, 58 Sudanese and 120 Americans.

Mouth. Eating led, but 39% of Americans and only 14% of Sudanese said talking. On the other hand, 50% of the Sudanese said eating and drinking, but only 3% of the Americans.

Father. Working and earning money, said 76% of the Lebanese, but only 10% of Sudanese; providing care and assisting family said 45% of Sudanese but only 9% of Lebanese.

Boy. Going to school or working, said 61% of Lebanese, 39% of Americans, but only 24% of Sudanese. Playing, said 34% of Americans, none of the Sudanese, and only 9% of Lebanese.

Trees. Food, said 69% of Lebanese (in a land of olives, dates, and almonds); and 34% of American children living in the same land. For climbing, said 12% of Americans but virtually none of the others.

Cats. For catching mice, said 50 to 60% of Lebanese and Sudanese; for pets, said 52% of Americans.

Birds. For eating, said 37% of Lebanese; for enjoyment, said 33% of Americans.

Source. Wayne Dennis, "Uses of common objects as indicators of cultural orientations," *Journal of Abnormal and Social Psychology,* 55:21–28.

Goals of a Class: Immediate or Delayed?

Children of the middle class are taught to value success for its own sake, often by fathers themselves who have, through a combination of hard work and luck, risen to a more affluent state than that of their fathers. Children of the working class, on the other hand, except a more immediate payoff, in money rather than promotions. These expectations are acquired early enough in life to show up in the classroom and affect performance there.

High school pupils in this study were given two tasks—one involving anagrams and the other motor skills—and told that they'd be given a chance to compare their scores afterward with the high school average. (Averages reported were higher than any pupil had achieved.) In addition, a third of the pupils were told that those whose score reached a certain value would get $10.

Following this, all students wrote stories concerning a series of pictures, the stories being scored on the amount of "motivation to achieve" which they showed—the extent to which the stories concerned success and failure and dealt with it in emotional terms.

Scores were high (8.3 and 8.1) for both middle class and working class children under the $10 prize condition. They remained high for middle class children but fell markedly for the working class children under the no-prize conditions (7.6 and 4.9).

Source. Elizabeth Douvan, "Social status and success strivings," *Journal of Abnormal and Social Psychology,* 52:219–23.

Seller and Buyer Disagree on Goals

Four sets of goals are involved when a woman sets out to buy a gift for a man. There are, to begin with, the goals of the man himself and then the goals which the woman thinks the man has. In the store she shops, the prospect will find two more versions: those of the designer of the product and those of the retailer who thought it would sell.

How do these sets of goals mesh? Not very well, in this study of 18 different gift package designs.

Men and women agreed on which packages looked most *expensive,* their ratings correlating .92. They were in fair agreement as to how *masculine* the packages looked, with a correlation of .70. But when asked how *appropriate* a design was as a gift for a man, the correlation fell to .58. (Women, incidentally, perceived an expensive look and a masculine look as being contradictory: these ratings correlated — .73. They preferred an expensive-looking package as a gift, correlation of .53, rather than a masculine-looking one, correlation — .21.) Package designers and employees of the advertiser agreed, to the extent of a .55 correlation, as to which packages were appropriate for a man. Unfortunately, men didn't agree with them; men's preferences correlated only .14 with the designers, and — .42 with the advertiser. Women also disagreed: correlations of advertiser and women were — .21 and designer and women were — .48.

The technique used in the ratings was the Q-sort, which sets quotas of 1-2-3-6-3-2-1 at the successive steps in a seven-point scale of appropriate—inappropriate.

Source. Milton L. Blum and Valentine Appel, "Consumer versus management reaction in new package development," *Journal of Applied Psychology,* 45:222–4.

Additional Research Readings

Buyer vs. seller. How important are price, style, service, gadgets, and ease of use in refrigerators, ranges, and washers? In this study 82 retailers differed from 280 customers by overrating price and downrating other attributes and in their ratings of three different brands—Frigidaire, GE, and Sears. **Peter J. McClure and John K. Ryans, "Differences between retailers' and customers' perceptions," Journal of Marketing Research, 5:35–40.** Agreement by 40 drug salesmen and their 103 pharmacist customers on how a salesman *should* behave has no effect on salesmen's success, but differences between ideal and actual behavior *do* affect number of drug firms purchased from. **Henry L. Tosi, "The effects of expectation levels and role consensus on the buyer-seller dyad," Journal of Business, 39:4:516–29.**

Ad effects. Newspaper split-run tests in six cities showed a 14% increase in purchases of advertised brands. **Leo Bogart, et al., "What one little ad can do," Journal of Advertising Research, 10:4:1–13.** Interviewees recalling a single magazine ad show twice as much intention to buy and complete twice as many actual orders as do respondents who fail to recognize the ad. **Jan Stapel, "Sales effects of print ads," Journal of Advertising Research, 11:3:32–6.**

Alternatives are so important a concept in decision making that progress through stages of the decision process will be halted at three different points for a view-in-depth of alternatives.

This is the first such pause.

In the next three chapters, we take a closer look at three different ways of conceptualizing alternative goals.

In Chapter 4, goals are viewed as *meanings* that are shared between seller and buyer. (Examples cited range from the studies of how adults and children learn categories to rules concerning the syllogism and date from Aristotle to modern set theory.)

In Chapter 5, goals are viewed as *attitudes* that sellers and buyers have toward products and services, brands and firms. (Again, examples range from Aristotle's ancient triad of belief, affect, and action to recent rival "balance" theories.)

In Chapter 6, the origin of goals is sought in human *motives*, in individual *personality*, and the multitude of conflicting *roles* that individuals play, in the consuming household and at work.

Chapter 4 Synopsis

● Definitions are arbitrary divisions of a continuous reality made by people for a purpose. They can be understood only if we know who has made them for what purpose.

● Traditionally, definitions consist of two steps: placing an object into a class or category and naming the attributes that distinguish it from other members of the category. The operational definition describes the object in terms of how it is measured or brought into being.

● Meanings can be defined in six ways: as categories, by the methods used to measure them, in terms of the functions they are designed to perform, as attitudes, as intermediate between given antecedents and consequences; meanings differ by the persons holding them.

● The seller needs to know what his prospects' categories are, how they are formed, how to change them, and how to determine when they have been changed. He himself in his decision making must form categories of products, prospects, and symbols.

● A category has three components: a set of attributes that determines what objects belong to the category, a label, and a value. The seller can work directly on the value, assuming that values influence prospects' behavior, or he can work indirectly, by attempting to change label or attributes.

● Attributes are of two kinds, formal and functional, which

may be combined in three ways: as alternatives, jointly, or as relationships.

● Some attributes will be combined into categories because of their nature, particularly their proximity in space and time. Other combinations depend on the perceiver, particularly how he has learned to generalize and discriminate through rewards.

● Small categories become elements in larger categories and so on. A seller may try to split up or combine categories already in prospects' minds or demonstrate that overlap exists. Attributes have varying effects on the combinations of which they are a part; the order of presentation affects their influence.

● Systematic combination of attributes and dimensions is useful in devising new products, in constructing messages, in devising media-message combinations, and in grouping prospects into markets and audiences.

● Scientists differ on how the values of attributes in a category should be summed up. One theory says the combination will have a value more extreme than its most extreme attribute; another says the value of the combination will lie between values of its extreme attributes.

● The syllogism represents a classic norm of how categories and statements about categories should be combined. Human behavior often departs from these norms; scientists are searching for patterns and principles that describe and explain how people actually think and reason.

Research Articles

Attributes.   Housewives indicate important attributes for cleanser and coffee (Banks); and for dry milk (Corey); evaluation of product depends on adding or averaging values of its several attributes (Anderson, Triandis).

Labels.   Removing brand names makes beers taste alike (Allison); adding brand names makes identical loaves of bread taste different (Tucker); labels influence recall (Carmichael).

Language.   Appears to affect perceptions of world (Carroll), but changes to fit shifts in society's values (Brown).

Fallacies.   Readers defend fallacious inferences as serving intentions of advertiser (Preston), but may not believe their invalid inferences (Kilbourne); style of discourse causes invalid inferences (Mehling); as time passes, beliefs become more logically consistent (McGuire); psychologists find meaningful patterns in men's lack of logic (DeSoto).

Categories.   Some categories are more quickly discovered than others (Heidbreder).

Chapter 4 Goals of the Communicator: Meanings

Before the wheels of the moving van stop turning, a milkman is on hand to sign the family up for every-other-day delivery. A clerk in a clothing store stamps a customer's account number on the sales slip. The route man for a soap company checks supermarket shelves and fills out an order blank. The "detail man" for a drug company brings news of a new drug to a physician who will neither buy it nor sell it. An engineer advises the manufacturer on equipment needed in his new plant and advises on repairs in his present factory. A new mother comes home from the hospital to find an insurance man and an encyclopedia salesman waiting on the doorstep.

Are all these people—milkman and clothing clerk, route man and detail man, and engineer and insurance man—*salesmen*? The differences among them are obvious; what do they have in common?

Or, look at these messages: a free notice in a neighborhood shopping guide offering giveaway kittens at an address in the next block; commercials that drive you nuts when you try to watch a late-late-late movie; Smokey the Bear looking at you from a billboard; a calendar from your friendly, local mortician; a full-page appeal in the *New York Times*, urging repeal of the draft; a list of this week's loss-leaders in the supermarket; a soft-drink jingle on a teenager's transistor radio; a paid announcement in *Fortune* announcing that, following a recent merger, WXYZ Co., has changed its name; a warning in *Editor and Publisher* that "Coke" should be spelled with a capital "C".

Are all these *advertisements*? Again, the differences are obvious. What, if anything, do they have in common that we can use in a definition of advertising?

How Does One Define a Definition?

One much-quoted definition says that advertising is *a paid form of nonpersonal presentation of ideas, goods, and services by an identified sponsor.* Do we agree? Well, yes and no . . . sometimes . . . under certain conditions . . . it depends. Nobody *paid* for the ads about free kittens and Smokey the Bear. The "friend" who buys advertising space in a student yearbook is certainly not an *identified* sponsor. The sales clerk often seems less *personal* than the movie star making a pitch on TV, though the latter is advertising and the former is not.

Definitions are arbitrary divisions of a seamless reality made by people for a purpose—usually the purpose of influencing the behavior of someone else. If a source knows what he wants his definition to accomplish, and if he knows something about the audience he's trying to influence, he can probably produce a definition that gets the response he desires. It's a "good" definition if it does what he wants it to do.

If one wants to distinguish between selling and advertising, he can refer to the latter as *nonpersonal*. (In communications, we spell out this same distinction in more detail by noting that personal selling involves *face-to-face relations* between buyer and seller with *immediate feedback*.) If he wants to distinguish an advertisement from a publicity story, he can define advertising as being *paid* and having an *identified sponsor*.

Since definitions are arbitrary, it's not surprising that there will be cases on the borderline that won't fit neatly into the categories we are constructing: "advertising" and "not-advertising." The same is true of selling: it involves a wide variety of functions of which any given salesman performs only a part. Some salesmen handle delivery, credit, and collections, but non-salesmen may also perform these functions. Keeping customers satisfied by providing prompt service is a key to repeat sales and thus is an important part of the selling operation; some persons charged with this function are called salesmen and some are not. Terminology varies by industry, firm, and individual.

Variation by User

Our point is this: one can construct a definition of advertisements or salesmen that will include or exclude any of the examples we have given. This means a seller can choose the definition most likely to make prospects respond as he wishes them to. It also means that if he wants to change the meanings other people have for a word, he needs to know their *present* definitions. Let's consider the word *advertising* as an example.

To an editor, advertising is what editorial copy is wrapped around, appearing in space purchased by erratic individuals whose whims determine whether he will be permitted to continue serving the needs of large and loyal audiences. To an accountant, advertising is a current expense, even though a firm's image, built by advertising, may be a more enduring and valuable "investment" than its obsolete plant and equipment, and goodwill, created by advertising, more "real"—less dependent on public opinion—than depreciation. To an economist, advertising is a poor substitute for price competition, a force that threatens his conviction that free competition is the proper path to the general welfare by making consumer wants subject to, rather than dominant over, the businessman. To some buyers, some advertising is entertaining, other advertising is not; some informative, other not; some believable, other not; some helpful, other not; some persuasive, other not. Discovering why, when, and to whom it is each of these is the key to success in advertising.

Each of these definitions contains a strong evaluative element reflecting how much the person involved likes or dislikes advertising. Some of the definitions also reflect an individual's perception of the causes or the consequences of the thing being defined. Some suggest the attributes or properties that all examples of the term defined must possess.

Variation by Purpose

Definitions may be used as goals for the communicator. The advertising industry would like *legislators* to define advertising as a cornerstone of free enterprise that should not be taxed. It would like *prospects* to define advertising as expert and trustworthy information. It would like *sellers* to define advertising as a powerful persuasive force that can make any product profitable. Each purpose and group requires a different definition emphasizing different attributes of "advertising."

To avoid the confusion that arises when one word can be defined in so many different ways, it helps to assign a different label to each definition, distinguishing between *missionary salesmen* who persuade prospects but don't actually write up orders and *order takers* who do little but write orders, differentiating *point-of-purchase advertising* from a *TV commercial,* and recognizing that although a package, a publicity story, or a word-of-mouth message perform advertising functions, they are *not* advertisements.

Confusion is not always a disadvantage, however; a communicator may use it, deliberately or unconsciously, as a means to his goals. By subtly shifting the content of a category while leaving the label unchanged, he may induce a receiver to accept something he previously rejected, or to like something he previously didn't know existed.

Six Kinds of Definitions

Traditional definitions are constructed in two steps. The first is to put an example, such as a soft-drink jingle (ad) or a milkman (salesman), into a large category such as *means employed by a seller to increase the sales of his product*. The second is to distinguish each item from all other members of the category. Thus, to some, the jingle is *a set of rhythmic, rhyming words set to music which seeks to insure brand-name recognition; originally transmitted by radio or TV, the jingle depends upon subsequent word-of-mouth transmission for its effects*. The milkman is *a man who solicits patronage from householders on a continuing basis but spends the major part of his time in delivering goods previously ordered*. (New definitions would be necessary if one wanted to combine into a single category the milkman and the routeman who delivers bread or beer to retailers or to distinguish a two-line "Winston-tastes-good" jingle from a 60-second poetic paean to product perfection.) *The combining of small categories into larger ones or the splitting up of large categories into small ones is fundamental to the process of persuasion.*

However, traditional definitions have their shortcomings. They do not recognize that any definition applies to a given time and place. (Before radio and TV came along, for example, advertising was fairly adequately defined as *salesmanship in print;* broadcasting made this definition obsolete.) They require that objects be one thing or another. (There may be considerable news content in an advertisement for a new product—and considerable advertising in a news story about the same product, even though most definitions try to make a sharp distinction between the two.) Often traditional definitions lead users to suppose that if something can be defined, it must actually exist. (Angels and unicorns do not exist in the experience of most of us, even though each can be defined—at length.)

Many persons therefore prefer *operational* definitions that permit someone to make a cake, to select a cake from a bakery shelf, or experience the process of cake-eating. They feel such definitions are less likely to mislead by ignoring time and place, differences of degree, or the unreality of imaginary things.

Operational definitions tend to deal with things that can be measured such as time, space, quantity. In making a cake, certain quantities of certain materials are combined in certain ways in a specified order. Intelligence becomes what an intelligence test *measures:* advertising effectiveness is defined by measures of recognition and recall.

We have suggested that definitions vary with their users and the functions the definition is to perform for them. The "meaning" of an object, event, person, or idea consists of the beliefs and feelings people have about it, and the way they behave toward it. Focusing on an *object,* we can say it has certain *meanings* for a specific group of people; focusing on the *people,* we can say that they have an *attitude* toward the object.

Meanings can be defined in six ways.

As categories—with attributes, labels and values;

By the methods used to measure them;

In terms of the functions they are designed to perform;

As attitudes, comprising beliefs, feelings, and action tendencies;

As the result of certain antecedents, and the cause of certain consequences;

Differently, by the persons using them. (In this book, by buyers and by sellers.)

Since so much has been written on attitudes, the next chapter will be devoted to them. Cause-and-effect relationships and measurement are such complex subjects that they will be dealt with separately. That leaves categories, functions, and user differences for *this* chapter.

Buyer's Categories

We begin with categories by noting that a buyer's categories are important to a seller, who needs to know the following.

What they are. Some of the categories in the minds of prospects and those categories inherent in language constitute part of the seller's *environment,* factors he can't change and therefore must adjust to.

How they are formed. If categories depend primarily on the objects categorized, persons are likely to agree on their categories; if they depend on the user, we expect wide variations in categories.

How they change. Since categories determine behavior, the seller can evoke the buyer behavior he desires by changing categories. He can change categories by changing their labels, values or attributes. Which is easiest to change? Which is most likely to produce the greatest change in buyer behavior most quickly?

When he's succeeded. The seller must be able to detect and measure changes in a buyer's categories, to assess his success in changing them so that he can adjust to them.

In making decisions, sellers construct categories of their own. They group *persons* seeking similar consumer benefits into *market segments* and *audiences.* A retail outlet finds itself categorized as a clothing store or grocery store or department store because of the assortment—the categories—of products

it stocks. Sellers select *symbols* from a category of words-and-pictures-likely-to-evoke-favorable-responses-from-a-buyer, creating a new category—*messages*. The seller seeks to give his brand meanings—to get the buyer to put it into the category of brands-I-prefer.

The Three Elements of the Category

Every category has three aspects: a *value* (which is usually what one is trying to change), a name or *label,* and the *set of attributes* used to decide what objects belong to the category.

Names perform a double role. They reflect the attributes that have been put into a category; "beer" is a liquid with a particular alcoholic content made of certain raw materials by certain processes. Names thus determine what items will be permitted into the category. (To a buyer, margarine may be indistinguishable from "butter" in form and function, taste and nutritional value, but by law it may not bear the same name. Sellers of the "high-priced spread" see that the two remain in separate categories with separate labels.)

In addition, names both reflect and affect the value attached to the category. (A "town house" may be indistinguishable architecturally from a "row house" but the price is likely to be very different.) Sometimes the same object bears different names that reflect different values put on it by different persons. Sometimes, use of the same name may conceal the fact that users attach very different values to the object in question. (To a housewife, *broccoli* may belong to the category of *nutritious-green-vegetables-that-should-be-eaten-every-day;* her children may say *broccoli* with that special intonation that suggests that *they* are relegating it to the category of *spinach: to-be-fought-off-at-all-costs.*) Thus, a change of name by the seller may represent an attempt to change the value of a category;

acceptance of the new name by the seller will mean that the attempt has succeeded. A name bears no necessary or inevitable relationship to the category to which it's attached. By giving a dog or a rose a new name, one can try to change its meaning; if people change the way they respond to the renamed dog or the rose, we know the attempt has succeeded.

Two Kinds of Attributes

A decision maker may choose from two kinds of attributes in designing a product or a message.

Form. All shovels fall within a range of shapes and sizes; color and weight are critical attributes for other objects. (Fine cabinetwork may suffice to change a radio from an appliance to a piece of furniture; miniaturization may change it from furniture to a constant companion; combining it with a record player may save it from obsolescence.) Such changes in form are likely to be the cause or result of changes in:

Function. All shovels, regardless of shape and size, can do certain things—typically dig holes and fill them up again. By more sharply defining both form and function, one can distinguish between spade and shovel. By focusing on the function—holes —and ignoring the method—digging—he can incorporate shovels into a larger category that includes fence-post augers, both hand and motor-propelled, the hydraulic power of a hose, and the explosive power of dynamite.

Categorizing any product usually requires one to combine several attributes of both form and function. Attributes may be combined in three ways.

As alternatives. In baseball, a strike may be a pitch that the batter swings at and misses, *or* one that he hits but falls foul, *or* one that passes over the plate at a height between knee and shoulder. Any one of these attributes assigns the event to this single category.

Jointly. Three sides and *one* 90-degree angle are needed to make a right triangle; a human being must be female *and* have a child to be classed as a mother.

Relational. Some categories depend on the relationship between two or more attributes: a fat man is one whose weight is above a certain ratio to his height.

Let's look now at studies of category-formation in "real life," which represent the environment the marketer must adjust to, and then at category-formation in the laboratory, which more closely resembles the seller's attempt to manipulate categories.

How Categories Are Formed

How does a person, in a world containing millions of objects, decide which to put into a given category? Research suggests two kinds of guidelines.

The first is found by studying similarities in the way people behave. When the attributes involved are very simple, with little "meaning" of their own, people group objects together because they are *similar* in form, or *near* one another in space. Categories are determined by attributes rather than by the persons forming the categories.

Some types of similarity are easier to grasp than others. Shown a series of pictures, one at a time, children found it easiest to learn the name for objects.[1] Children were slowest to abstract the concept of a number like *five*. Outside the laboratory, children see similarities in terms of functions—what they do with an object or what the object does to them.[2] Next, they identify objects as to the place they are found.

Later, they group objects by form: the material they are made of, their parts, their attributes. (A bed begins as "something you sleep in" (*function*) which you "find in a bedroom" (*site*), that's "made of metal" (*attribute*) and "has a pillow and blankets" (*constituent parts*). Later it will become part of a *class*, "furniture," a meaning transmitted to the child by adults, furniture being something that's found in a furniture store and that, for the most part, just sits there and doesn't *do* anything in contrast to major appliances.)

Bruner sees the child as progressing through three stages of concept formation.[3] His first categories are based on *motor* responses: throwing balls, smelling flowers, digging holes. His next are based on *perceptual* responses: he can give names to things pointed to or described. Finally he passes from this iconic stage to a *symbolic* stage in which he can categorize and label things that can't be visualized or pointed to.

The second guideline in category formation comes from learning studies of *generalization* and *discrimination*. Pavlov's dog, induced to salivate to the ringing of a bell which preceded the presentation of food, at first *generalized*—he salivated to such similar sounds as the burr of a buzzer or the beat of a metronome. (In similar fashion, a human's sweat glands, ordinarily beyond his control, "learn" to respond when a certain tone indicates that electric shock will follow. At first, the glands react to similar sounds although the strength of the response—its size, frequency and so on— falls off as one moves up or down the scale from the test tone used as a cue for shock.) As trial follows trial, and food or shock fails to follow any but the original bell or tone, responses to nearby stimuli weaken and "extinguish." Dog and man, we say, have learned to *discriminate*. (The child who calls all animals "dogs" and all men "father" soon finds that his labeling is confirmed and rewarded only in some cases and not

in others. Thus, he learns, without being formally instructed, what attributes a member of the named category must possess.)

After a boundary line has been drawn between one category and another, perceptual mechanisms tend to accentuate the differences between categories. (The "yellow" on the yellow side of a yellow-orange mixture begins to look yellower, the political views of a person categorized as belonging to the right-wing begin to look more extreme.) Labels aid the process: a piece of banana-shaped paper looks yellower than a piece of the same paper cut in the shape of an orange.[4] In short, our perceptions shape our categories and our categories shape our perceptions.

Why Are Categories Formed?

We've described *how* categories are formed; it's time to ask *why* they come into existence. There is a limit to the number of objects, however similar or familiar, that may be perceived as a unit. At one-tenth of a second, subjects can correctly perceive, without counting, from six to 11 dots—the average being eight. In the same one-tenth of a second they can perceive five *groups* of five dots each, or a total of 25[5]—although they may not notice if a dot is missing from one or two of the groups. Subjects can see only four or five unrelated letters, in a brief exposure, but as many as 20 when put together in a familiar word, although they are likely to overlook typographical errors. They can read a four-word sentence in the same time it takes to read four unrelated letters. The ways in which categories can be combined become a highly significant aspect of the "meanings" that are the goal of marketing communications.

How Sellers Manipulate Categories

There are three basic operations a seller can perform on categories in influencing buyer behavior.

He may argue that his product or brand is different from a competitor's: that it belongs to a separate category. (This is the strategy of advertising "Uncola," caffeinfree coffee, low nicotine cigarettes, Metrecal milkshakes and sugarless pops, all of which lack an important, but presumably undesirable attribute. It's the strategy of the V8 slogan: *It looks like tomato juice, but it sure doesn't taste like tomato juice.*)

He may try to show that his product or brand belongs in the same category as one already on the market. (Thus, margarine duplicates the color and taste of butter, and plastics imitate wood or china or metal.) Usually this strategy is adopted by products that have a price advantage over those they're being compared with.

He may show that his product overlaps with several other categories—that it shares attributes with them. This is typically the strategy followed with a major product innovation, like radio or TV.

Change in a single attribute may have marked effects on the way a brand, a product, or a person, such as a salesman, is evaluated. This has been demonstrated in a classic experiment in which subjects were given the list of adjectives shown at left below, describing an individual, then asked to check which adjectives on another list of 18 they thought also applied to this person.[6] A second group of subjects got the same list with one change, the word *cold* being substituted for *warm*. As the second list shows, this change of a single word led to less favorable ratings on six traits.

	Effect of Changing *Warm* to *Cold* on Second List	
Original List of Attributes	Decreased Choice	No Effect
Intelligent	Generous	Reliable
Skillful	Happy	Important
Industrious	Good-natured	Good-looking
(Warm)	Humorous	Persistent
Determined	Popular	Serious
Practical	Imaginative	
Cautious		

A later study[7] showed that the attribute "warm/cold" made a difference even when subjects were rating a live lecturer and not just a hypothetical person.

The order in which attributes are presented also has an effect: those first on the list create an impression into which others must then fit. This has been demonstrated by reversing the order of adjectives in the warm/cold experiment. In another study,[8] when the word *skyscraper* began a list consisting of "prayer, temple, cathedral," 60% of subjects let it remain, creating a "building" category that excluded "prayer." When "skyscraper" came second on the list, 70% of the subjects crossed it out.

Choosing Categories

Since every object has many attributes, more than needed by any single category, every object can be categorized many different ways. To a man who can swim, the depth of the river may be less important than its width or temperature. If the man goes to the river for a drink, he may ignore depth, width, and temperature, and concern himself with its visible sediment or invisible bacteria. If a man wants to hit someone on the head, granite and sandstone will serve his purpose. If he wants to carve a tombstone for his victim, he will find that a category which includes both granite and sandstone is not very useful.

Most of us treat an automobile as a *consumer durable* and a *shopping good*. High in price, relative to our income, we buy it carefully and use it for several years. A stunt driver, on the other hand, may treat it as a producer's *raw material*, using up a different car at each performance. Some people treat a car as a *specialty good*, refusing to drive anything other than a Volkswagen or a Lincoln, and a wealthy person may buy a car on *impulse*, as the rest of us buy popcorn or peanuts.

A book may be put, at various times and

by various persons, in the same category as a sofa cushion, a refrigerator, a newspaper, or a pail of sand. If one wants to prop open a door, either a book or a pail of sand will serve. If he wants to bring a youngster's head above his plate at supper, he can seat the child on a book or on a sofa cushion. If he wants to read while his wife does the dishes, he can hide behind a newspaper or bury his nose in a book. If he is paying a personal property tax or collecting fire insurance, books and refrigerators go on the same list.

Note that in each instance, the category into which the book is put depends on a different attribute. When used to prop open a door, the attribute is *weight*, shared with the pail of sand. When used to elevate a child at the table, the important attribute, shared with the cushion, is *thickness*. *Verbal content* becomes important when the book is regarded as reading material; its *cost* becomes important for taxes and insurance. These critical attributes are often referred to as dimensions; a category is formed where dimensions intersect.

The fact that an object may be assigned to many different categories is of great importance in marketing. Until a seller knows which category buyers assign a product to, he cannot easily influence their behavior.

Research has found that some smokers see cigarettes as something to manipulate; the attribute of *firm-packing* interests them. To others, the cigarette is a means of comfort; they want *strength*. Those who seek oral sensation value *taste*, and those who seek relief for nervous tension don't seem to care what the cigarette tastes like. Some buyers put gasoline into a category with fuels like electricity, and others put it into a category of transportation along with bus tickets, but more than half the respondents in one survey classed it with items for personal consumption such as bread, boots, or beer. This suggested to researchers, who also knew that drivers perceive all brands of gasoline as being alike, that there was a great potential for personal involvement with gasoline which might be tapped through introducing magic additives, through advertising, or both.

Before marketing a product, a seller will do well to determine which attributes of existing products are most important in influencing brand choice and purchase. He may find that certain attributes are taken for granted; his brand must have them if it is even to be considered. He may find others are decisive: the purchaser values them and perceives differences among brands along these dimensions. He may find other dimensions, characteristic of "dissatisfied" users, on which existing products are seen as uniformly undesirable.

Combining Value Scores

The value of a category (which is reflected in the name given it and which influences the way prospects will behave toward it) is based on the values of the attributes or dimensions that enter into it. How should attribute scores be combined to obtain a composite value for the category? Some studies suggest that the category will have a value somewhere between the highest valued attribute and the lowest.[9] Others suggest that each positive-valued attribute raises the value of the category, so that it is always more highly valued than the best attribute. (Or, if all attributes are disliked, the category will be more disliked than the worst of the attributes.) Of course, attribute values are not independent of product categories. *Soup, beer, cold,* and *hot* can be valued separately as words, but cold beer and cold soup and hot beer and hot soup are very different things.

Three Basic Dimensions

There are so many possible attributes, and so many potential ways in which they can be combined, that one might despair of ever finding any patterns or principles at all. In fact, however, such patterns do exist and turn out to be fairly simple. They have been found by using the semantic differential,[10] a seven-point scale whose ends are marked by polar-opposite adjectives like these:

Good —:—:—:—:—:—:— Bad
Soft —:—:—:—:—:—:— Hard
Active —:—:—:—:—:—:— Passive

Using a great many such adjectives to rate 100 different concepts in a variety of languages and cultures, researchers have found the three basic dimensions represented by the scales above: evaluative (the most important), potency, and activity.

Since languages deal mainly with human beings, a sample of adjectives and nouns from any language will contain a high proportion of terms relevant to personality.[11] When such scales as *fair-unfair* must be applied to a concept like *tornado,* or concepts like *power, peace,* and *mother*

City	Schumacher	Crabb	Dooley	Maier
Albany, N.Y.	4	2	5	1
Bangor, Maine	5	1	6	2
Cleveland, Ohio	1	3	4	3
St. Louis, Mo.	2	4	3	4
San Diego, Calif.	3	6	1	5
Santa Fe, N.M.	6	5	2	6

must be rated as *hard-soft* or *hot-cold,* adjectives must be used metaphorically. Since metaphor is based on the emotions, Osgood regards his three basic factors—evaluative, potency, and activity—as measures of emotional meaning. He states that even facial expressions, the mirror of emotions, can be classed into these three factors.[12]

Categories of People

Although we have focused thus far on product and brand categories, people, too, must be classified into *market segments* and *audiences.*

A seller may categorize people by their demographic attributes, and then see whether people in different categories of income, education, age, and occupation respond differently to marketing, media, and message mixes. Or he may use buyer responses to categorize persons as light-, heavy-, and nonusers, and then ask whether members of these categories have different demographic characteristics or media-use habits.

Some buyers agree that an attribute is crucial to a decision but disagree on whether that decision should be "yes" or "no." We call such buyers, who agree on attribute but clash on their value for it, *collinear.*[13] Here is an example of what happened when four persons were asked to rank cities on their *livability.*

Schumacher likes big cities; he ranks cities in order of population. Crabb's rankings are just the reverse of Dooley's; apparently both are based on geography. (Unfortunately, north and east are correlated on this list: Bangor is at once the most eastern and the most northern city, and San Diego the most western and southern. We can't be sure whether Crabb likes Bangor because it's farthest north or farthest east or both. If we'd constructed the list more carefully—substituting Portland, Ore., for San Diego, for example, we should know). And Maier apparently didn't take the request seriously; there's no reason to suppose the alphabetical order has anything to do with livability.

Collinear individuals like Crabb and Dooley may find it easy to communicate with one another. The public relations man who's trying to lure industry to St. Louis will presumably refer to it as "gateway to the West" when he's talking to Dooley but reverse ground and emphasize its nearness to the East when he's addressing Crabb.

Categorizing Symbols and Sentences

Important as attributes are in classifying products and people, they are crucial in constructing messages. Advertising copywriters on automobile accounts, for example, stress speed, comfort, and beauty but avoid such other, inescapable attributes as rush-hour traffic jams and parking problems. Illustrators are more likely to show an auto speeding through open country or at rest in front of a mansion than parked on a city street.

Theories that attempt to explain how words fit together in a language range from simple to complex. One of the simpler theories is that of Osgood's *semantic interaction* technique.[14] *SUDDEN surprise,* Osgood suggests, makes sense, but *melancholy* is *enduring* rather than sudden in its onset. In fact, he suggests that most parts

of speech can be classed as continuous or terminal, whether they are verbs (*believe* vs. *happen*), nouns (*infinity* vs. *a moment*) and adverbs (*incessantly* vs. *abruptly*).

Far more detailed theories range from very old to very new: from Aristotle's logic to Chomsky's transformational grammar.

Syllogisms

The key concept in logic is the *categorical syllogism,* with rules for combining sentences into valid statements and avoiding fallacies. The syllogism has three parts.

(The element of such a syllogism is also called the minor term, the category the middle term, and the value, which forms the predicate in the conclusion, the major term.)

Here is a very simple message, designed to convince an audience that all advertising is good. The laws of logic say that the audience is bound to accept this conclusion if it can be convinced of two things: (1) that both premises are true and (2) that the conclusion logically follows from the premises.

A *premise*, naming the category to which an element belongs:	**All advertising is free.***
	(element) (category)
A *premise*, making a value statement about the category:	**All free things are good.**
	(category) (value)
A *conclusion* in which the category vanishes and the value attaches directly to the element:	**All advertising . . . is good.**
	(element) (value)

---

* The reader who rejects this premise out of hand as obviously untrue is looking at it from the standpoint of a seller to whom advertising may be very expensive. A sophisticated buyer will realize that the ultimate consumer pays for advertising, whether he sees the ad or not. A reader who enjoys an ad but fails to buy the product is being subsidized by the buyer who pays for the product but doesn't see or enjoy the ad.

An audience in real life may, of course, and often does accept a conclusion without regard to the truth of the premises; its approval of a conclusion may sometimes lead it to accept the premises as well. The logician, however, says that a reasonable man will first make a check of logical validity in this sequence: First, he classifies each sentence into one of the following types, traditionally given the labels, A, E, I, or O.

conclusion must also be distributed in the premises. (If we want to say that all advertising is good, we must also say all advertising—not just some—is free, and that all free things, not just some of them, are good.)

3. If the two premises are negative, no conclusion can be drawn.

4. If one premise is negative, the conclusion must be negative.

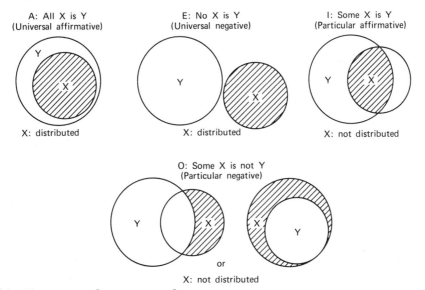

Figure 4.1   Four types of sentences in logic.

Next, he applies these rules for the categorical syllogism.

The three sentences of our syllogism each take the "A" *form* and these diagrams show that our reasoning is valid.

1. The middle term—"free things" in our example—must be distributed at least once; that is, the words *all* or *none* must modify it. (We must make a statement about the entire category, not just part of it.)

2. Any term that is distributed in the

(Notice that the premises are not symmetrical; one is not permitted to say that all free things are advertising or that all good things are free.)

Sometimes messages that violate the laws of logic are, nevertheless, effective. A list of such violations, called *fallacies,* may serve as protection for the wary receiver and scrupulous copywriter, or guidebook for the adman who wants results, however they may be achieved.

Types of Fallacies

Formal fallacies represent violations of the rules; *informal fallacies* include a list of debaters' tricks and propaganda techniques. Below are examples of the former, with diagrams to show why they are invalid.

Undistributed middle. This violates the rule that the middle term must be distributed (stated in all or none form) at least once: *Some poison is medicine. Some medicine is healthy. Some poison is healthy.*

Illicit term. This violates the rule that says no term may be distributed (stated in all or none form) in a conclusion if it is not distributed in the premises: *Some admen are intelligent. All good men are intelligent. All admen are good men.*

Exclusive premises. This violates a rule that says both premises may not be negative: *No retailers are manufacturers. No consumers are manufacturers. Therefore some retailers are consumers.*

Still another rule bars drawing an *affirmative conclusion from negative premises.*

1. *Cause-and-effect* or *hypothetical syllogisms* involve relationships in time, rather than space. The major premise contains an antecedent (*if it rains*) and a *consequent* (*we will be soaked*). The minor premise affirms the antecedent (*it IS raining*). The conclusion follows (*we will be soaked*).

The other types of syllogism concern alternatives; a logician's rules concerning their interpretation differ from those of the layman.

2. The *alternative syllogism* begins with a statement such as *either the driver has a Chevrolet or he has a Ford.* One checks to see if he has a Chevrolet:

Fact	Conclusion
He does not have a Chevrolet	
	therefore he must have a Ford.
He has a Chevrolet	
	therefore he does not have a Ford.

The first conclusion is valid, the second is not; the conventions of logic allow a third possibility: the driver may own both makes.

3. The *disjunctive syllogism* says *a driver cannot own both a Chevrolet and a Ford.*

Fact	Conclusion
He does not own a Ford	
	therefore he must own a Chevrolet.
He does own a Ford	
	therefore he cannot own a Chevrolet.

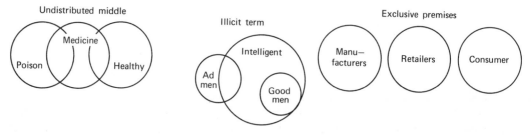

There are three kinds of syllogisms in addition to the categorical syllogism we have been discussing, each with its attendant fallacies.

The first of these is invalid, the second valid, since the logician's rules interpret the original statement to permit the driver to own *neither* type of car.

The fallacies associated with these two types of alternative and disjunctive syllogisms constitute the fallacy of *ignorance,* in which a speaker argues that having proved one alternative is not true, its opposite must be true.

Other frequently found *informal fallacies* include the following.

Division. This suggests that an attribute of a group necessarily attaches to each individual in a group. (A rich union may be made up of poor members, however.) Its opposite, *composition,* implies that attributes of individual members necessarily characterize the group. (An organization of wise men, however, may behave unwisely.)

Black or white. This suggests that a thing must be A or B, rather than a mixture of the two or something else entirely. (The opposite of this, the fallacy of the *beard,* implies that since it is hard to say when the addition of a single hair brings a beard into being, no such thing as a beard can exist.)

Several informal fallacies involve misuse of evidence: a rule may be applied to a case where it is inappropriate, or a single case or inadequate set of cases may be used as the basis for a rule. When one argues that because Market Segment A resembles Market Segment B in six attributes it must also resemble B in attributes 7 through 11, he is committing the fallacy of a *misused analogy.* Another fallacy is involved when one argues that a course must be correct because it lies midway between two extremes.

Other fallacies, related to the *source* of a message, occur when *authority* is substituted for evidence, fame for expert knowledge, or an expert in one field testifies in another. And it is a fallacy to argue that a course is correct because "everybody" is doing it. On the other hand, the *ad hominem* fallacy attempts to discredit a message by attacking its source as unqualified or biased or by showing that his words contradict themselves or are contradicted by his behavior. (Evil men may produce both valid and invalid arguments.)

Still other fallacies relate to the *style* of a message. Sometimes they beg the question—taking for granted the real issue in the matter. (Thus a lawyer demands, "When did you stop beating your wife?" and the salesman asks "Cash or credit?" before you've agreed to buy.) Little phrases, such as "You haven't . . ." or "Didn't you . . . ?" assume an answer.

Responding to Fallacies

Ultimately, of course, a buyer's experience with a product and brand will test the validity of its claims. Moreover, men's attitudes and beliefs resist change, even if this means they must accept fallacies or change premises to fit their prior conclusions.

Scientists seeking order in men's illogic have come up with a theory of "psycho-logic"[15] in which categories are related to one another in one of four ways: *positive* (like, equal, own, affirm), *negative* (opposite, prevent, to be incompatible with), *ambivalent* (both positive and negative), or *irrelevant.* These relationships may exist between two persons, an action and its outcome, and so on, according to the rules of psycho-logic. Two such rules lead to this interesting situation, which is quite contrary to ordinary logic.

AnB and BnC imply ApC	*ApD and DnC imply AnC*
Margaret (A) dislikes (n) trips to the dentist (B).	Margaret (A) likes (p) brushing her teeth (D).
Trips to the dentist (B) are a means of fighting (n) tooth decay (C).	Brushing teeth (D) is a way of fighting (n) tooth decay (C).
Therefore: Margaret (A) likes (p) decayed teeth (C).	Therefore: Margaret (A) dislikes (n) decayed teeth (C).
In common-sense terms: "We like someone who dislikes the same things (or people) whom we dislike."	In common-sense terms: "We dislike things that are disliked by people whom we like" or "We share the dislikes of our friends."

Thus, by plausible sounding associations, one comes to contradictory conclusions! The contradiction is plausible: such ambivalent feelings appear to be quite common in daily life. A seller who knows of such ambivalent feelings can often exploit them to his own advantage.

Thought, Talk, and Action

1. Imagine that you are running for governor. List all the attributes you can, including both experience and your positions on public issues. From this list, select attributes you would emphasize for these situations: a breakfast for party workers, an evening meeting of uncommitted members of the public, and a luncheon with a hostile group.
2. Using the six different kinds of definitions in this chapter, define yourself, the institution you are attending, an auto you have driven, and your present residence.
3. For each of the audiences listed in No. 1 above, pick one proposal that would be accepted, one rejected. Now, by combining and splitting categories, try to reverse attitudes on these proposals. Then do the same for cigarettes and vodka—making users reject them, and non-users accept them.

Notes

Chapter 4

1. E. Heidbreder, "The attainment of concepts: 1. Terminology and methodology," Journal of General Psychology, 35:2: 173–89.
2. Jerome Kagan and Ernest Havemann, Psychology: An introduction (New York: Harcourt, Brace and World, 1968), pp. 199–200.
3. Jerome S. Bruner et al., A study of thinking (New York: John Wiley and Sons, 1956).
4. Jerome S. Bruner et al., "Expectation and the perception of color," American Journal of Psychology, 64:216–27.
5. Robert S. Woodworth and Harold Schlosberg, Experimental psychology, rev. ed. (New York: Holt, Rinehart and Winston, 1964).
6. S. E. Asch, "Forming impressions of personality," Journal of Abnormal and Social Psychology, 41:258–90.

7. Harold H. Kelley, "The warm-cold variable in first impressions of persons," Journal of Personality, 18:431–9.
8. A. J. Judson and C. N. Cofer, "Reasoning as an associative process: 1. Direction in a simple verbal problem," Psychological Reports, 2:469–76.
9. Gardner Lindzey and Elliot Aronson, editors, The handbook of social psychology, 2nd edition (Reading, Mass.: Addison-Wesley Publishing Co., 1968), Vol. I: pp. 187–93; Vol. III: pp. 154–5.
10. Charles E. Osgood et al., The measurement of meaning (Urbana: University of Illinois Press, 1957).
11. Charles E. Osgood, "On the whys and wherefores of E, P, and A," Journal of Personality and Social Psychology, 12:194–9.
12. C. E. Osgood, "Dimensionality of the semantic space for communications via facial expressions," Scandinavian Journal of Psychology, 7:1–30.
13. P. J. Runkel, "Cognitive similarity in facilitating communication," Sociometry, 19:178–91.
14. Same as No. 11.
15. R. F. Abelson and M. J. Rosenberg, "Symbolic psycho-logic: A model of attitudinal cognition," Behavioral Science, 3:1–13.

Attributes That Affect Buyer Choice

Before a seller puts a new brand on the market, he needs to know what attributes he should build into his product and stress in his advertising. One way of finding out is to ask housewives.

Interviews with Chicago housewives revealed that they looked for 6 key attributes in buying cleanser and 4 in purchasing coffee. Shown these attributes, a new set of 465 housewives then scored competing brands on each attribute, indicated brand preferences on a 9-point, satisfactory-unsatisfactory scale, and told interviewers which brand they had bought.

An arbitrary score of 1.00 was given to the attribute that correlated highest with preference and purchase—*ability to clean* for cleansers and *flavor* for coffee. *Number of cups per pound* had more to do with preference than *price* (.10 to .05) but price (.43 to 0) had more influence on purchase. *Grittiness* was given as an explanation of cleanser preference, but only *price* and harshness on hands influenced purchases.

Source. Seymour Banks, "The relationships between preference and purchase of brands," *Journal of Marketing*, 15:2:145–7.

In Los Angeles, 50 housewives rated 10 attributes of dry milk on six-point scales, with scores on each attribute being correlated with total scores for all attributes. Here are sample figures.

Instant Nonfat Dry Milk Is:	r	r^2	Mean
Better than skim milk	.70	.81	3.6
Economical	.76	.58	4.9
Appetizing	.49	.24	3.0
Kids like it	.25	.06	3.1
Best with snacks	.17	.03	3.1

(The r^2 column means that "economical" ratings explained 58% of total ratings for dry milk and "best with snacks" only 3%.)

Two ads were then devised, one stressing the two attributes at the top of the list and the other those at the bottom. Given a choice of two brands, 94% of respondents chose that advertised as *better than skim milk* and *economical,* compared with 6% who chose it because *kids like it* and *it is best with snacks.*

Source. Lawrence G. Corey, "How to isolate product attributes," *Journal of Advertising Research,* 10:4:41–4.

Combining Attributes

After a seller finds out what attributes buyers want, he would like to know how various attribute combinations will affect brand preference and choice. One theory says that overall preference depends on the *average,* another that it depends on the *sum* of the values of the individual attributes. The first theory favors two high-rated attributes against a combination of four high and two medium attributes; the second theory favors the four-attribute combination.

In this study, subjects were asked to rate individuals on two or four adjectives; results shown suggest that adding two more *moderate* adjectives did little to reduce the impact of two extreme adjectives.

Adjectives	Mean Scores
2 highly favorable	73
2 highly, 2 moderately favorable	71
2 moderately favorable	58
2 moderately unfavorable	42
2 highly unfavorable, 2 moderately so	26
2 highly unfavorable	24

Four adjectives of the *same* value, however, consistently showed greater effects than two.

Value of Adjectives	Mean Scores for:	
	2 Adjectives	4 Adjectives
Very favorable	73	79
Favorable	58	63
Unfavorable	42	39
Very unfavorable	24	18

Source. N. H. Anderson, "Averaging versus adding as a stimulus-combination rule in impression formation," *Journal of Experimental Psychology,* 70:394–400.

In another study, 100 undergraduates rated characters on 5 seven-point evaluative scales, read a message about one of them, Mrs. Williams, and then rated the characters again. Five messages were used. One didn't mention Mrs. Williams, another described her as *honest,* a third added that she was *friendly,* and a fourth that she was *helpful.* (The fifth repeated the adjective *helpful.*) Each subject also rated the adjectives on the same scales used to rate Mrs. Williams.

Thus Mrs. Williams had two scores: one based on the values of the adjectives used in describing her, the other an overall rating.

For the total group of 100 subjects, the predicted score obtained by *averaging* scores for the adjectives correlated .38 with actual ratings. Correlation with actual ratings for the score obtained by *adding* correlated .66.

Source. Lynn R. Anderson and Martin Fishbein, "Prediction of attitude from the number, strength and evaluation aspect of beliefs about the attitude object," *Journal of Personality and Social Psychology,* 3:437–43.

Another experiment supporting the additive rather than averaging theory began by asking 25 students to rate eight descriptive terms on a seven-point good-bad scale. The terms concerned color (white, Negro), occupation (bank manager, coal miner), nationality (French, Portuguese), and religion (same as the subject or different). Various combinations of terms were then rated by the students and the ratings correlated with predictions based on averaging or on adding scores of the several attributes. In five out of six cases addition gave the higher correlation.

Correlation of Obtained Ratings
with Predictions Based on:

Color	Nationality	Job	Religion	Averaging	Adding
White	French	banker	same	.80	.77
Negro	Portuguese	miner	different	.78	.84
White	Portuguese	miner	different	.63	.77
Negro	French	banker	same	.60	.70
White	Portuguese	miner	same	.53	.73
Negro	French	banker	different	.41	.65
Average				.65	.75

Source. Harry C. Triandis and Martin Fishbein, "Cognitive interaction in person perception," *Journal of Abnormal and Social Psychology,* 67:446–53.

A Rose by Any Other Name Would Probably Smell Terrible

By changing the label on a category one can change the "meaning" it has for an individual: I am *firm,* you are *stubborn,* he is *pigheaded.* Expectations as to flavor, texture and other sensory rewards, are summed up in a brand name. *Remove* the brand name and you may discover that the brand differences you thought you could taste have vanished with it.

Free six-packs of beer, from which brand identification had been removed, were given 326 beer drinkers to test and rate on nine three-point scales, involving such qualities as aroma, lightness, and after-taste, and one 10-point, poor-to-excellent scale. Each pack contained three of the five brands—two regionals and three nationals—being tested. There were no significant differences on the 10-point scale. Drinkers agreed that none of the unlabeled beers had enough aroma, body, foam, or strength and that all of them were too bitter. Drinkers were not able to identify their favorite brand, when sampled "blind." With labels restored in a second six-pack, all brands got higher ratings and ratings of aroma, body, foam, and strength all rose. Significant differences in ratings showed up for four of the five brands, and drinkers showed clear-cut preferences for their usual brand.

Source. Ralph I. Allison and Kenneth P. Uhl, "Influence of beer brand identification on taste perception," *Journal of Marketing Research,* 1:3:36–9.

To nail down this evidence of the significance of brand names, another researcher took identical loaves of bread, and attached meaningless labels: the letters L, M, P, and H. Each of 42 women made 12 consecutive choices. Twenty-nine of the women used their first four choices to try each "brand" in turn; a few of them never picked the same brand twice in succession. One woman, however, proved "brand loyal" on the third trial, and 21 were consistently favoring one brand by the end of the experiment. Six more consistently rejected one of the brands as being inferior. The study also tested *strength* of brand preferences. As soon as a woman had picked the same label three times in a row, a penny was attached to the brand she had picked least often, and another penny was added each trial until she switched to

this brand: six women switched to this brand, for rebates of two to seven cents, but not everyone was persuaded by price. One woman said: "No wonder you put the special on Brand P. It is the worst one of all."

Source. W. T. Tucker, "The development of brand loyalty," *Journal of Marketing Research,* 1:3:32–5.

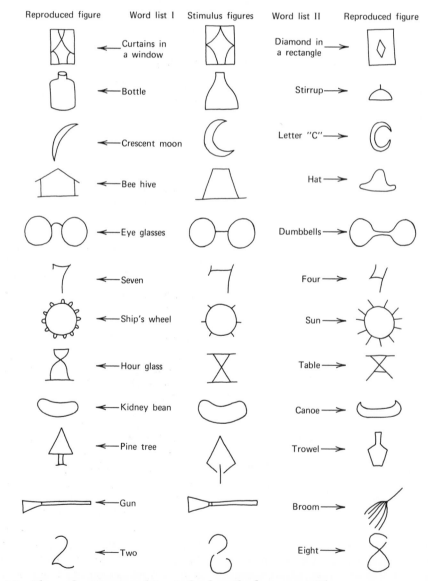

Figure 4.2 These drawings used in study described on page 95.

In these studies, when brands of beer lost their labels, they lost their distinctive tastes, yet when identical loaves of bread were marked by different labels, they began to taste different. Meanings attached to labels through advertising apparently affect perceptions. Labels also affect memory.

Subjects were shown the pictures shown in the center column of Fig. 4.2, bearing labels shown at the right or the left. When asked to reproduce what they had seen later, their drawings (first and third columns) were influenced by the labels attached to them. They seem to have forgotten the pictures shown them and made their drawings match the remembered labels.

The center column of figures represents those shown to subjects. Columns on the side show the figures that subjects later reproduced and the effects of the labels attached to them.

Source. L. Carmichael, H. P. Hogan, and A. A. Walter, "An experimental study of the effect of language on the reproduction of visually perceived form," *Journal of Experimental Psychology,* 15:73–86.

The Whorf-Sapir hypothesis holds that English and other Indo-European languages deal in entities rather than events, in a world of dichotomies and extremes rather than degrees. English speakers, it is argued, tend to view the world in these terms more than do users of such other languages as the American Indians'.

In English, one speaks of 10 days as if they could be assembled in one place, like 10 salesmen or 10 magazine ads; the Hopi, instead, speak of the 10th day. Anglos say that *John Jones is dying,* implying an act of will, whereas the Navaho say, *Dying is occurring in John.* In English, *lightning* is an entity which *flashes;* to Navaho, there is just a flashing. In English someone must pick up something; the Navajo drop both subject and object but attach one of 12 suffixes to the verb to indicate whether the thing picked up is a single animate object, long and slender, rope or fabric, and whether the agent is animate or inanimate.

Language differs; do perceptions also differ? To answer this question, Navaho children were shown two objects, differing in size, color, or shape, and asked which most closely resembled a third, which matched the shape of one, the color of the other.

Navaho language emphasizes shape, and the test showed that Indian children speaking Navaho were more likely than those speaking English to match on shape.

	Original Pair	Test Object
A.	Yellow rope/blue stick	Blue rope
B.	Yellow stick/blue cylinder	Blue stick

Percent Matching on Basis of Shape	
Navaho-speaking	English-speaking
A. 71	40
B. 71	44

When color was contrasted with size, size not being stressed in Navaho verbs, 85% of both groups matched a medium blue cube with a large blue cube rather than a medium white cube.

Unfortunately for the hypothesis, English-speaking children tested in Boston out-Navahoed the Navaho-speakers: from 83 to 100% matched on the basis of shape!

Source. John B. Carroll and Joseph B. Casagrande, "The function of language classifications in behavior," in Eleanor Maccoby et al., *Readings in Social Psychology* (New York: Holt, Rinehart and Winston, 1958).

Labels reflect cross-cultural differences in categories; whether they *cause* differences in categories is arguable. Labels also reflect differences in time; language changes to accommodate historical changes in technology and social relationships.

One of the most interesting examples of the way that language changes to reflect social change is that which began in early Latin with two second-person pronouns: *tos* for one person and *vos* for more than one. In the fifth century, the V-form began being used in speaking to the emperor, who replied with the T-form. By the Middle Ages such usage between persons of unequal status had become general: parents said T to children and got V in return, noblemen said T and vassals replied with V, angels said V to God and T to men, men addressed animals as T. (Even animals conformed: big animals gave T to small ones in folk tales and got V in return.)
However, the two pronouns also began to express the degree of intimacy existing between speakers: T being used between friends, V between strangers.
These two "meanings" began to conflict. Should daughter speaking to her mother use T for intimacy or V for respect? (The mother has no problem, since T expresses both meanings—intimacy and status.) Growth of the democratic ideal of equality resolved the problem in languages like French, German, Japanese, and Yiddish: T came to symbolize intimacy, ceased to express differences in status. The change continues (only since World War II have French army regulations required officers to address enlisted men as V) and is not yet universal. A study of six unequal-status relationships, three between intimates (parent-son, master-servant, siblings of different ages) and three between strangers (customer-waiter, officer-soldier, employer-employee) found that 27% of Italian replies as compared with 12% of those

by Germans, retained the T/V status distinction, most often between master and servant.
English saw a somewhat different development. The pronoun *thou* was lost; the need for the T-V distinction remained and was met in the form of address: first-name (FN) for intimates or title-and-last-name (TLN) for strangers. Status, however, still affects usage. A graduate student may give his professors TLN and get last-name-without-title in return whenever Dr. Brown and Smith confer. Very dignified, prestigious, or ancient professors may be TLN-ed to the end of their lives.

Source. Roger Brown, *Social Psychology* (New York: The Free Press, 1965).

Interesting remnants of the conflict between status and intimacy abound: beauty shop operators have their first names stitched on their uniforms, but address their clients as "Madame." Insurance salesmen, often address clients by their first name, to the frequent discomfort of clients who feel such usage is justified neither by friendship nor status. The salesman may use FN deliberately to create an atmosphere of pseudo- or quasi-friendship. Or he may be rebelling against remnants of a master-servant relationship in the purchase-sale encounter or, he may seek to dominate the conversation by asserting the higher status that FN symbolizes.

Fallacies Aid Seller

The ad says *99 and 44/100% pure . . . it floats* but the reader who replaces the dots with a *therefore* commits a *post hoc, propter hoc* fallacy. How often does a reader commit fallacies so beneficial to the seller?

Two sets of 15 advertisements, chosen to illustrate 13 different logical fallacies, were shown to 60 college students. Five statements accompanied each ad, students being asked to check which of the five represented an accurate rephrasing of its content. In actuality, only one statement in each set of five was an accurate paraphrase; students checked it an average of 13.3 times out of a possible 15. But they also checked logically *invalid* inferences nearly as often as they checked logically valid inferences.

Type of Statement	Average Frequency Statement Accepted as Accurate
Accurate paraphrase	13.3
Logically valid inference	11.6
Logically invalid inference	9.8
Irrelevant to ad content	5.0
False	2.0

Among the types of logical fallacies presented (and accepted) were the following.

If X then Y: If Y then X. The ad said a Salem cigarette is different. The invalid inference said that Salem is the ONLY cigarette that is different.

Some X are Y: All X are Y. Indianapolis 500 winners use Champion spark plugs. Invalid inference: such plugs are best for ordinary driving.

If X then Y: Assumes X is in fact true. The ad said you need Geritol if you have tired blood. The invalid inference was that you do, in fact, have tired blood.

In discussions afterward, subjects admitted that the ads didn't actually make the invalid inferences in so many words but argued that this must have been the intent of the ads. Why, they asked, should Bayer report that doctors recommend bed rest and aspirin in case of colds unless they wanted readers to interpret the message as meaning *Bayer aspirin?*

The illogical inferences, in short, were quite valid *interpretations* based on what readers perceived to be the intentions of the source.

Source. Ivan L. Preston, "Logic and illogic in the advertising process," *Journalism Quarterly,* 44:231–9.

Although readers may have correctly perceived what the advertiser wanted them to believe, however illogical, this does not necessarily mean that they believed it.

To check on this possibility, texts of 15 of the ads used in the previous study were given to 110 students at the University of Houston, along with the five statements. As shown in the table below, students responded in this replication much as they had done in the earlier study. However, when the statements were given to the students two days later with instructions to check on their *believability,* acceptance of the invalid inferences dropped notably, acceptance of valid inferences somewhat less.

Type of Statement	Mean Number of Statements Checked as: Accurate Paraphrase	Believable
Accurate paraphrase	12.9	10.4
Valid inference	10.5	7.4
Invalid inference	10.7	5.6
Irrelevant to ad content	3.4	11.9
Reversal of ad content	1.3	3.6

Both valid and invalid inferences dropped in acceptance, the valid inferences having a slight advantage.

Source. William E. Kilbourne.

An earlier study revealed that the way premises were stated predisposed students to accept some conclusions and reject others, without regard to their logical validity.

In this study, 31 university students were given the major and minor premises of seven syllogisms, with five possible conclusions for each, only one of which was logically valid. In three examples invalid conclusions were preferred, because of an "atmosphere" effect. (A negative premise led to a preference for negative conclusions; a "some" premise caused a preference for "some" conclusions.)

Over Time, Beliefs Become More Logical

Over time, apparently without any conscious effort, individuals' conclusions do tend to come into line with premises, as shown in this study.

Thirty high school seniors and 90 college freshmen rated 48 statements as to their likelihood of being true, on a 0 to 100 scale, and as to their desirability, on a 5-point scale.

Each statement was taken from a syllogism like the following.

Form of Premise		Percentage Favoring Invalid "Atmosphere" Conclusion	Percentage Favoring Valid Conclusions
Major	Minor		
Some are	Inversion of some are ...	87	7
All are	None are	49	39
All are	Some are not	62	32

The three in which a majority of subjects preferred valid conclusions were these forms: A and converse of O, O, and E, and E and converse of O.

Surprisingly, when letters were substituted for meaningful words in the test (supposedly removing the misleading influence of subjects' attitudes toward the premises), *fewer* valid conclusions were checked for six of the seven syllogisms.

Students who violate any regulation that has been made to safeguard the lives and property of other students will be expelled. (Major premise)

The regulations against smoking in the classrooms and corridors were made to safeguard the lives and property of the student. (Minor premise)

Students who violate the regulation against smoking in the classrooms and corridors will be expelled. (Conclusion)

(The three statements in a syllogism were separated and interspersed with statements from other syllogisms.)

As expected, conclusions which students ranked as more desirable than their premises were more likely to be rated as true.

Source. Reuben Mehling, "A study of non-logical factors of reasoning in the communication process," *Journal of Communication,* 9:118–26.

Desirability of Conclusions	Joint Probability of Premises	Probability of Conclusions
Lower than premises	33.7	35.9
Higher than premises	30.1	47.3

One week later, students were given messages of 200 to 300 words which sought to raise probability ratings for 16 of the original premises. Ratings rose not only for the premises, but for the conclusions. Two weeks later, students repeated their ratings. Probability of the premises treated in the messages dropped sharply in the interim, from 17.6 to 9.1, but probability of the conclusions fell very little, from 6.0 to 4.5. Ratings for conclusions rose 52% as far after one week as they would need for logical consistency with ratings of premises; in two weeks they had made 90% of the change (11.6 and 4.9).

Messages most effective in changing probability ratings concerned either major premises or conclusions.

Source. William J. McGuire, "Cognitive consistency and attitude change," *Journal of Abnormal and Social Psychology*, 60:345–53.

Looking for Sense in Men's Illogic

Logicians despair of man when they observe how frequently he violates the rules they've laid down for rational thought. Persevering psychologists find, however, that there are intelligible patterns to be found even in illogical man. Here is an example.

Each of 117 students was given a deck of 64 cards. Each card contained two premises of a linear syllogism plus a conclusion stated in the form of a question which students were expected to answer in 10 seconds.

Logicians assumed that these two forms of the syllogism would be easiest to answer, since they proceeded consistently.

Premise
A is better (>) than B
C is worse (<) than B

Premise
B is better (>) than C
B is worse (<) than A

Conclusion
A is better than (>) C
C is worse than (<) A

Six other sequences were possible: the better or the worse premise could come first, with the sequence going worse-better, better-worse, middle-to-ends, ends-to-middle.

Contrary to the logicians' expectations, of eight possible combinations, the second (C < B, B < A) proved one of the three most difficult. Here are the results.

The authors cite two principles of learning to explain the results. (1) It's easier to learn in better-to-worse direction than the reverse, which explains the first four figures in this table, and (2) people learn the ends of a series before they learn the middle

Initial Element

Statement		Within Premises	Between Premises	Percent Correct
A > B	B > C	Better	Better	61
B > C	A > B	Better	Worse	53
B < A	C < B	Worse	Better	50
C < B	B < A	Worse	Worse	43
A > B	C < B	Ends	Better	62
C < B	A > B	Ends	Worse	57
B < A	B > C	Middle	Better	42
B > C	B < A	Middle	Worse	38

(which explains the second four figures).

Respondents said they solved the problems by visualizing the men's names (which were substituted for letters) in space, with the best man highest in a vertical array. This tendency was tested in a second study in which subjects were given printed statements like these, one at a time.

Tom is better than Bill
Bill is worse than Tom
Tom has darker hair than Bill
Bill has lighter hair than Tom

Accompanying each statement was a sheet of paper, with a cross on it, with boxes at each end of the cross in which the names were to be written as they were read. Sure enough, out of 25 subjects given *better* first, 23 entered the first name (the *worse* man) at the bottom. This wasn't true of hair color, however. The first adjective given, whether *lighter* or *darker,* was put into the lefthand or topmost box. It appears that time sequence determined placement of hair color in left to right sequence, but that evaluative terms were located in terms of higher and lower.

Source. Clinton B. DeSoto, Marvin London, and Stephen Handel, "Social reasoning and spatial paralogic," *Journal of Personality and Social Psychology,* 2:513–21.

Some Categories Are Easier to Learn than Others

By the time most of us get to the door of a psychological laboratory, we have learned so many categories that considerable ingenuity is required to devise sets we have not yet learned.

In this study, subjects were shown a picture, heard it named by the experimenter, then repeated the name. Five of the 16 series presented are shown on page 101. Each series consisted of nine pictures, one for each category to be learned.

Labels for the first column, reading from the top, are *ling, fard, relf, pran, leth, pilt, stod, mank,* and *molp.* Labels for the second column, same order, are: *pran, relf, pilt, molp, ling, fard, leth, stod,* and *mank.* Can you label the third, fourth, and fifth columns correctly? As the text notes, objects are easiest to learn, number concepts hardest.

Additional Research Readings

Attributes. Ratings of 10 attributes of dry milk, with results subsequently tested in model ads, showed 94% preference for "better than skim milk," compared with 6% "best for snacks." **Lawrence G. Corey, "How to isolate product attributes," Journal of Advertising Research, 10:4:41–4.**

Labels. Given identical slices of turkey, only 34% of subjects chose those labeled with an unknown brand. Given tough and tender slices, 63% identified the tender with the known brand. **James C. Makens, "Effect of brand preference upon consumers' perceived taste of turkey meat," Journal of Applied Psychology, 49:261–3.**

Fallacies. Evidence that readers tend to add to ad content was obtained by giving the same 12 messages four different identities. When invalid statements were identified as ads, they were accepted by 63% of subjects; when they were identified as letters, they were accepted by 54% and as news stories by 49%. **Ivan L. Preston and Steven E. Scharback, "Advertising: More than meets the eye?" Journal of Advertising Research, 11:3:19–24.**

Some Categories Are Easier to Learn than Others

Series I	Series II	Series III	Series IV	Series V

Source. E. Heidbreder, "The attainment of concepts: I: Terminology and methodology, 2," *Journal of General Psychology*, 35:2: 173–89.

Image Building by Firm and Industry

Most advertisers select *media* that reach a high proportion of prospects for their products, and *messages* that will persuade them to buy the products and services they want to sell. Here are six exceptions from an outstanding campaign by the St. Regis paper company: ads directed to consumers, even though the firm sells to industrial buyers, and containing no product information whatsoever. The beauty of the full-color ads, only hinted at in black and white reproduction, provides one *reward* for the reader. The interesting information about forest life contained in the ads provides another. These goals substitute for the aid in making a purchasing decision which most ads provide their readers.

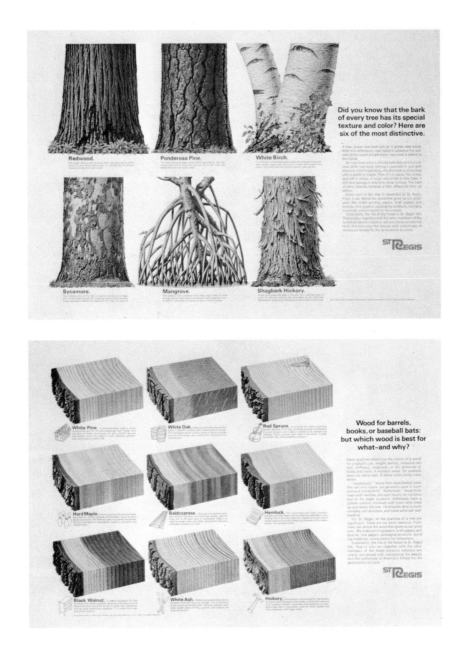

Print Ads Live Longer

Although a TV commercial vanishes as one watches it, print ads like these may survive for years on the walls of a child's bedroom or a classroom, continuing to work for the advertiser years after he's paid the media for running them. Surely few can read them without being awakened to the wonders of the world they live in, or without feeling that St. Regis must share their love for living things. Only in the bottom ad are we reminded that trees are useful when cut down, as well as when standing in the forest, but even this ad lacks any plea for St. Regis products.

102b

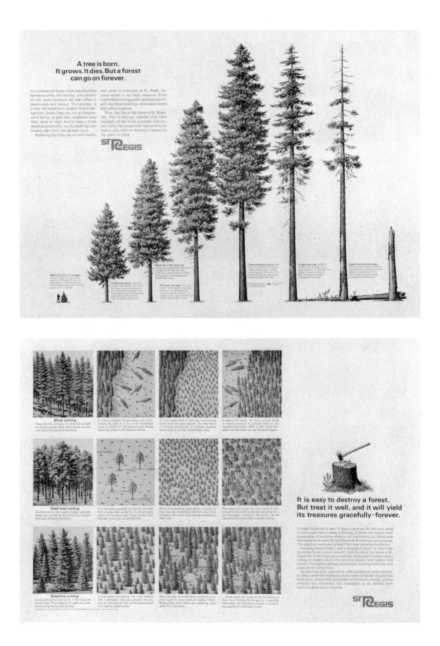

Indirect Reply to Critics

Few industries have been subject to more sustained attacks from conservationists than the pulp and paper industry—first for cutting down trees and then for pollution incident to the manufacture of paper. If the industry tried to meet its critics head-on, the ads might *boomerang* by spreading the critics' message to people who hadn't heard it. In these ads, St. Regis points out that all trees must eventually die, but that tree-farming can constantly renew a forest. Without acknowledging that foes of clear-cutting exist, St. Regis informs the reader that lumbering methods must vary with the kind of trees involved.

Chapter 5 Synopsis

● Two problems are involved in using research to guide a seller's decisions: the scientific problem of being sure that cause-effect relationships exist, and the practical problem of finding causes that can be manipulated by the decision maker.

● Feasible as a goal from a scientific viewpoint, sales often fail to meet decision-making criteria, being too late in time and not specific enough to guide decisions at all points in an organization or for all audiences.

● Surveys that ask prospects to report past behavior or predict future behavior may be useful, depending on whether buying is directed by habit or by planning. But, by themselves, neither type of survey explains why buyers behave as they do.

● Comparison of users and nonusers, projective techniques, and a combination of reports from laymen and experts may uncover answers to the why question by discovering motivations of the buyer.

● The method applicable to the widest variety of seller's problems is loosely defined as attitude research. Just as *meaning* discussed in Chapter 4, emphasized goals from the standpoint of the message, *attitude*—the flip side of meaning—emphasizes goals from the standpoint of the person receiving the message.

● A wide variety of techniques for measuring attitudes exists, ranging from physiological measures, suitable to the feeling component of attitudes, to measures of abstract beliefs. Measures of action-tendencies, the third component of attitude, are also needed. Changes in any of these components will produce changes in the others; messages usually operate primarily on the belief or cognitive components.

● Inconsistencies among a set of beliefs tend to be reconciled over time; balance and congruity theories suggest how a communicator can best proceed given a specific state of inconsistency by indicating which belief changes are most strategic.

● To determine which beliefs are most vulnerable to change, one needs to look at the beliefs themselves, at the persons who hold them, and at the forces that brought them into being.

● Messages are only one of the forces that introduce inconsistency into a belief system and only one of the influences that lead to beliefs being expressed in action. Attitude change is a goal to be sought and an effect to be measured when one is devising media and message mixes, but attitude change may not produce a measurable change in buying behavior.

Research Articles

Belief Change. Minimum rewards cause more change in beliefs
to match actions (Festinger); hypnosis-induced change in
feelings followed by change in beliefs (Rosenberg).

Cause, Effect. Attitudes instrumental to values accepted more
readily (Rosenberg, Carlson); one tends to perceive what
one wants to (Hastorf); six factors affect power of attitudes
to determine behavior (Dollard).

Balance Theories. Deprived of sensory input, subjects seek
novelty—challenging theories of attitude consistency and
selective perception (Jones).

Chapter 5 Goals of the Communicator: Attitudes

Even if one were to repeat as a litany at three-hour intervals throughout the day the rubric, *meanings are in people,* the very word *meaning* would still suggest that every object has a singular correct meaning —however errant individual perceivers may be. A term like *attitude,* on the other hand, implies attitudes *of* someone *toward* something; since we know people vary, we expect their attitudes to differ. Thus, even though *meanings* and *attitudes* apply to the same phenomenon, a relationship between perceiver and thing perceived, *attitudes* seems the better term, being used oftener and more easily in correct fashion in studying buyer behavior.

The seller has three ways of studying the buyer. He can observe the buyer in action in a store. He can observe the results of such action, in the form of emptied store shelves or filled pantry shelves. Or he can ask questions of buyers—questions about what they know, feel, and do. All answers that buyers give reflect buyer attitudes to a degree varying with interviewer, respondent, and question. This chapter is concerned with the questions asked prospects, buyers, and users.

One of the most important questions a seller can ask a prospect is, *What do you plan to buy in the future?* Answers to such questions about buying intentions, suitably interpreted, can guide seller decisions. Intentions can also be forecast by asking, *What have you bought in the past?* When one asks prospects what they've bought in the past, he testifies to the importance of *habit* and assumes they will continue to buy the same brands in the same quantities at the same intervals in the future. When he asks prospects what they plan to buy, he assumes that purchases are *planned,* not made on impulse. Together, these two questions include most of the purchases that concern a seller.

Habit. A study of diaries in which consumers recorded past purchases, for example, has found that repeat purchases of a given brand vary by product over a three-year period from a low of 33% for one product to a high of 100% for another. (Loyalty to retail outlet appears higher than loyalty to brand.) But repeat purchases reflect many variables, such as availability, sales, cents-off coupons, etc., which have little to do with the meaning of a brand—the *attitude* of brand preference implied by the term loyalty. *Attitudes,* too, need to be measured. When they are, brand preferences sometimes prove remarkably long-lasting.

In one study, brand preferences, first measured in school children, persisted for 12 years and averaged about 33%—or 10 times higher than chance.

Planned Purchases. These occur in industry and when consumers purchase such durable goods as automobiles and refrigerators. Regular surveys of consumer intentions were begun in World War II by the U.S. Department of Agriculture and continued, at the war's end, by the Survey Research Center at the University of Michigan. Both government (Census Bureau, Department of Commerce) and private organizations (National Industrial Conference Board, McGraw-Hill Book Co.) survey consumer or industrial buying intentions from one to six times a year. A typical study[1] found that 52% of those who said they intended to buy a new car in 1948 actually did so, that 10% bought a used car, and 38% failed to behave as intended. Another study[2] suggests that wives are better able to predict what the family will buy than husbands.

Just as sales have their limitations as a guide to decision making, so do these two questions about buyers' past and future behavior. Past behavior is no guide to the seller of a major product innovation. Asking a prospect if he'd buy a product he's never seen or heard about, as is done in *concept testing,* is a very different thing from asking his intentions concerning a product or brand he has bought before, read about, talked about, and used. Business conditions affect the predictive value of *what-will-you-buy* questions: prosperity or fear of rising prices may cause intentions to be surpassed, a recession may frustrate them. Faulty memories invalidate *what-did-you-buy* questions, particularly if such questions specify a very long time span for purchasing; few of us bother to record or add up our purchases except at income tax time if we think they're deductible.

The Question of Why

Moreover, both questions fail to shed light on *why* the buyer bought what he did where and when he did. Neither question is suitable in studying a prospect who hasn't bought the product and, being in an early stage of the persuasion process, has no present intention to buy. Before the seller can plan his marketing mix, choose his media, or create his messages, he needs answers to this question of *why*.

He can, of course, ask the user, buyer, or prospect—except that often they don't know; the question may never have occurred to them before. The answers they give may have nothing to do with any variable that the seller can control. (*We bought a new car because the old one broke down . . . . My aunt died and left us $50,000 so we bought a house with a swimming pool.*) Even if the buyer does know why he bought, he may not be willing to say, figuring it's nobody's business but his own.

Instead of asking a *why* question, a seller may compare attributes of users and nonusers, and find the two groups differ in income, education, social class, job, or stage in the family life cycle. Or he may find that buyers are more ambitious or aggressive

or venturesome than nonbuyers. Knowing buyers' socioeconomic attributes, a seller can use the census to pinpoint geographic areas and media abounding in prospects. Personality differences between users and nonusers may help a copywriter.

Special techniques, such as *projective questions,* can even uncover motivations of which the prospect himself is unaware.[3] Although lengthy probing into buyers' repressions seems unproductive, a good analysis of respondents' answers may turn up information they were not aware of. (Housewives, for example, showed interviewers children's shorts which they liked and others which they disliked, but it took an expert in shorts' manufacture to discover how the "good" differed from the "bad." The housewives knew what they liked but not why.)[4]

The seller needs research methods that can be used to seek out *why's* wherever they occur, in buyer or seller, in prospect or user, in product or brand, in retail outlet or salesman or advertisement; for both new and old products and for planned, impulse and habitual purchases; while the product is being designed and after it is on the market; and for any aspect of the marketing mix, including price, or of the communications mix, including the media that carry the message.

Attitudes and Meanings

Such methods exist. They employ a wide variety of questions, ranging from an open-ended, *How do you feel about . . . ?* to a highly structured, forced choice of specific alternatives. Whatever the technique used, the method is loosely called—very loosely, as we shall see—attitude research, and it has spawned a vast and growing literature.

Attitude was originally defined as a *predisposition to act*—such as buying intentions. In practice, however, most attitude studies have concerned emotions and feelings—what psychologists often call *affects*. Recently, interest has risen in beliefs and ideas—what psychologists call *cognitions*. (Some students prefer to call all three of these elements—action-tendencies, feelings, and beliefs—components of attitude. Others prefer to think of attitudes as representing feelings, which are presumed to correlate highly with both actions and beliefs.)

Our own use of the term is based on the arbitrary nature of all definitions, the equivalence of meaning and attitude, and a preference for operational definitions.

The word *attitude*, we feel, emphasizes the *response* to a message: a feeling response, which in its most intense form has a strong visceral and sympathetic-nervous-system component, and a belief response, which appears to be based largely in the brain. The word *meaning*, we feel, emphasizes aspects of the *message* that evoke such responses. The attributes of a category, our unit of meaning, tend to evoke *beliefs*; its values tend to evoke *feelings*; labels tend to evoke both beliefs and feelings. But, of course, the matter is not that clear-cut. Thus, attributes may evoke both feelings and beliefs; beliefs are not free of values; feelings are not unrelated to a category's attributes. We can devise separate measures of feelings or beliefs or action-tendencies but this separation exists in our measures and not in the things measured—not in the messages and not in the receiver of the messages. In short, we are well advised to adopt an operational definition—to say that attitudes are defined by the instruments that measure them. This means that we have many definitions rather than one.

At one extreme in this list of operational definitions lie the measures of physiological responses (which appear to report the strength and intensity of feelings more than their direction). These responses arise largely in the autonomic system, which is linked to the viscera and glands, largely independent of the brain, and prominent in the emotions. There are 10 such responses.[5]

Galvanic skin response. A sharp change in the electrical conductance of the skin occurs.

Blood pressure. Vessels constrict and we turn pale in fright; blood floods to the surface and we flush in embarrassment and anger.

Heart. Rate of beating increases.

Breathing. Rapid inspiration and expiration indicate excitement; a slow rate indicates tension.

Eyes. Pupils dilate (our "eyes widen") in anger, pain, or excitement; eyes may blink.

Salivation. Mouth becomes dry.

Goose pimples. The hairs of our skin bristle.

Visceral changes. We suffer nausea or diarrhea, and the flow of stomach acids may produce ulcers.

Muscles. When we cannot decide what to do, opposing muscles try to contract simultaneously and our muscles tremble.

Chemistry. The composition of the blood changes as adrenalin and blood sugar increase. Urine is affected.

At another extreme are such feeling-free measures of beliefs as intelligence tests dealing with mathematics or logical relationships.

Between these extremes lie a wide variety of techniques for measuring attitudes. Among the best known are the following.

Thurstone's Equal-appearing Intervals.[6] Judges sort 100 or more statements concerning the attitude object into 11 piles, ranging from highly favorable to highly unfavorable. Then, 200 to 300 subjects indicate whether they agree or disagree with each item. A final scale is constructed by (1) selecting items with median scores, based on judges' ratings, ranging from 1 to 11, or as near that as possible, and (2) rejecting items which, when given to subjects, had low correlations with total scores. (This last step, item analysis, is often used to develop objective examinations. Not originally used by Thurstone, it is an improvement suggested later.)

Likert's Summated Ratings.[7] This eliminates Thurstone's judges, and takes the attitude statements directly to subjects. Each statement becomes a miniature scale; instead of checking agree-disagree, subjects must indicate whether they strongly approve, approve, are undecided, disapprove, or strongly disapprove. Item analysis indicates which statements correlate best with total score; these are kept and others discarded.

Guttman's Cumulative or Unidimensional Scale.[8] Through an elaborate procedure, programmed for the computer, statements are selected on the basis of responses by trial subjects, so that if one knows an individual's score on the scale, one also knows which items he checked to achieve that score. (Since most attitudes appear to have several dimensions, each of these would have to be identified and a scale developed for it under the Guttman system.)

Bogardus' Social Distance Scale.[9] This scale has a strong intention-to-act element in it, since it requires an individual to predict the degree of intimacy he is willing to accord another nationality, religion, or ethnic group. In its original form, it offered these seven degrees: close kinship by marriage, as a chum in my club, to my street as neighbors, to employment in my occupation, to citizenship in my country, as a visitor to my country, as someone who should be denied permission to enter the country.

Osgood's Semantic Differential.[10] This scale is easily constructed by separating such polar adjectives as *good-bad* by a line marked off in seven segments, and printing above the scale the name of the object or idea one wants rated. Each subject then checks the segment of each scale that represents his attitude: in the segment closest to *good* if he thinks the object is very good, in the middle segment if he has no opinion

or thinks the object is neither good nor bad or a mixture of both. (In part, because of its ease of construction, this scale has been widely used, and misused, in marketing and communications.)

Applying Scales to Buyer Behavior

How can such scales as these be used to predict or influence buyer behavior? Let's look at the housewife's purchase of a package of cake mix. To begin with, the housewife probably has attitudes toward "instant" foods in general, toward cakes, and toward prepared mixes. (The combination, "instant cake mix," may mean a quick, economical way of fulfilling a duty or of pleasing husband and children. Or the same set of three words may mean too cheap-and-easy a method, one that doesn't allow her to show off her skill as a cook.) All these attitudes can be summed up in the term *product image;* we suspect that any large increase in sales for such items as oatmeal, spinach, and prunes depends on drastic changes in their product images.

The housewife also has attitudes toward the firms that make cake mix. One firm may "mean" reliability and quality; another firm's brand "means" a low-cost, even risky product that is good enough for family but not for guests. These attitudes can be summed up in the term *brand image;* favorable experiences with several of a firm's products may lead a housewife to buy others bearing the same brand name.

Next, the housewife has attitudes toward the stores that stock cake mix. Even if she likes a brand, the maker won't make a sale if it's stocked only by a store that she shuns —and she may have many reasons for avoiding a store that have nothing to do with the cake mix itself. (Surly clerks, an inadequate variety of brands, low-quality meat, an unattractive produce department, an inconvenient location—all these attributes contribute to an unfavorable store image.) Store image becomes important when the housewife is buying new products, unfamiliar brands, and items whose quality she has difficulty in judging, either because of infrequent purchase or because of the intrinsic nature of the product. By helping reduce perceived risk, both the store's reputation and its policy of taking back unsatisfactory merchandise encourage buying behavior in such situations.

Still other attitudes affect purchasing behavior: attitudes toward the media in which a seller advertises, his advertising messages, the personality of his salesmen—all these affect brand and store images.

In Thurstone and Likert scaling, each of these many attributes would be represented by a separate statement; in Guttman scaling, each of these attributes would be represented by a separate, multistatement scale. Osgood's method needs no statements, only labels for the concepts themselves, plus several scales for each concept.

Using any of these methods, one could get separate ratings for each department in a supermarket, as well as for such attributes as location, clerks, prices, quality, etc. Through factor analysis one could then determine the number of independent attitudinal dimensions that these attributes represent. By selecting one concept to represent each dimension, one could, through multiple regression, obtain a predictive formula indicating how much influence each aspect of the store image had upon some criterion, such as proportion of purchases made at this store in preference to others or an overall evaluative rating for the store itself.

Obviously, a great many attitudes may affect brand preference and product purchase. Two questions are of great theoretical and practical importance: How do ratings on these separate elements combine into an overall rating? (Do they *add* or *average*?) And which elements, if changed,

are most likely to affect overall preferences?

Definitive answers to either question are not yet available, but contesting theories do highlight some of the problems involved.

Consistency Theories

These theories are based on the idea that the human mind, without its owner being conscious of it, seeks consistency. This consistency may be among what we have called beliefs, feelings, and action-tendencies, or it may be consistency among elements within each of these categories. When one belief is inconsistent with another, or feelings and beliefs conflict, such theories say that processes of resolving the conflict set to work.

(If an advertising message changes one attitude element, and the change sticks, then other elements must change to restore the consistency that previously existed. Common sense suggests, and for years we have been acting on the suggestion, that by changing a man's beliefs you can induce subsequent changes in what he feels and how he behaves. One value of consistency theory is its insistence that this is not the only way change can be accomplished.)

Sometimes behavior changes first, causing subsequent changes in feelings and beliefs. This *fait accompli* effect appeared during World War II when racial integration was imposed on the army. It occurs after every election when those who voted against the winning candidate tell themselves maybe things won't be as bad as they themselves were predicting a few days earlier. The effect has been duplicated in the laboratory, with subjects induced, by force or bribery, to behave in a manner contrary to their beliefs. (Contrary to common sense expectations, experimenters have found that to obtain the greatest possible change in beliefs and feelings, one should use the least possible bribe or threat. It is as if the subject can explain away behaving in a way inconsistent with his beliefs if bribe or threat are big enough, but when they are small, he can justify his behavior to himself or others only by changing the attitude inconsistent with it.)

In the laboratory the change process has been initiated by manipulating feelings, ticularly dissonance theory, have spawned an ingenious and exciting array of experiments, too voluminous for review here.

Figure 5.1 is an example in diagram form derived from balance theory, which illustrates relationships between three attitude-objects, each point of the triangle repre-

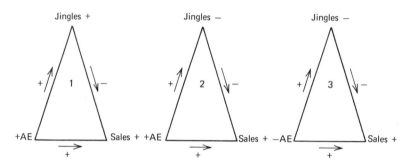

Figure 5.1   Three kinds of attitude imbalance.

either through injection of a drug that affects autonomic processes associated with the emotions, or by telling a subject, while under hypnosis, that when he awakes he will feel a certain way.

(By giving away free samples or offering a free trial of car or TV, a seller may get a behavioral change—product trial—without first obtaining strong beliefs or feelings about his brand. However, any resultant changes in attitude probably stem from the experience itself rather than users' knowledge that they have behaved in a manner inconsistent with their beliefs.)

Cognitive Consistency

A seller operating in the real world operates primarily upon beliefs. He is primarily concerned, therefore, with theories concerning consistency among cognitive elements. There are three such major theories, Heider's balance,[11] Osgood's congruity,[12] and Festinger's dissonance,[13] the first two of which are backed up by an impressive array of formulas and diagrams. All three, but par- senting an object, each side a relationship. (A positive sign at one of the points means that the person whose beliefs the triangle represents is favorable toward the object bearing the sign. A positive sign on a side of the triangle means that the objects it joins are seen as causing, liking, or owning one another; the arrow in each case indicates the direction of this relationship. To illustrate all combinations of positive and negative signs possible with three attitude-objects would require 64 triangles [2 × 2 × 2 × 2 × 2 × 2]. We have selected three.)

The first triangle represents attitudes of a brewer toward the account executive (AE) in his ad agency, a man whom the brewer respects (positive sign). The AE has just advocated (positive sign) the use of radio jingles, which the brewer likes (positive sign) himself, but feels will hurt (negative sign) rather than help sales of his beer. At the same time, he knows that the account executive has helped increase (positive sign) sales. (It goes without saying that the brewer regards sales positively.)

The inconsistency here is that something the brewer likes (jingles) will hurt something else he likes (sales). Consistency can be restored if the brewer will change his belief about the effect of jingles on sales from negative to positive.

(Since juggling three objects of belief and three relationships can get complicated, it helps to define balance before looking at the other triangles. Balance exists whenever:

Elements of *identical* sign are linked by *positive* relationships, or

Elements of *opposite* sign are linked by *negative* relationships.)

A different problem is presented in triangle 2—now the brewer dislikes jingles and balance can most easily be achieved by changing one sign—by making the brewer believe that the account executive does not really plan to use jingles to advertise beer. This means that both the brewer and the adman, whom he likes, now share a dislike for jingles. The brewer's belief that jingles are ineffective or harmful in selling beer remains untouched.

The third triangle pictures the brewer as disliking the adman. Here balance can be achieved by changing the sign at the base of the triangle: if the brewer comes to believe that he was wrong, and that the account executive really hasn't increased sales in the past, then it is entirely consistent for the brewer to perceive that a man he dislikes is in favor of something (jingles) that the brewer hates and that hurts sales.

In each triangle, we have suggested changes based on the supposition that balance will be achieved by changing the fewest signs possible. Balance can be achieved in other ways. In the first triangle, for example, balance can be attained by changing signs of the relationship on the left side and of jingles. (The brewer decides that he dislikes jingles and that the account executive doesn't really plan to use them.) In the second triangle, we can get balance

by making sales negative (the brewer decides he doesn't want them increased) and the relationship between jingles and sales positive (the brewer decides jingles will increase sales).

Some *objects* may be so important, as we suspect sales are in this instance, that an individual will *not* achieve balance by changing their signs. Some *relationships* may be so firmly established, in physical reality or in the individual's perceptions, that they resist change. Although balance theory recognizes only differences in *direction* (positive or negative), congruity theory allows for variations in *intensity*.

We have used triangles to suggest what would happen in the mind of the brewer, on the assumption that the fewer changes of sign required, the more likely a given means of achieving balance will be adopted. The triangles can also be used to plan communications strategy to influence the brewer's attitudes. In the third triangle, for example, if the account executive wants the brewer to like him, he might tell the brewer that jingles disgust the adman. (This means changing the positive sign on the left side of the triangle to negative, producing a temporary imbalance that the brewer can resolve by deciding he likes the adman. Both men will be thrown together by a shared dislike for jingles!)

Which Beliefs Are Vulnerable?

Consistency theories can pinpoint which beliefs are strategic, and so suggest what the goal of advertising and sales messages should be. How can one determine which beliefs are vulnerable to change?

One way to answer this question is to look at the attitudes themselves. Another is to look at the persons who hold them. A third is to look at all of the forces that tend to create attitudes in the first place, and ask whether these forces are likely to change.

A belief closely linked to many other beliefs is likely to resist change, since change in it would require the others to change as well. Beliefs about objects closely linked to an individual's beliefs about himself tend to resist change, as do beliefs about the standards of authority and evidence by which other beliefs are to be judged. The beliefs dealt with in advertising are perhaps among the easiest to change, being lightly held on little evidence.

The durability of beliefs that serve as a means to other goals will depend upon how highly these goals are valued and how close the cause-effect relationship is seen to be. Public commitment to certain beliefs may be required of members in certain groups; if membership in such groups is valued, such beliefs will resist change. (Once in a group, interaction with like-minded members will reinforce such beliefs, making them still more resistant to change.)

As for individuals, intelligence tends both to facilitate and retard change. (It facilitates change by enabling an individual to better understand the messages he receives. It makes him more critical of these messages and more resistant both to them and to group pressures.) Attempts to demonstrate that some persons are naturally persuasible across a wide range of topics have not been very successful although woman's role in our society tends to make them, as a group, more persuasible than men.

Extreme views on any attitude scale appear to be held more intensely than moderate views; extremity and intensity make them resistant to change. Some authorities suggest that it is always easier to move persons away from a neutral midpoint of a scale, than toward it.[14] Others feel that the most difficult movement to obtain is that which takes an individual *across* the neutral point, forcing him to "change sides" on an issue. (Part of the problem arises from the ambiguity of the midpoint on such scales as Osgood's semantic differential, which fails to distinguish between two kinds of neutrality—the neutrality of ambivalence and the neutrality of indifference. Ambivalent neutrality, in which pro's and con's are evenly balanced, is often unstable and temporary; messages, for example, may shift the balance one way or the other. If the category is an important one, the conflict of pro's and con's may cause the person in such a position to repress the attitude-object or flee from situations in which he is under pressure to express a clear-cut choice.)

In the neutrality of indifference, the communicator must show the receiver why a decision is important. (One way to do this is to show that it is a means to some goal that he already regards as important.) In the neutrality of ambivalence, the communicator must relieve anxiety caused by recognition that the issue *is* important.

A small change that moves a person across the neutral point may be much more significant, practically, than a larger change that occurs on one side of the neutral point.

Once committed, however lightly, to the opposition, the factor of *selective exposure* begins to operate. The person who has changed sides tends to seek out messages and persons who support his new position, and avoid those who support his previous position.

Usually we think of the process of attitude change as involving a gradual movement of the person toward and across the neutral point. However, in cases of *conversion* an individual passes quickly from one extreme view to its opposite. In such cases, it may help to view the attitude scale not as a straight line but as a circle with a slight gap in it. Thus the distance between the two ends of the line which makes up the circle is less than the distance from either end to the midpoint of the line.

Every scale has several neutral points. There is the arbitrary point designated by the scale maker. (On a seven-point scale, the fourth position represents such a point.) Three different locations are determined by actual responses: the midpoint of the range actually used (if actual ratings on a seven-point scale ranged from three to seven, then this midpoint will be position number five); the mode, the most popular value; and the point on the scale which best separates persons who perform a criterion behavior predicted by the scale from those who do not.

Individuals vary as to the point on a scale that separates "acceptable" from "unacceptable" positions. They differ markedly in the number of positions they find acceptable.[15] (Persons of extreme views, for example, tend to have very narrow *ranges of acceptance* and very wide *ranges of rejection*. Unless another's view comes very close to their own, extremists will tend to see him as an opponent, although persons of less extreme views would lump the two together. Persons at both extremes of an attitude scale tend to hold their views intensely. The neutral point may be determined by plotting intensity scores on a vertical scale, extremity of views on a horizontal scale. When this is done, some attitudes are V-shaped, others U-shaped. In the former, intensity rises steeply on either side of the neutral breaking point between pro and con. In the latter, or U-shaped attitudes, intensity may be low for some distance on either side of the neutral point; neutrality is a zone rather than a point.

The neutral point, viewed as an index to a receiver's range of acceptance, helps answer the question of whether a source should advocate a large change, on the theory that his results represent a constant fraction of what he attempts, or ask a small change, on the theory that if he asks too much, he may get nothing.

Recent research suggests that the source should advocate the largest possible change that falls within his receiver's range of acceptance but avoid advocating a position that falls outside this range. Since persons of extreme views have narrow ranges of acceptance, the source should advocate small changes for them. He can seek larger

changes, however, with persons elsewhere on the scale.

Inputs that Cause Inconsistency

If, as consistency theories postulate, there is a tendency toward cognitive consistency, why hasn't everyone in the world moved to a completely consistent position and stayed there? (This question becomes even more cogent when one recalls other psychological mechanisms that tend to protect the individual from events that might create imbalance: *selective exposure*, which protects him from publications he's likely to disagree with; *perceptual defense* and *selective attention*, which keep him from seeing upsetting news in the publications he does read; *wishful thinking*, which distorts the meaning of what he does see; and *selective forgetting*, which eliminates any inconsistent and undesirable material.)

Decisions, themselves, cause imbalance in a belief system. The conflict among alternatives that precedes a decision does not completely vanish once a choice has been made. Often one still regrets the advantages he had to forego. (For this reason, advertising is not infrequently directed at persons who have already purchased the product. Such advertising helps dissipate "cognitive dissonance.") Inconsistency seems to be built into our environment, from the contending goals within an individual, to contending groups in society. The world changes, upsetting consistency in a set of beliefs. An individual moves geographically and socially, through time and the family life cycle, exposing himself to new influences.

Deliberate attempts to introduce inconsistency through advertising and other forms of propaganda represent only a small part, and often the least important part, of the inputs that lead to imbalance in a belief system. Such messages can be more effective if they take advantage of imbalance that already exists. Theory suggests that change in beliefs can affect behavior. And there is a good deal of evidence that beliefs are related to voting, purchasing, college attendance, job choice, and so on. (Brand preferences, for example, correlate with purchases: 56% of those who listed a given make of automobile as their first choice actually bought it within six months, as compared with only 22% of those who considered it favorably, 9% who said they'd consider it, and 3% who said they would not consider it.[16] Only 8% of current users of a dental product rated it as "poor," whereas only 8% of nonusers rated it as "excellent"; 78% of users rated it excellent although 76% of former users rated it poor.) But caution is needed in using such figures as evidence that messages can affect behavior. Brand purchase and use may be the *cause*, not the result, of brand preference ratings, and although existing attitudes may be related to present purchasing, a change in attitudes may not produce a change in buying behavior.

In an experimental laboratory, messages produce marked differences between before-and-after scores on attitude tests, but these involve subjects who are used to doing what they're told, smart enough to guess what the experimenter wants, and obliging enough to give it to him. In the everyday world, however, where individuals have free choice as to what messages they'll receive and every message is countered by a host of competitors, such changes are much harder to obtain. Attitudes are formed by a wide variety of influences, including the personality of the receiver of a message and the influence of his associates. Changing only one of these influences—the informational input from messages transmitted by the mass media—can hardly be expected to produce dramatic, easily measured changes in behavior. If attitudes are already favorable to a product or brand, sales and advertising messages may provide the final push that evokes a purchase. If attitudes are not yet at this point, marketing communications may help move them toward it.

Thought, Talk, and Action

1. To penetrate an existing market with your new brand, you must upset the balance of existing attitude structure. Describe actions you might take to cause such upset by changing the affective, the cognitive, or the action-tendency element. Next describe what you would do in the alternate role of seller of the brand which now dominates this market to resist such upset and restore the original balance.
2. Draw an attitude triangle to depict this relationship: As a media buyer you feel that billboards are an effective way of making a political candidate known, but you're afraid that women, whose votes he needs, resent billboards. Is this a balanced relationship? If not, propose two different ways of achieving a balance favorable to your client.
3. As research director, you must plan a series of studies related to the introduction of a new brand of shaving lotion. Select one physiological measure, one of the five attitude-scaling techniques described in this chapter, and a measure either of past buying behavior or present intentions. Specify when and how you would use each technique.

Notes

Chapter 5

1. George Katona, The powerful consumer (New York: McGraw-Hill Book Co., 1960), p. 83.
2. Elizabeth H. Wolgast, "Do husbands or wives make the purchasing decisions?" Journal of Marketing, 23:151–8.
3. A good basic work on motivation research, written in its heyday, is George Horsley Smith, Motivation research in advertising and marketing (New York: McGraw-Hill Book Co., 1954); pp. 75–166 give types of projective questions.
4. E. L. Quenon, "A method of pre-evaluating merchandise offerings," Journal of Marketing, 16:158–71.
5. S. S. Stevens, Handbook of experimental psychology (New York: John Wiley and Sons, 1951), pp. 479–81.
6. L. L. Thurstone and E. J. Chave, The measurement of attitude (Chicago: University of Chicago Press, 1929).
7. Rensis Likert, "A technique for the measurement of attitudes," Archives of Psychology, 1932, No. 140.
8. L. Guttman, "A basis for scaling qualitative data," American Sociological Review, 9:139–50.
9. E. S. Bogardus, "Measuring social distance," Journal of Applied Sociology, 9:299–308.
10. Charles E. Osgood et al., The measurement of meaning (Urbana, Ill.: University of Illinois Press, 1957).
11. F. Heider, The psychology of interpersonal relations (New York: John Wiley and Sons, 1958).
12. Same as Reference No. 10.
13. Leon Festinger, A theory of cognitive dissonance (Evanston, Ill.: Row and Peterson, 1957).
14. P. H. Tannenbaum, "Initial attitudes toward source and concept as factors in attitude change through communication," Public Opinion Quarterly, 20:412–25.
15. Muzafer Sherif and Carl I. Hovland, Social judgment (New Haven, Conn.: Yale University Press, 1961).
16. Leo Bogart, Strategy in advertising (New York: Harcourt, Brace & World, 1967), p. 309.

Consistency Theories

Consistency theories may be viewed as a special case of combining two or more small categories into one larger one; they focus on how a person's values for the new category relate to this value for the original categories. In congruity theory, source of message and subject matter of message combine in their impact on the receiver, his response depending on his evaluation of each. In dissonance theory, contradictory beliefs about a thing, person, or event must be reconciled. In other balance theories, actions, feelings, and beliefs must be brought into harmony. These distinctions among consistency theories blur, however, when one realizes that dissonance may be created by a man's belief that he ought to act one way and his knowledge that he has acted in another.

In each case one is concerned as to how disparate values will be combined. If both original values are on the same side of the neutral point on one's scale, will the value of the new combination be more extreme than either or lie midway between the two? If one element changes in value, which elements will change to restore the original balance?

These questions become important to the retailer or manufacturer who is trying to influence the several attitudes which make up a store or brand image, and to any seller who is trying to induce action in a prospect by working on his beliefs and feelings. Less obviously, consistency theory also applies to the retailer, who has gotten a consumer to try his product by offering him a free sample or a cents-off coupon, in hopes that this *action* will be followed by appropriate changes in beliefs and feelings.

Changes in Behavior Affect Beliefs

Salesmen and advertisers try to change prospects' attitudes, hoping to change their behavior. In the laboratory, the reverse is also possible: change people's behavior, by threats or bribery, and their attitudes may change as well.

Common sense suggests that it's *cheaper* to use the minimum bribe or threat that will get the job done. Re-

search suggests it's more *effective.* If a threat is overwhelming or a bribe is huge, the subject has a rational explanation as to why he did something he really doesn't believe in. If threat or bribe is small, however, he can "explain" his behavior to himself or others only by changing his belief to conform to his new behavior. Here is a classic study of this phenomenon.

Students at Stanford spent an hour at such boring tasks as putting spools into a tray and dumping them out again. Then 20 subjects were offered $1 and another 20 offered $20 apiece to tell another subject that the task they had just finished was "enjoyable, a lot of fun, interesting, and exciting." Both of these groups plus a control group of 20 students rated the experiment on 11-point scales, low scores indicating dislike.

Mean Ratings		
Control	$20 Group	$1 Group
Were the tasks boring or enjoyable? (−5 to plus 5)		
−.45	−.05	1.35
Would you participate in a similar study? (−5 to plus 5)		
−.62	−.25	1.20

Source. Leon Festinger and James M. Carlsmith, "Cognitive consequences of forced compliance," *Journal of Abnormal and Social Psychology,* 58:203–10.

Changes in Feelings Affect Beliefs

Most messages try to change beliefs, in the expectation that a change in beliefs will produce subsequent change in feelings and actions. Some admen argue that it may be more effective to change feelings first since, according to balance theory, beliefs then will change so as to restore consistency between the two.

At Yale, 11 subjects were located who could be hypnotized to the point that, when awakened, they would carry out suggestions made under hypnosis without realizing why they were doing so. Each of the 11, plus a matching control group, filled out a questionnaire on seven social issues, including Negro movement into white neighborhoods and the city-manager plan. A week or so later, each of the 11 was given suggestions under hypnosis to reverse the feelings he had reported. (One subject, for instance, might be told that on awakening he would feel happy about neighborhood Negroes and full of loathing and disgust about city managers.) After awakening, each subject re-took the previous tests.

On a 16-point scale, there was only a .07 difference between control and experimental groups on *feelings* not manipulated under hypnosis, but differences of 3.3 (for high interest attitude objects) and 3.8 (for low interest objects). As for *beliefs,* experimental subjects averaged a score change of 2.62 points more than control subjects for high-interest objects, and one of 3.87 for low-interest objects.

Source. Milton J. Rosenberg, "Cognitive reorganization in response to the hypnotic reversal of attitudinal effect," *Journal of Personality,* 28:39–63.

What Functions Do Attitudes Perform?

Most of the things that people buy are valued because of what they will do. Is this also true of the *ideas* that people buy? The copy platform seeks to relate a product feature to a benefit that buyers desire; are public policies, like private purchases, valued for their effects? Two studies suggest the answer to both of these questions is *yes.*

When asked whether Communists should be allowed to speak in public, Michigan collegians checked a five-point scale as follows: 17 strongly opposed, 31 moderately opposed, 44 moderately approving, 25 strongly in favor. Three to five weeks later they were given 35 cards, each containing a value or goal such as "people being well-educated" and "keeping promises made to others." These were sorted twice: first, on a 21-point scale indicating how satisfying each value was to the student, and second, on an 11-point scale indicating whether allowing Communists to speak would aid or hinder the value. These two scores were then combined. Thus a student might rate the value of a steady income as 10 on a scale of importance. If he felt that free speech for Communists would completely block his attaining a steady income, and gave it a rating of -5, his total score would be -50. If, on the other hand, he felt that free speech for Communists would guarantee him a steady income, rating it $+5$, the combined score would be $+50$. These combined scores were then summed over all 35 of the values or goals.

The combined scores proved best in predicting attitudes toward the free speech issue.

Source. Milton J. Rosenberg, "Cognitive structure and attitudinal affect," *Journal of Abnormal and Social Psychology,* 53:367–72.

First asked whether Negroes should be allowed to move into white neighborhoods, University of Michigan students then indicated on 11-point scales the amount of satisfaction attached to 25 values, and the extent to which they saw Negroes in the neighborhood as fostering or blocking these values. Next subjects were required to listen to a talk by the experimenter and to write messages indicating that Negroes in white neighborhoods would tend to aid four goals, represented in eight of the value statements.

America having high prestige in other countries.

Having the value of property well protected.

Being a person who is experienced, broadminded, and world-wise.

Everyone having an opportunity to develop himself and his capacities.

Moderate subjects were most affected by the experience: from 60% to 70% become more favorable toward Negro neighbors as compared with 50% of those located nearer either the pro- or anti-Negro extremes on the scale. Messages did convince subjects, particularly midscale subjects, that integrated housing would affect the four key values. Opposition to Jewish or Negro army officers being placed over non-Jewish, non-Negro enlisted men, and to Jewish neighbors decreased. The messages did not appear to affect attitudes toward Mexicans, however.

Source. Earl R. Carlson, "Attitude change through modification of attitude structure," *Journal of Abnormal and Social Psychology,* 52:256–61.

Attitudes Affect Perceptions

A product or an event acquires meaning from the skills and attitudes that the people who perceive it bring with them. Since these vary, so must the perceptions; as perceptions vary, so may responses.

In 1951, Dartmouth and Princeton played a hard-fought football game

which resulted in one broken nose, one broken leg, 95 yards in penalties, and a Princeton victory.

Some 69% of Princeton students polled characterized the game as rough and dirty; 86% said Dartmouth had started the rough stuff. Only 42% of a Dartmouth sample (which included many fewer actual spectators since the game was played at Princeton) declared the game rough and dirty, and only 36% agreed Dartmouth had started it. (Another 2% blamed Princeton and 53% blamed both sides.)

Two weeks following the game, a motion picture of it was shown to men at Dartmouth; about a month after that, the film was shown at Princeton. Students looking at the same film were asked to count the rule infractions that they observed. These are the results.

Group Observing Film	Average Number of Infractions Committed by Each Team	
	Dartmouth	Princeton
Dartmouth	4.3	4.4
Princeton	9.8	4.2

High feeling at Princeton, "scene of the crime," apparently distorted judgments, even after a month.

Source. Albert H. Hastorf and Hadley Cantril, "They saw a game: a case study," *Journal of Abnormal and Social Psychology,* 49: 129–34.

But Do Attitudes Determine Actions?

Sales, for the reasons given in an earlier chapter, do not provide a good measure of the effectiveness of marketing communications. Instead, we tend to use measures of comprehension, recall, and attitudes. Such measures help us to devise better messages and also to provide a baseline from which progress can be measured. But how good are attitudes in predicting behavior? Sometimes they are good and sometimes they are not, suggests a noted psychologist.

1. They are good predictors if the subject is aware, when his attitude is measured, of all of the elements that will affect his later behavior. (A man who has never faced an armed robber may not be aware of the unconscious tendencies that will come to the fore in him when this happens.)
2. Persons with poor verbal skills, those of low intelligence, and the inarticulate may not have the words needed to forecast their own behavior.
3. Opinions of people who think before they act, and seldom think without doing something concrete about their conclusions, are likely to predict their behavior.
4. Previous experience with a given kind of behavior makes one's predictions of future behavior more likely to come true.
5. The attitude test should not include behavior-influencing elements which will not be present when the behavior itself is to be evoked.
6. Prediction is best when no new experience that might affect behavior intervenes between the attitude test and the behavior itself.

Predictions can be improved by eliminating the unpredictable types of people—those with unconscious tendencies, the inarticulate, the daydreamers, and the inexperienced—and by making both the attitude-testing situation and the attitude-forming situation which precedes it as similar as possible to the final, behavior-evoking situation.

Source. John Dollard, "Under what conditions do opinions predict behavior?" *Public Opinion Quarterly,* 12:623–32.

Challenge to Attitude-Consistency Theories

When the temperature rises or falls, the body responds with processes which maintain a steady state within the system. A great many studies suggest that a similar process occurs within man's mind. If messages force themselves through the perceptual defenses erected against them (itself a debatable point), the theory suggests that beliefs shift to restore balance. However, other studies suggest that man and monkeys seek the very novelty which upsets balance, that they seem to have a "curiosity drive." See what happens when man is subjected to *sensory deprivation.*

Eight male volunteers at the University of Pittsburgh were paid $12.50 a day to spend 12 hours lying quietly on a bed in a blacked-out room. Sound was cut off by earplugs and special earmuffs. By pressing a button, subjects could, at will, cause dim ceiling lights to flash 24 times, at 1-second intervals.

Four different sets of lights were used; a different set for each of the five days in which volunteers stayed in the room. The sets varied in the amount of "information" (or novelty) they contained:

Zero information. All 24 flashes were the same color.

One-third information. Two-thirds of a given color, the rest being randomly assigned to red or green.

Two-thirds information. One-third of a fixed color, the rest randomized.

Total information. All color selection was randomized (and, therefore, unpredictable from one trial to the next).

As expected, subjects under the last condition pressed the button most often. (Button pressing increased steadily for the first 9 hours, then fell off for the last 3, and was higher on the first day than subsequently.)

Experimenters realized that these results could be the result of a need for information, or an increase in habit strength with reinforcement. So they tried a second experiment, in which 26 undergraduates were paid $12 for a single 10-hour session. This time subjects were forced to spend some time in the room before they were allowed to push the button. Half of them had to wait one hour, and half had to wait five hours. This time a dial allowed them to pick the zero, one-third, two-thirds, or total information conditions, as well as a new condition— one in which red and green lights alternated. This last condition, contained the maximum of *variety* in stimulation in contrast to the "total" condition, which included both variety and *novelty*.

This time responses rose steadily with the amount of novelty in the light patterns; the average proportions of responses to each pattern were:

Zero information	10%
Alternating lights	15
One-third information	20
Two-thirds information	25
Total information	30

The group that had to wait five hours made many more responses than the other group—twice as many during the first hours.

Source. Austin Jones, H. Jean Wilkinson, and Ina Braden; "Information deprivation as a motivational variable," *Journal of Experimental Psychology*, 62:126–37.

Additional Research Readings

Attitudes. To predict behavior one needs to determine attitudes toward church-related *behaviors* rather than toward the church itself and to ask what impact extraneous events would have on such behavior. **Allan W. Wicker, "An examination of the 'other variables' explanation of attitude-behavior inconsistency," Journal of Personality and Social Psychology, 19:18–30.** Methods and likelihood of converting attitudes into action in politics depend on whether one seeks stability or change and whether he is dealing with local or federal levels and executive or legislature. **M. Brewster Smith, "A psychologist's perspective on public opinion theory," Public Opinion Quarterly, 35:36–43.** Price deals, out of stock, and similar factors reduce the ability of attitude scores to predict brand purchase. **William D. Barclay, "The semantic differential as an index of brand attitude," Journal of Advertising Research, 4:1:30–3.** Small changes in attitude but large changes in behavior were produced when, under distracting conditions, subjects read aloud speeches opposed to their own views on legalizing psychedelic drugs. **Philip G. Zimbardo and Ebbe B. Ebbesen, "Experimental modification of the relationship between effort, attitude, and behavior," Journal of Personality and Social Psychology, 16:207–13.**

Chapter 6 Synopsis

● Motives select the attitudes to be expressed in action; they represent buyer benefits in the copy platform. Dominant motives make up an individual's personality. Role emphasizes the part that social setting (associates, organizations) plays in determining behavior. Role emphasizes similarity among individuals in similar situations; personality emphasizes similarity of an individual's response to a variety of situations.

● Personality is general, inflexible, and represents an environmental factor rather than a manipulable variable in buying and selling. Firms select salesmen because of their personality; salesmen select messages on the basis of prospects' personalities. Traits vary in stability and scope; personality has been divided into role, sociometric and expressive aspects.

● Personality scores are based on observations of behavior or ratings by the individual or his associates. Questionnaires, which may include nearly 500 items, may measure from 15 to 18 different traits, reported in the form of *profiles*. Designers of such measures may begin with a theory or a dictionary. The trait of persuasibility, if it exists, would be of interest in communications.

● Traits are based on inherited IQ, physique, and emotional responsiveness and are learned early in life. One theorist suggests seven stages, all of which may operate simultaneously in adulthood. The chapter lists five defense mechanisms used in frustration.

● Every man's repertoire includes many roles, played consecutively and concurrently. Eligibility for occupancy of a given role is affected by physiology (sex and age), by experience (formal and informal learning), and by a degree of personal choice. Four roles interest the seller; member of a family, employee, member of informal group, customer.

● Conflict of roles affects behavior. There are four kinds of conflict, depending on whether roles are contradictory or irrelevant, separable or inseparable. Some men (sales managers) face conflict within a firm; others (salesmen and account executives) are in the middle of conflicts between firms. They have several ways of coping with conflicting claims upon them. A man is subject to penalties for inadequate performance of *ascribed* roles (those he is born into) and to rewards for adequate performance of achieved roles (those he chooses).

● Being multiple, motives (like roles) often conflict both within and between individuals. Knowing motive strength, one can predict outcome for individuals; for decision-making groups, one must know motive strength and power of each individual to influence decisions.

● Conflict between two desirable goals is more easily resolved than conflict between two undesirable goals: avoidance motives tend to persist and give rise to emotions that inhibit choice and action. Learned motives are more important than innate physiological motives in buying and selling, but little is known about identifying and measuring them, how they are caused and their effects. Maslow's hierarchy of needs represents an interesting theory of motive development, backed by little research.

Research Articles

Personality. Four traits related to use of seven products (Tucker); personality fails to distinguish owners of two popular automobiles (Evans), but three traits differentiate owners of two different auto *models* (Westfall).

Fear Appeals. Low-threat message best in dental behavior (Janis); high threat changes attitudes but not behavior on tetanus shots (Leventhal); high and low threat cause different actions on smoking-cancer issue (Leventhal); threat in message interacts with anxiety level of respondent (Nunnally).

Salesmen. Functions and customers determine traits of successful salesman (McMurry, Mayer); faking on test correlates with success as salesman (Ruch).

Role. Demands of role override personality differences (Berkowitz); output best when role and personality are congruent (Smelser); status in group determines response of monkey to aggressive stimulus (Delgado); sales suffer when ad appeal conflicts with housewife's perception of role (Haire).

Chapter 6 Goals of the Buyer: Motives, Personality, and Role

Three advertising campaigns are spread out on the conference table—all of them designed to pave the way for the recruiters your firm is sending to interview college students next spring. One talks about quick promotions and a chance to make important decisions. Another tells the student that he'll be working in a team that includes men like himself—eager, intelligent, friendly. The third gives down-to-earth details about starting pay and fringe benefits. Each appeals to a different kind of *personality*. Your problem: Which type of personality does your firm need on its engineering and its sales staff? Which type should your advertising appeal to?

On your desk is a research report, summarizing a six-month study of car buyers. The report says that your new import has two distinct advantages over the competition: (1) It's inexpensive to buy and to operate. (2) It's convenient to use, seldom being laid up for repairs. Your problem: Should your advertising appeal to drivers' desire to save money or their desire to save time and trouble? Or should you forget both and stress speed and style? Which *motive* will make prospects decide in your favor?

You've already decided that *McCalls* magazine will carry ads for patterns and fabrics intended for women who find they like clothes they make for themselves better than those they can buy ready-made, and *Parents'* magazine will advertise your line of children's fabrics. But how should your commercials be placed—which TV programs provide the most appropriate context for your appeal to prospects in their

role as women and which to their *role* as mothers?

Three Kinds of Goals

Goals of the buyer can be expressed in these three different ways—in terms of motives, personality, and roles.

A *motive* represents an inferred link between an attitude and an act. At any given moment, a person has a great many attitudes or preferences stored in his mind but a *motive* must be present before any is expressed in action. We infer the presence of a food motive, for example, if we know that a white rat has gone without food for 24 hours, if we see him moving about restlessly, if he speeds toward the goal box containing food when put in a familiar maze, and if he eats the food when he gets there. Motives energize and direct: they sensitize a receiver to certain stimuli, they trigger action, and they guide action toward an appropriate goal. Motives tend to be specified in terms of the goals for specific acts: they are the response counterpart of what, from the viewpoint of the message, we call an *appeal*, or *buyer benefit*.

The set of motives that guides an individual's behavior over long periods of time (or are perceived by others as so doing) represent his *personality*. If a person consistently seeks security in a wide variety of situations, or behaves aggressively toward a wide variety of objects, we think of him as having an insecure or aggressive personality. We tend to explain why two persons behave differently in the same situation as being the result of personality; we attach the term to persons rather than specific acts.

When we want to stress similarities in the way persons respond in a given situation, we often do so in terms of *role*, defined as a set of rights and duties attached to a specialized function. We can speak of the role attached to a specific position in an organization—the role of treasurer of an advertising club, for example, or that of marketing vice-president in a retail chain. We can also speak of the roles of member and employee. A woman plays the role of wife and of mother, of daughter and of sister, of housekeeper and secretary, all part of the larger role of *woman* in 20th-century Western culture.

Roles explain behavior in terms of the demands of the environment upon the individual; personality explains behavior in terms of the demands of the individual upon the environment. In seeking the motives for any given act, we must look to both role and personality.

An Example: The Salesman

A salesman may have an aggressive, dominating, or outgoing, extraverted personality; this may be why he became a salesman. Regardless of his personality, however, the salesman is forced to act as if he were outgoing; such behavior is expected of him both by his employer and his customers. His motives in any given encounter with a buyer will be many, and they will vary from one salesman to another, from one buyer to another. Some of these are controlled by the employer, who can fire him, promote him, or raise his pay. Many, however, are *not* controllable by the employer. A salesman has many felt needs of his own, and plays many roles; he hesitates to be too aggressive, perhaps, lest he lose the friendship of his fellow salesmen or the goodwill of the customer, both of which he finds rewarding. He became a salesman in the first place because, in his role of father, he must earn a living for his family; in case of serious conflict between the demands of the two roles, his duties as father will probably have priority.

If a relationship between personality and role can be established and there are enough applicants for the job to give him

any choice, the employer will *select* men whose personalities best fit the role. He will *train* new men in the rights and duties that go with being a salesman. And he will do what he can, perhaps through a system of incentive pay, to *motivate* his salesmen.

Similarities and Differences

Although the layman tends to explain behavior by referring to "personality," social psychologists, marketing men, communications experts, and others who deal with men in the aggregate tend to regard role as more significant. By definition, personality refers to long-standing, firmly rooted behavioral tendencies that can be changed, if change is possible, only by long and intensive therapy. Every person plays so many roles and has so many motives that his behavior can be influenced by directing messages to and offering rewards for different combinations of them. A person shifts from one motive to another and from one role to another many times each day. Some roles are abandoned and others assumed in the normal life cycle; motives appear and disappear as circumstances change and as an individual ages. Personality represents an environmental variable to the seller; he can identify the types of personality in his market and adjust his mix to them, or he can decide which types of personality he wants to reach with his mix and his messages, but he cannot change personality itself.

The methods used in studying and measuring these three kinds of goals differ. Motives have been extensively studied in white rats and other laboratory animals: relative strengths of food, sex, and avoidance of shock as goals have been measured. Roles have been studied both in real life and in laboratory, conflict among roles being of particular interest. Personality has been studied primarily through questionnaires, usually with the subject revealing his own personality by reporting on his feelings or preferences although self-ratings may be checked against ratings by friends or associates.

In overview, the three goals are defined as follows.

	Motives	Roles	Personality
1. Is the stress on similarities or differences among individuals?	Similarities	Similarities	Differences
2. Which is seen as antecedent and controlling: individual or environment?	Individual	Environment	Individual
3. Is change hard or easy?	Easy	Easy	Hard
4. Does an individual have one or many?	Many	Many	One
5. Does the concept embrace many acts or is it specific?	Specific	Specific	Many
6. Is the communicator's choice within an individual or between individuals?	Within	Within	Between

Personality as a Goal

Sometimes the word *personality* is used to sum up the total effect of a man's habits and attitudes, motives and perceptions, roles and statuses. At other times the word is used to label the leftover behavior that these other concepts fail to explain or predict.

It helps to think of personality as one extreme on a scale of *generality*. When a person is friendly or hostile or indifferent to a wide variety of objects, we tend to say that he has a personality trait of friendliness, or aggressiveness or apathy.

A person who is thoughtful of others, a personality trait, may express this trait by very different habits, depending on the setting: he may eat with both hands in one country, but with only his right hand in another; he may avoid belching in one country but belch out of courtesy to his host in another. A person may have a habit of deference to his parents, or the more general personality trait of submissiveness to many kinds of authority: parental, governmental, ecclesiastical, educational, and peer group.

Personality also represents one extreme on a scale of *flexibility*. Ordinarily, changes

in personality require a close relationship between subject and therapist over a considerable period of time. Even then the therapist may limit himself to interpreting the patient's behavior to the patient himself. (His behavior remains as it was but his attitude toward it changes.) The therapist may help the patient find new means of nonverbal and verbal behavior, leaving the motives that such behavior expresses untouched.

The industrial salesman, who sees a few customers regularly, can spend a good deal of time studying their personalities and reshaping his communications to be most effective with them. The door-to-door salesman or the sales clerk who seldom sees the same customer twice must develop a workable set of personality-type categories, a set of symptoms by which customers can be pigeonholed into such categories, and messages for each of these categories.

Three Types of Measures

Basically, there are three ways of measuring personality.

Observation. We can observe an individual's behavior in many different situations, either natural or created for the purpose of testing him.

Ratings by Others. These are especially useful in communications, since they tell us what personality an individual communicates to others. (Usually we also want to know what personality he thinks he is communicating or wants to communicate.) Such ratings tell us something about the persons doing the rating. Friends may be too generous, strangers may be too uninformed, and all of us are likely to judge a person's most obvious traits and then assume that he has other traits consistent with the obvious one. Students can best rate one another on traits like sociability, but teachers can do a better job in rating students on scholarship. A soldier can do a better job of rating officers on leadership than their fellow officers can.

Self-ratings. These are perhaps the easiest, cheapest, and therefore the most common way of measuring personality. Usually they put the individual rated somewhere between what he "really" is (e.g., how he appears to others) and what he would like to be.

One Trait or Many?

Some measures involve only a single trait. One such measure is the introversion-extraversion scale. This distinguishes the person who is turned inward, who prefers to read about something rather than experience it, and is self-conscious and retiring in groups. Unfortunately, such measures encourage users to forget that everyone is a mixture of many different traits. Moreover, because our language tends to deal in polar opposites, such tests tend to divide a world of almost infinite gradations into only two groups.

Measures that involve several traits come closer to giving a complete picture of a personality, but make a personality harder to understand. They make it harder for us to determine what kind of messages will most influence behavior.

Here are brief descriptions of three such multitrait questionnaires.

*California Psychological Inventory.** This consists of 480 items which in scoring produce 18 different personality traits. An individual is asked to mark "true" or "false" on such statements as the following.

> *Lightning scares me.*
> *I usually feel poised at parties.*

Edwards Personal Preference Schedule.† This consists of 225 pairs of statements about things people like or feel which are reduced to 15 traits in scoring. In each case, the individual must choose one of the pair:

> *I feel depressed when I fail at something.*
> *I feel nervous when giving a talk before a group.*

Cattell's Sixteen Personality Factor Form. This consists of 187 statements, each of which offers three responses, usually "yes," "in between," and "no," although occasionally other choices are offered.

> *I prefer people who (a) are reserved, (b) are in between, (c) make friends quickly.*
> *Money cannot bring happiness. (a) yes (true), (b) in between, (c) no (false).*

This form reduces in scoring to the 16 traits mentioned in its title.

Since it is hard to keep 16 or 18 scores in mind, psychologists put the scores on a graph and compare personality "profiles." Such profiles are especially useful in guidance and counseling, since they enable us to compare an individual with other persons of his age, or with other members of the group or category to which he belongs.

Theory or Dictionary?

Psychologists construct personality questionnaires in two ways. Some make up statements that reflect the traits called for in a theory. Others start with a dictionary and draw up questions to tap as many different words reflecting personality as possible. Cattell began his questionnaire with 4000 such terms. Allport estimates that of 18,000 words for distinctive forms of personal behavior, 4500 are relevant to measuring personality.[1] (He arrived at this figure by omitting some 5500 evaluative words—angelic, disgusting—that describe a person's effects on others; another 4500 words that describe a temporary mood or activity—rejoicing, frantic; and some 3500 words that he calls metaphorical—alive, prolific.)

How does the psychologist reduce such a list of 4000 or 4500 adjectives to the 480 items of the California inventory or the even smaller number of other questionnaires?

One way is to retain the statements that differentiate between groups of persons known to differ in the particular trait being measured. The other way is through factor analysis. If two statements are highly correlated with one another, this means either of them can be used to measure that trait.

The psychologist who begins with a single trait often finds it breaking up into several smaller parts. Factor analysis has identified five different introvertive traits: a tendency to withdraw from social contacts, a preference for meditation and self-analysis, feelings of guilt, strong fluctuations in mood, and lack of a carefree, impulsive nature.[2] Some introverts may show all of these, others may not. (Three sociable behaviors —being gregarious, liking friends, attending parties—correlated only .44 and four punctual behaviors—returning a book, meeting assignments, keeping appointments, handling course-change slips—correlated only .19.)[3]

Categorizing Traits

Traits may be grouped by the kind of behavior which they call forth. One theorist puts traits into three classes, based on the kind of response to other people they imply.[4] The sociable and gregarious person is classed as one who moves *toward* others. The hostile and aggressive personality moves *against* others, and the withdrawn and isolated personality moves *away* from others. Another three-class grouping is this.[5]

Role dispositions. Ascendance, dominance, social initiative, independence. These represent the behavior one exhibits toward others.

Sociometric dispositions. Acceptance, sociability, friendliness, sympathy. These are essentially the feelings we have toward others.

Expressive dispositions. These seem to be matters of individual style in behavior; a person may be competitive, aggressive, self-conscious, or exhibitionistic.

A third system classifies traits by the way they function.[6]

Stability. Some traits appear to change more easily under the impact of time and experience than others. (In one study, 446 subjects were rated twice, with 20 years intervening between the two ratings. Self-confidence appeared to be relatively stable; the two ratings produced a correlation of .60. Sociability appeared less stable, with a correlation of only .45.)[7]

Scope. Some traits are exhibited only in specific situations or toward specific persons; others are more general. Some traits, such as poise, can be observed only in the presence of others.

Persuasibility as a Trait

If persons could be scored on persuasibility (the ease with which they can be influenced on any issue regardless of variations in message, channels, or source), a source could adjust his efforts to his audience. Most of us, however, are more easily persuaded on issues that are not ego-involved, and in areas where we lack information or the information we have is ambiguous. We are more easily persuaded by highly credible sources and by suggestions that conform with norms of a reference group. Research[8] suggests the following.

Girls tend to be more persuasible than boys. This appears to be a result of the sex roles that our society demands, rather than innate, biological differences. (Since boys' sex role does not affect their persuasibility, personality variables exert more effect on them than on girls.)

The source of a message seems to have little effect upon young children. Children of seven, if persuasible at all, are equally responsive to persuasion from both peers and adults. By the age of 13, however, a general trait of persuasibility has disappeared: by this age the source does make a difference.

Persuasibility and low self-esteem tend to accompany one another. The person who feels inadequate and socially inhibited tends to be easily influenced. (We do not know which of these characteristics is the cause of the other; both may be the results of a third characteristic. Guilt feelings may lead to both low self-esteem and high persuasibility.)

Stages of Development

A child's first attempt to become independent of his parents, and establish a personality of his own, occurs at about the age of two. His next move in this direction occurs when he enters school, and spends much of his waking hours with another adult. The third, and final move, comes at adolescence, as he becomes influenced by others of his own age. Allport sees seven stages in this growth toward self-hood.[9] All seven may coexist in a student preparing for an exam.

Bodily self. The student senses that his heart is beating faster.

Self-identity. He has a history; the student who takes the quiz today is the same one who studied yesterday and will study tomorrow.

Self-esteem. He has an attitude toward this person: he takes pride in his ability to handle the test.

Self-extension. He sees himself as part of a group; he wants to do well on the test to please his family.

Self-image. He wants to do well so that he can continue to think of himself as intelligent.

Rational agent. He can observe and compare his techniques in answering the exam questions.

Goal-directed. He realizes that success in this exam will help him achieve his goal of becoming a lawyer or doctor.

Roughly speaking, the first three of these aspects of self appear by the age of three; the next by the age of six. The sixth appears by the age of 12, and the seventh during the teens.

If our needs are satisfied as we grow up, we tend to be confident and self-assured but may be at a loss when we face a problem or meet frustration for the first time, since we have had no experience in dealing with it.

Something quite different happens, however, if our wants are completely and consistently frustrated. (Such frustration may arise from physical conditions about us; from our own biological makeup; from the social environment in which we find ourselves; or because we simultaneously experience several conflicting wants.) When this happens we may attack the source of frustration, seek a way around whatever is blocking our way, or give up the effort to satisfy our wants. Or we may resort to one or more of several *defense mechanisms*,[10] such as the following.

Projection. We may attribute to others aspects of ourselves that cause anxiety. Desiring public praise ourselves, we may accuse others of being vain and conceited.

Reaction formation. We may react against the feeling that threatens us, by expressing a completely opposite attitude. Fear of our own sexual impulses may lead us to censor literature that arouses such impulses.

Rationalization. To conceal the real feelings that motivate us, we may seek to explain our behavior in reasons that we, or society, find more acceptable.

Compartmentalization. We remove the conflict between two opposed feelings or tendencies by giving expression to them at different times and in different circumstances.

Denial and withdrawal. We pretend that the feeling does not exist, or we refuse to think or talk about it.

All of us show each of these occasionally to a mild degree under suitable circumstances. When we tend to show a few of these responses frequently and under many circumstances, they become a part of personality. In extreme form, used inappropriately, they require therapy.

Role as a Goal

Personality emphasizes the effect of an individual's *past* history on his current behavior; role emphasizes the impact of *present* surroundings on that same behavior. Role tells a man *what* he should do, personality affects the *way* he does it.

In the course of a day, each of us plays many roles, and each of these roles itself consists of many smaller roles. The insurance salesman who, during working hours, simultaneously enacts the roles of employee of his firm and financial adviser to his clients, stops on his way home at an automobile salesroom; as he steps through the door he shifts roles, from salesman to customer. As he continues on his way, he assumes the role of patient, in a chat with his physician; of voter, in talking politics with a friend; of layman, when he meets his pastor. At home, as he steps through his front door, he finds himself playing the roles of husband and father.

The salesman's wife also plays many roles: wife and den mother, PTA executive and daughter-in-law, back-fence gossip and cook. Even so routine an act as a trip to the supermarket may involve many roles: that of good mother, when she buys oatmeal; indulgent wife, as she purchases cigarettes; hostess, as she buys cheese dip; individual, as she selects a mystery story; neighbor, as she chats while queued up at the cash register.

One's choice among his role repertoire and the way he defines any given role is affected by expectations of other actors in the scene that's being played—members of the *role set*. (Few roles can be performed in isolation. To be a salesman, a man must have someone who will play the role of customer; to be a wife, a woman must have a husband; to be a mother, she must have a child.)

Three sets of expectations influence the way a role is played: those of the role-player himself, those of his role set, and those of "outsiders." These expectations define acceptable ranges for three kinds of behavior: acts, attitudes, and interactions. Some of these are required, some permitted, and others forbidden to occupants of a given role.

Eligibility for a given role is determined by three things: physiology, experience and individual preference.

Physiology

Sex is basic. Only a woman can be a wife and mother, although many women are neither. In most societies, men specialize in functions of task performance and women in those of group maintenance—although societies vary markedly in the way they assign occupational roles. (In the United States, women are more likely than men to become typists, teachers, and dental technicians, but less likely to become lawyers, doctors, or sandhogs. In Russia, more women than men serve as physicians—and street sweepers. Sex-linked assignments vary in time as well as space: the first typists were men, not women, and when veterans returned to campus and wives worked to put food on the table, men discovered they could cook and change diapers.)

Aging forces continual changes of role, some of which are taught in school and others which are not. When the United States was a farming country, both boys and girls could learn their future occupational roles by watching and assisting their parents; no sharp change of role was required as one moved from childhood through adolescence to adulthood. In some societies, such *role continuity* still exists.[11] In our society, expectations as to acts, attitudes, and interactions change frequently. A boy who, in preschool years, is expected to inhibit aggressive impulses in the home, is expected to be reasonably aggressive with playmates at school. Parents who tolerated careless work habits in a boy attending an undemanding high school show alarm when the first grades are received from a college that expects a student to show self-disciplined study.

When roles change so drastically, a ceremony signalizing the change to the individual and society makes the shift easier. (Sociologists call such a ceremony a *rite of passage*—the passage being from one role and status to another.) Ceremonial induction following formal training characterizes military, medical, and legal professions, where drastic changes in rights and duties occur. When a change of role is less clearly marked, tension often arises. In the United States, for example, a teen-ager doesn't know where he stands for years. At home, he may have to behave like an adult, so far as duties are regarded, but finds himself treated like a child when he seeks adult privileges. (As home becomes unrewarding, he turns increasingly to his peers to learn the rights and duties of his emerging role and to gain the emotional support needed in such learning. This makes word-of-mouth a powerful sales force among teen-agers.)

Experience

Formal training both tests and changes the ability of an individual to perform a role and gives him a clearer picture of its rights and duties. Informal contact with role occupants reveals the variety of roles available, their costs and rewards; it thus affects level of aspirations for jobs and for the training needed to achieve them. (Children whose parents and parents' friends have only unskilled jobs are slow to learn that other jobs exist and to aspire to them, and find it difficult to discover what abilities are required and whether they have those abilities.)

It is never possible to teach in formal fashion all the rights and duties involved in any role. The more important a role, the less specific teaching tends to be. This is true, for example, of the vital roles of *customer* and of *parent*. The number and variety of rights and duties involved in such roles is so wide and the skills involved need so much practice that it would be difficult to include them in formal training.

Some of the experiences that prepare individuals to fill a role are common to everyone in a given society at a point in time; others are common to members of a class within that society; others are highly individual. Of two sons in a family, the younger is likely to find his parents more relaxed; experiences with the first child have taught them parental roles. Growing up in a relaxed atmosphere, the second child is likely to be more relaxed in later life, while the first son—who has been forced to share parents he once had to himself—may develop an anxious and tense *personality*. The two sons are likely to perform their later role as fathers in rather different fashion.

Choice

Within the limits set by physiology and the insights as to role demands and his own ability to meet them provided by experience, an individual has some choice. He does not aspire to all of the roles for which he is eligible. On the other hand, acceptance of one role may foreclose choice of another, either because of formal rules or popular attitudes. In the United States in 1971, a priest of the Roman Catholic church could not also play the roles of husband and father, but he could be a college president. At one time, barbers were also surgeons, but no more. We would be uneasy if our physician were also an undertaker, but find undertaking and selling furniture congruent occupations. Most persons can become parents but only a few can become concert pianists.

Four Major Roles

Four kinds of roles are of particular interest to the marketing communicator. These are the roles associated with the family decision-making unit, those of husband or wife; the role of the employee; roles in the informal group; and the role of customer. Nearly everyone plays all of them.

Family

The roles of husband-father and wife-mother are *difficult* because they involve diverse, virtually unlimited obligations. Parents must feed and clothe their children, praise them and admonish them, motivate them and teach them 24 hours a day, seven days a week. The roles are *basic*, in that others derive from them. Most men would work less hard and less steadily, and some would not work at all, if they were not husbands-and-fathers.

Society's survival depends upon communicating to each generation the knowledge and values accumulated over time. Parents do much of this job and force the children to attend the schools and churches which complete the job. As the basic decision-making unit of society, the family interests both politician and advertiser.

Employee

Although men and women take on the role of employee as a means to an end, the means may become an end in itself. (Anything to which one gives a third of each day comes to be seen as important.) As a man rises in a business organization, rewards become objectively as well as subjectively greater. At upper levels, the firm may provide social and emotional rewards of interaction which other men receive from their families.

Informal Group Member

At lower levels in the firm, employees may seek rewards through membership in informal groups, either in the firm or outside. Since most advertisements are prepared by one business organization (an advertising agency) on behalf of another business organization (a manufacturer) and transmitted through a third business organization (one of the mass media) to either households or a fourth business organization (a retailer or another manufacturer), the roles of employee and informal group member within the business organization are important to the marketing communicator.

Customer

The marketing communicator needs to know what customers expect of themselves and what they expect of advertiser and salesman. An industrial society converts many of the role relationships that previously depended on kinship or friendship to buyer-seller relations. (We expect services not because people are friends or relatives, or because we have done them favors, but because we pay for their services.) Recently the social rewards obtained through friendly interaction have vanished from large areas of the market. The role of customer has changed in functions and rewards.

The employer trying to influence the behavior of his salesmen seeks to make the role of employee dominant. The salesman trying to influence the behavior of his prospects seeks to make the roles of customer and consumer dominant.

To do so, however, both employer and salesman must know how to heighten salience of roles consistent with their aims and reduce salience for those that conflict.

An encyclopedia salesman hopes that his prospect's wife will be on hand and children nearby, since these help remind the prospect of his role as father. He is distressed, however, if the prospect's hunting and fishing companions are present, to remind him of another role and another way of spending funds that might go for a set of encyclopedias. (Of course, the appeal to the parental role can aid manufacturers of sports equipment, too. Their ads may remind the prospect that he ought to take his son hunting and fishing!)

There are four types of role conflict, representing the intersection of two dichotomous variables: (1) whether demands of the roles are unrelated or contradictory and (2) whether the roles are separable or not.

In the simplest form of conflict, two (or more) roles compete for a man's time and money: he can't attend a PTA meeting and participate in a bowling meet if both are scheduled at the same time, but he is free to give up one or the other role. (This form of conflict is sometimes called *role strain.*) A second type of conflict involves similar competition for time and money but between two roles that are not easily separated: as a husband, he should take his wife dancing, but as a father, he should take his son to a ball game. Giving up either role diminishes his ability to perform the other. Still keener is the conflict that arises when one role says an action must be performed and another that it must not. (This is often called *interrole* conflict.) As a member of the PTA, a father is expected to vote for higher school taxes, but as a member of the taxpayers' league, he may be expected to vote against a tax increase. (He can, of course, quit either organization.) The fourth type of conflict arises when members of a role set expect different behavior from the role occupant. (This is labeled *intrarole* conflict. Note that the distinction between interrole and intrarole conflict is primarily one of definition. That is, if one divides the superintendent's role into two intersecting roles, one involving relations with teachers and the other with school board, what was intrarole then becomes interrole conflict.) A student proctor is expected by the teacher who appoints him to enforce rules against cheating to the letter; his fellow students may expect a measure of leniency.[12] A school board expects a superintendent, as an administrator, to keep teachers' salaries as low as possible; teachers expect him, as a fellow educator, to push them as high as possible.[13] (There is an important distinction between proctor and superintendent, however. The duties of student and proctor can be separated but those of superintendent cannot be.)

Superintendent and proctor are *men-in-the-middle*. The factory foreman must get along with both management and workers and the army sergeant with officers and enlisted men. The man-in-the-middle, to get the cooperation of his subordinates, may have to water down the orders given to him from above. More common in marketing are the men who mediate between the firm that employs them and outsiders, men like the account executive, salesman, reporter, and waitress. The account executive faces demands from clients and from both superiors and subordinates in the agency. The reporter must gain the cooperation of his news sources, while satisfying his editor. The salesman must gain the confidence of his customers, while pleasing his employer. The waitress must satisfy customers without violating orders of the manager.

Formal superiors do not always "win" in role conflict involving either type of man-in-the-middle. The power of superior, subordinate, and outsider depends on how easily each can detect rejection by the man-in-the-middle, and how willing each is to impose sanctions. Since the man-in-the-middle frequently spends more time in face-to-face interaction with outsiders and subordinates than he does with superiors, he is more subject to their influence and more rewarded by such interaction.

The man-in-the-middle may play one group off against the other, using pressure from one to excuse deviant behavior to the other.[14] He may seek support from his peers in resisting the demands of both superiors and outsiders. He may be able to conceal his resolution of conflict from observation. (Society itself legitimizes such concealment in the case of law, medicine, and the ministry in the form of privileged communications with clients. The American Association of University Professors protects the privacy of the classroom as a means of defending academic freedom.) The man-in-the-middle may delay a choice, in hopes that the dilemma will vanish or one of the antagonists lose interest. If lucky, he has a clear-cut set of priorities, endorsed by society, which say that some obligations (such as those of a parent) take precedence over all others.

An individual may escape by giving up membership in one of the groups. Thus reporters can get away from an editor's pressure by taking a public relations job with one of their news sources. Salesmen can go to work for a former customer, the account executive can switch sides and become an advertising manager, and a waitress may marry an affluent patron.

Conflict, even for the man-in-the-middle, is often less acute than our discussion to this point might suggest because of differences in individual expectations concerning a given role. Teachers, for example, differ as to how big an increase they expect the superintendent to win for them and how far they expect him to stick his neck out in getting it. Members of the school board, on the other hand, disagree on the degree of miserliness appropriate to a superintendent. A canny superintendent may find an area of overlap between expectations of some teachers and some board members, if necessary playing teacher off against teacher and board member against board member.

Motives as a Goal

Certain roles are *ascribed;* these roles, which an individual attains by birth and parentage, tend to be broad in scope: age and sex roles, and ethnic, kinship, and class roles. Good performance in such roles which tend to be learned in childhood, is taken for granted; poor performance is punished. Other roles are *achieved;* poor performance in these gets a neutral response, and good performance is rewarded.

Buyers' motives are usually discussed in terms of product use, but a prospect must also be motivated to search, to shop, and to bargain. Many advertisements are read and many commercials viewed for their own intrinsic interest; the receiver of such messages may *not* be motivated by any interest in the product advertised. Shopping and bargaining are enjoyable in themselves.

Motives, like roles, are always multiple— and often in conflict. This conflict may occur within the mind of a single prospect. (One commentator notes that home buyers often want a home that's modern inside, but has used bricks and prewarped shingles on the outside, that they want to "rough it" with foam mattresses and propane stoves, that women want to be both neat and messy with a "windblown" hairdo, and that suburbanites want all the conveniences of the center city.)[15] When the decision-making unit consists of more than one person, conflict in motives becomes interpersonal and visible. The outcome of such conflict depends on both the strength of the motives and the power of the persons in whom the motives exist.

Since life situations may reward or punish, there are two basic motives: a motive to avoid punishment and a motive to approach reward, and four kinds of conflict.[16]

Approach-approach. When two goals are equally attractive, the conflict is fairly easily solved; a step toward one goal makes it appear closer and therefore more attractive than the other.

Avoidance-avoidance. When both goals are undesirable, a solution is harder. The step that brings one nearer one of these goals makes it appear more unpleasant. An individual hesitates, halts, reverses direction; he may try to escape conflict by withdrawing, physically or mentally.

Approach-avoidance. A single goal usually has both pleasant and unpleasant aspects. A child may want a cookie but fear punishment for robbing the cookie jar; he may hate to practice the piano but enjoy the praise he gets for practicing. At some point short of the goal the two forces will be in balance and movement may halt. Prospects who desire a product but hate to pay for it, postpone purchase.

Double approach-avoidance. This is the typical decision-making situation, with at least two goals each of which has both positive and negative aspects. Avoidance is a strong kind of motivation that does not seem to extinguish. (If we fail to give a monkey grapes in exchange for poker chips, he will eventually stop working to get poker chips; his motivation to work will *extinguish.* But a dog continues to avoid a grill where he had been shocked, even when the electricity is turned off.) However, aversive stimuli arouse strong emotions, which may spread widely to remote stimuli so that behavior becomes increasingly hard to predict. Subjects may try to escape not just the painful stimulus but the situation in which it occurs. (Instead of teaching them to buy our product and avoid halitosis, body odor, and tooth decay, our commercials may teach them to avoid TV commercials, if not TV itself.)

As emotions spread beyond the original situation that aroused them, vague fears may arise; their vagueness prevents us from doing anything about them. Such a state, called *anxiety,* may be produced by fear of one's own aggressive impulses. (When such anxiety prevents aggression, a "natural" response to frustration, the frustration remains while the frustrated desire to aggress adds to anxiety. Before anxiety can be relieved, it may have to be momentarily increased by making the anxious person aware of his desires to aggress. Common in therapy, this technique is difficult to use in marketing.)

Any motive can find several means of expression; any behavior can express several different motives. (One child may steal because he wants to impress his peers, another to get even with the victim, and a third because he needs the money.)

Psychologists recognize that the goals of individuals tend to be multiple, complex, contradictory, and varied. A firm assigns its employees goals meant to serve the superordinate goals of the firm itself. The employee, however, has goals of his own; these goals, and his success in achieving them, determine whether he stays with the firm and the quality and quantity of his output.

The employee's goals are often vaguer, less verbal, *and* more intense, more persistent, and less amenable to change than those of the firm. We call them *motives* rather than *goals* to emphasize these differences.

An individual may express his goal in words or use words to conceal and disguise his motives. (For this reason, observers prefer to infer his motives from observation of what he says and does not say, what he does and does not do, and the manner of his saying and doing.)

To communicate, an individual must express his feelings in terms another person can understand. This means modifying them. Further modification occurs if a source wants his receiver to accept him as *rational*. Goals, because they are communicated, tend to appear more reasonable than motives.

Motives that are not verbalized, even in thought, are also subject to less control by the individual himself. Accidental juxtaposition of two events in time or space may cause an individual to respond as if one were cause and the other effect.

If we merely see a rat run from one end of a maze to the other, we do not know whether it is running away from an electric shock at the starting point or toward a reward at the other end. We need to see the rat hop about in agitation at the start of the maze or munch food pellets at its end. If it slows down as it draws away from the starting box, we suspect it is running away from something. If it speeds up, we suspect it is running toward something. If it always runs to the same end point, regardless of where it starts, we suspect its goal lies in the end box. If, on the other hand, it runs in various directions from the same starting point, we suspect it is running away from rather than toward something.

To predict how the white rat will behave, it is usually enough to know:

Situation. A maze, with a food box at the end.

Drive state. The rat has had no food for 24 hours.

Behavior. Restlessness in the starting box, rapid running down the maze.

Goal box adjustment. Rat eats and becomes quiescent.

With this much information, we would *explain* the rat's behavior as being motivated by hunger. If we knew that the rat had previously been in this maze while hungry and had learned to run it and find food at the end, we could *predict* its behavior. In men, we may find motives for present behavior in events that occurred 60 to 70 years ago at the age of five.

Learned motives, those dependent on experience, differ from one person to another. These are the motives of most concern in marketing communications and the ones we know least about. *Physiological motives* are the same from one person to the next and even from man to animals; we know a great deal about them. For example, experiments with animals tell us that discomfort may arise either internally, as in the chemical changes and stomach movements that follow a period without food, or because of intense, pain-producing external stimuli, such as loud noises and electric shock. Discomfort may cause restlessness, or sensitize the animal to stimuli that cause restlessness—the question is being debated. As it moves about, the animal may escape a painful stimulus or attain something, such as food, which ends internal imbalance. Through experience, it learns to end discomfort quickly and even to avoid conditions that might cause discomfort; in unfamiliar situations, however, restless, searching behavior will recur.

When the balance of sugar in the blood is upset by fasting, this imbalance sets off stomach contractions that are interpreted as hunger pangs. Asleep or awake, when our stomach contracts, the rest of our body tends to become active. Yet because of experience, hunger persists even if the stomach is removed and so can no longer contract or if the nerve that reports its contractions to the brain is severed. Hunger is a strong motive. After one day's deprivation, a female white rat's strongest drive is to reach her young, followed by thirst, sex, and hunger in that order. After two days' deprivation, however, hunger becomes stronger than thirst or sex.

In contrast to our knowledge about physiological drives, we have little experimental evidence—but a great deal of speculation—about learned motives. Some theorists seek a single basic motive; others offer a dizzy proliferation of motives. (The latter may be useful to a marketing communicator, by suggesting a wide variety of appeals to use in his messages. But it is hard to identify such motives in an audience, or measure their strength. All motives of such a list are not equally likely to occur, nor equal in strength, nor necessarily independent of one another. It is dangerous to isolate a motive from the situation in which it

occurs, the behaviors it produces and the goals toward which it directs such behavior.) We don't know whether motives that aren't easily observed are more powerful than those that can be. They are harder to control.

Why do motives so basic as hunger and thirst, which affect all men, play so little part in everyday behavior—and in selling and advertising? A plausible explanation, so far with little evidence to support it, is offered by theorist Maslow in terms of a five-item *hierarchy of needs*.[17]

1. Physiological needs. These are the needs that seem to exist in all cultures: hunger, thirst, sleep, elimination, breathing, activity.
2. Safety.
3. Love and belonging.
4. Esteem, in our own regard and in the regard of others.
5. Self-actualization, to become all one is capable of being.

The *order* is important. Maslow argues that no need on the list can affect behavior until needs previous to it have been taken care of. (If the need for food is 90% satisfied, a need for safety, which is only 30% satisfied, may dominate behavior. Meanwhile, a need for belonging is just beginning to make itself felt. As the need for safety is satisfied, the belonging needs take over.) In our society, the physiological and safety needs have little effect; they are satisfied before they can be felt. Maslow suggests that our society defines the person with major needs for love and esteem as psychologically sick and in need of therapy. Thus the need for self-actualization becomes dominant.

There are critical periods in the life of an individual, however. A child whose need for safety is not satisfied may permanently lose the desire or the ability to give or receive affection (a higher need); safety needs may dominate his adult life.

Thought, Talk, and Action

1. Think of 3 different products, one of which would benefit from an appeal to personality, one to role, and one to motive. Can you also think of an appropriate media vehicle (magazine, TV program) for each? Think of a fourth product which might use all three of these appeals.
2. How many different motives could you appeal to in advertising a house? a car? a restaurant? Are some of these motives contradictory? Are some likely to be associated with certain personality types? Certain roles?
3. Taking each of the types of role conflict in turn, show how it might be used to *aid* in selling a particular product or brand. Next, show how each kind of conflict might *inhibit* sales. Finally, suggest how an adman or a salesman might work to create each kind of conflict, and how he might try to reduce each kind.
4. From your experience as customer or salesman, describe instances in which personalities of buyer and seller clashed with one another. What did the salesman do to reduce this clash? Did he succeed or fail?

Notes

Chapter 6

1. Gordon W. Allport, Pattern and growth in personality (New York: Holt, Rinehart and Winston, 1961), pp. 353–6.
2. J. P. Guilford, An inventory of factors STDCR (Beverly Hills, Calif.: Sheridan Supply Co., 1940).
3. G. J. Dudycha, "An objective study of punctuality in relation to personality and achievement," Archives of Psychology, 1936, No. 204.
4. Karen Horney, Our inner conflicts (New York: Norton, 1945).
5. David Krech et al., Individual in society (New York: McGraw-Hill Book Co., 1962), pp. 106–7.
6. *Ibid.*, pp. 111–2.
7. E. L. Kelly, "Consistency of the adult personality," American Psychologist, 10:659–81. Quoted in Reference No. 5, pp. 111–3.
8. Irving Janis et al., Personality and persuasibility (New Haven, Conn.: Yale University Press, 1959).
9. Same reference as No. 1.
10. Ruth L. Munroe, Schools of psychoanalytic thought (New York: The Dryden Press, 1955).
11. Ruth Benedict, "Continuities and discontinuities in cultural conditioning," Psychiatry, 1:161–7.
12. Samuel A. Stouffer, "An analysis of conflicting social norms," American Sociological Review, 14:707–17.
13. N. Gross et al., Explorations in role analysis (New York: John Wiley and Sons, 1958).
14. Warren Breed, "Social control in the newsroom: a functional analysis," Social Forces, 33:326–35.

15. James U. McNeal, editor, Dimensions of consumer behavior, 2nd ed. (New York: Appleton-Century-Crofts, 1969), p. 8.
16. Carl I. Hovland and Robert R. Sears, "Experiments on motor conflict, 1. Types of conflict and their modes of resolution," Journal of Experimental Psychology, 23:477–93.
17. A. H. Maslow, Motivation and personality (New York: Harper & Brothers, 1954).

Does Personality Predict Purchase of PRODUCTS?

The hypochondriac personality, one would suppose, would be a sitting duck for green, pink, and yellow pills, and the gregarious type a poor prospect for the Book of the Month Club. With few exceptions, however, attempts to link personality types to product preferences have failed. Here is one of the exceptions. Note, however, that predictions actually were made from use to personality rather than the reverse.

In Texas, 101 men students filled out questionnaires concerning the use of 9 different products and a 4-trait personality scale, the Gordon Personal Profile.

Subjects were divided into 2 groups on the basis of their use of each product in turn; there were 31 students, for example, who "never" used mouthwash versus 70 who used it. Mean personality scores on each of the 4 traits— ascendancy, responsibility, emotional stability, and sociability—were then compared for each pair of product-use groups. Of 36 such comparisons, 13 produced statistically significant correlation ratios.

Two products, cigarettes and deodorants, showed no significant relationship to any of the personality traits.

Source. W. T. Tucker and John J. Painter, "Personality and product use," *Journal of Applied Psychology*, 45:325–9.

Does Personality Predict Purchase of BRANDS?

Take the two most popular makes of automobile in the United States. Both, one might guess, appeal to such a broad cross-section of the population that their drivers would be indistinguishable. Has advertising created an image of each car and its owner which would show up on a personality test? This was the problem a University of Chicago professor set out to study.

Questionnaires sent to 100 Chevrolet and 100 Ford owners in a suburb 30 miles south of the Chicago loop, and completed by 70% of the drivers included these items.

Twenty-one brief descriptions of people, drawn from a personality

	Ascendancy	Responsibility	Emotional Stability	Sociability
Headache remedies	.46		.32	
Vitamins	.33	.30	.09	.27
Mouthwash		.22		
Chewing gum		.29	.33	
Alcoholic drinks		.36		
Automobiles		.28		
Accepting new fashions	.33			.57

inventory. Example: *Likes to travel, aggressive driver, always telling jokes, thinks himself physically attractive to women.* Each car owner was asked to check the phrases he thought applied to him and to indicate which automobile was suited to the person described.

Twelve objective variables, such as age, income, religion, politics, home ownership, and miles driven per year.

Only 5 of the 21 personality descriptions showed statistical significance at the .05 level. Both Ford and Chevrolet owners agreed that Chevrolets were suited to the cautious person and Fords to the aggressive, car-loving, nonconformist collegian. Ford owners said that the Chevrolet type was *always seeking advice from others.* Chevrolet owners rejoined that the Ford driver *wanted to be boss, was always telling jokes, thought himself attractive to women.*

A linear discriminant function calculated from test scores misclassified 37% of the sample, as compared with flipping a coin, which would have misclassified 50%. Objective variables produced a discriminant function which misclassified only 30%. Neither statistic was significant at the .05 level, however. Because of the nature of the sample, the range of readings on the objective variables was limited.

Source. Franklin B. Evans, "Psychological and objective factors in the prediction of brand choice: Ford versus Chevrolet," *Journal of Business*, 32:340–69.

Does Personality Predict Purchase of CAR MODELS?

The Big Three of the automobile industry boast that they have cars to fit any purse and purpose. If so, auto make (brand) is unlikely to distinguish one personality type from another. But within each make, aren't there differences in *model?* Motivation researchers thought so when they suggested that the owner of a convertible looked on it as he would a mistress. This study used a personality test.

In California and in Illinois, 27 students interviewed over 18 male owners of convertibles, compacts, and standard autos, persuading them to fill out a 140-question personality inventory which, when scored, rated seven traits. Three of the traits showed significant differences (*.05 level or better) for car owners; one proved significant in regard to preference for car type.

Trait	Preference	
	Compact	Convertible
Active	11.03	12.85*
Impulsive	11.47	12.27
Sociable	11.94	13.06

Trait	Ownership	
	Compact	Convertible
Active	11.45	13.34*
Impulsive	11.11	12.50*
Sociable	11.96	13.45*

The remaining traits—vigorous, dominant, stable, and reflective—did not differentiate car owners.

Source. Ralph Westfall, "Psychological factors in predicting product choice," *Journal of Marketing*, 26:2:34–40.

Does Fear Sell Products?

Most products promise the prospect a pleasurable experience—the soft drink will refresh the trip, and the shaving lotion force a man to fend off females with a karate chop. Other products promise that they'll help the prospect *avoid* something unpleasant. They create a felt need by arousing fear.

The classic study of a *fear appeal* exposed groups of 50 high school freshmen to messages about dental care. A "strong threat" group were told that poor care of teeth could lead to paralysis or blindness and were shown some gruesome slides; their messages contained 71 threatening details. A "moderate threat" group received messages with 49 such items, and a "mild threat" group heard 18 items and were shown slides of healthy teeth only.

The messages affected attitudes as one might expect, the percentage of students agreeing with statement varying by condition.

Strong Threat	Moderate Threat	Mild Threat

I feel worried about care of teeth

66%	36%	34%

Scores on a before-and-after, five point, not worried-very worried scale showed the following increase in worry about decay.

Strong Threat	Moderate Threat	Mild Threat
42%	26%	24%

(Only 8% of a control group, which heard a lecture on the human eye, showed an increase in worry about teeth.)

However when students' actual behavior was studied, the low-threat message was found to be the most effective, both in inducing conformity to proper teeth-brushing procedures and in making an actual visit to a dentist. Here are the results (in %).

Strong Threat	Moderate Threat	Mild Threat

Net increase in counseled practices

8	22	36

Proportion visiting dentist

10	14	18

(Only 4% of the control group visited a dentist in this period.)

The authors suggest that a message which arouses fear but fails to relieve it will be forgotten or minimized. A receiver can escape the threat by rejecting the source and blanking out his message rather than accepting his cure.

Source. Irving L. Janis and Seymour Feshbach, "Effects of fear-arousing communications," *Journal of Abnormal and Social Psychology,* 48:78–92.

More recent studies—dealing with smoking and cancer and injury stemming from failure to use seat belts—have tended to disagree, finding that the stronger the fear appeal used, the greater the response. Giving clear directions has been found to be essential to getting action, as distinguished from mere verbal compliance.

Seniors at Yale were given booklets on tetanus varying in two dimensions. A *high-threat* version described convulsions and showed a gaping tracheotomy. Students reading it turned pale and, on a series of 21-point scales, reported that they felt anxious, nervous, tense, angry, and nauseated. Reactions to the low-threat version were less extreme. Booklets also varied in advice as to what students could do to avoid tetanus: some said the University would give free shots whereas others provided a time schedule and map showing where and when one could get shots.

High fear led to greater change in

attitudes, as in the previous study, but *action* depended on how detailed the instructions for action were.

Detailed Directions		General Directions	
High Threat	Low Threat	High Threat	Low Threat
Number of subjects reporting for shots			
4	4	0	1

Although high threat and low threat were equally effective with regard to action, a subsequent study showed that merely providing detailed directions, without any threat at all, was not sufficient to get students to take shots.

Source. Howard Leventhal, Robert Singer, and Susan Jones, "Effects of fear and specificity of recommendation upon attitudes and behavior," *Journal of Personality and Social Psychology,* 2:20–9.

The effect of fear appeals appears to vary with the specific kind of action sought. A *high-threat* message appears to be best in getting subjects to reduce the amount of smoking, but a *low-threat* appeal is most effective in getting smokers to take a chest X-ray to check on the possibility of cancer.

Three sound-and-color movies were used. Diagrams in the *low-fear* version showed the relationship between smoking and cancer. In medium fear, an editor was shown visiting a doctor, the camera following to the door of the operating room. In high-fear, viewers actually saw ribs being opened, the heart beating, and a lung removed. Subjects were classified as "low" (10 cigarettes or less a day) or "high" in smoking, and rated on how susceptible they felt to illness, lung cancer, and auto accidents. Three effects were measured: intentions to stop smoking, actually stopping, and submitting to an X-ray. This design produced three multicell tables.

	Intention to Decrease Smoking	Fear Present in Message		
		Low	Medium	High
Light smokers	High susceptibility	4.0	4.5	4.8
	Low suspectibility	3.4	3.7	3.7
Heavy smokers	High susceptibility	3.3	3.3	3.7
	Low susceptibility	3.3	3.6	3.1

Actual Decrease in Smoking	Fear Present in Message		
	Low	Medium	High
High susceptibility	53%	57%	83%
Low in susceptibility	62	56	75

Had Chest X-Rayed	Fear Present in Message		
	Low	Medium	High
Nonsmokers	46%	41%	45%
Light smokers	56	25	0
Heavy smokers	50	63	7

The authors suggest that taking an X-ray would increase fear, whereas stopping smoking would decrease fear and that predicting results requires one to estimate total fear present in terms both of message and of the actions it urges.

Source. Howard Leventhal and Jean C. Watts, "Sources of resistance to fear-arousing communications on smoking and lung cancer," *Journal of Personality,* 34:155–75.

The fear which a threatening message induces depends not only on the content of the message but on the person receiving it. A given message may be highly threatening to an anxious person but only mildly threatening to a calmer individual.

Three different aspects of the message were varied: degree of anxiety (high vs. low) as shown by depicting persons in pain; personal vs. impersonal (second or third person pronouns); and the presence or absence of a solution. All possible combinations of these were used with each of eight messages concerning treatment for mental illness: shock, analysis, psychodrama, and hypno-, occupational, hydro-, drug, and group therapies.

Messages were mailed to 288 members of a public-opinion panel who were asked to rank the messages in order of interest, from 1 to 8. Mean ranks were:

4.1 Nonanxious-solution-personal
4.1 Nonanxious-solution-impersonal
4.3 Anxious-solution-impersonal
4.4 Nonanxious-no solution-personal
4.7 Nonanxious-no solution-impersonal
4.7 Anxious-solution-personal
4.8 Anxious-no solution-impersonal
4.9 Anxious-no solution-personal

Source. Jum C. Nunnally and Howard M. Bobren, "Variables governing the willingness to receive communications on mental health," *Journal of Personality,* 27:38–46.

Since no mass medium would accept advertisements reproducing the high-threat appeals used in these laboratory studies—rotting teeth, bleeding gums, tetanic convulsions—marketing communications deals with low or moderate fear conditions. Consider how gingerly advertisers edged into the mention of bad breath, by inventing the word *halitosis.* Advertisers would do well to remember, however, that buying behavior is stimulated—or inhibited—by the total threat in a situation, which means not just that built into the message, but that inherent in the receiver's personality, in the action advocated, and in the time and place of exposure to the message.

What Personality Traits Make a Good Salesman?

Personality colors three decisions of the seller. He tries to find prospects whose personalities his products will appeal to. He tries to devise messages which appeal to those personalities. And he tries to pick salesmen with persuasive personalities.

What traits must a salesman have? One expert lists six: a desire for superficial affection, based on the feeling that no one can ever truly love him; energy, self-confidence, love of money, industrious habits, and a tendency to aggression rather than withdrawal when he meets resistance.[a]

A hundred college students in Texas, when asked to note what they liked and disliked about salesmen's "speech and deportment" ignored speech and emphasized friendliness. Nearly 70% of them said they disliked high pressure and salesmen who were overly helpful; 75% said they liked courtesy, helpfulness, a friendly attitude, and interest. Only 10% praised knowledge of the product being sold, and only 10% condemned lack of product knowledge.[b]

Two experts, summarizing seven years of field observations, said two traits were enough—an ability to put themselves in the customer's shoes and a strong desire to make a sale for its own sake, not just for the money involved.[c]

The search for any set of traits common to successful salesmen is unlikely to succeed for several reasons. One is that in any combination of traits, strength in one may compensate for weakness in another.

Another reason is that the functions to be performed differ so widely by firm and industry, depending on how the salesman's job is to be performed, that it is unlikely that any single set of traits will fit so wide a variety of desired behaviors.

Third, the personality and methods that work with one customer may prove obnoxious to another. A good salesman may be sensitive enough to deduce what customers want and have a repertoire of skills sufficient to give it to them.

Fourth, an employer may devise techniques which, applied uniformly in selling situations, without regard to customer differences, have a reasonable ratio of success. When this is true, differences in salesmen become unimportant. The method—plus selection, training, and attrition—makes all salesmen behave much the same.

Sources

[a] Robert N. McMurry, "The mystique of super-salesmanship," Harvard Business Review, 39:118.
[b] Author has lost reference and would appreciate help in finding it.
[c] David Mayer and Herbert M. Greenberg, "What makes a good salesman," Harvard Business Review, 42:119–25.

A good salesman needs the flexibility of an actor, so that he can assume the personality required by the customer he is dealing with. The Minnesota Multiphasic Personality Inventory (MMPI) has a device, called the K scale, which detects attempts to fake a "good" score. Persons who score high on this scale are said to have *the social skills and experience to cover insecurities under a facade of imperturbability.* That sounded to the psychologists like a good description of the salesman's role, so they ran a test.

They gave the MMPI to 182 industrial salesmen working for nine different employers and compared test results with ratings which employers had previously made of their salesmen's skill.

Without exception the raw scores on the MMPI proved a better predictor of success in selling than adjusted scores obtained after corrections for faking had been made.

Here's an example, using the schizophrenia scale.

	Better with Faking	Better with Faking Eliminated
Good salesmen	56	32
Poor salesmen	36	56

Before correction, most of the scales had validities high enough to make useful parts of a set of tests in selecting salesmen; after correction, validities dropped to zero.

Source. Floyd L. Ruch and William W. Ruch, "The K factor as a (validity) suppressor variable in predicting success in selling," Journal of Applied Psychology, 51:201–4.

Role vs. Personality: Which Determines Behavior?

The personality of most individuals is so multifaceted that they can meet the demands of any situation they are likely to encounter. Role, therefore, tends to be more useful than personality in predicting and in influencing human behavior.

This has been demonstrated by putting persons rated low in *ascendancy* (desire to lead) in positions of leadership; within 40 minutes they could not be distinguished from "natural" leaders in similar positions.

To be scored as being high on ascendancy, a student volunteer had to pass two tough tests of leadership. First, he had to land in the upper-third of the Guilford-Zimmerman Temperament Survey on this trait. Second, in a team which included one other high-scorer and two persons low in ascendancy, he had to spend 30 minutes assembling precut lumber into the framework of a house. At the end, he had to be ranked, both by his fellow-workers and by two outside observers, as one of two subjects making most attempts to lead.

New four-man teams were then assembled, consisting of one low, one high, and two moderates on the ascendancy ratings. Three members of the team sat in cubicles with a slot permitting them to communicate only with the fourth member, who thus had the job of coordinating their efforts. In half of the teams, this fourth member was the one with a low ascendancy rating; in half he was the one with a high rating.

Each team was given three problems to solve, and 16 to 20 minutes to solve them in. Eight pieces of information were needed for a solution, each team member being given two of them. (A typical problem was: How many trucks are needed to move a firm's chairs, desks, typewriters, and files to a new office in a single trip?) Success was measured by speed in finding a solution.

On the first trial, teams in which a high-ascendant person occupied the leader's position had a distinct advantage. By the second trial this advantage had been nearly cut in half, and by the third trial

it had disappeared. Not only did low ascendants rise to the occasion but high ascendants occupying nonleadership positions *decreased* in the rate of message transmission (the means by which leadership was exerted) from the first to third trial.

This table shows the average number of 10-second intervals needed to solve the problem.

| | Leadership Position Occupied by Person Rated as | |
	High Ascendant	Low Ascendant
Trial I	71	88
Trial II	45	35
Trial III	38	37

Source. Leonard Berkowitz, "Personality and group position," *Sociometry*, 19:210–22.

In another study, ROTC students at Berkeley were given a personality test which identified those high or low on a scale of dominance. Students were then paired off in a cooperative task: operating model trains over a track with two bypass sidings. Each partner controlled one train; both trains had to complete a trip before either trip was scored.

Seven kinds of two-man teams were formed. In three, nothing was said about role. These teams were made up of two dominant members (D-D), two submissive members (S-S), or one of each (D-S). In the remaining four types, one student was labeled dispatcher and the other told to carry out his orders. Again, there were teams made up of dominant members, the small letters indicating the *role* assigned them: Dd-Ds, and submissive members, Sd-Ss. In one of the dominant-submissive pairs, Dd-Ss, the roles assigned were appropriate to the personality-test scores (indicated by capital letters). In the other pairs, Ds-Sd, roles were inappropriate.

Here is how the groups scored on the task:

Dd-Ss	160
Dd-Ds	153
Sd-Ss	143
D-D	142
S-S	141
D-S	130
Ds-Sd	116

As one would expect, scores were highest when role and personality were congruent and lowest when they were in conflict. Dominant subjects outperformed submissive subjects, even when one had to take a submissive role. When roles were not assigned, requiring dominant and submissive personalities to work together on a cooperative task apparently cut down achievement.

Source. William T. Smelser, "Dominance as a factor in achievement and perception in cooperative problem solving interactions," *Journal of Abnormal and Social Psychology,* 62:535–42.

Dramatic evidence of the dominance of role over "personality" has come from experiments in which the brain has been electrically stimulated.

Such stimulation can prevail over "free will" and make a person, in turn, fearful, anxious, enraged, aggressive, alert, voluble, in pain. It induced aggression in a monkey—but the effects varied with the social environment. When the monkey had lowest status in a group with three others, she attacked once and was attacked 24 times. In a similar group, where she ranked second, the same electrical stimulation caused the same monkey to attack others 79 times, while she herself wasn't even threatened once.

Source. Jose M. R. Delgado, *Physical Control of the Mind* (New York: Harper & Row, 1969).

Does Role Affect Purchase of a New Product?

Many an advertiser (male) has said in the past, or seemed to say, "If I were a housewife, I would want to be efficient" and talked about the speed and convenience of his brand. Such an appeal may work, if a task is something a woman detests, like mopping floors. But sometimes such an appeal runs counter to the housewife's definition of her role.

One of the chief rewards a housewife receives is praise for skill as a cook. When she says that prepared foods "do not taste as good" as others, although neither she nor anyone else may be able to tell them apart, it may be because of a half-sensed threat to her role from the "instant" foods and mixes.

One way to reach such hidden feelings is to ask questions about the people who *use* products. Mason Haire did this in 1950, when he asked 50 housewives to describe the woman who made out this shopping list:

Pound and a half of hamburger
2 loaves of Wonder bread
Bunch of carrots
1 can Rumford's Baking Powder
Nescafé instant coffee
2 cans Del Monte peaches
5 lb potatoes

Another group of 50 housewives got the same list with one substitution: 1 lb Maxwell House coffee (drip grind) instead of Nescafé.

Almost half of the women who saw the list with instant coffee on it described the woman who drew it up as being lazy and a poor planner. Very few of the women who got the list with drip grind coffee on it used such words about the hypothetical shopper.

Haire checked respondents' pantries and found that 32 of the housewives who got the Nescafé list had instant coffee on their own shelves; 72% of the comments these housewives made were favorable, compared with only 21% of those made by the 18 housewives who did *not* have instant coffee on their shelves.

Source. Mason Haire, "Projective techniques in marketing research," *Journal of Marketing*, 14:5:649–56.

Additional Research Readings

Fear appeals. Authors cite four reviews of literature, note effects of audience segment, source credibility, repetition, and curvilinearity and distinguish between social and physiological threats. **Michael L. Ray and William L. Wilkie, "Fear: The potential of an appeal neglected by marketing,"** Journal of Marketing, 34:1:54–62. Reassurance is more important in halting than in preventing behavior. **Ronald W. Rogers and Donald L. Thistlethwaite, "Effects of fear arousal and reassurance on attitude change,"** Journal of Personality and Social Psychology, 15:227–33. Fear worked better in inducing a purchase (deodorants) than in changing a habit (smoking). **John R. Stuteville, "Psychic defenses against high fear appeals: A key marketing variable,"** Journal of Marketing, 34:2:39–45. Reassurance was needed to change beliefs for women with high anxiety about medical exam, threat worked for others. **Stanley Lehmann, "Personality and compliance,"** Journal of Personality and Social Psychology, 15:76–86.

Role vs. personality. In the prisoner's dilemma game, cooperative persons turn competitive and low authoritarians behave like high authoritarians. Thus neither insight nor interaction reveals the possibility of cooperation to the naturally competitive. **Harold H. Kelley and Anthony J. Stahelski, "Social interaction basis of cooperators' and competitors' beliefs about others,"** Journal of Personality and Social Psychology, 16:66–91.

Chapter 7 Synopsis

● Constraints force redefinition of goals for buyer and seller but make it easier to predict the other's behavior. A decision maker needs to know how much choice is possible within existing constraints and how easy it is to alter them. Technology can alter objective constraints; messages can alter perceptual constraints.

● Constraints arise from the physical environment, of which technology is a part; from the social environment, including such cultural institutions as law and economics; from characteristics of the individual buyer or seller; and from the nature of the decision-making process itself, in which every choice made limits subsequent choices.

● Although space and time constraints of the physical environment seem inflexible, they can be altered through both technology and messages. (Culture affects perceptions of both time and space.)

● Economic theory, economic conditions and a buyer's own resources all constrain choice, by saying what goals should be or by limiting resources available to achieve them. However, even the buyer's resources can be altered by messages that affect perceptions.

● The law consists of five subsystems: courts, legislatures, regulatory commissions, prosecutors, and adversary counsel. Its function is to resolve conflict without violence, and balance change against stability. Three factors tend to favor stability against change (and so constrain seller adjustment to change): reliance on precedent, the adversary system, and methods of recruitment of members to the five subsystems. Knowledge of these factors helps in predicting how the law will be affected by changes elsewhere in society.

● Sellers need to know how cultures differ and change if they plan to do business in other countries or with subcultures within this country, such as those of youth and the Negro. They also need to be aware of changes in customs and in values.

● In selecting his marketing mix, each choice a seller makes is limited by technology and buyer perceptions and each choice, in turn, is limited by all previous choices.

Chapter 7 Constraints on Decision Making

After a buyer or seller has specified his goals, but before he begins seeking alternative means of attaining them, he must assess the *constraints* that limit his search.

A buyer's goal may be a car that will take him to work and to the country club; his bank balance tells him that car can't be a Rolls Royce. A seller's goal may be a million dollar annual profit or a 65% share of the market, but his present market share, his competition, and the state of the economy tell him this goal can't be achieved next year. Constraints thus force redefinition of the goals themselves. Highly constrained behavior is highly predictable. When buyer constraints are tight, a seller need not continually check back on his prospects. Fewer constraints on buyer behavior mean more opportunity for a seller, gained at a cost of more effortful decision making. (If prospects always bought the cheapest brand available, for example, sellers could forget about consumer research and concentrate on their competitors. The fact that they do not creates work and opportunity for the seller.)

Change in constraints may be induced by a seller's messages, his competitors' messages, or other causes. (Buyers, in turn, distinguish between changes that result from their efforts and all others.)

We can identify at least two dimensions: the variety of choice permitted within the existing set of constraints (its *width*), and the resistance to change of the set itself (its *rigidity*). Each of these has both an objective and a perceptual character. One man "feels" poor and the other "feels" rich, although their net incomes are identical. The variation in perceptions probably causes the latter to spend more freely than the former. *Technological* developments in both production and distribution can increase (or decrease) the number of objective alternatives available; *messages* of advertiser and salesman can widen or narrow perceptual boundaries.

Four Causes of Constraints

Constraints are produced by four different causes.

Physical environment, including time, space, and the material universe, and such man-made, changeable "givens" as the current state of technology. The movement of goods through space and time from producer to user accompanied by change of ownership and paralleled by a flow of messages is the core of marketing. Technology can relax constraints of time and space through improved transportation (railroad, truck, airplane), improved communications (telegraph, telephone, radio, TV), and improved information handling (the computer); technology itself is a constraint since an individual seller cannot alter it.

Social environment, including cultural institutions such as economics, law, and language and the influence of reference groups, one's work situation, and his family.

Individual characteristics, which vary between individuals as well as from one time to another within each individual. ("Laws" based on the senses and memory appear to be fixed and invariant for all men; sex, intelligence, and personality are relatively fixed for an individual.)

Decision-making process. When buying decisions are made by several persons, as in a purchasing committee or in the family, each participant is constrained by all the others. Each step in decision making limits the alternatives available in each subsequent step.

A decision maker may accept constraints or decide that they limit his choices too severely and suspend decision making while he operates upon the constraints.

His choice will be affected by the following.

The source of the constraints—physical environment, social environment, characteristics of the individual or of the decision process.

Who is attempting to change constraints —the decision maker, a message source, or someone/something else?

Whether the constraints are primarily objective or primarily perceptual.

Constraints of Time and Space

If one is five minutes late to a business appointment in the United States, he apologizes; 50 minutes late and he has no appointment left, and has insulted the person he was to see in the bargain.[1] Diplomats in a foreign country, on the other hand, regard an hour's tardiness as the equivalent of the American's five minutes; to appear earlier would put in question their own self-respect and independence and show a servile nature. Even in the United States, definitions of tardiness vary by time of day, one's role, and section of the country. Mormons and the military interpret an 8:30 A.M. invitation as meaning "not later than 8:30," and so arrive between 8:00 and 8:27, with 8:25 being the peak point. Other persons interpret 8:30 as meaning between 8:25 and 8:45. Ten minutes late is the maximum permitted for a dinner party in New York City, but a "5 to 8" cocktail party will find guests arriving between 6 and 7:30 P.M. and leaving only when thrown out.

Perceptions of space also vary. Latin Americans cannot talk comfortably with one another unless they have approached a physical closeness which, in North America,

suggests sexual or hostile intent. In North America, confidential matters are discussed at a distance of 12 to 20 inches, personal matters at a distance of 20 to 36 inches; in Latin America distances are much less. The army in World War II ordered reports to be made to superior officers at a distance of three paces—8 feet or more—which, in American culture, calls for the loud voice one uses to address a group. As a result, junior officers found themselves shouting at their superiors in a most disrespectful tone of voice.

The salesman who has learned American standards of time and distance, faces serious difficulty abroad and may never know why. As he backs off, to restore the distance North Americans regard as comfortable for a business conversation, his behavior will be interpreted as reflecting a cold and unfriendly personality. (And the salesman who finds his prospects overly friendly will wonder why they refuse to buy from him.)

Terrain and traffic affect perceptions of distance between buyer and seller. A store on this side of a dangerous highway will be perceived as nearer than one that requires bucking traffic; a customer on this side of a steep mountain will be regarded as nearer in space, as he may be nearer in time, than one on the other side.

Social Environment: Economics

Three aspects of economics—theory, business conditions, and a buyer's resources—constrain the decision process.

Economic theory provides a goal for the seller (profit maximization) and a means of achieving that goal (marginal analysis). If one assumes diminishing returns, for example, investment should cease when the return received on the last unit just equals its value, previous units of investment being presumed to have returned more than their value. [Attempts have been made to provide a similar norm for the buyer, by suggesting that he tries to maximize *utility* measured by curves that identify points at which the buyer doesn't care ("is indifferent to") which of two products he buys. These efforts have not been convincing to the behavioral scientist.]

Economic conditions, either persistent or temporary, constrain decision making. In underdeveloped nations all of a man's earnings must go to keep him alive, sharply limiting choice of goals. The same is true in this country for many persons during periods of depression and all of the time for the poor. A buyer's choice of means is constrained in periods when goods are short, as in wartime under rationing.

Economic resources of the individual buyer, the third and most obvious type of constraint, are not as purely objective or predictable as they at first may appear. Falling prices may stimulate buying—unless still lower prices are anticipated. A fall or a rise in income will affect purchasing if it is seen as permanent but not otherwise. Sharp increases in income may go unspent while one is developing new tastes and felt needs. Good relations with old friends may make one avoid conspicuous spending. The idea that *you can't spend what you don't have* is becoming obsolete, thanks to installment purchases, credit cards, and *fly now, pay later* plans, and as a result of such sales messages, as *you owe it to yourself . . . you owe it to your family,* or the slogan, *you can't afford not to.*

Thus, all three types of economic constraints—prescriptions as to ends and means, the general level of the economy, resources of the individual buyer—have perceptual components that make them amenable to manipulation by the seller.

Social Environment: The Law[2]

In introductory textbooks, the label of "law" is usually applied to a list of *statutes*, with dates, passed by Congress or the state legislatures. More advanced courses recognize the role of *the courts* in making laws that control selling and buying, and refer to the quasi-judicial functions of *administrative bodies* like the Interstate Commerce Commission and the Federal Trade Commission. Much less attention, however, is paid to two other sources of law—the discretionary powers of *officials* charged with bringing law violators into the courts, and the relative skill of *legal counsel* defending businessmen against criminal charges brought by such officials, or representing businessmen in legal conflict with one another. Of these five subsystems of law, the courts are preeminent since they, not legislators, determine what the language of a statute signifies, and they determine the rules by which legal conflicts are waged between counsel.

In addition to their somewhat limited definition of *the law,* traditional business law courses often fail to ask what functions law performs. To a behavioral scientist function, perceived and actual, is basic. The law's function is not primarily or even minimally one of getting at the "truth" in a situation; law is a means of resolving controversies without violence. Contending parties need not feel that the law's resolution of problems is just or equitable—only that it is final. This means that legal decisions dare not depart too widely from the actual distribution of power in society and that losers in a legal contest must feel that the costs of resorting to violence are higher and the risks greater than their acceptance of defeat. (This judgment may depend, in part, on how soon they expect the contest to be resumed and on what terms.)

To be sure, the beneficiaries of any legal system conscript to their service all of the most valued symbols of their culture and benefit from the great number of unexamined beliefs that everyone takes for granted. Property rights are an example. Legal protection of a man's property is both more thorough and more ancient than protection of his person. (Indeed, the law often makes protection of the person incident to protection of his property; witness the laws against unlawful entry, requirement of a search warrant, etc.) Property rights, although dependent upon government, are often regarded as antecedent to it. (So sacrosanct is a man's right to pass on to his son the material evidence of his life's labor, that craft unions justify exclusion of Negroes by arguing that members have a property right to their jobs which they pass on to their sons through apprenticeship priorities.) The right to possess and use property, to enjoy the income from it and to dispose of it to another is, of course, basic to marketing.

Law thus puts a boundary around the area of marketing by defining what constitutes property. When slaves ceased to be property and became labor, they ceased to be of interest to marketing men. (Even ideas can become property and so marketable when patented and men's labor despite the abolition of slavery is converted into property by a contract that binds a man to work, if he works at all, for only one employer.)

Distribution of Power

Law reflects the distribution of power in a society. To understand how law affects buyers and sellers, we must take a look at such aspects of power as the *locus of aggregation*. Few consumers buy in sufficient volume or with sufficient frequency for any purchase to be very important to a buyer. In the aggregate, however, these purchases become a matter of life or death to the seller. The courts have refused to entertain claims by disaffected buyers, saying the injury they suffered was trivial. Not until the late 1960s did courts begin to permit aggrieved individuals to act on behalf of similarly unhappy buyers in a *class action*.

When business firms buy, order size changes. DuPont is powerful, whether buy-

ing from a local gravel pit or selling synthetic yarns to a carpet manufacturer. Sears is powerful; manufacturing firms will pare margins to the bone to sell to Sears. (However, since such sales could make a firm's continued existence dependent upon Sears, it may also market under its own brand name. By investing in advertising, it may be able to sell this brand at a higher price than equivalent merchandise sold under the Sears' label, hoping the *consumer franchise* established through advertising will ensure continued survival should Sears shift its patronage.)

Recognizing that law reflects power, the United States Congress has attempted to limit power through laws such as the Sherman Antitrust Act (1890), prohibiting monopolies and conspiracy to restrain trade; the Clayton Act (1914), banning price discrimination and interlocking directorates; the Robinson-Patman Act (1936) and the Antimerger Act (1950). It created the Federal Trade Commission as a quasi-judicial body to halt "unfair" competition. Such actions were not infrequently represented as being designed to aid the consumer but in practice have operated to protect business firms against one another. (This effect was obviously intended in the Miller-Tydings Act (1937), which legalized a ban on price-cutting by retailers which, at least in the short run, would have benefited the consumer.)

As one would expect from the *locus of aggregation* analysis, administration of these laws has often ignored or been hostile to consumer interests. Reasons for this may be found in the function of the courts in a world of change where frequent industrial revolutions affect the distribution of power.

Three Factors and Stability

The courts balance change with stability, since frequent change upsets any activity, such as business, which must be planned over a fairly long period of time. Three characteristics of the judicial system tend to favor stability against change.

The first is the courts' reliance upon *precedent* as a standard of legitimacy so that the past is made a guide to the future, and traditional ways of operating and the existing distribution of power are preserved.

The second factor, the courts' dependence upon the *adversary system,* gives an advantage to those with the larger present resources, who can hire more and better advocates to represent them, continue a judicial battle longer, and return to the fray more often. This fact gives an advantage to whoever is wealthier—more often defender than challenger of the status quo.

The third factor is that of *recruitment* of members to the organizations whose interaction creates law: legislatures, the courts, administrative tribunals like the FCC, federal and state attorneys general, and the bar itself.

Recruitment to the bench, as one might expect from their role in creation of law, tends to favor stability and/or size, since most lawyers are concerned with property rights and work for corporations. Comparatively few lawyers are trial lawyers; even fewer get famous enough or rich enough in such pursuits to be able to win an appointment or an election as a judge. Prosecutors, not defense lawyers, tend to be picked as judges, some as a reward for loyal service to a political party; others because, as media news sources, they have become sufficiently familiar to get elected as judge. Attorneys come to the bench with far more experience in prosecuting unpropertied persons for crimes against property, than in prosecuting propertied persons for crimes against the unpropertied. Few white-collar criminals are ever arrested or tried. Winning elections involves campaigns whose costs must be met by the candidate or monied friends, another selective factor favoring stability-minded judges. Lifetime tenure, whose manifest function is that of freeing judges from political pressure, tends to create an aged judiciary, another factor working against change.

One might expect legislators to be responsive to change and to the felt needs of the great mass of consumers rather than to a comparatively small group of sellers. In practice, however, they are sometimes even more devoted to the status quo than the courts.

There are several reasons for this. State legislators are poorly paid for part-time work; few wage or salaried workers have jobs they can leave for the duration of a legislative session. Campaign costs screen out advocates of change. During a session, legislators—whose work can get highly technical—must depend on lobbyists for information. (If strong lobbies operate on both sides of an issue, as when railroad and trucking lobbies battle, we have an analogue to the adversary system of the courts and expect similar consequences.) However, few business interests face any consumer opposition.

Members of the public, lacking lobbyists of their own, often don't know what's happening in a legislature. Although the press have historically acted as watchdogs of government for the public, few newsmen cover any state legislature and those few have to protect their news sources. Newspapers have never shown equal zeal in protecting the public against big business and the immunity extended to business covers most lobbyists. Publishers, themselves big businessmen, are better able to empathize with their peers than with dissidents desiring change. The media themselves tend to ban the most obvious abuses with the effect (and possibly the intent) of making laws against such practices unlikely, if not unnecessary. Thus, state legislatures tend to impose few constraints on the businessman; they are often just another of the variables he manipulates.

The same is true of Congress, but for

slightly different reasons. In many parts of the South, only a small proportion of the population votes; this makes it easier for businessmen to control the men who get elected. In addition, the South's single-party system tends toward few election contests and long, uninterrupted terms in Congress. The seniority system means that such long terms give southerners control of important committees. Finally, the impact of an electorate that might upset business by demanding either rapid changes or response to consumer interests is mitigated in the Senate by the numerical equality that deserts like New Mexico and Nevada have with populous states like New York and Illinois.

Commissions like the FCC and ICC, the third type of law-making organization, were originally established to handle technical matters that got bogged down in courts relying on precedent and the adversary method. However, since the courts retain the right of reviewing commission actions, procedures of these commissions have tended to become more courtlike. (The number of commission members who are lawyers accentuates this tendency.) Commission members tend to be drawn from the industries they regulate—and to obtain jobs in these industries when they leave the regulatory commissions. Thus, commissions, too, are less a constraint upon the businessman and more one of the variables he manipulates.

Enforcement of federal antitrust and other laws regulating business depends largely on the zeal of the man whom the president appoints as *attorney general*. (In the states, this post is usually elective.) The courts can't act until someone brings a case before them. Few congressmen will complain if an attorney general fails to prosecute; few will know he's passed up an opportunity. Every prosecution, however, will bring congressmen to the defense of firms based in their district and executives who have contributed to their campaigns.

(If a telephone call or letter doesn't succeed in mitigating a prosecutor's zeal, a cut in his appropriations may.)

Predicting the Impact of Social Changes

The businessman who recognizes the complexity of the law-making process and the forces—precedent, adversary procedures, and recruitment—which determine its direction is in better shape to predict future constraints than the one who regards "the law" as something sacrosanct, eternal, immutable, and beyond a layman's comprehension. He is less likely, for example, to feel himself at the mercy of capricious and arbitrary forces; he can ask how social changes will affect the law-making process and adjust to them.

Will registration of Negro voters in the South, for example, break the stranglehold on Congress held by southern congressmen? Will nationwide reapportionment under the Supreme Court's one-man, one-vote decision make legislative bodies less respectful of the rights of property? Will rising standards of living and increased education make men more aware of their own self-interest? Answer "yes" and one would predict *more* legal constraints on business and more rigid constraints.

Cultural Constraints

Law and economics are part of a larger category of constraints called *culture*—the things and ideas so universally shared that a people take them for granted.

Our knowledge of culture has come to us from anthropology, which began with scientists who sought out primitive tribes, isolated enough to have developed distinctive cultures, and lived with them. Their reports were fed into a cross-cultural library at Yale University, which expanded into a cooperative venture of 15 universities. Here scholars searched for universal patterns of behavior and thought, common to all men. They found that all people seem to have clothing and shelter—but the variations were more notable than the similarities, particularly to a marketing man. They assumed that most cultural patterns originated as a meaningful response to the environment. In our society in these days, technology causes such rapid changes in environment (and people move from one environment to another in such large numbers) that the ideas in their heads frequently fail to change in tempo with changes in their environment, technology, and behavior.

Some kinds of cultural adjustment have ceased to be important in the United States. A halt to immigration has removed the problem of immigrants who found a shift from a rural, foreign culture to urban America so difficult that sometimes only their children were able to make the change. Some types of adjustment continue. In the process of becoming adults, adolescents tend to develop a subculture of their own. Other kinds of cultural adjustment appear. Life styles of the rural southern Negro have been changed by immigration to the urban North, producing a new kind of subculture which businessmen know little about.

Sellers usually think of subcultures such as those of Negroes and youth as market segments for which special products and messages must be designed. They collect figures that show that the Negro male purchases nearly twice as many shoes at a cost one-third again as high as that of the general population.[3] (Seeking an explanation, they realize that although job discrimination has put a lid on Negro incomes, other forms of discrimination prevent Negroes with money from spending it on suburban homes and country club memberships. As a result, Negroes both save more and spend more on luxuries than whites of the same income level. They discover that Negroes,

having less extensive social contacts than many whites, are more dependent upon advertising and more prone to pick advertised brands.)[4]

Discrimination has concentrated Negroes, more visible than most market segments, into geographic areas; this, and restricted mobility, make them reachable by interested retailers. Special media, both print and broadcast, are available to reach the market.

The seller is interested in cultural *customs* and how they change over time. Changes in hair length affect barbers; changes in length of skirt affect the garment trade and retailers. Some changes destroy a market; others create one. Clark Gable's appearance without an undershirt in a single scene in a movie is said to have distressed underwear firms for years afterward. On the other hand, until trench warfare in World War I liberated men, cigarettes and wristwatches were considered effete if not epicene.

More important than such changes in customs, but harder to observe, are changes in cultural *values*—changes that may affect both products and messages.

Some observers[5] see six values as characterizing society in the United States: a strong personal sense of moral responsibility rooted in religion (whether an individual attends church or not), a high value for personal achievement, a desire for security, sensitivity to the views of others (to the point of not wanting to offend via nonconformity), a desire for leisure, and a distaste for old age. Others[6] see a trend away from the traditional Protestant ethic, with its emphasis on hard work, and toward an easy life in which wife and children rule the home, pleasures demand immediate gratification, spending is more to be lauded than saving, security is superior to independence, sexual chastity gives way to free love, and formal religion is deemphasized. Any of these may have marked effects on buying habits and response to messages.

Constraints Inherent in Decision Making

In any system or process, each decision limits the alternatives available for subsequent decisions. Let us suggest a few, with both objective and perceptual aspects, in the seller's choice of a marketing mix.

Product. Science and technology limit form and function in a product. Thus, fuels, metals, and theory all had to converge before airplanes could be produced and marketed; the computer revolution would have been aborted if transistors had not been invented to replace vacuum tubes in the nick of time.

Price. There are three constraints on price: the costs of labor and materials used in making and distributing a product; prospects' ability and willingness to pay; and competitors' decisions. As buyer affluence rises, such constraints relax.

Place. Realities of time, space, and costs constrain choice of sites for plants, warehouses, and retail outlets and of the means of transportation used to convey products from one to the other. One's choice of participants in the process of distribution and sale is constrained by their willingness to sell and stock one's product which, in turn, is affected by the opportunities offered by competitors.

Prospects. There must be enough prospects, dissatisfied with current offerings, within a geographic area that can be reached by one's channels of physical distribution and of message flow, and with the resources to purchase one's product. Developments in the technologies of production, distribution, and communications may relax these constraints by reducing the size of the market needed. Birth, death, and migration rates,

all beyond the seller's control, affect market potential.

Promotion. The arrival of TV as an advertising medium greatly increased the minimum budget required, both to produce and deliver messages. At the same time, development of regional and demographic editions of mass magazines, and a proliferation of special interest publications relaxed constraints of cost on use of printed media. Automobiles, freeways, and airplanes relaxed constraints of time and space that had previously limited the area a salesman could cover; computer techniques increased the flexibility of direct mail; closed-circuit TV and the WATS line extended the communications facility of the salesman.

As important as the constraints that affect each element individually, are the constraints that arise from interaction among these elements of the marketing mix.

Price, for example, may be interpreted as a cue to produce quality. Too low a price may hurt the sales of products, such as perfume and drugs, whose quality the buyer is rarely able to judge. (A high price may reassure a husband that the perfume is a suitable anniversary gift, or that the cough medicine is safe for his children. Under conditions of high risk, involving the buyer's health or the opinions that others hold of him, a buyer may seek assurance by paying a high price rather than a low one, when offered a choice.)

Thus, an expenditure on advertising directed at consumers may relax constraints on place by increasing the number of alternative outlets available to the manufacturer. The nature of the product limits seller choice as to place variables: perishable products set limits as to time and/or mode of transportation; gravel, gasoline, and women's garments offer different kinds of constraints.

Thought, Talk, and Action

1. Give examples of objective and perceptual constraints arising from the physical environment, the social environment, and the decision maker. Suggest measures to alter each kind of constraint in each of the three areas.
2. Looking in turn at each of the five legal subsystems, prepare a forecast for your employer as to whether constraints will be more or less rigorous 10 years from now. Do this separately for these employers: a pulp mill, a strip miner, a billboard company, an auto manufacturer, a department store.
3. The text mentions the subcultures of the Negro and youth. The aged also represent a subculture. Describe how attitudes of this group vary from the general population; describe differences in purchasing and consumption behavior. (For purposes of this question, assume one becomes aged at 65.)

Notes

Chapter 7

1. Edward T. Hall, The silent language (Garden City, N.Y.: Doubleday & Co., 1959).
2. Among references giving a behavioral scientist's view of "the law" are these:
   (a) Philip Selznick, "The sociology of law," in Robert K. Merton, Leonard Broom and Leonard S. Cottrell, Jr., Sociology today (New York: Basic Books, 1959).
   (b) June L. Tapp, "Psychology and the law: the dilemma," Psychology Today, 2:9:16–22.
   (c) Hans Zeisel, "The law"; Arnold Rose, "The social scientist as an expert witness in court cases," and David J. Bordua and Albert J. Reiss, Jr., "Law enforcement," all in Paul F. Lazarsfeld et al., The uses of sociology (New York: Basic Books, 1967).
3. James H. Myers and William H. Reynolds, Consumer behavior and marketing management (Boston: Houghton-Mifflin Co., 1967), p. 229.
4. Raymond A. Bauer, Scott M. Cunningham, and Lawrence H. Wortzel, "The marketing dilemma of Negroes," Journal of Marketing, 29:3:1–6.
5. James F. Engel et al., Consumer behavior (New York: Holt, Rinehart and Winston, 1968), pp. 241–50.
6. Philip Kotler, Marketing management (Englewood Cliffs, N.J.: Prentice-Hall, 1967), pp. 37–8.

Chapter 8 Synopsis

● No search for alternatives need occur if past experience, with product or messages, solves problems the instant they arise, or if a prospect is unable or unwilling to delay a decision while search proceeds. Because of this a seller trying to influence buying behavior needs to know how past experience is stored; he needs to study *learning*.

● When search does occur, it is more likely to be internal than external; it depends upon retrieving from memory information already stored there. Again, *learning* is the key. External search, the active seeking of new information following identification of a specific problem, depends upon *perception:* the translation of sensations into rewarding experiences or the use of input from one sensory receptor to indicate probability of another type of sensory reward. Perception emphasizes similarities among men and current stimuli; learning emphasizes differences and past stimuli.

● Messages are stored in memory even though, at the time of exposure, motivation, response and reward are absent. (Latent learning). Three kinds of evidence are available as to message attributes which aid learning. We know something of how variations among receivers affect message reception and retention.

● Internal search has advantages of speed, reliability and security. External search is more efficient, avoiding irrelevant and outdated information.

● Internal search requiring no new information input also occurs within the firm, but since it requires communication among multiple decision makers it is more susceptible to observation than the inside-the-head internal search of the consumer. Size of firm and number of competitors affects amount of search undertaken.

● The firm selling to consumers, in contrast to the firm selling to other manufacturers and retailers, must process information on more buyers, must work harder to uncover dissatisfaction, has more free information available. It is questionable whether consumers themselves would benefit by undertaking more extensive external search before making buying decisions.

● Three apparent exceptions to the observation that consumers typically engage in very limited external search involve shopping as recreation, survival of price bargaining in auto purchases, and purchase of investments and farm supplies. These may be more apparent than real.

Research Articles

Information Seeking.   Varies with topic (Wright). Seeker tends
to read more ads, make more shopping trips: methods do not
substitute for one another (Bucklin). Word-of-mouth source
changes with age of seeker (Feldman). Sources other than
advertising and salesman often preferred (Udell). Source
sought varies with stage in process of adopting an innovation
(Copp).

Messages.   Messages we agree with are learned faster, remembered longer (Levine). Some scholars urge taking an extreme
position (Hovland, Weiss) while others urge moderation
(Hovland). Extremity affects extent to which message changes
evaluation of topic and source (Aronson).

Cooperating.   By cooperating, consumers and experts can isolate
product attributes that determine buyer choice (Quenon).

Chapter 8 Seeking Alternatives

In analyzing buyer behavior as a preliminary to trying to influence it, a seller must answer two key questions concerning the search for alternatives.

Does the prospect engage in search of any kind or are problems solved (opportunities seized) the instant they present themselves?

If he does engage in search, what kind is it—internal or external?

Search is not likely to occur if satisfactory past experience provides an instant solution. Such past experience is of two kinds.

Product. If the buyer is satisfied with the brand he's used previously (or, however dissatisfied, sees no brand that promises greater satisfaction), he will engage in repeat purchasing. *Habit* will determine his behavior.

Messages. No choice will be necessary if the prospect *knows* of only one brand and is not able or willing to delay his purchase while he seeks alternatives.

A prospect is not *able* to delay his purchase in many emergency situations, as when a car breaks down in the desert or a furnace in midwinter. He is not *willing* if he thinks the possible brand differences he might discover would not repay the costs of search and comparison. (Much *impulse* buying is of this kind. Sight of a brand at a check-out counter awakens a latent need—solution *precedes* problem, in this instance —which is satisfied instantly. The likelihood of such purchases is increased if only one brand is offered; lack of opportunity for comparison prevents a delay that might lead to no purchase at all.) Sometimes external constraints prevent search. In times of severe shortage, for example, a buyer had better grab the first opportunity of purchase he encounters. In a ghetto, persons lacking transportation and needing credit may have to buy their groceries at a high-priced, "mom-and-pop" store on the corner.

When search does occur, more of it tends to be internal than external. (Internal search consists of calling up from one's memory two types of experiences: experience with products and experience with messages.) All external search involves some internal search, but the reverse is not true. A prospect may be sure of the brand he wants, and use the yellow pages of a telephone directory to find the nearest or cheapest outlet handling the brand. Or he may fix upon a particular retail outlet and restrict his search-and-comparison to the brands it offers. (In one study, 42% of buyers visited only one retailer before purchasing such an expensive, infrequently bought durable as a refrigerator, and 82% bought a lower-priced electric iron at the first store visited.)[1] Sometimes *only* internal search is involved, a decision being made on the basis of memory with no input of new information.

A buyer's experience thus is a factor in all buying and the determining factor for many purchases. The seller, therefore, has a vital interest in *any relative permanent changes in behavior that occur as a result of experience.* (Since the above phrase is a definition of *learning,* the seller needs to know about different kinds of learning, how they are measured and how they can be produced. He needs to know how experience gets into memory and what can be done, then and later, to increase the likelihood that one memory will be retrieved in preference to another. Chapter 9 discusses these problems in some detail.)

When past experience does not suffice for a decision, and active search is required, the seller must *use his senses to gain knowl-*

edge from his environment, an environment that includes brands and messages about them. (Since this phrase is a definition of *perception,* the seller needs to know how light and sound waves are converted into sensations that the mind experiences as products and brands. He is concerned with two kinds of sensations: those that are rewarding in themselves, such as the sound of a stereo or the taste of candy, and those that serve as cues to such rewards, such as the red-and-white color that identifies peppermint candy or the illustration that suggests beautiful music. Chapter 10 deals with these questions.)

Perception emphasizes message-response relationships that are common to all men, current stimuli rather than past experience, and guides the active, information-seeking behavior of the buyer engaged in external search. *Learning* emphasizes differences among individuals, arising from their varied past experiences, and affects the information-retrieving and processing activities of internal search.

If the brain stored only the results of actual experience with products, rather than the vicarious experience provided by messages about them, advertising would vanish. (Manufacturers might distribute free samples to induce storable consumer experiences.)

If consumer decisions were based on information gathered in a search that began only after problems had been identified and goals set, most advertising messages and media would be useless. Only a few members of any mass media audience can be facing a buying decision at the time of exposure; unless messages are stored in memory, most will be wasted. (Salesmen would continue to be useful, since most of their contacts are actively seeking information for specific decisions.)

Because message content *is* stored in memory, advertisers bathe prospects in a sea of messages most of their waking moments. They know that the few who are

seeking information will be sensitized to relevant messages, and that some will pay attention because they seek reassurance for purchases they have made recently. Advertisers try to construct messages that will appeal to the rest, either by arousing a latent need or by being rewarding in themselves—style and format arousing interest even when content does not. Neither they nor the prospect, however, know how long a time will elapse before either will receive any benefits from sending or receiving the advertising message. (The message will never be stored in some brains and in others a subsequent influx of other messages will bury it so deep that it is not likely to be retrieved when needed.) Chances of storage and retrieval rise as a message is repeated or given greater initial impact and to the extent the situation of original exposure matches that of eventual use.

Most persons are exposed to advertising when they have too low an interest in the product advertised to seek out or attend to messages on the basis of content. Most exposures occur at times when a host of other advertisements are competing for attention and retention. Media may be picked because they have a high proportion of potential prospects; messages are designed to overcome receiver apathy and competitors' noise. Principal elements in this design are repetition and stylistic quality.

Some admen argue that repetition to the point of irritation can penetrate apathy without much risk, since the feeling (irritation) will dissipate over time while the attendant cognition (memory of brand name) will remain to guide buyer choice. Others suggest that a successful ad is one that slips past a prospect's defenses, one he never really becomes aware of. There is evidence to support both viewpoints. Admen also disagree on how close a relationship is required between attention-getting devices in a message and the message itself. If the two are unrelated, a prospect may turn off when he discovers the trick; if no attention-getting devices are used, he may never notice the ad.

Three questions about learning, memory, and perception are of particular importance to a seller trying to influence buyer behavior.

Will a message be stored in the memory if, at the time of exposure, the subject is not motivated, does not respond, and is not rewarded?

What are the qualities in a *message* that make it stand out from other messages competing with it for attention so that it is stored in memory?

What attributes of an *audience* predispose them to pay attention to an advertising or sales message?

Latent Learning

In most learning experiments, motivation, performance, and reward are all present: a hungry rat runs the maze to a food box. Most advertising, however, reaches persons who are not hungry, who do not run down to the corner store to buy it, and who may not consume it for weeks. Most advertising is received under conditions similar to those in *latent learning* studies, in that no visible behavior is produced; the learning is *incidental*, unrelated to the task at hand, unmotivated, and unrewarded. Learning does occur under such conditions. (Rats allowed to wander aimlessly in a maze without reward do run the maze subsequently, when hungry and with food at the end of the maze, as fast as those who have only run it under conditions of motivation and reward.)[2] However, learning in the absence of felt-need, reward or practice is often less efficient than when all three are present. More trials are needed—15 times as many in one study.[3] (There may be situations in which learning without awareness is more

efficient. If the message *contradicts* a belief or attitude held by the receiver, he may resist it; if it is stored in his memory, a negative value will be attached to it. Distracting his attention might allow the message to "sneak by" his defenses. The argument sounds plausible, but experimental evidence is mixed.)

Message Qualities

Three types of evidence suggest how message characteristics may increase learning: (1) study of man's sensory receptors, (2) findings of Gestalt psychology concerning the ways in which stimuli combine and conflict, and (3) attempts to determine what features of advertisements are correlated with high recognition scores or other measures of advertising effectiveness.

Receptors

Ordinarily, the brain receives several cues concerning the location and nature of any object, such as an orange: sensations that the brain interprets as smell, taste, appearance, and feel of the orange; and within the single sense of vision, shape, size, distance, and color. (There are seven separate visual cues as to distance; the ears provide no less than five separate cues to direction.) These multiple cues usually permit us to identify an object correctly, even when viewed from various angles, and even when visual or auditory distraction is present. Ordinarily, these several sensory cues are consistent with one another; by introducing inconsistencies in the laboratory, we can see which cues are most persuasive. Within the range of stimuli encountered most often, there appears to be a consistent relationship between physical properties of the cue and the sensations reported to the brain. Beyond these limits we lose the ability to tell one cue from another or to detect any cue at all.

Gestalt

Cues near one another in space or time tend to be perceived as a group or sequence. Up to a point, repetition of a cue increases the chance that it will be noticed; beyond, repetition may cause the same stimulus to recede into the background. A cue that contrasts with its spatial or temporal context is likely to be noticed. (Usually this gives an advantage to a sudden, loud noise, to a bright color, or to a moving object. In a context of noise, color, and movement, however, a sudden hush, absence of color, or an object that does not move will stand out.) One important contrast is that between what a receiver expects to see and hear and the messages actually sent him. Minor discrepancies will be overlooked; the receiver will see and hear what he expects. Larger discrepancies, however, will seize his attention.

Message Elements

Men have tried to relate ad content characteristics to readership scores, but recognition of an ad is just one measure of memory and memory is only one of the effects that ads are supposed to produce. Even recognition scores are likely to vary from one audience segment to another. (Interest in the product being advertised, for example, is likely to affect both attention and recognition scores, and interest obviously varies from one person to the next.)

Objective counts of ad attributes that can be counted or measured, tend to reflect *amount* of advertising rather than quality. (In one such study, for example, 15 *mechanical* variables and 19 *content* variables produced predictions that correlated from .58 to .80 with actual recognition scores. But the predictions were based on only three variables: number of pages, number of colors, and size of illustration.)[4] If, on the other hand, one tries to score ads on stylistic variables, scores must be based on

independent ratings by several judges; the number of judges, the population from which they are chosen, the method of choice, and the kind of instructions and training given them then become crucial.

Finally, as we have seen, contrast appears to be associated with, and perhaps even essential to, attention getting. But contrast arises from the interaction between a message and its context; no formula that ignores context can predict whether an advertisement will benefit from contrast. Novelty is important too: an ad that reproduces the high-scoring qualities of previous ads may bore buyers and boomerang on its sponsor. (The first firm to use a given copy platform or emphasize a product feature may make its brand name so closely related to that theme that it wins a *consumer franchise*. If a rival firm attempts to use the same theme, its ads may be misperceived or misremembered as belonging to the original advertiser.)

Receiver Variations

Our third question—the attributes that sensitize an audience to a particular marketing message—has already been dealt with in our discussion of role, motives, personality, and attitudes. A prospect's chance of exposure to a message depends on the amount of time he gives to media use in general, as well as the portion of this time given to its advertising content; the kind of media he uses; the number of contacts he has with salesmen; the number of contacts he has with friends, and the extent to which they relay messages received from salesmen and advertising. Individuals vary, even when exposure is controlled, in the extent to which they understand, accept, and recall the messages received. All these factors, as well as attention, are affected by prospects' age, sex, education, and occupation. Persons with a college education and employed in business or the professions show greater media use than do others. Women probably process more advertising than men, and young adults more than retired persons.

So far, we have been talking of internal search as that which occurs within the head of an individual buyer. Search that requires no new input of information and is not very visible to the seller also occurs within the firm. Internal search of this kind, however, usually involves communications between decision makers and so is potentially observable in a way that search by the individual buyer is not.

Internal Search by the Firm

Such internal search in the firm is taken seriously: even a few cents per unit become significant when hundreds or thousands of units are being bought and sold. By basing executives' rewards upon the balance sheet, firms make such decisions important to the men who make them. It's easier to tell good decisions from bad; it's important to do so; routines for doing so exist.

Internal search in the firm depends on a continuous flow of information into the decision-making system geared to routine decisions, often programmed like habits. At relatively little expense, in-house records and secondary data can be fed into a computer's memory continuously. This information process may itself identify a problem —as well as seek out and compare alternative solutions to it. (Analysis of daily sales records can spot products, salesmen, territories, or customer types who fail to match their potential.) Quality-control techniques encourage marketing men to express goals in terms of upper and lower limits; crossing these boundaries permits *management by exception:* a problem-centered decision process.

The rigor of computer programming helps in spotting informational gaps. By handling of routine data, the computer frees employees to seek and process such new information.

However, there are important differences between firm and family. Firms are likely to get most of their information from salesmen skilled in diagnosing problems and suggesting solutions for them, whether they concern punch-press capabilities or forecasts of consumer response to fad and fashion. Industrial buyer and seller are willing to spend more time than the typical consumer in exchanging information. High costs of idle men and machinery and of customer dissatisfaction make a buyer want to have backup sources of supply on tap if present ones fail. Failure to see a salesman with a product innovation might give the buyer's competitors a significant advantage. The supplier wants salesmen to make repeated calls, sale or no sale, because of the potential size of the order that might come his way. For the same reason, he is willing to spend a good deal of time diagnosing a prospect's problems and providing him with a wide variety of services.

Internal search—defined as a review of information stored prior to recognition of a problem—has several advantages. One is speed; when a consumer's air conditioner breaks down or a warehouse fire destroys the raw materials one's plant was to process next Monday, there is no time for any very thorough search for alternative sources of supply. Another is reliability; there has been time to check out such information; its source couldn't distort it to fit needs not known at the time. Internal search that keeps prospective suppliers from knowing the urgency of a buyer's present needs improves his ability to bargain.

External Search

External search takes time: time in seeking and evaluating new information, time in doing without the product. External search involves information-seeking costs and the psychological cost of wrestling with an increased number of alternatives. Against these costs are the possible gains from extended external search: greater efficiency of search with less likelihood of collecting irrelevant information and of not gathering important information, since a problem has been defined. Internal search involves the risk for both firm and family that stored information may be out of date.

Consumers probably spend less time, effort, and money than do business firms in external, problem-initiated search. They have no need to do so, since sellers inundate them with "free" information and they lack the ability to search intelligently. Consumer brands may be more similar than alternatives open to the firm; even where they differ, the consumer may not be aware of this or have any confidence in his ability to detect such differences.

Although a firm, either as buyer or seller, tends to take more time in searching or trying to influence search processes than does a consumer, firm size is important. A large firm has greater resources than a small firm to use in exploring alternatives, but perhaps less need to use them. Both seller and buyer have directories and other services that will help to locate their opposite numbers and assess their credit; consumers lack such resources. The number of competitors also affects search: a firm with few competitors has less reason to seek the best alternative than one that faces many, vigorous rivals.

The liveliest search of alternatives is likely to be exhibited by the firm that sells to consumers. Much more information is needed, consumers being more numerous than purchasing agents, and more is available from governmental and commercial sources of information to a firm and its competitors. Some kinds of consumer information require more effort: a purchasing agent who is sold an unsatisfactory product is likely to yell loud enough to be heard back at the plant but customers are likely to take their patronage down the street. This means business firms must survey consumers' attitudes, intentions, and actions.

Consumers' limited external search may represent a rational recognition that possible gains are unlikely to justify costs. Legal constraints, the need for satisfied customers who will make repeat purchases, and the damage that dissatisfied customers can do through word-of-mouth communications with their peers all tend to eliminate dangerous and worthless products. Competition, as reflected in the product life cycle, tends to make between-brand differences small. (Within-brand variations tend to be small, too, thanks to the techniques of mass production and quality control.) Techniques of mass distribution tend to make offerings similar. (Mass marketing requires a one-price system. Neither consumer nor retailer in an industrial, urban society can afford to take the time required to negotiate price in each purchase.)

Perhaps the two most important signals in the whole search process, external and internal, are *halt* and *resume search*. A prospect can seldom examine ALL the alternatives available in any market—but when has he examined enough? If he sets minimum criteria for each relevant product attribute and adopts a *satisficing* strategy, his search can halt whenever a brand reaches these minima. Or he may halt when it appears that examining new brands will add nothing new or superior to the alternatives he's found. Cost affects the decision between these strategies. If no brand meets all the minima of the satisficer after a reasonable expenditure of time and energy, he may relax his standards. Similarly, the buyer who wants something better will not continue hunting for it forever, even though he risks missing a better brand just around the corner.

A buyer knows that the data stored in his memory need to be updated now and again. A change in ownership is likely to cue such search or a buyer may make a trial revisit to a rejected retailer at intervals of six months or a year to see if things have changed, even though he is fully satisfied with present suppliers.

Although we make a conceptual distinction between the search for alternatives and other stages in decision making, in real life the housewife who walks into a department store to buy a new bra may spot a new gadget in the housewares department or an on-sale fabric, or check prices of fine china. Evaluation of alternatives does not wait until the search process is completed; the housewife sniffs scents and quizzes the perfume counter clerk, rejecting one brand out of hand, and adding another to a list of "possibles" for the gift she will not buy for three more months. Goals are seldom set without regard to reality; search for the available often precedes and causes goal setting rather than following it. External search may occur in an information-storing rather than problem-solving and decision-making context.

Thought, Talk, and Action

1. Compare the internal search processes of business firm and of household. Now compare the external search processes of each. Explain the differences you find between firm and family.
2. The text says that consumers seldom engage in extended external search. Reconcile this statement, if you can, with the extended search that appears to occur in the purchase of an automobile, among women, and in the purchase of investments.
3. Compare the costs of internal and external search by putting hypothetical dollar values of your own choosing onto the advantages of each. (It helps to have a specific product in mind.) Sum them up so as to decide which of the two you would employ.

Notes

Chapter 8

1. William P. Donnermuth, "The shopping matrix and marketing strategy," Journal of Marketing Research, 2:128–32.
2. Jerome Kagan and Ernest Havemann, Psychology: An introduction (New York: Harcourt, Brace & World, 1968), pp. 70–2.
3. G. W. Faust and R. C. Anderson, The role of incidental material in programmed instruction (Urbana: University of Illinois, 1966). Mentioned in Annual Review of Psychology, 1967, p. 142.
4. Dik Warren Twedt, "A multiple factor analysis of advertising readership," Journal of Applied Psychology, 36:207–15.

Information Seeking

There have been thousands of studies of the information and persuasion peddler, but few studies of his opposite number, the information-seeker. Here's one example.

Graduate students in five departments (political science, journalism, philosophy, meteorology, and Italian) were quizzed on four topics: foreign affairs, success in graduate school, controversies in their field of study, and questions about their field of work. Students were then classified as leaders or followers and as information seekers or avoiders.

	Percentage of Leaders Who Are Also	
	Seekers	Avoiders
Foreign affairs	68	6
Controversies	54	18
Student success	25	18
Field of work	21	27

	Percentage Who Are Also Leaders	
	Seekers	Avoiders
Foreign affairs	53	4
Controversies	56	21
Student success	55	19
Field of work	48	24

Half of those seeking information were leaders, but only one-fourth of those avoiding information. When leaders were classified, differences were much smaller, and in the opposite direction— 21 and 27%. (And 52% of the leaders were neither seekers nor avoiders.)

Source. Charles R. Wright and Muriel Cantor, "The opinion seeker and avoider: Steps beyond the opinion leader concept," *Pacific Sociological Review* 10:2:33–43. Data reprinted by permission of the publisher, Sage Publications, Inc.

Turning to marketing, here is a study that found that advertisements and shopping trips are not substitute means of gathering information; as use of one increases, so does use of the other.

Quizzing 506 women who had purchased at least one nonfood item costing more than $5 during the month (a total of 891 items were involved), interviewers asked how many had looked at advertisements beforehand. They found wide differences by product involved, from 9% for shoes to 52% for furniture, with an average at 24%. Looking at ads was more common, as one would expect, for items which were expensive (14% if under $5, 46% if over $50) or purchased infrequently (18% if within 3 months, 30% if over 18).

Apparently women read ads for *product* rather than brand information: ad checkers did *not* show higher brand loyalty than ad skippers, and 51% of those who checked ads said they knew what features they wanted in the product purchased; only 38% of those who skipped ads were this confident. Apparently, reading ads is *not* a way to avoid going from store to store.

	Percentage Who	
	Checked Ads	Did Not Check Ads
Have a favorite store	28	47
Shopped more than one store	25	14
Regard price as important	46	34

Source. Louis P. Bucklin, "The informative role of advertising," *Journal of Advertising Research*, 5:3:11–5.

The search for information took another form when persons began looking for a physician, for whom advertising is forbidden.

Members of 415 households were classified into eight occupational groups, and six age groups. Results showed that the source of information on doctors changed with the patient's age.

Information Source	Median Age of Patient
Relative	28.1
Acquaintance	32.9
Professional	33.9
Nobody	39.2

The older one gets, the more likely he is to know someone outside his own kin and other medical persons or to have had enough experience with doctors to need no informants at all.

Source. Sidney P. Feldman, "Some dyadic relationships associated with consumer choice," in Raymond M. Haas, *Science Technology and Marketing* (Chicago: American Marketing Association, 1966).

Another study suggests that buyers do not spend much time in going from store to store in search of information. They spend more time reviewing their own experiences or in word-of-mouth communications with friends than they do in looking at ads.

Interviewers in the three weeks preceding Christmas visited four Wisconsin appliance stores. They approached 770 persons who had bought small appliances, most of them (in 1964) priced between $7.51 and $22.51; 90% of the buyers answered questions.

Many customers mentioned more than one source of information but few *shopped* in more than one store.

Advertising	
Newspaper	25%
Direct mail	21
Magazine	15
TV	14
Radio	7
	82%
Previous experience	50%
Word of mouth	34
Consumer Reports, etc.	9
Phone inquiry to store	4
	97%
Single store	60%
Two stores	16
Three or more stores	24

Purchasers, 60% of whom were males, said they had not spent much time in thinking about the purchase: 22% had made the decision to buy that day, another 28% within the week, and 33% more within the month. Only 28% of persons buying appliances costing $7.50 or less shopped in more than one store, as compared with 63% of those buying appliances priced at over $50. There was only a 3% chance that a person who left the store would come back to buy an appliance costing under $7.50, but a 57% chance that he would do so if it cost over $50.

Source. Jon G. Udell, "Prepurchase behavior of buyers of small electrical appliances," *Journal of Marketing*, 30:4:50–2.

When an innovation appears, different types of information may be sought through different channels at different stages in the persuasive process.

Interviewers asked 175 dairy farmers in Pennsylvania about three new farm practices: grass silage, hay drying, and control of spittle bugs.

Farmers were classified as to which of 5 stages they had attained: awareness, interest, acceptance, trial, and adoption. Here is the percentage of mentions which each channel received at each of the first 3 stages.

Stage	Awareness			Interest			Acceptance		
Practice[a]	a	b	c	a	b	c	a	b	c
Source				Percent					
Farm magazine	31	36	33	23	19	17	9	22	27
Radio	5	3	2	2	2	0	0	0	0
Extension: print	36	17	21	14	15	13	16	10	18
Extension: oral	10	14	11	25	26	24	27	20	23
Peers	14	28	25	34	33	38	45	46	27
Commercial	1	0	4	1	2	6	2	2	5
Total	97	98	96	99	97	98	99	100	100

[a] a is spittle bug control, b grass silage, c hay drying.

Printed messages had an advantage in early stages. Face-to-face messages were important later, in legitimizing and making specific application to the individual's farm.

Source. James H. Copp, Maurice L. Sill, and Emory J. Brown, "The function of information sources in the farm practice adoption process," *Rural Sociology,* 23:146–57.

Messages We Agree With Are Learned Faster, Remembered Longer

A good many of us can avoid being exposed to any message, from the media or our associates, with which we strongly disagree. What happens when we are forced, as in a laboratory experiment or a classroom, to expose ourselves to such material?

Ten students in New York City, 5 of them pro-Communist and 5 anti-Communist, read two prose passages over twice. One of the passages was anti-Communist, referring to mass arrests, executions, and barbarous deportations. The other was somewhat pro-Communist, referring to Russian elections, its "bright clean cottages" and feeling of unity.
Students read one of the passages, spent 15 minutes chatting with the experimenter, and then were asked to reproduce the passage they had just read before going on to read the second message. The learning trials were repeated for 4 weeks; tests of students' memories continued for another five weeks.

The graphs on page 169 show that students tended to learn faster and retain longer messages which matched their own attitudes.

Source. Jerome M. Levine and Gardner Murphy, "The learning and forgetting of controversial material," *Journal of Abnormal and Social Psychology,* 38:507–17.

Should One Ask for Too Much or Just Enough?

One of the most important choices facing a marketing communicator is this: how big a change should a message advocate—more than the source expects to get or the minimum that he will settle for? Two studies, among many, suggest taking an extreme position.

In the first study, 51 high school pupils gave their views on a dozen issues ranging from the chances that atomic-produced electricity would be lighting homes within five years to the

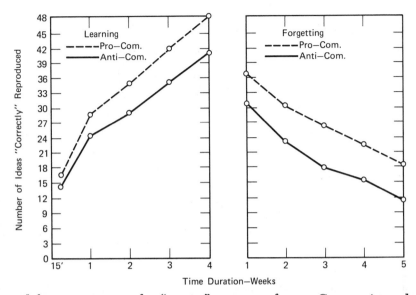

Learning and forgetting curves for "correct" responses for pro-Communist and anti-Communist groups on the pro-Soviet Union selection.

desirability of forcing persons to vote in presidential elections. They also indicated whose opinion they would respect most on each issue.

A month later, they were given the same questionnaire again, this time with a check mark next to each question indicating the opinion of their favorite authority. (A third of the pupils were told the authority was close to their own position, a third that he was somewhat distant, and another third that he was quite distant.)

Extreme sources caused greatest amount of change, although change as a percentage-of-change-sought fell.

Distance of Authority from Student Position

Short	Moderate	Marked
Mean difference, before-after on seven-point scale		
.88	1.25	1.75
Change obtained as percent of original distance between authority and pupil positions		
88%	62%	58%

Source. Carl I. Hovland and Henry A. Pritzker, "Extent of opinion change as a function of amount of change advocated," *Journal of Abnormal and Social Psychology*, 54:257–61.

Any position can be made to appear "moderate" by bracketing it between extremes. This device, here called *anchoring,* was used in the second study.

One group of subjects read an appeal by an anonymous source for a punitive policy toward delinquents. A second group read the same message preceded by two "anchor attitude statements" representing extremes of leniency and harshness. Both groups then checked scales to indicate their own attitudes and what they perceived as the attitudes of the source. "Anchors" caused the source to be perceived as less extreme or more trustworthy, and resulted in subjects with a higher punitive score even though this represented a smaller movement in proportion to movement advocated. (In this after-only study, both groups were assumed to have had the same views, before exposure to the message, as a control group which received no message.)

	Subject's Estimate of Source's Position	Average Change as Percentage of Change Sought
Subject's Mean Score		
Group given "anchors"		
6.2	10.7	15
No-anchors group		
5.2	13.3	21

Source. Walter Weiss, "The relationship between judgments of a communicator's position and extent of opinion change," *Journal of Abnormal and Social Psychology,* 56: 380–4.

On the other hand, "extreme" messages in other studies produced less effect than moderate ones.

After completing a nine-statement scale of attitudes toward alcohol, subjects listened to a 15-minute tape-recording. The 183 "drys" heard arguments against prohibition, either strong or moderate, and 25 convinced drinkers heard either "dry" or moderate "wet" arguments. A middle-ground set of 290 subjects heard dry, wet, or moderately wet versions. "Extreme" messages were seen as unfair and subjects were little influenced by them, compared with those who received "moderate" messages. Here are the net percentages of subjects moved by each message.

	Wet Message %	Dry Message %	Moderate (Wet) Message %
Drys	4.5	—	12.3
Moderates	28.3	13.8	—
Wets	—	4.0	—

Source. Carl I. Hovland, O. J. Harvey, and Muzafer Sherif, "Assimilation and contrast effects in reactions to communication and attitude change," *Journal of Abnormal and Social Psychology,* 55:244–52.

How can these differing results be reconciled? The person who receives such a message *can* change his opinion about the topic it treats, presumably toward that of the source, or he can keep his view of the topic unchanged and think less of the source of the message. If the communicator is credible, the first is likely; if he isn't, the second can be expected.

At the outset, 112 coeds ranked nine alliterative stanzas of poetry; then each read a two-page critique of the stanza she had ranked next to last. A third of the subjects were told this stanza was average; a third that it ranked third; and a third that it was the best of the lot. Half of each of these groups were told the critique's author was an expert, T. S. Eliot, the others that he was a student. In short, distance and credibility were both varied. Effects of the critique were measured by asking students to rerank the original passages, and to evaluate the critique itself on 14 seven-point scales.

Here are the results, in average attitude change toward the poetry and toward the source of the critique.

	Poetry Discrepancy Between Source and Subject Rankings		
Source	Small	Medium	Large
Expert	2.50	4.06	4.14
Fellow-student	1.19	2.56	1.41

	Derogation of source Discrepancy Between Source and Subject Rankings		
Source	Small	Medium	Large
Expert	31.8	29.3	32.4
Fellow-student	60.1	58.0	56.0

Source. Elliot Aronson, Judith A. Turner, and J. Merrill Carlsmith, "Communicator credibility and communication discrepancy as determinants of opinion change," *Journal of Abnormal and Social Psychology*, 67:31–6.

Expert Can Find Attributes that Determine Laymen's Choices

Consumers often resemble the visitor to the art gallery who "doesn't know anything about art, but I know what I like." They may be able to report that a product pleases or displeases them, without being able to say why. But with this much of a clue an expert can then track down the particular product features that have affected buyers' attitudes.

Interviewers asked housewives to let them examine two pairs of their children's boxer shorts—those they regarded as "best" and "worst." Using a check list of product attributes, interviewers found that 95% of the "best" shorts but only 61% of the "worst" were made of four pieces of cloth. Here are other attributes which seemed important, percentages representing difference between good and bad.

Good shorts more likely to have	(%)
Sanforized	50
Double-needle stitch	37
Close-weave fabric	32
Solid pattern	22

Bad shorts more likely to have	(%)
Raveled seams	73
Crotch bind	56
Fading	50
Small seat	36

With this information, a discriminant function was devised, importance of each feature being represented by weights outside the parentheses. [Inside the parentheses was entered a "1" (if good qualities absent) or a "0."] Here's the formula.

$$1.59 \text{ (close weave)} + .60 \text{ (solid color)}$$
$$+ 1.37 \text{ (absence of shrinkage)}$$
$$+ 1.01 \text{ (absence of fading)}$$
$$+ .97 \text{ (cut from 4 pieces)}.$$

Thus a "perfect" pair of shorts would have a score of 5.54, representing the sum of the weights. The predictive formula was then tested against a new set of shorts obtained from housewives; it identified 80% of the best and 65% of the worst shorts.

When scores on this formula were correlated with prices charged for the shorts, a coefficient of .88 was obtained, meaning that 77% (.88 × .88) of variations in price were explained by variations in quality—or vice versa. The author used this relationship, along with sales data, to construct charts predicting expected sales, sales, and gross profits at different price levels.

(Data reprinted from the *Journal of Marketing*, national quarterly publication of the American Marketing Association.)

Source. E. L. Quenon, "A method for pre-evaluating merchandise offerings," *Journal of Marketing*, 16:2:158–71.

Additional Research Readings

Diffusion. Alumni of 17 management training programs taught over four years in India were quickest to adopt financial budgeting (62%), slowest to adopt market analysis (32%). **Howard Baumgartel, "A survey approach to measuring the penetration of modern management practices in India," Public Opinion Quarterly, 34:458–9.** In Honduras, information and influence occurred simultaneously with 38% of those who accepted smallpox immunization; processes were separate for the 44% who took longer to decide. **Nan Lin, "Information flow, influence flow and the decision-making process," Journalism Quarterly, 48:33–40, 61.** Study of 148 farm wives' use of nylon, orlon, and dacron suggests mass media inform but don't influence, that commercial sources induce trial, and that trial results affect adoption. **George M. Beal and Everett M. Rogers, "Informational sources in the adoption of new fabrics," Journal of Home Economics, 49:47–52.** Touch-tone phone experience suggests ads should induce emotion as well as inform and depict innovation as socially acceptable. **Thomas S. Robertson, "Purchase sequence responses: Innovators vs. non-innovators," Journal of Advertising Research, 8:1:47–52.** Subjects who habitually use narrow categories were less likely to accept new product features such as radial-ply tires, shoe synthetics, and freeze-dried coffee. **Donald T. Popielarz, "An exploration of perceived risk and willingness to try new products," Journal of Marketing Research, 4:368–72.**

Again, examination of the decision-making process is interrupted for a longer look at alternative methods that buyers and sellers employ in the search for alternative products or markets, suppliers or buyers.

Chapter 9 concerns the *internal* search for alternatives. It discusses how, through learning, facts and preferences are put into the memory and how they are retrieved from it, when needed in decision making.

Chapter 10 concerns the *external* search, to which buyers and sellers turn when stored memories prove inadequate. Here we look at the way in which man's senses provide rewards and also cues as to product attributes that will be rewarding.

The seller who knows how the senses accept incoming cues, how such cues are interpreted, how they are stored, and how they are retrieved from storage, can devise effective messages for the buyer. Similar knowledge on the part of the buyer may protect him from being misled, whether by his own inadvertence or the seller's design.

Readers desiring a quick overview of the decision process itself may prefer to skip these chapters for the moment and proceed directly to Chapter 11.

Chapter 9 Synopsis

● The adman, as educator, may find that before buyers can use his clients' products they must learn perceptual-motor skills, perceptual discriminations, word associations, new attitudes. To make the purchase that precedes product use, they must learn to associate bodily sensations with the names of products and brands, must learn how to compare rival products and brands, and how to act upon the choices they make.

● As teacher, the adman must discover how the goals of learning vary not only with products but also with the learner himself; he must help them unlearn the inhibitions that prevent product purchase and use. Doing this may require changes in the marketing mix, as well as creation of relevant messages.

● Buyer responses may be based on habit, on internal search, or on external search; storage of experience through learning and retrieval through memory are essential to all three kinds of response.

● Input of sensations, which initiate learning, and their deposit in the brain have been studied by use of electrical currents, drugs, surgery, and experiments in which stimuli and responses are sharply restricted.

● Three seminal experiments are those of Pavlov, in which a dog's old response became associated to a new stimulus; of Thorndike, in which errors were eliminated in a series of trials by cats responding to an aversive stimulus; and of Skinner, in which pigeons developed new behaviors through a rewarded series of successive approximations to behaviors specified by the experimenter. Skinner's studies specify the optimal proportion of rewards for original learning and for persistent performance.

● Extent and speed of learning can be measured by the size of response, its accuracy, and its latency; by frequency of response, number of trials to a criterion, and persistence in the absence of reward. Degree of memory can be measured by recall, recognition, reconstruction, and relearning.

● Degree of learning can be influenced by varying tasks, rewards, and respondents. Manipulating rewards requires six dichotomous choices: immediate or delayed rewards, intrinsic or extrinsic, complete or partial, random or regular, positive or negative, and definition by source or by receiver. Punishment suppresses performance but leaves learning intact; denial of reward "extinguishes" learning.

● Aspects of tasks that affect speed of learning include length and spacing of rest periods, amount and kind of transfer possible from previous learning. Intelligence is the respondent attribute that most affects speed and degree of learning; it comes in various types which correlate to varying degrees with respondent age and sex.

● Although a respondent may be unable to retrieve an experience from memory, it has not vanished but been overlaid by more salient experiences. The adman or teacher can increase the salience of a memory either at the time of original learning or at the time of retrieval.

Research Articles

Habit. Brand preferences persist longer than repeat-purchase habit (Cunningham, Guest); repeated exposure to paired labels and value words affect attitudes without subject being aware (Staats, Rhine).

Reinforcement. Partial reinforcement makes habits persist (Rhine); punishment less effective than reward in teaching a habit or than its denial in eliminating a habit (Kelley, Ring); pupils feel rewarded by teacher's punishment (Hamblin); supplying of reward and motivation evokes latent learning which occurred in absence of motive, reward, and response (Blodgett).

Content. Affects speed, extent, and retention of learning (Hunter).

Chapter 9 Learning and Memory

Two years from the day you left college, degree in hand, you find yourself part of an educational system that operates coast to coast, 24 hours a day—the advertising business. You "teach" a more varied student body than ever showed up in a classroom— all ages, from 2 to over 100; illiterates and Ph.D.'s; ghetto residents and multimillionaires. You have less control over your "students" than the most permissive principal in the land; to drop out, all they need do is flick a TV switch. They never see you in person and you never see them; there's none of the face-to-face feedback that tells a teacher whether he's getting his message across. Your curriculum is as wide-ranging as life itself, for you sell everything from cribs to caskets. You accomplish all this in "class periods" which, on TV, may last all of 30 seconds. And if the students don't learn, *you* flunk—they don't.

The partner in your two-man ad agency handles client relations, leaving you with only two hats to wear: you are the agency's creative department and its research department. At the moment you have only four small local accounts: a flying school, a French restaurant, a political candidate, and a shop selling learn-a-foreign-language-in-the-privacy-of-your-own-home records.

Types of Learning

Shifting hats rapidly, you, as creative director, ask what lessons are to be taught your clients' customers: What must prospects learn if your clients are to prosper? How many different types of learning are involved? As researcher, you reply as follows.

Flight lessons. Student pilots must learn the "meaning" of a whole new set of cues: cloud movements, dials on an instrument panel, messages from a control tower. These cues must cause their fingers to move quickly and smoothly on the controls of the plane. (As in the training of a swimmer, skier, or tennis player, the sensations created by the first muscle movement must act as stimulus for the next muscle movement, which stimulates a third, and so on.) Pilots learn a *perceptual-motor skill*, through practice, with progress measured by an increase in speed and a decrease in errors. Feedback from an instructor helps eliminate errors; length of practice sessions and of rests between them is important. Since most pilots have previously learned to drive automobiles and will alternate between piloting plane and car, the question of *transfer* arises: how much do driving skills help and how much do they hinder piloting a plane?

Gourmet diners. To really enjoy champagne, caviar and soft music, diners must learn *perceptual discrimination*. Those who now think that champagne tastes sour and caviar salty must develop a finer set of categories, with new values and labels: "sour" must become "dry" and "salty" become "piquant." Customers must learn to distinguish one type of wine from another, and "good" years from "bad," just as stereo prospects must learn how to distinguish Mozart from Haydn and Scarlatti, and art lovers must learn to distinguish Monet from Manet, early Manet from late, a Manet copy from an original.

Record buyers. The tourist or businessman who buys a set of language records so he can speak French-like-a-native in 30 days must learn perceptual discrimination, must learn to hear the difference between the sounds he makes and those on the record. He must also learn to *associate words* in new ways: he may think *dog* but he must say *le chien*. As the skier learned to link muscle movements together, so the language learner links sounds: *Il n'y a pas de quoi* soon trips off his tongue in response to another's *merci*. Principles of learning like these are important to users of this product: the speed of verbal learning depends on how meaningful the words learned are or whether a student tries to learn a part in its entirety or bit by bit and how he divides his time between reading and reciting the words being learned. Your client needs to know whether future learning makes it harder to remember present learning (retroactive inhibition) or whether past learning gets in the way of present learning (proactive inhibition).

Voters. Since polls indicate that voters want lower taxes, more courteous cops, and fewer potholes in the streets, your agency's mayoralty candidate promises all these things. (His image—which is another way of saying voter *attitudes*—becomes the target of your advertising campaign.) You remind voters of the city's problems, try to get them to associate the present mayor with the problems and your man with their solutions, hoping they'll pull your candidate's lever on election day.

To *use* your four clients' products, your students must demonstrate the four major types of learning: perceptual-motor skills, perceptual discriminations, word associations, attitudes. But purchase must precede use and before purchase can occur, a lot of other things must be learned.

Diners must learn to appreciate new sensations of taste and to associate with them visual cues of product and brand. Five separate associations must be tied together in an instant: a feeling in the throat gets a label, *thirst; thirst* becomes associated with the name of a product, *champagne; champagne* is associated with a brand name, *Dom Perrier;* and brand name becomes associated with an anticipated sensation. With repetition, this chain may become so firmly fixed that *Dom Perrier* appears the moment thirst is experienced. (*Habit* takes over.)

In contrast, *voting* is a one-shot deal; a series of messages must build up a preference that will persist until election day. Voters must be taught the criteria for a good candidate and convinced that the agency's candidate meets them better than his competitors. External search is involved since awareness of a problem precedes messages.

A decision to learn French may follow the offer of a job overseas, or a wife's decision on a vacation abroad. Motivated to learn, the prospect's decision involves a comparison of *products:* records save the cost of time, travel, money, and possible ridicule involved in the alternative of enrolling in a class or hiring a tutor. Pilot training, on the other hand, may involve comparison of neither brand nor product but a choice between action and inaction: "To fly or not to fly?" The adman must convince prospects that little skill and no danger is involved in learning to fly.

This, then, is the agency's curriculum: you must get prospects to remember associations among bodily state, product, and brand; you must teach them how to compare competing products and brands; you must move them to make choices and act upon them. Having purchased, buyers then must engage in still other kinds of learning if they are to use (and enjoy) the things they buy.

Types of Learner

Different products, as we have seen, involve different kinds of learning—but learning also differs with the person learning. Before you as adman can prepare messages about restaurants, candidates, records, and flying schools, you need to look at the prospects you want to respond to such messages. They differ and your plans must adjust to those differences.

Student pilots. Most present students are in their late teens, you discover, self-confident and with a strong sense of adventure. Older men, with money to buy their own planes (and use them in business and in sports) hold back: flying appears too dangerous and too difficult. They need a new self-concept; if ads, salesmen, and a free flying lesson can once get these older men up in the air, the experience may change their attitudes toward flying (*It's easy*) and themselves (*I can do it*).

Diners. Champagne and caviar salesmen have taught prospects that appreciation of fine wines signifies sophistication, and that caviar signals affluence. But salesmen have done too good a job: prospects despair of being able to distinguish the subtle nuances of a vintage wine and avoid buying wine for fear that their ignorance would be revealed. You reassure them with labels that picture the foods that a wine may accompany. "Vintages-schmintages," say your ads; California's climate is so steady that one year's crop is identical to every other's. You teach prospects what attributes are important and what cues reveal a brand's "score" on those attributes.

French students. Research uncovers three problems: (1) the handful of buyers who complete the course find their accent can't be understood when they get overseas; (2) most buyers haven't the willpower to finish the course; and (3) few people see any reason why they should learn a second language in the first place. You sell the first group a tape recorder and a monthly checkup lesson with a live language tutor. You offer group lessons, social reinforcement to the weak-willed second group which acts as an interim reward. To the third group, you and a travel agent make a package offer: language lessons and a conducted tour led by a guide who refuses to speak English. In short, learning theory has led you to provide guidance and *feedback* from the teacher and *interim rewards.*

Voters. The candidate based his platform on what people told pollsters they prefer and a follow-up survey shows his image has moved from nowhere to favorable, but you realize that attitudes are not necessarily actions. *Apathy* will keep some voters at home, unless door-to-door and telephone "salesmen" see that they get to the polls, driving them there if necessary. Other voters will be immobilized by *cross-pressures;* they like your candidate, but he belongs to the wrong party, church, or ethnic group. Leaders of such groups must endorse him publicly, teaching voters new *group norms.*

You began by specifying, for each account, what kind of learning was required to serve your client, the seller's purpose. You next specified the buyer's goals, the motivation that would induce him to act as the seller wished. (You suggested product modifications that would better help him attain such goals: first-hand experience to reassure student pilots; a label to give confidence to novice connoisseurs; tie-in sales of tape, tutors, and tours to improve performance and strengthen motivation of the language learners; personal contact to convert favorable attitudes into action among the voters.) Only now are you ready to select the media and create the messages which, like the teacher's lectures, move buyers toward desired ends.

Such movements, we know, are of three kinds. The ad may trigger a *habit;* it may induce an internal search of *memory;* it may stimulate and guide *external search* of stores and the media. Learning, the process by which experience is stored in the brain, and memory, through which such experience is retrieved, are essential to all three kinds of response.

In internal search, memory supplies answers as well as questions. In external search, memory tells the prospect where to look for answers, in what stores, and what media; search itself will turn up answers and new questions.

Techniques of Research

Memory and habits are produced by learning. How is learning itself produced?

Learning begins when light and sound waves reach eye and ear, sending nerve impulses speeding to the brain, where they set off chemical changes, such as protein synthesis. We've traced this process in the following ways.

Mild electrical currents have enabled men to chart the brain, determining where each sense reports and which points send impulses to control muscles of arm, hand, foot, tongue.[1]

Drugs have been used to suppress activities of different parts of the brain; in lower animals, parts of the brain have been excised and changes in behavior observed.

Flatworms, having learned to respond to a stimulus, have then been ground up and fed to other flatworms; the untutored cannibals have thereupon performed the behaviors learned by the worms they have just eaten.[2]

Some of the most fundamental principles of learning can be observed at work throughout the animal kingdom, from paramecium to human. (It is not always necessary to study middle-aged housewives to discover facts about memory and the learning process of value to the seller.) Earthworms and cats show similar avoidance behavior after destruction of part of the brain, for example; reindeer, whales, and raccoons have been trained to perform in commercial displays. In experiments that reward only occasional responses, similar effects have been observed in mouse, horse, vulture, and guinea pig. However, dolphins have proved superior to monkeys in switching electrical currents on or off, and goldfish quicker to learn to avoid harmful stimuli than fighting fish. Different strains of mice and pigs, or the same strain bred by different suppliers, show different responses on some tasks. (On simple tasks, two species may respond differently. On complex tasks, efficiency in learning appears to rise as one ascends the scale of backboned creatures toward man.)

Relevance of the vast literature on learning derived from animal experiments has been challenged as "illusory" and "untenable." Lockard asserts that the only animals behaviorally relevant to man "are those related by common ancestry or . . . similar selection pressures: apes are relevant by relatedness, wolves for ecological reasons."[3] Problem-solving ability, he asserts, is a response to ecology. Birds like the crow, which occupy a broad ecological niche, are more intelligent than mammals like the mountain beaver. "Wasps are superior in delayed response problems to Norway rats," he argues, "and pocket gophers better than the horse at maze problems."

"Pick any animal species, study its behavior in its normal habitat through its life cycle," he argues, "and you will discover an intricate set of behaviors . . . (which match) demands of the environment like a lock and key."

He cites the relationship of 60 behaviors of the gull to its nesting on cliff ledges, including lack of ability to identify its own young—an ability possessed by ground-nesting gulls, whose young can stray.

The extent to which inferences about human behavior can be drawn from experiments with animals has been questioned. Certainly the three research methods employed with animals are not transferable to man. Man's brain cannot be operated on at will, either with drugs or a surgeon's knife, and currently cannibalism is frowned upon. Harmless electrical stimuli have been used on man, but only within limits.

Most of our knowledge of human learning comes from experiments in which the environment is so restricted, either physically or by verbal instructions, that a subject can perceive only a very few stimuli and make only a few responses. Such control of input and output permits the experimenter to infer that responses observed must have been produced by the stimuli manipulated, that a relation between message and act has been learned.

Such inferences may be wrong, since learning is necessary—but not sufficient— to performance. Lack of response may arise from lack of motive to respond, not failure to learn. A buyer may fail to respond as a seller wishes because other responses get in the way: the seller's boat has a fine brand image but the buyer needs a car; anxiety over a job or tonight's date hurts a student's score in a laboratory test or the classroom examination. When performance fails, this may be the result of inferior original learning (usually measured immediately), inferior retention of what was learned (measured at varying lengths of time), or both. Other experiments fail because subjects regard the goal set for them by the experimenter as trivial and substitute one of their own, without telling the scholar they have done so. More obliging subjects may guess what the experimenter wants and provide it, ignoring the gadgets he is flashing and buzzing for their benefit. Nevertheless, most of what we know about learning in man and other animals has been obtained in laboratory experiments in which input and output are sharply controlled. Three of the most important experiments, which set off thousands of subsequent studies, involved animals.

The first was by Ivan Pavlov, who became head of a Leningrad laboratory in 1890 and won the Nobel prize in physiology in 1904.[4] He strapped a dog into a harness, put food powder in its mouth, and measured the subsequent flow of saliva produced through built-in reflex action. Physiological research became transformed into psychology, however, when Pavlov then accompanied or preceded the food with a sound—bell, buzzer, metronome, or tuning fork. Now saliva began to flow when the dog heard the sound, whether or not food followed. The dog was said to have become *conditioned* to the sound.

Subsequent experiments with a great number of other stimuli, responses, and subjects, have agreed that a new stimulus can substitute for—but not replace—an old one; that learning proceeds most efficiently if the new (conditioned) stimulus precedes the old (unconditioned) stimulus by a half second and the two end at the same time; that backward conditioning, in which the old stimulus begins and ends *before* the new stimulus appears, seldom works.

The second experiment was by Edward Lee Thorndike, who, as a graduate student at Columbia University shortly before the turn of the century, put cats in a box from which they could escape by pulling the right string or pushing the right lever. He found the animals engaged in a wide variety of random activity until they stumbled on the answer. On successive trials, the cats engaged in less and less irrelevant behavior, committing fewer "errors." The first escape did not eliminate subsequent errors; one-trial learning did not occur. (In similar fashion, a housewife who enjoys the "escape" of a pleasant vacation may not know just which aspect caused the pleasant feeling: beautiful scenery, meeting interesting people, not having to wash dishes, or a chance to spend some time with her husband.)

The third experiment was by B. F. Skinner who, about 1930, began putting rats in boxes in which, by pressing a lever, they could obtain food as a reward. Later he expanded his horizons, and ours, by putting pigeons in his boxes and rewarding them for pecking at a spot on the wall or twirling around in circles. Whereas Thorndike's cats managed to escape an unpleasant situation by operating on their environment,

Skinner's rats and pigeons could be induced to perform almost any behavior that the experimenter wished to reward. (The parallel between pigeon and buyer, experimenter and seller should be obvious.)

Skinner didn't reward his pigeons for every peck; he also used schedules of *partial reinforcement*. Sometimes a reward came after a set number of responses, as a piece worker is rewarded in a factory or a salesman who works on commission. Sometimes the reward came after a given period of time, like a salesman's salary, without regard to what the pigeon had been doing in the interim. Sometimes he rewarded every 10th response or every fifth minute. Sometimes he kept the proportion of rewards constant but varied the timing—10% of responses chosen at random, being rewarded. And sometimes he changed the proportion of rewards itself, increasing or decreasing it in a series of trials. Partial rewards, Skinner discovered, lead to slower learning but better retention than a 100% schedule.

Through the method of *successive approximation*—rewarding an animal only if each step took it closer to the behavior the experimenter had planned for it—Skinner's livestock added new behaviors to their repertoire: pigeons whirled in circles and squirrels played ping pong. Unlike Pavlov's dog, who gave an old response to a new stimulus, Skinner's pigeon gave a new response to an old stimulus. The pigeon made its move; if the experimenter approved, he rewarded the pigeon with a bit of grain; the reward increased the probability that the pigeon would repeat its move.

When Skinner paid no attention to what the pigeon was doing, but instead rewarded it every five minutes, such *fixed interval reinforcement* caused the pigeon to repeat whatever it happened to be doing at the time of reward. Thus new behaviors were built up which the experimenter himself couldn't predict in advance. Skinner's approach has often been called *instrumental conditioning*, meaning that the behavior involved is a means to an end—the reward. Both Pavlov and Skinner, as well as Thorndike, also used unpleasant stimuli: dogs lifted their paws in reflex action to a shock; rats fled from one side of a cage to the other to obtain the rewards that go with escaping from the reality or the threat of electric shock. Learning responses to unpleasant or aversive stimuli differ from approach responses to pleasant stimuli in many ways; as one example, such responses persisted much longer in the absence of shock than did Pavlov's food-conditioned reflexes or Skinner's food-rewarded behavior in the absence of food. In psychological jargon, the new behaviors resisted *extinction* much longer.

Measuring Degree of Learning

Almost anything *can* be learned; nearly everything we do *has* been learned. (Even the wired-in reflexes, such as salivation, which men ordinarily are unaware of and have no control over, can be conditioned. A man's palms can be made to sweat, his eyes to blink, and his brain waves to alter by cues which, after appropriate conditioning experiences, can take the place of the bodily processes that ordinarily produce such responses.) Teacher and adman alike need to know *when* learning has been accomplished, *how rapidly* it has taken place, and to *what degree* their teaching goals have been attained.

There are six ways to measure learning, three of which can be used with a single subject.

Size. How *big* is the response? (How much saliva did Pavlov's dog produce?) This measure is used most often when teaching an old response to a new stimulus.

Accuracy. How far or how long a time is the subject off target?

Delay. The response occurs much more quickly after the cue is given; the *latency* or delay decreases.

The other three measures of habit strength require several trials, several subjects, or both.

Frequency. How many subjects give the desired response on a given trial, or how many times does a single subject give the response on a set of trials? The higher the frequency of response, or the fewer the errors, the greater the learning.

Practice to a criterion. How many minutes or how many trials does it take subjects to reach a standard, such as two successive repetitions of a list of words without error? This is useful for comparing different teaching methods or the learning abilities of different subjects.

Persistence without reinforcement. How long does a subject persist in behavior after withdrawal of the reinforcement that originally brought the behavior up to criterion?

This rise in the strength of a relationship between stimulus and response is what we mean by learning. Since the line between *learning* and *memory* is an arbitrary one, the following four measures of memory are also measures of habit strength.

Recall. Can the subject reproduce what he has learned—can he supply the name, recite the list? This method takes a good deal of time. Pure recall scores are often so low that comparisons between two advertisements are impossible. Various aids to recall can be provided. Instead of asking *What advertisements did you see in this magazine?* an interviewer may ask *What soap advertisements did you see?* Or he may name the product and a slogan and ask for the brand name.

Recognition. The subject is shown a list of words or a portfolio of advertisements and asked which he remembers having seen before. (Scoring must take account of chance success. To make sure that subjects could have seen the ad only in the magazine being studied, an unpublished ad is often included. Subjects who claim to have seen such an ad can be dropped from the study as unreliable.)

Reconstruction. Scrambled parts of an original message are given the subject who is asked to put them back in their original order. (Rarely used in advertising, this method works only when there is no natural or logical order that would be apparent even to someone who hadn't seen the message previously.)

Relearning. When a subject relearns something he has forgotten, the *savings score*—the reduction in time or trials required for the second learning—is sensitive enough to reveal traces of learning where other measures will not. (Conversely, the savings score is inferior to recall if we want to discover small amounts of *loss*.)

Looking for Causes

In an experiment, these 10 measures represent the results we are trying to produce. What variables do we manipulate to bring about these results? There are three.

Stimuli. The task itself, the stimuli and messages the experimenter uses, and the physical and social setting in which the experiment is staged. (These variables are discussed at length in chapters on perception, symbols, and messages.)

Respondent. The subject's physical and emotional state, his previous learning and current mood, his personality and motives, his ability to receive the stimuli and interpret them, his attitudes toward the task and the experimenter. These are controlled both by selection of subjects and by experimenter behaviors before the experiment and during it. Subjects may be chosen on the basis of age, sex, attitude, or personality. They may be deprived of food or companionship. They may be drugged, hypnotized, or given instructions (which may or may not mislead them as to the purpose of the study).

Rewards. Since rewards follow an act, rather than precede it, they would seem to represent consequences rather than the antecedent conditions that "cause" behavior. However, even when learning occurs on the first exposure to a stimulus there must be at least one additional trial to measure the learning that has occurred, and usually learning requires a long series of trials. Since the reward that follows one trial necessarily becomes an antecedent to subsequent trials, it does serve as their cause.

Manipulating Rewards

Rewards may be defined, and varied, in six ways.

Source or Receiver? A learner's (customer's) goals, not those of the teacher (advertiser), determine what is learned. A teacher may set understanding as the goal of learning, but pupils work for passing grades. An advertiser may talk about shoes, when he should be selling comfort; toys, when he should be selling parents' delight in happy children; or tires, when he should be talking about worry-free driving.

Food is rewarding to a rat that is hungry but not to one that has just eaten. A given score on a test will reward or punish a student depending on his expectations. These in turn are based on his previous scores and on the scores of other students he deems similar to himself. Failure on a task

will cause a subject to lower his *level of aspirations,* making a lesser achievement rewarding on the next trial and making success more likely. Success, on the other hand, may cause a student to raise his sights. A teacher can make a student succeed or fail by his selection of tasks, the way he matches task to student ability, by the feedback he provides—or by providing false information concerning performance by the student or his peers.

Many purchases provide multiple rewards by satisfying physical needs, winning friends' approval, or serving as a means to still other goals with their own rewards. A prospect may enjoy a message in its own right, because it helps him make a better buying decision or because it provides a topic for conversation with his friends.

Timing. Every individual has many goals, some of which may conflict with one another; offer him the one he's interested in at the moment of exposure. (If you make cake mix, this may mean broadcasting commercials at a time when individuals are likely to be hungry.) Immediate rewards are more effective than delayed ones. Thus, it is well to provide smaller rewards along the way—grades each term in college, not just a bachelor's degree at the end of four years, or trading stamps to paste in a book, not just a premium a housewife must wait a year to obtain.

Since rewards serve as feedback to a learner, telling him whether he's on the right track, the quicker they follow his response, the better. (In a typical study, students who had quizzes corrected before they left the room did better on a final exam than those who had to wait until the next class session.) Moreover, in learning as in accounting, future expectations must be discounted to obtain present values.

Intrinsic or Extrinsic? Children often learn things because of rewards that are extrinsic to (outside of) the learning itself. (A boy practices piano so that he can play softball or he does his homework for a dish of ice cream.) But extrinsic rewards have their disadvantages. (Let rain drown out the softball game or the store run out of ice cream, and the boy will stop playing the piano.) Once the task itself becomes rewarding—once rewards are intrinsic to the learning process—learning maintains itself.

Complete or Partial? Learning proceeds faster when every performance of the task being learned is followed by a reward, but also vanishes more quickly when rewards are cut off. The best strategy is to teach under a 100% schedule of reinforcement, and then shift to partial reinforcement provided at random intervals. Performance then will persist long after the rewards themselves cease, or when the frequency of reward is very low. (Skinner, for example, has taught pigeons to respond at the rate of 6000 pecks an hour for only 12 rewards —one for every 500 pecks.)[6]

Random or Regular? Reinforcement can be regular, with every *n*th trial being rewarded or with a reward being provided after every *n*th interval of time, or the rewards can be at irregular intervals, as indicated by a table of random numbers or the flip of a coin.

Positive or Negative? Escape from the threat of punishment acts as a positive reward, but actual punishment may interfere with learning. Although punishment indicates what should not be done, it does not suggest any alternative types of behavior. It does cause the subject to engage in more variable behavior, during which he may stumble upon the desired behavior, but even then it does not tell him which of several alternatives is preferred. Punishment tends to suppress performance but doesn't cause a response to be unlearned; once punishment ceases, performance may resume. Moreover, punishment may generalize, inhibiting more aspects of behavior than one intended, and inducing consider-

able emotional upset that blocks action and thought. A subject may try to avoid and escape punishment, not by giving up the habit punishment seeks to disrupt, but by changing his attitude toward the source of punishment (rejecting the teacher or the advertiser who alarms him with scary symptoms), or by fleeing from the situation in which punishment occurs (giving up school rather than spitballs, turning off television rather than buying the sponsor's headache remedy.)

Breaking Up Old Habits

By offering bigger rewards faster and more frequently, teachers and advertisers can speed up learning and teach new habits. But an advertiser also wants to break up old habits—to stop purchase of competitors' brands as well as to induce purchases of his own. Punishment won't do this, even if a seller could punish a prospect. Forgetting can be induced by removing rewards previously associated with the habit.

When a bell or a buzzer continued to sound, but Pavlov failed to follow sound with food, his dog's saliva eventually ceased to flow; in technical terms, the conditioned response *extinguished*. Similarly, when Skinner stopped rewarding his pigeon with grain, pecking or twirling extinguished; this occurs rather quickly if the habit has been established under a 100% reinforcement schedule of reward on each trial, and more slowly otherwise.

Effects of Varying Responses

The task that an experimenter sets for his subjects and the responses he permits them to make influence speed and degree of learning.

Long tasks may be divided into smaller parts for easier learning, but the time spent in learning to link the parts to one another must be added to the total. (From 30 to 80% of learning errors occur at this stage.)[7] In lengthy tasks, whether they involve a rat running a maze or a child learning a poem, the beginning and end are learned first and remembered longest. This may be one reason why a salesman does well to concentrate on the opening and close of his pitch!

Once a task has been broken up into meaningful units, it helps to alternate rests and practice sessions: six 10-minute sessions are often more efficient than a single 60-minute period, whether one is learning a poem or practicing a perceptual-motor skill such as typing. (Bumstead memorized nine 50-line excerpts from *Paradise Lost*, looking at the text when his memory failed, and continuing until he could recite it without error or prompting.[8] If he allowed only an hour between learning sessions, it took him 43 readings and a total of 140 minutes. If he let a day pass, it took him 19 sessions totaling 60 minutes. If he let 8 days intervene, he needed only 13 sessions and 46 minutes.) Rests allow a subject to forget *wrong* stimulus-response relations faster than he forgets *correct* ones, and they may also allow physical fatigue and boredom to dissipate. Several studies find that the brain requires 3 to 18 seconds to move a memory from temporary to permanent storage; rests allow time for this shift to occur.[9]

(Electrical disturbance of the brain waves during this interval can erase memory, but similar disturbance later will not. Injection of a stimulant during this period enhances memory, but injection of an antibiotic prevents it, apparently by inhibiting the formation of new protein, believed to be the key to long-term memory.) A test following a rest period or sleep tends to get a higher score than one immediately following a learning trial. This phenomenon—called *reminiscence*—suggests that errors and fatigue that reduced test performance have dissipated in the interim. (Reminiscence is often observed with young subjects and meaningful material. Meaningful material is easier to learn and remember than nonsense. As material becomes more meaningful, rests tend to be less helpful.)

Proper length and spacing of practice and rest periods varies with subjects and task. (Subjects who can learn 50 words of prose in 2.25 minutes, take four times as long to learn twice as many words.[10] Subjects asked to add and subtract series of three, four, five, and six digits have found that the time required for learning rises as the cube of the number of operations to be performed.)[11] Rests as short as one minute between trials have been found helpful; periods of 20 minutes, 12 hours, and 24 hours have been found better than either shorter or longer periods.

To make sure that subjects are not continuing to practice mentally while supposedly resting, they may be given an alternative activity during rest periods. This, however, may give them an advantage, by maintaining a learning set, or a disadvantage, by conflicting with their principal task. Other solutions are: compare the group at rest with a control group that continues active practice or use animals, presumably incapable of mental practice. Learning of motor skills, where mental exercise during rest should be of little help, provides a baseline for verbal learning in this respect.

Graphs that plot learning as an increase in proficiency or a decrease in errors show that progress is rapid at first, then slows down. Sometimes the graphs show *plateaus* in which little improvement is made; the spurt that ends these plateaus may represent a renewal of motivation, or a shift in learning strategy (as when an individual who has been translating a language word by word begins to grasp the meaning of entire phrases.)

The more variable an individual's behavior, the more likely he is to stumble upon a solution. Being exposed to many different stimuli helps; so does rapid abandonment of inadequate responses. Since search must not stop, high motivation helps unless it leads to anxious persistence in inadequate responses. If previous habits hinder problem solving by persisting in inappropriate responses, anything that can temporarily suspend the former habit (such as sleep or another activity) will help. Habits help learning when problems can be solved by combining parts of old responses in new ways. Experience in making new combinations itself can lead to a problem-solving habit called "learning to learn."

In addition to letting rests interrupt learning periods, it's also well to let a student test himself periodically. Such tests provide interim rewards, help eliminate errors and identify difficult parts that need attention, and give subjects training in the final exam that will measure their success. It's been suggested that 80% of time spent in learning should be devoted to such recitation.

Transfer of Learning

So far we have talked as if we were working with entirely new stimuli and responses. Adult learning is more likely to involve substituting a new stimulus or a new response in the old stimulus-response relationship. Does this old relationship make it easier or harder to learn the new one? In psychological terms, is *transfer positive* or *negative?*

Negative transfer arises if one is trying to associate an old stimulus with a new response and positive transfer occurs if the response is old but the stimulus is new.

Trouble arises if a new response is opposed or antagonistic to the old one. (Rats have learned to turn right when a light is on and left when it is off, in an average of 286 trials.[12] When the signals are switched, it takes them an average of 603 trials to unlearn the old S-R relationship and substitute the new one. Similar difficulty occurred in military airplanes where switches for communication and ordnance were located left-and-right for the pilot and right-and-left for the co-pilot; whenever the two men changed seats, trouble developed!) If changes in S-R relations occur frequently enough, however, something new happens: we get nonspecific, positive transfer. Learning a specific action, such as stepping on the clutch, may cause one to tromp down meaninglessly in a car with an automatic transmission. Learning how to attack a new problem or discovering a principle or rule that can be applied to a series of similar situations may speed up learning tremendously. (In the short run of a single learning period, we call such transfer *warming up* or *persistence of set.* In the long run, we refer to it as "learning to learn.") Moreover, a rule or principle is briefer than the variety of experiences it covers and, therefore, more easily remembered.

Transfer is important for three reasons. One is that the same task is never performed twice under identical circumstances; the conditions under which a task is learned and those under which it is used will always differ. Another reason is that almost all adult learning involves transfer since it requires taking parts of old habits and putting them together in new combinations. The third reason is that the phenomenon referred to as forgetting, or memory loss, is itself an example of negative transfer. (Mere passage of time does not produce forgetting. Ancient events long below the level of awareness can be brought to the surface of articulate speech again by hypnosis or electric stimulation of the brain. When subjects are put to sleep immediately after a learning trial, memory losses are less than when activity follows trial, particularly if such activity resembles the task being learned.)

Effects of Variations in the Learner

The decisions that a teacher or an adman make about rewards and their task-related predictions about speed of learning must take account of differences in the individuals doing the learning. For example, learning "wholes" rather than "parts" becomes more advisable as the intelligence of the learner increases, just as it does when the intrinsic meaningfulness of the material to be learned rises.

Advertisers often use the simplest language possible, tailoring it to the prospect with the poorest verbal facility. However, such a message may offend or amuse educated persons; to reach them, the advertiser may transmit more complex messages through more selective media, such as the *New Yorker* or *Harper's*.

It's obvious that a prospect's intelligence will affect his ability to receive and respond to messages. What is less obvious is that there seem to be many different kinds of intelligence, many ways of measuring them —and bitter arguments about both.

The number of separate abilities a researcher finds depends on the research methods he employs and on the use he hopes to make of his results. (The question is which scholarly uses best resemble the problems of a particular seller or market segment.)

Some scholars find two kinds of intelligence, based on their *origins:* one that is inherited, which appears to increase until the age of 15, and another arising from environment, which appears to increase until the age of 30. (One expert, summarizing many studies, suggests that 75% of the variations in school children's intelligence test scores is explained by heredity, 21% by environment, and 4% by "accidental factors.")[13] Some scholars find a general factor, which affects all learning tasks, accompanied by varying numbers of special abilities which are related to specific tasks. Both laymen and experts distinguish between physical abilities and mental abilities. Tests divide mental abilities on the basis of the symbols manipulated—words and numbers; both verbal and mathematical abilities themselves have been further subdivided.

Thirty years ago, for example, factor analysis of results from 60 tests suggested the existence of a speed-of-perception factor plus six others related to learning.[14] Four of these six showed high correlation with *general intelligence*—word comprehension, word fluency, reasoning, and ability to handle numbers. Two showed low correlation with the general factor or one another: memory and spatial perception.

A more recent theorist has proposed a three-dimensional matrix with 120 cells ($5 \times 4 \times 6$), each cell presumably calling for a separate kind of mental ability.[15] His dimensions are as follows.

Operation performed. Cognition, memory, divergent and convergent production, evaluation.

Content. Figural, symbolic, semantic, behavioral.

Results. Units, classes, relations, systems, transformations and implications.

(Not all of the combinations called for in this matrix have been discovered and measured and, of course, many of those that have been measured show high correlation with others, suggesting that the distinction between them may not be truly necessary or meaningful.)

Tests can be multiplied to proliferate distinctions; their scores, in turn, can be correlated and factor analyzed to simplify the picture. In his search for simplicity, the psychological theorist tends to emphasize the latter. The buyer and seller may be more interested in looking at the full range to find the results best suited to the decisions they have to make and the variables they can manipulate.

To be useful in selling, intelligence test scores need to be related to the demographic variables used to describe markets and audiences. Men, for example, show superiority in areas where society says they should be superior—mathematical reasoning, mechanical aptitude, and relations of objects in space. Women appear to excell in size of vocabulary, fluency, and memory. Thus, there's a question as to whether these differences are biological in any sense or the result of society's sex-linked reward system. Cross-sectional studies show that mental ability grows rapidly until adolescence, more slowly in the twenties, declines gently thereafter only to drop sharply at 65. The decline is fastest on tests that depend on speed, slowest on those that measure judgment and verbal skills or are affected by experience. Longitudinal tests, in which the same individual is scored at successive points in time, show a rise in intelligence continuing into the fifties for those at the high end of the scale. (Few at the low end have been studied in this fashion.)

Retention and Retrieval

Labels like *memory* and *learning* may seduce us into thinking that the two are separate processes. They are not. Unusual stimuli aid attention, learning, and recall. Rests aid all three. Repetition aids all three. It is best to think of responses to stimuli as involving a three-stage, continuous process: (1) a message is repeated until it reaches the threshold of attention and is perceived, (2) passes from short-term perceptual memory into long-term memory, (3) is called up from memory into awareness and expressed in verbal or motor behavior. Once in memory, do changes occur in information that is stored?

The brain continues active even when new input is minimal. Electrodes attached to the scalp reveal that even in sleep or under an anesthetic, the brain remains active—10 alpha waves per second passing along the neural circuits. (Although such waves were long thought immune to conscious control, electronic gadgets that supply visible feed-back have in the last few years enabled individuals to control even these waves.)[16] Rapid eye movement during sleep reveals that people average four to five 20-minute dreams a night, a fifth of sleep being spent in dreaming, although few dreams are recalled on waking.[17] (These dreams are made up of bits of remembered experiences, often combined in new ways.)

Despite such evidence of activity, we have no studies yet which show systematic and predictable changes occurring in stored information.

We do know that memories which appear to be lost can be recovered. But why are some memories more easily retrieved than others? Why are some habits easier to reinstate than others? Answers to these questions would be of great importance to the seller.

Once an experience passes from temporary to permanent storage, it is apparently never forgotten, even though it may not be easily retrieved. (The fact that one can relearn a forgotten task in less time than original learning required is evidence that *something* must have been retained. Under hypnosis, subjects can report past events as if they were reexperiencing them. Relaxed on a therapist's couch, rewarded by a listening ear, patients can recall long-forgotten events. Even an interviewer can get viewers to recall TV programs they've watched by first getting them to recall more important events of the previous day, such as the time they went to work or came home.)

A person fails to retrieve a stored experience not because it has been "lost" but because it has been overlaid by more salient —not necessarily more recent—associations, or because an old stimulus-response association has been overlaid with an antagonistic habit of avoiding the stimulus or refusing to respond to it. (Support for this theory has been found through use of a drug that blocks strong habits and so allows weaker habits to emerge—strength being measured in terms of task difficulty, number of learning trials, or recency of learning.[18] In one instance, rats had learned to avoid a light, then had this response extinguished. The drug removed the extinction, restoring the habit of avoidance—and making it hard to teach the rats a new response of approaching the light despite a sugar-water reward.)

Salience—the likelihood that a given association will be retrieved from memory —is affected by many things. An unusual experience, particularly one related to an individual's attitudes toward himself (his *self-concept*) is likely to be salient. An association linked to a great many other associations which can serve as a cue to call it up is salient. A task which has been *overlearned*—repeated over and over again well past the point of perfect performance —is salient. (This explains why perceptual-motor skills like swimming and bicycling can be picked up again quickly after years of disuse. Since they took a long time to acquire and got a good deal of use, they were overlearned. Another reason is that new words flood in upon us every day to compete with those already in storage, but we learn new motor skills only at infrequent intervals.)

The seller has two opportunities to increase salience of memories that serve his goals: at the time of original learning and at the time of recall. Anything such as recitation or rests which aids learning thereby improves recall. Periodic reminders, a kind of relearning trial, extend the length of memory. (The number of such reminders and the lapse of time between them is of major concern to a media buyer. In one study, only 14% of housewives remembered an ad with a single exposure, but 63% remembered the same ad, when it had been mailed to them weekly for 13 weeks.[19] None of these women remembered these ads 9 months later, as compared with 48% of housewives to whom they were mailed 9 times but a month rather than a week apart. This is not surprising, since the delay between exposure and test was six months for the first group, one month for the second.)

Of course, the activities that occur between learning trials or between the last trial and a test of learning affect speed of learning and extent of memory. In general, the more similar intervening tasks are to the task being learned, the more likely interference becomes. In one study, university students learned lists of adjectives, engaged in another task, and then were tested.[20] Six different kinds of activities were allowed to intervene, with the following results.

Intervening Task	Percent of Original Adjectives Recalled
Adjectives synonymous with first list	12%
Adjectives opposite in meaning to first list	18
Adjectives unrelated to originals	22
Nonsense syllables	26
Three-digit numbers	37
Reading (not memorizing) jokes	45

Thought, Talk, and Action

1. Think of a product whose use involves all four types of learning listed in this chapter: motor skills, perceptual discrimination, word associations, and new attitudes. Then for each pair of these types (there are six pairs in all) think of a product whose use would require the two skills.

2. Suggest three sales or advertising campaigns in which the prospect would successively play the role of Pavlov's dog, Thorndike's cat, and Skinner's pigeon.
3. As sales manager, show how you would make each of the six dichotomous choices concerning rewards so as to maximize learning by the salesmen in your charge.

Notes

Chapter 9

1. W. Penfield and T. Rasmussen, The cerebral cortex of man (New York: Macmillan, 1950).
2. References to these and subsequent studies concerning animals are cited in J. M. Warren, "The comparative psychology of learning," in Annual Review of Psychology, vol. 16 (Palo Alto, Calif.: Annual Reviews, 1965).
3. Robert B. Lockard, "Reflections on the fall of comparative psychology: Is there a message for us all?" American Psychologist, 27:168–79.
4. Most students will find as much detail as they need of Pavlov, Thorndike, and Skinner's work in an introductory psychology textbook. The more ambitious may seek out I. P. Pavlov, Conditioned reflexes (London: Oxford University Press, 1927); E. L. Thorndike "Animal intelligence," Psychological Monographs, vol. 1, No. 8, 1898, and B. F. Skinner, The behavior of organisms (New York: Appleton-Century-Crofts, 1938).
5. S. S. Stevens, editor, Handbook of experimental psychology (New York: John Wiley & Sons, 1951).
6. Ernest R. Hilgard, Theories of learning, 2nd ed. (New York: Appleton-Century-Crofts, 1956), p. 92.
7. John A. McGeoch and Arthur L. Irion, The psychology of human learning, 2nd ed. (New York: Longmans, Green and Co., 1958), p. 504.
8. Ian M. L. Hunter, Memory (Baltimore, Md.: Penguin Books Ltd., 1964), pp. 133–4.
9. David Krech et al., Elements of psychology (New York: Alfred A. Knopf, 1969), pp. 472–4.
10. Same reference as No. 7, p. 489.
11. Reference No. 7, p. 494.
12. Reference No. 7, p. 323.
13. Bernard Berelson and Gary A. Steiner, Human behavior (New York: Harcourt, Brace & World, 1964), p. 217. Original source: Frank K. Shuttleworth, "The nature versus nurture problem: II," Journal of Educational Psychology, 26: 655–81.
14. Ibid., p. 212. Original source: L. L. Thurstone and T. G. Thurstone, Factorial studies of intelligence (Chicago: University of Chicago Press, 1941).

15. Edwin A. Fleishman and C. J. Bartlett, "Human abilities" in Annual Review of Psychology, vol. 20 (Palo Alto, Calif.: Annual Reviews, 1969), p. 350. Original source: J. P. Guilford, The nature of human intelligence (New York: McGraw-Hill Book Co., 1967).
16. Reference No. 13, p. 177.
17. Reference No. 13, p. 175.
18. J. A. Deutsch, "The physiological basis of memory," in Annual Review of Psychology, vol. 20 (Palo Alto, Calif.: Annual Reviews, 1969), p. 92.
19. H. A. Zielske, "The remembering and forgetting of advertising," Journal of Marketing, 23:3:239–43.
20. Reference No. 8, p. 260. Original study by J. A. McGeoch and W. T. McDonald.

Habit: Repeat Purchases of the Same Brand

Perhaps none of the "relatively permanent changes in behavior resulting from experience" which occur in a buyer is more important to sellers than his habit of repeated purchase of a given brand.

A buyer is said to be "loyal" to the brand that he purchases most frequently, or purchases most consistently, or says he prefers. There are several difficulties with the label brand loyalty, however.

First, the word loyalty suggests the behavior is a good thing. (It may be, for the dominant brand in a market; it may not be for other sellers or for the buyer himself.)

Second, it does not distinguish between an attitude—brand preference—and an action—repeated purchase of the same brand.

Third, it attributes an additional cause for repeat-purchase behavior which may not be correct. If a buyer carefully compares brands, chooses, uses, and is satisfied by one of them, and checks alternatives from time to time but sticks to his preferred brand, he would appear to be "loyal" in all the connotations of the term.

On the other hand, if he sticks to a brand merely because it's stocked by his favorite store, his loyalty is to the retailer not the brand. Or a buyer may be "loyal" because he sees all brands as being so similar that there would be no point in even trying another, or because any slight gain in switching would be offset by costs of search and comparison. Sometimes brand loyalty is contractual, the buyer being bound by a lease, a subscription, or a membership in a "club" of some kind. If a sale causes a buyer to switch brands temporarily, his basic "loyalty" hasn't changed; one has merely discovered its limits.

The significance of repeat purchases depends on the opportunities to switch brands which, in turn, depend on how frequently a buyer purchases a product and how many brands are available. Study of buyers switching to and away from his brand will tell a seller to which market segments he appeals. By comparing his brand's attributes with those of these two classes of competitors, and attributes of his message and media with theirs, a seller can revise his marketing strategy.

If a seller finds prospects who prefer his brand but never buy it, perhaps his advertising is creating brand preferences but his distribution is poor or his price too high. If his steadiest users show very little preference for his brand, the seller may be benefiting from good distribution, but is likely to be highly vulnerable to a competitor's attack. Such comparisons help a seller decide whether his product or his advertising needs refashioning; drowning the distinction between attitude and action by labeling both "brand loyalty" would prevent this.

Only 66 families qualified as "loyal" across all seven products. Loyalty to store was higher: the 10% most-loyal families made more than 90% of their purchases in a single store; the least loyal 10% made a third of their purchases in a single store. Loyalty to store was highly correlated with brand loyalty for coffee and peas.

Correlation Between Repeat Purchase of Single Brands of Two Products

Second brand	First Brand						
	Soap	Cleanser	Coffee	Peas	Margarine	Juice	Headache Tablets
Cleanser	.30						
Coffee	.23	.17					
Peas	.02	.12	.07				
Margarine	.14	.13	.12	.27			
Juice	−.06	.02	.06	.22	.19		
Headache tablets	—	.10	.09	.13	.08	.02	
Retail outlet	.20	−.05	.43	.42	.30	.39	.05

Some people are "loyal" purchasers of one kind of product, others of another; few tend to be across-the-board repeat purchasers.

A *Chicago Tribune* panel of 402 families kept purchase diaries which permitted "loyalty" to be measured over a three-year period. Minimum purchase levels were set for each product. (Minima were needed to avoid inflating loyalty estimates, since the person who purchased the product only once during the three years would be given a meaningless "100% loyal" rating; such a low rate of purchase would not interest a seller.) Nearly all of the families achieved the minimum for soap, but only about half the families for headache tablets and frozen orange juice.

Source. Ross M. Cunningham, "Brand loyalty: what, where, how much," *Harvard Business Review,* 34:1:116–28.

If purchase behavior shows little loyalty over so short a period as three years, what might one expect of brand attitudes over a period of 12 years? Beliefs and values may be more consistent than behavior, perhaps because behavior has more causes.

A list of 5 brands for each of 15 products was given pupils in grades 3 through 12 in a public school near Washington, D.C. in 1940–1941; 813 pupils picked their favorites. Twelve years later, responses from 20% of the original groups were obtained to a mail

Product	Minimum Purchase	Number of Families Qualifying
Toilet soap	18 cakes	390
Scouring cleanser	15 cans	319
Regular coffee	20 pounds	359
Canned peas	13 cans	325
Margarine	10 pounds	290
Frozen orange juice	10 cans	211
Headache tablets	4 purchases	208

questionnaire which again asked their brand preferences.

Although on a chance basis only about 3% agreement was expected between the two ratings, average for the 15 products was 32%, the range being from 23% for cereal to 38% for razors. Preferences in 1953 showed 63% agreement with actual brand use in 1953; preferences in 1940–1941 agreed only 28% with actual use in 1953.

Source. Lester Guest, "Brand loyalty—twelve years later," *Journal of Applied Psychology*, 39:405–8.

How Do Values Become Attached to the Labels We Use?

Before a new product is marketed, it must be named. The name must be chosen carefully, for labels express values even as they point to an object. The process by which values become attached to labels has been duplicated in the laboratory, without subjects being aware of what was happening.

Two groups of a dozen students each were given a two-part learning task: to learn the names of six nationalities which they saw flashed on a screen, and to memorize words which they heard the experimenter speak. In one group, a visual *Swedish* was always paired with spoken words like *bitter* and *ugly,* whereas the visual *Dutch* was paired with words like *gift* and *happy.* (In the other group, to allow for any preexisting attitude toward the nationalities, the pairings were reversed: negative words paired with Dutch, positive words with Swedish.) After 18 such trials, students were given a list of six nationalities and asked which names they'd seen; on a 7-point, pleasant-unpleasant scale they indicated how they felt about the nationality.

	Mean Rating for:	
	Dutch	Swedish
Group I: Swedish paired with negative words	2.67	3.42
Group II: Swedish paired with positive words	2.67	1.83

The experiment then was repeated with the names of people: *Bill* and *Tom.* These were the results.

	Tom	Bill
Group I: Bill paired with negative words	2.71	4.12
Group II: Bill paired with positive words	3.42	1.79

None of the subjects indicated they were aware of the nature of the pairings; 17 who "saw through" the study were dropped from the analysis.

Source. Arthur W. Staats and Carolyn K. Staats, "Attitudes established by classical conditioning," *Journal of Abnormal and Social Psychology,* 57:37–40.

Unfamiliar, even nonexistent categories can be given favorable and unfavorable evaluative meanings—without subjects being aware of what is happening.

Students were shown a list of 50 personality traits and asked to guess, after each trait, whether it applied to a little-known tribe. After each guess they were told whether anthropologists and missionaries familiar with the tribe agreed.

In actuality, the list consisted of equal numbers of desirable traits (*active, gifted*) and undesirable (*boastful, lazy*), presented in random order. On the first 50 trials only *undesirable* traits were confirmed. Next, 25 traits were presented, without comment by the experimenter. Finally, a series of 54 randomly ordered traits were presented; this time the experimenter confirmed the *desirable* traits.

Five trials were enough to fix the response: undesirable traits were attributed to the tribe for an average of 44.6 trials in the first series and on 24 of 25 test trials. The association was quickly reversed on the third set of trials: an average of 49.6 trials by 54 students giving favorable judgments.

These were the results when the experimenter confirmed every undesirable trait in the first series and every desirable one in the third series— but he didn't always follow this 100% schedule of reinforcement.

Four groups of students got confirmation for from 50 to 92% of the traits in both "unfavorable" and "favorable" trials. Those getting only partial confirmation were slower to attach unfavorable traits in the first trial, but more likely to persist in giving such traits on the third trial, despite the experimenter's change of direction.

A recent study suggests that the superiority of *partial* reinforcement may depend on the learner seeing his success as a result of chance. Subjects guessed the identity of a hidden card, with the outcome assumed to depend on luck, and they pulled a string to raise a platform with a ball balanced on it, with the outcome assumed to depend on skill. When they perceived skill to be involved, the habit resisted extinction better under 100% than under 50% reinforcement.

Source. Julian B. Rotter, "External control and internal control," *Psychology Today*, June 1971.

How Do Reward and Punishment Affect Learning?

Reward encourages an individual to repeat the behavior for which he has been rewarded. Punishment has more complicated effects. It may encourage

Proportion of Traits Confirmed	Mean Number of "Correct Responses" Under Various Levels of Reinforcement		
	92%	80%	50%
50 training trials (Negative confirmed)	36.6	29.2	25.5
25 test trials (No confirmation)	20.2	17.2	13.5
54 habit-change trials (Positive confirmed)	39.8	41.2	44.5

Source. Ramon J. Rhine and Betsy A. Silun, "Acquisition and change of a concept attitude as a function of consistency of reinforcement," *Journal of Experimental Psychology*, 55:524–9.

The ability of *partial reinforcement* (in which rewards do *not* follow every trial) to fix habits firmly has been used to explain why gamblers find it so hard to shake the habit. Its effects on habits of brand preference and repeat purchase have still to be explored.

an individual to conceal his acts from the punisher, if he can. It may discourage him from acting at all, if that is possible. Even if it halts an action that is not desired, punishment may not motivate the subject to seek out what acts are desired and rewardable, and gives him little guidance in such search.

Given pairs of statements, one reflecting depression and the other anxiety, students were asked to indicate which statement indicated greater psychological illness. They could check each choice with a psychologist, if they wished, by leaving a light lit; a subject who didn't want his choice known could turn the light off.

Half of the subjects, assigned to a "trusting trainer," were rewarded every time they were right, whether they let the tell-tale light burn or not. If their choice was wrong, and they let the light burn, they were punished with an electric shock. However, if they were wrong and turned the light off, supposedly hiding their choice from the trainer, only a fifth of their wrong choices were punished. The rest of the subjects were assigned a "suspicious trainer." He punished every wrong choice, hidden or not. He rewarded all correct choices, if the light was left burning, but only a fifth of right choices if the subject tried to conceal them by turning off the light.

Suspicion was more effective, both in getting subjects to show their choices and to adopt the "right answers" as specified in the trainer's reward-and-punishment scale. The trusting trainer, it appears, rewards for and thereby builds up a habit of concealment which prevents the subject from learning by experience.

In the second study, a "rewarding" trainer praised correct choices and passed off wrong choices in friendly fashion, while the "punishing" trainer gave a noncommittal nod for correct choices, but was harshly critical of errors. This time punishment got the results that trust had in the earlier study. Subjects' hesitation to reveal their choices prevented them from learning the "correct" answers. The authors suggest that the best teaching strategy is to punish attempts to conceal choice, provide mild punishment to let the subject know when he's made wrong choices (but revealed them), and reward all choices which are both revealed and correct. (When punished the subject fails to discover the right answers and, indeed, doesn't much care what they

are or feel any urge to accept them.) They suggest that punishment is least effective when the task being learned produces many errors at the outset for then the teacher is most likely to adopt a punishing mode and it is then that punishment is likely to be most detrimental.

Sources

H. H. Kelley and K. Ring, "Some effects of 'suspicious' versus 'trusting' training schedules," *Journal of Abnormal and Social Psychology,* 63:294–301.

Kenneth Ring and Harold H. Kelley, "A comparison of augmentation and reduction as modes of influence," *Journal of Abnormal and Social Psychology,* 66:95–102.

It's Not Always Easy to Distinguish Penalty and Reward

Advertisers and teachers are sometimes surprised to discover that what they thought was rewarding to prospects and pupils doesn't work, or works in reverse. The opposite also occurs: sometimes actions that are intended to penalize act like rewards.

Punishment may suppress behavior, destroy rapport between a pupil and the punisher, or lead to ingenious attempts to escape from situation, punishment, or punisher. Sometimes the victim actually seems to enjoy what was intended to dismay him.

An experienced teacher tried everything she could think of with five highly aggressive 4 year olds: strict discipline, wise counsel, clever arbitration, sweet peacemaking. By the end of eight days a "normal" 15 sequences of aggression per day had escalated to 150. The boys seemed to enjoy the battle, for they always won. No matter what the teacher did—scold, hit back, get angry, cajole—*they* were in charge.

Period:	1	2	3	4	5	6	
		Reward Cooperation				Reward Cooperation,	
	Normal Teaching	Ignore Aggression	Penalize Aggression	Ignore Aggression	"Normal" Teaching	Ignore Aggression	Control
Cooperative acts	56	115	115	140	90	181	60
Aggressive acts	150	60	110	16	120	7	15
Percent of time pupils pay attention to teacher	8%	—	—	75%	23%	93%	—

But then, psychologists watching through a one-way window began coaching the teacher via wireless. They told her to turn her back on an aggressor and ignore him, but to reward any cooperative child with plastic discs which could be exchanged for a movie, Playdoh, etc. Then the rules changed and she began imposing plastic-disc fines for aggressive acts. After this came a period in which, once more, she ignored aggression. Then "normal teaching," without any use of discs, was followed. Finally the ignore-aggression but reward-cooperation-with-discs routine was restored. Like puppets on a string the boys responded to each change.

Note that even when cooperation was rewarded, penalizing rather than ignoring aggressive behavior tended to increase it. (Top of page.)

Sellers are less likely to encounter an aggressively hostile audience than they are to face an apathetic, immovable one. The same St. Louis classrooms that saw taming of the aggressor also witnessed arousal of the apathetic, and by the same reward—plastic discs simulating coins.

About half of the 22 3-to-5 year olds in preschool sat like vegetables, refusing to talk. (Most youngsters, whether from the ghetto or the upper middle class, talk about 40% of the time in such circumstances. These children spoke only about 8% of the time, and then only a word or two at a time.)

Then plastic discs were offered for talking. (With four of them, a child could sit on the floor to watch a movie; for eight, he could sit on a chair; for 12 he could sit on a table!) Here are the results, scores representing proportion of 15-second observation periods in which the youngsters were recorded as talking.

"Normal" Teaching	Rewards for Talking	New Teacher But No Rewards
8%	48%	23%

New Teacher Plus Rewards	New Teacher, No Rewards
60%	47%

In short, over time rewards could be dropped, but above-normal talking continued.

Source. Robert L. Hamblin et al., "Changing the game from 'get the teacher' to 'learn'," *Trans-Action*, January 1969, 20–31.

Memory Span Varies With Content

The number of items that can be perceived, learned, and remembered varies with the nature of the items themselves.

Number of Binary Digits in Group	Number of Labels Required by Code
2	4
3	8
4	16
5	32

Students who have a memory span for 8.5 digits tend to retain only 7.5 consonants, 6 nouns or geometrical figures, and 3 word pairs or nonsense symbols. When one asks "how much" can be retained he must specify "of what."

With practice, short-term memory span can be increased: after 50 days of practice, two students who could originally repeat back sequences of only 9 or 10 digits were able to echo sequences of 13 to 15.

By grouping symbols into larger units, a man who has the ability to remember "the magic number seven, plus or minus two" expands the scope of his memory. He can remember either seven single-digit units, or seven units made up of three digits each. More work is involved with the latter: he must devise a "code"—a set of symbols representing three-digits—and he must translate single digits into this code and vice versa. Such a code, however, enables him to retain 21 symbols rather than the original seven.

Here is how such a code works.

Using the two digits, 0 and 1, of the binary system, an experimenter found he could remember random sequences of 12 units. He then broke the sequences into pairs of symbols, such as 00, 01, 10, and 11, and labeled them with their decimal-system equivalents of 0, 1, 2,

and 3. He was still able to remember 12 unit-sequences in the decimal system—and to convert them back to their 24-unit binary-system equivalents. And so on, with these results.

Number of Binary Digits Retained	Number of Labels Retained
24	6
36	12
40	10
40	8

Note that increases in the size of the vocabulary (the number of labels in the code) led first to a reduction in the number of *labels* retained and then to a leveling-off of the number of *digits* into which these could be decoded. (The difficulty is twofold: more labels to be kept in storage, and a longer wait until the label can be applied—while one ear is attuned to the continuing stream of digits.)

Putting labels on categories of symbols is perhaps the most fundamental operation performed in communications and thinking, in learning, and in remembering. Every course a student takes involves subsuming a variety of events and things under such labels as *audience, feedback,* and *advertising media.* This experiment gives concrete evidence of how much this process of classifying and labeling can increase efficiency.

Source. Ian M. L. Hunter, *Memory* (Baltimore, Md.: Penguin Books, 1964), pp. 59, 67, 69–72.

Latent Learning

Ordinarily we know that learning has occurred because, in response to our stimulus, an animal's behavior changes. If we see no change, we infer that no learning has occurred. However, the animal may be too tired to respond or, in the absence of a reward, have no reason to respond. Proof that learning has occurred will appear in behavior when the animal ceases to be tired or a reward is offered.

Rats run in a foodless maze—dinner being delayed until an hour after they'd been removed from the maze—showed little learning when compared with rats which found three minutes worth of edibles at maze end. However, these same idle rats performed as efficiently as the others when, two to seven days later, food was provided in goal boxes for the first time.

In no-reward conditions, rats injected with a stimulant made as many mistakes in the maze as those not stimulated. When the stimulant was cut off and rewards added, both groups improved in performance—but the group previously stimulated proved superior. Both groups *had* stored something in memory, which rewards evoked, but the stimulated group had stored more of it.

In human experiments, with one student presenting material that another is to learn, subsequent tests show that both (including the "teacher" who hadn't expected to be tested) have learned, but that the "teachers" have learned less. Apparently students work harder in constructing categories, attaching labels to them, and forming associations. Latent learning is less efficient than learning that is motivated.

Source. H. C. Blodgett, "The effect of the introduction of reward upon the maze performance of rats," University of California Publications in Psychology, 4:113–4. Cited in David Krech et al., *Elements of psychology* (New York, Alfred A. Knopf, 1969), p. 308.

Additional Research Readings

Size of reward. The bigger the incentive offered for advocating a viewpoint one opposes, the more reprehensible such action appears to be; small rewards accomplish more attitude change. If payment is made *after* the act, *big* rewards achieve more change. **Duane R. Kauffmann, "Incentive to perform counter-attitudinal acts: Bribe or gold star?" Journal of Personality and Social Psychology,"** 19:82–91. When students were given a choice as to making a counter-attitudinal public statement, 50¢ rewards produced more attitude change than $2.50; when they were forced to act, $2.50 produced more change. **Steven J. Sherman, "Effects of choice and incentive on attitude change in a discrepant behavior situation,"** Journal of Personality and Social Psychology, 15:245–52.

Punishment. Highly anxious preschool children proved more effective in a marble-dropping game when confronted with a critical, punishing experimenter. Children with low anxiety, however, performed best for a positive experimenter. **Mark R. Lepper, "Anxiety and experimenter valence as determinants of social reinforcer effectiveness,"** Journal of Personality and Social Psychology, 16:704–9.

Memory. Subjects shown mutilated slogans, then complete versions, remembered 21 of 30 compared with a score of only 18 for those shown complete slogans on both trials. Added effort improved learning. **Norman Heller, "An application of psychological learning theory to advertising,"** Journal of Marketing, 20:248–54. Asked to write down pleasant and unpleasant experiences, students found the unpleasant decreased in intensity faster than pleasant ones and that this fall in affect reduced recall. **David S. Holmes, "Differential change in affective intensity and the forgetting of unpleasant personal experiences,"** Journal of Personality and Social Psychology, 15:234–9.

Unusual Cues Attract Attention

By using a camera angle that distorts familiar objects, advertisements catch viewers' *attention.* But *distortion* also serves other purposes. It helps BOAC emphasize the amount of leg room in its planes. It provides PG&E tasteful art as a lead-in for an ad that discusses manure disposal!

Kraftco adapts the split-face technique, often used to show conditions before and after product use, to a very different purpose. Ethnic differences emphasize the firm's new worldwide scope and the broadened product line which have forced it to change its old, familiar name.

198a

Antiquity
INLAND COPPERPLATE

Delicate
BERNHARD MODERN

Firmness
CENTURY NOVA

Oriental
REINER SCRIPT

Boldness
FRANKLIN GOTHIC

Dependability
GARAMOND BOLD

Gaiety
P. T. BARNUM

PATRIOTIC
SAPHIR

Character
CRAW MODERN

Dignity
MELIOR

Luxury
CASLON OPEN FACE

Progressive
AMERICANA BOLD

Conservatism
EUROSTYLE

Ecclesiastical
OLD ENGLISH

Masculinity
FORTUNE EXTRA BOLD

Reliable
GOUDY OLD STYLE

Continental
BERNHARD TANGO

Femininity
FUTURA LIGHT

Movement
BRUSH

Strength
COOPER BLACK

Type Face Functions

Type faces, if carefully chosen, can add subtle *connotative nuances* to the denotative meanings conveyed by the words which employ them, as shown at the top of this page. (Heavy type may suggest strength but most of these nuances reflect ways such type faces have been used in the past.) *Metalworking News* uses unusual headline type both to *attract attention* and to suggest a not-quite genuine fear of anti-trust action. In an ad for local dealers, the American Newspaper Publishers Association first isolates *auditory cues* to such desirable car qualities as good tires, solid construction and soft seats and then finds *visual cues* to represent these sounds.

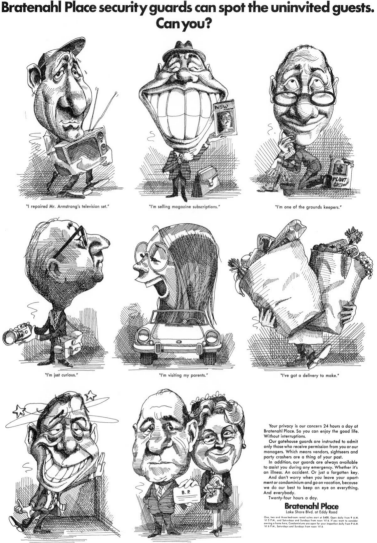

Bratenahl Place security guards can spot the uninvited guests. Can you?

"I repaired Mr. Armstrong's television set."

"I'm selling magazine subscriptions."

"I'm one of the grounds keepers."

"I'm just curious."

"I'm visiting my parents."

"I've got a delivery to make."

"My dear, old friend is having a party here tonight."

"We've made reservations at the restaurant. Here's our card."

Your privacy is our concern 24 hours a day at Bratenahl Place. So you can enjoy the good life. Without interruptions.

Our gatehouse guards are instructed to admit only those who receive permission from you or our managers. Which means vendors, sightseers and party crashers are a thing of your past.

In addition, our guards are always available to assist you during any emergency. Whether it's an illness. An accident. Or just a forgotten key.

And don't worry when you leave your apartment or condominium and go on vacation, because we do our best to keep an eye on everything. And everybody.

Twenty-four hours a day.

Bratenahl Place
Lake Shore Blvd. at Eddy Road

One, two and three-bedroom rental suites start at $480. Open daily from 9 A.M. til 5 P.M., and Saturdays and Sundays from noon 'til 6. If you want to consider owning a home here, Condominiums are open for your inspection daily from 9 A.M. til 6 P.M., Saturdays and Sundays from noon 'til 6.

Cartoons Achieve Many Goals

Cartoons in this ad serve two functions: the rarity of their use in advertising provides attention-getting *contrast,* and they promise the *rewards* of humor. The *distortion* involved in over-large heads helps attract *attention,* and, by emphasizing man's most expressive feature, it allows more *meaning* to be packed into a small space. The faces arouse *curiosity* which is only partially satisfied by reading the one-line captions under them. Full satisfaction requires one to read the copy block itself. Talking about burglars and muggers as a lead-in to the value of 24-hour guards might scare readers away; reducing such fears to the status of nuisances avoids dangers inherent in the *fear appeal.*

Chapter 10 Synopsis

● Senses provide both rewards (example: the taste of a lemon) and cues to rewards (example: the lemon's color). This relationship may be very close, as in the relationship between taste and smell, or arbitrary, as in the relationship between words that are seen or heard and the objects they symbolize.

● Sellers need to know how many different stimuli will produce a given sensation, how the situation of exposure to a stimulus affects sensation, how senses vary in their ability to perceive any stimulus and to differentiate between two stimuli.

● The seller in manipulating cues has more than 20 sensory dimensions to play with including 4 of taste, 4 to 6 of smell, 4 of touch, 3 each of vision and hearing, plus organic aches, muscle feedback, and the sense of balance. A variety of cues from ears and eyes place an individual in time and space by providing cues of direction and distance.

● Relations between physical input and sensation perceived vary among the senses, between individuals and, over time, within an individual. The Weber-Fechner fraction suggests a constant relationship between input and perception that distinguishes each sense.

● Sensory cues to one or more receptors behave, when combined, in ways that cannot always be predicted from their individual effects. If relationships remain unchanged, despite absolute changes in input, perceptions remain stable. Multiple cues help prevent error under "noisy" conditions of reception.

● Expectations affect speed and accuracy of perception in ambiguous situations. Expectations and desires sensitize and inhibit perceptions.

● Perceptual phenomena of interest include figure-and-ground, category formation, effects of contrast and change on attention, adaptation and object constancy. All are important to a seller seeking favorable perceptions of his product and message.

Research Articles

Packaging. Influences choice of product, perception of flavor (Banks), misleads in judgment of freshness (Brown).

Thresholds. Three methods of determining them compared (Cornsweet); studies disagree on whether we are quick to perceive things we like, slow to perceive things we dislike (McGinnies, Lazarus, Naylor, Postman, Lambert, Bruner).

Correlates. Psychological set determines perception of ambiguous words (Siipola) and so does physiological state (Postman).

Chapter 10 Sensory Cues and Rewards

A lemon sits in the center of a table. Seated around the table rim, a motley crew: you, creative director for an ad agency; a plant breeder; the representative from a citrus growers' cooperative; a home economist; a psychologist; and a housewife.

The housewife has just finished speaking. Her lemons, she has said, must be medium dark and medium heavy; vision and touch tell her what taste her tongue can expect. Her lemons, she has said, must be fresh; she knows they're fresh when her finger tips touch the fruit. If it feels too soft, she perceives it has passed its prime. Scent, too, she says, signals freshness: if the fruit doesn't give off a faint, lemony odor when she picks it up, it goes back on the grocer's display. Of course, she adds, one kind of lemon is best for lemon pies and another for lemonade. Each use requires a special combination of whatever chemicals—and she hasn't the faintest idea what they are—make a lemon taste sweet, sour, and a bit bitter, all at the same time, and make one kind of lemon taste slightly different from another.

The botanist says he can come up with a new lemon, given a year's time and $50,000, but he wants the home economist to tell just which of these three tastes—sour, bitter, sweet—he needs to alter and by how much. The home economist points out that the question is complicated, since the lemon won't be taste-tested until it has gone into a wide variety of finished products, but she hopes that the botanist won't alter lemon's Vitamin C content.

When the plant breeder comes up with a new lemon or the grower succeeds in altering its appearance, what words and pictures can you, as creative director, use to suggest flavor, scent, and texture? What

radio jingle will symbolize freshness? How can your ads make people thirst for a lemon?

Many of the answers each of you seeks will be found in a psychological laboratory. There you discover how many *tastes* a lemon can have, how many a housewife's tongue can detect, and which tastes will please her. If your client manufactured automobiles, you'd be concerned with speed and how people perceive time and space and movement through time and space. If he manufactured perfume, you'd have to study the subtleties of *scent;* how skilled women and men are in detecting the presence of the perfume and in telling one perfume from another. Color *vision* is of concern to the paint manufacturer, interior decorator, and the owner of a fabric shop. The man who makes or sells hi-fi sets will find it's folly to offer gradations in *auditory stimuli* beyond a human's ability to hear.

Rewards and Cues

Senses are significant, therefore, in that they provide *rewards* to the consumer. Expectation of such rewards converts a prospect into a purchaser.

The senses are also important as *cues* that produce these expectations. This distinction between cue and reward is seen most easily when one sense provides the cue and another the reward: when vision and touch suggest the taste of a lemon, and when touch and smell testify to its freshness.

Sometimes the relation between sensory reward and sensory cue is very close; such a close relationship exists between the chemical senses, between *taste*, whose receptors are on the tongue, and *smell*, whose receptors are in the nose. (Sensations from the nose may be perceived as taste. The tongue alone, for example, cannot distinguish apple from potato or ground coffee from crumbled crackers. On the other hand, taste buds can make vinegar "smell" sour. Pain receptors in the nose give household ammonia a *biting* "smell" and cold receptors in the nose can make a menthol shaving soap or cigarette "smell" or "taste" *cool*.)

Often the relation between sense-as-reward and sense-as-cue is not wired-in but learned; the relation then may differ from one buyer to another, or from one situation to the next. A delicate scent on stockings may never be detected *as* a scent but, rather, as a finer knit.[1] Short weight in a package of potato chips, sensed subconsciously by vision or touch, may be perceived as a difference in taste and may result in a decision not to buy the brand again.[2]

Still looser are the arbitrary relations between the symbols used by the adman and the sensory rewards they promise to his audience. (To people who speak English, the word *lemon* may suggest color, shape, size, scent, and taste more powerfully than would a picture by Picasso or a wax replica. To people who do not speak English, the word—in contrast to the picture or the replica—may convey no meaning whatsoever. More than most cues, therefore, words must be selected with regard to the particular audience addressed.) Knowing how arbitrary this relationship is, buyers may put more faith in such sensory cues as smell and sight. (Sellers may react by using chemical baths to improve the color and texture of the lemon and make it appear more uniform.)

Sometimes the same sense may serve as both cue and reward, as when a demonstrator in a supermarket hands out samples of cheese. But an advertisement in blues and greens may provide visual cues to suggest non-visual experience—the cool "smell" or "taste" produced when menthol molecules in a cigarette hit sense-of-touch receptors in the nose.

A seller needs to know how many different ways there are of producing a given sensation, so that he can select the one that is the cheapest and has the fewest undesirable side effects. (When he converts his lemons into lemonade, how is he to induce the user to say, "How sweet it is!"? Sugar is fattening, saccharine has a bitter aftertaste, and cyclamates have been banned.)

A seller needs to know how users differ, for this will tell him how fine he must segment his market. (Knowing that taste buds atrophy as a person ages, he may decide to put out a strongly flavored brand for senior citizens.)

The seller also needs to know the circumstances in which his product will be consumed. (Lemonade sold in movie theater may need less sugar than lemonade served at lunch: the popcorn eaten along with it will accentuate its sweetness. Lemonade served under fluorescent lights may have to have color added to restore the cue of richness bleached out by the light.) The advertiser needs to know the time and space context in which his message will be exposed. (Volume on his commercial may need to be stepped up if it's being broadcast to teenagers deafened by rock-and-roll music. Crass or banal copy may be disastrous if placed amid the sophisticated editorial and advertising content of the *New Yorker*.)

The seller needs to know the limits to man's ability to perceive his environment: when are cues too weak or too strong, too high or too low, to be picked up by his senses? Within this range, how big a change in a cue is needed for him to notice a change? (Taste, so important to food manufacturers, appears least sensitive of all the senses: 10,000 molecules are needed to produce a sensation of taste for every single molecule that produces a sensation of smell.)

Specialties within psychology have been developed to answer these questions. *Psychophysics* relates physical events—temperature, pressure, light and sound waves, molecules of liquid and gas—to sensations.

Physiological psychology studies the receptors that convert these physical events into neural impulses speeding toward the brain. *Experimental psychology* studies *absolute thresholds* (the minimum amount of a physical or chemical event that can be sensed, and the ceiling frequency that passes beyond sight and hearing, the taste or smell that becomes painful). It also studies *differential thresholds* (the amount of physical and chemical change required for a change in sensation).

Scholars in these areas help us appreciate the extent to which a clever seller can manipulate perceptions by identifying more than 20 sensory dimensions.[3]

Taste. Taste buds on the tongue report four sensations—*sweet, sour, bitter,* and *salty.* The taste sense seems more dependent than other senses and more likely to decrease in sensitivity over time, because of continued stimulation or such natural processes as aging.

Smell sensations, reported when particles of gas reach the nose, are more complex and controversial. Psychologists distinguish *six* different sensations of smell, whereas chemists distinguish *four* sensations of smell and classify the chemical elements that affect smell into five groups. (These five groups include 16 elements; the remaining 100 elements appear to have no effect on nasal receptors.)

Touch includes cues from four kinds of skin receptors that report *pressure, pain, warmth,* and *cold.* (Pain differs from other skin senses in that the sensation does not disappear under continued stimulation because involuntary bodily movement exposes new pain receptors; pain is cued not only by pain receptors but also appears by intense stimulation of pressure, warm, and cold receptors.)

Hearing is cued by air movements produced by a vibrating object and reported via a complex series of mechanisms in the ear: a drumlike membrane, a series of three tiny bones, a tube filled with fluid and some hairlike cells. The ear produces three sensations—*pitch, loudness,* and *tonal quality*—which reflect the frequency, intensity, and mixture of frequencies of the air waves.

Vision, like hearing, has three dimensions corresponding to cues contained in the waves reaching the eye. These are *hue* or color, *brightness,* and saturation or *purity* which reflect wave length, wave height, and the number of different wave lengths contained in the stimulus.

At least three other sensory cues are important to marketing, although little is known about any of them: (1) Least known are the cues that receptors within the human body report of aches and pains from organs and tissues; these aid the physician's diagnosis and supply prospects to the man who sells pain-killers. (2) *Sensory feedback* from muscles and joints, in combination with visual and other cues, is necessary to the learning of perceptual-motor skills but, again, is virtually inaccessible to study. (Such feedback has a label, *the kinesthetic sense,* but that's about all.) (3) The anatomist's knife has given us a good deal of information about receptors for the *sense of balance* in the "vestibule" of the ear. When a man's position in space changes, fluid in three tubes—one for right-left movement, one for up-down movement, and one for forward-and-back movement—move hairlike cells which trigger nerve impulses that inform the brain that the astronaut, automobilist, or ocean voyager has been tilted, jerked, or spun. Men who design vehicles or tranquilizers can presumably profit from such information.

Position and Distance

Two of the most important perceptions are those of *position* and *distance* which allow men to relate themselves in time and space to other objects like tigers and crazy drivers and so aid survival. Men lack special receptors for these perceptions but depend on fail-safe messages provided by combining several cues of vision and hearing.

The eyes provide seven distinct cues to distance. Two are provided by feedback from muscles that control the eye. (For distances up to 20 feet, the muscles that make the lens of our eye thicker or thinner provide a cue. For distances up to 70 feet, the muscles that cause our eyes to turn toward one another aid distance perception.) Although the eyes are only about 2.5 inches apart, the slight disparity between images on the two retinas provides cues of depth.

A single eye, by itself, provides four cues to distance.

1. *Overlap.* When a bush blots out part of a tree or a person masks a doorway, we know that the bush and the person must be between us and the tree or building.

2. *Perspective.* As every artist since the Renaissance knows, whether his art shows it or not, distant objects produce a smaller image on the retina than do nearby objects of the same size. Railroad tracks converge to a point on the horizon; detail blurs, brightness decreases, and colors tend to gray out with distance. Objects in the distance appear to be higher than those near at hand. In a field or on a beach, particles of dirt and sand look smaller and closer together in the distance. Since the air transmits light imperfectly, distant mountains become hazy and blue.

3. *Shadows.* Since solid objects cast shadows, shadows suggest solid objects. Shadows permit us to "see" three-dimensions on a two-dimensional printed page. On the assumption that light comes from above, as usual in real life, the position of the shadows will tell us whether the surfaces seen are convex or concave, whether we are looking at gentle hills or craters.

4. *Movements.* When a person moves his head, nearby objects appear to move backwards, but distant objects appear to move in the direction the head is moving. (Thus, telephone poles beside a railroad track fly backward as the train passes, but a distant tree or the moon overhead tag along.)

When these cues conflict, what does a person perceive? Two kinds of evidence are available. In a laboratory, two balloons at a fixed distance were made brighter or bigger; either change made them appear to move closer and both changes brought them still closer.[4] When these two cues were in conflict, what little movement occurred responded to *size* rather than *brightness*. (This reflects everyday experience: the amount of light falling on an object changes much more often than does the size of an object.) Another experiment, in which a cut-out corner on a playing card made it appear to be behind rather than in front of another card, indicated that overlap is a most powerful cue,[5] even when it forces one to perceive giant and miniature playing cards in an array. Hearing also provides cues to direction and distance, three of which require both ears.

Time. Since sound waves travel only 1100 feet per second, the width of one's head is enough to make a difference of as much as 1/2000 of a second between the time sound reaches the near and the far ear. (Although this cue would not seem to help for a sound directly overhead, behind, or in front of us, we have learned to compensate for this by shifting our head, usually unaware that we are doing so.)

Intensity. The slight amount of sound absorbed by the head or by the air as sound travels around or through the head tells which ear is nearest the sound.

Timing. If the distance between peaks of a sound wave is sufficient (i.e., if the pitch is low enough), the top of the wave will reach the near ear before the far ear, providing still another cue to direction.

Two single-ear cues reveal distance:

Intensity. Distant sounds are usually weaker than near sounds. Having recognized the identity of a sound, the loudness we hear, compared with the loudness we know was emitted at the source, reveals its distance.

Frequency. Most sounds are made up of several different frequencies. As sound travels, high frequencies are absorbed more readily than low; a low-pitched rumble reaches more distant ears than a high-pitched screech.

Knowing how cues substitute for one another and interact with one another, a communicator can select the strongest cues. Knowledge of how space is perceived helps in developing stereophonic record players and in making a small room appear large. If moviegoers refuse to wear Polaroid glasses to watch a 3D movie that depends on the *disparity of image* cue, we give them Cinerama, which creates a similar sensation through *gradients* of *texture and movement* of an enveloping screen and through *stereophonic sound.*

The world that man perceives is even more complex than the 20 sensory cues suggest, thanks to two factors. First, as we have seen, the visual and auditory senses have receptors at more than one location. Second, each of the sensory dimensions reports cues quantitatively. The 100 million receptors in the eye can respond 1000 times a second, pouring 100 billion bits of information into the brain during that time.[6] Receptors in the nose can combine odors in 16 million different ways. Such reports go to a central switchboard, the brain, whose 10 billion cortical cells can provide a number of circuits that it would take 8 billion digits to specify.

Combining Cues

So vast a number of cues does not complete the story. Cues can be combined and effects of their combinations cannot be predicted from knowledge of their individual effects.

Relations between physical stimuli and sensation vary. Some of these relationships appear unalterable, wired in, common to all men: these limit what a seller can do. Others, although fixed for a given individual, show marked differences from one person to the next: these affect a seller's freedom to segment the market. Finally, there are those that change from time to time within individuals. These cause concern for the context in which a product will be bought and consumed.

More than 100 years ago, two Germans— E. H. Weber and G. T. Fechner—developed a *law* that predicts (within the midrange of most sensory dimensions) how big a change in stimulus is required for a change to be sensed. The increase is expressed by a fraction, different for each dimension, which remains constant through this range. Taste, touch, and smell require the largest increases: one-fifth for salty tastes, one-seventh for skin pressure, one-tenth for loudness—compared with only 1/333rd for changes in pitch. (More recently, S. S. Stevens[7] has suggested that equal stimulus ratios correspond to equal ratios of sensation, the range being from .33 for brightness in vision to 3.5 for electric shock.) The respondent's sex makes a difference: women are quicker to detect small amounts of sweet and salty substances and men better at detecting degrees of sourness. Individuals vary widely in their ability to detect tastes at all and to detect small differences among them.

Sensory Combinations

Most sensations, both consummatory and cue, are produced by multiple stimuli. Since sensed stimuli interact, the combinations often behave differently from their individual parts. These interactions among sensory cues are of two kinds.

The dimensions within a given sense are not independent of one another. In hearing, the physical intensity of a sound tends to be perceived as loudness and wave frequency as pitch. However, a 1000-cycle-per-second sound wave sounds louder than a 100 cps wave of the same physical intensity. As intensity rises, high frequencies sound higher and low frequencies sound lower even though wave frequency does not change. (The producer of a TV commercial may argue that his soundtrack hasn't become louder (more intense): if the pitch of the pitchman's voice is higher than that of the performer he interrupts, he will *sound* louder.) These relationships between cues from a single set of receptors seem to be wired in.

Quite different interactions are those learned through experience involving cues from different senses that converge to help us perceive constant objects in a changing world. (A lemon remains a lemon even in the dark when we have nothing to go on save the size, shape, and texture that our fingers report to us. We look for our car at the curb in moonlight and at high noon; we can identify it from front or rear, at street level, or from a fifth-story window. We can recognize a friend's voice in the jungle's cacophony or the silence of an arctic waste, the stillness of a cork-lined office or the noises of cocktail party, busy street or boiler factory.) Men perceive objects as a relationship among cues; so long as the relationships are unchanged, whatever the *absolute* level of stimulation, the object will still be perceived correctly.

Minimal and Redundant Cues

Multiple cues may be on different sensory dimensions or provided by repetition of a single stimulus—both help a stimulus get through the competition from other stimuli or in unfavorable contexts, as when lighting is poor.

When we speak of multiple cues, we imply that under ideal conditions some smaller, minimum number would obtain a receiver's attention and understanding. *Information theory* provides a definition for this ideal number.

Such theory begins with a problem: we must find one coin in a hundred and we can ask only one kind of question: *Is it in this group of coins?* Seven questions will find the coin; any message that will locate the coin in one trial is said to contain seven *bits* of information, each bit representing the content of one of the seven answers.

(How is it done? On the first trial, the coins are divided equally; a "yes" or "no" answer eliminates 50 coins. On subsequent trials the same procedure narrows alternatives to 25, 13, 7, 4 and 2; each trial reduces alternatives by half. In more formal fashion, the theory says that when alternative choices are equally likely and independent of one another, the amount of information is proportional to the logarithm to the base two of the number of alternatives.)

Such a strategy is, of course, highly congenial in conversations with a computer that has only two states of being ("current on" and "current off") and a language with only two symbols, 0 and 1. If we want to use two-digit words in talking to the computer, our vocabulary consists of 00, 01, 10, 11; if we misspeak or the computer "mishears," meaning has changed. To prevent this, we can use three digits to transmit two-digit meanings. From our larger three-digit vocabulary pool, we accept only four combinations: 000, 110, 101, and 011. Now, two errors, not one, are necessary for a shift in meaning. Any of the three digits can be missing or changed, since a single error produces a nonexistent word. (We must use care, however, to avoid combinations in which an identical digit performs no security function, examples being 000 and 100 or 010 and 110.)

Attributes of the stimulus, such as those just described, affect the ease and accuracy with which it may be perceived. So do attributes of the receiver, including his current needs and his previous experience.

Expectations Ease Perceptions

The speed and accuracy with which one can perceive a message depends on how many different messages he expects to see. If his task is to distinguish whether the letter "A" or "B" is coming, he can do so quickly and without errors; if he doesn't know which of the letters from "A" to "Z" may appear, it takes longer exposure. (If animal names are being shown and one is *prepared* for animal names, he does better than if he just expects words in general and much better than if he expects to see the names of flowers or vegetables.)

Given a choice of two figures, or a figure that is vague or ambiguous enough to be interpreted in two ways, one tends to see what he *expects* to see or what he would *like* to see. Expectations may be based on a lifetime of experience, as in object constancy, or on a very short period of activity, in the phenomenon called *psychological set*. (If we have been looking at a series of letters, we are likely to interpret an ambiguous figure as the letter "B," whereas if the figure has been preceded by a series of numbers, we are likely to report seeing the number "13.")

Just as we tend to see what we have been rewarded for seeing in the past, we tend, when given a choice, to see the reward most relevant to our current needs and desires. (For example, 100 sailors were shown a dimly lit, smudged screen, and told that it showed a picture of "three objects on a table" or "a group of people enjoying themselves." Only 15% of the sailors who had

eaten an hour previously reported seeing pictures of food on the screen; but 23% of sailors who had not eaten for 16 hours reported seeing food.)[8]

Suppose, now, that we are exposed to pictures that are threatening or unpleasant rather than rewarding. What happens then? Some experiments suggest that we are more likely to see such signs of danger than we are to see neutral cues. On the other hand, so many experiments show resistance to the perception of such stimuli that the resistance has been given a tag of its own— *perceptual defense*. A smoker does not see newspaper stories about the relation between cigarettes and cancer.[9] If he sees them, he does not read them. If he reads them, he distorts the message. And if he understands the message, then he proceeds to forget it as rapidly as possible. The suggestion has been made that perceptual defense occurs when the threat is one that the subject is not ready to cope with, but that increased perceptual sensitivity occurs when the subject can do something to avert the danger. Perception thus would mobilize the individual for dangers he can do something about, but suppress anxiety-producing cues that would make him less able to cope.

Details may be suppressed or distorted as a result of our desires, as in perceptual defense, and also as a result of our expectations. An inexperienced proofreader will miss a great many typographical errors; his eye sees what it expects to see. Cues may also be overlooked for a third reason. Those that persist unchanged over time tend to fade into the background; it is a sudden silence, not the constant noise, which is heard.

If we tend to perceive brands that are familiar, and avoid brands that are unfamiliar, how is it possible for a new brand to get through our defenses? How can brand switching occur?

There are two kinds of evidence that show how this can happen.

The first comes from a laboratory where

normal letters, which subjects had been familiar with since they could read, were exposed for brief periods of time, interspersed with reversed letters, which they had never seen before. As expected, longer exposures were necessary for recognition of the novel stimuli. However, when subjects were warned ahead of time that reversed letters might be included, the difference disappeared.[10] A psychological *set* or expectation overcame years of experience.

The second comes from a classroom where college students were given a list of such complaints as insomnia, indigestion, and bad breath—themes of many an advertisement—and asked to report what remedy first popped into their heads and which brand, if any, they actually used.[11] Nearly half the students named a specific brand; not quite 40%, usually those who hadn't had to deal with the problem, named a product. Of the 50% who named a brand, 18% were apparently reflecting familiarity with advertising, since they hadn't used the brand and another 8% reported a bad experience that had stopped them from using the brand again. Thus only half of the subjects who voluntarily associated a brand with a problem actually *used* the brand named. Advertising by a competitor, a better price, or a more convenient retail outlet might well induce purchases at variance with preferences.

Five Questions

Buyers respond on the basis of what they perceive. Nearly every action a seller takes is aimed at influencing buyers' perceptions. Sellers must understand the basic processes involved if they are to be effective. They must ask *why* people behave in ways which most of us take for granted. For example:

How do we separate objects from their surrounding and background? What makes an object, individual, or ad stand out? (*Figure and ground.*)

What determines how we group objects into categories? (*Gestalt.*)

What focuses our attention on an object? (*Contrast and change.*)

Once focused on an object, why does our attention relax, allowing us to attend to another object? (*Adaptation.*)

Why do we perceive objects as objects, even though the cues of shape, size, and color they emit are constantly changing? (*Object constancy.*)

Here are brief answers to these questions.

Figure and Ground

Change, in time or space, stimulates man's senses. He pays attention to a sudden noise or a sudden silence—a snag in a stocking or a stationary stone in a moving stream. The boundary between an object and its background, representing a change in meaning, attracts his eye. (In technical language *figures* stand out from *ground*; they appear closer and more three dimensional.) In a laboratory, scholars construct stimuli that make this separation difficult: a wavy line can be interpreted as a face looking either right or left; two lines can be seen as outlines of a vase or of two profiles facing one another; a picture is that of a young girl or an old hag. Ordinarily, we see only one of the possibilities. Once we realize both are present, our attention fluctuates from one to the other. In real life, some behaviors stand out from others; a new employee who fumbles on his first day may be identified as a fumbler to the end of his days.

The ability to see figure and ground appears wired in rather than learned, since it is found among rats reared in darkness and persons, blind from birth, who later gained vision. It is found in hearing as well as in vision: a melody "stands out" from its accompaniment.

Categories

Given an environment with many objects, we tend to put them into categories. Why? One possible reason is that categories permit us to perceive more stimuli, in a given time period. Subjects who can correctly perceive 6 to 11 dots, the average being 8, at one-tenth of a second, can perceive 25 dots, in groups of five, in the same period.[12] Subjects who can see, on the average, only four or five unrelated letters, will perceive as many as 20 when joined in a familiar word. (In both instances, they may ignore a missing digit or a typographical error.)

But what determines *which* category an object is put into?

Objects of the same size, shape, or color tend to be grouped together, as do those near one another in time and space. The object or event that precedes another in time tends to be seen as causing the one that follows. When *similarity* and *proximity* are manipulated in a laboratory to produce antagonistic perceptions, similarity seems a more powerful influence.

In real life, small gaps in a geometrical figure and typographical errors in a word tend to be overlooked. If they are seen at all, it is as a circle with a gap rather than a figure without a name made up of curved lines and as a misspelling of a familiar word rather than as a new word. In both of these instances, of course, the problem of what a subject actually perceives is overlaid by the problem of how to report what he sees; it's certainly easier and quicker to say "circle" than to describe what's there.

This tendency to fill in gaps, called *closure*, is powerful; it can overcome the effects of proximity. For example, closure resembles the advantage that symmetrical groups have over asymmetrical groups and that continuous lines and curves have over those that are interrupted. Information theory has been used in an attempt to define the "goodness" that gives one shape predominance over another in a way that could be programmed for a computer. The good shape, in this version, is the shape that can be defined with the least amount of information.[13] Less information is needed when areas of a given color are contiguous, boundaries simple, and objects symmetrical. In these terms, rectangles are "better" figures and should be perceived more easily than trapezoids.

Once boundaries have been seen that separate one collection of stimuli from another, sensory displacement takes place, away from the border and toward the center of the group. The effect is to strengthen and preserve the differences created by boundary drawing.

Having put objects into a category, we may then perceive that they have more or less of the attribute on which the category is based. How do we perceive differences in quantity?

Sometimes subjects are given a standard in the middle of the range of objects whose weight or size or color they are to judge; their judgments of quantity become less accurate as they move away from this standard. If subjects are not given such a standard, they supply their own—the high and low ends of the series. Again, errors increase as they move away from these standards—this time errors accumulate in the middle of the range. If a new stimulus just outside this range is now introduced, subjects tend to underestimate its distance until it gets too far away; then they begin to overestimate it. The new stimulus may also change judgments of others in the original set.

If a weight, a light, or a heated object is at the heavy, bright, or hot end of the set of objects, it feels and looks heavy, bright, and hot. Extend the range, however, by adding a heavier, brighter, or hotter example of the same kind of object and the first ones judged will begin to feel and look light, dull, and cold. If, on the other hand, the new object is of a different kind, it will not affect the original set; comparisons appear to occur only among similar objects, within the same categories. A heavy, new box thus will cause a subject to revise judgments of the weights of boxes previously estimated, but lifting a typewriter of exactly the same weight will cause no change. Attitudes as well as sensory judgments follow this rule: people exaggerate the similarity of persons within a group and their differences from persons in other groups.

Contrast and Change

Why does an advertiser so often use sound to attract our attention, rather than light and color? Why do fire engines have sirens?

Advertisers today depend on sensory responses which, in the days of the caveman, may have helped men escape the sabre-toothed tiger.

Sound does not travel far and it does not travel fast but it can travel around corners, unlike light, and so can operate as an alarm both night and day. It alerts us to a moving object near at hand; the nearer the object, the larger it is, and the more violently it is moving, the louder the noise it makes.

Sound alerts us—but is poor in providing cues as to direction or detail. Although at a cocktail party we can "tune out" one conversation and "tune in" another, our ability to focus our ears is less developed than our ability to focus our eyes.

Unlike the ear, one's eye reports a great deal about objects both far and near, in motion and at rest. The most complex messages come from six million cone-shaped visual cells located near the center of the eye; such messages cannot be received in dim light. Much more numerous are the 125 million rod-shaped cells that extend to the outer edge of the retina, reporting only light and dark. These rods serve an *alarm* function, since they operate in very dim light and are sensitive to motion glimpsed out of the corner of the eye—or, in more technical terms, the periphery of vision.

Alarm or Subtle Distinctions?

The better job a sensory system does of serving an alarm function, the poorer it seems to be at making subtle distinctions. This is true of taste: the presence of bitterness is easy to detect, but differences in bitterness are not. It is true of vision: rods are quick to report motion but cannot report different colors. In color vision, finest distinctions among colors are made at middle ranges: a sense of green, and wave length of 500 millimicrons in dim light, a green-yellow sensation of 550 in bright light. And in nature, disregarding the civilized subtleties of Mozart and the Beatles, sound is primarily an alarm system, a clue to danger rather than a sensation to be enjoyed.

A moving object sets off the alarm system; but an individual may also cause his receptors to move as an aid in identifying objects that do not move of themselves.

Since the direction of a sound depends upon it reaching one ear sooner than the other, sounds directly in front of, or behind, or above an individual cannot be distinguished from one another. He seldom is confused, however, since without realizing it he shifts his head and restores the cue he needs.

A change in a stimulus will attract attention. Such change may be accomplished by moving up or down one of the sensory dimensions, by stopping or starting stimulation, by altering an object's attributes. The change may occur in either time or space or both.

Intensity. A change in sound level or the intensity of light will be noticed, so will a marked change in size—a subject that is much smaller or much larger than others around it will be noticed. (Print media buyers have long used a rule of thumb, based on the Weber-Fechner rule: to double an ad's attention value, they spread it across four times as much space.) Repeating a stimulus in time or in space may increase its total intensity to a point where it will be noticed.

Movement. Since most elements in a landscape are static, a car moving along a lonely highway attracts attention. However, in a stream of traffic, it may be the stalled car that is seen first just as it is the unmoving rock in a brook that draws the eye. Thus, flashing lights and signs that revolve invite us to stop and buy and stop-motion photography at the movies emphasizes a director's message.

Color. In a black-and-white newspaper, an infrequent ad in color tends to stand out (as it should, considering its higher cost.) In a brightly costumed crew on a color TV screen, however, a single actor dressed in black and white will stand out.

Novelty. A cue that contrasts with our expectations is likely to be noticed. Such expectations may be produced in many ways: by previous experience in time and space, by instructions from a message source, by elements in the message itself. One italicized word stands out in a page; a discord in a melody will be noticed; an obscenity that would pass unnoticed in a barracks may hush a cocktail party. The very word "new" has been so overworked in advertising that novelty can be achieved by denying that there's been any change in the product. We *expect* sellers to puff their own products; the man who advertises "white elephants" gets high attention and credibility. In pages of close-packed print, white space wins attention for an advertiser but in a picture magazine, an occasional all-text ad will draw the reader's eye.

Adaptation

If a stimulus persists unchanged, the senses *adapt* (become less sensitive), saving the receptors from possible damage and permitting the individual to attend to a new threat or promise. (Like the quality-control man in a factory or a trouble-shooting marketing executive, the receptors respond to exception.) Surround a viewer with a smooth, single-color surface and he sees space rather than a surface, even if it is only six inches away. Focus the image of an object on a single spot on his retina and the object vanishes. Deprive a subject of nearly all sensory input, with goggles and earmuffs and cardboard cuffs, and he becomes disturbed to the point of imagining things that aren't there and losing his ability to solve problems.[14]

Both sense organs and the nerves that carry their reports to the brain need time to recover after being stimulated; their sensitivity decreases temporarily; we say that the sense has *adapted*. Absolute and differential thresholds rise, so that greater intensities and differences are required for a response.

Nerve impulses travel on the surface of the nerve, the speed varying with the circumference of the fiber—from 100 meters per second down to one meter per second for thin-fibered, cold-blooded animals. Before the nerve can fire again, surface energy must be replenished from inside the nerve, a process that may take 12 milliseconds for a large fiber. Meanwhile, other fibers (and there are several to serve each receptor) take over the communications job. The more intense a stimulus, and the larger the area stimulated, the longer recovery takes.

Vision. If one's gaze is fixed on a single object in either light or dark, it will fade out after a brief time. If the eyes move so as to let the image fall on new areas of the retina and cortex, the image will reappear in a second. Three seconds are required if a new area of the retina but not the cortex is involved, and 10 seconds if both retina and cortex areas are unchanged.

Hearing. For a brief period at 200 to 300 milliseconds, loudness sensed for a given intensity increases over time. Then the ear fatigues so that after a pause of 80 milliseconds, a higher intensity is needed to produce the same loudness. However, this effect lasts only about half a second.

Touch. With respect to pressure, the skin seems to report this sensation only while it is actually bending, a period varying from 2 to 20 seconds, depending on the size of the weight used and the part of the body, hand, arm, forehead, or cheek being stimulated. Adaptation to warmth and cold operates primarily through varying the size of the neutral range in which neither sensation is felt. The time taken varies from 30 seconds to 3 minutes, increasing as we move away from normal skin temperatures to points as extreme as 41°F and 113°F. On the other hand, if the changes take place slowly enough, at a rate of .36 degrees per minute, the temperature can move 18 degrees up or down without producing any sensation. Surface skin pain produced by a single needle will cease in 10 to 100 seconds; when several needles are applied to a small area, the process may take as long as 5 minutes. Pain from heat does not adapt; it begins to be felt when tissue damage begins, at about 113°F.

Smell. Most odors consist of chemical mixtures, whose parts adapt at varying rates, causing the odor smelled to vary over time. Nitrobenzol, which originally smells like bitter almonds, tends to take on a tarry odor over time. Both the kind of odor and its intensity affect speed of adaptation.

Taste. The decrease in sensitivity varies markedly with the substance involved. Acids shows least change, adaptation requiring an increase of only 1.6 times in the amount that can be used without detection. Bitter substances show a change of 2 to 3 times, sugar a change of 6 to 20 times, and salt one of 300 times. Interestingly enough, as taste buds become less sensitive to salty or sour tastes, they become more sensitive to sweetness.

Object Constancy

Although an object may recede into the background through adaptation, it does not change its identity even though there may be marked changes in the reports that our senses receive from it.

Four types of *constancy* are important in vision, the sense we most depend upon in understanding our environment.

Shape. The top of a milk bottle or a cup is perceived as round and a book or a door continues to be seen as rectangular, whether viewed from the top or side. Cues from object and context position the bottle or book in relation to the eye; cues of position combine with the actual image falling on the eye's retina to tell us what it is and how it's tilted. Artists know that when a glass is viewed from the side, its top must be drawn as an ellipse and the swinging door must be drawn as a trapezoid; when this is done, our senses and brain will convert the physical cues received into circles and rectangles.

Brightness. Coal looks black under a bright sun at high noon, and snow remains white even in dim light although the frequencies that coal reflects should appear much whiter. This is true, however, only so long as we know what we are looking at. In real life we perceive *albedo:* our perception is based on the percentage of light falling upon the object that is reflected. This percentage remains constant for any given object: if it reflects 80% of sunlight, however bright, it will also reflect 80% of moonlight, however dim. Adults and children have been able to pair off two sets of 48 different shades of gray paper, even though one set had 20 times as much light thrown upon it, thanks to albedo.[15] In a laboratory, however, one can remove contextual cues and so prevent a subject from sensing the amount of light falling on an object. When this is done, perceptions tend to vary with the actual amount of light reaching the eye.

Color. Even the colors we see tend to be appropriate to the objects they represent. Pieces of gray paper, cut in the shapes of a banana, lemon, carrot, and tangerine, were mounted on blue-green backgrounds and covered with a ground-glass screen; laws of color contrast say all four should have appeared identical, gray against blue-green being sensed as brownish orange. But shape made a difference: the banana and lemon were perceived as yellowish; the tangerine and carrot as having an orange tinge.[16] The illusory colors persisted even when subjects watched the objects being cut out of the same piece of paper. In similar fashion, blue paper under a yellow light is seen as blue unless it is viewed through a peephole which prevents both object and background from being identified; then it appears gray as laws of color mixture say it should.

Size. If we see two men, one 10 times as far from us as the other, we do not report the distant man as being one-tenth as tall as the man nearby. Knowing men and given a choice between perceiving them as differing in size or location in space, we choose the latter; men, we know, more often move about in space than they differ in size. The size we perceive helps us estimate an object's distance; if the object is unknown, so that we have no idea of its size, we may first estimate distance and base judgment of size on that. Distance judgments are often accurate—pilots have erred less than four inches, on the average, in judging the height of a six-foot stake from a distance of a mile.[17]

Thought, Talk, and Action

1. Draw up a list of common ailments—headaches, indigestion, insomnia—and interview a variety of subjects, asking them what remedy first popped into their minds. After completing the list, go back and ask what brands, if any, they actually used. Compare the original mentions of the products vs. the brands used; compute the extent to which the brands named were actually used, and how many respondents used more than one brand.
2. How many different attention-getting devices can you think of that could be used in print advertising? on radio? on TV?
3. Listen to ten radio commercials, counting the number of mentions of the brand names. Now view ten TV commercials, counting the mentions on the audio track of brand names. If you have an opportunity, view the TV commercials a second time and record how long the brand name appears on video. Summarize and explain any differences between repetition on radio and TV.

Notes

Chapter 10

1. Donald A. Laird, "How the consumer estimates quality by subconscious sensory impressions," Journal of Applied Psychology, 16:241–6.

2. James C. Naylor, "Deceptive packaging; are the deceivers being deceived?" Journal of Applied Psychology, 46:393-8.

3. Basic references for observations regarding the senses are S. S. Stevens, editor, Handbook of experimental psychology (New York: John Wiley & Sons, 1951) and Robert S. Woodworth and Harold Schlosberg, Experimental psychology, rev. ed. (New York: Holt, Rinehart and Winston, 1964).

4. Charles E. Osgood, Method and theory in experimental psychology (New York: Oxford University Press, 1953), p. 263.

5. Ibid.

6. Alfred Kuhn, The study of society (Homewood, Ill.: Richard D. Irwin, 1963), p. 113.

7. S. S. Stevens, "The surprising simplicity of sensory metrics," American Psychologist, 17:29-39.

8. D. C. McClelland and J. W. Atkinson, "The projective expression of needs: I. The effect of different intensities of hunger drive on perception," Journal of Psychology, 25: 205-22.

9. Charles F. Cannell and James C. MacDonald, "The impact of health news on attitudes and behavior," Journalism Quarterly, 33:315-23.

10. M. Henle, "An experimental investigation of past experience as a determinant of visual form perception," Journal of Experimental Psychology, 36:1-21.

11. E. L. Brink and W. T. Kelley, The management of promotion (Englewood Cliffs, N.J.: Prentice-Hall, 1963), p. 128.

12. George A. Miller, "The magical number 7, plus or minus 2; some limits on our capacity for processing information," Psychological Review, 60:81-97.

13. David Krech et al., Elements of Psychology, 2nd ed. (New York: Alfred A. Knopf, 1969), p. 156. Original articles cited are: J. E. Hockberg and E. McAlister, "A quantitative approach to figural goodness," Journal of Experimental Psychology, 46:361-4, and F. Attneave, "Some informational aspects of visual perception," Psychological Review, 61: 183-93.

14. Reference No. 13, p. 507. Original study cited: W. Heron et al., "Visual disturbances after prolonged perceptual isolation," Canadian Journal of Psychology, 10:13-8.

15. Reference No. 3, Woodworth and Schlosberg: p. 434.

16. Jerome Kagan and Ernest Havemann, Psychology: An introduction (New York: Harcourt, Brace & World, 1968), p. 176. Original study cited: J. S. Bruner et al., "Expectation and the perception of color," American Journal of Psychology, 64: 216-27.

17. Ibid., p. 178. Original study cited: J. J. Gibson, The perception of the visual world (Boston: Houghton-Mifflin Co., 1950).

What Cues Suggest Attributes?

A housewife will buy a cake that *looks* fresh; she will repurchase a brand that *tastes* fresh. Packaging material can help both appearance and flavor, as Adman Seymour Banks has demonstrated in an artful combination of consumer survey and sales test.

To check on appearance, he had interviewers show 230 consumers two packages of layer cake and two packages of Danish pastry and ask them which package in each pair they preferred. Respondents were then asked to bite into two slices of each product and compare their flavor.

The new packaging material, designed to resist grease and moisture, would have been preferred 50% of the time on a chance basis. Actual results, significant at the .10 level, showed that 67% of the customers judging *appearance* picked the Danish pastry wrapped in the new material, and that 65% of those judging *flavor* picked the layer cake in the new wrap. (Some consumers tasted day-old samples, others slices four to five days old—the normal time packages stay on the shelf. Flavor preferences for the new wrap rose as the cake in it aged.)

Since shoppers can't nibble a cake to test it for flavor before buying, only looks

of 17%. However, he notes, attributes other than appearance probably influence customer purchases; only if appearance had a weight of at least 80% would the preference found in his survey have been sufficient to be detected in his sales test (17.4% $\times$ 80% = 14%). He suggests that surveys may be useful in reducing a large number of alternatives so that a sales test may be run on the remainder.

Source. Seymour Banks, "The measurement of the effect of a new packaging material upon preference and sales," *Journal of Business*, 23:71–80.

Housewives have told researchers they look for two qualities in bread: freshness and flavor. Judgments of flavor require a taste test but freshness is often judged by touch, a cue which sellers can manipulate.

Fifty housewives were approached in a supermarket and asked to judge the freshness of bread, hidden from view behind a screen, solely by feel. They compared two samples at a time. Stiff paper, results showed, suggested age. Housewives could tell the difference between fresh and day-old bread by feel, but not between day-old and two-day-old.

	Percent of Preferences			
Kind of Wrapping	Fresh	Day Old	2 Days Old	Average for Wrap
Cellophane	42	40	42	42
Cellophane and wax	40	33	32	34
Wax paper	18	27	26	24

could be given a sales test. This was done by having bakery route men alternate new packages and old in deliveries to matched sets of retailers, who were not told about the test.

Banks' sales test was sensitive enough to detect an increase in pastry sales of 14%; his survey detected a preference

Difference in wrappers was statistically significant for each age of bread.

Source. Robert L. Brown, "Wrapper influence on the perception of freshness in bread," *Journal of Applied Psychology*, 42: 257–60.

Measurement of Thresholds

When a marketing consultant reported that he had boosted popcorn sales 57% and Coca-Cola sales by 18% by flashing sales messages on a movie screen for 1/3000th of a second—well below the threshold of awareness—the nation became alarmed. When subsequent attempts to replicate the results failed, the nation relaxed.

Knowledge of how thresholds are determined might have eased some of the fears. They are averages—a threshold varies from one trial to the next for any single subject and from one subject to the next. These averages may be obtained in three different ways.

Method of limits. Starting with a stimulus well below the threshold, an experimenter increases intensity, trial by trial, until it is perceived. Then he starts with an above-threshold stimulus and gradually reduces intensity until it ceases to be perceived. He alternates such trials and averages the results.

Method of constant stimuli. The experimenter uses a set of 5 to 8 intensities ranging from one that will rarely be perceived to one that will always be reported and presents them in random order for as many as 100 trials. The intensity that is reported half of the time is dubbed the threshold.

In the first method, expectations may affect perception, since the subject knows that the next stimulus will be either higher or lower than the last one. The second method is inefficient since it requires repeated use of stimuli that may be distant from the threshold. As a result, a new method has been devised.

Double-staircase method. The experimenter simultaneously employs both an ascending and descending series, deciding by random means on each trial which series his stimulus will come from. Thus he gains all the advantages of the "limits" method but, through randomization, prevents the subject from anticipating whether the next stimulus will be higher or lower than the last. As soon as either series reaches the threshold, it goes into reverse. The three methods do not produce identical results, even for a single subject.

Source. T. N. Cornsweet, "The staircase-method in psychophysics," *American Journal of Psychology,* 75:485–91.

Vigilance, Defense, and Subception

If we want to predict what a person will perceive and how quickly, it helps to look at the thing to be perceived, the person, and the relationship between the two.

When we do this, it appears that an individual's needs, moods, and interests may make him see some symbols sooner than we'd expect him to (vigilance), and prevent him from seeing other symbols as soon as we'd expect (defense). It also appears that even when he doesn't admit in so many words that he can recognize the symbols being "shown" him, bodily reactions beyond his conscious control, such as the sweating of his palms, reveal that something is getting through.

Sixteen students in Alabama, half of them coeds, were shown a series of 18 words, beginning with exposure of each for .01 second and increasing by .01-second intervals until subjects reported the word they had seen to an experimenter.

Included in the 18 words were seven words with sexual implications—words not ordinarily used in mixed company. Everyone of these seven words required longer exposure than others on the list:

whore requiring an average of nearly .16 second to about .05 for words like *apple* and *sleep*.

The "vulgar" words which subjects are slow to admit seeing, even though their sweating palms suggest that they have

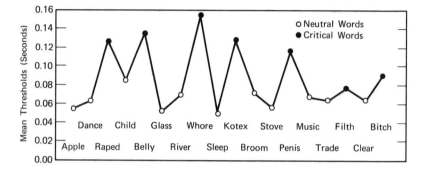

Mean thresholds of recognition of the observers to the neutral and emotionally charged words.

Source. Elliott McGinnies, "Emotionality and perceptual defense," *Psychological Review,* 56:244–51.

Since subjects in the vulgar-word study may have been reluctant to repeat such words to an experimenter of the opposite sex, another study was attempted using 10 five-letter nonsense syllables, half of them accompanied by an electric shock which caused the palms to sweat. Sure enough, when these syllables were shown to subjects at speeds below their recognition threshold, the five nonsense syllables conditioned to shock caused an increase in sweating—even though the subjects "saw" no syllables at all. Here, again, was evidence for what experts call "subception."

Source. R. S. Lazarus and R. A. McCleary, "Autonomic discrimination without awareness," *Psychological Review,* 58:113–22.

Although there is little doubt that perceptions are affected by characteristics of both message and perceiver, these relationships are complex.

seen them, also tend to be longer and less familiar. A review of 25 studies in which both word length and frequency were controlled revealed that only 18 of them had found perceptual defense. When experimenters controlled both of these factors plus the dirty-word factor, which would inhibit reporting aloud to an older person or a person of the opposite sex, only 5 of 12 studies reviewed found perceptual defense to operate.

Even less support is found for the phenomenon of "subception"—perception below the differential threshold. The problem here is in the definition of this threshold as the point at which a difference in stimulus is perceived half the time.

All three studies which had controlled for partial recognition showed negative results; none of the seven which supported subception had introduced such controls.

Source. J. C. Naylor and C. H. Lawshe, "An analytical review of the experimental basis of subception," *Journal of Psychology,* 46: 75–96.

Subjects appear to be quick to recognize symbols that they find rewarding.

Twenty-five students first were scored on the six values of the Allport-Vernon scale: theoretical, economic, social, religious, political, and aesthetic. Then 36 words representing these values were shown in brief exposures. Sure enough, a student with a high score on a given value was more likely to detect words consistent with that value at brief exposures. One with a high score on *religion,* for example, was quicker to see the word *sacred* and more likely to misperceive the word *scared* as *sacred.*

Source. L. Postman, J. S. Bruner, and E. McGinnies, "Personal values as selective factors in perception," *Journal of Abnormal and Social Psychology,* 43:142–54.

A high-valued symbol may not only be seen more quickly; it may also be seen as larger.

Children from rich and poor families were asked to adjust a circle of light until it matched the size of various coins: a penny, a nickel, a dime, a quarter, and a half-dollar. All children overestimated the size, but rich children overestimated the size of a quarter by only 20% as compared with 50% for poor children. Subsequent debate suggested that memory, not perception, was involved, and that poor children merely had less experience with quarters and so tended to exaggerate their size rather than exaggerating because quarters meant so much more to them. However, another study revealed that value could be induced experimentally, by allowing children to "buy" candy with poker chips, and that the size of valuable chips was overestimated.

Sources

W. W. Lambert, R. L. Solomon, and P. D. Watson, "Reinforcement and extinction as factors in size estimation," *Journal of Experimental Psychology,* 39:637–41.

Jerome S. Bruner and Cecile C. Goodman, "Value and need as organizing factors in perception," *Journal of Abnormal and Social Psychology,* 42:33–44.

Psychological Set

Differences in subjects need not be as fundamental or long lasting as variations in values or wealth to affect perception. Psychological set can be induced by a word from an experimenter.

Eighty subjects were told that they would be shown, at exposures of a tenth of a second, words concerning animals and birds; another 80 were told that the words would concern travel. Included in the lists were six nonsense words which could, with slight alteration, be put in either list:

Nonsense Word	Similar Word in Assigned Category	
	Animal-Bird	Travel
chack	chick	check
sael	seal	sail
wharl	whale	wharf
pasrot	parrot	passport
dack	duck	deck
pengion	penguin	pension

As expected, subjects tended to "see" nonsense words consistent with set:

Instructions	Responses	
	Animals	Travel
List of animals and birds	63%	11%
List of travel terms	14	74

Source. E. M. Siipola, "A study of some effects of preparatory set," *Psychological Monographs,* No. 210.

What happens when characteristics of symbols and perceiver tend to reinforce one another? One study suggests that symbols are more influential, at least for the moderate degree of hunger involved with these subjects.

More than 700 undergraduates were asked to fill in missing letters in a series of mutilated words such as *pick- -* which could be completed as a food (*pickle*) or not (*picket*). Five different 21-word lists were used, each with a different subset of the subjects. Before seeing these lists, one group of subjects was given a single "practice" word perceived as food related: lun-h (*lunch*). Each subsequent group was given an additional food-related, set-producing word so that the fifth group practiced all the words on this list: d-ss-rt (*dessert*), che-s- (*cheese*), b-n-na (*banana*), c--kie (*cookie*), and lun-h. With the rise in cues for food, the number of food-related completions rose. Students' actual hunger, as measured by their own reports and by the number of hours since last eating, showed no significant effect: hungry students averaged fewer food-completions—8.8 to 9.3.

	Number of Food Completions in Practice Set				
	1	2	3	4	5
Number of food completions in 21-word test set	6.3	6.7	8.9	9.2	10.9

Source. L. Postman and R. S. Crutchfield, "The interaction of need, set and stimulus-structure in a cognitive task," *American Journal of Psychology*, 65:196–217.

Additional Research Readings

Sensory needs. Subjects with a high need for stimulation preferred complex, 2109-element tartans to simple, 91-element ones, retained more of a message heard under distracting conditions, and talked more in groups. **Stephen M. Sales, "Need for stimulation as a factor in social behavior," Journal of Personality and Social Psychology, 19:124–34.** After having a homogeneous group rate 236 odors and a heterogeneous group rate 10 odors, this expert drew up 124 "rules" about the sense of smell. **R. W. Moncrieff, Odour Preferences (New York: John Wiley & Sons, 1966).**

Vigilance. The name of a brand one prefers is glimpsed more quickly in exposing 83 kids by tachistoscope to names of 7 brands of toothpaste, 14 of soap, 10 of deodorant, 14 of detergent, and 8 of headache pills. **Homer E. Spence and James F. Engel, "The impact of brand preference on the perception of brand names," in David T. Kollat et al., Research in Consumer Behavior (New York: Holt, Rinehart, 1970).**

As soon as a decision maker has collected a sufficient number of alternative courses of action, he must begin a new kind of search: for the data and the criteria that will enable him to make a choice among them. He seeks to determine which set of causes is most likely to achieve the kind of results to the degree he wants them in the time available.

The scientist tries to focus upon the strongest, most probable of alternative causes. The businessman adds two additional criteria: he seeks causes that he can control and methods of study that will reap gains, from improved decision making, greater than the costs of the study itself.

Chapter 11 deals with research design, asking how many causes are to be studied and whether at one or several points in time. It recognizes that a single cause is seldom either necessary to or sufficient for a given effect. It also recognizes that unnecessary and insufficient results are usually attained by any given set of causes.

Chapter 12 deals with data-gathering choices: manipulation of causes versus observation of natural events; before-and-after tests versus control and experimental groups; alternative methods of sampling subjects and behaviors; the avoidance of interference by study methods with the causes and effects being studied. It suggests that usually more than one technique of either data-gathering or analysis is advisable.

Chapter 13 asks what can be done when a study produces unexpected results, including a review of assumptions and an examination of drop-outs and deviant cases. It also takes a look at the cost-and-benefit problem as handled by Bayesian statistics.

Chapter 11 Synopsis

● Eight questions need to be answered in specifying unknowns in preparation for gathering and analysis of data.

a. Are we concerned with the behavior of groups or individuals?
b. Which individuals (or groups) should be studied?
c. With which behaviors of these persons are we concerned?
d. Do we observe behavior itself or its products?
e. How long should we wait after a causal event before measuring its effects?
f. How far back in the causal chain should we search?
g. How should we present our findings: mean, mean difference, correlation coefficient, index number, table?
h. Which causes will we study?

● Effects in human behavior have multiple causes, both concurrent and consecutive. (And causes have multiple effects, both concurrent and consecutive.) The choice of how many causes one should study and how far back one should go in the chain depends on two factors: the strength of the cause-effect relationship, and the seller's ability to manipulate the causes. Just as we have two ways of summarizing the relationship between a single cause and effect, so we have two ways of summarizing the relationship between multiple causes and an effect. Analysis of variance, an extension of the comparison of two means, is one; multiple regression, an extension of the correlation coefficient, is the other.

Research Articles

Causes. May be sought in characteristics of individual or of aggregate.

Choice. Eight different statistics summarize meanings of table (Zeisel).

Effects. Recognition scores and sales records used to isolate characteristics of effective ads (Starch); hypothetical example shows how effects of message operate on topic and on source according to congruity theory (Osgood).

Chapter 11 Selecting Unknowns as Goals for Data Gathering and Analysis

Halfway through the decision-making process is the stage labeled *specify unknowns.* Behind lie problem recognition and definition, goal setting, determination of constraints, and the listing of alternatives. Ahead are collection and analysis of data, choice of alternatives, product purchase (or sale), and product use.

It is true that each of the stages before and after involves unknowns: the problem (opportunity) itself was an unknown until defined; the pleasures and pains of using a product became known only in the process. At this stage we are concerned with a very special kind of unknown: what we need to know about the alternatives we have discovered before we can make an intelligent choice among them.

When goals were set we specified the effects we wanted to obtain; the alternatives we listed represented ways of obtaining these effects. Now we ask whether the causes we manipulate will produce the effects we desire.

Seven Questions Concerning Data

We make this assessment through research into the response of prospects to products and to messages.

Three kinds of questions concern the seller: questions of technology, of costs, and of behavioral response. In making *place* decisions, the marketer must compare speed and costs of factory, warehouse, and retail locations and alternative means of transport among them; he must also determine how retailers will respond to manufacturers' efforts and customers to those of retailers.

He must make sure that *prices* cover costs, but he is also concerned with the responses customers and competitors make to them. Technology and costs limit the attributes that can be built into *products,* but those attributes must provide sensory satisfaction to the consumer and cues to such satisfactions. *Promotion* is concerned not only with how many persons competitive media can expose to a message per advertising dollar but also with the responses customers and retailers and manufacturers make to those messages. Marketing communications is concerned with the human responses to the variables of price, place, product, and promotion. In studying such human responses, we must answer seven questions.

1. *Are we concerned with groups or individuals?* Until recently, most marketing research concerned itself with individual characteristics: reading habits and buying habits, attitudes and personalities, demographic and geographic location. Increasingly, however, it is recognized that buying decisions frequently result from interaction of husband and wife in a household or a new product committee for a chain of supermarkets. We must study interaction among decision makers and between buyer and seller.

Individuals may be given a score based on their membership and activity in one or more *groups;* we predict their behavior because they belong to the PTA or the GOP. Groups may be characterized by the sex or age of their *members,* by members' average score or the dispersion of their scores. One group, we say, has a high average IQ or income, another is closely knit; a third has high turnover of membership and little influence on what members think, say, or do. If we choose to observe group responses, it may appear that our advertising messages have had no effect. A closer look might show, on the contrary, that messages made some individuals more favorable to our brand but boomeranged with others, so that the two effects cancel one another. [Knowing this, we can prepare *two* messages (or two products) for these two different audience segments.]

2. *Which individuals should be studied? How many?* By studying a small number of people, a sample of his market and audience, the seller hopes to devise a more effective marketing mix or message. The formulas of sampling statistics tell him how many he needs; in general, the more people vary in regard to the causes and effects he is studying, the more of them he will have to study. Even more important than the number he studies, is the way he chooses his subjects. He must, for example, know the probability that any individual in the population will be selected. (In a simple random sample, this probability is the same for every individual. Such sampling is often wasteful. To contrast the buying behavior of millionaires and factory workers or of politicians and white-collar workers, a seller requires a minimum number of each. Since a random sample will contain the same proportion of each as does the population, the seller might be well advised to employ a stratified random sample that includes 100% of the millionaires in the city or state being studied but only 1% of more ordinary folk.)

Unhappily, not all doors open to an interviewer's knock; not all persons invited to participate in a laboratory experiment actually show up; and many a mail questionnaire is dropped into the recipient's wastebasket. Worse, such refusal to cooperate is not distributed randomly through the population: it is more common among the very rich and very poor, the aged and persons with little schooling. Such groups tend to be underrepresented in most studies so that care is needed in collecting and interpreting data.

Studying a small sample often produces better results than taking a census of an entire population. More detail can be obtained from a small sample without increasing costs. The fewer interviewers needed can be selected with more care, and trained and supervised more carefully. Results can be obtained faster.

3. *Which behaviors of respondents should be probed?* The seller observes a different kind of action than those he seeks to influence; he must use one kind of response to predict another kind—always risky. (He may have no choice: the act he's interested in hasn't occurred yet or can occur only once—a first house, a first car, a first baby.) Often the seller uses verbal responses to predict nonverbal behavior: it's much cheaper and much faster. A seller could stand in a supermarket, observe housewives' behavior, and predict, on the basis of his observations, how they would respond to a questionnaire. He is much more likely to do the reverse. A sociologist who is interested in the effect of behavior upon attitudes may use nonverbal behavior to predict verbal responses, and find that customers just waited on by a Negro clerk deny any knowledge of that fact, or that innkeepers who have accepted Chinese as guests respond to a letter of inquiry by saying that they would refuse them a room.[1]

4. *Does one observe behavior or the effects of behavior?* An observer can stand in a supermarket and watch housewives remove items from the shelves. He will usually find it more efficient, however, to check invoices and inventory shelves at stated intervals. An interviewer can ask housewives what cake mix they use; an inventory of their pantry shelves may be a better check upon their behavior. Memory often errs. A housewife may not remember what she bought and name the brand that is heavily adver-

tised, or the one she usually buys, or the one with a high-status image. A researcher interested in family power structure may get the private opinions of husband and wife, and then see whose opinions win out in actual purchases, or observe the decision-making process itself, actual or simulated.

We sometimes compare various methods of research in terms of accuracy, speed, and cost, acting as though the results obtained from in-house data, secondary data, experiment, and survey were identical. Such comparisons are dangerous: different methods necessarily involve changes in *what* is being studied, obvious or subtle, large or small. Sales records tell us which customers are responding to a given product or salesman and help us decide which salesman to promote or discharge, which product to drop from our line or push in our promotion. Feeding cost data into the computer will provide even better information; it will tell us which customers cost us more than they are worth and spot the product providing the best combination of volume and profit margin. Such analyses are likely to be faster, cheaper, and more accurate than if we were to ask customers how much they'd bought or salesmen how much they'd sold. Some won't reply; some will err; and some will lie.

The ease of asking questions often prevents us from seeing how difficult it is to answer them. *How many tubes of toothpaste did you use last year?* is a question few can answer; Who keeps records of such behavior? If a question concerns too remote a period, a respondent is likely to answer in terms of his current beliefs and feelings. On the other hand, using trend lines on sales graphs to predict the future is risky; we'd do well to add some answers from customers about their buying intentions. It helps to determine *why* the action occurred. Sometimes reasons are clear: a housewife patronizes the nearest grocery store. Sometimes reasons are revealed when we cross-tabulate questions: ownership of a hi-fi set and possession of a college degree are related. Sometimes a direct reason-why question gets results. When all three kinds of data converge on a single explanation, we feel more confident.

Usually questions used to elicit *beliefs* are not disguised, although privacy for respondent and permissiveness by interviewer may be required to elicit expression of unpopular beliefs. A yes-no or multiple choice question may allow a respondent to express an opinion on an issue he's never heard of before. To prevent this, an interviewer may use an information-type question or may ask a question twice, in different ways, so that self-contradiction exposes the uninformed.

Although an interviewer can ask a respondent what his *feelings* are, the interviewer is more likely to put credence in the hesitation, stammer, or blush that accompany the answers than in the answers themselves. In the laboratory, a variety of instruments are available to measure the physiological components of emotion. Feelings are often diffuse; a respondent may not have the words needed to express them, may not accept the feelings himself, or may feel that they would not be acceptable to a stranger.

5. *How long should one wait after a cause before measuring effects?* Enough observations of human behavior need to be made at enough different points in time to distinguish strong, permanent tendencies from more temporary ones. On the other hand, the *shorter* the time that elapses between events observed and events predicted, the better the predictions tend to be. A long period of observation may make the research cost more than its results are worth; too short a time lapse between observations and predictions may not allow careful decision making.

Usually, memory loss following exposure to a message, advertising or otherwise, is rapid; delay as much as a day and it may be difficult to detect any effects at all. On occasion, however, effects may actually increase over time in what has been called a *sleeper effect.*[2]

An advertisement or a news story may sensitize a reader, making him more likely to notice subsequent advertising; the total effects traceable to the original ad may then be greater than the immediate results. Public commitment to a point of view may "freeze" an individual's attitude; admiring consistency, he may not want to backslide. Overt action following a message makes its effects more enduring. (If this action involves joining a group, the group provides messages and rewards that intensify effects of the original message. If this action involves purchase of a product, its use may be so satisfying as to result in repurchase.)

Media and ad agency may encourage *immediate* measurement of advertising effects, when they are likely to be at their maximum. A client needs to know whether effects will persist from ad exposure to time of next product purchase; this may require a *delay* in measurement but, unfortunately, little is known as to how long this delay should be.

6. *Which causes will we select for study?* Characteristics of message and medium, respondent and situation, are important;

Appearance

Many billboards
↓
Distract drivers
↓
And produce accidents

most of these can be influenced by the seller.

An important tool in such selection is the method of factor analysis. Such analysis begins by assuming that if two causes are highly correlated with one another, only one need be measured. It assumes that when subjects respond in similar fashion to different variables, variables (or subjects) have something in common; this something-in-common represents the "factor" of factor analysis.

The method has been used to categorize scents, personality traits, and intelligence tests, as well as message variables in advertising. It permits a wide variety of tests to be collapsed into a smaller number of factors. TV programs can be grouped into categories based on viewer reactions. Individuals can be grouped together on the basis of similarities in buying behavior or response to advertising.

7. *How far back in a causal chain should one's search go?* Satisfied customers tend to be repeat-purchasers; do we need to find out why they made their *first* purchase? If the amount of beer one drinks affects the brand one prefers, need we determine how a beer-drinking habit forms and why it varies in strength?

We may find that two variables that appear to be cause and effect are instead the results of a third variable further back in the causal chain. Here are two examples.

Highway locations with many billboards cause a lot of accidents because drivers, distracted by billboards, crash into one another.

Reality

Heavy traffic on highways
↙ ↘
Increases chance of accidents | Attracts advertisers who want high ad exposure

The more fire engines there are at a blaze, the more property damage results, proving that damage is caused by firemen, not fires.

Appearance	Reality

Appearance
Many fire engines bring
↓
Many firemen
↓
Who damage property

Reality
Big, dangerous fires
↙ ↘
Bring many   Cause much
fire engines   property
and firemen   damage

In other instances, there are two possible causal chains.

Salesmen have more automobile accidents than men in other occupations. Apparently selling attracts aggressive and unstable personalities who are accident prone.

Explanation A

Salesmen are aggressive
↓
Aggressive persons tend to
cause traffic accidents
↓
Salesmen cause traffic
accidents

Which explanation is correct? A table like this may tell us.

Score on Aggressiveness	Amount of Driving	
	High	Low
High	40%	12%
Low	40	8
		100%

(These hypothetical figures indicate that those who do a lot of driving tend to be involved in more accidents, regardless of their aggressiveness. Other figures might show that both explanations are true but that one is more important than the other.)

Sometimes introduction of a third variable eliminates the cause-effect relationship that appears to exist between two variables. Here is an example of what at first seemed clear-cut evidence that educa-

tion increased men's willingness to serve in the military during World War II.

	Education	
	High (N: 1761)	Low (N: 1876)
I feel I should be deferred	12%	30%

Explanation B

Salesmen use their cars a lot
↓
Persons who use their cars a lot are
more likely to have accidents
↓
Salesmen are likely to be involved
in accidents

Clearly, persons with low education were more likely to feel they shouldn't have been drafted. But why? Did their lack of education make them fail to appreciate the nation's war aims? Or was it the fact that most persons with low education couldn't pass screening tests and were deferred?

Here are hypothetical figures showing the percent in each group which felt it should have been deferred:

Friends Were Deferred		Friends Were Drafted	
Education		Education	
High (N: 335)	Low (N: 1484)	High (N: 1426)	Low (N: 392)
37%	37%	6%	5%

These figures suggest that men whose friends had escaped the draft were the ones who felt resentful. It is doubtful that any number of messages on war aims would overcome this feeling of *relative deprivation*—although other kinds of messages might.[*]

---

[*] Based on Herbert Hyman, *Survey design and*

Here is another example in which the introduction of a third variable strengthened one relationship, and specified the circumstances in which another occurred.

In the days before television, Lazarsfeld asked how choice of radio programs was affected by a person's age and his education. At first, it looked as if there were marked age differences in the percentage listening to three types of programs.

Type of Program	Young	Old
Religious	17%	26%
Discussion	34	45
Classical music	30	29
	(N: 1000)	(N: 1300)

However, *old* persons were also *less educated:* only 30% of those over 40 were high school graduates compared with 60% of those under 40. Was it the difference in age or the associated difference in education that determined listening habits?

In the case of religious programs, apparently it was education; age had no effect.

	Young	Old
High school graduate	9%	11%
Nongraduate	29	32

As for classical music, education made a difference but only among older people.

	Young	Old
High school graduate	32%	52%
Nongraduate	28	19

For discussion programs, both age and education influenced listening.

	Young	Old
High school graduate	40%	55%
Nongraduate	25	40

---

analysis (Glencoe, Ill.: The Free Press, 1955), pp. 279–80. Reprinted with permission.

In media-selection, as in all communications, one variable is seldom enough to explain an event or guide decision making; an advertiser who chose his radio programs on the basis of age alone would have missed the mark.*

8. *How should one's findings concerning cause-and-effect relationships be presented?* The previous questions must be answered before one can start collecting data to answer them. This question *should* be answered even earlier, since the answer it gets affects the way the others are answered. Its answer depends on what ways of summarizing findings are permitted by scientific logic, which alternatives the decision-maker can understand and which he sees as relevant to the choices he must make.

Usually we try to reduce each complicated, multidimensional, cause-and-effect relationship to a single, summary figure: an average, an index or a simple, four-cell table.

(There are exceptions. A shoe manufacturer or a haberdasher has little use for an "average" shoe, shirt, or hat size: he needs a frequency distribution showing the number of men in each size category.)

One's choice of an average is limited both by the data, and the way one plans to use it. When one's scores form the normal, bell-shaped curve beloved by statisticians and psychologists, all three measures of central tendency—mean, median, and mode—fall at the same place—the midpoint and peak of the curve. When data are not "normal," however, extreme values will distort the *mean:* a mean income of $10,000 may re-

---

* Paul F. Lazersfeld, "Interpretation of statistical relations as a research operation," pp. 115–25. Table reprinted with permission of The Free Press from *The Language of Social Research* by Paul F. Lazarsfeld and Morris Rosenberg. Copyright 1955 by The Free Press, a Corporation.

flect a neighborhood in which incomes range from $9,000 to $11,000 or one containing a single millionaire and a host of relief clients. The *median* discounts the millionaire by choosing the income of the man who falls at the midpoint of the distribution. The *mode* reports the most common income, without regard to either range or size of incomes. (The mode, however, is subject to manipulation: by breaking up large categories or combining low-frequency categories, one can shift it up or down the scale.) Although all three measures may be used to *describe* a group, the mean is most frequently used in making *inferences* about cause and effect. To make such inferences, one must take account not only of the mean itself but also of the variation in scores.

Cause-effect inferences are expressed in two ways. One is by comparing the mean scores of two or more groups which are made up of different kinds of people or have been subjected to different kinds of experiences, events, or messages. We ask whether the difference in means is statistically significant. (To be significant, variation in scores *between* the two groups must be greater than the variation of scores *within* them.) The other method is through a correlation coefficient, which may range from -1.00 (a perfect negative correlation) through zero (no relationship) to a maximum score of 1.00 (perfect positive correlation). This has two advantages over the mean difference as a summary figure: it disregards the size of the original scores making comparisons easy and, when squared, tells how *good* the relationship we have found is. (If beer sales and temperature correlate .60, a respectable coefficient in the behavioral sciences, we conclude that temperature "explains" only 36% ($.60 \times .60$) of the fluctuations in sales of beer—and that we must keep looking for the other 64% of the explanation.)

(Analysis of variance extends the significance test for mean differences to cover several causal variables. Multiple regression extends simple correlation to tell how much of an effect is caused by each of several variables (and the whole set)—and how much of causation still has to be determined. Both techniques are best understood by studying examples that accompany this text.)

Useful as the mean is, it is only one way to summarize data for a decision maker. Another favorite is the *index number*: the combining of means or other figures, through addition or subtraction, multiplication or division. One must decide what figures to put into an index and how to combine them. The choice may not be easy.

The *Houston Chronicle* printed a *split-run* edition: some subscribers receiving a black-and-white test ad, others the same ad in two colors.[3] Three to five days after publication, a recall study obtained these results.

	Percent of Respondents Recalling Ad	
	Black and White	Two Colors
Small ad	13%	26%
Full-page ad	26	39

Was color more effective in increasing recall for a small or a large ad? The simplest and, in terms of readers-per-dollar, the most appropriate index was obtained by subtracting black-and-white scores from color scores. By this standard, page size makes no difference; color increased readership by 13 percentage points in both instances.

However, a researcher who believes that once readership reaches a *floor* of 25% further increases in recall are easy to achieve, would prefer to use black-and-white recall scores as a base in calculating the percentage of gain caused by color. By this standard, color is twice as effective with small ads as with large ones: 13%/13% or 100% as compared with 13%/26% or 50%.

A third researcher argues that 25% recall is close to the *ceiling* that an ad can receive, so that the full-page ad, starting with 26% recall, is at a disadvantage. His index takes as its base the possible increase in readership: 100%–13% or 87% for small ads and 100%–26% or 74% for large ads. Dividing the 13% gain by these figures, he shows that color in the full-page ad reaches 21.3% of possible, obviously superior to the 14.3% of possible score of the small ad.

Often, of course, indices simplify rather than complicate decision making. Here is an example suggested by Zeisel.[4]

The firm that wants to reward the "most efficient" batsman on the Little League team it sponsors can do so on the number of home runs alone. Or it can try to take into account an overabundance of data like this.

Slugging Averages

Maier	319/502	.635
Dooley	274/578	.474
Crabb	306/500	.612

Marketing communications uses a host of such indices—ranging from the complex calculation of a consumer price index to such equally controversial indices of media performance as readers-per-dollar, program ratings as percentage-of-sets-in-use, and advertising costs as percentage-of-sales.

Some persons like index numbers; others prefer tables. Here is an example of a table, based on a report made for *Reader's Digest* in 1962, which classified subscribers on three dimensions: sex, age, and geographic

Player	1 Base	2 Bases	3 Bases	Home Runs	Times at Bat
Maier	101	23	12	34	502
Dooley	133	36	11	9	578
Crabb	73	8	11	46	500

An index, the slugging average, reduces each boy's record to a single figure. It is calculated by multiplying each hit by the

location.[5] Buried somewhere in it may be information as to why people subscribe to the magazine. Can you find it?

Percentage Who Receive *Reader's Digest*

Region	Age: 10–17 Men %	Women %	18–34 Men %	Women %	35–54 Men %	Women %	55 and Older Men %	Women %
Northeast Metropolitan	15	16	16	17	21	24	23	22
New York	14	16	19	18	23	25	22	22
Pacific Metropolitan	15	20	16	16	25	29	27	32
Los Angeles	20	16	18	23	23	29	28	28

number of bases it won and dividing by total times at bat:

By going back to the original data and calculating new percentages, one can reduce this monstrosity to three tables, each summarizing one of the three variables that might affect coverage.

It is hard to see any pattern in these scores, but means suggest that the student underestimated "noted" scores but did a fairly

Percentage Who Receive *Reader's Digest*

By Region %		By Age %		By Sex %	
Northeast	19	10–17	13	Men	17
Metropolitan New York	21	18–34	15	Women	19
Great Lakes	18	35–54	22		
Southern	13	55–up	22		
North Central	19				
Southwest	16				
Pacific	23				
Metropolitan Los Angeles	24				

Or one can produce two-way tables such as this:

good job of predicting the smaller "read most" scores.

Percentage Who Receive *Reader's Digest*

Region	Men %	Women %
Northeast	19	20
New York City	20	21
Los Angeles	22	25

Average Discrepancy Between Student Estimates and Actual Scores

	Noted %	Read Most %
Men	−16	−1.3
Women	−15	0

Another way of simplifying a complicated table is to report averages. Below, for example, is a comparison of one student's predictions with actual Starch measurement of readership for a series of advertisements in the *Saturday Evening Post*.

Tables showing percentages can clarify cause-and-effect relationships if they use the right base.

Below is a table, based on hypothetical figures for a small town in the Midwest, which provides very little information be-

Student Estimates Compared with Readership of Selected Advertisements

	Men		Women	
Advertisement	Noted %	Read Most %	Noted %	Read Most %
Rambler	+ 8	− 13	− 7	− 9
Plymouth	− 42	− 15	− 32	− 5
Cadillac	− 35	0	− 22	+ 2
Longines	− 13	+ 3	− 19	+ 2
Admiral TV	− 26	+ 3	− 24	+ 2
Kent cigarettes	+ 11	+ 14	+ 14	+ 8

cause the percentages are figured the wrong way.[6]

Home Ownership and Income

	Own Home %	Rent %
High income	25	5
Medium income	40	30
Low income	35	65
	100	100

What is wrong with this table? The *causal* variable should appear at the head of the columns; clearly income determines home ownership rather than the reverse. (Only if we happen to know that the high-income group represents about 10% of the population and the middle-income group about 30% can we see the effect of income on ownership.)

Sometimes, either way of figuring percentages makes sense. Here is an example, with car-sale figures for a hypothetical midwestern town.[7]

Make	Sedan	Convertible	Hardtop
Chevrolet	36	16	31
Ford	31	17	28
Plymouth	27	12	30
Total	94	45	89

If you, as an automobile dealer, want to know which of your *models* is most popular, this table will tell you.

Percentage of Automobile Sales by Make and Model

	Chevrolet %	Ford %	Plymouth %
Sedan	43	41	39
Convertible	19	22	17
Hardtop	38	37	44
Total	100	100	100

On the other hand, if you are interested in how big a *share of market* your brand of automobile gets, use models not makes to head columns.

Percentage of Automobile Sales by Make and Model

	Sedan %	Convertible %	Hardtop %
Chevrolet	38	35	35
Ford	33	38	31
Plymouth	29	27	34
Total	100	100	100

Three Difficulties: Interactions, Thresholds, and Probabilities

Study of cause-and-effect relationships in human behavior is difficult because of three factors: interaction, curvilinearity, and probability.

Interaction

Items in a package of causes are seldom independent of one another: variable B may be twice as effective when combined with variable C as when combined with variable A. A drop in price may increase a brewer's sales to a low-income group, for example, but cause sales to drop in a high-income group if its members use price as an index of quality. Ads that talk about "gusto" may attract the hearty male drinker but may suggest to women that beer is fattening. When variables *interact* with one another, the researcher must test all possible combinations of a given series of variables for definitive results. Such tests require a great many subjects and are costly.

Curvilinearity

Most variables can be quantified; one must not only decide whether to study variable A but also how much of variable A to study. Frequently a researcher finds a *curvilinear relationship*. Up to a certain threshold, variable A seems to have no effect. For a time, increasing the amount of A increases the effects; then, beyond a certain *ceiling*, increasing the amount of variable A has a diminishing effect, fails to have any effect at all, or even reduces the effects produced by a smaller amount. (A brewer may find that this curvilinear effect operates on everything from flavor to price to repetition in advertising. That is, up to a point, an increase in dryness may attract customers, an increase in price may suggest an increase in quality, and repetition of a slogan may increase retention of a brand name. Carried too far, dryness may be perceived as bitterness, a high price may be interpreted as extravagance, and repetition may cause annoyance or indifference.)

Probability

The third difficulty is that cause-effect relationships in the behavioral sciences are never certain, only probable. Even the best set of causative variables, each present to an optimum degree, cannot produce effects 100% of the time.

Predictions can be improved by increasing the number of variables studied, the number of subjects studied, or by extending the study over a longer period of time. If one decides this gain in predictability is worth the cost, he must then choose between probability and precision. He can increase the probability of being right in his predictions or he can increase precision. He makes a choice between these alternatives.

Chances are 95 out of 100 that the recognition score for advertisement A is 9 to 11% higher than the score of advertisement B.

Chances are 99 out of 100 that the recognition score for advertisement A is 5 to 15% higher than the score of advertisement B.

(This choice may be visualized in the form of a target: the larger one makes the circles around the bull's eye, the more chance that an arrow will fall within them. If one chooses to count only the hits that come close to the target, he must be content with a lower count.)

Other difficulties in research arise because variables in the marketing mix interact with those in the environment, and because some important variables are hard to identify and measure.

A product that sells like hotcakes in Mobile may sink like a lead balloon in Minneapolis for a dozen reasons, ranging from climate to competition to per capita income. The advertisement that scores today may have been a disaster yesterday and may be a catastrophe tomorrow, depending on everything from the current state of the business cycle to the mysterious shift of fad and fashion. Product and ad have meaning only in relation to the context in which they are perceived; they must *conform* to some aspects of this physical and social environment to be *accepted* and *contrast* with other aspects to be *observed*.

A business firm is happiest when it can deal with figures: pounds, degrees, feet, dollars. Decision making in an organization is easiest when results are predictable. It would be nice to be able to say: *If we double our advertising budget, we will double our sales.* It would be convenient to say: *If we double our advertising budget, we will reach peripheral prospects, and sales will go up only 25% to 50%.* It is not much fun to have to say: *The size of our advertising budget doesn't matter nearly as much as the quality of the adver-*

tising it buys. We don't know how to get the agency's creative staff to produce better advertising. In fact, we aren't even sure we can recognize better advertising when they do produce it. At least not until we've run it on TV and in the newspapers and the public begins to respond to it.

A Second Look at Multiple Causes and Effects

In human behavior, it is rare that any effect has a single cause, or that any cause has a single effect. One must decide how far back in the chain of causation to go, and how many concurrent causes of a given effect to study.

In the behavioral sciences, rarely is any cause *both* sufficient and necessary. Indeed, it is hard to find any cause that is *either* sufficient or necessary.

Looking at causation from the standpoint of a *buyer*, let's consider the man trying to decide whether to light up a pipe. The smoking habit, the advertiser's messages, the presence of an easy chair and a newspaper, news stories about cancer and cigarettes, an "oral" personality in the smoker, and his feeling that a pipe is the thinking man's smoke—all favor smoking. Holding back the smoker are the cost of the pipe, his difficulty in keeping it lit and, perhaps, of keeping it clean. His wife's objection to the smell of the pipe and the ashes it produces may be a pro or a con—depending on the man's attitude toward his wife!

A pipe manufacturer would like to know how much weight each cause has in a man's decision and how weights differ for men of different demographic groups. Studying all of them, however, may be costly. As the number of variables rises, the number of subjects required rises even more rapidly. An advertiser who wants to study how sex, four different age levels, and three degrees of education affect re-

sponses to his messages must fill a table of 24 cells $(2 \times 3 \times 4)$. If he follows the rule of thumb that calls for 30 persons per cell, this will require 720 persons. (Some of the combinations called for, the Ph.D. aged 20 to 25, for example, may be hard to find, and even harder to lure into a laboratory.) Adding five income levels to the study would mean expanding the table to 120 cells and require 3600 subjects.

Difficulty of interpreting results also increases with the number of variables studied. One statistician, for example, points out that using more than five or six independent variables in a multiple correlation formula does not increase its predictive power very much.[8] The difficulty of interpreting interactions among variables in analysis of variance suggests that the number of variables used there, too, should be limited.

In the past, many researchers have preferred to study a single independent variable at a time: computation was simpler; statistical formulas for more complex analyses were lacking; it was easier to understand what one was doing and communicate it to others. The first two of these problems have been solved: computers now perform the computations, and statisticians have developed techniques for multivariate analysis. The third remains: it is still hard to communicate complex research designs and their conclusions!

Looking at causation from the *seller's* viewpoint, consider the brewer who knows that a hot spell in July will cause his sales to soar. Hot weather is an unsatisfactory kind of "cause." The brewer can use weather forecasts to plan production, shipping, and advertising, but he can't *produce* a hot spell. So he looks further. He may ask how many people, during a hot spell, seek solace in soft drinks rather than beer. Or he looks beyond the hot spell: people drink something at meals, even if it is only water, and serve something, even if it is only coffee, when their friends drop in. Or the brewer asks why beer seems to be a lower-class drink; is it solely a matter of price? Why does beer tend to be a man's drink? A drink for young people? Why do some people prefer nationally advertised, more expensive premium beers to his regional brand? Why do some prefer a competing regional brand to his?

If the brewer finds that social class and income don't separate beer drinkers from the hard liquor crowd, he may have to look to subtler personality differences. Or he may ask how a taste for beer was learned or how one's family and friends influence beer drinking.

Just as a brewer must decide how far back he wants to go in looking for causes, so must he decide how far forward he wants to go in measuring effects. Ultimately, profit and sales test the wisdom of a seller's choices, but a host of other measures are needed as well. Prospect preferences are used as an effect in *concept testing* when a seller goes to prospects with the description of a new product or the theme for an advertising campaign. Samples of a new brew can be *taste-tested* in a laboratory; trial ads can be tested in door-to-door interviews or be thrown on a screen for captive audiences. Once the product is in production or the ads have been written, they can be placed in *test markets* with inventory checks to test sales, and recognition scores to see whether people remember the ads.

Having specified the causes and results that interest him, a seller (or buyer) must then determine whether in fact the two *are* related. Even if he finds they are, he may have a problem in telling which of the two variables is cause and which is effect.

Sometimes it's easy: we know that biological sex influences selection of TV programs, and that age causes income differences rather than the other way around. Other relations seem probable: if income and magazine readership rise together,

most of us would agree that income is the causal variable. (Even then, we'd be happier if we knew the *process* involved; if we knew that a given income is necessary before one can afford the magazine, or that the job which gives a man his income requires him to read magazines.) Sometimes, however, only research can answer the question.

Once cause and effect have been identified, one must measure the strength of the relationship. Controls are necessary, both in real life and in the laboratory, to make sure that the effects observed are the result of the causes one is studying. These controls are of two kinds. A researcher may test a group before and after exposure to a message, or he may compare the behavior of an experimental group, exposed to the message, with that of a control group, identical in all respects except exposure. Often he does both. The purpose, of course, is to eliminate all possible causes except those one is interested in. (If experimental controls fail, the researcher may be able to use statistical tools to eliminate the undesirable variables.)

In a laboratory, subjects can be assigned to groups by random methods. Since this may not be possible outside the laboratory, a *before test* is used so that each individual can serve as his own control. But if it sensitizes subjects to cake mix ads, a before test will ruin an experiment that seeks to determine the attention-getting power of such ads. A before test may teach subjects new attitudes or cause attitudes to firm up and become resistant to change, rather than determining their existence and strengths. Subjects may try to make answers on the after measure consistent with earlier answers rather than reflect their true opinions. After-test responses may be affected by subtle interactions between the "cause" one is studying, outside events, and the before and after tests. Elaborate research designs, employing several control groups, may be needed to solve these problems.

Problems of the before-test design multiply in a *panel survey* involving a series of interviews with the same persons. *Attrition* sets in: in addition to subjects who refused to participate at the outset, others drop out at each stage through sickness, lack of interest, change of residence, or absence. Usually, factors that cause dropouts are related to what one is studying: persons who lack interest in the subject matter drop out and so do busy and mobile individuals, though these may be of great importance in the study. Attrition, therefore biases results.

Thought, Talk, and Action

1. After outlining at least two alternative responses to these problems, answer the chapter's eight questions concerning unknowns.

   (a) The FTC has ruled that 25% of your advertising space and time for the next year must admit that previous advertising has been ruled untruthful.

   (b) A new water softener boasts that it needs to be serviced only once a year in comparison with yours, which requires monthly service calls.

   (c) An ingredient used in your soft drink has been found to cause cancer in white rats.

2. For each of the problems listed under No. 1, prepare hypothetical findings and present them in two different ways (such as cross-tabulation, average, correlation, index, etc.).

3. Taking each problem in No. 1 as a midpoint in a causal chain, trace it backward at least two steps and forward at least two steps.

Notes

Chapter 11

1. R. T. LaPiere, "Attitudes vs. actions," Social Forces, 13:230–7.
2. C. I. Hovland et al., Communication and persuasion (New Haven: Yale University Press, 1953).
3. James C. Becknell, Jr., "Comment on Webb's case for the effectiveness index," Journal of Advertising Research, 2:4: 42–3.
4. Hans Zeisel, Say it with figures (New York: Harper and Brothers, 1947).
5. *Ibid.*
6. *Ibid.*
7. *Ibid.*
8. Quinn McNemar, Psychological statistics, 3rd ed. (New York: John Wiley & Sons, 1962), pp. 186, 340.

Where Do Causes Lie, in the Individual or the Group?

Sometimes a communicator will use data about groups to characterize their members and sometimes he will gather data about individuals so that he can characterize the groups to which they belong. Sometimes he uses data about individuals to classify groups and then categorizes individuals on the basis of the groups to which they belong.

Here is a hypothetical example which asks which has more influence, the

Individuals	Aggregates

Independent Variables

1. *Housewife.* What is her age, education, personality? What does she know about Brand X? Does she like it? Has she bought and used it? How often and how much?

1. *Nominal data.* How many types of personality are there in neighborhood? What is modal personality?

2. *Other persons.* What is husband's age, education, personality, occupation? What are his beliefs and feelings toward it? Has he used it? How many children and what ages?

2. *Percentages.* What percent of families have children and own home? What percent of wives have college degrees? What percent have *used* Brand X? What percent of husbands *like* Brand X? In what percent of families do wives make decisions? In what percent is husband older than wife?

3. *Interpersonal relations.* Who makes buying decisions about Brand X? How much weight does decision maker give to others' feelings? How much difference in spouses' ages and education?

3. *Averages.* What is average age of housewives, average years schooling, average number of children? How much Brand X is used, on the average, during a year? What is average difference in spouses' years of schooling and age? What is average length of residence in neighborhood?

4. *Household.* (a) How long has family lived in neighborhood? Does it own its home? (b) Are housewife and household typical of neighborhood?

4. *Variation.* What is range of housewives' age and number of children, residence in neighborhood, and use of Brand X?

5. *Demographic.* (a) How is family classified along ethnic, racial, and socioeconomic lines? (b) Does family live in a homogeneous or heterogeneous neighborhood?

5. Are one or several ethnic, racial, and socioeconomic categories represented in neighborhood?

6. Is household located in a neighborhood with many barriers to external communication, but few barriers to internal communication?

6. Does neighborhood aid or impede communication? (a) Do highways, hills, or rivers impede communication outside of neighborhood? (b) Are houses close? Is there a lack of barriers within neighborhood? (c) If present, are neighborhood facilities, such as schools, parks, water supply, roads, adequate? If lacking, does the lack create a motive for interaction?

Dependent Variables

7. (a) Does the housewife see herself as influencing others or being influenced by back-fence communication? How many persons influence her? How many does she influence? How many of the influences in either direction are within and how many outside the neighborhood? (b) Does housewife live in a neighborhood with a high or low rate of influence given or influence received?

7. What is average and range of influence given and received in neighborhood? Are most of messages given or received from inside or outside?

housewife herself or her neighborhood, on the number and kind of messages exchanged and the effects they have on housewifely behavior.

The first four variables listed under *individuals* may be expressed as a type, a percentage, an average, or a measure of variability. These include demographic variables, beliefs, feelings, and behavior. Both raw data, such as age and education, and derived indices, such as similarity between husband and wife in education or age, are included.

With Data in Hand, How Do We Summarize It?

Continuing with the examination of communications among housewives, what does one do with the data that is collected?

Suppose six housewives were allowed to send a minimum of one written message and a maximum of five messages to each of the others. A simple table, like the following hypothetical one, might then report the actual number of messages sent (down columns) and received (across rows).

preferred receiver? The standard deviations show that agreement was highest on Housewife C, lowest on Housewife E.

3. *Which housewife exerted the most pressure on her neighbors?* As the totals at the bottom indicate, F sent 22 messages. D was least "talkative," sending only 13 messages.

4. *Which housewives picked their targets carefully, and which sent out an equal number of messages in all directions?* Standard deviations indicate that D was most careful in choosing her targets, whereas E tended to treat her neighbors alike.

5. *How closely does the number of messages a housewife sends correspond to the number she receives?* This is shown by a coefficient of rank correlation between the 2 sets of scores. It is low and negative ($-.26$) for the group as a whole, and varies from one housewife to the next. (Correlation coefficients for individual housewives are: A.69, B-.22, C-.51, D-.85, E-.29, F-.48.)

6. *How closely do the messages which*

Each Housewife Sent Messages as Shown in Columns:

		A	B	C	D	E	F	Total Received	Standard Deviation
Each Housewife Received	A	—	5	3	3	3	4	18	.80
These Messages from	B	5	—	5	5	4	4	23	.49
Others:	C	3	3	—	3	3	4	16	.40
	D	4	3	4	—	4	5	20	.63
	E	3	4	2	1	—	5	15	1.41
	F	3	4	2	1	3	—	13	1.02
Total sent		18	19	16	13	17	22	105	
Standard deviation		.80	1.43	1.17	1.50	.49	.49		

At least seven comparisons can be made among housewives in this single hypothetical neighborhood.

1. *Which housewife got the most messages?* As totals in the next-to-last column indicate, Housewife B got the most, and Housewife F the fewest.

2. *Did housewives agree on their*

each housewife sends to others correspond with the total number of messages the others receive? Another rank correlation coefficient answers this question: A.27, B.72, C-.74, D-.63, E-.59, and F-.33. Housewife B tends to get many messages from the housewives she herself sends messages to. The reverse is true for C, D, and E.

7. *Do certain pairs of individuals tend to communicate a lot, and others only a little?* This is answered by taking each possible pair, and adding up the messages each sent to the other: A and B are closeknit, with the highest possible score (10); CE and DE are low with mutual scores of only 5.

8. *How "communicative" is this group as a whole?* Its members could have sent 25 messages each, or a total of 150. Actually, they sent a total of 105, or an average of 17.5 each. (They attained 70% of possible.)

Source. Illustration suggested by pages 110–4 of Hans Zeisel, *Say It With Figures* (New York: Harpers, 1957, 4th edition).

Using Readership Scores to Identify Winning Ad Themes

By counting the number of magazine readers who recognized a given advertisement and then quizzing readers on whether they've bought the product advertised during the past week, Daniel Starch obtains what he calls a Netapps (*NET-Ad-Produced-PurchaseS*) score. The score is calculated in this fashion.

Starch suggests that this score can be used to compare new and old campaigns, competitors' campaigns, or media, and in deciding how often to repeat an advertisement. Scores alone, even for a single product, do not predict effectiveness in dollar terms. (See next page.)

The Netapps technique was applied to scores for some 45,000 advertisements in *Life* and the *Saturday Evening Post,* with 400,000 interviews over a 16-year period. As evidence of its validity, Starch reports that the average score for the 352 brands studied was 13.9%, which compares closely with scores in five other studies:

1. A 12.3% average rise in purchases found when a publication began to carry advertisements—ten products.
2. A 14% fall in purchases when a publication stopped carrying ads—80 products.
3. A rise of 11.3% in purchases by readers of an issue with ads as compared to an issue without advertisement—250 cases.
4. Sales 14.3% higher for advertisement readers than nonreaders—426 products.
5. Sales 14.5% higher for advertisement readers than nonreaders, the two

Step One	
Readership score of ad	30%
Percentage of readers who bought product within week	15
Percentage of nonreaders who bought product within week	10

Step Two	
Percentage of buyers among readers (30 × 15)	4.5
Percentage of buyers among nonreaders (10 × 70)	7.0
Total buyers	11.5

Step Three	
Readership x percentage of readers who bought (30 × 15)	4.5
Readership x percentage of readers who would have bought even if they had not seen advertisement (30 × 10)	−3.0
Net percentage assumed to have bought because of advertisement	1.5

Final Step	
Divide net percentage who bought because of advertisement by total number of buyers (1.5/11.5) to get—	13% Netapps Score

Theme	Seen-Associated Score	Netapps Score	Sales Return per Ad Dollar
Colgate toothpaste			
Romance	15.5	.77	$3.80
Brush after eating	10.1	1.06	5.59
Romance and research	10.4	.71	4.23
Campbell's soup			
Frozen soup	38	2.0	$2.99
New soup	64	6.5	6.56
Children	64	5.5	5.47
Ingredients	57	2.3	2.51
Large picture	64	5.1	5.21

groups being paired on preexposure buying rates—898 cases.

One caution in interpreting the Starch results is necessary: the reminder that correlation is not causation. Purchasing a product can lead to readership, or vice versa. A person who has bought a product may be more likely to remember an ad, and memory of an ad may increase the chance that he will remember making the purchase.

Source. Daniel Starch and Staff, *Measuring Product Sales Made by Advertising* (Mamaroneck, New York: Starch, 1961).

Parsnips, Pecan Pie, and Mothers-in-Law

Predictions as to how messages will affect attitudes toward topics and sources are offered by Osgood's *congruity* model, with attitudes measured on a seven-point scale that runs from strong dislike (− 3) to strong like (+ 3). Here is an example, dealing with attitudes toward seven different foodstuffs and seven different message sources, each source being able to argue for (+) or against (−) a given food.

These are the author's attitudes *before* any messages are transmitted:

	Product	Source
3	Pecan pie	Wife
2	Ice cream	Doctor
1	Hamburger	Advertisement
0	Bread	Stranger
−1	Turnips	Waitress
−2	Liver	Brother-in-law
−3	Parsnips	Mother-in-law

Balance is achieved when source and object have identical point scores. If the source says he *likes* an object, then the two scores will be on the same side of the neutral midpoint; if the source says he *dislikes* an object, the two final scores must be on the opposite sides of the neutral midpoint.

In achieving balance, Osgood suggests that the one which is farthest from the midpoint—the one toward which I have most extreme opinions—will move *least*. He hypothesizes that the *source's* proportion of the total distance from the midpoint determines how far the *object* travels and vice versa. One first figures the amount of movement necessary to achieve balance. (When linked positively, by a word such as "cause" or "like," this is the original distance between the two items on the scale. When linked negatively, by a word such as "dislike" or "prevent," assume that one item remains fixed and that the other moves to the same value on the opposite side of the midpoint. This indicates the total distance to be shared between the two items.)

To calculate the *proportion* of this distance that each item must travel, one adds scale points of the two items ignoring signs. This represents 100%. If an item's percentage of this total is labeled *p,* then the proportion of the distance it travels is represented by 100-*p.*

No movement occurs if the objects are already in balance: if my wife (3) praises pecan pie (3) or my brother-in-law (— 2) praises liver (— 2). If the stranger, toward who I am neutral, praises ice cream, he takes on its value (2); if he praises liver, he falls to its level (— 2).

On the other hand, if my wife praises anything less desirable than herself, she falls slightly and it rises slightly. Let us suppose she praises hamburger; balance requires a total movement by both wife and hamburger of two points. My wife has a 3-point rating and hamburger rates 1-point distant, for a total of 4 points. My wife moves one-fourth (100–75%) of the distance; since one-fourth of 2 is a half-point, she falls from a rating of 3 to 2–1/2, and hamburger rises to meet her.

If my doctor (2) praises liver (— 2), they share the distance between them equally and both end up at the midpoint. However, if my doctor (2) praises turnips (— 1), turnips benefit most: they move 2/3 of the distance which separates the two, crossing the midpoint to a rating of 1.

Balance exists and no change occurs if my doctor disapproves liver, my wife dislikes parsnips, or my mother-in-law dislikes pecan pie. The stranger, however, who rose to 2 when he said he *likes* ice cream, falls to — 2 if he *dislikes* it. Similarly, the neutrally valued object,

bread, falls to — 2 if disapproved by my doctor (2) or rises to 2 if rejected by my brother-in-law (— 2).

Statements of disapproval or rejection make me more favorable toward a source and an object I originally disliked, and less favorable toward a source and an object I liked.

Suppose, for example, that my mother-in-law (— 3) were to turn up her nose at liver (— 2). Since something my mother-in-law dislikes must have some good in it, my opinion of liver changes. In fact, liver, being in the less extreme position, would gain most. When a mother-in-law (— 3) rejects liver, liver must move from its original position of — 2 across the midpoint to 3 or my mother-in-law must move to 2. (In either case, a distance of 5 points.) However, liver will move only three-fifths (100–40%) of this distance to a scale reading of 1. My mother-in-law will move 2/5 of 5, to a scale reading of — 1; thus balance, defined as equal-but-opposite scores, is achieved.

Let my doctor (2) sneer at pecan pie (3), however, and both will fall: pie by 2/5 of the distance, and the doctor by 3/5, so that he arrives at a new reading of — 1 and pie at a reading of 1. By similar reasoning, if an advertisement should attack pecan pie (3), the advertisement will suffer most; it will travel three-fourths of the 4-point distance, so that it lands at — 2, while pie falls to 2.

Real-Life Complexities

In real life, of course, the situation becomes immensely more complex. Osgood has made adjustments for two such complications. One is an adjustment for sheer disbelief; I may disbelieve a message in which my doctor praises parsnips, or my mother-in-law rejects them, or one in which an advertiser condemns his own product.

When a highly credible source is credited with a message that seems inconsistent with our attitude toward the source, we may suspect that the source has been misquoted. Or we may reinterpret what was said.

The second adjustment Osgood made, the *assertion constant,* allows greater attitude change toward the object of the message than its source. My attitude toward the waitress is more affected— Osgood suggests .17 of a scale point more—when she is praised by my brother-in-law than when she praises him.

The congruity model shows how salesmen, starting at a neutral position with a new customer, gradually build up their own position by finding out what the customer likes and indicating that they like it, too. Sharing customer dislikes will have similar effect. Then the salesman can transfer some of his attitude points toward new objects which are neutral or lower on the scale than he himself.

Source. Based on Charles E. Osgood et al., *The Measurement of Meaning* (Urbana: University of Illinois Press, 1957).

Additional Research Readings

Creativity. When asked how to lure more tourists to the United States and how to meet a need for teachers, individuals working alone averaged 64 suggestions. Those who started in a group and then worked alone averaged 55; those who began alone then went into groups averaged 53; and those who worked only in groups produced 43. **George S. Rotter and Stephen M. Portugal, "Group and individual effects in problem solving," Journal of Applied Psychology, 53:338–41.** Inferiority of group to individual in suggesting benefits and problems of an extra thumb became more marked as groups increased from five to seven to nine members. **Thomas J. Bouchard, Jr., and Melana Hare, "Size, performance and potential in brainstorming groups," Journal of Applied Psychology, 54:51–5.**

Consistency. Ratings of TV commercials predict attitudes to products better than do previous product ratings, attitudes, or product-commercial congruity predictions. **James J. Mullen, "The congruity principle and television commercials," Journal of Broadcasting, 7:35–42.** Balance theory was upset when 95 students predicted outcome of a prison escape attempt, a druggist's recommendation of a drug for arthritis, or a newcomer's selection of laundromat and dry cleaner. **Robert S. Wyer, Jr., and John D. Lyon, "A test of cognitive balance theory implications for social inference processes," Journal of Personality and Social Psychology, 16:598–618.** When messages increased belief in the minor premise of a syllogism, consistency was restored by increased belief in its conclusion but not by the theoretical alternative of decreased belief in the major premise. **Sam G. McFarland and Donald L. Thistlethwaite, "An analysis of a logical consistency model of belief change," Journal of Personality and Social Psychology, 15:133–43.**

• Business firms spend far more time and money in a conscious, detailed, and systematic study of more causes, more effects, and more complex combinations of the two than do consumers. Business firms, therefore, will be the focus of this chapter.

• They use more diversified sources of data: secondary sources, in-house sources, surveys, field experiments, and laboratory experiments. The more of these sources they use in a study, the better results they are likely to get, from a scientific point of view. From a business viewpoint, they should use as many sources as will pay off in improved decision making.

• A major problem in data gathering is that of preventing the measurement process from affecting the responses one is measuring. Bias may arise from the respondent, the interviewer, and the questions used. Each of the five sources of data has its advantages and disadvantages; each produces different results, subtly changing the goal of research in the process of attaining it.

• Concealment of sponsor is important in a survey; concealment of purpose is important in an experiment. Without concealment, each, however elaborate, tends to collapse into a simple question: *Do you like me?*

• To prove that he has eliminated bias or to compensate statistically for what bias remains, the experimenter varies his treatment of randomized groups so that he can separate the effects of concurrent environmental change, experimental events and any tests which, occurring prior to the experimental events, may interact with them to magnify effects. Comparable results are achieved in surveys by using different types of questions and comparing the results achieved by different interviewers and different coders of the responses to "open" (unstructured-response) questions.

• Bias that either magnifies or minimizes a cause-effect relationship may be introduced in either survey or experiment by the way the study selects subjects or the way subjects select themselves at the start of the study or while it is going on; elimination of subjects during analysis may also introduce bias as may failure to eliminate them.

Research Articles

Lab vs. Field.   Results differ because of differences in receivers, sources, issues, and time span (Hovland); results alter when study moves from home to laboratory (O'Rourke).

Hawthorne Effect. Knowledge that they are subjects alters individuals' behavior (Homans), but design using three control groups can isolate effect (Selltiz).

Self-Reports. Subjects' report of change in own views fails to match reality (Fink).

Chapter 12 Data for Decision Making

Nowhere is the contrast greater between the firm—either buyer or seller—and the consumer—either individual or household—than in the gathering of data to satisfy the "unknowns" of the decision-making process. The firm gathers more diversified kinds of data and analyzes them more systematically than the consumer, who lacks both the ability and the desire for extended and systematic search and analysis.

A consumer decides that this lemon "tastes good" or that record "sounds nice" and makes a simple, two-valued decision: he buys or he does not. The firm, however, must know exactly what amounts of which chemicals produce what degree of liking on a "tastes-good" scale among how many prospects; it then can fashion a number of different alternatives at different costs (and prices) for different market segments.

A consumer takes his tastes for granted, whether wired-in at birth or acquired through experience; barely conscious that they exist, he seldom attempts to analyze them. The firm, however, profits from understanding how the consumer's sensory apparatus works and may systematically vary prospect, stimuli, situation, and method of measurement in a study of the tasting process.

A consumer often spends little time in search and comparison since he perceives that rival brands really don't differ very much on the dimensions of choice that he feels to be important. Similarly, he seldom spends much time in trying to determine whether the cues he uses to index the presence and measure the degree of such dimensions are either accurate or optimal. The firm, on the other hand, finds the cumulative effects of offhand consumer decisions to be very important. It gives a great deal of attention to the "minor" differences between its brand and rival brands. Its chemists work hard to develop accurate indices of product dimensions. Its consumer research staff works equally hard to discover what cues the buyer uses.

The consumer tends to favor simple cause-and-effect relationships; his causes tend to be few in number and direct and immediate in their effects. The firm, on the other hand, usually recognizes that any given effect has many causes, some remote in time and operating through intermediates. In designing research, as well as in actual decision making, the firm must decide how many causes to examine and asks of each possible cause: How much impact does this cause have on the result? How much is it subject to my manipulation?

Therefore, the discussion in this chapter will apply primarily to the firm rather than the consumer.

Decisions in Designing Research

The goals of research, the causes and effects to be examined, are specified when one lists unknowns. He then must decide *how* this examination is to be made. Sales—a measure of the effects of a marketing mix—can be counted by subtracting a grocer's current inventories from original supplies and shipments, by counting brands on pantry shelves, by asking consumers to keep monthly diaries of their purchases, or by sending interviewers from door to door. Each method is likely to give a different result. Which method is *best* depends on how the results are to be used. (Usually several methods provide more information than any single one; whether such additional information improves decision making sufficiently to recapture its cost must be determined.)

Here are three examples of data collection by means of the survey.

The phone rings, and, after a suitable introduction, a voice at the other end asks: *Do you believe that washing machines need fewer repairs today than they used to, about the same, or more?*

There is a knock at the door, and an interviewer asks: *How did you feel the last time your washing machine broke down?*

A questionnaire arrives in the mail: *Do you plan to buy a new washing machine within the next twelve months?*

Three methods of asking questions: telephone interview, mail questionnaire, face-to-face poll. Three types of attitudes: beliefs, feelings, actions. Three time periods: present, past, and future.

Which method of gathering data is best? Each is appropriate for some functions, inappropriate for others.

The survey is only one research method. Data also may be gathered in laboratory experiments and experiments in the field, from the United States census and other secondary sources, and from such in-house data as sales reports and warranty cards returned by purchasers. Each has its place: the *laboratory experiment* allows a researcher to introduce and exclude stimuli at will and specify the order in which they will appear. He can create laboratory analogues of real-life situations or use novel tasks and novel situations to eliminate the effects of previous habits.

He can get subjects to play a role, in favor of a point of view contrary to their own and see how this affects beliefs. He can induce feelings, through hypnotism, to see how they affect actions, or he can create stressful situations and see how they affect feelings. With a tachistoscope, he can determine the "readability" of a new brand name by exposing it for a few seconds. The major drawback of the laboratory experiment is that many subjects cannot be induced to come. (The great majority of laboratory subjects are college sophomores and white rats.) This limits the experiment to problems in which audience differences are not important.

In a *field experiment,* an experimental message may be delivered to real-life audiences in real-life settings by ordinary channels, without their knowing that anything unusual is going on. (The *split-run,* which randomly divides the mailing list of a newspaper or magazine into comparable audiences, and sends each audience an issue with a different advertisement, is an example. This is a good method of determining advertisements' attention-getting ability. A laboratory in which subjects can be forced to attend to the advertisements may be better in studying ad credibility.)

Allowing people to decide whether or not they will expose themselves to a message means that audience differences as well as variations in the message will affect results. Yet if one asks a random sample to receive a message, it becomes impossible to measure the attention-getting power of the message. In addition, readers may start acting as they think "experts" are supposed to act. An ingenious solution to this problem is to ask a random sample *not* to receive the message. They then can act as a *control* group for the rest of the population. Both field and laboratory experiment help a researcher find which variables are most important from a cause-and-effect standpoint. To discover which variables are frequent or rare, he must use the survey method.

Most advertising research, in fact, has been *survey research.* The researcher needs to be sure that all relevant variables are present, but does not care too much whether he knows what they are since he is less interested in establishing long-run principles than in settling an immediate problem.

Obtaining representative audiences, a drawback of the laboratory experiment, is also a problem in surveys. Interviewers, whether face-to-face or telephone, have even more difficulty than salesmen in getting past a secretary to see a business executive; a mail questionnaire may land on his desk but this does not mean it will get answered.

Secondary data is often used to determine how many prospects live in a given market area; the United States census reports their occupations and education, income and age—which help one estimate how much of a product they will buy or provide one with the information needed to design the sample for a field survey. (*Sales Management's* annual survey tells us what proportion of the nation's buying power resides in a given market area by combining three percentages: the area's percent of population, given a weight of two; its percent of retail sales, given a weight of three; and its percent of buying income, given a weight of five.) Most magazines, many broadcasters, and some newspapers will supply details about their audiences, even to the point of their actual product and brand purchases. (Such data must be used with caution since no advertising medium is likely to finance an audience survey that will reveal its shortcomings.)

Past events, such as pottery making among the prehistoric cliff dwellers or trade in medieval Germany, can only be reconstructed through surviving artifacts or documents. Designed for other purposes, such records include much irrelevant data and omit much that is needed in decision making. Moreover, surface appearances may be deceiving, such a sudden rise in births, deaths, or crime may merely reflect improvements in gathering data. Current records often provide a check upon the validity of survey data.

In-house data, the sales and other records that a firm accumulates in the normal course of business, provide data that is free, except for the analysis. (Balance sheets and other summaries, designed for comptroller, tax man, or production engineer, may not serve marketing needs; usually original data must be reanalyzed.) Analysis of in-house data and review of available secondary data should precede the design of the survey or the experiment. A successful experiment or survey may lead to routine collection of new types of data by the firm or, more often, by purchase from a commercial research firm.

Research itself is a form of communications. In selling, one selects source, message, and channel so as to have maximum impact upon a receiver's responses. In research, one does just the opposite: if one's research messages (questions) are to measure the effects of marketing mix or advertising, questions must be as neutral as possible. This means one must determine what is going on inside the mind of a respondent, either by comparing his answers to different kinds of questions and interviewers or by comparing different persons' responses to question and interviewer.

Every question, Getzels suggests, arouses two responses: an internal response, followed by an overt one.[1] Sometimes the two are identical; sometimes they are not.

An interviewer asks, *Do you like meeting strangers?* and the respondent thinks, *No, strangers make me feel nervous and inferior.* What he says aloud depends on who is asking the question.

To his psychiatrist he says, *Strangers make me feel nervous and inferior,* for he anticipates a permissive reaction. The pollster, asking the same question, gets an equivocal answer: *It depends on the strangers.* (Obviously the pollster doesn't object to meeting strangers and the respondent hesitates to admit his own weakness.) But the personnel man, who is interviewing him for a job, gets a forthright: *Strangers are all right. Actually, I enjoy meeting them.* (Again, the respondent disguises his true feelings, fearing he wouldn't be hired if the interviewer knew how he really feels.)

Just as questions must be carefully worded, so must interviewers be carefully selected, trained, and supervised—a turn of phrase, a tone of voice, or the lift of an eyebrow may alter a respondent's answers.

If an observer merely notes the results of behavior that is already over and done with by a person no longer on the scene, obviously the observer cannot influence that behavior, although his own biases will affect his report. (An example in point is an assessment of the popularity of museum exhibits based on the frequency with which floor tile in their vicinity has to be replaced.)

Bias is also minimized when persons whose behavior is being observed are not aware of the observation. Thus a *participant observer* mingles with a work group or a gang of delinquents; in Britain, inconspicuous bystanders near newsstands and on subways watched people purchase and read publications. Concealing themselves behind a one-way window, which looks like a mirror to their subjects, psychologists observe children at play, adults leafing through magazines, and group conferences.

One ingenious experimenter measures attitudes toward offbeat groups by "losing" letters addressed to them on the street, and then counts the number of letters that passersby pick up and mail, rather than destroy.[2] Others send a confederate ahead to sit on an already occupied park bench, then approach in the guise of an inquiring reporter. They first question the naive subject, then the confederate, who ridicules the first speaker's views.[3] The purpose, of course, is to determine natural reactions to ridicule. In neither example is the respondent likely to realize he has participated in an experiment; respondent bias is thereby eliminated.

By choosing time and place carefully, a researcher may not need to intervene—merely observe. Some events recur regularly: the traffic jam at quitting time is an example. Other events are announced in advance: the student of mob behavior can count on sales at certain large stores in New York to produce grist for his mill. When a researcher would have to wait far too long for an event to occur naturally, he may intervene, either by causing events to happen (an experiment) or asking questions (a survey).

The events that he makes happen in a field experiment are ideal, in that they happen to people representative of the population and they occur in a real-life context. The events themselves are identical with those his findings will affect and the subjects are unaware that any experiment is being conducted. However, such events require the cooperation of businessmen, which may be hard to get even if they are paying for the research. As a result, field experiments are rare and often costly. Although the laboratory experiment uses unrepresentative subjects and events that simulate rather than duplicate real-life happenings, it is inexpensive and fast, and can be replicated over and over to verify results and develop theory. Random assignments of subjects and control over the order of events can prevent confusion between cause and effect or entry of a third variable.

Cause and Effect in the Laboratory

To stage an experiment, one must find laboratory equivalents of real-world events: powerful causes and sensitive effects that will reveal measurable cause-effect relationships in a brief time with a relatively small number of subjects. Hunger has been manipulated by letting a subject drink milk, injecting milk or a salt solution into his stomach, or slicing through part of his brain.[4] An unpleasant initiation into a fraternity can be simulated by requiring coeds to read obscene words aloud to a male experimenter or making subjects do 30 push-ups.[5] Results also have several laboratory analogues. Degrees of hunger, for instance, may be indexed by counting stomach contractions or the rate at which an animal will press a bar that delivers food, by measuring the amount of food consumed or the amount of quinine in food that will be tolerated.[6]

A plausible cover story must then be devised that makes the manipulations and measures seem sensible without revealing what the experiment is all about. (Most subjects, particularly college students, are docile to the point of disbelief. In one study, subjects performed a very dull task, tore their answer sheets into 32 pieces, and so on for several hours, making few errors, continuing at a steady rate of speed, and showing little outward hostility. In others, subjects have been willing to continue administering electric shocks to a confederate of the experimenter while he screamed, kicked, and begged to be turned loose.)[7]

Asking housewives to rate TV commercials or other advertisements is unwise: their answers may reflect what they think they should like and one fails to assess one of the most important factors in a commercial's success: its ability to attract attention. Instead, Schwerin asks audiences into a theater to preview TV pilot *programs*. Should you win a prize in our drawing, they are asked, which of these products and brands would you choose? At the end of the viewing, the question is repeated. Since a commercial for the sponsor's brand has been shown along with the "test" program, any increase in preference for this brand is attributed to this commercial.

It is difficult to vary only one factor in an experiment. When electric shocks were substituted for obscene words in the severity-of-initiation study, the study had to be described as one of emotionality rather than embarrassment and the discussion topic shifted from sex to cheating. Both obscene words and electric shock, it was assumed, would make subjects uncomfortable. Those most uncomfortable, it was hypothesized, would value membership in the group more than those given a milder initiation. Electric shock and obscenity *did* increase attraction to the group, but was discomfort involved? Asking subjects might reveal the purpose of the experiment, but a physiological indicator of discomfort, like sweating palms, is one that subjects cannot consciously control and usually are unaware of.

Another choice for an experimenter is that of *show* or *tell:* should he *tell* subjects that his confederates are likable people, or *show* them these assistants doing likable things? Showing presumably has greater impact—provided subjects interpret events as intended, something the experimenter needs to check on.[8] Similarly, one needs to see if subjects really expected to get a promised reward or give a threatened speech. The way effects are measured may determine whether a given experiment succeeds; a face-to-face interview has found significant results although a self-administered questionnaire did not.[9]

Concealing a Study's Purpose

Whether given a plausible explanation or not, the subject is likely to supply his own explanation, which may enhance, inhibit, or have no effect on the results. One solution is to make the subject think he is participating in *two* experiments, not one. (In one such study, subjects were paid varying sums to perform a dull task.[10] A little later another experimenter asked them to rate various pop records. Explaining that their current moods would affect their ratings, he asked them what they'd done during the day and how they enjoyed it, as a means of controlling for mood. In actuality, these ratings, a measure of subjects' response to the dull task, were the real purpose.) Another solution is to persuade a subject that he is a confederate of the experimenter and that someone else is the real subject.

It is often necessary to conceal the purpose of an experiment from those *running* the experiment since, without knowledge or desire to do so, experimenters may misread results or mislead subjects through subtle cues that indicate what they expect to happen. (One study asked subjects to rate 20 pictures of people.[11] Half the experimenters were told the persons pictured were successful and half that they were failures. Subjects rated the photographs in line with the experimenters' expectations, even though a study of sound films of the experiments could detect no cues to such expectations.) Even rats randomly assigned have proved "bright" or "dull" in a learning task, in line with what experimenters had been led to expect.[12] A good solution to such bias is to tell an experimenter the general purpose of the study but conceal whether the particular subjects he is running are in a control or experimental condition. This *double blind* design is used when sugar pills are mixed with real drugs so that neither patients nor their doctors know who is getting which.

All these precautions may fail, however; it is important to measure effects of extraneous features so that what one has failed to control experimentally can be controlled after the fact through statistical adjustments.

The scholar seeking cause-and-effect relationships has a choice of starting his search with an observed effect or a possible cause and of observing differences in space or time. If an individual buys one brand today and another one next week, the scholar can ask what happened to cause this change. Or, starting with a cause, he can ask whether, on a given day, senior citizens and teen-agers pick different items from a restaurant menu.

"Before" Tests and Control Groups

Perhaps the simplest way to determine whether reading an ad or using a product

has affected people is to measure their knowledge and preferences before and afterward. If we find that only 35% favored a brand before viewing a commercial or tasting a sample and 65% afterward, we may credit ad or sample with the change. We may be wrong: our biggest competition may have produced a product or commercial so foul it made ours look good!

To overcome this danger, the experimenter turns to the control group. Using a table of random numbers he divides his subjects into two groups; one sees the commercial, the other does not. He compares scores of the two groups.

For even greater certainty, the experimenter combines these two methods and gives before and after tests to experimental and control groups.

The *before* test, which tells whether experimental and control groups are equivalent to begin with (and allows one to adjust for any differences he finds), may cause trouble. It may sensitize members to the message or experience that follows and so increase or decrease its effectiveness. To settle this question, an elaborate design involving *four* groups has been devised. Effects in one group are caused only by outside events; in a second group by outside events and one's message; in a third by outside events and one's *before* measure. Subtracting effects of the first group from each of the others will isolate separate effects of the message and the *before* measure. All three effects—of outside events, message, and *before measure*—can then be subtracted from results observed in the fourth group. Any effects remaining must be a result of the interaction among the three elements.

Bias in Surveys

Even in experiments, with all their controls, experimenters, with all their training, may bias results without desiring to do so or realizing they have done so. This may occur even if experimenters are kept in the dark as to how subjects are expected to behave; their personality, skill, and sex may alter results. (Male experimenters, for example, appear more friendly toward subjects than do female experimenters.)[13]

In surveys, the danger of respondent bias due to the questions and the people who ask them is even greater. In addition, there is the danger of interviewer bias. Some examples: transients interviewed by a prohibitionist consistently blamed liquor for their plight; those interviewed by a socialist blamed social conditions.[14] Interviewers favoring prefab housing were more likely to find respondents favorable to such housing than were interviewers who opposed such housing.[15]

Age, class, color, and religious background of the interviewer all have been shown to influence the answers he gets.[16] Middle class interviewers, for example, found 59% of their respondents favored a law against sit-down strikes; only 44% of those interviewed by members of the working-class agreed. Adolescents admitted more disobedience of parents' rules to young interviewers than to older ones. When southern Negroes during World War II were asked, *Do you think it more important to beat the Axis or to make democracy work here at home?*, white interviewers reported 62% favored beating the Axis; black interviewers reported only 39%. Interviewers with Jewish names and Jewish appearance found less prejudice against Jews than did those who appeared Jewish but had Gentile names. Interviewers who lacked both Jewish names and Jewish looks found most prejudice of all.

Types of Questions

The extent to which an interviewer's attributes and attitude influence respondents varies with the kinds of questions he asks. A free-response or *open-end* question such as *What do you do when you have a headache?* or *What does the term "fair trade" mean to you?* invites the respondent to reply in his own words. The length of his answer will be limited by his knowledge and interest in the subject. The *amount* of encouragement an interviewer gives a respondent will affect the length of the answer; the *kind* of encouragement he gives will affect its nature. If the interviewer writes down the "sense" of the answer, rather than recording it verbatim, further bias creeps in. Still more bias is likely when such answers are coded into categories for punching on IBM cards.

Structured questions, such as *When you have a headache, do you take aspirin, some other medicine or nothing at all?* or *Do you favor or are you opposed to fair trade laws?*, eliminate much of such bias and save time for the respondent, who is more likely to continue to the end. They save interviewer time, and so are cheaper; they require less care in selecting interviewers and training them, which further reduces costs.

Both closed and open questions may suffer from ambiguity. (During World War II, persons who said they hoped postwar conditions would be the same as prewar were actually thinking of seven different kinds of conditions, ranging from technology to politics, employment levels to consumer goods. Obviously, it would have been better to ask seven questions rather than one.) The open-end question fails to get comparable data across persons and is difficult to code and summarize.

At least one open question is desirable in any interview, to give a respondent a chance to "sound off" in his own words; this opportunity may motivate him. Closed questions are bad if they omit a reply respondents want to make, or if the respondent lacks the knowledge or the attitude the researchers are seeking! The man without an opinion can always select an alternative at random to get the job over.

Perhaps the best data are obtained by using both types of questions, as suggested by George Gallup. Here is such a series.

1. *What does the term "fair trade law" mean to you?*

This is a screening question used to qualify a prospect. If the term has no meaning for a respondent, one can skip to the next topic. If a great many respondents have no meaning for the term, one may have to drop the survey or begin the interview by defining the term. Such screening questions are often used in opinion surveys and readership surveys.

2. *What if anything, do you think Congress should do about Supreme Court decisions declaring such laws null and void?*

Another *open* question, this is used in the early stages of a study to find out what responses need to be included in a structured questionnaire. It is also used to discover which response is salient—which first comes to mind. A salient brand name is likely to be purchased, but a salient belief need not dominate respondent behavior.

3. *Do you approve or disapprove of an amendment to the Constitution that would permit "fair trade" laws?*

This forced-choice question seeks to prevent an in-between or a don't-know response. (A less restrictive multiple-choice or "cafeteria" question might offer five responses instead of two.) Another way of handling the respondent who refuses to choose is to ask: *You say you have not decided which make of car you like best. But which do you tend to favor at this moment?*

4. *How strong are your feelings (or) how certain are you of your reply: very strong (or certain), fairly strong (or certain), not at all strong (or certain)?*

This *intensity* question helps predict whether approval will be acted upon and how likely a subject is to resist pressure from other messages, events, or sellers. The seller who wants to influence behavior, however, needs to ask one more question.

5. *WHY do you feel this way?*

Thus, Gallup's series ends as it began, with an *open* question which may reveal that persons who agree on what they want desire it for different reasons. The answers can lead to a new survey and provide hypotheses for further research.

As this example suggests, the *order* in which questions are asked is important; each question may be interpreted in the context of the questionnaire as a whole, the setting in which it is asked, and its sponsor.

The first questions asked should be easy to answer, interest the respondent, and impress him with the importance of the interview. Since the motivation the questions provide affects the rate of refusals, they should make the effort demanded appear as small as possible. Many interviews start by asking the respondent to express an opinion since this is easy to do and most persons like to do it. Related items should be grouped so that a subject does not have to switch frequently from one frame of reference to another.

Sensitive questions, such as those concerning the size of the respondent's income, are often left to the very end. If the purpose of a questionnaire is to gather facts, then starting with an opinion question may be unwise, since the subject may misperceive subsequent questions about facts as being requests for opinions.

Since there is a tendency to choose the first alternative offered, it is wise to alternate the order of responses. This is particularly important in polar-adjective rating scales such as "good—bad" or "like—dislike." Favorable and unfavorable ends should be reversed from one scale to the next and, for any given scale, from one questionnaire to the next.

Effects of Subject Matter

Respondents tend to exaggerate things they think society approves of—like gifts to the United Fund and airplane travel—and to be reluctant to report behavior that they perceive is disapproved. Reports of expenditures on rent, automobiles, and medical care tend to be accurate, but much less liquor use is reported than records show exists. (Such comparisons permit inferences as to how people perceive social norms.)

Knowledge of systematic biases like the following guides researchers in designing and interpreting questionnaires. When records are not available, asking the same question in several different ways may catch such distortions.

In World War II, 47% of upper-income respondents were willing to admit they'd cashed a war bond during the past week, as compared with only 7% of lower-income respondents, even though the only persons questioned were those who *had* cashed in bonds.[17] Upper-income respondents tend to be more accurate than others in reporting savings accounts, less accurate in reporting automobile and cash loans. Private opinions often differ from those that people are willing to express publicly. When Methodists in New York State were asked whether their bishop had made real efforts to help them, 92% of respondents told a pollster he had. But when they put their answers into a sealed ballot box, only 31% of them agreed.[18]

A check of interview results against store records shows that accuracy in reporting the purchase date of a washing machine or the date of household repairs decreases over time. The proportion of visits to doctors drops by one-third within two weeks; 93% of actual hospital visits are reported within the first 20 weeks, but only 70% after 41 weeks.[19]

Here are results of 900 interviews in a single community, showing proportion of respondents giving inaccurate reports.[20]

Contributions to Community Chest	40%
Voting and registration	25
Age	17
Ownership of library card, driver's license	10
Ownership of home, auto, or telephone	2–4

The way a question is phrased can shape results. A question such as *You like Del Monte pineapple, don't you?* demands an affirmative answer. But even a question such as *Do you like Del Monte pineapple?* has an affirmative bias; it would be better to add *or don't you?* (And a question that asks whether one likes Del Monte pineapple better than Ann Page pineapple, or Del Monte pineapple better than Del Monte peaches has more relevance to real-world decision making.)

Use of evaluative terms is an obvious way and thus perhaps the least dangerous way of influencing attitudes. A more subtle error occurs when a question joins into a single category elements that a respondent feels are very different, or splits up elements he regards as identical. Not everyone, for example, regards riots and strikes as the same thing, although some persons will have no difficulty in responding to the question, *Should strikes and riots be outlawed?* Others will find it difficult to make such a choice as *Would you rather buy a new car or send your son to college?* (A respondent may be willing to outlaw riots but not strikes or may have every intention of buying a new car *and* sending his son to college.)

If the set of responses provided omits an alternative that the respondent prefers, his response will have poor predictive power. If the response set includes responses that would not spontaneously occur to him, the question may change his attitude, rather than measure it.

Words cause trouble when they mean different things to different respondents or have so little meaning to any of them that they produce many *no opinion* and *don't know* answers.

Minor differences in wording may produce drastic differences in results. Here are three questions reported by Zeisel.[21]

1. Which of these three magazines is your favorite?
2. If you could have but one of these three magazines, which would you keep for yourself?
3. Which one of these three magazines do you like best?

They sound almost the same—but the first question gave top score to magazine A, the second to magazine B, and the third to magazine C!

Changing a single word changed the meaning of this question: *Do you think anything _____ be done to make it easier for people to pay doctor or hospital bills?*[22] When *should* was inserted in the blank, 82% said yes; with *could* inserted, 77% said yes; and with *might* inserted, 63% said yes. On another occasion, 92% of respondents said hospital insurance was a good idea, but only 66% said they themselves would like it. (The *good idea* question might be fine in a public opinion poll, but a salesman looking for prospects would certainly prefer the second.)

Words high on the ladder of abstraction, like industry and labor, permit a great deal of variation among respondents in the referents they include. To add to the difficulty, abstract words often have a high evaluative content—either positive, like "freedom" and "American," or negative, like "dictatorship" and "Communism."

Four Rules of Thumb

Four rules of thumb can help one choose the best word for a question, as in Payne's search for a suitable middle term in a set of three responses: *good, _____, poor.*[23]

1. How many different meanings does each alternative have? Barnhart's American College Dictionary lists 16 meanings for the adjective *fair*, in addition to the one, *moderately good*, in which we are interested. It lists one meaning for the adjective *medium*. Payne's rule: *Choose the word with the fewest meanings.*

2. What shades of meaning does each alternative term possess? The word *fair*, may *denote* an equitable state of affairs, a blonde complexion, a *state fair*, or a state between good and bad. The synonym *ordinary* has a below-average *connotation* while the synonym *normal* seems to carry a favorable connotation. Payne's rule: *Choose the word least likely to cause denotative confusion or connotative bias.*

3. How familiar is each alternative—how often do people use it? A count of 4.5 million words, taken from 12 issues of five popular magazines published from 1927 through 1938, found 1526 uses of *fair* and 119 uses of *medium*. Payne's rule: *Choose the most familiar word.*

4. How *long* is each alternative? Words of many syllables are usually harder to read and pronounce and usually appear well down on any list showing frequency of use. Payne's rule: *Choose the shortest word.*

To prevent people from overclaiming socially approved behaviors, such as reading good books and giving to charity, we may have to keep them from losing face: *Have you had time to read a book in the last week?* or *Have you made a gift to the United Fund yet?* We may be able to prevent them from concealing disapproved activity through questions which indicate that many people *do* get parking tickets or argue with their wives, and that the interviewer won't be shocked.

The nearer questions can come to suggesting the situation in which behavior will occur, the better. *You do not really expect* a raise in pay this year, do you? obviously suggests the answer "no"—but if that is the way the boss will phrase the question, then that's the way the interviewer may want to ask it. Or look at these questions:

Do you personally favor violent or nonviolent settlement of international disputes?

If war came, would you volunteer for military service, wait to be drafted, or seek alternative service as a conscientious objector?

Are you going to defend your country like a man or be a dirty draft dodger?

The second question seems to be the least biased. The first would probably produce a 99% majority in favor of nonviolence. If we are trying to predict the number of conscientious objectors during a war, however, the third question will probably be best, since it's the kind of language a draft board is likely to use. The man who can't face a question like this probably has not got what it takes to be a conscientious objector.

Privacy in an interview and anonymity in a mail questionnaire, as well as careful questions and a permissive interviewer, encourage truthful answers in sensitive areas. Sometimes, however, even these do not suffice.

In the laboratory, instruments can detect physiological indices of emotional reactions (such as sweating palms and widening pupils) which the respondent can't control and is often unaware he is making.

Another technique is that of *word association* in which respondents, given a series of stimulus words, are asked to respond with the first word that pops into their minds. Since statistics are available on "normal" responses, any unusual responses can easily be identified. If a respondent *blocks*—delaying his reply or being unable to think of a response—this indicates something out of the ordinary, too.

An indirect form of questioning some-

times used in measuring attitudes is that of *error choice*.[24] This measure appears to be a test of factual knowledge—asking how much a Rolls Royce costs, or how many different brands a supermarket stocks, or how far one has to travel to a lake resort—but none of the responses offered is correct. Some exaggerate and others underestimate. The choice that a respondent makes thus is assumed to reflect his attitude toward the object in question.

A third-person or *projective question* is also used in marketing. The prospect is asked how he thinks other people think, feel, or act about a given product. *Describe the sort of a person who borrows from a household finance company,* he is told. Or, *Why do you think some people refuse to ride in an airplane?* Since the ordinary person is unlikely to have any solid information on either of these subjects, it is assumed that his answers will reveal his own attitudes. Such questions can be asked in structured form by a checklist that asks which words best describe people who borrow from small-loan companies: *Extravagant, poor planners, thrifty, careless, rich, residents of a ghetto, uninformed, tightfisted.*

Questions may also be asked in the form of pictures and cartoons. Murray's *Thematic Apperception Test* presents a series of ambiguous-looking pictures and asks the respondent to describe the people and tell what they are doing. Rosenzweig's *Picture Frustration Test* offers a series of cartoons showing persons in frustrating situations and asks the respondent what he thinks they are saying to one another. (This test is particularly useful in a day when cars and appliances are prone to break down and service is likely to be costly, of indifferent quality, and hard to obtain.)

Even more unstructured are the *Rorschach ink blots*. Norms are available for Rorschach blots; unusual responses and blocking of response are useful cues to the therapist.

The researcher must translate his words and concepts into ones that are meaningful to his respondents. *How often do you experience role conflict?* would bewilder a housewife, but one can ask her whether she finds it hard to please both husband and children when she shops.

Respondent language is not always simpler than that of the researcher: often it is just different. (The housewife's vocabulary may contain a good many words not in the sociologist's vocabulary, such as *quiche Lorraine, overcasting, peau de soie,* and *quenelles,* and retailing has a jargon all its own.) Ignorance of respondents' jargon may cause them to doubt the value of a study or the competence of the persons making it. Constructing questions in a broadly based poll which will neither confuse the uneducated nor talk down to the Ph.D. is obviously not easy.

Three Channels for Questions

The type of questions one asks is influenced not only by respondents but also by which channel one uses: face-to-face interviews, telephone interviews, and mail questionnaires.

Face-to-Face Interviewing

Like personal selling, this channel is useful when one expects considerable difficulty in getting a response from his receivers. Persons of low income or little education are likely to have little interest in research and may find reading a questionnaire difficult. The aged may lack the flexibility or the hearing ability to respond to an interviewer. The rewards and pressures of face-to-face influence may be needed if a questionnaire is long, involves sensitive areas, or dull subject matter.

An interviewer can observe the hesitations that suggest answers should not be taken at face value and follow up with "probe" questions. The major disadvantage of such interviews is their cost, about $5 to get the interview and $10 to get and process it.

Mail Questionnaire

This channel is quick and cheap. It works fairly well if the respondents are interested in the survey and if the questionnaire itself is neither long nor complicated. Its big disadvantage is that many persons don't answer, even after one has mailed persons three separate copies of a questionnaire, and offered various kinds of small incentives. (It's usually safe to assume that the nonrespondents differ in ways that are related to the subject matter of the study. If nothing else, they seem to have less interest in its outcome.)

Telephone Survey

This method is fast, cheap, and suited to fairly brief schedules of questions. Although persons who do not have telephones are missing from one's sample (leading to underrepresentation of lower economic groups and persons with unlisted numbers), such surveys usually have fewer respondent refusals than the mail questionnaire. It is less polite to hang up a telephone than to throw away a questionnaire but, at the same time, it is easier to hang up the telephone than to slam a door in the face of an interviewer. The greater anonymity of the telephone makes it easier to get honest answers to some sensitive questions than do face-to-face interviews.

The opportunity for extraneous factors to influence survey results appears greatest when "open" questions are used in face-to-face interviews, and least when structured questions are used in a mail survey. The more leeway an interviewer is given as to follow-up "probe" questions and the more freedom he has in recording responses, the more his own views are likely to color the results.

Loss of respondents in the course of a survey is likely to occur and to bias results on all three channels.

Quota sampling in surveys was discredited when it was found that middle-class interviewers tended to avoid extremes of rich and poor and anyone else whose cooperation might be hard to obtain. Today, well-designed surveys not only specify which house on a block must be called upon but also which resident is to be quizzed when the doorbell is answered. But the bell may not be answered and some who answer may refuse to cooperate, just as many a mail questionnaire is thrown away unanswered. (This is why those who fail to respond to an original questionnaire usually get at least two more and why telephone and door-to-door interviewers are expected to make two or more callbacks,

on different days and at different hours, to catch those absent the first time.) When the same people must be quizzed on several successive occasions in a panel study, losses mount both because of refusal and, in a mobile society, of the fact that some original respondents have moved away and can't be traced.

Since the subjects in an experiment are a restricted, motivated group, and since many experiments are quickly completed, refusals and dropouts are less serious a problem. But what if subjects fail to respond to the experimental stimulus? What if shock or obscene words fail to make some subjects uncomfortable in a study that wants to show that a discomfortable initiation increases liking for a group. One's hypothesis concerns only uncomfortable people, to be sure, but if one's predictions are to be of practical use, one needs to know how many people can be made uncomfortable.

Thought, Talk, and Action

1. For the following firms, show how each of the five sources of data might be used as part of an information system; if you can, suggest a single problem-opportunity whose solution might require all five sources.

    (a) Maker of band instruments who finds interest in bands declines as size of high school increases.
    (b) Department store which, apparently because of recession, finds it is losing customers to nearby discounter.
    (c) Morning newspaper in big city which finds it is losing readers to evening paper and advertisers to smaller suburban dailies.

2. Show how interviewer, respondent, wording of questions, and their sequencing might lead to survey results at variance with behavior they are supposed to predict in the following instances.

    (a) Acceptance of open housing and fair employment.
    (b) Liquor purchases during past six months.
    (c) Donations to United Fund: actual or anticipated.

3. Show how use of other data-gathering methods, either as substitutes for or in addition to survey, might reduce bias in the three cases mentioned in No. 2.

4. Prepare hypothetical findings to show how subject selection might (a) exaggerate and (b) minimize strength of causal relationship. Compare effects of self-selection by subjects, of selective effects of data-gathering method, and of selection through attrition such as occurs in a consumer panel.

Notes

Chapter 12

1. J. W. Getzels, "The question-answer process: A conceptualization and some derived hypotheses for empirical examination," Public Opinion Quarterly, 18:80–91.
2. Stanley Milgram, "The lost-letter technique," Psychology Today, 3:1:30–3.
3. R. P. Abelson and J. C. Miller, "Negative persuasion via personal insult," Journal of Experimental Social Psychology, 3:321–33.
4. Gardner Lindzey and Elliot Aronson, The handbook of social psychology, 2nd ed. (Reading, Mass.: Addison-Wesley Publishing Co., 1968), Vol. 2, p. 15. Original study: N. E. Miller, "Experiments on motivation," Science, 126:1271–8.
5. Ibid., pp. 16–7. Original study, E. Aronson and J. Mills, "The effect of severity of initiation on liking for a group," Journal of Abnormal and Social Psychology, 59:177–81.
6. Ibid., p. 16. Original study: N. E. Miller, "Experiments on motivation," Science, 126:1271–8.
7. Ibid., pp. 23 and 62. Original studies: S. Milgram: "Behavioral study of obedience," Journal of Abnormal and Social Psychology, 67:371–8, and M. Orne, "On the social psychology of the psychological experiment," American Psychologist, 17:776–83.
8. Ibid., p. 44.
9. Ibid., p. 55. Original study: E. Aronson and D. Linder, "Gain and loss of esteem as determinants of interpersonal attractiveness," Journal of Experimental Social Psychology, 1:156–71.
10. Ibid., p. 64. Original study: J. M. Carlsmith, B. E. Collins, and R. L. Helmreich, "Studies in forced compliance: I," Journal of Personality and Social Psychology, 4:1–3.
11. Ibid., p. 67. Original study: R. Rosenthal and K. L. Fode, "Psychology of the scientist: V. Three experiments in experimenter bias," Psychological Reports, 12:491–511.
12. Ibid., p. 67. Original study: R. Rosenthal and K. L. Fode, "The effect of experimenter bias on the performance of the albino rat," Behavioral Science, 8:183–9.
13. Ibid., p. 66.

14. *Ibid.*, p. 549. Original study: S. A. Rice, "Contagious bias in the interview: A methodological note," American Journal of Sociology, 35:420–3.

15. *Ibid.*, p. 549. Original study: R. Ferber and H. Wales, "Detection and correction of interviewer bias," Public Opinion Quarterly, 16:107–27.

16. *Ibid.*, pp. 550–1. Five studies cited.

17. Reference No. 1.

18. Reference No. 1.

19. Reference No. 4, p. 542. Original study: C. F. Cannell et al., "Reporting of hospitalization in the health interview survey," Vital and Health Statistics, Series 2, No. 6.

20. H. Parry and Helen Crossley, "Validity of responses to survey questions," Public Opinion Quarterly, 14:61–80.

21. Darrell Blaine Lucas and Steuart Henderson Britt, Measuring advertising effectiveness (New York: McGraw-Hill Book Co., 1963), p. 224.

22. Stanley L. Payne, The art of asking questions (Princeton, N.J.: Princeton University Press, 1951), p. 9.

23. *Ibid.*, pp. 141–7.

24. K. R. Hammond, "Measuring attitude for error-choice: an indirect method," Journal of Abnormal and Social Psychology, 43:38–48.

Surveys versus Experiments

The laboratory experiment is most often used to study the relationship between causes and effects, the survey to locate and count causes and effects in a population. Theories developed in a laboratory tell a market researcher what to look for in his survey; survey findings may, in turn, suggest that theory needs to be modified.

Laboratory studies of communication commonly report that a third to one-half of subjects are influenced by experimental messages; a message that takes only 15 minutes to read may produce significant changes in attitude. Yet before-and-after surveys in the field find that communications in a political campaign change the views of as few as 5% of the population. Why do these two research methods obtain such divergent results? Four reasons have been suggested by Carl I. Hovland.

Different Receivers

Laboratory subjects are usually individuals, isolated from the group affiliations which, in real life, provide information and influence to counteract the effects of a seller's message.

Surveys usually concentrate on adults, whereas experiments use high school pupils and college sophomores as subjects who are accustomed to accepting what they hear and doing what they're told, especially in the academic setting.

Different Sources

An adult authority figure with high source credibility and rewards and penalties at his disposal usually administers the laboratory experiment.

Survey questions, in contrast, are asked by strangers whose status is seldom superior to that of a respondent who is free to cooperate or refuse.

Different Issues

Surveys usually concern issues with intrinsic or social significance on which respondents (and the groups they belong to) have firm, long-standing commitments. Issues dealt with in the laboratory are chosen to avoid such commitments. Some of them, like the nonsense syllables used in learning studies, may be without meaning; most of them are novel.

In real life, people tend to expose themselves only to messages with which they already agree. A survey either finds no effect at all, because respondents haven't been exposed to an attitude-changing message, or very little effect, because respondents are already close to the position advocated in the message. The laboratory subject is often chosen because, lacking any strong view on the subject, he is easy to sway. Moreover, he cannot avoid exposure to the experimental message.

Different Time Span

Experiments are usually so brief that effects must be measured minutes after a message is received and before any interference can occur. In the field, measurement is usually delayed; a message can be forgotten or its effects reduced by interference from competing messages.

Direction as well as degree of attitude change may differ; cause-and-effect relationships in surveys often differ from those found in experiments.

In experiments, the further a subject's attitude is from that expressed in the message, the more chance he has to change and the more he does change. An "extreme" message often boomerangs in surveys, since it is likely to concern an issue on which the respondent has committed himself.

When two antagonistic messages are presented, the first one appears to have an advantage in surveys; apparently the receiver takes a position after hearing the first message and then "blanks out" subsequent messages. This is less likely in the laboratory. The advantage of primacy even in the field is reduced when the situation itself is defined as controversial, when different communicators present each side, or when the communicators are identified as partisans. (All three of these conditions apply, it should be noted, in such situations as political campaigns, court trials, and debates.)

Source. Carl I. Hovland, "Reconciling conflicting results derived from experimental and survey studies of attitude change," *American Psychologist,* 14:8–17.

Hawthorne Effect

Watching people affects their behavior. Repeated interviews with a "representative" group of housewives soon makes them unrepresentative: they get to know so much about whatever is being studied that they start acting like experts. The same is true of experimental subjects, as was discovered at the Hawthorne works of Western Electric in 1927.

Six girls, average workers, were selected and put in a test room divided from the rest of the shop by an eight-foot partition. As they finished assembling a telephone relay, it slid down a chute; for five years a record of each girl's output was recorded on tape automatically.

After a five-week getting-settled period in the test room, observers introduced a series of changes which they thought might increase or decrease output.

Five-minute rest periods were introduced in midmorning and afternoon.

Rest periods were increased to 10 minutes each.

Six five-minute rest periods were substituted.

Free lunches were provided in midmorning and midafternoon.

Girls were released a half-hour early—at 4:30 P.M.

Girls were released an hour early—at 4 P.M.

Quitting time was returned to the original 5 P.M.

The five-day week was introduced.

All of the changes were removed: rest periods, lunches, early dismissal, the five-day week.

Daily output rose during each period, even the period when all the special "incentives" were taken away. Two reasons were suggested. One was that the girls had become a group: they

being singled out for special attention—a room to themselves, meetings with the superintendent, and interviews by the researchers—acted as an incentive. The girls felt less closely supervised and less anxious—even though more people were watching them more of the time. This change in behavior resulting from observation has become known as "the Hawthorne effect."

Source. George Caspar Homans, "Group factors in worker productivity," in Eleanor E. Maccoby et al., *Readings in Social Psychology* (New York: Holt, Rinehart and Winston, Inc., 1958).

How can one keep the "Hawthorne effect" from invalidating the results of his study? By using four different experimental groups or conditions, one can assess the separate as well as the combined effects of outside events, experimental events, and "before tests."

All four groups receive an "after" test following the experimental event. Subjects are assigned to all groups by random means.

	Group 1	Group 2	Group 3	Group 4
1. Is there a "before" test?	Yes	Yes	No	No
			(Average of scores for groups 1 and 2 is used as a substitute.)	
2. Is group exposed to experimental event?	Yes	No	Yes	No
3. Which are any changes found attributed to?				
Before measure	Yes	Yes	—	—
Experimental event	Yes	—	Yes	—
Outside events	Yes	Yes	Yes	Yes
Interaction of above	Yes	—	—	—

chatted freely while working, observed one another's birthdays, spent time together off the job. A leader emerged, who saw a chance to advance through higher output, and a group norm developed favoring increased production. The other reason was that

The elaborate design shown on next page can be broken up into four simpler, less adequate designs.

Three-group design. This eliminates group 4; it assumes that outside events are unimportant.

Before-after design. This uses only groups 1 and 2. By subtracting scores of group 2 from those of group 1, one obtains a measure of both experimental event and interaction.

After-only design. This uses only groups 3 and 4. By subtracting the score of group 4 from group 3 one eliminates effect of outside events. Remaining results reflect three causes: before measure, experimental event, and interaction.

Still other designs are possible. For example.

One-group design. This uses only group 1, assuming that the "before" measure will not affect responses either to the experimental event or the "after" measure, and that outside events will have no effect.

Interchangeable groups. One group corresponds to group 4 above in that it gets no "before" test and is exposed to outside events. This group is paired with another which gets a "before" test but, unlike all those pictured above, gets no "after" test. Thus each group is measured just once, either before or after exposure. It's assumed, since subjects are assigned randomly, that the group receiving only the after test would have scored the same on the before test as did the group that got it. This design fails to measure the separate effect of outside events.

Intact groups. When it isn't possible to assign individuals at random, so-called "intact groups" may be used. This may also be done when one wants to study the differences between existing groups. In such cases, a "before" test and the technique of covariance will enable one to adjust final results on the basis of original group differences. This precaution fails, of course, if unsuspected and nontested differences in the two groups influence results.

Source. Based on page 110 of Claire Selltiz et al., *Research Methods in Group Relations* (New York: Holt, Rinehart and Winston, 1961; revised edition).

Effect of Setting on Results

Most researchers are aware that a slight rewording of a question, or a nuance in an interviewer's tone of voice can cause drastic differences in the responses one gets. Less known and more surprising are the differences that a change in the setting of an experiment can make. In this instance, a study of family decision making shifted from home to laboratory.

Twenty-four couples were recruited from two churches near Yale University, half of them being accompanied by a son aged 15 to 17 and half by a daughter of the same age. Each group began by looking at a pair of TAT pictures for 20 seconds, spent 25 minutes discussing a story about the family shown in the pictures and 10 minutes writing up a summary.

Each group then was given two problems concerning the family in the picture and asked to discuss six alternative solutions to each problem. (*Example.* A 10-year-old lets his homework go until the last minute. Solutions suggested were: ignoring the problem, making a daily check, explaining the importance of good work habits, setting a definite time each day for homework, helping the child with his work, punishing him for not working harder.)

The experimenter coded all comments made during the discussion into one of three classes: task-centered, positive social-emotional, and negative social-emotional. (He hypothesized that adults would dominate their children, that men's comments would be task-centered, and women's aimed at relieving tension.) Each family participated in two experiments: one in their own home and one in a university laboratory. (The experimenter hypothesized that the number of task-centered comments would increase in the unfamiliar laboratory setting.)

The table shows scores on a positivity index—excess of positive social-emotional comments over negative expressed as a percent of total comments. Thus a high index indicates attention to social and emotional content; a low index indicates task-centered discussion.

As predicted, scores on the index were higher in the home than in the laboratory for fathers and sons who gave emotional support to one another in the home but became highly task-centered in the laboratory. Presence of a daughter tended to minimize the difference between laboratory and home and reverse its direction. Change from home to laboratory had little effect on mothers.

Can People Report Accurately on How Their Own Attitudes Have Changed?

When one asks people what they used to think, feel, or do, there is always the danger that the answers one gets will be affected by their *present* feelings and beliefs. Does it help to recognize this possibility in one's questions, by asking them how they've changed?

At Cornell University, students were quizzed on their religious attitudes in 1950 and again in 1952. In 1952 they were also asked, *How have your beliefs changed?* and their answers compared with actual differences in their 1950 and 1952 answers.

On a six-item scale of theistic belief, ranging from *God the Creator knows my inmost thoughts for which one day I will be accountable* to an atheistic position,

	Scores of Individuals			
	Fathers	Sons	Mothers	Daughters
Home	771	347	634	291
Laboratory	598	216	720	308

	Scores for Groups		
		Couples with	
	Total	Sons	Daughters
Home	722	431	291
Laboratory	558	218	341

Source. John F. O'Rourke, "Field and laboratory: The decision-making behavior of family groups in two experimental conditions," *Sociometry,* 26:422–35.

many of those who *said* they had become more "religious" actually showed no change between 1950 and 1952.

Actual change (1950 vs. 1952)	Perceived Change: I Have Become:		
	More Religious %	Less Religious %	No Change %
More theistic	21	15	20
No change	63	38	58
Less theistic	16	47	22

There are three explanations for these differences between measured and perceived change. One is that perceptions were based on religious beliefs not covered in the questions. Another is that students who scored at the top of the theism scale in 1950 may have become still more theistic, but the test could not detect such change. A third is that in both 1950 and 1952 students were comparing themselves with their associates. Unchanged beliefs may have appeared more "religious" or "theistic" in an unreligious university atmosphere than they had to a younger person in his home community.

Source. Raymond Fink, "The retrospective question," *Public Opinion Quarterly*, 24: 143–8.

Additional Research Readings

Field or lab? Since nearly all existing organizations are authoritarian in structure, insistence on a real-life setting for research prevents one from finding out how balance, attribution, and social evaluation variables would work in nonauthoritarian situations. **Chris Argyris, "The incompleteness of social-psychological theory . . . ,"** American Psychologist, 24:893–908. Interviews with 1500 English housewives in their homes revealed more sensitivity to prices of coffee than a matching study of 3000 housewives at supermarkets. **Andrew Gabor et al., "Real and hypothetical shop situations in market research,"** Journal of Marketing Research, 7:355–9.

Subjects. Quizzed on personality, physique, and work-study habits, male volunteers proved readier at self-disclosure than nonvolunteer subjects. No such difference showed up for females, all of whom apparently were accustomed to such disclosure. **Thomas C. Hood and Kurt W. Back, "Self-disclosure and the volunteer; a source of bias . . . ,"** Journal of Personality and Social Psychology, 17:130–6. Willing subjects produced more Type I errors, and drafted subjects more Type II errors following pretests which gave clues to experimenter's intentions. **Ralph L. Rosnow and Jerry M. Suls, "Reactive effects of pretesting in attitude research,"** Journal of Personality and Social Psychology, 15:338–43.

Interviewer. Factor analysis disclosed that apparent differences in length of respondents' replies to questions on voting intentions were actually caused by the interviewer. **Michael J. Shapiro, "Discovering interviewer bias in open-ended survey responses,"** Public Opinion Quarterly, 24:412–5. Although five interviewers were supposedly recording respondents' words, one interviewer recorded "enjoyment" 8 times to another's 30, and the word "interest" appeared from 9 to 41 times. **W. Andrew Collins, "Interviewers' verbal idiosyncracies as a source of bias,"** Public Opinion Quarterly, 34:416–22.

Physiological response. As the difficulty of a series of color-naming tasks increased, so did the sweat on subjects' palms—while their heartbeat slowed down. Palms also reflected anticipation of shock. **Rogers Elliott et al., "Differences in the motivational significance of heart rate and palmar conductance . . . ,"** Journal of Personality and Social Psychology, 14:166–72. Sweat but not heartbeat reflected arousal least for reading silently words related to subject's life, next for listening or writing, highest for speaking and evaluating them. **Loren D. Crane et al., "The physiological response to the communication modes . . . ,"** Journal of Communication, 20:231–40.

● When data fail to guide decisions, one asks whether data deviated from plans, which statistical test fits data *and* aids choice; whether more data gathering will repay its costs. Search of data may disclose unforeseen relationships.

● Different data are often needed to satisfy goals of different sponsors, of the persons who do the research and those who use its results; what satisfies one may not satisfy the other.

● Bayesian analysis offers a decision-making tool that guides design and use of research and helps one determine whether to decide now or await still further research.

Research Articles

Analytic Choices. Housewives' drawings of supermarket produce three different indices of effective layout (Krugman); five statistics used in estimating market for dog coats (Massy).

Chapter 13 Analysis of Data

If unknowns have been specified in the detail suggested in Chapter 11 and data gathered with the care prescribed in Chapter 12, a decision maker should be able to fit numbers provided by his computer into blank tables drawn up in advance and pick the best alternative. If he's attained statistical significance for the cause-effect relationships he hypothesized, his analysis is complete. If he can't and hasn't, search must be resumed.

More often than not, hypotheses are confirmed in part, rejected in part, and in part plagued by residual ambiguity. Or one statistical test shows significance and the other does not. One alternative appears best in some respects, worst in others. This poses three tasks for a decision maker.

He must check to see whether data were gathered according to plan. Did the weather, a dip in the stock market or a competitor's sale swamp the variables he chose for study? Did his random sample of subjects become de-randomized during the study? (How many mail questionnaires were not returned, how many housewives dropped off a consumer panel, what kinds of subjects failed to report to the laboratory?)

He must ask which of the conflicting statistical tests best fits the data, as gathered, and which best guides his choice of alternatives. (If neither test meets *both* criteria, he may have to seek a new statistic.) Operational definitions of causes and effects may have drifted away from the original conceptual definitions designed to aid decision making. More sensitive measures of effects and more precise definitions of causes may be required. (Recall may

have been insensitive to differences in ads; perhaps recognition should have been used. A check of pantries might have been more accurate than housewives' diaries, or perhaps use rather than purchase should have been noted.)

He must determine whether the results of further research are likely to improve decision making enough to repay the costs of obtaining them—costs not only in dollars but also in time.

Unexpected Results

Ideally, all these questions would have been answered in advance. Exploratory studies would have pinpointed causes and effects, and pretests would have ensured that instruments were reliable, valid, and sensitive. Confounding factors would have been excluded or measured so that they could be controlled during gathering or analysis of data. But life confounds textbook maxims and creative researchers discover facts and relationships they did *not* anticipate. For example: what they thought of as a single "cause" may be revealed by the study as two different variables. (Working at cross purposes, each might cancel out the effects of the other to make it appear that there is no causal relationship rather than a complex one. Or failure to separate the variables may lead to significant results in one study, contradictory or insignificant results in another.)

Suppose that a manufacturer or publisher who has always assumed that his product is one of interest only to the well educated is confronted with the following survey results.

	Users	Nonusers
Educated	50%	50%
Uneducated	50	50

At first glance, this suggests that the product has a mass appeal—that everyone wants it. But the analyst remembers that education is only one of the factors that might affect product use. The survey also obtained data on *age,* and a second computer run produces results showing appeal to youth.

	Users	Nonusers
Young	80%	20%
Old	20	80

By cross-tabulating on both age and education, the manufacturer discovers that the two variables interact, so that effects of age are most marked with the uneducated.

	Educated		Uneducated	
	User	Nonuser	User	Nonuser
Young	35%	15%	45%	5%
Old	15	35	5	45

Useful as simple cross-tabulation is in illustrating the process by which one searches for meanings in his data or designs new data-gathering enterprises, the decision maker often employs more powerful tools. He fits ingenious curves, seeks underlying dimensions, devises complex predictive formulas. Analyst and computer may engage in a real-time dialogue as they search for meaning and design research; exploratory heuristics are becoming a real art, well beyond the scope of this book.

Different Goals

In attempting to predict how the results of one's data gathering and analysis will be received, we see a fundamental difference in the response made by businessman and academic researcher to the unexpected or inconclusive result.

Academicians tend to find disconfirmation of previous findings, particularly those of a colleague, both stimulating and re-warding. The discrepant result and the deviant case aid theory building and help the scientist describe the conditions under which a relationship holds. However, greatest prestige goes to those who can gather together many separate findings into a more general formulation, organizing the world's complexity into the simplest possible set of principles. Unless the deviant result can be incorporated into a theory of its own, it is likely to be neglected.

To the *marketing decision maker,* the scientists' concern with detail may be irritating since it delays *his* task of making choices now. He may prefer a faulty theory to no theory at all, if it helps him get on with the job. The scientist wants to extend theory to larger and larger areas; the seller wants to apply existing theory to particular, rather small areas of choice.

Advertising media and media vehicles want to show that they are superior to their competitors in some characteristic of potential value to an advertiser. *Life* argues that subscribers pass along their copies after reading them so that the total audience is several times that which the advertiser pays for. *Better Homes and Gardens* boasts that its issues are saved, not shared —that readers clip and file articles and ads. If such a sponsor fails to find competitive advantage in one direction, he's likely to look in another.

Consumers seldom engage in formal research since it would cost more than it might save. When products are purchased frequently, trial and error substitutes for research. Some consumers feel that the risks of marketing a bad product are so great, both in halting repeat purchases and in stimulating antagonistic word-of-mouth communications, that research is not necessary. Others feel that the big differences among brands needed to justify research just don't exist. Some feel that where competition exists, seller's research, however self-interested, will make all brands tend to serve buyer interests.

Industrial buyers find it worthwhile to seek out alternate sources of supply and compare their offerings. A buyer's research laboratories may find better, cheaper ingredients and manufacturing methods, but so may a seller's laboratories. (Which laboratories supply most of the research data probably depends more on relative size of the firms than on which is buyer and which seller.) Such research may be problem-centered and sporadic, rather than an opportunity-seeking, continuous research-and-development program.

Retailers, with the rise of multiple-ownership, are finding resources to do research matching their need for it, whether the focus be location of a new outlet or evaluation of a firm's ads. A retailer needs to compare his store's image with his competitors', discover which services attract and hold customers, and what variety and depth of product line buyers require.

In designing research, the seller must make a trade-off between a choice of causes that have a high probability of producing desired effects and a choice of causes that he can manipulate. Having done this, he must then determine whether research into such causes will cost less than the improvement in decision making which results of such research make possible.

For example: experience may suggest that a 20¢ mailing piece sent to 1000 persons will produce 200 orders. The 200 orders provide a profit of $1.50 each or a total profit of $300—minus the $160 cost of mailings to the nonresponsive 800. If research could identify nonrespondents in advance, these 800 wasted mailings need never take place. The resulting savings would justify a seller in paying up to $160 for such research.

The seller needs to estimate the value of research in his original decision to gather data and again when research results are in: should he go ahead on the basis of present findings, inconclusive as they may be, or engage in further research?

Bayesian Analysis

Bayesian analysis tries to answer this question by asking the decision maker to estimate the probability that each alternative course of action will achieve a given goal.

First, all possible outcomes (or *states of nature*) must be listed, including that of taking no action at all. He must estimate the profit or loss attached to each, and the probability of each outcome. The two estimates are multiplied together and the results summed, losses being subtracted from profits, to get an *expected monetary value.* With a computer, it's comparatively easy to perform a *sensitivity analysis*—to alter one's several estimates and see how big a change in outcome any given change would make.

Such analysis may occur at three points in time.

Prior. This means making a decision now, on the basis of present information.

Preposterior. This involves a decision as to whether one should gather additional data. Would the improvement that research could make in one's choice be worth more than the cost of the research?

Posterior. Once research findings are in hand, should one choose an alternative (prior analysis) or make another preposterior analysis, preparatory to gathering additional data?

Using hypothetical figures suggested by Bass,* let us suppose a marketing vice-president sees three possible buyer responses to a new bifurcated widget. (See next page.)

Prior analysis ends here with a decision to put the widget on the market. But the marketing research staff urges further research.

Perfect information as to future outcomes would permit the seller to forget about the

---

* Frank Bass, "Marketing research expenditures: a decision model," *Journal of Business,* 36:77–90.

TABLE 13.1

Market Share Likely to Be:	Probability of Getting This Market Share:	Profit or Loss in Millions	Expected Value (Col. 2 × Col. 3)
10%	70%	$10	$7
3	10	1	.1
1	20	−5	−1
	Expected value of putting new widget on market:		$6.1
	Expected value of *not* putting new widget on market:		0

widget if he were certain it would gain only 1% share of the market. Substituting a zero in the profit-or-loss column for this alternative would eliminate the − $1 million in the "expected value" column. Since this million dollar savings represents the maximum gain to be achieved through research, it sets a ceiling on the research budget.

Research is never perfect, however, so the marketing vice-president asks his research director to estimate how likely it is to be correct. These estimates suggest that there's a 60% chance that research which predicts a market share of either 10%-or-more or 3-to-9% will be correct; the chance is 80% if research predicts less than 3% share.

The first set of figures, based on the experience and intuition of the marketing vice-president, has already suggested that there's a 70% chance of achieving a market share of 10% or more, a 10% chance of a market share of 3%, a 20% chance of a market share of less than 3%. So now each column of the research director's table is multiplied by the matching vice-president estimate to give the data in Table 13.3.

The figures in the cells of the table thus represent the combined intuitions of two men—the vice-president's estimates of the product's potential market share, and the research director's estimate of the accuracy of his research. (In the barbarous language of the Bayesian, these are *preposterior* figures: advance estimates [pre] of what research results [posterior] would show.)

Next, he divides the figures in each cell above by the total for their row. He gets the figures for the first column thus: 42/47

TABLE 13.2

If Research Indicates Sales of:	These Are the Conditional Probabilities That Actual Market Share Attained Will Be:		
	10%	3 to 9%	Less than 3%
10% or more	60%	30%	10%
3 to 9%	30	60	10
Less than 3%	10	10	80

TABLE 13.3

Research Director's Estimates Sales of:	Marketing Vice-President's Original Estimates of Likelihood of Market Share Are:			
	10%	3 to 9%	Less than 3%	Totals
10% or more	42%	3%	2%	47%
3 to 9%	21	6	2	29
Less than 3%	7	1	16	24
Totals	70%	10%	20%	100%

TABLE 13.4

When Research Produces Estimates of:	Ultimate Sales Levels		
	10%	3 to 9%	Less than 3%
10% or more	89.4%	6.4%	4.2%
3 to 9%	72.4	20.7	6.9
Less than 3%	29.2	6.9	66.6

= .894, 21/29 = .724 and 7/24 = .292, and ends up with the data in Table 13.4.

He now uses these nine figures to recalculate the expected values of the first table, as follows.

TABLE 13.5

Estimated Profit or Loss of Widget Decision:		When Research Puts Market Share at:	Using Cell Values of Last Table, Calculate Thus:	Expected Value of Introduction
Don't sell	Sell			
0	$10 million	10%	89.4% (10 million) + 6.4% ($1 million) − 4.2% (−$5 million) =	$8,794,000
0	1 million	3	72.4% (10 million) + 20.7% ($1 million) + 6.9% (−$5 million) =	7,102,000
0	−5 million	1	29.2% (10 million) + 4.2% ($1 million) + 66.6% (−$5 million) =	368,000

The rational person will *not* introduce a product when a market share of 1% is forecast, and so will save himself $368,000. Expected value after research is therefore obtained by multiplying the first two expected values above by the appropriate total probabilities from Table 13.3 as follows.

47% ($8,794,000) + 29% ($7,102,000) + 24% ($0) = $6,193,000

By taking this new expected value of the optimal act after research and subtracting the original expected value before research of $6,100,000, one gets $93,000 as a value for the amount of improvement in decision making that the research described above will produce.

Often research can make a larger contribution. As Banks* suggests, research makes a greater and greater contribution as the cost and probability of failure rise. In this instance, if there were a 10% chance of a market share of 10%, a 20% chance of a market share of 3 to 9%, but a 70% chance of a losing market share of 1%, the expected value *without* research would be an actual loss of $2.3 million, the expected value *with* research a profit of $1.2 million, and the ceiling for "perfect" research $3,500,000!

Bayesian analysis is helpful in deciding whether to undertake any research at all and in deciding whether to do more research. It helps determine how many respondents to quiz by estimating the value of greater precision achieved through a larger sample.

* Seymour Banks, Experimentation in Marketing (New York: McGraw-Hill, 1965), Ch. 1

Occasionally, time pressures do not permit delaying decisions while research is undertaken. Often research can contribute only a very small improvement in decision making; research can easily cost more than it is worth. Even with a computer, alternatives proliferate to the point where both computation and understanding of results become difficult. And, often, expected monetary values are a poor guide to actual choice; many of us would rather have a certain $50,000 than a 50% chance of getting $150,000.

Having specified unknowns, gathered and analyzed data, and applied Bayesian techniques, a seller now knows what alternative to choose; his decision process is complete. He offers a product for sale. Whether a sale takes place, however, depends on the outcome of the *buyer's* decision process and what happens when buyer and seller encounter one another.

Thought, Talk, and Action

1. In this book, find a simple table showing a cause-effect relationship. Using hypothetical figures of your own devising, suggest how cross-tabulation on a third variable might alter the relationship shown.
2. Using the model of this chapter, suggest a problem involving preposterior analysis, and work it through, using figures of your own.
3. Reviewing the research summaries presented in Chapters 1 through 12, which seem designed to achieve academic goals and which to aid decision makers? Which would be most useful to buyers and sellers? to consumers, manufacturers, retailers? Be prepared to defend your point of view.

One Question: Three Answers

Here is a novel attempt to determine the relative "importance" of different "departments" in a supermarket, a question of importance in designing store layout, and three different ways of analyzing the results.

Fifty New York housewives were asked to draw a supermarket. The importance of a given element in the retailer's mix was then assessed in terms of which department was drawn *first,* which was drawn *largest,* and which was least likely to be *omitted* altogether. Meat scored high on two measures, second on the third.

Omitted completely. Meat by 10% of the subjects, produce by 20%, dairy 20%, dry groceries 25%.

Drawn first. Produce by 40%, meats 20%, dairy and dry groceries less than 20% each.

Size. The meat department, in actuality only a third the size of the space given dry groceries, was drawn 50% larger than them. Produce, also given only one-third their size, was drawn only 20% smaller than dry groceries.

Source. Herbert E. Krugman, "The 'draw a supermarket' technique," *Public Opinion Quarterly,* 24:148–9.

One Problem: Many Techniques

Here is a systematic attempt to bring the full range of statistical tools to bear on a hypothetical problem: What constitutes a good market for dog coats—and is Kansas City such a market?

The seller began by taking real figures on income from Sales Management's survey of buying power for 18 standard metropolitan statistical areas, temperature readings from the Rand McNally Commercial Atlas and Marketing Guide, and hypothetical figures on dog-coat sales in selected markets.

SMSA	Sales per 1000 Licensed Dogs	Income per Family ($000)	January Temperature
1. Atlanta	2.9	7.15	44.0
2. Baltimore	4.5	7.31	35.5
. . .			
18. Philadelphia	5.4	7.97	34.4

Cross-classification. By grouping the 18 areas into five income classes, the seller finds that sales of dog coats rise with income. In rural areas no such relationship holds so that weighted average of rural-urban dog owners obscures the cause-effect relationship.

Income Class	Average Sales per 1000 Dogs		
	18 SMSAs	Rural Areas	Total
$5500–5999	1.8	.2	1.5
$6000–6499	2.9	.3	2.0
$6500–6999	3.4	.4	2.2
$7000–7499	3.6	.5	2.3
$7500–7999	5.3	.7	2.0
$8000–8499	5.0	.8	2.2

Correlation. Using his original figures, the analyst obtains three correlation coefficients:

Income and sales	.89
Temperature and sales	−.45
Temperature and income	−.57

More dog coats are sold in high-income areas than in low, and fewer dog coats in cities with high temperatures than with low. But the third figure introduces a problem: why should incomes fall as temperatures rise? Does cold weather produce more sales because dogs are shivering or because owners in northern cities are wealthier? Partial correlation produced these figures:

Income and sales (temperature held constant)	.85
Temperature and sales (income held constant)	.16

Not only is the relationship of temperature to sales much *lower* when incomes are held constant, but the negative sign has changed to positive. Dog coat sales *rise* with a rise in temperature! (The analyst may find that there are more sensitive dogs, such as Mexican hairless, in Southern climes.) Squaring the correlation coefficients reveals that 74.8% of variance is explained by temperatures and incomes (in contrast with the 99.5% suggested by the two earlier figures).

Multiple regression. The seller can now predict sales for a new area, Kansas City, where dog coats are not currently sold. Using income figures for Kansas City (7.05) and the mean January temperature (26.7), he gets this prediction.

3.52 + 1.51 (7.05-6.96) + .0086 (26.7-40.9)
= 5.06 sales per 1000 dogs

Discriminant analysis. Any city with a score above .809 is clearly a good market, and any below .746 is clearly a bad one. Between these two points are two bad markets and four good ones whose sales are *not* predicted by income and temperature. Kansas City, with a function of .778, is within this twilight zone.

If sales figures shown in the first table were not available, a seller could still decide on whether to enter the Kansas City market, provided he could class each of the 18 cities as *good* or *bad*. Using income and climate data, he now gets a score (discriminant function) that indicates which class Kansas City is likely to fall into.

Factor analysis. If the seller had a dozen or more independent variables, instead of just temperature and income, he might first want to reduce his variables to more manageable proportions.

The first column below represents a "marketing" factor—things like sales and income, and the second column a "climate" factor. With more variables, other geographical features might load onto this factor—and additional factors might appear.

By squaring each loading and adding across rows, one determines the percentage of variance explained by all of the factors. (The "marketing" factor explains 96% of the variance in sales.) By adding down columns, he determines the percentage of variance in all variables explained by each factor. (Marketing explains 60%.)

Source. William F. Massy, "Statistical analysis of relations between variables," in Ronald E. Frank et al., *Quantitative Techniques in Marketing Analysis* (Homewood, Ill.: Richard D. Irwin, 1962).

	Rotated Factor Loadings		
	"Marketing"	"Climate"	Communalities
Sales	.959	−.195	96%
Income	.906	−.353	95%
Temperatures	.264	.964	100%
Percentage of total variance explained	60%	36%	96%

Additional Research Readings

Techniques. Nine techniques of assessing the relationship among several variables simultaneously are discussed. Included is canonical analysis, used when a cause produces multiple effects. (Techniques listed in this text measure the impact of many causes on a single effect.) Jadish N. Sheth, "Multivariate analysis in marketing," Journal of Advertising Research, 10:1:29–39.

Hypotheses. Why did the ratio of Cadillacs among Negroes run 14:4 that of whites in a study of 600 Chicago families? This study discards two explanations—upward mobility and relative income—but supports a third; higher personal involvement. Fred C. Akers, "Negro and white automobile-buying behavior: New evidence," Journal of Marketing Research, 5:283–90. Rival theories of cause and effect determine the way impulse buying is defined and measured and tend to exaggerate it. David T. Kollat, "A decision-process approach to impulse purchasing," in Raymond Haas, editor, Science, Technology and Marketing (Chicago: American Marketing Association, 1966).

Bayesian approach. Psychological costs of delaying a decision cause subjects to eschew techniques of choice prescribed by Bayesian analysis. Paul E. Green et al., "An experiment in information buying," Journal of Advertising Research, 4:3:17–23. As subjects shift from artificial to more realistic problems, they adopt more "conservative" strategies of choice than Bayesian techniques prescribe. Harry A. Alker and Margaret G. Hermann, "Are Bayesian decisions artificially intelligent?" Journal of Personality and Social Psychology, 19:31–41.

Artifacts. Sure enough, teachers told that training school inmates were "late bloomers" induced better exam scores from them than teachers who thought they were poor students. **Donald H. Meichenbaum et al., "A behavioral analysis of teacher expectancy effects," Journal of Personality and Social Psychology, 13:306–16.** When 39 students were asked to rate photos, high expectations among 15 experimenters produced better performance only for subjects made to feel ego-involved in the task. **Marshall W. Minor, "Experimenter expectancy effect as a function of evaluation apprehension," Journal of Personality and Social Psychology, 15:326–32.**

Comparing methods. A graphic rating scale of teaching effectiveness produced lenient scores and reflected different instructions but a forced-choice scale avoided such bias. **Amiel T. Sharon, "Eliminating bias from student ratings of college instructors," Journal of Applied Psychology, 54:278–81.** After a 30-minute coke date, student-coed attraction was measured by their physical proximity while speaking to experimenter and by paper-and-pencil measures. **Donn Byrne et al., "Continuity between the experimental study of attraction and real-life computer dating," Journal of Personality and Social Psychology, 16:157–65.**

● Choice of an alternative involves reconciling many goals, each of which can be provided by many product features and each feature of which may be signaled by many cues.

● Choice occurs throughout the decision process.

● The choice involved in a purchase-sale involves three decision processes—those of buyer, seller, and between buyer and seller. These processes are of three types: within-the-head, bargaining, and breaking down into subdecisions and then recombining. These types occur in two stages: evoking a set of alternatives, and selection of an alternative from this set.

● Buying decisions may be made in families or in organizations; organizations may be governmental, business firm, or voluntary group. Business firms may be distinguished by use of purchase (consumption, resale, processing); organizations by their beneficiaries (owners, members, nonmembers, society at large).

● Decisions may be made by command or by conflict/bargaining; the latter kind seems to be increasing.

● Most decisions today are group decisions and so involve bargaining. Group decisions differ from individual decisions in riskiness, creativity, acceptability, speed.

● Behavioral concepts affect the command structure, too, as shown in the concepts of span of control, gatekeeper, and in systems of recruitment and reward.

● An individual's response to rewards varies with what he expects, what he perceives his peers to have received and what alternatives he sees. Group influence over the individual's response varies with its size, duration, and scope, and its ability to observe and desire to influence individual decisions.

● Group members tend to begin similar and grow more so over time; lack of diversity may reduce productivity, as may appearance of status systems when the group becomes an organization.

● Knowledge of how groups and organizations function and how they differ enables a salesman to choose, to manipulate and adapt to the firm which employs him and those he sells to. He needs to vary his behavior among customer firms, between customer and employer, and to his employer at different points in time.

Research Articles

Family Decisions. Housewives report on how decisions are
   made; family patterns vary with job, income, education
   (Blood); reports of husbands and wives compared (Wolgast).
Business Firm. Flow chart shows how firm fixes price (Cyert);
   computer uses eight factors to split $80,000 ad budget among
   3 magazines over 4 months (Kotler).
Perceptions. Irrelevant cues influence housewives' choices
   (Laird); quantitative differences are perceived as differences
   in quality (Naylor).
Influentials. Handful of expert informants guide decision
   making (Wilson), but salesmen prove poor channel for
   information input to employer (Albaum); five types of
   influential discovered in group decision processes (Bales).
Man-in-Middle. Sergeants' attitudes match position between
   officer and men (Stouffer); on some issues officers and men
   think alike (Merton).

Chapter 14 Choosing Among Alternatives

Viewed from the standpoint of either buyer or seller, choice is a complex matter. Below, for example, are three factors that complicate the *buyer's* choice.

Most purchases are expected to satisfy a variety of goals: a car buyer may want economy, speed, dependability, and style but find no model superior on all four dimensions.

Each goal or consumer benefit may be provided by different product features. The desire for economy may be met by low operating cost of one make of auto or by the infrequent repairs that another demands.

Cues to each of these product attributes may conflict. A friend may report that his car averages 18 miles to the gallon, a rival manufacturer cite tests that back his claim and *Consumer Reports* favor a third.

The following is an example showing how complex a problem may face a *seller*.

His detergent is mild enough not to harm the most delicate dress but strong enough to undo the worst that a 10-year-old can do to his denims on a busy weekend. But tests show that buyers feel these two qualities are contradictory. They find it hard to believe a product can have both. The seller can gain two advantages by packaging them under separate labels.

Wives who would balk at a high price for workaday wash may gladly pay more for the psychological reassurance that the detergent won't harm delicate fabric.

Two products seize more space on a supermarket shelf, freezing out a competitor.

Thus, a manufacturer may make a product that is chemically the same look like two different products. He markets the "strong" version as a powder, in large boxes printed in bold colors and labels it "Tuff Job." He adds a sudsing agent, for women who think suds mean strength, and an unpleasant, antiseptic smell for others, who associate sweet smells with delicacy. In contrast, he markets the "mild" version as a liquid in small bottles whose size (and price) suggest delicacy; the label is in pastels and the scent supplied is mild. He supplies cues that reflect the way his product will be used, not its chemistry. Retailers respond by shelving the "mild" detergent with hand soaps, and the "strong" version with laundry supplies. Buyers respond by putting the "mild" detergent in the bathroom, and the "strong" version on a shelf in the utility room. Thus the seller profits by going along with buyer perceptions rather than by trying to change them.

Choice of Many Stages

Not least of the complexities involved in choice is the matter of isolating it in space or time. To the degree that decision making is a *process*, there can be no distinct act of choice or time and place of choosing; choice occurs all along the way.

Choice occurs when buyer or seller chooses to ignore some problems. It occurs again when either admits some alternatives to an evoked set, from which a "final" choice will be made, and rejects others. It continues even after purchase-and-sale; while a product is being used, the purchaser is deciding whether to buy it again; when a product is being sold, its seller is deciding whether to restock.

Two Stages, Three Processes, Three Methods

However, we can distinguish two stages in the choice process. The first occurs when made by an individual or group, and then combining the results. (The division and the recombination may be performed by either individuals or groups.) Figure 14.1 illustrates these processes.

Decision Method	Decision Maker		
	Buyer	Seller	Buyer-and-Seller
Individual			
Joint			
Partial			

Figure 14.1   Buyer and Seller Decision Methods.

either buyer or seller decides he has examined enough alternatives and is prepared to make a choice. The seller, for example, lacks time or money to pursue the search for alternative mixes—marketing, media, message, market segments—or foresees a low probability of success of finding new alternatives. Or the buyer finds that ads, salesmen, and retail outlets are beginning to repeat themselves. Sellers included in this *evoked set* of alternatives will, of course, try to hasten this decision; excluded competitors will try to delay this end to search. The second stage is the selection of a single alternative from this evoked set; often this occurs during the encounter between seller and buyer, and depends on the overlap between each participant's set of acceptable choices. This choice is followed by purchase-and-sale.

Every purchase-sale involves three decision processes: that of the buyer, that of the seller, and that of buyer-and-seller. Each of these processes may involve three different methods of arriving at a decision. One of these occurs within the head of a single individual. A second occurs by bargaining among two or more individuals. The third consists of dividing the decision into several parts, each of which may be

The importance of each cell in this table depends on two factors: (1) How many acts of purchase and sale-purchase dollars does each cell contain? (2) How available to study and manipulation are events in each cell—how readily can we determine causes and consequences of each entry and how alter them to suit our purposes? (Note that *column* totals must be identical, since every sale-purchase involves all three types of decision maker, but that *row* totals may vary.)

Bargaining or Command?

Joint and partial decisions can occur in two settings: within a family or within an organization. Organizations, in turn, may be differentiated by type, such as business firm, government, or voluntary group; business firms may be further distinguished by purpose of purchase: use, resale, or further processing. Organizations may be distinguished in terms of who benefits from their activities: *owners*, for the business firm; *members*, of labor unions and veterans groups; *nonmember clients*, for schools and hospitals, and *society at large*, for the internal revenue service or the police.[1] Problems vary with organizational type; in the labor union, leaders seek power and members tend to be apathetic; schools tend to assume that their clients aren't capable of knowing what is good for them. All four types of organizations may initiate seller decision processes, either because they represent market opportunities or because they operate as constraints upon the seller.

Within each organization and each type of business firm, two processes of decision making occur. One is that of *command,* characteristic of the hierarchical organization; presumably, "partial" decision making and command are closely associated. The other is that of *bargaining,* best occurring among peers; such decision making occurs at levels within the hierarchical organization and characterizes decision making in voluntary groups and the family.

When status differences, which characterize the hierarchical organization, intrude into the group, they cause trouble. Persons of low status are reluctant to criticize persons of high status and tend to be ignored if they do, even when they are right.[2] (As a result, productivity drops.) On the other hand, low-status members may seek to increase their status by messages to high-status members, whether such messages are relevant to the task at hand or not. (For this reason, groups where status differences are fixed may be more productive than those in which change is possible.)

Earlier chapters, such as those on perception and learning, have contributed to an understanding of decision making by individuals; individual decision processes per se are not readily accessible to study. In theory, at least, decisions in a hierarchical organization are susceptible to the highly "rational" goals of the economist's marginal analysis and the tools of formal decision theory and linear programming. (Prescriptions of the *system* may approximate actual decision processes.) The bargaining that occurs among peers is something else. Bargaining is of major interest

in marketing and something that the behavioral sciences have studied. It is the concern of this chapter.

Game theory deals with bargaining as a prescriptive system, providing rules for efficient play. Our concern is with process: with the actual behavior of real groups.

We know, for example, that groups often tend to adopt riskier courses than do individuals, although we are not yet certain why.[3] We know that groups are less creative than the same number of individuals, working separately, so that groups are not as good at generating alternatives as are individuals.[4] Reasons for this are better known, including the common sense observation that in a group only one man can talk at a time. Workers are often more likely to cooperate enthusiastically with a decision if they feel they have had a part in making it,[5] but group participation does not always lead to a better decision per se. Sometimes conditions such as a need for speed prevent group decisions.

A free flow of messages within a group can increase productivity in three ways. It encourages men to share their insights by removing inhibitions via provision of *social support.* Diversity of viewpoints, if shared, helps the group *detect errors.* Competition for group approval gained through participation *motivates* men to offer suggestions. Support from the like-minded and challenge from the unlike-minded both help.

Group processes of decision making are found in the family, the voluntary organization, government, and in the most hierarchical, command-oriented business firm. They affect decision making of the buyer and the seller; by definition, the encounter between buyer and seller is a group activity.

Bargaining Encounters Increase

How important are group decision processes and bargaining? For one thing, a growing proportion of decisions seem to take this form. The one-man firm is less common than it used to be; committees replace the boss. As large firms swallow up small ones, one would expect more business decisions to be made by processes of command, but *profit centers* within such firms have introduced bargaining here, too.

When a given individual is subject to contrary pressures from a superior in the command structure and a bargaining partner in the marketplace, the former does not always come out on top. The salesman, who must satisfy both boss and customer, *may* favor the latter. Friendships with customers not only build sales but are rewarding in themselves, to the point that the salesman battles his own firm's credit and shipping executives on behalf of the customer.

Behavioral problems beset even the command structure. The power an individual has to influence decisions may be more or less than his position on the formal organizational chart suggests; moreover, he may increase this power through strategic coalitions with other employees. As a result, it is often difficult to tell, in such a structure, where crucial decisions are made. Each person or *gatekeeper* on the chart tends to limit the decisions of his superior by the way he screens information flowing upward. (Yet, he must screen if the firm is to survive.) Similarly, as orders flow down the chain, gatekeepers tend to eliminate explanations, reasons, and qualifications. (This may result in actions at variance with intended goals and is likely to lower morale.)

The taller an organizational chart and the more numerous the gatekeepers, the more possibilities of distortion in message flow both up and down. If the chain is shortened, by increasing a gatekeeper's *span of control* (the number of subordinates reporting to him) he can spend less time with each of them. This is good, since too-close supervision prevents a sub-

ordinate from developing initiative, but it is also bad, since it deprives him of the reward of frequent interaction with a superior.

Lack of time for interaction hurts communications in the flat chart; distortions occurring in a long chain of self-interested gatekeepers limit communications in the tall chart. (The appropriate span of control depends on the number and kind of decisions required, the number of routine decisions to be made, and the personalities of superiors and subordinates. One study found that presidents of 100 firms of over 5000 employees each had from one to 20 subordinates reporting directly to them.[6] A study of 500 manufacturing plants in Ohio found executives' span of control ranged from one to 17; 20% of firms reported a span of six subordinates, and 18% reported a span of five; top men in 94% of headquarter plants had spans of less than nine.)[7]

Personal friendships affect communications both inside and outside the command structure or firm and may determine where purchases are made. And, of course, such human factors affect selection of men for positions, as well as influencing their behavior once they achieve them. As Tucker points out, Wendell Wilkie was made president of Commonwealth and Southern, which in turn made him a candidate for president of the United States, on three conditions: "That he stop biting his fingernails, get his suits pressed more often and have the gold in his front teeth replaced by porcelain."[8] Both hiring and firing may depart from simplistic prescriptions of the *systems* approach. At top levels, executives are more likely to get kicked upstairs than to be fired or demoted. Competitors, customers, and suppliers might interpret more drastic action as a sign of real trouble; the delicate network of human relations within the firm would be threatened and every other executive made to feel insecure. Even if an executive's contribution to profit could be isolated, relating the two might deny the stability and the symbols which authority requires to function.

Reward systems like personnel decisions function rather differently than economic theory supposes: "The model . . . suggests that pay be based on the labor market, the individual's contribution to profits or some combination . . . There is little evidence that corporations operate this way."[9]

In summary, then, although the command structure may appear more "rational" and less behavioral than the bargaining encounter, it is by no means immune from behavioral influences. Behavioral processes affect not only the group decisions involved in bargaining but the piecemeal decision process characteristic of command structures.

Responses to Group Pressures

To understand how group decisions are made, we must look at how individuals respond to rewards that the group offers. The impact of a reward depends on each individual's perceptions of three factors: the rewards received by his peers, the rewards he can obtain through alternative behaviors (or alternative groups), and the rewards he had expected to receive. The individual who fails to receive rewards that have been given to those he regards as his equals undergoes *relative deprivation;* his performance is likely to suffer. Expectations are still more complex. Each time a person succeeds, he tends to raise his *level of aspirations;* each time he fails, he tends to lower his level; thus, predicting the impact of a given reward upon a given individual may require knowing his history of success and failure.

Second, we must ask how much influence the group can exert upon its members. Equal participation by members tends to make groups productive, but participation tends to become unequal as the life of the group or its size increases since both factors create status differences that inhibit interaction. (As soon as a group has four members, some begin to participate more than others, the change being marked and consistent until the group has eight members.[10] Experiments have shown that group pressures for conformity reach a peak when one is faced by a unanimous trio.)[11]

Persons who join a group tend to be similar at the outset; this in itself reduces the diversity of information and outlook needed for high productivity. Their similarity increases over time, since the group screens cues from the environment, offers an "official" interpretation of ambiguous cues, and exerts pressure on members to conform. Pressure to conform increases to the extent that the group has clear-cut goals and means of detecting failure to conform to them.

Organizational Pressures

As groups grow in size, they tend to become organizations with formal roles arranged in a status hierarchy; roles and status lead to longer life—life that exceeds that of the original members. The prescribed functions, rights, and duties that go with role and status introduce impersonality both within the firm and toward clients or customers. Division of labor may reduce motivation, as a worker fails to see how his task fits into a larger picture. Communication suffers as low-status members hesitate to criticize superiors and find it hard to get a hearing for their ideas.

Status differences, of course, involve inequality of power; exercise of power creates tension. Rules which emphasize that power belongs to role rather than role occupant may relieve some of this tension. Rules also provide guidance and a warning that legitimizes exercise of power. They reduce uncertainty and protect a subordinate from inordinate or capricious demands.

They keep the subordinate out of trouble —but may stifle his initiative. They make the environment predictable, but tend to deprive the firm of insights from the lower ranks. Role, status, and rules, of course, are the earmarks of the command structure; to the extent they exist and work they reduce the use of bargaining in the firm.

The differences between groups and organizations at a given point in time are fairly easy to visualize. We are often unaware that a given organization changes over time, either because of growth and aging or in response to its environment; were we aware, we could more easily make compensatory changes in our own behavior —or leave the organization.

Such changes over time mean that the firm, like the family and the product, has a life cycle. For example, the founder of Sears Roebuck, Richard Sears, believed in changing environment rather than adapting to it.[12] Through advertising and low prices, he expanded sales from $1 million to $40 million in a decade. This rapid growth meant the firm often was unable to fill orders; this failure, plus a depression, made cost-cutting advisable under Sears' successor, Julius Rosenwald. The third chief, Robert E. Wood, increased retail outlets from 27 to 630 by adapting the firm's structure to changes in the environment. Under Theodore Houser, Sears returned to Sears' original policies of trying to change the environment: it began treating its suppliers as partners rather than antagonists, establishing scores of factories in the rural areas, at home and abroad, from which its customers came.

Analysts suggest than an organization can be typed at any point in time by the relative emphasis it puts on the three functions illustrated in Sears' history—adapting to the environment, operating upon it, or regulating internal affairs. (Leaders with personnel skills are happiest and most effective in the third phase, an "idea man" in the second, and a mixture of both types in the first.) The successful industrial salesman needs to know which of these phases a given customer-firm is in at the moment. Usually these three styles of leadership coexist within each firm; a salesman must know how to approach each as well as knowing which type is likely to be dominant because of the current stage. A salesman who seeks to advance into executive ranks also needs to know what *his* leadership style is, and whether that style will be needed when he's ready to advance. Cyert and March[13] suggest that management decisions often result from bargaining among executives, each trying to maximize his individual goals, rather than being made by a single man at the top of the heap who then tells his subordinates what to do. To the extent that a salesman can employ within the firm which employs him the same bargaining techniques he uses with customers, he may be more effective and comfortable than if he has to shift back and forth between bargaining and command structures.

Thought, Talk, and Action

1. Think of three purchases you've made recently: one involving a joint decision with at least one other person; one involving bargaining with the seller; the third decision occurring in your own head. How *long* did each take? How much did each cost? How many alternative brands did you consider? How many sources of supply did you visit? How many separate decisions concerning product attributes did each involve? How many times had you purchased each of the products before?

2. Reviewing your answer to No. 1, how would you behave *as a seller* to maximize your chances of making a sale to other persons like yourself?

3. Why have profit centers, which convert employees into quasi-entrepreneurs, caused a shift from command to bargaining? Do you think a similar shift has occurred in the American family during this century? How does this change affect the behavior of salesmen selling for the firm? Those selling to the firm?

Notes

Chapter 14

1. Peter M. Blau and W. Richard Scott, Formal organizations (San Francisco: Chandler Publishing Co., 1962), pp. 45–57.
2. Harold H. Kelley and John W. Thibaut, "Experimental studies of group problem solving and process" in Gardner Lindzey, editor, Handbook of Social Psychology (Cambridge: Addison-Wesley Publishing Co., 1954), Vol. 2, pp. 772–6.
3. Roger Brown, Social psychology (New York: The Free Press, 1965), pp. 656–62.
4. Harold H. Kelley and John W. Thibaut, "Group problem solving," Gardner Lindzey and Elliot Aronson, editors, Handbook of Social Psychology, 2nd ed. (Reading, Mass.: Addison-Wesley Publishing Co., 1969), Vol. 4, pp. 61–71.
5. Lester Coch and John R. P. French, Jr., "Overcoming resistance to change," Human Relations, 1:512–32.
6. Justin G. Longenecker, Principles of management and organizational behavior (Columbus, Ohio: Charles E. Merrill, 1964), p. 177.
7. *Ibid.*
8. W. T. Tucker, The social context of economic behavior (New York: Holt, Rinehart and Winston, 1964), p. 113.
9. *Ibid.*, p. 110.
10. Reference No. 2, p. 762.
11. S. E. Asch, "Effects of group pressure upon the modification and distortion of judgments," in Eleanor E. Maccoby et al., Readings in social psychology, 3rd ed. (New York: Holt, Rinehart and Winston, 1958), p. 181.
12. Abraham Zaleznik and Anne Jardim, "Management," in Paul F. Lazarsfeld et al., editors, The uses of sociology (New York: Basic Books, 1967), pp. 222–4.
13. Richard M. Cyert and James G. March, A behavioral theory of the firm (Englewood Cliffs, N.J.: Prentice-Hall, 1963).

Decision Makers in the Household

Before advertisers and salesmen can influence decisions, they must know who is making them. Detroit housewives reported that they did more grocery-buying and bill-paying than their husbands.

	Proportion of Families (%)	
	Bill-paying	Grocery-buying
Husband	25	14
Wife	41	56
Both equally	34	29

But doing chores is not the same as making decisions. These same wives reported four different patterns of decision making shown in Table 14.1.

Occupation

Professional	5.52
Unskilled	5.07

Income

Over $10,000	5.83
Under $3,000	4.58

Education

5 years *more* than wife	5.36
5 years *less* than wife	5.05

Two factors tended to make wives dominant, as indicated by the lower scores.

Location of Home

Center city	4.79
Suburbs	5.44

Race

(Percent of homes that wife claims to dominate)

Negro	44
White	20

Table 14.1 Family Decision Making

	Husband Dominates (%)		Wife Dominates (%)	
Choice Made by	His Job	Family Car	Her Job	Food Budget
Husband	94	68	31	12
Both equally	3	25	18	32
Wife	1	5	48	52

	Choice Made Jointly (%)		Choice Split: Joint or One Spouse (%)	
Choice Made by	Vacation Site	House	Family Doctor	Life Insurance
Husband	18	18	10	42
Both equally	68	58	45	41
Wife	11	23	42	14

On a 10-point scale, with husband's dominance represented by scores above 4, 22% of the wives said their husbands dominated decision making and 22% said *they* were dominant.

Since no seller can make a family-by-family study of his prospects to determine where decision-making power lies, the *causes* of power distribution become important. Three factors, for example, tended to make *husbands* dominant, as shown by higher scores.

Wives were more dominant when they held jobs outside the home.

Source. Data reprinted with permission of The Free Press from *Husbands and Wives* by Robert O. Blood, Jr. and Donald M. Wolfe, Copyright © 1960 by The Free Press, a Corporation.

Determining where decision-making power lies by interviewing only one class of participants—wives—may produce biased results. However, the Survey Research Center which interviewed both husbands and wives, found little disagreement among them.

Decision Making in the Firm, I

Routine business decisions can be turned over to computers—after someone has put down on paper, in

	When to Buy Car, as Reported by: %		When to Buy Household Goods, Reported by: %		When to Save, as Reported by: %	
	Husband	Wife	Husband	Wife	Husband	Wife
Wife decides	4	4	36	35	29	32
Husband decides	56	63	8	11	47	49
Both decide	31	23	53	51	21	17

An objection to both this study and the previous one is that what people *say* they do is not necessarily what they actually do.

By conducting five interviews over 2.5 years, the Survey Research Center was able to compare couples' prediction of purchases and actual buying behavior. Husbands and wives who said they would *not* buy a stove, refrigerator, or washing machine were equally accurate —although 33% of wives and 38% of husbands who said they would *not* buy a car went ahead and did so. However, wives who predicted the family would buy appliances were correct 57% of the time, husbands only 38%. Wives who predicted purchase of a TV set were right 76% of the time, husbands only 39%.

As incomes rose, it appeared that fewer decisions were made jointly.

the form of a flow chart, the step-by-step processes of rational decision making. On page 283 is an example showing how prices might be set.

Source. Richard M. Cyert and James G. March, *A Behavioral Theory of the Firm* © 1963 by permission of Prentice-Hall, Inc., Englewood Cliffs, New Jersey.

Decision Making in the Firm, II

Not all choices are so routine that they can be programmed for a computer. Some have to be hammered out by executives in committees. When such groups are simulated in the laboratory, valuable insights are gained about such decisions.

In a typical study at the Harvard laboratory in which Robert F. Bales

	Under $3000 (%)	Over $10,000 (%)
Car: Husband chooses	45	61
Savings: Wife decides	36	9
Household goods: Wife decides	24	31

Source. Elizabeth H. Wolgast, "Do husbands or wives make the purchasing decisions?" *Journal of Marketing*, 23:2:151–8.

studied group behavior, 5 freshmen, recruited by mail and paid $1 an hour, were given 40 minutes to arrive at a

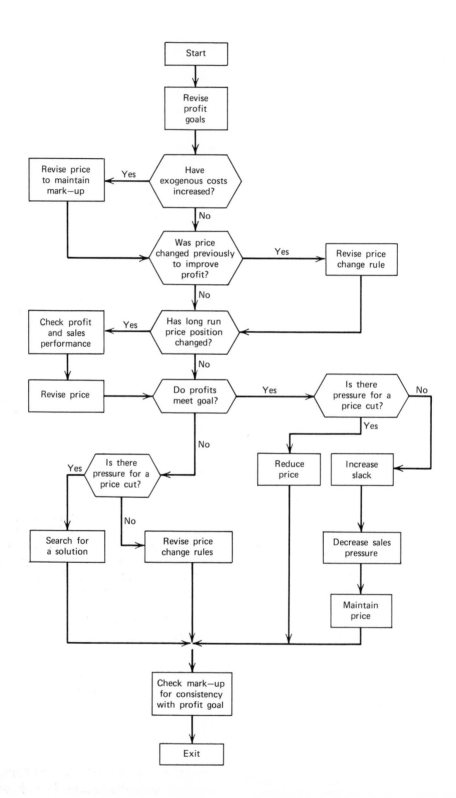

group recommendation concerning a solution to a human relations problem. Their discussion was recorded on sound tape, and observers noted who made each remark to whom and whether its purpose was to get the assigned task performed or to help maintain the group as a going organization. Members rated one another, after each session, on which participant had the most ideas, which one was best liked, and which one most disliked.

In the first session, about 56% of the men ranked high as having ideas tended also to be well-liked. By the fourth session, the two ratings went together only about 8% of the time.

Bales concluded that a group member may be active in trying to solve the problem, be rated by others as being able in problem solving, or be rated as likeable.

If ratings on each of these qualities are split between high and low, theoretically there should be eight different types $(2 \times 2 \times 2)$ of persons in the group. Bales reports finding five of them. The *good leader,* high on all three, is probably rare, he says, although the man who is low on all three, a kind of *scapegoat,* may be fairly common. Two other types, who often operate as partners, are the *task specialist* (low on likeability but high on activity and ability) and the social specialist (high on likeability but low on activity and ability). The man who dominates rather than leads the group is active, but low on task ability and likeability.

Source. Robert F. Bales, "Task roles and social roles in problem-solving groups," in Eleanor Maccoby et al., *Readings in Social Psychology* (New York: Holt, Rinehart and Winston, 1958, 3rd ed.), pp. 437–47.

Consumer Decisions: Emotional or Realistic?

Consumer decisions often appear to be based on error and lack of infor-mation. A closer look at the evidence, however, may indicate that consumers are behaving more sensibly than they've been given credit for. Here are two examples.

A house-to-house survey asked 250 housewives in Utica, to judge 4 pairs of hosiery. Interviewers encouraged housewives to feel them, look through them, stretch them, examine the seams, and do anything else that they would ordinarily do in shopping.

Although the four pairs were identical, housewives *explained* their choices on the grounds of texture, first of all, and then fineness of weave, feel, better wearing qualities, lack of sheen, heavier weight, and firmer weave.

A truer explanation of their choices was provided by the experimenter, who had given each of the 4 pairs a different scent. One pair was left with the natural "rancid" scent from castor oil and sulphates used in lubricating yarns to facilitate weaving. Although only six housewives noticed the scents and commented on them, their preferences for stockings were actually responses to scent:

Scent	Percentage of Choices
Natural	8
Sachet	18
Fruity	24
Narcissus	50

Source. Donald A. Laird, "How the consumer estimates quality by subconscious sensory impressions," *Journal of Applied Psychology,* 16:241–6.

But why shouldn't housewives prefer pleasant to unpleasant smells, particularly since it didn't cost them anything? If they hadn't cooperated with the experimenter by accepting his suggestion that the stockings *were* different, would the study ever have been published? Let a salesman try such shenanigans, however, and be caught at it and he's in trouble.

Three sets of packages of potato chips were prepared: 48 of the regular, 9-ounce weight; 48 with only 8 ounces; and 48 with 7 ounces. Anyone who purchased a package in either of 2 stores—an independent, suburban grocery and a metropolitan chain store—was given an experimental package, and asked to compare it with the one he had purchased.

Most consumers perceived the two packages as equal in weight.

weight packages, although identical with those in 9-ounce packages, were more likely to be described as greasy, bitter, stale, and limp and less likely to be described as crisp, delicious, and flavorful.

Source. James C. Naylor, "Deceptive packaging: Are the deceivers being deceived?" *Journal of Applied Psychology,* 46:393–8.

Actual Weight of Experimental Pack	Pack Judged Heaviest		No Difference
	Experimental	Regular	
9 ounces	9	4	30
8 ounces	5	8	22
7 ounces	7	8	25

Consumers also rated both packs—the one purchased and the one given free—on a 9-point terrible-to-excellent scale. When both packs weighed 9 ounces, the free pack was preferred; when the free pack weighed only 7 ounces, however, the purchased pack was preferred.

A third question asked which pack persons would buy on their next shopping trip. Again the short-weight packages lost out.

Sometimes a Handful of Cases Is Better Than a Carload

There are several occasions in which large, representative samples aren't needed. Sampling isn't necessary when only a few decision makers are involved; all of them can be quizzed. Funds and time may be available to question only a few, but this may be enough to improve decision making.

Actual Weight of Experimental Pack	Pack I Would Buy Next Time		
	Experimental	Either	Regular
9 ounces	22	7	11
8 ounces	13	14	6
7 ounces	12	8	15

The fourth question asked consumers to provide 3 words to describe each pack. The 109 words or phrases given were rated by 10 judges on a 5-point scale of favorability. The 8-ounce and 7-ounce packages were described less favorably than the 9-ounce package. Chips in short-

And sometimes a single member is enough to tell what each relevant audience is thinking. Here is a series of case histories which suggest the value of informal, "qualitative" research.

In 1959, when there were 450,000 TV

sets in the United States, interviewers asked 135 families how television had affected other kinds of leisure time activity. The results for a mere 135 families pointed up a problem which the entertainment industry woke up to a year later when the number of TV sets had tripled.

Went to movie	−64%
Went to boxing matches	−45
Went bowling	−12
Visited friends	−29
Entertained friends	81% up
Went to wrestling matches	22 up

After the war, a firm wanted to know whether there was a postwar market for a device that adjusted the fuel supply in airplanes. Researchers interviewed 75 engineering consultants in New York and Detroit, turning up so many uses that a device which management felt had no peacetime uses had soon boosted its wartime employees from 50 to 300.

Another study, by a weekly news magazine, discovered the existence of two types of purchasing procedure on the basis of 60 interviews in two cities. Purchases that affected technical production standards and, indirectly, the reputations of specialists in design, development, and production involved so many persons that a technically skilled and persuasive salesman was needed to bring them together. Nobody seemed to care about other purchases, such as office equipment and floor coverings. Here advertising had a real role to play.

The need for reaching a wide variety of audience types, rather than a large number of individuals of any single type, was illustrated by a study of surgical instruments. It included 40 interviews with hospital purchasing agents and superintendents, group purchasing agents, operating room supervisors, group insurance accountants, surgical chiefs of staff, resident surgeons, and makers of surgical equipment. Operating room supervisors did not like the stainless-steel instruments then in use, because they were hard to keep sharp. Surgeons did not like other kinds of instruments because their surfaces corroded. Researchers did not like the high cost of stainless steel instruments. Surface corrosion was eventually traced to the use of unskilled personnel to handle sterilization. Better selection or training here and everyone was happy— with sharper, cheaper instruments.

Source. Allan R. Wilson, "Qualitative market research," *Harvard Business Review,* 30: 1:75–86.

Decision Making by a Computer

Some choices can be made by a computer—although the computer input itself may include a good many subjective judgments by experts. Here's an example of how an $80,000 budget was divided among three magazines over a period of four months.

Ten operations were required. The first five adjusted the magazines' audiences up or down on the basis of overlap between magazine audience and target market, suitability of media and media vehicle to product, effects of color and time or space on message effectiveness, and effects of repetition.

1. *Audience.* The adjusted audience for Magazine X is arrived at by this formula, which represents an upward adjustment of 7.6%. (Figure 14.2)

6,000,000 (Actual audience)	× 1.09 (Age index)	× 1.05 (Income index)	× .94 (Regional index)	= 6,454,980 (Adjusted audience)

Figure 14.2

These three indices give more weight to segments which show high purchase of the product and the brand. The age index, for example, is formed by taking these figures from market and census reports.

| | Distribution of Women by Age (%) | | |
Age Group	In Population	For Product Sales	For Brand Sales
18–34	33	35	49
35–49	30	40	36
50 and up	37	25	15

The population percentage is divided by the product sales percentage (33/35% = 1.06) and the brand sales percentage by the product sales percentage (49/35% = 1.40). These two ratios are averaged for each segment. Multiplying by the average ratio then adjusts the actual audience figure to give more weight to high purchase segments. (See Figure 14.3).

(unidentified) product in this example alter adjusted audience figure (6,454,980) of step No. 1.

Media Weights		Readjusted Audience
Magazines	1.15	7,423,227
Television	1.00	6,454,980
Radio	.85	5,486,733
Newspapers	.80	5,163,984
Billboards	.60	3,872,988

3. *Vehicle.* Within the medium of magazines, vehicles such as *Good Housekeeping* and *McCall's* differ in the extent to which their advertisements are noted or believed, and how much the vehicle's prestige "rubs off" on advertisements. Subjective weights assigned to magazines readjust the audience again.

4. *Message variables.* Audience figures obtained in Step 3 are now multiplied by indices which reflect the relative effectiveness of 20-second vs.

Age Group	Product Index	Brand Index	Average Index	Actual Audience	Audience Adjusted for Age
	(Col. 1 ÷ Col. 2)	(Col. 2 ÷ Col. 3)			
18–34	1.06	1.40	1.23	3,000,000	3,690,000
35–49	1.33	.90	1.11	2,000,000	2,220,000
50 and up	.68	.60	.64	1,000,000	640,000
				6,000,000	6,550,000

Figure 14.3

Finally, one divides the adjusted audience (6,550,000) by the actual audience (6,000,000) to get the age index of 1.09 used in the formula shown above. A similar process is repeated for each index and for each magazine.

2. *Medium.* Next, subjective weights are needed to reflect the fact that magazine color may be best suited to a product like food, and the live demonstration possible on TV to a new gadget. These subjective weights for the

60-second commercials, or full pages vs. half-pages, or color vs. black-and-white.

5. *Effect of repetition.* At some point, diminishing returns set in as an ad is repeated in the same vehicle. If we assume a 10% loss per issue, then the audience of Magazine X (boosted from its actual audience of 6,000,000 to an adjusted audience of 7,500,000 by the four steps just described) would decrease thus.

Insertion	Adjusted Audience
First	7,500,000
Second	6,750,000
Third	6,075,000
Fourth	5,467,500

After five successive modifications of audience numbers, the next three steps consider *dollars,* splitting an ad budget of $1,200,000 among media and months of the year.

6. *Split among media.* The client or history or brand strategy dictate spending 80% of the budget on television and 20% on magazines.

7. *Quantity discounts.* Magazine X has a constant rate of $9000 per insertion. Its three competitors offer discounts as number of insertions rises.

Number of Insertion	Rate of Insertion		
	Magazine V	Magazine W	Magazine Y
First	$9,500	$10,000	$10,000
Second	9,000	10,000	9,000
Third	8,000	10,000	8,000
Fourth	8,000	7,000	7,000

8. *Readers per dollar.* Audience figures in Step 5 are now divided by the cost figures of Step 7, showing number of persons per dollar for each insertion in each of the magazines.

Month	Total Audience	Total Cost	Persons per Dollar
January	15,500,000	$19,000	816
February	6,750,000	9,000	750
March	14,200,000	19,500	728
April	18,855,000	28,000	673

Magazine	1st Insertion	2nd Insertion	3rd Insertion	4th Insertion
V	737 (March)	700 (April)	709	638
W	800 (Jan.)	720 (March)	648 (April)	833
X	833 (Jan.)	750 (Feb.)	675 (April)	607
Y	600	600	608	625

9. *Advertising schedule.* Some advertisers run heavy schedules in the months preceding the time they expect high-purchase rates; others try to counter such tendencies. In this illustration, $20,000 of the $240,000 magazine budget will be spent in January, $10,000 in February, $20,000 in March, $30,000 in April. Using the table in Step 8, these amounts will be divided among the magazines as follows.

January.	First insertions in Magazines X (833 persons per dollar) and W (800). Total cost: $19,000 (from Step 7).
February.	Second insertion in X (750). Total cost: $9000.
March.	First insertion in V (737) and second insertion in W (720). Total cost: $19,500.
April.	Second insertion in V (700); third insertions in X (675) and W (648). Total cost: $28,000.

10. *Summary.* Here is a summary of the effects of this schedule over these four months of January through April.

These totals do not consider duplication. If 30% saw *both* magazines used in January, the number of different persons reached would be 10,850,000 instead of 15,500,000. Dividing the larger figure by the smaller gives 1.43 as an index of frequency—the number of times the average viewer is exposed to the advertisement.

Source. Philip Kotler, "Toward an explicit model for media selection," *Journal of Advertising Research,* 4:1:34–41.

Feeding Information Into the Firm— And What Happens After It Gets There!

Marketing communications has emphasized message output by the seller, but has overlooked the input of information to him. Salesmen can bring a seller news about prospects, competitors, and suppliers. Here is an experiment which suggests they could be doing a much better job of message input.

At the request of an electrical manufacturing firm, but without the knowledge of the firm's salesmen, purchasing agents for its customers planted 6 rumors with the salesmen during their regular calls.

Three to 18 days later, the manufacturer sent a questionnaire to managers and staffs of 10 product sections, managers of 57 operating units within these sections, and field personnel. (Replies were received from 36%.)

In each case, the appropriate target for the rumors was Operating Unit A. Two of the rumors were planted with salesmen for this unit, 2 with salesmen for another section of the same branch, and 2 with salesmen for a different branch of the firm.

Only one of the rumors was passed on to the appropriate target without distortion. Two accidental factors probably explain this. The salesman had formerly sold widgets and was a personal friend of Unit A's sales manager.

Another rumor was passed on in distorted fashion. No trace was found of the other 4 rumors. Two concerned competitors: a low price quotation for a widget made by a Japanese company, and news that a competitor was to construct a new widget factory in California. Another concerned the conversion of military radar and the fourth the development of a competitive widget from a new, previously unused material.

Source. Gerald Albaum, "Horizontal information flow: an exploratory study," *Journal of the Academy of Management,* 7:1:21–33.

The Man in the Middle

Many a man in many an organization must appear to be "one of the gang" to his subordinates but a "member of the management team" to his superiors. Superiors laud him for enforcing rules; subordinates hope he will bend a regulation when necessary. The role of the man in the middle is defined quite differently by the man himself, by those from whom he gets orders, and by those to whom he gives orders, as shown in attitude studies in World War II.

	Percentage Agreeing with Statement		
	Privates	Noncoms	Officers
Off-Duty Behavior			
A noncom will lose the respect of his men if he pals around with them off-duty.	13	16	39
A noncom should not let the men in his squad forget he's a noncom even off-duty.	39	54	81
Discipline			
A noncom has to be very strict with his men or they will take advantage of him.	45	52	68
On the Job			
A noncom should keep his men busy even if he has to make them do unnecessary work.	16	22	39
On a fatigue detail, the noncom . . . should not help the men under him do the work.	36	37	68

Source. Samuel A. Stouffer et al., *The American Soldier, Studies in Social Psychology in World War II*, I:48 (Princeton, N.J.: Princeton University Press, 1949).

In any organization, some attitudes are widely shared, since they are not affected by differences in status, but views as to relations between subordinate and superior vary markedly with the place the viewer is standing.

Issue	Average Difference in Percentage Points Between Views of Officers and Enlistees
Feelings in combat	11
The army itself	25
Relations between officers and men	44

Source. Robert K. Merton and Paul F. Lazarsfeld, eds., *Continuities in Social Research* (New York: The Free Press, 1950), pp. 106–32.

Additional Research Readings

Choices. Thanks to Wisconsin law, which requires cash redemption of trading stamps, and proximity of Superior, Wis., to Minnesota, whose laws do not, experimenters contrasted cash-only (Madison), premiums (Rockford, Ill.), and choice of either (Superior/Duluth). They found only 3% of Duluth sought cash, while 87% of Superior sought premiums. **Jon G. Udell, "Can attitude measurement predict consumer behavior?" Journal of Marketing, 29:4:1 46–50.** A computer simulated information and choice processes which are suitable to choice of college or doctor and to training of auto salesmen or purchasing agents. **G. David Hughes and Philippe A. Naert, "A computer controlled experiment in consumer behavior," Journal of Business, 43:354–72.** In choosing a physician, 28 year olds sought the advice of relatives, 34 year olds that of professionals, and 40 year olds depended on their own judgment. **Sidney P. Feldman, "Some dyadic relationships associated with consumer choice," Ray-mond M. Haas, editor, Science, Technology and Marketing (Chicago: American Marketing Association, 1966).** Faced with choices of vacation site, auditor candidate, secretarial applicant, and varieties of rice, subjects were offered information about the alternatives, about their attributes, or about a third attribute. (Each alternative was superior on one attribute, inferior on another.) **Steven H. Chaffee et al., "Experiments on cognitive discrepancies and communication," Journalism Monographs, 14:55–74.**

Risk. Business students were less cautious than businessmen in making decisions about innovations, but matched them in judging salesmen's skills. (Engineering students were *more* cautious than engineers.) **Inder P. Khera and James D. Benson, "Are students really poor substitutes for businessmen in behavioral research?" Journal of Marketing Research, 7:529–32.** If firms want to increase shopping by phone, they must reduce risk perceived by housewives, especially for clothing and appliances. **Donald F. Cox and Stuart U. Rich, "Perceived risk and consumer decision-making . . . ," Journal of Marketing Research, 1:32–9.** A high-risk lab group, asked to choose one of three unfamiliar hair sprays, took nearly three times as long to choose as a low-risk group and sought much more information from other persons. **Jagdish N. Sheth and M. Venkatesan, "Risk-reduction processes in repetitive consumer behavior," Journal of Marketing Research, 5:307–10.** On a five-point scale nearly 500 housewives chose brand loyalty over 10 other methods as the best way of reducing risks to time, money, health, and ego. **Ted Roselius, "Consumer rankings of risk reduction methods," Journal of Marketing, 35:1:56–61.**

Although decisions by either buyer or seller *may* take place within the head of a single person, the purchase-and-sale event requires at least two persons. Moreover, many decisions to buy or to sell, including the most important ones, involve group decisions. So we pause again for an in-depth look at the significance, in marketing communications, of the fact that messages are often sent by and to several persons.

Chapter 15 examines three types of people categories: *aggregates,* whose members resemble one another but do not interact; *groups,* which consist of similar persons communicating with one another; and *organizations,* in which role, examined earlier in Chapter 6, determines individual behavior. The audiences for advertising messages tend to be aggregates; groups provide channels for word-of-mouth messages; organizations prepare and transmit messages.

Chapter 16 focuses on the effects of status upon communications, emphasizing the matter of *social class,* viewed either as aggregate or group.

Chapter 17 completes the picture with a look at the *organizations* in which most of us earn the incomes that qualify us as buyers; in which some of us are employed as salesmen and others as purchasing agents.

Following these three chapters is Chapter 18, the culmination of the decision processes in a purchase-and-sale that involves interaction of individual or organizational buyers and sellers.

Chapter 15 Synopsis

● Three people categories—aggregates, organizations, and groups—affect message style and content, provide channels, determine audiences, and influence responses in marketing communications.

● *Aggregates* exist within an observer's mind, being made up of individuals linked together by common attributes who, for that reason, are expected to show similar responses. *Groups* are made up of members who, originally similar, tend to become more so through interaction with one another. *Organizations* consist of large numbers of persons whose interactions are specified for them by role and status. (Some people categories, like *social class,* may be defined as either aggregates or groups.)

● The goal of any group is made up of the goals that individual members hope to accomplish through it, as modified by interaction among them. Such goals are of two kinds; in *task performance,* the group is the means to a goal external to the group; in *group maintenance,* group activity is an end, enjoyable in itself. Every group has elements of both, requires leaders with both kinds of skill, offers both types of reward.

● In groups, communication among members tends to produce differences in role and status; in organizations, members are recruited for particular roles and statuses which impose different communications patterns on their occupants. Groups exist within organizations where they may aid or impede organizational goal achievement.

● Although productivity is enhanced by equal participation among members of varying viewpoints, viewpoints tend to become more similar and participation more unequal through interaction in the group, and emergence of role and status differences. The ability of a group to enforce conformity depends upon clarity of norms, size of rewards, ability, and desire to enforce the norms. Groups may also be compared, in estimating their effects, in terms of size, duration, cohesion, and priority and scope of claims upon the member. A seller can seek the support of the most powerful groups in his messages to the buyer.

● Salesman and account executive resemble one another and differ from the sales manager in that they are influenced by two organizations: the one that employs them and the one that employs the persons with whom they must bargain. All three, however, find themselves engaged in both competitive and cooperative activities, in zero-sum and nonzero-sum games.

Research Articles

Participation.   Group discussion appears superior to lecture in changing product use (Lewin), but commitment and perception of consensus prove key (Bennett).

Conformity.   Study isolates effects of selective recruitment and of interaction (Siegel); group's value for individual and individual's value for group affect extent of conformity (Jackson).

Norms.   Contradictory expectations of faculty and students tug at student proctors (Stouffer); group norms made salient by experimenter's instructions (Charters) or makeup of group (Shomer).

Chapter 15 People Categories: Aggregates, Organizations, and Groups

Throughout this book we have dealt with two kinds of people categories: *aggregates* of buyers and of sellers, and the simple two-person *group* that is formed whenever buyer and seller confront one another.

Most advertising messages are fashioned by small *groups* of persons, interacting with one another. These messages then fight their way up and down the perilous levels of a client's *organization* for approval. The client firm turns them over to other organizations (the media) to be transmitted to an *aggregate* or collectivity, called an audience, which overlaps another aggregate called a market segment. Individual members of this audience may relay the message, in turn, to a *group* of friends, of fellow workers in their employer's *organization,* of fellow members of such voluntary organizations as their church or lodge, or of members of the most basic group of all, the family.

Finally, the family in council assembled responds to the message. *Every other girl my age is wearing them,* says daughter—calling to her aid that important *reference group,* an adolescent's peers. *But your father's a physician,* says Mother. *What will people in this neighborhood say? Educated people just don't do that sort of thing.* Thus does Mother remind her daughter that the family has certain *class* standards to maintain, views one must respect if one wants to associate with persons of similar occupation and education. *It would be all right if we lived in the jungle,* Father chimes in. *But, after all, this is a civilized country.* Father apparently feels even more strongly than Mother; the latest teen-age fashion offends not just class but modern-industrial,

Judeo-Christian, western European, majority-American *culture* itself.

Thus do other people, visible and invisible, determine the style and content of a seller's message, provide the channels through which it is transmitted, set bounds to the audience-market it can reach, and affect the response the message receives when it finally hits its target.

We have encountered such influences several times already in these pages. In the very first chapter, we discovered that one of the seller's most crucial choices is that of deciding what market segment (*aggregate*) he will seek to serve. Then, in Chapter 2, we found that every person involved in a purchase has goals he seeks to satisfy, and that these must be reconciled in the (*group*) decision process. The utility of any definition (Chapter 3) depends upon the number of persons who can agree on it, and attitude scales (Chapter 4) are validated by comparing the scores of groups known to vary on the dimensions they measure. Personality (Chapter 5), a source of individual goals, comes into being when an individual interacts with others; role, another source of goals, symbolizes the differentiation of functions that can arise only within a group or organization. Of the four major types of constraint (Chapter 6) that affect decisions in marketing communications, the social environment—as we have just seen in Daughter's Dilemma—is often the most important, whether codified in the institutions of "The Law" or as casual as a neighbor's frown. Finally, after the decision is made, buyer and seller interact (becoming a temporary *group*) in the social event called a purchase-sale.

Members of an aggregate (market segment and audience) may never see one another or even be aware that they are part of a category. (The aggregate may exist only in the mind of the seller who finds some common attribute in persons unknown to one another that enables him to send them a single product or message.) Members of a group must, by definition, interact with one another. (The family, a relatively permanent group in which membership is determined both by birth (for the children) and by election (husband and wife), imposes rights and responsibilities that touch upon nearly every aspect of human behavior.)

Aggregate, Group, Organization

In estimating the impact of people categories on individual behavior, we must make a distinction between categories that exist only within an observer's mind (convenient groupings of persons on the basis of some similarity) and categories of real people who interact and so influence one another (in ways that may aid or hinder the outsider trying to shape their behavior).

Aggregates that exist only in an observer's mind can be reshuffled at will, the market segment being an example. A group made up of real people, like the family, is as likely to constrain a seller's decisions as to help implement them. A social class can be either group or aggregate. (A class in a small town may consist of people who associate with one another, particularly in the kind of leisure time activities that may eventuate in marital ties. A class in a large city, a nation, or the world may consist of persons who merely share similar characteristics.) Marketing is more likely to deal with social class as a perceptual aggregate rather than an interacting group. The *reference group* that influences an individual's decisions may be an actual group to which he belongs or one that he would like to join or it may exist only in the mind, an aggregate of persons regarded as experts and standard setters or as people to be despised. (In the first instance, the individual will emulate their behavior; in the second instance, he will shun it.)

A distinction must also be made between the goals that individuals bring to a group and the goals they arrive at in the course of the group experience itself. Tom joins a teen-age dance combo because he likes to play drums. Dick joins because he wants to earn money. Harry joins because he enjoys being with the other two. Each will remain in the combo so long as it proves an effective means to his individual goals, a means more effective than any alternative available to him. (Dick may quit if another combo offers him higher pay. Tom may lose his place to another drummer who Dick thinks can attract better-paying dates.) Individual members' goals may cause changes in the group; changes in the group may bring about a new mix of goals. (Addition of an attractive, blonde, female singer could set off competitive tendencies that would break up the group.)

Most groups are formed and most persons join groups because they expect division of labor in the group to accomplish more effectively what each individual separately desires. (Each may seek the same goal, such as money, or each may have a different goal.) Whatever these goals are, every group engages in two kinds of activities: those of *task* which help the group move toward its goal(s) and the *social* or *group maintenance* activities which keep the group together by easing tensions and building cohesion. Frequently, a group will have two leaders, one skilled in each of these areas. Matching these two types of activities are two kinds of rewards: (1) success in the task it was organized around, and (2) the less visible reward of having a good time in the process. Some persons are primarily interested in the latter; some groups proclaim having a good time as their aim. (Such protestations need not be taken at face value. Groups that speak most loudly of "good fellowship" may be very effective in bringing buyers and sellers together on golf course and in locker room.)

Individuals with a strong need to achieve are interested in moving toward the formal goal. Those with a need for affiliation are more interested in pleasurable interaction. (Young men may league together in groups one writer calls *cabals* to exchange information that will help them advance in an organization. Older men, content with their positions, may form *cliques* which provide the alternative rewards of group maintenance.)

Individuals also differ in their ability to perform the activities involved in task performance and in group maintenance. In an informal group, each of these tends to be best performed by a different man. In a formal organization, one man usually performs both functions. The amount of supervision a leader supplies reflects the amount his subordinates want. (The amount they want increases as one descends the organizational chart, since employees at the bottom tend to have less interest in task performance and less confidence in their own ability.) It also reflects the behavior of the leader's own superior whose supervisory methods suggest what the organization wants and what it will reward.

Even the simplest group tends to develop one specialist skilled in moving the group toward some specific goal (beating a sales record, building a bridge, winning a golf tournament, or mastering Beethoven's Ninth Symphony) and another who eases the interpersonal tensions incident to such efforts.

Specialization Rises with Size

As groups grow larger, in members and activities, and as their life expectancy lengthens, jobs become more and more specialized. The duties attached to a role are prescribed more precisely so that if the occupant of a role leaves, someone with similar abilities can be fit into it without changing the slot. As jobs become more specialized, they must be coordinated: work flows must be planned through time, and a chain of command and communications set up. Jobs tend to be arranged vertically, with decisions being made at the top and orders flowing down and rewards diminishing as one descends the organizational chart. All these differences—in the power, responsibility and reward attached to a role—we label with the name *status*. Differences in *status* tend to distinguish the organization from many groups.

Indeed, business firms may be categorized by their number of levels of status. (Job applicants want to know how many rungs there are on a firm's career ladder, and how many subordinates report to each manager.)

In contrast, groups tend to be small. (One definition, which says that each member must be able to communicate face-to-face with every other "regularly," imposes a practical ceiling on membership of 15 to 20, with the most effective groups appearing to be half that size.) Groups tend to be short-lived, to have less well-defined roles and statuses, and to have fewer of them. Groups often grow up to become organizations; most organizations contain several groups within themselves.

Channels of communication are an independent variable in the group and a dependent variable in the organization. In a group, an individual's communications with other members determine the rules and roles that develop. If a member must adjust to patterns already established, he has joined an organization. (If Henry leaves his gang of bowlers, for example, and members look for someone to take his place who is as much like Henry as possible, the group has become an organization. If members of a college gang try to insure the gang's survival, despite their own graduation, by converting it into a club or society, then it becomes an organization.)

Informal Groups in Organizations

Small groups of peers, the seed from which organizations grow, persist within the most bureaucratic organization, to provide, informally, the rewards of group maintenance that the larger organization often neglects. In doing so they develop norms of their own which may be hostile toward, irrelevant to, or, on a few happy occasions, actually contribute to the task-performance goals of the larger organization. (In a factory, workers league together to hold down production, frustrating incentive plans. In an office, workers circumvent regulations which, if observed, would bring operations to a grinding halt. In a clothing store, salesmen find the competition which management seeks so threatening that they cooperate to frustrate it.)

Individuals seek out groups and are sought by them because they already share the characteristics, values, and goals of the group. (The concept of *anticipatory socialization* suggests the worker most likely to become foreman is the man who has already begun thinking like a foreman. Through *selective recruitment,* a group insures that new members resemble old ones.) After they join, members become still more like one another. Groups screen the information that members receive: members respond similarly because they get similar messages. A member will emulate the behavior of his colleagues because he seeks the reward of their approval. (Should he fail to behave as expected, other members attempt, through persuasion, to bring him back into line; if this fails, they will punish him by ostracism and, ultimately, by actual expulsion.)

The effectiveness of such pressure on an individual depends on how much he values membership. If the group has a clear goal that he values, if the group has the resources needed to attain the goal, and if it is following a path that seems likely to achieve that goal, the member is likely to value the group and respond to pressure from its members. (Equal participation by members representing a variety of abilities and viewpoints tends to increase productivity. But just as equality of participation tends to disappear from a group over time, so does variety among its members.)

The increase in similarity among members over time means that the seller's messages can emphasize values that members share; that members will relay and endorse his messages; that a product which meets the needs of one member will probably suit others.

Control Over Members

A group's ability to enforce conformity depends upon clarity of norms, size of rewards, surveillance, and desire. Has the group clearly distinguished between member behaviors that are *musts, must-nots,* and *mays* and made sure that members understand? How easily can a group detect a member's deviation from such standards or norms? How quickly does it reward conformity and punish deviance? How much are its *rewards* desired and its penalties feared? (What alternative opportunities does the member have elsewhere?) How much does the group *desire* conformity; how willing is it to impose its rewards and penalties? Do all members help enforce its norms or is enforcement delegated to certain role occupants?

By comparing groups on these four dimensions, a seller can predict which will most influence an individual and adapt his messages to the norms of the more powerful group.

A seller must consider not only how much power a group has over its members, but how many members it has and how many of their behaviors it is concerned with. (These factors may be summed up as *size, duration,* and *scope.*) The degree to which a group can influence members' behavior is affected by *cohesion* and *priority*. (The effects of *cohesion* have already been noted; members tend to value any group that provides them with the rewards they seek. They respond to persons similar to themselves, similarity being related to liking.)

A large group obviously affects more members than a small one, but *size* must be measured in time as well as space. An organization that persists over a long span of time, or whose members remain loyal through most of their lives, obviously has more influence than a short-lived group or one in which members change frequently: *duration* is important. Some groups affect only a few behaviors, others influence what members think, wear, eat, and say. (Membership in the American Civil Liberties Union or the Daughters of the American Revolution affects few sales, except perhaps of copies of the Constitution; membership in a congregation of Orthodox Jews will both proscribe and prescribe many purchases.) *Scope* of this kind differentiates aggregates as well as groups. An open class society like that of the United States permits the individual greater freedom of action; a caste system such as that in India limits freedom over a wide range.

Finally, the larger society recognizes that the norms of some groups should have *priority* over those of others. Most persons are expected to put the welfare of their families above that of their employers, in case of conflict. (In some parts of the world, kinship priorities extend even to finding soft jobs for incompetent third cousins. In western culture, definition of one's family is restricted to one's parents, the family one is born into (*orientation*) and one's spouse and offspring, the family one produces (*procreation*), limiting the demands of family.) However, priorities vary with status: the higher one's position in a firm, the more legitimate its demands appear to be.

An industrial salesman must determine where decision-making power is located on each organizational chart; the number of levels involved and the number of roles at each level. (Which transactions must a purchasing agent buck upstairs for approval? Who in a firm favors a purchase? Which decision makers must be reached indirectly through informal word-of-mouth messages from a member of the firm whom the salesman can reach?) Sometimes the men a salesman can reach, those who can be influenced and those who have power of decision, have little overlap.

An advertising manager, in contrast to a sales manager, tends to be involved in external processes of bargaining and conflict, rather than internal processes of conflict and command. Many of his communications are with peers, rather than formal superiors or subordinates, in outside organizations (usually the firm's ad agency, less often, with representatives of media and research groups.)

The sales manager needs an accurate, adequate flow of information from the field, knowing that each participant, whether salesman or independent distributor, will tend to pass on only news that reflects favorably on himself. He must pass down directives from above, giving each man as much of the big picture as he needs (although often less than each would like to have).

The advertising manager supplies information to employees of the ad agency and has veto power over their actions but neither rewards nor supervises them directly. Incoming messages, hurdling few hierarchical levels, may give him a picture less distorted than that of the sales manager. (The marketplace seems freer than the command structure, as shown by the frequency with which agency-client and agency-employee relations are severed.)

Inside the firm and out, both ad manager and sales manager find themselves engaged in both competitive and cooperative activities. In the former, a kind of zero-sum game, one man's gains represent losses for the other. Such competitive games are played with one's colleagues in the firm at budget time and in the field with one's competitors. Sales manager and sales staff, on the other hand, cooperate to attain sales quotas; ad manager and agency creative team strive together to get a winning campaign by deadline. In both examples, all members benefit when the team wins.

Thought, Talk, and Action

1. List the groups that you belong to or have been a member of during the past five years. Rank them in terms of the similarity of their members, in demographic characteristics, viewpoints, etc. Now rank them in terms of the frequency, duration, and intensity with which members interact with one another. How much do the two sets of rankings coincide? (With "D" representing the difference between ranks for each group, you can get a rank correlation with this formula:

$$1 - \frac{6\,D^2}{N\,(N^2 - 1)}$$

2. Now list the organizations to which you belong. How could you, as seller, use these group and organizational memberships to reach and influence prospects? Think in terms of specific products and brands.
3. Imagine a situation in which two of the groups listed in No. 1 made demands on you which conflicted, either because you couldn't find time to serve both or because they demanded antagonistic acts of you. How would you try to keep in favor with both? If forced to choose, which would you favor? Now compare the two groups in the characteristics listed in the fifth paragraph of the chapter synopsis.

Using Groups to Change Attitudes

Perhaps no human habit is as hard to change and as resistant to rational argument as men's choice of food. Rice-eaters in Asia go hungry rather than eat the wheat shipped in from overseas, and ethnic preferences for spaghetti and sauerkraut persist into the third and fourth generation in the United States. Like most other preferences established in early childhood, food preferences are hard to change. The attitudes that support them are multidimensional; one may object to the taste, the smell, appearance, and texture of an unfamiliar food. Moreover, before they can use new foods, housewives may have to learn new methods of preparing them.

Yet changes do occur over time—olives and tomatoes, once shunned as poisonous or dangerous aphrodisiacs, are now openly sold in our supermarkets. To benefit from such changes is one thing; to try to produce them usually takes more time and money than a marketer can afford to spend. To suppose that deep-seated aversions to using intestinal meats could be overcome in 45 minutes seems optimistic, to say the least.

At the State University of Iowa in World War II in the midst of the meat shortage, home-nursing volunteers heard lectures advocating use of beef hearts, sweetbreads, and kidneys for reasons of health, economy, and the war effort. A checkup later showed that only 3% of the women who heard the lectures, but had never tried the meats before, actually went home and served them to their families. Meanwhile, other volunteers held a group discussion, with an expert to tell how such objections as cooking smell and husbands' attitudes might be overcome. Follow-up interviews found that 32% of this group tried the meats for the first time.

The lecture method, which closely resembles advertising in lack of feedback, was subsequently pitted against the discussion method in two more studies. In one, housewives were urged to use more fresh or evaporated milk. Follow-ups at the end of two weeks and of four weeks showed greater increase in use of milk among discussion group subjects than in lecture audiences. In the third study, a nutritionist conferred individually with farm mothers who had just had their first child, urging them to give the baby orange juice and cod liver oil. She also met with other mothers in groups of six for 25-minute discussions in which the same practices were urged. Discussion proved more effective.

Volunteers in the meat experiment belonged to groups which met regularly; housewives in the milk study knew one another but had not met as a group. Mothers in the orange juice discussion groups had never met one another previously.

Source. Kurt Lewin, "Group decision and social change," in Eleanor Maccoby et al., *Readings in Social Psychology* (New York: Holt, Rinehart and Winston, 1958).

Tupperware rewards housewives for inviting their neighbors to a "party," and developers of resort property often invite strangers to enjoy a free dinner and listen to their sales pitch. Sellers may assemble groups of prospects, as did Lewin, either to obtain a consensus effect, the presence of other prospects reassuring purchaser,

or to obtain a competitive effect, as at an auction, with each prospect hastening to act before someone snatches a choice lake lot away from him.

A closer look at Lewin's studies showed that at least four different variables might account for the success of group discussion.

The discussion itself as a channel of information: questions were raised that supplied feedback to the leader.

Individuals were asked to commit themselves, to make a decision.

Their commitment was public.

Individuals could perceive the existence of consensus in the group.

Which of these were most important? At the University of Michigan, four degrees of commitment were studied: no decision at all, an anonymous decision, public commitment by raising one's hand (as in Lewin's study), and commitment by raising one's hand and having one's name recorded. Each kind of commitment was tested in a lecture group, a discussion group, and a control group which heard no arguments at all.

The action sought this time was that of volunteering as a subject in a psychological experiment. A few days after subjects got the "please volunteer" message, they received a letter asking them to sign up as subjects. A week later, a classroom questionnaire asked whether they had committed themselves at the original session, whether they had responded to the letter, and how many other students they thought had signed up. The results were as follows.

Group discussion: no effect. (About 75% in both lecture and discussion groups volunteered.)

Public commitment: no effect.

Decision making: 22% of the groups asked to make a decision did not volunteer, as compared with only 15% of those not asked to decide.

Perception of consensus: The proportion volunteering ranged from 41 to 100%, with the average at 72.5%. Those who volunteered perceived a higher rate of volunteering than did those who refused.

Thus, deciding to volunteer and perceiving that others were doing the same appeared to be the decisive factors in the study. Discussion and public commitment did not appear important.

Source. E. B. Bennett, "Discussion, decision, commitment, and consensus in 'group decision,' " *Human Relations,* 8:251–74.

Use of discussion to change attitudes works in real life as well as in the laboratory. It has helped reconcile workers to a job change which they had resisted for fear it would reduce their earnings.

A pajama factory in Virginia employing 500 women and 100 men on a piecework basis was in trouble. Records showed that during the relearning period after shifts to a new job, 62% of those shifted either quit or got stuck at a substandard rate of output. Apparently groups in the factory exerted pressure on members to hold down production. (One presser was harassed when she began to exceed her group's rate of 50 units a day; her output thereupon fell from 56 to 48 units. When members of the group were transferred, freeing her from their pressures, her output shot up to 92 and stayed there.) Experts suggested that if group norms could be changed, so as to favor higher output, the firm would benefit. But how to do this?

Three groups, matched in terms of efficiency and cohesion, were used. One group of 18 pressers heard time-study man explain a new piece rate, which he said was required because of

competitive pressures. A second group of 13 heard a similar explanation but then elected members to be trained in the new methods, whose subsequent performance would determine the piece rate to be paid all members. (These representatives also trained the persons who had elected them.) The third group of subjects met in small groups to hear of the need for change, then *all* of their members participated in designing the new job, with new piece rates being based on all their performances.

In the first group, conflict and hostility broke out immediately and 17% of the group quit. Production averaged about 50 units. Members of the second, "representative" group were cooperative. Nobody quit, and the entire group soon hit an average of 61 units within two weeks. Output in the "total democracy" group slumped for a single day, then hit a level 14% higher than that prior to the change. Again, nobody quit.

In all three groups, variability of output among workers markedly decreased after the change. Average daily standard deviations before the change were about 10 in all three groups. Afterward they were 1.9 for the no-participation group, 3.8 for the representative group, and 2.7 for the total-democracy group. In the first group, the change produced an agreement to restrict output; change plus participation (and training) was enough to get uniform output at a high level in the other two groups.

Source. Lester Coch and John R. P. French, Jr., "Overcoming resistance to change," *Human Relations,* 1:512–32.

How Groups Influence Members and Would-Be Members

Two factors tend to produce homogeneous attitudes in any group: selection of members and the interaction within the group. Here these two effects were isolated.

At the time of the study, coeds at Stanford University were required to live in a large dormitory during their freshman year. At the end of the year, a lottery was held with winners being allowed to move into former sorority houses whose high prestige was a lure. Twenty-eight such applicants were followed during their sophomore year.

Nine who had won admission to the prestigeful houses.

Eleven losers who renewed their applications at the end of their sophomore year.

Eight losers who decided *not* to seek admission to the former sorority houses.

Earlier studies had found that during their careers at Stanford, coed's scores on a scale of authoritarianism decrease, the decrease being least noticeable for residents of the former sorority houses.

The nine women, whose original scores had ranged from 70 to 143, changed least during the year thanks to their daily interaction; their scores dropped an average of only 3.89 points.

Scores for the second group of 11, who still considered the nine winners their reference group, although they had little chance to interact with them, dropped an average of 11.18 points during the year.

Scores for the third group, for whom inmates had ceased to be a reference group, dropped an average of 19.75 points.

Source. Alberta Engvall Siegel and Sidney Siegel, "Reference groups, membership groups and attitude change," *Journal of Abnormal and Social Psychology*, 55:360–4.

The person who values his membership in a group is more likely to conform to its norms. He is likely to value his membership if other members reward him and if he regards the group as important.

Three scores were obtained for 46 professional employees of a midwest child welfare agency and 26 nonprofessional workers (such as typists and housemothers).

Benefit. The extent to which each felt rewarded by working in the agency.

Social worth. The frequency with which other members listed him as a valuable employee.

Contact. Frequency of contacts he reported with fellow employees.

Analysis showed low but statistically significant correlations between benefit and social worth for *professional* workers both within the organization as a whole (.30) and within one of the six work groups earlier found to exist in the agency (.37). Neither of the correlations (.16 and .11) for nonprofessionals attained significance. This correlation for professionals was obtained only for those who reported high contact with other members; correlations for these members were .55 for the agency and .66 for the work group. Worth-and-benefit correlations fell to .15 for professionals out of touch with their colleagues.

Source. Jay M. Jackson, "Reference group processes in a formal organization," *Sociometry*, 22:307–27.

Often a person faces contradictory pressures from two or more different groups. Students are subject to cross-pressures (from peers and from school authorities); so are reporters, advertising men, and factory foremen. Here's a study which shows what happens in such a situation.

In an anonymous questionnaire, 196 Harvard and Radcliffe students were asked to imagine they were proctoring an exam, saw a fellow student cheating, and that the student admitted it. They were asked to check which of five actions they would take, ranging in harshness from reporting him for cheating to acting as if nothing had happened.

In all they answered this question six times.

1. The student was a stranger, and neither the authorities nor their own friends would know anything about the situation unless they themselves took action.

2. The student was a stranger and there was little chance their friends would find out—but a good chance that authorities would.

3. Next, they were asked how authorities and how their friends would feel about each of the five possible actions.

4. Then they were asked how they would behave if the cheating student was their roommate and close friend.

5. Next the conditions of Number 2 were repeated but under the close-friend situation.

6. Finally question Number 3 was repeated under the close-friend condition.

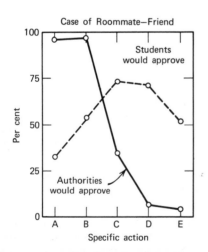

Case of Roommate—Friend

Students thought that the authorities would accept all but the two most lenient positions (both of which let the cheating

student finish the exam and failed to report him), but would take little account of the stranger-friend difference. Students indicated that although few of their friends would expect them, as proctors, to take the most lenient course for a stranger, about 50% of them would expect them to follow this course for a cheating friend.

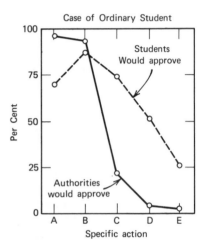

Case of Ordinary Student

Source. Samuel A. Stouffer, "An analysis of conflicting social norms," *American Sociological Review,* 14:707–17.

Two Methods of Evoking Reference Group Responses

If the norms of a reference group are to influence a decision, the buyer must be reminded of the group and its norms at decision time. When group norms conflict, a source must try to bring one of them into the receiver's awareness and keep the other out. Here are two methods of doing so.

While other members of their psychology class met together in an auditorium as usual, 46 Catholic students, 58 Jewish students, and 33 Protestant students, mostly Lutheran, met in three rooms, one for each faith.

Students were asked to complete a 72-item questionnaire, which contained 7 statements dealing with Catholic doctrine, 7 with Protestant beliefs, and 9 with Jewish beliefs. In the auditorium the questionnaire was described as concerning values on which students differ. In the separate rooms, students were asked to construct a questionnaire on religious beliefs, it being noted that all those in any given room shared the same faith. (This point was emphasized in two other ways: in a discussion emphasizing basic assumptions underlying beliefs of the particular faith involved, and on the questionnaire, where students were asked to check which statements they believed important to their faith. Their answers, however, were to be their own personal statements for Jews and 1 of 16 for Protestants, however.

Source. W. W. Charters, Jr., and Theodore M. Newcomb, "Some attitudinal effects of experimentally increased salience of a membership group," in Guy E. Swanson, Theodore M. Newcomb, and Eugene L. Hartley, *Readings in Social Psychology* (New York: Henry Holt & Co., 1952), pp. 415–20.

Twenty years later, a similar study was undertaken, using sex instead of religious preference to segregate subjects and a scale of attitudes toward women's rights instead of religious orthodoxy to test reference group effects.

This time there was no deliberate attempt either by discussion or on

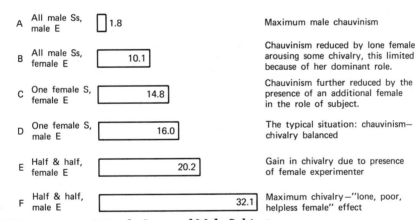

A	All male Ss, male E	1.8		Maximum male chauvinism
B	All male Ss, female E	10.1		Chauvinism reduced by lone female arousing some chivalry, this limited because of her dominant role.
C	One female S, female E	14.8		Chauvinism further reduced by the presence of an additional female in the role of subject.
D	One female S, male E	16.0		The typical situation: chauvinism—chivalry balanced
E	Half & half, female E	20.2		Gain in chivalry due to presence of female experimenter
F	Half & half, male E	32.1		Maximum chivalry—"lone, poor, helpless female" effect

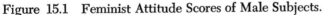

Figure 15.1 Feminist Attitude Scores of Male Subjects.

opinions, with anonymity assured.)
Catholic students responded as expected, showing greater orthodoxy on 7 Catholic-doctrine questions, 9 "general religious" questions, and 24 questions on attitudes toward the church, than did non-Lutheran Protestants and students in the auditorium. The experiment obtained significant differences on only 1 of 18

questionnaires to emphasize group membership, obvious cues of gender being thought sufficient. Three kinds of groups were formed: equally split between the sexes, made up of a single sex, or all but one member of the same sex. A second variation was introduced by varying the sex of the experimenter.
As Figure 15.1 shows, opposition to women's rights (*male chauvinism*)

was highest where all subjects and the experimenter were male. However opposition was least (and *chivalry* highest), in groups with a male experimenter and a single female subject.

In the earlier study, failure of Protestants and Jews to respond to norms of their supposed reference groups was attributed to one of two causes: weakness of group norms, as compared with those of Catholicism, or the possibility that members reacting *against* the evoked norms of their religious affiliation cancelled out those responding favorably to them. In this study, the *chauvinism-chivalry* continuum was offered as an explanation and, of course, as a hypothesis for future study.

Source. Robert W. Shomer and Richard Centers, "Differences in attitudinal responses under conditions of implicitly manipulated group salience," *Journal of Personality and Social Psychology,* 15:125–32.

Additional Research Readings

Group influences. Cohesive groups influenced choice of beer and cigarettes but not of deodorants. **Robert E. Witt and Grady D. Bruce, "Purchase decisions and group influence," Journal of Marketing Research, 7:533–5.** When three stooges confidently and unanimously chose one of three identical suits as best, 52% of subjects agreed. When stooges appeared less certain, only 30% did so. **M. Venkatesan, "Experimental study of consumer behavior conformity and independence," Journal of Marketing Research, 3:384–7.**

Membership. In 1955, 64% of adults reported no membership in voluntary associations, in 1962, 57%. Nonmembership rates were 76% for incomes under $2000 versus 48% for over $7500; 77% for 8 years education versus 39% for 4 years of college. **Herbert H. Hyman, Charles R. Wright, "Trends in voluntary association memberships of American adults," American Sociological Review, 36:191–206.**

Cultures. Learning programs giving four responses to incidents involving Americans and a foreign national proved effective in teaching foreign cultures to persons headed for Honduras, Thailand, and Greece. **Fred E. Fiedler et al., "The culture assimilator: An approach to cross-cultural training," Journal of Applied Psychology, 55:95–102.**

● Class membership affects an individual's goals, both desired and achieved; it affects men's interaction, acts, attitudes, and product purchases. Differences in income, education, and associates have an impact in decision making on information gathering, choice among alternatives, and the purchase-sale encounter. Symbols of status, wrongly used, have caused trouble for retail stores and advertisers.

● Within limits, a low "score" may be offset by a higher score on another of the six dimensions of social class: style of life (possessions), occupation, job performance, associates, beliefs, and class identification. Class membership may be assessed by objective attributes, by self-ratings or by ratings of associates. Class membership influences the number of classes an individual perceives; he tends to be insensitive to distinctions for classes distant from his own.

● Occupation appears the most basic dimension of class in industrial countries. However, the measure one uses varies with the use he wants to make of the concept. Because of the many dimensions of class, an individual's overall status may be ambiguous. Where scores are inconsistent, he will seek to equalize them upward.

● Behavior is affected by the mobility permitted in a society, and by the mobility achieved by an individual. Of four scores of mobility, which has tended to concentrate individuals at middle levels of the class system, at least three are expected to continue causes. Some theorists see class distinctions as necessary and inevitable if individuals are to be recruited for vital functions; others see them as being neither, but due, rather, to conflict for power.

Research Articles

Occupations. Fall into six social classes (Edwards), vary in prestige and its stability over 16-year period (Hodge); vary in rank on different scales of values (Gusfield).

Numbers. Of persons in social classes reported (Kahl, Hollingshead).

Effects. Social class influences level of aspirations (Rosen), ability to induce others to violate law (Lefkowitz), or to accept new farm practices (Lionberger). Innovators may appear in any class, depending on nature of innovation (Graham).

Status Systems. Found to affect behavior in restaurant kitchen (Whyte) and in jury room (Strodtbeck). Correlation between ascribed and achieved status studied by comparing *Who's Who* and *Social Register* (Bendix).

Chapter 16 Social Class

Social class affects the goals and aspirations of individuals. Wives of workingmen, we are told, having known little security in their lives, seek security, including the security of a well-known brand name.[1] They value respectability. They tend to associate more with relatives than with friends. Seeking escape from the drudgery of household chores, they try to transform the home where they spend most of their lives into a pleasant, "pretty" place. Their husbands are geared more to present pleasures than future achievements, their horizons and interests are limited in both space and time. Workingmen are uninterested in abstractions, preferring things they can touch and see. They feel they have only limited control of their environment, that the choices which affect their lives are made by others rather than themselves.

In contrast, members of the middle class are said to be more self-confident, to have a clearer picture of a larger world which they feel they can influence. They look further into a future in which they expect their children to have higher social status than their own, and take steps, such as stressing the importance of a college education, which will make that future more likely. The Protestant Ethic, which encourages the giving up of present pleasures for larger future rewards, continues to flourish in the middle class.

These perceptions have a basis in fact. Class affects the probability that an individual will attain his goals. A member of the upper class is likely to live longer: during a 20-year period just prior to World War II, for instance, although life expectancy in the lowest social class began catching up, rising from 50 to 57 years, longevity in the upper classes remained ahead, rising from 61 to 65.[2] Mental illness is far less common in the upper classes, at least as measured by public records. Following World War II, 11 cases of schizophrenia were reported for every 10,000 persons in the two highest categories of a five-class system; the lower class reported 89 per 10,000.[3] Sons of upper class men are five to eight times more likely to succeed their fathers than chance would suggest; and the sons of professional men have 3.5 times chance probability of becoming business leaders.[4] This is not too surprising. Even ignoring any possibility of superior genetic inheritance, children of the well-to-do are likely to be born into a more stimulating home environment and to develop higher aspirations and self-confidence in it, likely to attend better schools, and likely to benefit from their fathers' friendship with prospective employers or "fat-cat" customers.

An understanding of social classes other than their own is important to members of the upper class whether they choose to earn a living in selling and advertising or in industrial management. The majority of the customers they must influence or employees they will supervise will be of a lower class. Such understanding is even more important to the young executive who has risen to a class higher than that he was born into. He must learn and practice the attitudes and behaviors of his new class without forgetting or rejecting those of the class from which he has come.

Differences in Acts, Attitudes, and Associates

What are some of these class differences that must be understood? Social class affects the number and kind of persons one *associates* with and the nature of one's interaction with them. For example, it affects the church one joins.[5] In the Roman Catholic church, class differences are reflected in the congregation to the extent that residential segregation affects parish lines. In

Protestant churches, however, whose worshippers may be drawn from wider geographic areas, denominational memberships reflect class differences. A typical study in one California town found a Congregational church to have highest prestige, followed by the Methodist, Baptist, Adventist, Nazarene, the Assembly of God, Church of God, and Pentecostal churches.[6] Professional men and business managers made up 50% of Congregational membership; unskilled labor made up 80% of Pentecostal membership.

Social Class Affects Men's Acts

A comparison of 15 studies of child-rearing practices made over a period of 25 years and involving a total of 11,000 cases, has shown clear-cut, but changing, class differences.[7] From 1930 until the end of World War II, middle-class mothers were less permissive toward infants than working-class mothers: less likely to breast feed or to feed a baby when it cried, and more insistent on early weaning and toilet training. Since then, middle-class mothers have become more permissive. (In both periods, prewar and postwar, middle-class mothers apparently were better informed and more susceptible to infant care fads currently fashionable among the experts.)

In dealing with older children, middle-class parents were more insistent than lower-class parents, over the whole 25-year period, on good grades in school and acceptance of responsibility at home. They used less physical punishment, controlling children more by making the middle-class child feel guilty and afraid of losing his parents' love. At the same time, middle-class parents were more willing to treat the child as an equal and less insistent upon obedience. These practices, in turn, caused middle-class children to be more self-controlled than children of the lower class. High-status farmers are more likely to innovate and to induce others to innovate, too.[8]

Social Class Affects Attitudes

In two studies, prejudice has been found to be related to mobility, the effects varying with the type of mobility: single generation or between generation. Among 150 war veterans in Chicago, those whose postwar occupations were lower in status than their prewar positions showed a considerable prejudice against Negroes and Jews.[9] The authors, hypothesizing that prejudice is the downward-mobile person's way of venting his frustration, found, as they expected, that upward-mobile veterans were less prejudiced than those whose status had not changed.

In contrast, two other authors[10] predicted that a man whose status is different from that of his father, whether higher or lower, will feel insecure and that this feeling will make him prejudiced. They, too, found what they expected, in an analysis of 664 residents of Elmira, New York. They used three measures of prejudice. These were dislike of having a member of a minority group as a neighbor ("keep out"), agreement that the minority in question is obtaining more power than "is good for the country" ("power"), and agreement with statements that Jews are dishonest in business and Negroes are ignorant and lazy ("stereotype"). Results of their analysis are shown in the table on page 310.*

Social class affects product preferences, but in complex ways. Beer has long been considered a lower-class product and hard liquor the drink of the upper-classes, yet Negroes account for 25% of the nation's sales of Scotch, a share far beyond their proportion of the population, to say nothing of the proportion of disposable income. (One reason suggested for this is that discrimination prevents well-to-do Negroes

---

* Data reprinted from Reinhard Bendix and Seymour Martin Lipset, *Class, status and power*, Copyright 1953 by The Free Press and The Macmillan Co.

Status of Son's Occupation		Percentage Taking Prejudiced Position Toward:					
		Negroes			Jews		
		Keep Out	Power	Stereo-type	Keep Out	Power	Stereo-type
Higher than father's	154	71%	9%	45%	15%	29%	36%
Same	415	59	7	39	11	20	28
Lower than father's	95	63	16	39	13	27	42

from buying the kind of homes in the kind of neighborhoods to which their incomes entitle them. Another is that they seek the social security provided by high-prestige products and high-prestige brands.)

Research studies, almost invariably made by members of the middle class, report that members of the lower classes prefer "sweet chocolate, fabrics with a rubbery touch and strong-smelling flowers" while upper-class buyers have more refined preferences for "bitter-dry tastes, irregular weaves and less pungent fragrances."[11] Upper-class buyers are said to prefer "controlled" product designs, and lower class "sentimentalized" designs.[12] Lower classes are said to prefer "borax" style furniture.[13] Automobile executives in the 1950s, we are told, thought splashing chrome trim all over their vehicles was vulgar, but went ahead anyway and discovered that chrome would sell cars to the masses.[14]

Three Causes for Behavioral Differences

Can some pattern or order be found in such data, some explanation of these apparent variations in preference and taste? Are such differences in preferences the logical outcome of more basic differences?

Income. By and large, upper-class individuals have more money than those in the lower class, despite the storied plumbers who outearn the equally storied college professors. Upper class families save a larger proportion of their incomes not just because they value future goods more than present delights but because they have larger dis-

cretionary incomes—more surplus funds after necessities have been purchased. Buying stocks requires more knowledge and involves greater risk than putting savings in a sock or a local bank; upper-class persons have the knowledge and usually can better afford to take the risk. Persons who have incomes higher than the average for their class, whatever that class may be, tend to be innovators when innovations cost money: they were the first to buy color TV, for example.[15] On the other hand, they were among the last to turn to such money-*saving* innovations as compact cars, both foreign and domestic.

Education. Before the days of movies, radios, and record players, nearly all drama and music critics came from the upper classes; only wealthy parents were able to expose their children to plays and symphonies at the early age necessary to develop the ability to make fine distinctions. Participant sports such as polo and fencing require skills that must be learned and leisure in which to learn them. Spectator sports like baseball, TV, and beer-drinking, on the other hand, require no such skills, only the cost of a ticket, a TV set, or a six-pack.

Associates. Members of the upper class belong to more organizations and are more active in them. One study of a small Midwest town of some 6000 persons found that every family in the upper classes belonged to at least one association, memberships per family averaging 3.6.[16] Only half of the middle classes belonged, with an average of one membership per family, and 30% of the lowest class, with an even lower average membership. Again knowledge, opportunity, and leisure may explain these differences. People join organizations because they think organizations can operate on the environment to their mutual advantage. Because of their occupations, their verbal and financial resources, and their contacts, most members of the upper class *do* exercise more control of their own lives than do members of the lower class. In showing respect for authorities, upper-class members are merely reciprocating the deference that authorities show them, just as lower-class persons often repay the disrespect shown them with distrust.

Class Differences in Decision Making

Class differences in education, income, and associates affect three stages of the decision process.

Information Gathering. Members of the lower classes have less money with which to buy magazines and newspapers, less time to read them, and less of the education needed to interpret what is read. Having less access to independent sources of information, they are therefore more subject to sources, such as advertising, which are controlled by the seller. A limited range of acquaintances, most of whom also lack access to the media, means that word-of-mouth channels are unlikely to supply information either relayed from independent media or derived directly from personal experience. Time and transportation for extensive comparison shopping may also be lacking.

Women of the upper classes may shop for both fun and profit; work, both outside the home and in, may prevent lower-class women from imitating their example. As a result, such women may welcome a door-to-door salesman as a visitor from the world outside, and fall victim to his wiles. Readership studies suggest that education and

income affect both the amount of news read and its nature.[17] As incomes rise, so does readership of editorials and news of public affairs. As education increases, the newspaper is used less for excitement and entertainment and more for information on public affairs. Education appears more powerful an influence on readership with women than with men; income affects men more than women.

Choice of Alternatives. Buying decisions in poor families tend to be made by wives. One reason for this is that most purchases are sheer necessities: food that the wife must cook, clothes for her children. The wife must decide whether she will "make or buy" such things. Another reason is that there may be no man in the house or that, being unemployed, the husband fails to bring in the resources that would entitle him to a voice in decisions. (Even in middle-class families, where decisions often are made jointly by husband and wife, wives who work tend to have more say about purchases than wives who do not.)

The crucial save-or-spend decision, which affects most major purchases, varies by class. Low-income families save primarily so that they can buy consumer goods with their savings; upper-income families' savings are invested. Since most consumer-good purchases in our society are delegated to the wife, she has a strong voice in the low-income family's decision to save. Choice of investments, on the other hand, is usually delegated to the husband; his job experience and business contacts are presumed to make him more expert on the subject than his wife.

Purchase-and-Sale. A customer seeks contradictory qualities in a salesman whom he wants to be both a trusted peer and an expert whose judgment he can respect. Social class gets in the way.

As members of the middle class, salesmen working in cut-rate stores may feel their status diminished by having to deal with lower-class customers. One observer sums up their attitude thus: *Look, I'm a busy man. Make up your mind and let's get it over with.*[18] Although these words themselves may never be spoken, the meaning gets across, if only by posture, pace, or lifted eyebrow. Threatened by the superior status of upper-class patrons, on the other hand, the salesman may try to emphasize his role as expert, saying defensively, *This is an absolutely perfect combination. If you don't buy it, I'll know that you either can't afford to or are completely lacking in taste.* (To carry off such a role, the high-fashion salesman must indeed have the expert knowledge he professes; acquiring such knowledge takes time and such salesmen tend to be well paid.) Finally, in dealing with members of his own middle class, the salesman may give up the role of expert, and assume a we're-all-in-this-thing-together stance, *Look, I'm a nice guy and I've tried hard. Won't one of the things I've shown you do at all?*

Differences in Use of Symbols

Subtle nuances of class can be conveyed by the pitch and rhythm of one's speech, his choice of words, his grammar, and his accent. *My Fair Lady* is not fiction; for years a rise to power in British government depended on the pre-teen acquisition of the accents of Eton, Harrow, and Oxbridge. Many other symbols, including the typefaces used in advertising, tip off a housewife as to whether a retail store is one in which she'll feel comfortable. (This has been proved by showing women ads for stores they'd never heard of; they tagged accurately the low, middle, and high-status stores.)[19]

In Houston, six separate firms, each with multiple outlets, compete for soft-goods trade, ranging from Penney's at the low-priced end of the scale to the world famous Neiman-Marcus at the top. Using a dozen techniques, including the length of their line (the number of price ranges offered in each clothing category) and the depth of line (the amount of stock and number of sizes available for each individual item), each firm has found its niche of class in the soft-goods market, the special segment it wants to attract. Even experts make mistakes, however, the worst of them being a tendency to underestimate their clientele. One Houston firm is said to have come to that brash, booming oil capital of the world with the attitude *Aren't you lucky to have us come to town?* That firm ran in the red, so it is said, for the next 11 years. Another department store set up what looked like a discount operation, complete with supermarket carts, in a less affluent section of the city. Affronted by the implication that they couldn't afford the kind of service offered at the firm's stores elsewhere in the city, persons in the area stayed away in droves, until heads rolled at headquarters and the ill-advised experiment was terminated. (Even supermarkets appear to suggest subtle class differences; Martineau has reported that one chain was patronized by the middle class and another by the masses.)[20]

Similar mistakes in the use of symbols in advertising are reported. One involved putting fox hunters on the label of a beer bottle. The picture was meaningless to the mass of lower-income beer drinkers and ridiculous to upper-income groups who might occasionally admit beer to a picnic, patio, or poolside party, but never put it in a stirrup cup at the hunt. A TV commercial, which was killed at the testing stage, showed beans and hot dogs served in a silver casserole. Low-income wives admired the dish but ignored its contents; upper-income wives scoffed that everybody knows that food like *that* belongs in a crockery pot.

Six Dimensions of Class

As such differences in product preferences, choice making, and response to symbols become increasingly apparent, the need to know more about classes in our society becomes increasingly acute.

To begin with, how is class itself defined? Class, like the family life cycle, is a multidimensional concept. There are six dimensions of social class; high rank on one dimension may, on occasion, compensate for relatively low rank on another, but always within limits.

Style of Life. A man's possessions reflect a man's income, which in turn is an index to the value of his occupational roles in society. Possessions also provide subtle indicators as to whether the man's status is one he has achieved or one he was born into. Only by being inside a group can we know what the group regards as acceptable in terms of furniture, clothing, and dozens of other products. Originally valued because they are a symbol of membership in a group, possessions may become rewarding in themselves and for this reason be advertised to and purchased by outsiders.

Occupation. This is the most basic status dimension. Two aspects of an occupation affect its status: the amount of general, systematic knowledge that it requires and the number of other persons whom it controls. As a Ph.D. in business, where Ph.D.'s are rare, Crabb has a status comparable to that of the president of a firm with hundreds of employees (whose status, in turn, may equal that of a government official with many subordinates). In academic circles, however, Crabb's practical orientation may give him lower status than the experimental psychologist, who commands greater breadth and depth of theory—and the latter, in turn, may enjoy lower status than the physicist, who has a mass of highly developed mathematical theory and a nice

governmental research grant to back up his claims to power.

Job Performance. How able is a man? How does he perform his job? Answers to these questions affect a man's reputation within an industry and within a business organization. (Occupations have prestige, performance has esteem, often known only to insiders.) Within any group—lawyers, chiefs, or thieves, for example—comparisons can be made on the basis of reputation or income.

However, income and reputation are poor indices to interoccupational status differences. (A sales manager may be paid more than a research director; businessmen in general earn more than educators; gangsters are often wealthier than legitimate businessmen. Television and movie actors are more widely known than most philosophers and college presidents.)

Associates. Occupation, job performance, and possessions often determine who a man and his family associate with outside of working hours. One's associates may become visible in the society pages of a newspaper, but highly important within-group differences are often visible only to insiders.

These first four dimensions of status reflect the indices by which others judge a man's status and so determine their behavior toward him. The last two reflect the way a man perceives his own status and so influence the way he behaves toward others.

Beliefs. Groups induce conformity in thought as well as action by original selection of members, by screening the cues members receive, and by direct pressures to conform. (Associates, both on the job and off, do this. So do occupations: we assume a millionaire steelmaker will oppose higher taxes on millionaires, lower tariffs on steel, and higher tariffs on iron ore.)

The man who aspires to rise in an organization is likely to fashion his beliefs to match those of persons higher on the organizational chart, who become his reference group. Knowing a man's status, we can often predict his beliefs; knowing his beliefs, we can often specify his present status and the status to which he aspires.

Class Identification. An alternative form of mobility is that in which a man tries to rise not as an individual, but as a member of a group, by lifting the status of the occupation or other group itself. Not only do persons in the group have similar beliefs but they also become conscious of both group and beliefs and tend to identify themselves with the group. If a new situation arises, they ask themselves what the group will think and do.

In the United States, a man's status tends to be determined by his job. His job's importance, in turn, depends on the scarcity of the abilities and the amount of training it requires, the number of subordinates, the wages, and the nature of the product. As occupations increase in number and variety, men find it more difficult to rank them and may use income as a common denominator.

All of us tend to see finer distinctions in status at our own level in society than at more distant levels. This means that persons at either end of the status level tend to see two levels—their own level and that of everyone else.[21] Persons in the middle, on the other hand, are likely to see at least three levels—their own, a higher level, and a lower one. Power appears to be the major variable used in judging status by persons at the bottom of the ladder. ("They" have it and "we" do not.) Prestige plays more of a part in judgments of status elsewhere in the system.

The scientist who wants to quantify these observations about class must choose which of these dimensions to observe, how much weight to give each, and how to gather his data.

He may let respondents themselves decide how many social classes they need to classify people and what labels to pin on these classes, or he may supply both the number of classes and their labels. (Given freedom to set up their own system of categories, 250 residents of Boston used an average of 6.9 categories to classify a list of 70 occupations in one study.[22] They placed more occupations at their own level: 21 as compared to an average of 13 occupations per level.) Most market researchers and sociologists prefer to use five or six classes; of these, the middle two usually account for about 80% of the population and the topmost class may include only 1% of the population.

A scientist may ask individuals to rate themselves or to rate one another, or he may use an objective measure of status. In small communities, where everyone knows everybody else and in stable societies where the various dimensions of status have had a chance to crystallize, ratings based on a man's associates may be a very good index to status.

W. Lloyd Warner, an anthropologist, asked informants chosen from different levels in "Yankee City" to report how many classes they perceived and to name representative members of each. Informants identified five classes, half the number that Warner himself had expected to find. Their agreement produced what he called the method of *evaluative participation* or EP.[23]

Even in a small community, however, it is often easier to discover what a man does for a living and where he lives, than it is to find out with whom he dines and plays bridge. (In a society such as our own, in which one-fourth of the population changes residence each year, measures of interaction are seldom worth the trouble.) Thus, Warner found it useful to supplement his measure of interaction with an *index of status characteristics* (ISC) which correlated .97 with EP.[24] Observers used seven-point scales to rate a man's source of income (investments, salary, and so on), his job, his neighborhood, and his type of house, then multiplied income source and house type by three, occupation by four, and neighborhood by two to arrive at a final score.

Scores of this kind are attractive to the marketing communicator because data they require to classify markets along class lines are available without charge in census and other published reports.

Occupation Is Basic

Intuitively, occupation seems the basic dimension of status: high-status jobs require ability and education, and provide the income that permits a high-status style of living. Job, income, and possessions give a man access to groups of high-status associates that foster class identification and shape a man's beliefs. Empirically, occupation has been proved basic through the technique of centroid factor analysis.[25] Taking 19 variables related to social class, Kahl and Davis extracted two factors. The largest included variables related to occupation —education, income, the occupations of best friends, and the interviewer's rating. The second factor centered on ratings for house and neighborhood. Most respondents saw a three- or four-level class system based on occupation and life style.

When the National Opinion Research Center asked a sample of 2920 American adults in 1947 to rate 90 occupations on a five-point scale of prestige, it found considerable agreement on the rankings.

Guttman scaling divided this list into eight groups, which produced scales with a "reproducibility" (a measure of predictive success) of .80.[26] (These eight groups were political occupations, professional, business, recreation-aesthetics, agriculture, manual work, military, and service trades.)

Residents of other industrial nations tend to rate occupations in similar fashion. Although data were scanty—ranging from

seven comparable occupations for Russia and Great Britain to 30 for Great Britain and New Zealand—correlations ranged from .74 for ratings by Russians and Japanese to .97 for New Zealand and the United States.

	Correlation with	
	United States	5-Nation Average
Russia	.90	.84
Japan	.93	.89
Great Britain	.94	.93
New Zealand	.97	.93
Germany	.96	.94
United States	—	.94

Reprinted from the *American Journal of Sociology*, 61:329–39, by permission of the University of Chicago Press. Copyright 1956.

Education, another index to status, is helpful in predicting a man's acts and his attitudes. In one study, education alone predicted 12 out of 22 different kinds of behavior, ranging from frequency of church attendance to foreign travel and listening to news broadcasts.[27] Education provided better predictions than a man's occupation, in answer to the question *What social class are you in?* or his self-assignment to one of four classes suggested by the interviewer: upper class, middle class, working class, and lower class.

Using Data on Class

The measure of status that one adopts will, of course, vary with the use one wants to make of class. Awareness and beliefs interest politicians and union organizers. A man's associates allow one to subdivide the upper class down to a fraction of a percentage point, and so interests anyone trying to study or influence a community's power structure. Performance on the job interests anyone studying opinion leaders and the spread of innovations within a profession.

All four of these, however, require original inquiry. Better suited to the audience assembling and market targeting of a seller is occupation, data on which can be obtained from the census. He can also locate cases of status inconsistency—persons whose occupation, income, and education, for instance, are out of phase.

Complex as social class itself is, with six dimensions each measurable in many different ways, determining the class of an individual is even more complicated. A college student can be ranked relative to his fellows as to height, weight, grade average, swimming ability, or dancing skill. His ranks on these dimensions will be inconsistent, yet are not completely independent of one another. An underweight, penniless student is not likely to have high prestige in football-playing and car-owning circles; low rank on all four dimensions may mean low rank in a dating status system.

A businessman's occupation, income, education, style of life, job performance, associates, beliefs, and class identification are seldom completely congruent. Inconsistency creates a problem for his associates, who aren't sure whether they are speaking to a high-status graduate of Yale, or a wretched bowler. A desire to equalize statuses upwards is considered a powerful motive in human affairs.

Societies differ in the number of classes they contain, the clarity with which these classes are defined, and the ease with which a man (or his children) can move from one to another. The ease of such movement affects the efficiency of a society and the attitudes of its members.

In a closed or caste system, members tend to remain with the status they are born into. Status is *ascribed* rather than *achieved*. Although most such societies seem able to prevent incompetent occupants of high-status positions from doing as much damage as one might expect, they also prevent persons of high ability but low status from giving society the full use of their talents. This loss of efficiency is offset to the extent that high-status members of such a society can prepare for responsible positions with some assurance that they will get them. If ambition is frustrated by lack of opportunity, members are also protected from the anxiety of failure.

In an open-class system such as our own, ability has an opportunity to show itself. The society gains in efficiency but at a price. Members who rise in status must leave friends and kin behind, and those who try to rise but fail are burdened with anxiety, disappointment, and self-blame.

Changes in the status of an individual—his social mobility—affect products purchased, and media use. If a man stays in the neighborhood of his youth, he may not be able to adopt the style of life that his income permits; to do so, would make it appear that he is "getting above himself." If a man moves into a higher-status neighborhood, on the other hand, he may be forced to spend more than he earns to keep up with his neighbors.

How much mobility actually exists in the United States? Experts estimate that over the last 100 years, both in the United States and the industrial countries of Europe, rates of mobility have been fairly constant.[28] Between half and three-quarters of the men in professional, business, clerical, and skilled jobs have risen slightly in status compared to their fathers. (Mobility is low at the bottom of the ladder and the top. At the bottom are youths who represent the third generation on relief. Some of the wealthy, on the other hand, have five to eight times as much chance to stay at the top as would be expected if neither talent nor wealth could be inherited.)[29]

Kahl estimates that, in 1950, 67% of the labor force held occupations at a different status level than those of their fathers. He attributes this change to four causes, giving the first three equal weight.[30]

Cause of Mobility	Percentage Labor Force Affected
Technological	20%
Step-by-step	20
Individual	20
Reproductive	7

Technology has changed the shape of the American class system. Mechanization and automation have reduced the need for unskilled workers at the bottom and increased the need for technical and white-collar workers at the top. As a result, society begins to look less like a pyramid and more like a diamond. (Between 1920 and 1950, as the labor force increased 27%, the number of professionals increased by 58% but the number of farmers dropped by 32%.)[31] Writing in 1956, Kahl predicted technology would continue to enlarge opportunities at upper levels of job status.

Step-by-step mobility occurs because each new professional position tends to be filled by someone whose father is in the next step down in the occupational structure. As he fails to follow in his father's footsteps, this creates a new opening at the owner-manager level and so on down the scale. Kahl predicts that this process will continue.

Reproductive mobility occurs when men in high-status jobs fail to have as many children as those further down the scale, and thus they create openings in high-status ranks. Kahl predicts that farm families will continue to be largest, urban blue-collar families next, and urban white-collar families smallest. The differences are small, however, and he predicts this source of upward mobility will disappear or even reverse itself.

Individual mobility represents an exchange of job occupants, rather than an overall change in the job opportunities at any level; one father's son slips down a notch, making it possible for another father's son to move up to take his place. This source of mobility is expected to continue.

Immigration, which once introduced large numbers of unskilled workers from overseas at the bottom of the occupational pyramid, has ceased to affect mobility although internal migration of Negroes from the rural South to the urban North continues.

Mobility for the Communicator

Figures of this kind help a marketing communicator envision future audiences and markets. What of his own chances to rise, however? How much room *is* there at the top?

There are some signs that the chances improved between 1928 and 1952, although sons of professional men and businessmen still had an advantage. In 1920, 4% of all men were professionals. By chance, therefore, 4% of business leaders in 1952 should have been the sons of professional men, instead of the actual figure of 14%. Thus, sons of professional men were 3.5 times (14 : 4) as likely to become business leaders as would have been true had they been unable to inherit either ability or improved opportunity. This ratio-of-advantage of 3.5, however, represented a decrease from the 1928 ratio of 4.3. The figures are given below.

	Ratio of Advantage	
Occupation	1928	1952
Professional	4.3	3.5
Business	9.7	4.7
Clerical, sales	.7	.8
Farmers	.3	.3
Laborers	.2	.3

W. Lloyd Warner and James C. Abegglen, *Occupational Mobility in American Business and Industry* (Minneapolis: University of Minnesota Press). Copyright 1955 by the University of Minnesota.

Two factors seem to explain this increase in high-status mobility. One is the increasing size of business firms; in large firms, ownership and management seem to be divorced. Another is the increasing number of college degrees obtained by the children of fathers lower on the status ladder, in a day when the degree has become a prerequisite to a job and advancement in the large corporation.

Class in Society: Whither Away?

Will class in the future have more or less effect on buying behavior than it has had? Will class differences themselves enlarge or wither away?

Mass marketing became possible when products, once the exclusive property of a favored few, were made available to a mass market. As a result, differences in life styles between rich and poor diminished. (In days of universal suffrage and the universality of suffering involved in income taxes, the wealthy also became more discreet; privacy, rather than possessions, has become the ultimate luxury.)

Class differences in style of life seem less visible and may be less marked than in the past, making class less relevant to marketing. What is likely to happen to class differences in the future?

Theorists disagree as to whether such differences are inevitable, because they perform functions necessary to society, or accidental and subject to control.

Some theorists argue that differential rewards, symbolized by and administered through status and class, are necessary to recruit and motivate persons of scarce talents to take the arduous training needed for and to perform onerous tasks crucial to society.[32] This theory sees social classes as coordinating activities for the benefit of both society and the individual and as distributing tasks, rewards, and power equitably. (Or that they once were so distributed and will evolve again in that direction.)

Individuals differ, they say, and any visible difference can form the basis of a class system (and probably has at some period and place on earth). Age and sex limit the groups a man may belong to and the roles he may acquire in those groups; in many societies, status rises with age. Unequal rewards are necessary to induce persons with rare skills to train for, accept, and perform roles vital to society. The family, basic unit of society, upsets rational relations between reward and performance because fathers try to pass on to their children wealth or improved job and educational opportunities. In time, however, incompetent heirs dissipate their wealth and power and the able poor achieve both so that in the long run, these theorists say, rationality is restored.

An opposing "conflict" theory argues instead that classes *prevent* a society from functioning at its best.[33] Classes, say these theorists, result from a power struggle, cause both tasks and rewards to be distributed unfairly, and can be changed only through conflict.

The layman who sees both justice and injustice in his society's class system thus has a choice. He can decide that injustices are temporary, probably the result of failure of the reward system to change rapidly enough to keep pace with technology. Or he can decide that equity and justice are mere accidents, that the natural tendency of any society is toward injustice, and that change can occur only through conflict.

One ingenious writer accepts both theories, arguing that men tend to be rewarded equally in an economy at the subsistence level since each depends on the others for survival.[34] As technology produces a surplus (which is more than needed for survival but less than enough to satisfy everyone if shared equally), power takes over so that privilege and prestige, the bases of class, are distributed unequally. How does this writer reconcile this theory with perceptions that class differences are less extree now than in earlier times? Perhaps, he suggests, holders of power have been willing to give up part of what they've seized to reduce hostility and increase their chances of hanging on to the rest. Or perhaps in a democracy men who are powerless as individuals have found ways to combine their forces. Or perhaps all we are seeing is a change in the source of power; technology may have reached the point where knowledge rather than wealth or arms forms the basis of class.

Thought, Talk, and Action

1. List the names of eight persons you know fairly well, including yourself, your father, father's employer (or client if self-employed), a neighbor, your closest friend, plus persons you have bought from or sold to. Using an arbitrary scale from 1 (low) to 7 (high), score each person on each of the six dimensions of social class. Compare the total scores of the six persons. How consistent are the scale scores for any given person? Where there is inconsistency, what changes would you expect over time?
2. It has been reported that foreign travel has become a status symbol in the United States, taking the place that the auto has in much of Europe—and that the fountain pen or eye glasses play in less developed nations. What reasons for these differences can you suggest? How would they affect your advertising?
3. Taking each of the six dimensions of social class in turn, suggest a different product whose sales would be affected by each. Then think of a single product and show how advertising appeals might be centered on each of the dimensions in turn.

Notes

Chapter 16

1. Lee Rainwater et al., Workingman's wife (New York: Oceana Press, 1959).
2. Albert J. Mayer and Philip M. Hauser, "Class differences in expectation of life at birth," in Reinhard Bendix and Seymour M. Lipset, editors, Class, status and power: A reader in social stratification (Glencoe, Ill.: The Free Press, 1953), p. 283.
3. August B. Hollingshead and Frederick C. Redlich, Social class and mental illness (New York: John Wiley & Sons, 1958), p. 236.
4. W. Lloyd Warner and James C. Abegglen, Occupational mobility in American business and industry (Minneapolis: University of Minnesota Press, 1955).
5. John L. Haer, "Predictive utility of five indices of social stratification," American Sociological Review, 22:541–6.
6. Walter R. Goldschmidt, "Class denominationalism in rural California churches," American Journal of Sociology, 49: 348–55.
7. Urie Bronfenbrenner, "Socialization and social class through time and space," in Eleanor E. Maccoby et al., Readings in

social psychology, 3rd ed. (New York: Holt, Rinehart and Winston, 1958).

8. Herbert F. Lionberger, Adoption of new ideas and practices (Ames, Iowa: Iowa State University Press, 1960).

9. Bruno Bettelheim and Morris Janowitz, The dynamics of prejudice (New York: Harper and Brothers, 1950).

10. Joseph Greenblum and Leonard I. Pearlin, "Vertical mobility and prejudice: A socio-psychological analysis," in Richard Bendix and Martin S. Lipset, editors, Class, status and power: A reader in social stratification (Glencoe, Ill.: The Free Press, 1953).

11. Robert A. Dahl et al., Social science research on business: Product and potential (New York: Columbia University Press, 1959), pp. 108–9.

12. James H. Myers and William H. Reynolds, Consumer behavior and marketing management (Boston: Houghton Mifflin Co., 1967), p. 216.

13. W. T. Tucker, The social context of economic behavior (New York: Holt, Rinehart and Winston, 1964), p. 74.

14. Reference No. 12, p. 212.

15. Ibid., p. 215.

16. W. Lloyd Warner et al., Democracy in Jonesville (New York: Harper and Brothers, 1949).

17. Wilbur Schramm, editor, The process and effects of mass communication (Urbana: University of Illinois Press, 1960), pp. 71–3.

18. Same reference as No. 13, p. 76.

19. James F. Engel et al., Consumer behavior (New York: Holt, Rinehart and Winston, 1968), pp. 304–5. Original study was Charles B. McCann, Women and department store newspaper advertising (Chicago: Social Research, 1957).

20. Pierre Martineau, "Social classes and spending behavior," Journal of Marketing, 23:121–30.

21. Elizabeth Bott, "The concept of class as a reference group," Human Relations, 7:259–85.

22. Joseph A. Kahl, The American class structure (New York: Holt, Rinehart and Winston, 1961), pp. 78–9.

23. W. Lloyd Warner et al., Social class in America (Chicago: Science Research Associates, 1949), pp. 36–9.

24. Ibid., p. 168.

25. Joseph A. Kahl and James A. Davis, "A comparison of indexes of socio-economic status," American Sociological Review, 20:317–25.

26. Paul K. Hatt, "Occupation and social stratification," American Journal of Sociology, 55:533–43.

27. Reference No. 5.

28. Reference No. 22, pp. 262–8.

29. *Ibid.*, p. 272.
30. *Ibid.*, p. 261. Original study reported in National Opinion Research Center, "Jobs and occupations: a popular evaluation," Opinion News 9:3–13.
31. *Ibid.*, p. 255.
32. Jack L. Roach et al., Social stratification in the United States (Englewood Cliffs, N.J.: Prentice-Hall, 1969).
33. *Ibid.*, p. 55.
34. *Ibid.*, pp. 60–4: Ralf Dahrendorf, "Integration and values versus coercion and interests," reviews Gerhard Lenski, Power and privilege: A theory of social stratification (New York: McGraw-Hill Book Co., 1966).

Using Occupation as an Index of Class

Several scales are available which assign an individual to a social class, given his occupation. Here is one.

1. Professionals: doctors, lawyers
2. Owners, managers, public officials
   (a) Farmers, both owners and tenants
   (b) Wholesalers and retailers
   (c) Owners and managers of smaller firms
3. Clerks
4. Foremen and skilled workers
5. Semiskilled workers
6. Unskilled workers
   (a) Farm labor
   (b) Factory workers; construction labor

(c) Other labor
(d) Servants

Source. Alba M. Edwards, "A social economic grouping of the gainful workers in the United States," *Journal of the American Statistical Association,* 28:377–87.

Behind this scale is considerable evidence that Americans do rank occupations in this fashion. In 1947, the National Opinion Research Center asked 2920 adults to rate 90 occupations on a five-point prestige scale. Shown below is a comparison of the 1947 rankings with similar rankings obtained in 1963, grouped into five categories suggested by Kahl.

	Rank	
1. Occupations requiring special technical knowledge of control over many subordinates:	1947	1963
United States supreme court justice	1	1
Physician	2.5	2
College professor	8	8
Banker	10.5	24.5
Lawyer	18	11
2. Educated men who are not professionals; managers of medium-sized organizations:		
Owner of 100-employee factory	26.5	31.5
Accountant for large business	29	29.5
Teacher in public school	36	29.5

3. Owners of ten-employee firms; white-collar workers;

| | Rank | |
highly skilled workers:	1947	1963
Farmer	39	44
Bookkeeper	51.5	49.5
Automobile repairman	59.5	60

4. Owner of two-employee firm; less skilled white-collar and manual workers:

Owner of lunchstand	62	62.5
Clerk in store	68	70
Farmhand	76	83

5. Unskilled laborers:

Restaurant waiter	79.5	80.5
Night watchman	81.5	77.5
Shoe shiner	90	90

Source. Robert W. Hodge, Paul M. Siegel, and Peter H. Rossi, "Occupational prestige in the United States, 1925–63," *American Journal of Sociology*, 70:286–302. Reprinted by permission of the University of Chicago Press © , 1964.

Further study suggested that the meaning of "prestige" varies with the persons doing the rating. Low-income respondents base their ratings on the *income* and *security* attached to a job; high-income respondents rate jobs on the *opportunity for self-expression.* Here is a study which shows that prestige is only one of the status systems that can be applied to occupations.

Occupations with NORC ranks ranging from 1 (scientist) to 15 (machine operator) were given to 337 students in sociology and architecture to be ranked and to be rated on 32 seven-point semantic differential scales. Some of the scales were evaluative (*honest, useful, dirty, insecure*), some were more factual (*working class, Democrat, urban, poor*), and some were both evaluative and descriptive (*religious, foreign, strong, tough*).

Results showed that adjectives like *successful, middle-class,* and *Republican* correlated well with occupational prestige rankings. Other adjectives, such as *emotional, people-oriented, masculine,* and *youthful,* did not.

For example, although the scientist and lawyer held the two top ranks in prestige, the lawyer was seen as much richer (second vs. seventh), the scientist as more useful (first vs. fifth). Teachers ranked sixth in wealth and seventh in prestige but first in honesty and second in usefulness. Lawyers ranked sixth in honesty, bankers eighth in usefulness.

Source. Joseph R. Gusfield and Michael Schwartz, "The meanings of occupational prestige," *American Sociological Review,* 28:265–71.

Most Everybody Ends Up in the Middle

Many analysts prefer a five-class analysis of social stratification in the United States. Here is one such system, based on 1955 dollars.

1%	Plutocrats with incomes over $15,000, largely from investments.
9%	Salaried income from business or a profession of $7500 to $15,000 a year; suburbanites.
40%	Earned income of $4000 to $7500, about half the time representing two working adults in the household. This group is about equally split between blue collar and white collar workers.
30%	Blue collar workers, without savings, and living on the installment plan with incomes of $2000 to $4000.
20%	Incomes of under $2000 a year, including both families in poverty and retired persons or childless newlyweds just beginning their careers.

Source. Joseph A. Kahl, *The American Class Structure* (New York: Holt Rinehart and Winston, 1961), pp. 120–1.

Here is another, based on a weighted three-factor index of residence (6), income (5), and job (9).

3%	Old families, top managers, and professionals; high incomes and education.
9%	Business managers, professionals; college graduates on the way up.
21%	Owners of small businesses, high school graduates.
49%	Blue collar workers, often members of ethnic minorities, did not graduate from high school.
18%	Low incomes, no savings, tenement-dwellers.

Source. A. B. Hollingshead and F. C. Redlich, *Social Class and Mental Illness* (New York: John Wiley & Sons, Inc., 1958).

What Are the Effects of Social Class?

The pervasive effects of social class are illustrated here in four very different settings and on four very different kinds of decisions.

First, an attempt to see whether social class motivates youth to get ahead and, at the same time, gives them the value orientations and the attitudes such aspirations require.

The researcher divided students in two Connecticut high schools into five social classes, based on fathers' occupation and education and neighborhood of residence. Then, with a slide projector, he showed them pictures like those in the Thematic Apperception Test (TAT) and asked them to write stories suggested by the pictures. Any story which both evaluated performance and expressed an emotion in regard to it was scored as representing motivation to achieve (*Example. The girl failed in an exam and feels miserable as a result.*) Finally, students filled out a 14-item questionnaire, agreeing with or rejecting three values assumed necessary to success. These are examples, questions stating values in reverse.

Value. It is possible and necessary for an individual to improve his status in society.

Question. All I want out of life . . . is a secure, not too difficult job, with enough pay to afford a nice car.

Value. Present sacrifices are necessary to future gains.

Question. Nowadays with world conditions the way they are, the wise person lives for today . . . .

Value. Family ties must give way to individual mobility.

Question. Nothing in life is worth the sacrifice of moving away from your parents.

Results indicated that the upper social classes, I and II, had a high need to achieve and tended to possess values assumed necessary to success.

| | Percentage in Class with High Scores on | |
	Achievement Motivation	Value Orientation
I and II	83	77
III	43	70
IV	30	33
V	23	17

Motivation scores, but not value scores, were related to school grades; value scores, but not motivation scores, were related to the desire to attend college.

Source. Bernard G. Rosen, "The achievement syndrome: a psychocultural dimension of social stratification," *American Sociological Review*, 21:203–11.

The second example shows that a person who, by his dress, appears to have higher social status, may influence the behavior of total strangers—even to the point of encouraging them to imitate him in violating the law!

An observer, 100 feet from traffic lights at 3 different street corners in Austin, Texas, watched 2103 pedestrians as they faced a 40-second "wait" signal and a 15-second "walk" signal.

For 5 trials, a confederate of the experimenter wore a freshly pressed suit, white shirt, tie, and hat. Then 5 observations were made while the confederate was absent. Finally, 5 trials were made while he appeared in low-status garb: scuffed shoes, patched and soiled trousers, and an unpressed blue denim shirt. Sometimes he would obey the signal; in another set of 5 trials, in the same garb, he would cross when the light said "wait."

Here are the results, showing percentage of pedestrians obeying the signal. (I indicates those in high-status garb, II those in low status dress.)

| | Behavior of Confederate (%) | | | |
	Obeys	Absent	Disobeys	Total
I	99	99	86	95
II	100	99	96	98

A few pedestrians were encouraged to disobey the sign when a person in low-status garb did so; 14% disobeyed when they saw a person in high-status garb do so.

Source. Monroe Lefkowitz, Robert R. Blake, and Jane S. Mouton, "Status factors in pedestrian violation of traffic signals," *Journal of Abnormal and Social Psychology,* 51: 704–6.

The third example, directly relevant to problems in marketing communication, found that high-status farmers were exposed to more sources of information, were in a better position to communicate such information to others, and in fact, were more influential in encouraging others to adopt new farm practices. They also were much more likely to adopt such practices themselves.

All 279 farm operators in a community in northeast Missouri were asked whom they talked to about farm problems. Each of the 279 was then rated in terms of the number of times other farmers said they talked to him.

The 22 farmers mentioned by at least five colleagues were put in Group A; they were more likely to belong to organizations, 41% to a civic club versus 4 to 10% for other groups; 59% to an adult farm school versus 4 to 13% for the others; 45% to a grain marketing co-op versus 4 to 12%; 64% to a farmers association, versus 28 to 40% for the others. They were more likely to be active in these organizations. (Participation was scored by giving 1 point for occasional attendance or membership, 2 for attending regularly, 3 for serving on a committee, and 4 for being an officer.) They were also more likely to belong to organizations extending beyond the local community.

Such membership gave Group A farmers an opportunity to influence a large number of their colleagues by passing on news they had read or by sharing personal experiences. Members of Group A had pioneered in 9 out of 10 new farm practices being studied.

Proportions of farm operations using designated improved farm practices are shown. Bars in each set represent A, B, C, and D groups reading down.

Although members of Group A did not differ from their colleagues in either age or education, they did differ on four other measures of social class.

| | Influence and Activity in Organizations | | | |
| | A | B | C | D |
Mentioned by	5 or More Peers	2 to 4 Peers	Single Peer	Not Mentioned
Number in group	22	60	72	125
Median participation score (local)	7.2	5.4	4.7	3.2
Percentage belonging to community organization	86%	65%	53%	39%
Percentage in extra-community organization	41%	23%	0	0
Percentage taking daily newspaper	91%	52 to 65%		
Average number of magazines taken	6.5	3.3 to 4.1		

	Group A (%)	Groups B, C, and D (%)
Judge's ratings: percentage in group ranked in top two of six classes	86	14–27
Possessions: running water in home	77	17–30
Wealth: average farm size	380 acres	178–229 acres
Income: average annual gross	$8000	$2500 to $4455

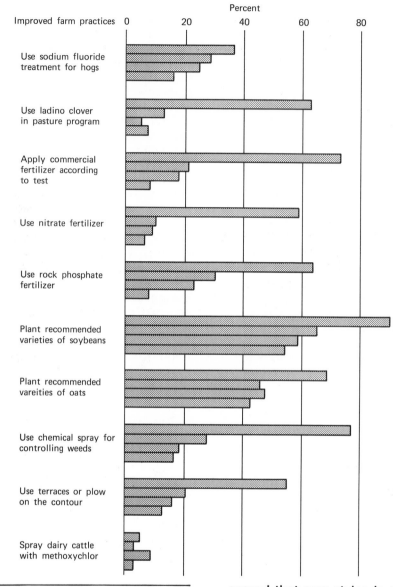

Percent

Improved farm practices

Use sodium fluoride treatment for hogs

Use ladino clover in pasture program

Apply commercial fertilizer according to test

Use nitrate fertilizer

Use rock phosphate fertilizer

Plant recommended varieties of soybeans

Plant recommended vareities of oats

Use chemical spray for controlling weeds

Use terraces or plow on the contour

Spray dairy cattle with methoxychlor

Source. Herbert F. Lionberger, "Some characteristics of farm operators sought as sources of farm information in a Missouri community," *Rural Sociology,* 18:327–38.

The fourth example moves off the farm and into the city, to trace the development of innovations, two of them involving marketing behavior.

New products were once thought to see their first adoption in the fad-prone, affluent upper classes and then "trickle down." Then someone ob-served that new styles in music often seemed to originate in the slums of Liverpool or New Orleans and work their way up. How can we tell which innovation will be popular at the top, bottom, or throughout a society?

A thousand telephone calls were made in New Haven, Conn., to locate 100 families, equally distributed through two upper and two middle classes, based on occupation. Fifty more families, representing the two lowest strata, were picked from inactive files of the state employment service. Interviewers asked each family whether they had accepted or rejected five innovations. Effects of social class were found for three of the five.

communications in a business firm is found in this study by William Foote Whyte. It begins like a novel: "It is 10:45 A.M. The chairs in Franklin's, one of Chicago's leading Loop restaurants,

	Upper Classes		Middle Classes		Lower Classes	
Percentages Adopting Innovation	1	2	3	4	5	6
The upper classes were slow to adopt television	24	44	48	52	84	72
The lower classes were slow to adopt canasta	72	72	44	20	32	12
Both lower and upper classes were slow to shop in supermarkets	52	80	56	80	52	48

Canasta, it was suggested, reflected upper-class preference for active participation; upper-class gregariousness also provided word-of-mouth channels through which the new card game was spread. Lower classes may have lacked the cash and transportation required to benefit from supermarkets, whereas upper classes may have lacked the time and desire.

Source. Saxon Graham, "Class and conservatism in the adoption of innovations," *Human Relations,* 9:91–100.

Status Rears Its Head in Kitchen and in Jury Room

The effects of class in society and of status in the business firm are well-known. However, status also has been studied in more exotic settings. Behind the scenes of a restaurant, a status system which sprang up without management being aware of its existence caused trouble.

Perhaps the most delightful introduction that a student can have to

are still empty, but the customers are already beginning to line up outside the locked front door."

Whyte takes his readers through that front door and behind the scenes, telling what he and 3 research assistants found as participant observers working in 12 Chicago restaurants during 1944 and 1945, and what they learned by interviewing workers in 13 other restaurants. He tells the story of the bartender who let customers go thirsty rather than take orders from a waitress, and of the waitress who suffered a nervous breakdown, caught between the conflicting demands of the management and the customers.

The kitchen in one restaurant included 45 workers arranged in a status system like this.

Cooks at the range
↓
Salad preparation
↓
Preparation of chicken and meat
↓
Cleaning chicken; preparing vegetables

Each of these levels in turn had its own strata.

Vegetable (8 persons)

Cooks (Nos. 1 and 2)
Halftime cook-preparation (No. 3)
Supervision of preparation (No. 4)
Others (Nos. 5, 6, 7, 8)

Chicken (7 persons)

Slice breasts for sandwiches (Nos. 1 and 2)
Weigh slices (No. 3)
Wrap slices (No. 4)
Pick white meat off carcass (No. 5)
Pick dark meat off carcass (Nos. 6 and 7)

Clean vegetables without odor were the sign of high status: only 6, 7, and 8 ever handled potatoes and onions. In chicken, white meat had higher status than dark.

What determined who was assigned to a given role? Age and seniority: Numbers 1 and 2 in the chicken hierarchy had been with the firm 9 years; Numbers 7 and 8, at the bottom of the vegetable hierarchy, were women of 72 and 65 who had to sit down while they worked. Education, social class, and marital status also played a part.

Source. William Foote Whyte, *Human Relations in the Restaurant Industry* (New York: McGraw-Hill Book Company, 1948).

The second example shows how jurors brought with them into the jury room status which affected their deliberations. The position a man takes at a table tends to reflect the status he brings with him. His position at the table, in turn, tends to determine the amount of deference others show him, and his influence over the group's activities. Status affects interaction and interaction enhances status.

Sixty-nine experiments were conducted in Chicago and St. Louis by drawing members from jury panels and inviting them to listen to a recorded trial. Their first job, before time for interaction, was to elect a foreman. Jurors seated at the ends of the table were most likely to be picked: figures at left indicate how often

foremen were chosen at each position around the 12-man table.

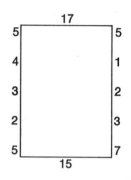

Position	Average Percent of Comments	Perceived Contribution to Decision (Votes)
End	10	300
Corner	7.5	241
Next-to-corner	7.8	358
Midtable	8.4	274

Jurors in owner-and-manager jobs took end positions about 15% more often than would have occurred by chance; they were twice as likely to be chosen foreman as were clerks and skilled workers, three times as likely as laborers.

The table indicates that persons in end positions were likely to originate more than their fair share of comments (10% rather than 8.4%) and were more often perceived as having helped the group reach consensus. Analysis of preferences indicated that end and middle positions were perceived as less socially distant. Their behavior could be observed more easily; such observations tended to produce a greater feeling of like-mindedness in the observer.

Source. Fred L. Strodtbeck and L. Harmon Hook, "The social dimensions of a twelve-man jury table," *Sociometry*, 24:397–415.

Social Prestige versus Job Status

The extent to which the prestige of a man's *occupation* coincides with his prestige as indicated by his *associates* has been studied by an ingenious use of published sources.

Using the *Social Register* as an index of associates and *Who's Who* as a measure of occupational status, E. Digby Baltzell compared listings in the two publications for 13 major cities as of 1940. *Who's Who,* biased in favor of educators and the clergy, listed 12,530 individuals in these cities, compared with 28,450 who made the *Social Register.* The percentage of *Who's Who* listings also found in the *Social Register* ranged from a low of 11% for Chicago to a high of 30% for Washington, D.C. The overall average was 23%.

In a society whose major decisions are made by financiers and businessmen, men in such occupations tend to be recruited from families at the top of the social structure. In Philadelphia, 75% of the 32 bankers in *Who's Who* were also listed in the *Social Register.* Intellectual ability, however, is passed on from one generation to the next less easily than wealth. Occupations in which success depends on a man's own wits show less overlap between the two publications. (Occupations of this kind thus represent a major channel of mobility which permits a man of low ascribed status to rise.)

Among such channels in Philadelphia are the church, only eight of the 80 *Who's Who* entries also being found in the *Social Register,* education (16% overlap), and public office (21% overlap). Physicians (37%) and lawyers (51%), perhaps as a reflection both of cost of their training and the wealth of their clientele, occupied a middle ground.

Source. Richard Bendix and Seymour Martin Lipset, *Class, Status and Power* (Glencoe, Ill.: The Free Press, 1953), p. 272.

Additional Research Readings

Skills. Choice of whole-or-part and description-or-inference processing of messages about faces and figures showed middle-class subjects to be more accurate communicators. **Eleanor R. Heider, "Style and accuracy of verbal communications within and between social classes," Journal of Personality and Social Psychology, 18:33–47.**

Bias. Product ratings and buying intentions gave biased results because lower-class consumers rated everything high, 42% being "yea-sayers" compared to only 20% of upper class. A change of instrument reduced bias. **Kevin J. Clancy and Robert Garsen, "Why some scales predict better," Journal of Advertising Research, 10:5:33–8.**

Self-esteem. When applicants for a research or computer programming job found themselves competing with a sockless student in a smelly sweatshirt, their self-esteem fell. It rose when their rival wore a dark suit and slide rule and carried a philosophy text. **Stan Morse and Kenneth J. Gergen, "Social comparison, self-consistency and the concept of self," Journal of Personality and Social Psychology, 16:148–56.**

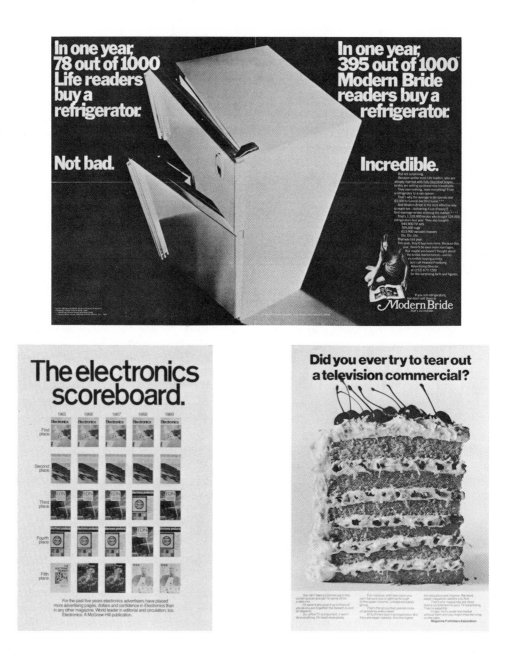

Comparing Alternative Media

Invidious references to one's competitors may invite retaliations from them and even cause government to frown. Some media forbid or discourage such comparisons—useful as they might be to a prospective buyer. The media themselves, however, show no such restraint, perhaps because they are dealing with a tougher-minded, non-consumer market. Thus *Modern Bride* doesn't hesitate to claim a 395:78 advantage over *Life,* nor do magazine publishers boggle at mentioning the rival medium, TV, which has driven some of them to the wall. *McGraw-Hill* uses a *band-wagon appeal* to demonstrate superiority of its magazine over four rivals.

330a

Name or Ignore Competitors?

Two advertisers help prospects compare brands but without naming rival brands. Uniroyal points to a specific product feature (six ounces less weight) which provides consumer benefits an unnamed competitor can't match. Honeywell, although not naming the "Mr. Big" of the computer market, uses the strategy Avis employed so well against Hertz of suggesting the little guy with the smaller share of market has to try harder. In contrast, Pearl, lower-priced, regional beer, gains points by claiming equality, if not superiority, as compared with two higher-priced, better-known, premium beers.

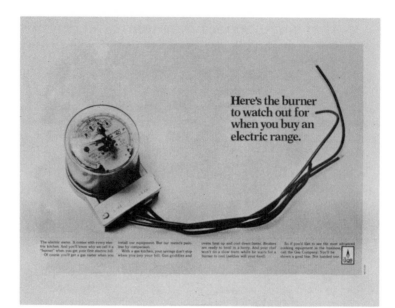

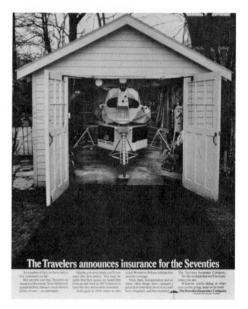

Reason Why or Flat Assertion?

Old Grand-Dad doesn't claim that any special process or ingredient distinguishes itself from six rival Bourbons—just uses its name in punning fashion to claim leadership. Text of the gas industry ad, in contrast, asserts three specific advantages: lower cost, faster heating, quicker cooling.

Its art illustrates the first of these, by showing an electric meter that looks as if it may have been ripped out by the roots by an irate user. Making no reference to any rival, Travelers claims superiority by having led the way in developing new forms of protection.

● The purchase-sale, culmination of buyer and seller decision making, is the least-studied stage of the process. Its beginning is vague, its length and nature vary, and it often occurs inside the head of the buyer, and so is difficult to observe.

● Mass marketing has shifted most information gathering and bargaining from a face-to-face encounter between buyer and seller to either a buyer's choice of retail outlets and a seller's choice of market segments or an internal dialogue between either buyer or seller and his imagined opposite number. This dialogue on the part of the consumer may be recaptured in interviews which ask why actual purchases deviate from previously stated intentions. Both product and type of retail outlet appear to affect extent to which product and brand plans are carried out. Through manipulating shelf space and store layout, retailers try to make purchases outrun intentions; through pricing and packaging, manufacturers try to encourage brand switching.

● Where negotiation about price remains possible, the outcome of the purchase-sales encounter may be viewed as determining which participant makes greater concessions within the range permitted to him by his employer (seller) or his resources (buyer). Considerations of knowledge, strategy, motivation, and definition of the situation all affect outcome. Strategies of both buyer and seller are often suboptimal.

● Social relations with peers are most rewarding; retail salesmen may be threatened by having to defer to lower-class customers and customers by associating with lower-class clerks. The salesman's role calls for deference, which is consistent with status relations of middle-class clerks and upper-class customers; in such encounters the strictly business nature of the encounter will be stressed. In relations with middle-class customers, equality of status tends to modify role-required deference.

● In industrial marketing, two additional types of purchase- and sale encounter are found: the auction (when many buyers face a single seller) and bidding (when many suppliers face a single buyer). Two questions of importance in distribution are who dominates the series of purchase-sale encounters that occur between manufacturer, wholesaler and retailer and where buying decisions are made within the retail firm.

Research Articles

Techniques. Buyer using "sophisticated" approach wins price concessions in auto purchase (Jung); seller uses small concessions to pave way for larger one (Freedman).

Interaction. Outcome of sale-purchase encounter predicted by observing interaction (Pennington, Willett); ethnic differences between buyer and seller affect price paid for TV (Sturdivant). Salesman finds it easier to switch buyers to cheaper than to more expensive brand of paint (Brock).

Chapter 17 The Purchase (and the Sale)

Perhaps the most puzzling of all stages of decision making involving buyers and sellers is that of the actual purchase itself. The first puzzle is why, although purchase-and-sale are the focus of both marketing and consumer behavior, this stage has been studied less than any other part of the process. It's as though one were to make elaborate studies of the breeding of bulls and follow dead bulls out of the ring to the butchers but ignore the "moment of truth" itself, just as Victorian novelists used to substitute asterisks for action at critical points in their narrative.

Possible explanations for this peculiar paradox include the following.

Since the crucial decisions occur in people's heads, they are hard to observe. (This also tends to be true of other stages, including problem definition, goal setting, and some kinds of product use.)

It is hard to determine when this stage begins. (This tends to be true of any process, whose stages are arbitrary conventions imposed to facilitate analysis.)

The length of the stage varies greatly, from the second it takes to put a coin into a vending machine to the months of negotiations involved in buying a new factory, a computer, or a guided missile. (This is also true of problem identification and the search for alternatives.)

The amount and kind of interaction between seller and buyer varies enormously, being absent for all practical purposes in both the vending machine and the modern supermarket, but being very intense in the sale of an insurance policy or a house.

The end of the sales-purchase stage is definite: it occurs when one participant, buyer or seller, makes an offer and the other accepts it. (Payment may be made at this time, or it may not. Physical possession may pass from one person to another or it may not. Exchange of title may have to wait upon legal formalities or completion of installment payments.) But when does this stage begin? Common sense suggests that it begins when the buyer seeks out a seller, or responds to a seller's invitation, and the two begin a process of bargaining and negotiations.

One problem, even with this definition, is that the process may abort at any time, forcing the prospect to resume his search for alternatives. (He may discover that the seller's offer is not what he had expected or that he cannot meet the seller's terms. He may threaten to resume search hoping to win concessions from the seller. A threat that fails may end the purchase stage; a threat that succeeds may be merely a part of it.) On the other hand, much of the interaction between prospect and salesman may concern earlier stages of decision making; the whole decision process can occur within a single encounter with a salesman.

Types of Process

It helps, perhaps, to think of the role of price in different kinds of purchasing: the bargaining in a village market; the interaction in an auction; shopping in a supermarket; and the face-to-face encounter between a salesman and a prospect.

Auction and supermarket represent extremes on a continuum of *price*. The auction deals with scarce, sometimes unique, products whose prices are set by competitive bidding. In the village market, each sale may be made at a different price depending on each buyer's skill in bargaining. The encounter between salesman and prospect shifts focus away from price; often the salesman has no freedom to alter price at all. In the supermarket, of course, price is fixed; if it were not, mass marketing would be impossible and mass production pointless. Does it make sense to talk about a purchasing stage or process in a supermarket?

Bargaining over price and other details, the essence of the purchase-and-sale, occurs at times remote from the actual transfer of ownership and within the heads of supermarket buyer and seller.

Before putting his brand on the market, *seller* engages in an interior dialogue with imaginary prospects, often seen as an aggregate on a demand curve. After it's been on the market, he studies sales figures and other data, trying to determine how far and why actual buyers deviated from the buyers he imagined in a "dialog" months or years earlier.

The buyer bargains by withholding his patronage, waiting for the seller or his competitors to respond with a sale. On both sides, bargaining is reduced to a binary choice: *Take it or leave it,* says the seller; *Drop your price or keep your product,* the prospect responds.

With interaction occurring at points distant in time, with each participant reacting with an imagined rather than real opposite number and with no observable events to record, the scientist must exhibit considerable ingenuity if he is to preserve and study the concept of a purchase-and-sale *encounter.* Yet he has no choice: such purchase-and-sale represents a large, increasing portion of all consumer transactions.

The scientist must observe buyer or seller responding to the *results* of the other's behavior rather than to the *person* of the other. He can listen to a housewife speak her thoughts aloud as she moves down the supermarket aisle, responding to seller decisions embalmed in prices, brand names, displays. Or he can infer such dialogue by comparing a housewife's intentions as she enters a supermarket with the contents of her cart as she leaves and asking her to explain the discrepancies.

When he does the latter, he discovers four types of discrepancy.

1. Some intended *products* weren't purchased: the store was out, the product couldn't be located, the price was too high, the quality was too low, or some more desirable item took its place.
2. *Brands* not listed were substituted for intended brands because sight of a preferred brand jogged the buyer's memory, the preferred brand was missing, or a price deal overrode brand preferences.
3. *Products* not listed were purchased; they or point-of-purchase advertising awakened latent needs or a special price triggered premature purchase.
4. Vague plans were made specific: *dinner for eight* became *meat* and meat became *steak; sausage* became *Oscar Mayer's.*

The customer benefits from a large number of purchases in category 4; he doesn't have to spend a lot of time drawing up lists in advance, but can use the store itself as a shopping list. If lack of a list increases his volume of purchases, then sellers also benefit.

The brand switching of category 2 may aid a retailer if the buyer shifts from a brand the store lacks to one it has, saving a sale, or if the buyer shifts from a nationally advertised brand to a private-label house brand. (House brands usually cost a few cents less, increasing total volume sold, but have larger markups.) A switch from one national brand to another, both of which he stocks, is a matter of indifference to the retailer—but of great importance to the manufacturer.

Both retailer and manufacturer benefit when latent needs are translated into a purchase, in category 3; both are injured if the category 1 purchases are not merely postponed but actually cancelled. (Evidence that this may happen was found during a two-day forced shutdown of stores in a Texas town. Grocery purchases were postponed but purchases of books and variety store items were cancelled.)

If many purchases fall into category 3, a retailer can stock a wide variety of products and brands and emphasize display, point-of-purchase advertising, and price deals. If category 4 is important, he needs to arrange his stock so as to facilitate the decision-making process. If category 1 is important, he needs to take immediate action; a customer disappointed too often may shop elsewhere.

Studies to date have tended to confuse categories 3 and 4. Instead of checking intentions on a reminder list of grocery products, housewives have drawn up their own lists. Low motivation for the task may have caused them to do a superficial job, underestimating the extent to which purchases are actually planned in advance and exaggerating the retailer's ability to influence buying behavior.

With this caution, here are figures showing differences by category among retail outlets and among products within the supermarket.[1] (Table 17.1)

It is not too surprising to find that liquor buyers have strong brand preferences—or that buyers seem to use supermarket shelves as a three-dimensional shopping

checklist. It seems unlikely, however, that purchases of meat and produce are completely "unplanned." More likely a housewife takes it for granted that everyone buys both on every trip to a supermarket. As one would expect, the proportion of unplanned purchases rises as shopping skills and habits increase (as indexed by years of married life) and the size of purchases increases (as indexed by either amount of money spent or number of items).

Changing Plans

Perhaps the most important in-store influence upon a buyer's behavior is the amount of shelf space given a product. If a seller gives a product less than two rows, a buyer may not notice it at all. One study reveals that 90% of the items stocked in a supermarket sell less than 24 units a week, and that 20 to 30% of them sell less than a unit a week.[2] It may take more than a month to get rid of the minimum supply needed to catch a buyer's eye on the ordinary supermarket shelf. (If slow-moving products were held down to this two-row minimum, it's been estimated that 35% of the typical supermarket's shelves would be freed for fast-moving items.) When number of shelves was systematically altered over a six-month period, sales of the 514

TABLE 17.1   Planning varies by store and product

Type of Stores	Category 2 (Switched Brands)	Category 3 (Unplanned)	Category 4 (General Plans)	Category 5 (Bought Planned Brand)
Supermarket	2%	50%	17%	31%
Drug store	7	22	15	56
Liquor store	10	8	20	62
Type of Product				
Produce	—	45%	13%	41%
Meats	3%	49	14	34
Baked goods	3	58	19	20
Frozen foods	3	61	17	19
Miscellaneous	1	67	8	25

items given more shelf space rose a net 33%, and net profits for 73 of the items rose from $53 to $103.[3] In another study, reducing the space for 65 slow-moving items caused no drop in sales; giving the space saved to canned fruit increased its sales by 35%.[4] Doubling the space given *slow-moving* items would have doubled expenses of pricing and stocking the goods, but increased profits only 11%.

Location as well as number of products displayed affects sales. A men's clothing store usually puts suits at the back, so that a suit buyer must pass displays of shirts, belts, and ties both coming and going. Produce, meats, and dairy products which appear on most shopping lists are positioned so as to maximize the number of other products a housewife will be exposed to on her way to them. Traffic-pattern studies show the proportion of shoppers who *pass* a display ranges from 30% for housewares to 94% for fresh meat.[5] The proportion of those who *buy* varies even more, from the 1% who buy records to the 80% who buy fresh meats.

In addition to shelf facings, housewives are influenced by special displays and point-of-purchase advertising. If one assumes that buyers know when they've switched brands, are willing to admit it and don't forget it, one can assess the effect of point-of-purchase materials on such behavior by a direct question. Such a question, asked of 2800 buyers in 16 drugstores in nine cities, found 18% had switched and 30% of the switchers—5% of all customers—said it was because of point-of-purchase displays.[6] Before-and-after measures with experimental and control groups in six different kinds of stores selling everything from beer to cameras found ordinary point-of-purchase ads increased sales 37% and moving displays increased them 83%.[7] (Customers may have been buying *sooner* rather than *more*: today's gains may be matched by tomorrow's losses. The fact that both studies were originally published by the point-of-purchase medium itself leads to a certain amount of skepticism. Were choices made in designing the study, perhaps unconsciously, which maximized

TABLE 17.2 Illustrative Results of Traffic Pattern Study

Product	Percentage Who		Percentage of Buyers Divided by Percentage of Those Who Pass
	Pass	Buy	
Fresh meats	94%	80%	85%
Paper products	64	37	58
Canned meat	64	19	30
Ice cream	61	14	23
Soft drinks	55	22	40
Dietetic foods	55	7	13
Candy	49	11	22
Records	39	1	3
Housewares	30	6	20

(Although such figures are useful in comparing pulling power of product versus location, we need a series of experiments in which housewives, whose specific buying intentions have been determined, are randomly assigned to different store layouts if we are to determine how layouts affect the number and nature of "unplanned" items purchased.)

chances that the studies would be publishable? It seems reasonable to suppose they were.)

Piles of cans at the end of an aisle increase the chance a product will be seen and suggest that it is on sale. Before-and-after measures in 20 stores, half experimental and half control, increased sales for a brand of coffee by a net of 115%, for gelatin by a net of 162% and for toilet paper by a net of 5%, in each case being accompanied by a decline in sales of competing brands.[8] (Reasons for the wide differences among brands and products remain to be discovered.) Another way of suggesting a price concession is to offer multiple units. Before-and-after sales audits have shown, for example, that offers of "two-for" and "three-for" can cause an average sales increase of 27%; a "six-for" combination caused a rise of 31%.[9] When the reverse was attempted—when products usually offered in multiples were priced by the unit—sales fell by 28%. (Again wide variation among products raises the question of how a retailer can use such data.)

Customer and Salesman Interaction

The delayed effect that the seller has on buyer behavior in the single-price, self-service retail outlet contrasts with the immediate and mutual effect of interaction that may occur between customer and salesman in a face-to-face sales encounter.

Sometimes, as we have seen, products and their prices are so uniform that skill in buying or selling becomes irrelevant. Advertising has great impact in such circumstances, inducing brand preferences when there may be no rational, objective grounds for preferring any one brand, saving time that would be lost in making a meaningless choice.

In other instances, although prices are fixed in each store at any point in time, they vary among stores and types of stores, or they change for a given store with seasons and sales. A buyer can benefit by search and comparison among different stores in the first instance or by shifting the time of purchase in the second case. Buyer skill pays dividends—but it is skill in discovering when and where bargains can be obtained, skill in choosing alternatives rather than the act of purchase.

Here there *is* face-to-face interaction between sales clerk and prospect: a clerk cannot alter prices or attributes but he can save a sale by helping the buyer find the style, size, and price he wants. Sometimes, the manufacturer enters the picture by offering the clerk and his employer special inducements to push his brand. In every case, retail sales provide delayed feedback to the manufacturer in the form of reorders (or failure to reorder). The buyer-seller interaction is split into three encounters separated in both space and time: customer-retail-clerk, clerk-buyer, and buyer-supplier-salesmen. (Such study is complicated by the fact that advertising may replace face-to-face interaction to degrees varying with product and people in the first and last of these encounters.) So far, such analysis has not been attempted.

A different situation may exist in the purchase of appliances, automobiles, insurance, and houses, since their prices may be subject to negotiation, either overt or concealed in bargaining over optional features, value of a trade-in or quantity and cash discounts.

To predict process and outcome in such bargaining situations, we ask how much influence each participant *can* exert and how willing each is to use this influence. What strategies does each employ? What costs will each incur to win what rewards?

One reward in the sale-purchase act is the exchange of product and money and a feeling that the price one has paid or collected is "fair." The other reward is in the process itself: pleasant interaction with a person one respects. (Needless to say, a sale-purchase may not be made, and customer-salesman interaction may be unpleasant.)

A firm might find it highly profitable if its salesmen managed to close only one sale in 30 attempts, a higher ratio than most advertising attains. It is doubtful, however, whether any salary can compensate salesmen for the sense of rejection produced by such a high rate of "failure." Similarly, some customers may postpone a purchase because they fear unpleasant interaction or they feel ill-equipped to bargain successfully.

If customers define the purchase-sale encounter as a combat situation, they will need to be very self-confident, even aggressive, before they will enter into it. A salesman must bolster such prospects' confidence or get them to redefine the situation. If a customer defines the encounter as a friendly game, he may need assurance that he and the salesman are evenly matched. (Most of us realize that salesmen have stronger motivation to win, have been selected and trained to win and have more experience than any customer with the product that is the focus of the encounter.)

Bargaining Strategies

A customer's success in bargaining depends on his resources, his strategy, and his knowledge of the freedom of negotiation possessed by the seller.

The poor are less aware of alternative sources of supply, more dependent on credit, and lack the power and skills needed in bargaining.[10] The very rich pay more because alternative uses of their time are worth more than the saving they might achieve through bargaining. Thus it is the middle classes who have the resources and the motivation needed for bargaining.

As for strategy, it's been found that college sophomores, white rats, and some media buyers often follow plausible but suboptimal strategies. Probably few sophomores would follow the strategy shown in Table 17.1[11] of sending an equal number of messages to market segments with widely varying proportions of prospects. In practice, however, subjects performing a wide variety of tasks *do* follow the stimulus-matching strategy in which messages are shared in proportion to prospects. A moment's thought or a glance at the table should convince one that it's better to send *all* messages to the high payoff market of segment I (or to choose the predominant color or suit in a game of guessing which card will turn up next in an altered deck).

(Interestingly enough, if a subject is rewarded for his correct guesses by giving him small amounts of money and penalized by fining him small amounts, he does shift to this optimal strategy, without realizing he has shifted or how.)

Even given the resources for bargaining and an optimal strategy, many customers lack the information needed for successful bargaining. A customer rarely knows the amount of markup for an individual product, a class of products, or a type of retail outlet. A seller is usually better able to

TABLE 17.3 Three Strategies of Dividing 200 Messages Among Four Market Segments

Market Segment (200 persons each)	Percent of Prospects in Segment	Number of Prospects Reached by		
		Strategy of 50 Messages per Segment	Stimulus Matching	All Messages to Top Market
I	80%	40[a]	64[b]	160[c]
II	60	30	36	0
III	40	20	16	0
IV	20	10	4	0
		100	120	160

[a] Since 80% of the 50 messages reach prospects, .80 × 50 = 40.
[b] Segment I has 160 prospects out of a total of 400 (160/4.00 = 40%) and so gets 40% out of 200 messages (80), which 80% reach prospects, so .80 × 80 = 64.
[c] Although all 200 messages go to Segment I, only 80% reach prospects, so .80 × 200 = 160.

estimate a buyer's range of acceptable alternatives than the buyer is able to estimate the seller's.

Finally, a customer's success in bargaining depends on the intensity of his motivations. Lack of any strong need or desire for the product gives him an advantage, since he can always withdraw from the game without any serious loss to himself. High motivation to bargain also gives the buyer an advantage.

Salesmen's Influence

The outcome of the bargaining depends, of course, on the salesman's skill and resources, as well as those of the customer. Some sales clerks are mere order takers. Other retail salesmen show much skill in probing customers' preferences, in subtly directing them to a more expensive line than they originally planned to buy or in inducing a man who came in to buy a shirt to buy tie, socks, and shoes as well.

If he is selling a product purchased frequently, the salesman is likely to forego immediate short-run gains in bargaining for the long-run advantage of repeat sales. If many competitors offer a similar product at a similar price, the customer's bargaining power is increased.

The most satisfactory social encounters are those that involve equals. If a salesman's status is clearly inferior to that of his customers, he is likely to lose control of the situation. If the salesman loses control, the whole communication process may break down.

Experience teaches most salesmen that they can communicate most successfully with persons like themselves, no matter how strongly their employers insist that *a good salesman can sell anybody*. In a retail store patronized by all classes, difficulties are likely. By definition, sales clerks are members of the middle class. The salesman's role specifies that its occupant is supposed to defer to and serve customers, yet every salesman knows that he must also control the encounter. In dealing with a middle-class clientele, middle-class clerks can adopt an informal stance that plays down the deference required by role and emphasizes equality of status.[12] If the shop caters to a wealthy clientele, the salesman must override status differences of wealth, occupation, or income by emphasizing product knowledge, an area where he is expert. Although a salesman may feel rewarded by associating socially with persons of higher status, they are likely to feel otherwise—another reason for stressing the strictly business atmosphere. A store serving a lower-class clientele creates even more serious problems. Middle-class clerks are likely to feel threatened by the role of salesman which demands that they defer to customers. Here the salesman may emphasize his superiority to lower-class customers by becoming brusque and impolite, losing sales but preserving status.

In industrial selling, problems of status become more complex since salesman and buyer belong to organizations with many levels of status, and a lot of competition for status and status symbols. A great deal of time may be spent in establishing satisfactory social relationships as a preliminary to sales, whether at lunch or on the golf course.

Industrial Marketing

In addition to the salesman-customer confrontation and the self-service substitute for a face-to-face encounter found in consumer sales, industrial marketing has two other kinds of means to accomplish purchase-and-sale.[13] When many buyers face a single seller, an auction sets the price at whatever the market will bear. When there are many suppliers and a single buyer, as often occurs in industrial marketing, buying by bid may determine price.

A manufacturer may decide to make rather than buy, because he has men and machines not being used, because he wants to maintain security on a new product or to protect quality and ensure delivery. He will be forced to make some parts if his account is too small to interest a seller; his costs are likely to be high, and lacking the research facilities of a large supplier, he may find it hard to adjust to change.

The manufacturer who decides to buy can negotiate, he can ask for bids, or he may combine the two. Bidding would seem to eliminate any opportunity for interaction between buyer and seller since specifications are released, sealed bids opened in public, and the contract awarded to the lowest bidder.

Sellers influence a buyer in drawing up specifications on which bids are to be asked. Only qualified firms are invited to bid; to qualify bidders, a buyer may talk to their salesmen, visit their operations, and talk to their customers. After a bid is accepted, its terms may be modified, which means still another occasion for bargaining.

The interaction between buyer and seller, which is not absent under bidding, is the essence of the negotiated sale-purchase.

Predicting the outcome of negotiations requires knowledge of how much room each participant has to make concessions, and knowledge of what each perceives the other's range of concession to be. The width of the range depends on the urgency of each participant's need. (How important is this sale to the seller and how important that it be made now? Does he have creditors demanding to be paid? Is this order an entering wedge either to further orders from the buyer or to other buyers in this market?) Width of range also depends on the number of alternatives open to buyer and seller if present bargaining should abort. (How many other suppliers and customers are available?) Width also depends on timing. (Does this order come during a slack time for the supplier? Will the buy-er's assembly line be forced to shut down if a decision is delayed?)

Some of the things a manufacturer buys, such as supplies and raw materials, may be so uniform in quality and price from one supplier to another that habit, a computer, or random choice would serve as well as bargaining. Other purchases, such as plant and equipment, which have to be custom designed, differentiate suppliers. Routine purchases can be made by one man well down on the organizational chart. Purchases that involve a long-time commitment and a large amount of money are likely to involve more men and men higher up in the organization. The seller also needs to know how much power each decision maker has at each stage of decision making, and what combination of advertising and personal selling will best reach and influence each.

Decisions in Retailing

Industrial marketing represents one end of the flow of products and messages that constitutes marketing; consumer marketing represents the other. Connecting the two are a series of middlemen of whom the retailer is most visible.

Two questions concerning these middlemen are of at least passing interest. One is where control lies: which type of firm dominates the series of purchases-and-sales that occur within these channels. The other is where purchase-and-sale occurs within the retail store itself, preliminary to the final encounter with the consumer.

At one time, large wholesalers dominated both small factories and small retail firms. Later, control passed to large manufacturers; they determined the rate of technological innovation and new product introduction and their messages dominated the advertising scene. Today large retail chains, like Safeway's over 2000 supermarkets and Sears' over 800 retail stores, are making more and more of the major decisions.

For years, success in retailing depended upon artful purchasing; the department head was also *buyer;* contact with customers, it was assumed, gave him the ability to purchase wisely. In department stores and supermarket chains, buying decisions have moved into the hands of central buying specialists and committees who, lacking direct day-to-day contact with consumers, must increasingly depend upon indirect feedback. A computer can provide daily reports on how the merchandise they have bought is selling; consumer research provides insights into buyers' desires and attitudes. The 80 separate departments, once centered around buyers, can be replaced by shops and boutiques, based on customer types and uses rather than product types. Sleeping or bathing products or products that meet the needs of high- or low-income groups, teen-agers, or matrons save shoppers the trouble of traipsing from one floor to another, increasing the number of clerk-initiated, tie-in purchases.

As mass marketing narrows the range of negotiation required of the retail clerk, the retailer reduces variability and risk involved in finding, training, and motivating salesmen. Routine tasks can be turned over to lower-paid groups lacking other opportunities, like women and ethnic minorities. Such tasks offer fewer chances of promotion and occupational status drops. (When Americans were asked to rate 90 jobs in terms of prestige in 1963, the retail clerk ranked 20th from the bottom, lower than a corporal in the regular army. Of 19 jobs ranked four times between 1925 and 1963, only two showed a steady drop in prestige: small retail store manager and clerk.)[14]

The lack of status, opportunity, pay, and interesting tasks in retail selling mean that stores apparently do not want or need skilled salesmen. This lack also means that clerks, like many production workers, are likely to place more value upon pleasant relationships with their fellow workers than they are upon sales-increasing interaction with customer. They may hold down sales, to avoid being rejected by less energetic co-workers, and are likely to give conversation with colleagues priority over conversation with customers.

In short, even where face-to-face relations still exist, as between customers and clerks, little can happen in such an encounter that will be rewarding to either.

Given such clerks, sales may rise (and costs fall) if one substitutes vending-machines and self service—and adds advertising to presell customers. As one observer notes.

. . . The mere presence of a salesman prevents large numbers of persons looking at things they are not seriously interested in, because of the presumed social obligation to buy. . . . Lack of such pressure in the self-service store . . . seems to do as good a job of suggestive selling as many experienced salesmen and more than the mediocre sales clerk at less expense.[15]

Thought, Talk, and Action

1. Suggest how the different goals of manufacturer, retailer, and customer may *conflict* in a supermarket, in a gas station, in a clothing store. Now list the three possible 2:1 coalitions that may arise in probable order of frequency. What implications would you draw from this list for the behavior of each of the three roles?
2. How would you recruit, train, reward, and supervise clerks if you were manager of a store in the ghetto, in the light of this chapter? What changes would you make if you were manager of a similar store in a middle-class neighborhood? Manager of a store in your city's wealthiest residential area?

3. Who would dominate distribution channels in a nation where both manufacturers and retailers are small? What changes might result if Sears Roebuck opened stores in the country? What changes if the Generals—Motors, Mills, and Electric—began operations there?

Notes

Chapter 17

1. James F. Engel et al., Consumer behavior (New York: Holt, Rinehart and Winston, 1958), pp. 487–8.
2. *Ibid.*
3. Douglas J. Dalrymple and Donald L. Thompson, Retailing: An economic view (New York: The Free Press, 1969), p. 291.
4. *Ibid.*, p. 289.
5. Reference No. 1, pp. 476–7, citing "Colonial study," Progressive Grocer (January 1964).
6. Reference No. 1, p. 478.
7. *Ibid.*, p. 479.
8. Mary L. McKenna, "The influence of in-store advertising," in Joseph Newman, editor, On knowing the consumer (New York: John Wiley & Sons, 1966).
9. Reference No. 1, p. 478.
10. David Caplovitz, The poor pay more (New York: The Free Press, 1963).
11. Suggested by Kenneth A. Longman, Advertising (New York: Harcourt Brace Jovanovich, 1971), p. 209.
12. W. T. Tucker, The social context of economic behavior (New York: Holt, Rinehart and Winston, 1964).
13. Ralph S. Alexander et al., Industrial Marketing, 3rd ed. (Homewood, Ill.: Richard D. Irwin, 1967), pp. 72–8.
14. Reference No. 3, p. 156.
15. Reference No. 12, pp. 76–7.

How Much Can a Car Buyer Gain by Haggling?

Mass marketing has virtually wiped out the kind of haggling that every purchase once involved except for a few products like automobiles. Here is a field experiment in which auto salesmen faced three different kinds of customers.

Customers trained to play three different roles called on all 30 new Ford dealers and all 28 new Chevrolet dealers within the Chicago city limits in a 10-day period in February 1959. One customer posed as someone who had just learned how to drive. Another played the role of a hardened shopper whose only interest was in getting a good price. The third played an intermediate role. Each salesman was told that he was the first one who had been contacted. No trade-in was offered. Customers using the "hard" approach countered the salesman's first offer with a counteroffer, set low enough so that it would be rejected, and then asked the salesman for his lowest price.

Of the 58 dealers visited, only one quoted the same price to all three shoppers. On the average, the *hard* approach got a lower price than the *soft:* $2577 versus $2610 for Fords and $2490 versus $2507 for Chevrolets. (The difference was not statistically significant.) In 23 cases the same salesman saw *two* test "customers." In 15 of these cases, the "harder" of the 2 approaches got lower prices. Four salesmen gave the same estimate to both customers. Four gave *lower* estimates to the "soft" approach.

The largest discounts were offered by the low-volume (500 cars a year) or high-volume (over 1000 cars a year) dealers.

Few salesmen offered demonstration rides or reasons for buying their make or from a particular dealer. Some 60% of the salesmen took the prospect's telephone number, but only a third of these actually telephoned. Salesmen tried to sell additional accessories in only 12 of the 174 sales interviews.

Markups for Ford dealers fell from 9.7%, the grand mean of all 90 prices obtained (3 customers $\times$ 30 dealers), to 6.9% after bargaining by the "hard" customers. Chevrolet dealer markups fell from 8.3 to 6%. The author speculates that a customer will gain more by bargaining with a dealer, after he has seen a few, than by continuing to see additional dealers.

Source. Allen F. Jung, "Price variations among automobile dealers in Chicago, Illinois," *Journal of Business,* 32:315–26.

Soften 'Em Up, Then Move In for the Kill

Salesmen are taught that by getting prospects to make a whole series of little decisions along the way, it's easier to get them to make the big decision—to buy and to buy here and now. Here are two studies, neither of them involving actual purchase of a product, which show how the technique works.

In Palo Alto, a half-dozen men asked housewives to let them go through their house and classify all of the household products in it. The percentage agreeing varied with the extent of previous cooperation.

Had answered eight questions	53%
Had agreed to answer eight questions	33
Familiar with interviewer only	28
No previous contact	22

In a second study, 105 women and 7 men were asked to post a small 3-inch sign or add their name to a 20-signature petition advocating traffic safety or keeping California beautiful. Two weeks later another experimenter asked if they would allow an enormous, ugly "Drive Carefully" sign to be put in their front lawn. Only 17% of the subjects approached cold agreed, compared with 76% of the subjects who had earlier agreed to put a small "drive carefully" sign in the window. Here are the results.

	Agreed to put ugly sign on lawn (%)
Had posted "drive carefully" sign in window	76
Had posted "beautiful California" sign in window	48
Had signed "drive carefully" petition	48
Had signed "beautiful California" petition	47

Source. Jonathan L. Freedman and Scott C. Fraser, "Compliance without pressure: The foot-in-the-door technique," *Journal of Personality and Social Psychology,* 4:195–202.

Encounter Between Buyer and Seller

First, scholars tried to predict purchase and sale by looking at characteristics of either the customer or the salesman. Next, they tried to relate characteristics of buyer and seller. (Dependent personalities and men prefer aggressive salesmen; women dislike hard-sell types.) Finally, they observed salesman and prospect behaviors during the purchase-sale encounter itself. Here are a survey and an experiment which show customers being studied in real-life settings without their being aware of it.

Concealed microphones in the pockets of 14 salesmen in 11 appliance stores in 7 midwest cities relayed their conversations with 210 customers (15 per salesman) to a tape recorder. Three days later interviewers asked customers whether they had bought an appliance; those who hadn't were interviewed again two weeks later.

Of the 210 customers, 58 bought before they left the store, and 74 more—a total of 63%—within two weeks. Analysis of the tape recordings revealed 10 bargaining variables that correctly classified, as buyers or nonbuyers, 80% of the prospects. There were an average of 11 bargaining acts per transaction: 60% of them being statements by buyer or seller of what they expected, 23% questions as to what the other person expected, 16% attempts to change the other's expectations. Of the encounters that led to a purchase, 75% lasted less than 30 minutes.

When a salesman's behavior was consistent across customers, but varied from that of other salesmen studied, he was assumed to be in control; salesmen did control most encounters, including the nature of questions asked by customers. (Customers asked four times as many questions as did salesmen.) Salesmen accounted for nearly all examples of disagreement, antagonism, and tension recorded.

Sources

Allan L. Pennington, "Customer-salesman bargaining behavior in retail transactions," *Journal of Marketing Research*, 5:255–61.

Ronald P. Willett and Allan L. Pennington, "Customer and salesman: the anatomy of choice and influence in a retail setting," in R. M. Haas, ed., *Science, Technology and Marketing* (Chicago: American Marketing Association, 1966), pp. 598–616.

Buyer and Seller Interaction

The outcome of a purchase-sale encounter does vary with the nature of the participants, at least if ethnic differences are involved.

Couples representing three ethnic groups—Negro, Mexican-American, and Anglo—went shopping for a portable TV set in Los Angeles. Each shopped in all three ethnic neighborhoods. Stores in Negro neighborhoods charged everyone the same price. Two of the three Anglo neighborhood stores charged minority couples more than Anglos, even though couples were carefully matched on their *credit profile* —age, job, income, savings, and debts. (However, Anglo prices were still no more or even less than those of their competitors.) Widest price variations were found in Mexican neighborhoods, possibly because bargaining is still prevalent in that subculture. Here are a sample of the results, with the *credit price* given in parentheses.

Location of Store	Ethnic Background of Shoppers		
	Negro	Mexican	Anglo
Mexican	$200 ($265)	$240 ($281)	$230 ($284)
Negro	$270 ($421)	$270 ($507)	$230 ($418)
Mexican	$210 ($245)	$210 ($250)	$204 ($258)
Anglo	$140 ($183)	$140 ($183)	$140 ($203)

Source. Frederick D. Sturdivant and Walter T. Wilhelm, "Poverty, minorities and consumer exploitation," *Social Science Quarterly*, 50:1064–71.

In this experiment, conducted in a real-life setting, a salesman tried to induce brand switching.

As customers stood at the cash register, waiting for their paint purchase to be rung up, a salesman said: "I wonder if I can give you some advice—two weeks ago I bought X gallons of Brand A. It costs a little (less/more) . . . than the Brand C you want to buy. I also got a little of the C . . . honestly, it didn't work out as well at all."

Over a five-month period, salesmen tried to switch half their customers, chosen at random, to a paint (A) costing *less* than the kind (C) they had already picked out and the other half to a paint costing *more.* The salesman emphasized his similarity to some customers by telling them he'd used the same quantity (X) of paint they were buying; he assumed a more "expert" role with others by claiming to have used 20 times as much.

It was easier to switch customers to a cheaper paint and "similar" salesmen were more effective.

Percentage of customers who followed salesmen's advice are shown below.

Tried to Switch Buyer to:	"Similar" Salesman	"Expert" Salesman
Lower price	73	45
Higher price	55	32

Source. Timothy C. Brock, "Communicator-recipient similarity and decision change," *Journal of Personality and Social Psychology,* 1:650–4.

Additional Research Readings

Choice of store. Customers varying in race (black, white) and dress (good, bad) found that prices in 12 Atlanta drugstores varied by type of store but not of customer. An analgesic cost $2.17 in "professional" pharmacies, $2.07 in "community" stores, and $1.63 at discount outlets. **Jeffrey A. Kotzan and Charles L. Braucher, "A multivariate analysis of retail prescription prices," Journal of Marketing Research, 7:517–20.** Analysis of purchase diaries for 240 households for 15 weeks suggested store loyalty to be good buying strategy since it saved search cost and allowed stocking up on specials. **James M. Carman, "Some insights into reasonable grocery shopping strategies," Journal of Marketing, 33:4:69–72.**

Bargaining. Study of 37 appliance dealers found that 20 varied prices with customer's bargaining skill. When sales volume was below $100,000, such price differences ranged from 15 to 45%; above that point differences were only 10%. **Walter J. Primeaux, Jr., "The effect of consumer knowledge and bargaining strength on final selling price . . . ," Journal of Business, 43:419–26.**

Internal choice. On five shopping trips, two housewives spoke their thoughts into a tape recorder; from 78 to 227 decisions per trip were tallied for one, 46 to 70 for the other. **James R. Bettman, "Information processing models of consumer behavior," Journal of Marketing Research, 7:370–6.**

Source and Receiver
Decision Processes and Interaction

A purchase-sale occurs when decision process of buyer and seller converge in an encounter and result in a transaction. Often, however, there is no face-to-face encounter between salesman and customer. To an increasing extent the seller's messages are transmitted via the mass media, and stored in the consumer's memory until a variety of conditions precipitates a decision to replenish depleted stocks or adventure in the purchase of a new product or an unfamiliar brand.

Sellers choose channels and media and frame messages for audiences chosen to be as congruent as possible to their target markets. Members of these audiences, in turn, attend to messages which interest them or promise to assist them in the buying decisions they expect to make, immediately or sometime in the future. Some day we may have courses and books which will help consumers seek out and select messages more efficiently and with greater advantage to themselves. That day, however, has not yet arrived.

The remaining six chapters in this book present an in-depth examination of elements of the communications process, from the viewpoint of the man who uses the process to sell products and services.

The four channels of communications, key to the process, are discussed in Chapter 18, with one of these channels, advertising media, examined in detail in Chapter 19. Channels collect an audience, the subject of Chapter 20, and channels limit the kinds of symbols that may be used and messages that may be transmitted. Chapter 21 looks at several symbol systems, emphasizing the two most important—spoken and written language. Chapter 22 then describes the ways in which symbols may be combined into messages, with a passing glance at the interaction between style and content.

Finally, in Chapter 23, we end with a glance at the seller himself—at how his attributes affect interpretation and acceptance of his messages, and of how the messages he transmits and audience reaction to them in turn affect the source. Source, we discover, is often hard to distinguish from channel, in terms of audience effects—but this, of course, is the essence of process. All five of the elements in these chapters interact with the others, influencing and being influenced, and often the distinctions among them are arbitrary interruptions of a seamless whole.

Chapter 18 Synopsis

● A seller seeks audiences that have enough prospects who want and can pay for his product to pay the costs of reaching them and messages made up of symbols that will bring desired responses from such audiences. His choice of channels determines audiences, limits messages.

● The seller chooses from two channels: personal selling and advertising. The buyer is influenced by these and two more: publicity and word of mouth. These channels vary on dimensions of mutuality, credibility, control, relevance, and cost. Channels both supplement and substitute for one another. Buyers and sellers must decide not only how much to use each but also in what order. Weight and order given each will vary with products, users, and stages of the decision process.

● For a variety of reasons, word of mouth tends to be the most persuasive of channels, and is crucial in the acceptance of major product innovations. It is probably less subject to distortion than commonly believed. The types of persons most likely to be active in this channel are known but sellers have not been successful in its use; the channel is more an environmental factor for them than a variable to be manipulated.

● Like word of mouth, personal selling is a face-to-face channel with most of its advantages, except the lessening of credibility caused by seller self-interest. Seller control of the channel is threatened by competing goals of the salesman and by his interaction with the buyer. Variability between and within salesmen limits predictability. The seller must specify the functions his sales force is to perform, the abilities required and recruit, assign and motivate salesmen. Varying weights given four sales functions lead to three distinctive types of salesmen. The buyer has ultimate veto over the weight given personal selling in communications and the type of salesman utilized.

● Publicity is, like word of mouth, important to the major product innovation. In using it, the seller must share control with the buyer and with a third party—an editor. Goals of publicity may be either product sale or company image. Since buyers are only one of the publics whom a public relations department must serve, the sales function of publicity is often slighted.

Research Articles

Word-of-Mouth. Channel's importance assessed in radio listening, choice of supermarket, product choice (Arndt, Atkin); information-seekers use channel to reduce risk

(Cunningham); distortion in channel found to have been exaggerated (Schachter); type of channel and participant's expectations affect its accuracy (Buckner).

Acquaintances. Strangers communicate across continent by chain of persons on first-name basis (Milgram).

Chapter 18 Choosing Channels

A seller expects communications to provide him with two things that will move him toward his goal of making a sale: audiences and messages.

Audiences must meet two criteria. First, they must provide the seller with certain *kinds* of prospects: those who desire his product and brand, and are able to pay for it. Second, they must contain enough of such persons to repay the costs of communicating with them.

Messages must be made up of symbols combined in such ways as will be perceived by desirable prospects and responded to in a fashion that serves the seller's needs.

By making one decision the seller affects both audiences and messages. This is his choice of channels of communications. He has two channels to choose from: advertising and personal selling. (Each choice he makes is only a preliminary to further choices. The budget a seller allocates to the advertising channel must then be subdivided among six *advertising media*—newspapers, TV, radio, magazines, direct mail, billboards. Funds designated for a given medium must be further distributed to individual *advertising vehicles*—specific stations and publications. A similar series of decisions must be made about the sales budget: what numbers and types of salesmen to seek, which individuals to hire, what territories to assign them to, and what method of compensation to adopt.)

The channels, media, and vehicles a seller selects determine what audiences he will reach, and limit the kinds of messages he may send such audiences. Of course, the effects are reciprocal. If one channel, media, and vehicle mix cannot provide the audiences and permit the messages a seller specifies, he will look for another.

Four Channels for the Buyer

A buyer has a wider choice of channels. His behavior is influenced by messages coming from four channels, not two.

Word of mouth. Conversations by housewives over the back fence or by businessmen over the Bacardis in which experience with sellers' products and sellers' messages is shared, compared, tested.

Publicity. News stories appearing in the daily paper, the weekly magazine, or the monthly trade journal, which may (or may not) have been stimulated by a news release issued or a "news" event staged by the seller.

Salesmen. Reassurances from the clerk in a department store, demonstrations by an Avon lady or a Fuller Brushman, the dire forebodings of an insurance man, and the bright prospects offered by the broker selling lots in Alaska or waterworks bonds from Walla Walla. Scores of statistics from an oil tool engineer or a space salesman.

Media. Radio jingles, TV commercials, double-page color spreads in consumer magazines, classified ads in the daily newspaper, a "you-are-a-winner" notice in the mails, and umpteen 24-sheet billboards masking trees and junkyards indiscriminately on the daily drive to work.

If a buyer is influenced by four channels, why do sellers typically employ only two? (Word of mouth plays a part in nearly all buyer decisions about products and brands. Word of mouth and publicity play a key role in the acceptance of major product innovations.)

The seller has found no way to put his messages on the word-of-mouth channel.

An explanation of seller failure to make more use of the channel of publicity is more complex. In part, it is because the seller has less control of this channel than he does of advertising and selling. (The buyer, too, has less control since a third party, the editor, decides what messages from the seller a buyer will be exposed to.) The business firm recognizes that advertising and selling both substitute for and supplement one another by putting these functions under a marketing vice-president. Publicity, on the other hand, is usually assigned to a public relations department, often reporting directly to the president. Since such departments must deal with many nonbuyer audiences, such as employees, stockholders, and government, they tend to neglect product sales and the buyer. Because public relations often assumes a defensive stance, trying to conceal or explain away practices that offend one or more of its publics, PR men may be ill-equipped to push products aggressively.

On campus, a unified approach to the four communications channels appears even more difficult than it is in business. Most advertising courses, students, and faculty are found in journalism schools; salesmanship, if found at all on the campus, is taught in business schools. Although public relations *is* taught in journalism schools, it is usually a major separate from advertising. Word-of-mouth communications tend to be split between at least two departments: speech faculties teach the techniques of face-to-face communications, and psychologists and sociologists study relationships of cause and effect in the word-of-mouth channel.

For these reasons, a seller tends to look on word of mouth as part of the environment to which he must adjust—often a hostile part. He tends to treat publicity as a chance factor: favorable publicity can boost sales, but unfavorable publicity can do a great deal of damage.

Differences Among the Channels

Both seller and student need to understand the world in which they function and to look at all four channels, both those that the seller uses and those to which he must adjust. How does each use each channel and when? What functions does he ask each channel to perform? What content does he depend on each channel to supply?

In answering these questions, we need to take a look at the dimensions that differentiate these channels from one another. There are five such dimensions, each of which affects the others: mutuality, credibility, control, relevance and cost.

Word of mouth is controlled by the buyer. In face-to-face relations with friends, the buyer determines when talk about products and brands will begin and end. The *mutuality* of such encounters tends to insure *relevance* and lead to high *credibility*. Rewards are high: not only is product information exchanged but such encounters tend to be pleasant in themselves and strengthen friendly relations among participants. Out-of-pocket *costs* are minimal or absent; social costs are indeterminate.

Control of *publicity,* as we have seen, is shared three ways: by buyer, by seller, by editor. Since face-to-face relations are absent, the buyer cannot exercise control and ensure relevance through mutuality; he may have to screen a great many news stories before he finds one that is relevant. Credibility varies with the medium that carries the publicity story: disinterest is often assumed in such media but expert knowledge may be perceived as being less than that of the ad or the salesman. To the extent that costs of the media vehicle are borne by the buyer, they are costs incurred for media content other than publicity, which is a free by-product.

Selling requires face-to-face relationships with the buyer who, through mutuality, gains a measure of control. (However, most of the control that a third party exercises over publicity probably lands in the hands of the seller on this channel.) On the other hand, buyers are able to influence a salesman more than they are an advertisement, making the salesman more relevant and, probably, more credible. Contact with a salesman usually costs the buyer more in terms of time and greater probability that he will be induced to make a purchase; to a seller, salesmen are the most costly channel.

A buyer has virtually no control over *advertising*, except in his ability to ignore it. The mutuality of immediate feedback is lacking, so that relevance is ensured only through selection. Credibility may be high or low, depending upon identity of the advertiser and the vehicle, expectation of repeated purchases from the same seller, and so on. Since any costs incurred by the buyer to obtain the vehicle are presumably justified by its nonadvertising content, costs from his viewpoint are minimal. (Indeed, since ads subsidize most media, a prospect's willingness to risk exposure to advertising means net profit rather than cost.) The importance of credibility varies with product and with prospect, and so do the importance of its two components: expert knowledge and trustworthiness. If purchase involves high risk, as is true of many drugs, most innovations, and all status symbols, credibility assumes special significance.

The seller must consider all these aspects of buyer behavior in making his channel decisions, as well as the kind of product he's selling and the kind of people he's selling it to. A seller advertises in mass-audience vehicles, for example, to sell products that nearly everyone buys and buys frequently. When prospects need assistance in diagnosing their needs and products must be custom-designed for the purchaser, the seller employs salesmen. In wartime and in some underdeveloped countries where goods are in short supply, a seller may depend upon word of mouth to empty his shelves.

Often, of course, one channel aids another. A publicity story, its reach extended by word-of-mouth communication, may cause buyers' doors to swing open to admit a salesman. A manufacturer introducing a bifurcated widget may use trade paper ads and salesmen to induce retailers to stock his product, while radio and newspapers inform consumers that it exists, tell them where they can buy it, and convince them they can't survive another 24 hours without it. The same manufacturer may send a news release to the business press and demonstrate the widget at a cocktail party for editors of women's magazines. If he's lucky, children will start singing his radio jingles and housewives will invite neighbors over to see their new widget.

In short, the seller usually employs more than one channel. Channels vary in effectiveness, depending on the stage of the complex communications process needed to produce a sale: Figure 19.1 shows a typical sequence of channel use. Note how assignment of a channel to a given stage is related to the degree of seller control and buyer credibility, of mutuality and of relevance to buyer needs.

Matching this model of seller behavior is Figure 19.2, which shows buyer responses.

Costs are harder to place in this diagram, although personal channels are costly. A single call by an industrial salesman may cost $50 or more, in contrast to a few cents per prospect that media-borne messages of advertising or publicity require.[1] The personal channel of word of mouth may involve very high costs to the buyer, but these are costs imposed upon him that he has little control over. He cannot *decide* to spend more or less on word of mouth, ordinarily, as he can with the other three channels. Costs bear a more predictable relationship to returns for budget inputs in

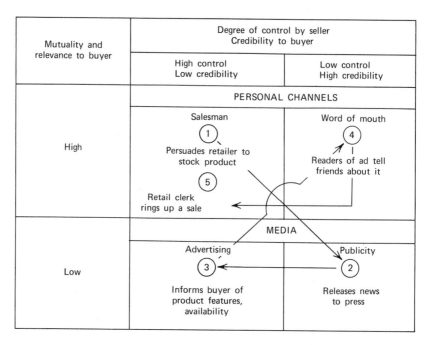

Figure 19.1

both advertising and selling than they do in publicity. However, this predictability should not be overestimated. Media may deliver an audience, but their responses depend upon the messages that media transmit; salesmen vary remarkably among themselves and from one day to the next.

Media are so important to advertising, just as advertising is so important a channel of communications, that an entire chapter, Chapter 20, will be devoted to them. That leaves the remaining three channels for discussion here.

Word of Mouth

Word of mouth tends to be the most persuasive of the channels.[2] There are many reasons for this. A prospect actively seeking

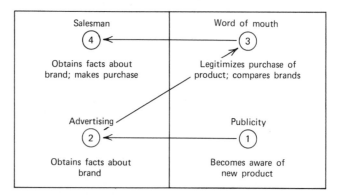

Figure 19.2

product information is more likely to perceive a message about the product. To the extent that conversations with friends about products tend to originate with a request for advice rather than the offering of an unsolicited opinion, word-of-mouth messages tend to be successful. Friends are closer at hand than a salesman and one can ask them a question without risking exposure to a high-pressure sales talk that persists after one's original curiosity has been satisfied. The give-and-take of true two-way communications is more common among friends than between salesman and customer, and so more rewarding to the information seeker.

Past acquaintance with one's friends enables one to estimate the extent to which they know what they're talking about, something one cannot always do with a salesman. On the other hand, just as one puts more trust in a salesman who hopes for a repeat sale than in the one-shot sales contact, so one tends to trust friends because they expect the relationship to continue. Friends tend to have needs similar to our own; if a product served them well it will probably do the same for us.

Product purchase and use forms so large a part of modern life that it would be odd, indeed, if talk about products did not make up a large part of modern conversation. Moreover, conversation with friends, unlike an encounter with a salesman, takes place when our defenses are down; we do not perceive that our friends are trying to sell us anything. In addition, having asked a friend's advice, we may be inclined to follow it because we hope to win and retain his good will. For these reasons, word-of-mouth messages tend to be persuasive. Such messages are particularly effective with persons who rate in the middle-range of a scale of self-confidence. They work less well with the very self-confident, who feel they know it all, and with persons low in self-confidence. Word-of-mouth channels are most

frequent and effective, wartime studies of rumor indicate, when the media fail to provide information concerning important and stressful events. Word of mouth also tends to supplement the news media following important events such as the death of a president.

The most persuasive messages on word-of-mouth channels are those that report personal experiences with a product; less effective but more frequent are reports that relay messages one has been exposed to. (Friends are likely to discuss a story in the newspaper that reflects a common interest or an exciting program on TV. Occasionally, an experience with a salesman or with an advertisement may stimulate a friendly conversation.) Unfortunately, from the seller's point of view, bad experiences with products and salesmen may provide more dramatic and interesting content than good experiences. Although a seller may argue that such experiences are interesting only because they are rare, this will not undo the damage he suffers from word-of-mouth communications. The seller may also fear that as the message is passed on from one person to another it will become increasingly distorted to his disadvantage.

This fear arises from wartime studies of rumor and reflects results caused by the messages chosen for study and the method used to study them.[3] Such studies used messages that were (1) false and (2) harmful to the war effort or public peace of mind. These messages were transmitted through a chain of rapid, compulsory, two-person exchanges in which any expansion or simplification of the message was scored as an error. This differs from real life where persons are free to let a rumor die, if they disbelieve it, and have time to check it against their own experience and with other persons and the media before they pass it on. Rumor in real life is probably less distorted than laboratory studies suggest, although rumors have caused runs on banks and caused consumers to shy away from everything from autos to aluminum cookware.

Seller Use of Channel

It is surprising, in view of the effectiveness of this channel, that sellers have not attempted more use of it, either offensively or defensively. One attempt was reported in 1948 by a firm operating in one Canadian and three U.S. cities which hired stooges to engage in loud conversations in subways, elevators, and football crowds. One client store, it is said, got rid of 7000 raincoats in this fashion.[4] There also have been attempts to stimulate conversations by offering prizes to anyone who makes the proper response, usually including a brand name, when accosted over the telephone or on the street. An automobile manufacturer, for example, is said to have offered 5000 taxi drivers in 67 cities $5 every time the passenger they queried about the 1963 Plymouth turned out to be one of the manufacturer's "mystery riders."[5]

Using a cabbie as the entry point into the word-of-mouth channel makes sense, in view of the large number of mobile people he encounters and, in this instance, his experience with the subject—automobiles. What guidelines are there for other sellers who want to use the word-of-mouth channel?

Gregarious people who have the need to communicate with others and frequent opportunity to do so are an excellent entry point. However, if a seller wants to reach all segments of the public, he will need to find separate entry points in each social class; research suggests that most word of mouth occurs within social classes and between persons similar in age, sex, and income.

At one time, it was assumed that fads and fashions originated in the upper classes and trickled down. It is true that, with the help of high-volume, low-margin garment manufacturers, designs originating with Paris couturiers do find their way to ready-made racks. Popular culture, on the other hand, appears to "filter up," originating in the speech and music of ghetto, slum, and prison.

The effects of word of mouth on buyer behavior were demonstrated most dramatically when interviewers asked 800 women in Decatur, Illinois what influenced their purchase of cereal, coffee, and soap.[6] Only 7% credited newspaper or magazine ads with such influence; 18% named sales clerks, 25% (in pre-TV days) named radio commercials—and 39% named friends.

Further questions revealed that the kind of friends consulted varied with the product involved. In every case, women consulted the friend likely to have had most experience with the product. The more children a mother had, the more often she was asked for her advice concerning cereal and soap; older women gave advice to younger women, and married women to single girls. These patterns of influence were reversed, however, when movies and fashions were involved. Eighty-eight percent of single girls in the survey went to movies at least once a month; 60% of them said they'd been asked to recommend a movie. In contrast, less than half of the wives over 45 went to movies monthly, and only a fourth of them had been quizzed about movies. Similarly, 80% of single women reported an interest in fashions, as compared with a third of the over-45 matrons—and it was the single women who most influenced choice of movies.

Salesmen

As a face-to-face communicator, the salesman enjoys many of the advantages of the word-of-mouth source: a small audience, immediate feedback, and the multiple dimensions of spoken and nonverbal symbols. In addition, he is usually perceived as more expert than the participant in the word-of-mouth channel. The salesman may emphasize this similarity of channels by first-naming a customer, mixing in a good amount of purely social chitchat with his product pitch, and passing on news of what others in the industry are doing. All these similarities tend to increase the salesman's effectiveness. Operating to his disadvantage, of course, is the fact that, unlike one's friends, he is paid to persuade prospects to purchase his products. The seller gains control of the personal selling channel, as against his limited ability to influence the word-of-mouth channel, at a cost of a loss of ability to persuade.

These similarities to word of mouth make the salesman superior to advertising. The small audience means he can tailor messages more precisely to listeners' needs and interests. Immediate feedback means he can alter messages to match listeners' responses, in contrast to delayed, expensive, often missing feedback from advertising. He cannot be turned off as easily as one flips a switch on an annoying TV commercial. Moreover, receivers feel an obligation because they have taken up his time and may buy because they like him.

Salesmen undoubtedly work harder at strategy in the purchase-sale encounter than do prospects. Some writers suggest that this strategy has five stages: the prospect must be induced to admit a need, then agree that this product meets the need. Next, he must agree that this brand is superior to others, that the price is acceptable and, finally, that the time to act is now. The length of each stage varies with product and customer. The salesman making a *cold canvass* must first gather information which he can use to convince the prospect that he *has* a need. The salesman on duty at a model home may take need for granted and begin by *qualifying* the prospect—making sure need is matched by ability to pay. An encyclopedia salesman may assume ability to pay by the looks of a house, and interpret a tricycle in the yard as indicating need; he will focus on *getting action* now.

Most encounters with salesmen begin with a social conversation that ends with the salesman taking control. (In other countries, this phase may continue over two to six meetings.) The salesmen encourage objections as pegs for additional sales arguments and because questions represent a kind of commitment. If price is brought up prematurely, a salesman may evade the question, lest it evoke brand comparison or provide a socially acceptable excuse for refusing to buy. Skillful questions as to preferences for product attributes may evoke a series of commitments which shade imperceptibly into the *close*. If resistance appears, the salesman may retreat to the type of social conversation used at the beginning. He may even pick up his briefcase and move to the door, only to stop on its threshold with a sudden inspiration that makes the sale. When gentler means of achieving a close fail, the salesman can be blunt: *We have spent two hours discussing these encyclopedias. I have answered all your questions. Shall I write up the order?*[7] Or, he can try to get the prospect to turn salesman with a sneer, *Of course, if you really cannot afford to give your children this protection. . . .*

Sometimes a customer can be led to believe that he and the salesman are in a coalition against a third antagonist. A salesman may promise a home buyer all sorts of changes, only to be overrruled by a cost-conscious builder's architect. (Defeats emphasize how far the salesman was willing to go in favoring friend against employer.) Auto salesman and prospect form a coalition against the hard-hearted man who appraises the trade-in.[8] More subtle interaction occurs when an insurance salesman encounters husband and wife. Talking to the two separately would give each a veto as well as doubling the cost of a sale. Separate encounters would allow a delay in which the prospect's sense of obligation to the salesman could dissipate, as well as risk exposing the prospect to rival brands and messages. So the salesman may side now with one, and then with the other in talking to husband and wife. And he will press for an immediate decision—mentioning the accident that could happen tonight, or the special rate that expires at midnight.

A seller's control over his salesman is never as absolute as his control over advertising, and tends to diminish over time, as a salesman gets to know his customers better. Interaction, more frequent with customers than with employer, is rewarding and influences behavior. The salesman knows that buyers must benefit from the encounter if he is to make the repeat sales his firm requires; to enlarge these benefits he may become an advocate for the buyer, seeking concessions from his employer in terms of price, speedy delivery, credit, etc.

Left to himself, a salesman may find contacts with some customers so pleasant that he sees them more often than necessary, while avoiding more obnoxious but potentially profitable types. An employer who responds by detailed specifications as to call frequency based on prospects' past purchases, their potential purchases, or competitors' vigor, may find such efforts self-defeating. Salesmen may close ranks, inventing ever more artful ways of circumventing supervision, or they may quit. Even if salesmen don't take their customers with them to a new employer, the employer they've left must now incur the costs of finding, selecting, and training replacements who, once they start selling, will respond to the situation in the same old way.

Detailed controls of salesmen deprive the employer of a major advantage of this channel: salesmen's ability to modify their messages to fit their prospects. Such modification can easily go so far that it acts to the employer's disadvantage. Experience and intuition may lead a salesman, without realizing what he is doing, to modify messages to the point that their cumulative effect violates company policy. But if policy is enforced so rigorously that it allows salesmen insufficient freedom of action to respond to prospect problems, prospects soon will stop talking to them. An employer who tries to prevent buyers from subverting his salesman by periodically shifting salesmen to new territories, risks a drop in customer satisfaction and purchases and in salesmen's income and morale—and gives his competitors a chance to get a foot in the door.

Buyer influence upon the salesman, inevitable in the face-to-face relationship, is only one factor that makes this channel less amenable to seller control than are advertising media. No two salesmen are identical; the effects of changes in personnel are much less predictable than are changes in the media. Indeed, the behavior of any single salesman varies from one customer to the next, from one day to the next, even from one item in the product line to the next.

Five Sales Force Decisions

Once a seller has decided what role salesmen will play in his communications program, he must then decide whether to "buy" such salesmen as manufacturers' agents, who work for several sellers, or to assemble his own sales staff. The first choice means surrendering management controls to the marketplace; the second choice retains control at the cost of taking on new management problems and making these five decisions.

Jobs to be performed. A salesman performs many different functions, the emphasis on each function being different for each type of salesman. Any seller may need several different types. How *important* is each of these functions to his sales? The answer will determine the abilities an employer seeks in his salesmen. How much *time* should a salesman spend on each? This answer will affect training and supervisory programs.

Abilities required. The abilities required to perform a specific sales function, and ways of identifying and measuring these abilities must be determined. The importance of selecting salesmen, either by screening applicants or eliminating the ineffectual, is shown by the wide range of productivity. One study showed that 27% of the salesmen employed by 500 firms made 52% of all sales.[9] Of those hired, 31% left during the first year, and another 20% were expected to have left by the end of the second year. Meanwhile, these firms estimated that in 1963 it cost them an average of $8730 to find, train, and supervise a salesman for one year. Add salary to this and sales expenses (which usually are equal to salary) and the cost of poor selection soon should disturb any employer, or stockholder.

Recruitment. Management experts suggest that screening of personnel is often overemphasized, great care being used to measure minor differences among applicants all of whom have a low level of ability. More is gained, they suggest, by attracting men of higher aptitude.[10]

Motivation. Reward systems must be devised to keep salesmen from quitting and encourage them to use their abilities. Methods of determining when they have done so must be devised to reward successful individuals, and get rid of those who fail to shape up.

Assignment of salesmen. If a firm's products are complex, numerous, or unrelated to one another, assignments may be based on products. If customers are diverse, salesmen may be assigned to particular firms, factories, or types of retail outlet. If buyers are distant from one another, salesmen may be assigned all customers, big and small, and all products in the firm's entire line in a given geographical area.

Regardless of the method of assignment used, two goals must be met. First, men must be assigned in such a way that *total sales* are maximized, rather than putting each man in the market where he could be most productive. Second, salesmen must agree that assignments are fair. If an able man gets rewards a great deal higher than other men, the others may become discontented. If, on the other hand, he feels his rewards are too low or his territory too poor, he may seek more attractive rewards elsewhere.

The following functions are among those often included in a salesman's job.

Identifying and gaining access to buyers and persons who influence purchasing decisions.

Diagnosing needs and making prospects aware of latent needs. Suggesting criteria to be used in comparing competitive brands.

Selecting appeals for individual buyers, answering questions, giving advice, demonstrating the product, helping them make a choice.

Writing up an order, expediting credit check and delivery, checking back to see if the product has been satisfactory in use and when it needs to be replaced.

Since salesmen's feelings affect their efficiency, an employer needs to know their attitudes toward paperwork and travel, how they react to a turn-down and whether they are patient enough to cultivate prospects over a long period of time or must be rewarded by an immediate sale. Salesmen, in turn, need to know what they are getting into—how much time they should spend on paperwork and travel, what proportion of refusals they're likely to get, and how many calls they can expect to make before a sale is negotiated. And they need to know which of these will have most effect on their pay and promotions.

Combined in various ways, these several functions produce three special types of salesmen.

Problem solving. "Advance men" advise doctors of new drugs or help a firm plan a new factory or a data-processing system, but do not actually clinch the sale. "Trouble-shooters," calling either on request or as a matter of routine, follow through on sales to insure buyer satisfaction.

Physical distribution. A route man delivers milk to the door before dawn or stocks shelves in the neighborhood grocery with bread, filling routine orders with a minimum of contact or conversation with the buyer.

Sale-clinching. A sales clerk helps a customer find the shelf holding a product he has already decided to buy and rings up the sale at the cash register. A more aggressive colleague may suggest a *tie-in,* selling socks to go with the new pair of shoes, or a *trade-up,* persuading the customer to buy a more expensive shirt than he originally intended.

Few of us would say that any of these three types represents a "real" salesman like the encyclopedia or insurance man who comes to our home or the salesman we meet in an automobile display room. To us, a real salesman is a mixture of all three types, a man we see when we aren't sure we really want to buy at all, or what brand we prefer, or how much we are prepared to pay, or think perhaps we should visit one or two more retailers. He's the man who dissolves our doubts in a flow of fact and fiction; he *sells* and we buy.

The Buyers' Veto

The decision as to what kind of salesman will be employed is one over which buyers have an ultimate veto. Sellers were slow to discover that housewives really didn't want or need a salesman in the grocery store. But buyers thronged into the supermarket when it appeared and caused "real" selling to vanish from a large part of the American scene. Its appearance meant increased emphasis on mass communications—on advertisements for packaged, branded merchandise.

In setting specifications for the salesman's job, sellers need to know how the buyer defines the purchase-sale encounter. Is he looking for a source of information, for someone to help him define his needs, for a partner in a bargaining game or just for someone to accomplish the rituals connected with transfer of title in our culture?

Often, a buyer takes the initiative: the housewife invites a salesman to call, or the shopper invites a clerk's *May I help you?* by stance, glance, or inquiring eyebrow. Some shoppers find it easier to quiz a salesman than to seek out and process the scanty information provided in much advertising, or in the labels on a store's shelves. Some prospects need help in analyzing their own needs, and relating them to available products. (Examples: the medical diagnosis that precedes surgery; the architect who lives with a family for a week to discover what design for living fits their needs.) Some persons' minds or families are so evenly divided that a decision to buy is impossible without the salesman's support, or feel so insecure that they delegate decisions to the salesman.

If a salesman's success is dependent upon his ability to meet so diverse a set of buyer motives and demands, it is unlikely that any search for the ideal traits of an all-purpose salesman can succeed. Instead, an insurance firm for whom every householder is an actual or potential customer may seek salesmen as varied as their prospects; the firm's training program and the men's own experience can then direct each man to the customer type with whom rapport is best. In a city, salesmen's paths may profitably crisscross to the point of each house in a given block being the target of a different salesman. For city folk may nod to their neighbors, but the friends whose names they give an insurance salesman are as likely to live crosstown as next door.

This strategy will not work, however, when a population contains only a few, widely scattered prospects. In such cases, one must seek salesmen with the ability to sense what kind of salesman each prospect wants and the flexibility to play the particular role each desires.

Publicity

If salesmen are not invited to call until a prospect has become aware of a problem or opportunity, how does a seller go about inducing such awareness? If his product is really new and different, publicity may provide an answer. An editor, like the editor of the *Reader's Digest,* may find DuPont's substitute for leather, Corfam, exciting enough to warrant a full-length feature. (We can be sure, when this happens, that a publicity man has been hard at work, helping him arrive at that conclusion.)

Such publicity stories have two advantages over advertisements. First, they may attract persons who ignore the advertising. Second, they may be more credible. They have one major disadvantage: loss of seller control. Many messages of great importance to the seller will fail to get through the editor-gatekeeper; those that do may be greatly changed in form. On the other hand, role conflict, which works to the disadvantage of an employer when his salesmen take sides with the customer, may work to his advantage where publicity is concerned. The reporter may take sides with his news source, the seller, to the disadvantage of his employer, the editor. To gain seller cooperation, a reporter may pretend to take his side but come to do so in reality for the informal rewards he receives from the interaction itself.

Marketing management benefits from two kinds of publicity: direct or product and indirect or image building. Indirect publicity is usually assigned to a separate public relations department; product publicity may be left to the firm's advertising agency. On occasion, messages to employees, stockholders, and the local community may urge purchase of the firm's product as a sign of "loyalty." The volume of such sales may be less important than a byproduct—spread of such messages via conversations over the back fence and luncheon table.

Publicity resembles advertising in that success depends upon an idea and not a verbal formula. The publicity man who can feed *ideas* to a newsman can be a great success without ever writing a word. He may even write a release that "buries" the news, so that a reporter will have the thrill and self-satisfaction of appearing to discover it for himself. (Sometimes, of course, a public relations man really does want to bury the news, since publication would damage the firm's image. Diversionary tactics are most likely to be successful in such cases. The publicity man may subtly play down the importance of the item, provide details that mitigate its damaging effects, or come up with two or three items of even greater news value which crowd the original item out of the paper.)

Publicity releases will take care of the routine new product, but more significant news is usually given out at a press conference where reporters have a chance to ask questions. A still more advanced stage of public relations employs the staged or created event.

The audience at such an event—the diners listening to a speech at an annual meeting of the Chamber of Commerce—may be far less important to the speaker than the audience that reads a news story about that speech the next morning. This is why every fund drive starts and ends with a ceremony. Presentation of an award for anything from life saving to longevity usually does more for the organization making the award than for the person who receives it.

These are routine devices, however. The real genius of the PR man appears in times of crisis.

When charges of monopoly and even fraud smeared public utilities in the 1930s, a jubilee was staged honoring Edison's invention of the electric light. Even the government cooperated by issuing a special commemorative stamp.

When motorists, angry after inching up a hill behind a slow-moving truck, began demanding curbs in the name of safety, public relations men pulled the human interest switch: they emphasized drivers' skill by staging annual "roadeos" and emphasized their safety records by requiring an accident-free history for entrants. Photographers and reporters for all the media covered the event, people began talking about it, and public opinion began to change. (Meanwhile, more direct PR tactics in the legislatures themselves slowed down anti-truck legislation.)

Staged events have an obvious advantage over the press release: they are harder for the opposition to counter, as well as more likely to persuade editor and reader. If the president of a truckers' trade association issues a statement, a reporter will ask their opponents—railroad or public—to reply both out of a sense of fairness and because a fight makes a better story. But what can opponents do when truckers get columns of news and picture space with an image-building "roadeo"?

Thought, Talk, and Action

1. Estimate what percent of impact might be attributed to each of the four communications channels in the following instances.

   (a) Persuading retailers to stock a new paper raincoat. Persuading women to buy the raincoat.
   (b) Announcement of a new electric automobile.
   (c) Opening of a new community college (two year).
   (d) Recruiting of peace corps volunteers in colleges; among retired persons.
   (e) A videotape recorder, recording in color, for $225.

2. Salesmen report that customers are asking retailers if it's true that a cancer-causing agent has been found in your brand of condensed milk. Your own program of quality control makes this impossible. What do you do about the reports?

3. Two agencies say they can stimulate word-of-mouth communications. One does so by telephone, and the other by enlisting members of local organizations to bring it up at meetings. Conceive of a product or situation in which you would use the telephone agency; conceive of another in which the other agency would be preferable.

Notes

Chapter 18

1. A mail survey of 3362 sales executives (and an 18% return) reported an average sales call cost of $49.30—and a range from $4.17 (motor carrier firm) to $650 (chemical processing equipment). No. 8013, "Cost of an industrial salesman's call in 1969," McGraw-Hill Laboratory of Advertising Performance, May 1970. This contrasted with 1967 average of 1.9¢ cost per subscriber for 697 business publications, whose page rates ranged from $48 to $2408. Same source, No. 8012, April 1968.

2. Johan Arndt, Word of mouth advertising (New York: Advertising Research Foundation, 1967). Cites D. J. Jacobson, The affairs of dame rumor (New York: Rinehart and Co., 1948) and R. Littell and J. J. McCarthy, "Whispers for sale," Harpers, 172:364–72.

3. Gordon W. Allport and Leo J. Postman, "The basic psychology of rumors," in Guy E. Swanson et al., editors, Readings in Social Psychology, rev. ed. (New York: Henry Holt, 1952), pp. 160–71.

4. Reference No. 2, p. 4.

5. *Ibid.*, p. 5.

6. Elihu Katz and Paul Lazarsfeld, Personal influence (Glencoe, Ill.: The Free Press, 1955).

7. W. T. Tucker, The social context of economic behavior (New York: Holt, Rinehart and Winston, 1964), p. 76.

8. *Ibid.*, p. 77.

9. Philip Kotler, Marketing management (Englewood Cliffs, N.J.: Prentice Hall, 1967), p. 507.

10. Saul W. Gellerman, Motivation and productivity (New York: American Management Association, 1963).

Word-of-Mouth Channels

The importance of word-of-mouth channels as compared with the media varies with the decision to be made and the persons making it.

	Percentage of Children Using Given Method of Choosing Radio Program
Word of mouth	42
Program listing	28
Dial twirling	24

In the days before TV, children in one study chose radio programs most often on the basis of friends' recommendations.

Similar behavior toward TV programs could be explained in terms of constraints—parents' objections to dial-twirling, for example, or children's inability to read or lack of access to a program log—or in children's use of TV experiences as a topic of conversation with their friends.

A more recent study reports that wives in housing projects for college students at Michigan State University tended to make word of mouth equal to media— 57 to 56%—in their choice of a supermarket. Many of these wives had to make the decision at the same time; proximity in status and geographical location stimulated word-of-mouth communication.

Word of mouth may be less important when proximity and simultaneity of need are absent. When asked what they most depended on in selecting new supermarket products, another group of housewives listed word of mouth as third.

	Percentage of Housewives Dependent for News of New Products
TV	58
Free sample	26
Word of mouth	18

When a product is first introduced, early users have little opportunity to talk with anyone who has had experience with it. More opportunities are open to laggards.

Hat Buyers	Percentage Reporting Word of Mouth "Most Helpful"
Early	3
Late	9
Non-buyers	13

Percentage of Housewives
Trying New Products

Source of Information	Rate of Trial	
	High	Low
Media	57	38
Word of mouth	27	50

Bad news (from a seller's viewpoint) may be transmitted more readily by word of mouth and be more effective than good news; word of mouth may cause lagging as well as result from it.

Nature of Messages Received About Product	Percentage of Persons Buying Product
Unfavorable	18
No messages received	42
Favorable	54

Unfavorable messages thus caused a drop in purchases of 24 percentage points (42 − 18 = 24); favorable messages caused a rise of only 12 points.

Evidence that word-of-mouth messages tend not to cross vertical barriers between classes was provided by the Decatur studies, in which two-thirds of all product discussions occurred between persons of equal status, and by a study of school elections, in which four-fifths of conversations occurred within one of five different groups— parents talking to parents, teachers to teachers, etc.

Sources

Johan Arndt, *Word of Mouth Advertising* (New York: Advertising Research Foundation, Inc., 1967).

K. L. Atkin, "Advertising and store patronage," *Journal of Advertising Research*, 2:4: 18–23.

Some discussions of word of mouth seem to assume that if enough information is forced on opinion leaders, they must share it or burst. Word-of-mouth channels often are opened up by persons seeking information rather than those having an oversupply of it.

A study of suburban gardeners, for example, found that two-thirds of all conversations began with a request for information. Such requests are likely when prospects perceive *risk*. A telephone survey of 1200 housewives found that 49% of the housewives who felt there was considerable risk involved in use of headache remedies sought information about such remedies from others—but that only 27% of those who saw little risk in such remedies initiated conversations about them.

Two high-risk products (headache remedies and fabric softeners) with one low-risk item (dry spaghetti) were compared, risk being assessed by taking the product of scores on two four-point scales. (One asked the amount of danger involved in trying a new brand, the other measured probability of such danger.)

	Percent Discussing	
	High Risk	Low Risk
1. Headache remedy	43	32
2. Fabric softener	50	42
3. Dry spaghetti	8	9

Percent Commenting on Brands			
Favorably		Unfavorably	
High Risk	Low Risk	High Risk	Low Risk
1. 62	46	6	1
2. 28	25	3	1

In this instance "bad" news, in the form of a warning against a brand, was *less* frequent than good news.

Source. Scott M. Cunningham, "Perceived risk as a factor in informal consumer communication," in D. F. Cox, ed., *Risk Taking and Information Handling in Consumer Behavior* (Boston: Graduate School of Business Administration, Harvard University, 1967).

Early studies of the spread of rumors in wartime emphasized the distortions that arise in word-of-mouth channels. A recent experiment suggests, however, that such distortion has been exaggerated.

Between 8:25 and 8:35 A.M., the principal of a private girls school stalked into each of four classrooms, pointed a finger at one of the pupils, and said, "Get your hat and coat and come with me."

The principal's actions created intense curiosity and a highly ambiguous situation—two factors in which rumors spread rapidly.

Each teacher was asked to keep a record of any questions asked; 198 were reported from 62 girls in four classrooms; they came so thick and fast that two teachers were unable to keep a count of them.

Meanwhile, a rumor which might serve as a plausible explanation had already been planted with two girls each from two classrooms from which girls were to be removed and from two other classrooms. Each teacher asked: "By the way, some exams have been taken from the office. Do you happen to know anything about this?"

Thus the experiment created three different types of subjects: the *U* or unclear group of 29 girls who had seen the incident but in which no rumor had been planted, the *R* group of 30 who had not seen the incident but in which a rumor had been planted, and a *U-R* group of 29 in which both incident had occurred and rumor been planted. Opportunities for the rumor to spread included a 15-minute morning recess, an hour lunch period, an hour gym period, and five-minute intervals while classes were changing.

At 2 P.M. each class in turn was brought to the lunchroom to talk to a staff of 20 interviewers.

Out of 96 girls interviewed, only two said they did not know of the principal's action, only one said she had not heard the rumor, and only 15% had failed to link the rumor and the principal's action.

Despite this widespread knowledge, the *R* girls in the two classes who had not seen anyone removed, spent an average of only 20 minutes talking about the removal compared with 100 minutes for the others. Moreover, 93% of the

	Uncritical	Transmission	Critical
Chain	Distortion rises	Sharp drop in information	Fall in accuracy
Network	Maximum rise in distortion	Slow drop in information	Rise in accuracy

Figure 19.3

U-R group mentioned the incident, without a probe question, during the interviews, but only 76% of the U group and 26% of the R group. The U-R group transmitted the rumor to an average of 2.9 others, the U group to 2.3, and the R group to 1.1.

In this experiment, not one of the 96 interviews showed any evidence of distortion. New rumors did spring up— 76% of U-R girls reported them, 65% of U girls, and 15% of R girls.

The author suggests that accuracy was increased by the simplicity of the rumor, high motivation among subjects (who operated on their own initiative rather than an experimenter's instructions), and that hearing a rumor from several sources tended to eliminate errors.

Source. Stanley Schachter and Harvey Burdick, "A field experiment on rumor transmission and distortion," *Journal of Abnormal and Social Psychology*, 50:363–71.

A more elaborate theory of word-of-mouth channels takes account of both the psychological set of the participant and the nature of the interaction.

This theory distinguishes between the *chain,* in which each person receives a message from only one person and transmits it to only one, and the *network,* in which each may have multiple sources and/or receivers. It recognizes three different types of motivation or set.

Uncritical. This participant may lack information, be unable to evaluate his source, lack critical ability because of personal insecurity or faulty education,

or have a need that the rumor meets. As a result, he warps a rumor's meaning to fit his own attitudes, modifies it to achieve closure, or invents a rumor of his own.

Transmission set. Participant is uninterested in subject matter of rumor. He may forget details but he will not consistently distort the rumor.

Critical set. Familiarity with subject matter leads to skepticism; this person will check on details and may refuse to pass on a rumor.

Combining these variables leads to the predictions in Figure 19.3.

In a survey respondents were asked whether they were familiar with nine news events, two of them imaginary. Interviewers also asked four factual questions about the trial of Eichmann (Nazi leader hanged for genocide) and how many persons the respondent had spoken to about the trial. Persons with a critical set (those who denied knowledge of the imaginary news events) and those who had spoken to more than one person about the trial were likely to have more knowledge about the case.

	Percent of Persons Answering at Least Two Factual Questions Correctly	
Number of Persons Talked to	Critical Set	Uncritical Set
Only one	66	56
Two or more	82	33

The more persons talked to by persons

with a critical set, the more knowledge they demonstrated.

Source. H. Taylor Buckner, "A theory of rumor transmission," *Public Opinion Quarterly,* 29:54–70.

Another study showed that information may travel outside the usual channels of the mass media or commercial sources.

A psychologist in Massachusetts asked himself whether a message could be carried across country by persons who knew one another on a first-name basis.

As ends of the chain, he picked a Boston stockbroker and the wife of a divinity school student in Cambridge. By mail, he recruited sources in Wichita, Kansas, and Omaha, Nebraska, who mailed a message to persons they knew by their first names.

Four days after the message started on its way, a seminary instructor walked up to the seminarian's wife and said "Alice, this is for you." The message, which had started with a Kansas farmer, went to an Episcopalian minister who sent it to a colleague in Cambridge: two links completed the chain. (The longest chain involved 10 links between source and receiver.)

Each participant filled out a roster, to prevent a chain from looping back on itself, and sent a postcard to the source, so that he could spot the point at which any incomplete chain broke off. (In all, of 160 chains which began in Nebraska, 44 were completed; the median number of links required was five.) Some chains extended 1000 miles and then broke, only a few hundred feet from the target person; geography in today's world is less a barrier than social divisions. A widowed clerk in Nebraska wrote a painter friend in Iowa who contacted a publisher in Bolton, Mass.—but it took five more residents of Sharon, Mass., including a tanner, a sheet metal worker, a dentist, a printer, and a clothing merchant, to reach that city's stockbroker. Half of the stockbroker's messages reached him via three men— two other Boston stockbrokers and a clothing merchant living in the same suburb.

Participants in the communications chains usually were members of the same sex. There were 56 female-female and 58 male-male links compared with 18 female-male and 13 male-female. It was estimated that each participant had a pool of 500 to 2500 first-name acquaintances on which to draw.

Source. Stanley Milgram, "The small-world problem," *Psychology Today,* 1:1160–7.

Additional Research Readings

Word of mouth. Favorable messages from friends in married student apartments tripled use of a cents-off coupon for a new food brand. **Johan Arndt, "A test of the two-step flow in diffusion of a new product,"** Journalism Quarterly, **45:457–65.**

Salesmen. Flooded by 2000 teen-age applications a week and a high dropout rate, a firm found middle-class boys most successful selling door to door. A 7-question screening device eliminated three-fourths of the failures. **Valentine Appel and M. R. Feinberg, "Recruiting door-to-door salesmen by mail,"** Journal of Applied Psychology, **53:362–6.**

Radio. In Finland, subjects read or listened to 2-minute speech excerpts which had been mutilated by deleting every 8th word. Number of right guesses of missing words was correlated with comprehension of written messages but not with understanding of those played aloud. **Osmo A. Wiio and Kaarle Nordenstreng, "Comprehension and interest of radio programs,"** Journalism Quarterly, **47:564–6.**

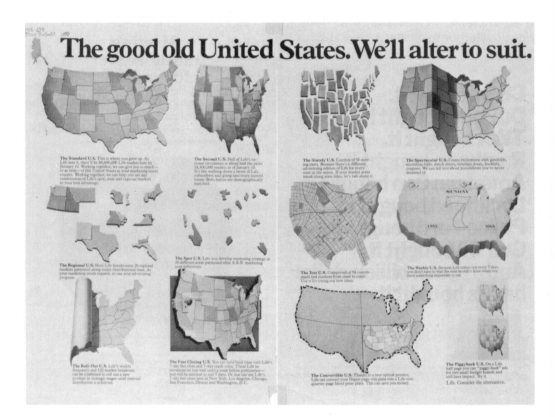

The good old United States. We'll alter to suit.

Matching Audiences to Markets

A prospect's location and income affect his *ability* to buy a product; his age, sex, occupation and education affect his *desire* for it—and also the chances that he will be *exposed* to an advertising medium and will *respond* to an advertising message. Media vie to demonstrate that their readers have the ability and desire to buy an advertiser's product and offer to segment their audiences to match the advertiser's market segments, whether these be based on geography, demography or rate of product and brand usage. Here *Life* suggests 11 different ways of altering the map to meet advertisers' needs.

Demography and Geography

At upper left and lower right, magazine publishers argue that their audience is superior, in demographic aspects, to that of TV. It contains, they say, a higher proportion of innovation-minded individuals who'll go for an avocado-colored refrigerator. Yet it's also superior in terms of such a common product as catsup. *Farm Journal* offers advertisers combinations of states based on a single crop like cotton or soybeans. An Oklahoma publisher, on the other hand, offers to split his state into five segments. (One can focus on given occupations, such as educators or doctors, by using specialized publications or special editions of such general-interest publications as *Life* or one can focus on subscribers in a single major city.)

Audience Selection by Message

In seeking a high-income target audience, Chemical Bank first selects such *media vehicles* as the *New Yorker.* For still finer focus, it then picks pictures, headline and copy that pull the "$500,000" man out of this audience. Other magazines, such as *True Story,* emphasize the sheer volume of purchases which blue-collar and other low income groups make each year, adapting both editorial and advertising content to such readers.

Overcoming Inhibitions

To enlarge its market, Allied Van Lines tries to reassure prospects who resist moving to another city because of the problems it will involve in finding new sources of supply for services. *Sports Illustrated* suggests that you don't have to be a superstar (or the parent of one) to enjoy its pages.

● Credibility and control, which are criteria for choice of channel, also affect selection of media that represent the advertising channel. Media choice also depends on weighing 7 other factors; selectivity, intrusiveness, sensory modality, space-time existence, permanence, number of concurrent symbol systems, and universality. The effect of these factors varies with the measure used: exposure, attitude change, recall, etc. There are also accidental differences, varying in space and time rather than inherent in the media, which affect choice.

● To select his media mix, a seller must determine, with attention to cost, which of alternative audiences is most congruent with his desired market segment. Media audiences vary in both size and shape. Media vary in the proportion of exposures that they convert into perception and retention scores; exposures in one medium do not have the same significance as those in another.

● In moving to the next decision, choosing the specific media vehicles that will transmit his messages, a seller must weigh 5 factors: impact vs. exposures, reach vs. frequency, continuity vs. impact, mass vs. select audience, and free vs. forced exposure.

● In weighing media vehicle factors, a seller needs knowledge of human behavior. The reach vs. frequency decision, for example, depends on knowledge that repetition affects recall in three different ways: by increasing probability that exposure will occur near point of buying decision; by increasing the number of persons exposed and by increasing the impact on the exposed individual.

● If the advertiser picks a vehicle with a large, unselected audience, he may still focus sharply on a more select target by the placement of his ad in space (print media) or in time (broadcast media).

Research Articles

Failures. Repeated exposure fails to halt circulation of hoax (Hall); publicity campaign fails to change attitudes toward United Nations (Star).

Success. Traits leading to success in selling vary with sales functions involved (Dunnette, Witkin).

Context. Program context affects audience reactions to TV commercials (Axelrod).

Chapter 19 Choosing Media and Media Vehicles

After a seller has specified the market segment he wants to reach, but before his advertising agency can devise messages for this segment, strategists must decide what media mix will assemble an audience that most closely matches the target segment. The market segment represents the goal *desired* by the seller; media audiences represent a *means* to that goal; the area in which segment and audience overlap represents the goal *achieved*.

One advertising medium—direct mail—can, in theory, collect an audience completely congruent with the segment: nobody left out, nobody not wanted. Ordinarily, however, the cost of doing so would be staggering. Instead, the seller usually turns to a ready-made audience, one already collected for him (and his competitors) by one of the media. He then must decide how many nonprospects in an audience he is willing to pay for—and how many live prospects he is willing to see omitted. Waste is most likely in the mass audiences of newspapers and TV; their cost per audience member may amount to only a few cents but their cost per live *prospect* to several dollars. Special-interest magazines and FM stations broadcasting Mozart reach much smaller audiences but audiences that some advertisers find contain a much higher proportion of lively prospects. (Direct mail lies somewhere in the middle, since it offers very specialized mailing lists as well as transmitting messages to "occupant.")

To a large extent the mass versus select audience choice occurs within media rather than between them. Magazines offer very select audiences, but a magazine like *Reader's Digest*, reaches a mass audience, and TV audiences run the gamut from Beverly Hillbillies to Bach.

Mass-audience vehicles tend to be used to advertise products that nearly everyone uses and uses frequently. On the other hand, sellers seeking select audiences may find that a mass vehicle can supply live prospects more cheaply than a selective vehicle, even though most members of the mass vehicle audience must be discarded. (Sellers who do so must prepare messages much more carefully than they otherwise would. Coin collectors may well miss an offer in a *Reader's Digest*, whereas they would turn to a coin collectors' digest expecting to see and looking for a similar offer. They might even suspect the expertness and good faith of a seller who would advertise to the presumably ill-informed and uninterested audience of a mass vehicle.)

Credibility, one of the criteria for choice among channels, also affects choice of media and of media vehicles; newspapers, magazines, and TV each have claimed that buyers perceive them as most trustworthy. By definition, no mass medium offers *mutuality,* another channel criterion; one of its aspects, personal intimacy, does differentiate media. TV is more personal than radio and radio more than print. The third channel-choice criterion, *control,* also has its counterpart in media and vehicle selection. Media vary in the speed with which a message can reach a prospect and vehicles vary in the extent to which an advertiser can influence the context in which his message will appear.

Seven Media-Choice Factors

There are, in fact, at least seven dimensions characteristic of media choice. The first and most important of these—degree of *audience selectivity*—we have already examined. A second is *intrusiveness*—the extent to which a seller can reach persons who are not actively seeking information concerning his product and, indeed, might even like to avoid it.

The telephone company's "yellow pages" are perhaps the best example of advertising which involves active information seeking by the prospect. Billboards represent the opposite extreme—their messages cannot easily be avoided. Billboard messages, however, must be brief—too brief to serve the needs of the seller of a new product who must arouse a hitherto unfelt need, provide a great deal of information about his product's attributes, tell how to use the product, and suggest criteria for comparing rival brands. Such new-product messages are better conveyed to an apathetic public in a context of entertainment, as on TV, or disguised as news, as in publicity. Skill is required to construct messages on such intrusive media: TV commercials must be brief enough so that the audience doesn't escape by switching channels; publicity stories must be subtle enough so that neither editor nor public penetrate their disguise.

Sensory modality represents a third dimension of media choice. This concerns whether messages reach the brain via eye, ear, or both. Sensory modality is related to intrusiveness, to the ability to be perceived in a noisy context, to intimacy, and to credibility. It is also directly related to the four remaining media dimensions.

Existence in Space or Time. Print media occupy *space*. Broadcast media, like a salesman's spiel and friends' word-of-mouth messages, occupy *time*. A message in time must be caught on the fly, at the convenience of seller rather than prospect. The receiver of a print message may peruse it at a pace which fits his own ability to read words and interpret pictures, but the receiver of a message in time must adjust to the pace of the sender.

Permanence. A printed ad can be reread time and again until its message is safely stored in one's memory or tucked away in a file folder for review when purchase becomes imminent. Few buyers, however, have film or tape libraries of TV and radio commercials! Permanence also affects the size of an ad's ultimate audience. Newspapers are more often used to wrap garbage in than they are shared with a neighbor but magazines have a high pass-along audience. On the other hand, both print and broadcast ads may gain added life spans on word-of-mouth channels.

Concurrent Symbol Systems. Media differ in the number of simultaneous symbol systems that they can transmit. Print carries both words and pictures and color, which employs the three visual dimensions of hue, saturation, and intensity. Radio carries words and sounds, which vary on three auditory dimensions of tone, timbre, and volume. Television uses all these print and radio dimensions—plus pictures-in-motion. Indeed, TV matches salesman and neighbor in the symbol systems it uses but, in addition, can telescope time and transcend limits of spatial movement as they cannot. The more concurrent symbol systems a medium permits to be used, the more choice its user has, either to emphasize, by putting the same message on each system, or to achieve subtle distinctions and unusual effects, by putting different content on each symbol system.

Universality. The symbol systems of speech are universally available to men, whatever their location in time and space. Before printed messages became possible, however, alphabets had to be devised, printing invented, and men taught how to read. In simpler times and places, this has often given higher prestige to print than to speech.

Implications for the seller of these seven media differences are not entirely clear. The fact that speech can be received with little effort on the part of a prospect may increase the chances that he will receive the seller's message, as contrasted with print. Dissonance theory, however, suggests that this very lack of effort may reduce the attitudinal effects of the message. The fact that radio transmits a limited number of symbol systems may be an advantage if simple messages achieve greater impact, either because they are more easily understood or because they require the receiver to fill in details of his own choosing. The fact that the ear can receive radio messages while the eyes are otherwise occupied permits the housewife to listen while ironing and the commuter to listen while fighting traffic, but divided attention may reduce the immediate impact of the message and the probability that it will be stored away in memory.

Since response to advertising is usually delayed, differences in media impact upon memory are important. Slight experimental evidence suggests that brief and simple messages directed to both eye and ear are better recalled than messages sent to either one of them.[1] If a choice has to be made between the two sensory targets, messages to the ear appear to be better remembered than those to the eye. Experiments in laboratory and in real-life settings suggest that a source face-to-face with his audience is more persuasive than one whose voice arrives via a loudspeaker and that the loudspeaker is more persuasive than a printed version of the same message.

Accidental Differences

The differences discussed so far represent inherent characteristics of the media. Other differences are peculiar to time and place, the result of historical accident and of business practices in a particular society. Thus, in many countries, movie-goers represent a captive audience for the advertiser; this is no longer common in the United States.

In nations without TV, radio continues to serve the entertainment function and collect the mass audience that it formerly did in the United States.

Although the consumer ultimately pays for seller messages, whatever medium transmits them, exposure to newspapers and magazines requires a conscious decision by the buyer to open his wallet. Billboards and direct mail, on the other hand, intrude on his attention without any effort on his part and even when he'd rather they wouldn't. TV and radio occupy a middle ground; once a person has paid for a set that will receive broadcast messages, the number of commercial messages he receives is limited by his leisure time rather than his income.

Market Segments and Media Audiences

Given the media differences just described, the seller can compare audience profiles of the media and vehicles available to him with profiles of the market segments he wants to reach.

Historically, broadcast networks and magazines have delivered nationwide audiences, whereas individual newspapers, radio and TV stations, and billboard companies have delivered local audiences. In the 1960's, large-circulation magazines, seeking to add regional advertisers to their list in the face of competition with TV, began offering regional, even single-city editions.[2] *Life,* for example, offered 26 editions, each corresponding to an A. C. Nielsen audience-survey area. Local media like newspapers did the reverse, cooperating with one another to offer advertisers convenient "package deals" of top newspapers in major cities. From its beginnings, TV provided both types of audience, with program sponsorship and commercial spots on a national network and local station basis.

Such geographic flexibility is important to the national advertiser who wants to use different message strategies in different regions, either for purposes of research or as a permanent policy. It is important to the seller who wants to introduce a new product region by region. And, of course, geographic limits are necessary for the seller whose products are not distributed nationally.

The shape as well as the size of the market is important. A broadcaster's signal can extend equally in all directions, ignoring political boundaries and many differences in terrain. In contrast, print media must take account of the same modes of transportation and limits of politics and terrain as do the products advertised in them. Much of the nonadvertising content of newspapers consists of news of politics and government; this fact, plus some legal realities, tends to influence size and shape of audience so that newspaper audiences often conform more closely to the shape of the market than do broadcast audiences.

Although all media and most media vehicles offer a wild variety of data to indicate that they reach "more" of the "right" kind of people than their competitors, comparisons are difficult—even when the figures are broken down to dollars per thousand.

The advertiser who buys future audiences on the basis of past experience may find his best-laid plans thrown akilter by unexpected events. Print media offer guaranteed circulations but cannot guarantee that their publications or the ads in them will be read. The audience for a given TV program is affected by concurrent programs on competing stations, as well as by the programs that precede and follow it both on its own and on rival channels. Quantity discounts are available on the media; bargaining, as well as the rate card, often determines actual cost.

Different methods of measuring audience size are likely to produce different totals even for the same vehicles; before a seller can decide which vehicle to use, he must weigh the merits of rival research organizations.

Across media, comparisons become even more difficult. People do not bring the same expectations to TV that they bring to their newspapers, nor do they make the same use of messages brought to them by these two media, even though the words used in the two messages may appear identical. (A woman weeping over the miseries of a soap opera is not the same decision maker as when she is making out a shopping list with the aid of newspaper grocery ads or looking up a plumber's number in the yellow pages.)

There are intrinsic, inescapable problems of audience comparison. The commuter who passes 100 billboards each morning on the freeway is "exposed" to 2000 billboard messages a month, even if traffic, car-pool chit-chat, and business worries prevent him from recalling a single one. Nielsen's audimeter records the minutes a TV switch is "on," even if the only individual in the room is a dog. The magazine that doesn't get lost in the mail may still be thrown away unopened. It is obvious that exposure opportunities tend to exaggerate audience size. It is less obvious that they also may underestimate audience size. In any case, they make cross-media comparisons difficult.

A broadcaster, for example, may suggest that one person exposed to a 60-second commercial, as measured by Nielsen, is equal to one person recognizing a full-page magazine ad, as reported by Starch. The salesman for print media will immediately observe that the print ad may accumulate an audience for weeks, whereas the TV commercial reaches its total audience at the time of broadcast. And he is likely to suggest that recall is a better measure of media (and message) effectiveness than exposure, or that ability to recall an ad is less important than a measured increase in brand preference.

Choice of Media Vehicles

After a seller has selected his media mix, by determining the relative importance of broadcast and print media and by dividing his budget among radio and TV, newspapers and magazines, he must then select specific vehicles within each medium. In doing so, he must answer five questions as he chooses specific media vehicles to carry his messages.

Exposures or impact? Lavish use of space and time may increase the impact of a given message at the cost of either more exposures or a larger audience. Through impact, a small firm may be perceived as being larger than it is; this method is also indicated when a small number of prospects have strong felt need for a product, and will buy if it is brought forcibly to their attention.

Reach or frequency? Does the seller want to reach a large number of prospects only once or to obtain repeated exposures of a smaller group? If a product is outstanding and felt need for it intense, a single exposure may be sufficient. In this somewhat rare instance, a seller will scatter his messages across a number of vehicles, rather than one, concentrating on vehicles whose audiences have a minimum of overlap.

Continuity or massed exposure? A seller's ads can appear hourly (on broadcast media), daily (on newspapers), weekly and monthly (in magazines)—or at longer intervals of time. A seller's choice here depends, in part, on whether need for his product is seasonal or not, and the frequency with which it is purchased.

Select or mass audience? Products like detergent, which every household uses, and firms like Procter & Gamble, with nationwide distribution, need the kind of mass audiences provided by the broadcast media (about 95% of United States households have radio and TV) and newspapers. Other sellers employ media, like magazines and direct mail, which pinpoint smaller audiences, either because only a few people want their product or because it is not distributed nationwide. (*Time* and *Life* have offered advertisers special demographic audiences, such as educators, physicians, or students, and special geographic editions, for individual cities.)

Degree of choice? It has been argued that the more freedom a prospect has to reject or ignore a media vehicle, the more impact the vehicles he selects are likely to have. In addition, publications that a prospect must pay for are more likely to be read; and publications bought at a newsstand are more likely to be read than those which, having been bought by subscription, are delivered in the mail. (Opponents counter with the argument that a magazine delivered to the home is likely to be more thoroughly read by more persons than one picked up at a newsstand and that the repeated impact of a subscription is worth more than the occasional impact of a single-copy purchase.)

There are similar arguments about whether the bull's eye audience targeting of a free publication, whose circulation is limited to prime prospects, is superior to the more diffuse (but presumably more highly motivated) audience targeting of a publication that anyone can buy who's willing to pay the price. Each is probably superior in some conditions, inferior in others.

These five factors of vehicle choice pose complex questions that may require considerable knowledge of audience behavior. Consider the advertiser who hesitates between additional exposures of a given audience and first exposure of an entirely new audience. His choice depends upon knowledge about the value of repetition. How much does each successive exposure increase chances that a message will be remembered? How rapidly do the effects fall off? At what point does excessive repetition boomerang by causing active dislike for the message? What interval between messages will most enhance perception and recall? Is repetition within a single issue of a magazine superior to repetition in several issues of one magazine, issues of different magazines, or in media other than magazines? Does strong original impact, gained by increasing size or duration of the advertisement, aid recall more than a series of smaller, shorter ads spread over a longer period of time?

The advertiser needs to remember that repetition achieves its effects in three different ways.

Timing

Only a small proportion of the population is actively seeking a product at any given time. Interviews made a week apart with 10,000 women in five cities, for example, found that 5% of respondents shopped for a dress during the week and 3% actually bought one. In an average week, ½ of 1% of the nation's families buy a car.[3] On the average shopping day, 6% of the nation's housewives buy coffee, 4% buy cornflakes, 1% buy cheese spreads and cocoa.[4] The more often an advertisement is run, the more likely it will be to reach someone who is about to buy the advertised product. Repetition thus increases the chance of reaching a prospect at a crucial stage in his decision making. This applies to first purchases as well as most recent purchases of a similar product.

At any given point in time, someone is buying his first engagement ring, car, house, or teething ring. Until need actually comes into being and rises from latency to awareness, ads may be ignored. The heaviest user and most brand-loyal purchaser eventually will leave the market, taking with him the habits and preferences produced by past advertising. He must be replaced by persons who have just become aware of new needs or who, although long aware of a desire for a yacht, have just now obtained the ability to indulge their desire.

Just as there may be a steady flow of persons into the market—the newcomer being sensitized to select one's ads out of the messages competing for attention—so is there a continual change in the persons exposed to the media. A teen-ager, for example, sees his first copy of *Playboy*. An expectant mother begins reading *Parents* magazine at the library. A child graduates from the comic pages to the sports pages of the newspaper, and so is exposed to a new advertising environment. Even after such milestones are reached, it is seldom that anyone reads every issue of a magazine or newspaper or manages not to miss any installment of a soap opera or situation comedy. Again, repetition increases the chances of exposure regardless of interest in products advertised, solely because of habits of media use. Repeated exposure to an ad in printed media may occur without repetition of the ad itself and, indeed, be beyond the control of both advertiser and medium. A monthly magazine is seldom read at one sitting; each time it is picked up there is a chance for repeated exposure by an individual reader as well, of course, as an increase in the number of different persons exposed.

Cumulation of Persons

The number of persons reached by a given magazine increases with the number of issues studied—but with wide variations from one magazine to another. Studies in 1966, for example, showed that 62% of *Time*'s audience were pass-along or secondary readers, as compared with 42% for the *Ladies' Home Journal* even though the total audience for each was about 15 million.[5] A study in 1964 showed that one issue of

Look then reached 14.7 million persons—but that four issues extended its reach to 24.1 million.[6] Ad readership increased even faster. Although an ad appearing in one issue of *Look* might be recalled by only 3.7 million persons, by the time it had been repeated four times it would be recalled by 11.6 million or nearly half of the total audience as compared with the original one-quarter. Ads with poor recall scores benefited most from repetition. Audience accumulation on TV, on the other hand, is slow. Bogart, for example, reports that a commercial placed between shows with an average audience rating of 20% would have to be repeated 20 times to ensure that 80% of households had seen it at least once.[7] Only 6% of newspaper readers are secondary readers, as compared with 60% of *Life*'s audience. A daily newspaper not read the day it is received is likely to be thrown away unread, whereas the readership for many magazines, including weeklies with a high pass-along rate, may continue to build up for six weeks.

Cumulative Effects in a Single Person

A large advertisement or a long commercial is more likely to attract attention than a small, short one, and several small, short ones are more likely to be perceived than a single small, short one. Repetition increases the chances that an ad will be perceived, and up to some limit increases the chance that it will be liked, remembered, and acted upon. The "size" of an advertisement thus must be measured both in space and in time when one measures its audience impact. Stimulus intensity, as measured by the response it produces, summates in both time and space.

This has been demonstrated in a wide range of studies and for a wide variety of responses. Mere repetition of a 1000-cycle tone while 11 kittens happened to be making their cage rotate induced such a strong association between sound and motion that sounding the tone subsequently caused the kittens to make their cages rotate five times as frequently as did kittens not previously exposed to the sound, even though no reward was offered at any time.[8] Repetition increases familiarity and familiar things tend to be favored. This has been demonstrated by playing unfamiliar music and showing subjects unfamiliar art. A second exposure to an advertisement has raised brand preferences from 29% to 38%.[9]

Even after an advertiser has determined what he wants in the way of repetition and which media vehicles will give it to him, he is not through. He still has the job of scheduling ahead of him—of specifying *placement* within a vehicle, particularly if the vehicle itself is not very selective.

One seller will advertise in *Jack and Jill* to reach children, *Harper's Bazaar* to reach upper-income women, *Good Housekeeping* for the middle majority, and *True Confessions* for women of the working class. Another will ship his commercials off to a TV station but specify Saturday morning cartoons as a context for his children's spot announcements, an afternoon soap opera for the middle-class and working-class wives, and a ballet "special" for the *Bazaar* types. A third may spot his ads on the Sunday comic pages of a newspaper for children, in the society section for middle- and upper-class women, and on the sports pages for their husbands.

Thus media choice and media-vehicle choice often represent alternatives to one another. A maker of band instruments may make a choice of vehicle by comparing four different magazines aimed at the bandmasters who influence parents and children in their purchase of an instrument. Or he may aim directly at parents by comparing two vehicles—*Reader's Digest* and a PTA journal—with one another and with another medium—spot commercials during a Thanksgiving Day or Rose Bowl parade.

Media vehicles are so numerous, data

concerning them so complex, and possible combinations so proliferate that the help of a computer is needed in comparing alternative vehicle mixes. Such programs exist, although the data fed into them lack comparability.

Media audiences, to say nothing of the audiences of particular vehicles, change so rapidly that the trade press rather than any text must guide decisions. As commuter trains vanish, morning newspapers lose a large part of their audience. As autos take their place, radio gains a new audience, to replace the mass audience it lost to TV. Old magazines die and new ones are born and a media buyer needs to be on top of the news.

Needs of any given advertiser vary so much by product, brand, and market share, and media rates and audiences are so affected by time, circumstance, and competition, that the specifics of selecting a vehicle mix are probably something the student had best learn on the job.

Thought, Talk, and Action

1. List the nine factors that affect media choice. Then, opposite each factor, list two magazines that vary widely on each factor. Do the same for two TV programs. Do the differences *within* a medium appear to be as great as the overall differences *between* media?
2. Now list the five factors that affect choice of media vehicles. Think of two products or selling situations, one which would require each of the choices involved. (That is: one would need impact, the other exposures; one would need reach, another frequency; and so on.)
3. Give two examples of ad placement in space to attract a select audience in a mass media vehicle. Do the same for placement in time. Suggest a product for each of the ways in which repetition affects recall; then suggest products that would benefit by each of the three pairs of methods.

Notes

Chapter 19

1. Joseph T. Klapper, "The comparative effects of the various media," in Wilbur Schramm, The process and effects of mass communication (Urbana: University of Illinois Press, 1960).
2. Magazine Advertising Bureau, Split run and regional advertising in magazines (New York: Magazine Publishers Association, issued annually).
3. Leo Bogart, Strategy in advertising (New York: Harcourt, Brace & World, 1967), p. 214.
4. *Ibid.*, p. 217.
5. *Ibid.*, p. 151.
6. *Ibid.*, p. 177.
7. *Ibid.*, p. 261.
8. Sarnoff A. Mednick, Learning (Englewood Cliffs, N.J.: Prentice Hall, 1964), pp. 25–6.
9. James F. Engel et al., Consumer behavior (New York: Holt, Rinehart and Winston, 1968), p. 578.

Media Perpetuate Hoax

A false story or hoax may survive for years, despite exposure, as one medium passes it on to another.

This item originally appeared in the *National Observer* on Nov. 16, 1964.

The Ten Commandments contain 297 words. The Bill of Rights is stated in 463. Lincoln's Gettysburg Address contains 266 words. A recent federal directive to regulate the price of cabbage contains 26,911 words.

More than 50 appearances of this item have been traced, since it was originated in the 1940s by some unknown critic of Office of Price Administration. The item has appeared in the *New York Herald Tribune,* the *Wall Street Journal,* the *Inland Printer,* a railway house organ, and on NBC. Rotary clubs and Walter Winchell have repeated it, and it has been cited on the floor of the House of Commons and in a senatorial campaign in Ohio.

Actually, no such order ever existed. (The OPA *did* have an order covering many fruits and vegetables, including cabbage.)

Along the way, the hoax spawned new variants. When the Chamber of Commerce of the United States found the cabbage order didn't exist, it substituted a "12,962-word order establishing the ceiling price of manually-operated fog horns and other items." (The "other items" not listed included 376 types of machinery, ranging from soot blowers to rock crushers. Even this qualification soon disappeared as this new version marched merrily onward.)

Source. Max Hall, "Case report: the great cabbage hoax," *Journal of Personality and Social Psychology,* 2:563–9.

Can Mass Media Change Attitudes?

By definition, the "mass media"— newspapers, radio, and TV—are *avail-able* to nearly everyone, but actual *exposure* tends to be highly selective. Few men watch soap operas; few women read the sports and financial pages. Thus, using the mass media to reach uninterested, indifferent, or hostile audiences is not likely to be very effective. This was demonstrated soon after World War II.

Two world affairs organizations conducted a 6-month campaign to sell residents of Cincinnati on the value of the United Nations. Newspapers cooperated by emphasizing news of the UN, 60,000 pieces of literature were distributed, and one radio station broadcast 150 UN spot announcements a week. Weekday church schools reached 14,000 children with the message, every school child received literature to take home, and PTA programs on the UN reached some 13,000 members.

At the start of the campaign in September 1947 a survey found that only 47% of respondents mentioned an *international* issue when asked to name problems facing the United States. A second survey at the end of the campaign in March found that 74% mentioned an international problem when asked the same question. It *looked* as if the campaign had made Cincinnati aware of international problems.

However, a nationwide survey showed that exactly the same rise in interest had occurred throughout the nation. A look at the headlines showed what had happened: the cold war, not the campaign about the UN, had caused the change.

As for the two groups sponsoring the campaign, after six months less than one-half of 1% of the public claimed membership in either of them and only 10% knew they existed.

Source. Shirley A. Star and Helen MacGill Hughes, "Report on an educational campaign: The Cincinnati plan for the United Nations," *American Journal of Sociology,* 55:389–400.

Salesmen: They Vary as Much as the Media Do

Although the differences between newspapers and TV or radio and magazines are obvious, men often talk and act as if all salesmen were alike. They are not. Attempts to discover the traits that make a good salesman, so that one may recruit and screen applicants, must specify what type of salesman and what sales functions one is talking about.

Using a checklist of 35 sales activities regarded as important to their jobs (activities ranging from replenishing stocks to giving technical advice), researchers identified 50 "retail" salesmen, and 70 "industrial" salesmen. The groups were then compared as to Strong Vocational Interest Blank scores, scores on a personality test (the Edwards Personal Preference Schedule), and choices from 36 groups of 5 adjectives which each man perceived as best describing himself.

Industrial salesmen perceived themselves as high in ingenuity, inventiveness, and exercise of wits; retail salesmen emphasized planning, hard work, and the ability to persuade others. Success of industrial salesmen was related to verbal reasoning ability, that of retail salesmen to their motivation toward selling, and toward being dominant in relationships with others.

Source. Marvin D. Dunnette and Wayne K. Kirchner, "Psychological test differences between industrial salesmen and retail salesmen," *Journal of Applied Psychology,* 44:121–5.

Scores on the Strong Vocational Interest blanks were obtained from 22 firms for 300 salesmen whom sales managers said, after a year's service, they would be willing to rehire. Of the number, 100 were specialty salesmen, 100 route salesmen, and 100 sales engineers.

Route men were highest on scores reflecting concern with business details: those for accountants, office workers, and purchasing agents. Sales engineers were most similar, in their scores, to production and personnel managers, and least like real estate and life insurance salesmen. None of the three groups ranked high on the advertising man scales.

Mean Standard Strong Score for Salesman Type			
	Route	Specialty	Engineers
A.	39	36	33
B.	40	39	45
C.	48	48	44

Strong Scale	
A.	Accountant
B.	Production manager
C.	Real-estate salesman

Source. Arthur A. Witkin, "Differential patterns in salesmen," *Journal of Applied Psychology,* 40:338–40.

Mood Created by TV Program Affects Products Advertised on It

The context in which an advertisement appears may affect the reception that the ad receives. Airlines would rather not have their ads appear on the same page with news of a fatal crash; *Holiday* magazine reminds advertisers that news of riots abroad are not its cup of tea. Some critics have even charged that TV programs are deliberately dull so as to make the commercials which interrupt them look good.

Before watching TV, 184 coeds completed four questionnaires.

1. *Attitudes.* Coeds used 10 semantic differential scales (bad-good,

dirty-clean, etc.) to rate such behaviors as "drinking a Daiquiri" and "Depositing some money in your checking account." Other products were savings bonds, a sewing machine, a typewriter, sterling silver, a liqueur, a deodorant, silk stockings, vegetable oil, and a pressure cooker.

2. *Desired mood.* Using the same 10 scales, coeds then indicated how desirable they felt each of nine moods was: aggressiveness, depression, anxiety, etc.
3. *Present mood.* On a 4-point scale, coeds indicated how appropriate each of 140 adjectives was in describing their present mood.
4. *Product and mood.* On a 7-point scale coeds indicated for each product in turn whether it made them feel more or less anxious, depressed, etc.

Coeds watched a documentary on Nazi war crimes, *The Nuremburg Trial,* then filled out the four measures all over again.

Moods changed on 8 of the 9 measures; coeds become more depressed, anxious, and aggressive and less affectionate and light-hearted. They also changed significantly in their ratings of moods they desired to have. Aggressiveness was rated more highly; coeds were less interested in feeling light-hearted, energetic, self-centered, and affectionate.

With the change in actual and desired moods, came a changed perception of the relationship between product and moods; the shift in moods and shift in perception of the product-mood relationships correlated .87.

All 11 products were less liked after the movie than before, nine of the changes being significant at the .05 level. Comparison of attitude predictions on the basis of mood, made before and after the movie, suggested such a downward shift in all cases.

Source. Joel N. Axelrod, "Induced moods and attitudes toward products," *Journal of Advertising Research,* 3:3:19–24.

Counting Noses

The ideal advertising vehicle would deliver all of the prospects for a given brand and product who live in the area where the brand is sold and have the money to pay for it—and only such prospects. It would meet audience specifications as to rate of use, brand loyalty, and stage of persuasion. It would concentrate on those who make the purchasing decision, but not neglect those who influence decisions.

No such vehicle exists.

Most of the samples on which audience profiles are based are so small that cross-tabs on even two dimensions, such as sex and job, reduce cell entries below the point of statistical stability. Even without such breakdowns, simple nose-counts may vary with the group that makes the count.

Here are the number of readers (in millions) reported by three surveys made within a few months of one another in 1964–1965.

	Politz	Simmons	Research Organization Data, Inc.
Woman's Day	13.31	10.96	15.54
Family Circle	15.55	12.44	16.54

Telephone reinterviews in 1964 of persons quizzed 10 days earlier about smoking found that 5% of the sample—equivalent to 6 million persons in the population—had changed their answers. Face-to-face interviews in the fall of 1964 found 24% of adults watching TV per minute during prime time compared with an average of 41% reported by a rival agency using a different method of gathering data. Weekly diaries in which families reported exposure of four media found radio audiences between 7 A.M. and 10 P.M. equal to 7% of adults in respondent households. Telephone calls which asked respondents *What are you listening to now?* boosted the 7-to-10 radio audience to 11%. Radio-only diaries, mailed in daily, raised the estimate to 14%. (Estimates of persons listening to radio any time during the day varied from 63% to 90% between the weekly four-media or the daily radio-only diaries.)

Differences in the methods of summarizing data also affect results—and decisions based on them. Single national rating for a TV program may conceal a range from 5 in one market to 40 in another. Time differences across the nation affect audience composition as well as size. With youngsters packed off to bed by 10 P.M., a program may attract an adult audience in the East—but lose this audience in the midwest where youngsters still "control the set." February's snow may deliver a captive audience to TV in Minnesota; insufferable humidity may make Gulf Coasters seek air-conditioned comfort at their TV set in July. Simple, national nose-counts do not reflect these differences. Summary figures also may not distinguish between 10 persons viewing a commercial 100 times and 100 persons viewing a commercial 10 times —a difference which is crucial to many advertisers. Media use, like use of many products, is often concentrated. A 1964 survey found, that 45% of woman-hours spent watching TV was accomplished by 17% of the nation's women and that another 44% of women did only 8% of female viewing.

Source. Examples cited in Leo Bogart, *Strategy in Advertising* (New York: Harcourt, Brace and World, 1967).

Demographic Profiles

Noses are not enough: the advertiser wants to know to whom the noses belong. Growing disinterest in mere body-counts is evidenced by the disappearance of magazines whose readers were loyal, but too diverse, too scattered, or too lacking in affluence to interest the advertisers who "subsidized" them. Thus *Collier's,* with 4 million subscribers, died in 1957; the *New York Mirror,* nation's second largest newspaper at the time, vanished in 1963, and the *Saturday Evening Post* was scuttled. At the beginning of the decade of the 1970s, trouble loomed not only for the handful of remaining mass magazines, such as *Life* and *Time,* but for network TV. With the cables of CATV offering cities a potential of 30 separate programs, it began to look as if, except for moon-landings and presidential assassinations, nationwide mass audiences might cease to exist!

Even if TV, taking the day's schedule as a whole, still has something for (nearly) everybody—this is *not* true of individual programs. Surveys have shown, for example, that westerns are half again as popular in low income groups as with viewers in the over $10,000 bracket (1967 dollars), whereas situation comedies have scored better in upper-income groups.

Who Pays for What

As advertising expenditures rose from $5.3 billion a year in 1949 to nearly $21 billion in 1959, the proportion spent by manufacturers increased to nearly half.

	1949	1959	1969
Manufacturing	41%	45%	47%
Retailing	29	24	24
Wholesaling	8	8	5
Services	9	9	10
All other[a]	13	14	14

[a] Construction, transport, utilities, extractive industries, finance, and real estate.

Source. Advertising Age, March 30, 1970. This and subsequent data from this publication for the dates indicated are reprinted with permission, copyright by Crain Communications, Inc.

About one-fourth of ad budgets went into message-preparation over this period; income to ad agencies took another 10%. The rest went to the media —newspapers getting the lion's share

We've just uncovered a rare species of the American Male.

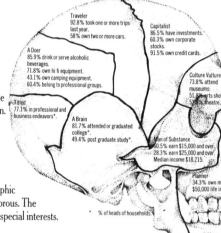

He's our subscriber.

There hasn't been a consumer like him since the dawn of civilization. Note data on his brain power, social behavior, material assets. The latest findings from an independent survey...still ink-fresh. Ever read of a life style like his? It follows our man's a psychographic phenomena, too. Inquisitive. Vigorous. The magazines he reads focus on his special interests. Ours, notably.

Natural History Magazine, the publication of The American Museum of Natural History.

200,000 of his breed make pretty strong circulation. He's no thumb-through reader. Needs no subscription discount inducements. We offer none.

Our recent articles explore the dangerous side effects of new technologies in underdeveloped countries, the problem of nuclear pollution, big city overpopulation. Dinosaurs, distant lands, exotic peoples, the ocean, the stars—a half hundred "ologies."

Most urgently—survival itself! These are the subjects that grab him.

Our man is no stay-at-home intellectual. He acts on editorials and ads.

Your message can send him off on a safari or auto trip. Down the corner to buy a new book, new camera, new boat. To the phone to inquire about more insurance, more stocks. Into his well-lined pockets to help save the American Indians. Or he may simply make a mental note to buy your product because you're doing research on air pollution or a project he's actively involved in.

Travel, educational, financial advertising. Corporate and product advertising of companies like BOAC, AT&T, Renault, Airequipt, Mexican National Tourist Council, Lincoln Continental, IBM, Nikon, Standard Oil of New Jersey. He responds to them all.

Come explore us. Discover a great market.

Write or call Harvey Oshinsky, Ad Director, collect for your confidential report on our rare species—Natural History Subscriber Characteristics.

Natural History Magazine
A rare discovery.
Central Park West at 79th Street, New York, N.Y. 10024 • (212) 873-1669

Magazine Presents Demographic Profile of Its Audience

because of their domination of retail advertising.

	1949	1959	1969
Newspapers	28%	24%	23%
Magazines	13	10	8
Direct mail	14	14	12
Radio	8	5	5
TV	1	10	14
Outdoor, etc.	6	5	6

Advertising Age, March 30, 1970.

Importance of advertising varied remarkably both by industry and by firm as indicated by ad expenditures as percentage of sales.

1968 Advertising Budgets		
	Millions of Dollars	Percentage of Sales
General Motors	199	1
General Foods	110	9
Procter & Gamble	199	10
Colgate-Palmolive	103	24
Bristol Myers	108	14
Avon	8	2
Coca-Cola	56	6
Royal Crown	13	20
Schlitz beer	18	7

Advertising Age, August 25, 1969.

Media preferences of the biggest *national* advertisers, those selling food, drugs, and automobiles, differ.

1969 Expenditures in Millions of Dollars

	Total	News-papers	Magazines	TV Spot	TV Network	Radio
Procter & Gamble	188	2	11	56	119	—
General Motors	160	23	46	13	41	29
Bristol Myers	110	2	25	18	59	6
General Foods	105	7	7	39	50	3
Ford Motor Co.	100	11	27	8	31	20

Advertising Age, July 13, 1970.

Eight U.S. agencies had total billings of more than $250 million, at least $200 million of this being spent within the United States.

	1970 Billings in Millions of Dollars World	United States	Number of Employees
J. Walter Thompson Co.	764	436	2830
McCann-Erickson	547	247	1110
Young & Rubicam	520	356	2165
Ted Bates & Co.	414	254	1779
Leo Burnett Co.	389	283	1557
Batten, Barton, Durstine & Osborn	350	324	1663
Doyle, Dane, Bernbach	291	250	1433
Grey	251	201	1324
Ogilvy and Mather	250	159	903

Advertising Age, February 22, 1971.

Clients also disagreed in how to split ad budgets among the media, both by product and by brand.

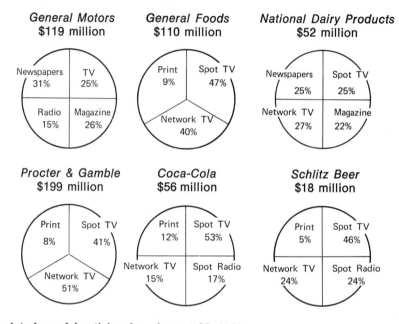

General Motors
$119 million

Newspapers 31% | TV 25%
Radio 15% | Magazine 26%

General Foods
$110 million

Print 9% | Spot TV 47%
Network TV 40%

National Dairy Products
$52 million

Newspapers 25% | Spot TV 25%
Network TV 27% | Magazine 22%

Procter & Gamble
$199 million

Print 8% | Spot TV 41%
Network TV 51%

Coca-Cola
$56 million

Print 12% | Spot TV 53%
Network TV 15% | Spot Radio 17%

Schlitz Beer
$18 million

Print 5% | Spot TV 46%
Network TV 24% | Spot Radio 24%

Based on data from *Advertising Age,* August 25, 1969.

Additional Research Readings

Involvement. Arguments that TV commercials do not involve the user while magazine ads do (and are therefore more effective) are countered by evidence that the difference is the result of message content and not medium. Of 916 commercials, 72% were for products (beer, soap, gas) whose brands are very similar; this was true of only 41% of 1612 magazine ads studied. **Ivan L. Preston, "A reinterpretation of the meaning of involvement in Krugman's models of advertising communication," Journalism Quarterly, 47:287–95.**

Effects. Ads, speakers, radio, and newspapers changed attitudes toward mental retardation in a community of 4400 population, as compared with a control community which saw no such publicity campaign. **Dorothy F. Douglas et al., "An information campaign that changed community attitudes," Journalism Quarterly, 47:479–487, 492.**

Chapter 20 Synopsis

● So that they can be matched, both market segments and audiences are defined in terms of geography and demography. Not all products are available nationally; not all prospects are located where it is profitable to reach them with products or messages. Geography and the demographic variable, income, help to define who in the population is *able* to buy a given product.

● Variables of age, sex, job, and education affect a prospect's desire to buy a given product, his chances of exposure to a given medium and the probability that he will respond to a given message. Data on such variables are available in the United States census, for region, state, city, and census tract. These variables are often combined into composite indices of social class and life cycle which are useful in identifying segments and audiences and matching the two.

● Sellers also need other data concerning audiences, such as how many are located at each stage in the process of persuasion, present brand preferences, how much influence individuals have in purchasing decisions, rate of product usage. Given such data, a seller can implement such strategies as drawing nonusers into the market, changing light to heavy users, and encouraging brand switching.

● Buyers may be differentiated on the basis of the purposes of their purchases: further processing, resale, or use in consumption. A seller may direct his messages to any or all of these audiences. Typically, industrial purchases involve more persons, take longer, and find buyer and seller bargaining more as equals than is true when buyers are consumers. The industrial buyer has more alternatives: he can make, he can reciprocate, and he can offer volume buying.

Research Articles

Audiences. IQ, an index to audience ability to understand messages, reported for population segments (Terman, Cronbach) and for occupations (Harrell).

Effects. Choice must be made among reach, frequency, and impact of message (Bogart, Engel).

Recall. Of TV commercial affected by its length (Barclay); of ads by their spacing through time (Zielske); optimal level of repetition varies by product (Stewart).

Chapter 20 Matching Audiences to Market Segments

The seller's strategy seeks market segments made up of prospects who want his product and are able to pay for it. The seller implements his strategy by choosing audiences made up of persons who can be exposed to his messages and will respond to them. He compares media on the basis of how closely audience overlaps segment and how cheaply.

A seller, however, cannot make a survey in every community where his brand is sold to determine who wants his brand and can pay for it, what media they see, and what symbols they will respond to. What he can do is to describe his market segment in terms which also are used to describe media audiences. These terms are *geographic* and *demographic*.

Geography affects product availability—not all manufacturers seek a nationwide market and most retailers, Sears Roebuck being an obvious exception, are interested in a single city or neighborhood. In some instances, limited distribution is a temporary phase, while a new firm or new product is trying to establish itself. In other instances characteristics of place impose permanent geographic limits on sales: oil furnaces sell poorly in a tropical climate, for example. Ability to pay has geographic correlates: few yachts are sold in urban ghettoes; Scotsmen's love of oatmeal and Southerners' liking for okra and hominy grits are not unrelated to low incomes in these areas. Some differences are historical: pizza flourishes in United States communi-

ties where Italians happened to settle and sauerkraut where German immigrants came. Other differences are inherent: some products are bulky and heavy in proportion to their price (and the cost of transportation), so that the scope of their markets is permanently limited.

Limiting markets geographically may hike profits. By concentrating on 22 standard metropolitan statistical areas, a seller can reach 36% of the nation's population, 37% of its households, and 40% of its retail sales; to reach this many people *outside* the nation's 199 SMSAs, which include all counties containing a city of at least 50,000 populations, he would have to ship products and send messages to 2745 counties![1] (By concentrating on the 199 SMSAs, a seller can reach 65% of the nation's households, which account for 69% of all retail sales.)

Of the demographic variables, *income* provides the best index to ability to buy; age and sex, occupation and education are correlated with a desire for the product.

Income

In 1960, of some 352 billion dollars in after-tax incomes, it was estimated that 25% had to be spent on fixed commitments such as mortgages and 40% to maintain existing living standards.[2] This left 35% as discretionary income; what people did with this 35% depended, in part, on the relative effectiveness of banks in designing messages urging that they save, and manufacturers and retailers in designing messages urging that they spend.

Family spending patterns vary with family income; higher income groups typically spend less on food and drink and more on furniture and automobiles.

Here are figures from a study made by *Life* magazine in 1957.[3]

Percentage of Annual Household
Expenditures

	Annual Income per Household		
	Under $2000 %	$3000 to $3999 %	$7000 to $9999 %
Food, drink, tobacco	36	30	26
Furniture	7	8	9
Automobiles	11	15	15

What happens when incomes change? This depends on whether the change extends to all society, to a whole class or occupation, or to an individual household. In the latter case, increased buying as the response to an increase in income is likely to be limited by the family's friends and neighbors; its full effects may not occur until the family moves into a new neighborhood. Current spending does not automatically reflect current income. A man can spend more than he is earning, by dipping into savings or by borrowing; he can spend less, by saving more. A temporary fall in income or a permanent rise in income, may lead a man to borrow and spend beyond his current income. His willingness to do so depends partly on his expectations concerning his own personal income and partly on his expectations as to general business conditions.

Income, like geography, acts as a constraint on seller choice, limiting the persons who are eligible for inclusion in his audiences. They are indices of ability to buy. Age, sex, job, and schooling, on the other hand, are correlated with buyer interest in product and in message.

Occupation

A man's job determines his income, influences where he lives and with whom he associates, and affects his way of life—the products he buys and uses. Figures in the bottom row of the table[4] at bottom of page show how job affects income; the effects of job (and income) on purchases are shown by the percentages.

The individual who changes his occupational level and thereby acquires a new group of friends is likely to show a great, rapid change in attitudes and buying behavior. Changes in buying patterns will follow the decrease in blue collar and farm jobs and the rise in service trades.

Education

The effects of education are twofold. Like occupation, education affects the kinds of purchases a person makes: books, wine, travel, and stereo sets tend to be popular with college graduates. But education also directly affects the channels and messages a marketing communicator must use. Mag-

Percentage of Annual Household Expenditures

	Occupation of Household Head		
	Professional	Clerical, Sales	Factory
Food, drink, tobacco	26	27	32
Furniture	8	8	8
Automobiles	14	16	15
Total average annual spending in 1957	$5626	$4845	$2002

azines in general and such specific magazines as *Harper's* and *Holiday* tend to reach the more educated purchaser who is likely to be more critical of advertising in general, more suspicious of it, and less dependent on it in making his decisions. He frequently judges the advertising message on its style and entertainment value, and he may resent its attempt to persuade.

As occupation is the chief determinant of income, so education is the chief means to a rise in the occupational scale in the United States today. The proportion of college graduates is increasing, with some employers insisting on a high school diploma for jobs where a sixth grader's ability to read may be all that is necessary. Since occupation, income, and education are related to one another, marketing communicators often find it convenient to combine these three types of data into an index of *social class*, using them as a basis for profiles of market segment and audience.

Sex

Although the proportion of men and women tends to be equal at birth, subsequent events may cause changes. When wars were fought on battlefields to obliterate opposing armies instead of cities, they tended to produce a deficit of males. In peacetime, the tendency of men to die earlier seems to produce a surplus of old women.

Sex differences affect both purchasing and communications behavior. Women use lipstick, listen to soap operas, and read the society sections of their newspapers. Men smoke cigars, watch westerns on television, and read the sports pages. Sex also affects the influence an individual has in household decision making. A husband may decide what is to be bought, a wife make the actual purchase, and children use the product. Or vice versa; particularly vice versa.

Age

Of all the demographic variables, age alone runs a continuous, predictable, and progressive course. Desire for products change with age, as one moves from a hunger for pablum to a need for false teeth. So does our role in purchasing change. Children, for example, influence purchasing decisions long before they become old enough to do any purchasing themselves, as every toy and cereal manufacturer advertising on television knows. Age affects progress in schooling and entry into the job market, and within any occupational level, it is not unrelated to income.

At least in the early years, age also determines the communications channels a marketer must use. Sesame Street reaches preschoolers, situation comedy seems to work with preteens, and disc jockeys on portable transistor radios are fine for the teen-ager, off in a world of his own.

As science lengthens life, the proportion of aged in the population increases. This is likely to decrease the total size of purchases, since both income and desire tend to diminish with age, as well as change the kind of products desired. Purchasing habits may grow stronger with age, attitudes more fixed, and marketing messages less effective in influencing purchases. As an older person's circle of friends constricts, word of mouth exerts less influence on purchasing.

Age and sex combined lead to marriage and the formation of a household, the basic decision-making unit in purchasing. In creating a two-person group, marriage itself leads to a great many new purchases, housing, furniture, and insurance prominent among them. The arrival of children intensifies these needs and creates new needs for such items as bottles and diapers.

All three of these demographic variables —age, marriage, and children—can be combined into a single index of purchasing behavior, called the *life cycle*. Like social class, life cycle is often useful in constructing and comparing profiles of market segment and of audience.

Behavioral Indices

Since both of the categories which the seller is trying to match—the audiences and market segments—are based on *behavior*, wouldn't behavioral measures make more sense than either geographic or demographic indices? Often they would. However, the data required to use demographic indices are supplied to the seller without charge by the government in the form of a census every 10 years. With the census, he can define markets in terms of regions, states, urban areas, and even census tracts within cities. Nevertheless, sellers are continually seeking alternative methods of comparing segment and audience. Sometimes these consist of indices which combine census variables, such as social class and life cycle. Sometimes these mean obtaining more up-to-date survey data between censuses. And sometimes these alternatives involve behavioral and attitudinal variables.

The seller of a major innovation needs to know how close members of his audience are to making the first trial purchase. The seller of a new brand needs to know preferences for present brands and which are most vulnerable to his appeals. The seller who seeks to increase sales by changing light users to heavy users needs to know how many buyers fall into each category. The seller of a big-ticket consumer durable needs to know how much influence each member of the decision-making unit has on the purchase itself.

If prospects have such strong brand preferences that they will refuse substitutes, a seller with a satisfactory share of the market may find that a listing in the yellow pages provides the audience he needs. If the product is bought frequently but brand preferences are weak, the advertiser may want to place his ad as near the point of purchase as possible—using a billboard the buyer will see or a radio commercial that he will hear while driving to the store, or a counter display within the store itself. If, on the other hand, a sale is made only after a joint decision following considerable deliberation, the seller may have to reach several audiences. He may, for example, make wives aware of his brand by spot announcements on daytime television, but move their husbands toward actual purchase by ads run on newspaper sports pages.

Common-sense attempts to match segment and audience do not always work: a *Good Housekeeping* survey found that 30% of housewives interviewed said they bought razor blades for their husbands and another researcher reported that one-third of all detergent purchases are made by men.[5] Perhaps Gillette should look beyond the male audiences of sportscasts and Lever Brothers beyond the female audiences of soap operas.

Similar questions arise when the seller's strategy requires him to distinguish prospects in terms of light and heavy product use or brand preference. Rate of use and brand loyalty tend to vary with product and brand. Data in Chicago, for example, indicate that a media schedule which reaches heavy users of bacon does not produce an audience of heavy users of instant coffee.[6] Ad researcher Twedt has concluded that a TV program needed a separate rating, in terms of potential prospects, for each prospective sponsor.[7] A comparison of two women's magazines with identical audiences found that one of them reached 24% of prime prospects for toothpaste, and the other 44%.[8] Brand "loyalty"—the tendency to repeated purchase of the same brand—appears to vary with both product and brand. One scholar found loyalty varied from 54% for cereal to 73% for margarine and 95% for coffee.[9] Another found that loyalty for toothpaste ranged from a low of 32% for one brand to a high of 74% for another.[10]

It is risky to aim at an audience of heavy users identified on the basis of a one-shot study. Here, for instance, are figures based on diaries for 1958 and 1960 showing how many purchasers of three different products behaved consistently during the two years.[11] Note variations among products and the volatility of the "medium users."

	Percent Appearing in Same Class in Both Years		
	Product A	Product C	Product D
Heavy user	57	48	74
Medium user	32	27	49
Light user	66	41	80
Did not use	59	69	52

In each instance, medium users were more likely to shift into the "light" than the "heavy" class. In one major product class, the same analyst estimated that 50% of the families in the market one three-month period had dropped out the next quarter and been replaced by families not purchasing the product the previous quarter.[12] He suggests that where such movement exists brand switching is unlikely to affect sales volume.

Role and Mood

Even if two media or two vehicles in the same medium should draw exactly the same persons into their audiences and expose them to the same messages, this does not mean that responses would be identical. For much depends on *when* exposure occurs and in what context, and part of that context consists of the medium or the vehi-cle that carries the message. (The medium *is*, sometimes and to some degree, the message.)

On any given day, for example, a woman is likely to shift back and forth between the roles of wife and mother, cook and cleaning woman, citizen, and purchasing agent for the family. There are moods appropriate to each role. As a mother, she may be indulgent or strict; as a cleaning woman, careless or diligent; as cook, proud; as purchasing agent, canny. A good housewife may not be comfortable watching a soap opera on TV in the morning, before breakfast dishes are washed and beds made. She may, however, be able to do her chores while listening to a radio quiz show or feel that a homemaker program on TV is consistent with her duties. The TV and radio programs, or the broadcast commercial itself, may evoke a role or a mood that is appropriate to its message, or one that utterly defeats it. Program context does affect response to attendant advertising.

Some of these relationships are obvious. Makers of fine perfume will advertise neither in *Parents* magazine, whose readers are interested in powder for baby's bottom, nor on morning broadcasts, when housewives' ears are attuned to talk about cake mixes. Other relationships are more subtle. When instant coffee was first introduced, its makers appealed to women in their role as guardians of the family budget, only to discover that when housewives think of coffee they see themselves in the role of hostess and wife.[13]

Nonconsumer Audiences

Although the buyers that have been discussed to this point have been consumers, other audiences are important in marketing. Manufacturers may sell to middlemen, such as wholesalers and retailers, or to processors, as well as to consumers; or to any combination of these audiences as well as to all of them. DuPont, for example, may urge consumers to buy from manufacturers who use raw materials supplied by DuPont. Messages must parallel the flow of physical product into the market; every point at which title is transferred represents a decision maker whom messages may influence.

The first of these diagrams shows two basic patterns of physical distribution: through middle-men or direct from factory to user via door-to-door salesmen, direct mail, or factory outlets. (Arrows from the side represent competition.)

manufacturers, salesmen talk to retailers about markups and turnover, newspaper ads talk about taste and smell to the consumer. Advertising in business papers helps the industrial salesman get a hearing or produces inquiries that a salesman can follow up. To obtain retail outlets, the manufacturer "pushes" his product through the channels by advertising to the retailer in business papers, and "pulls" it through channels by advertising that sends consumers to the store to demand his brand. His salesmen call on retailers to check on shelf displays, to show the retailer proofs of future consumer advertising, and to supply

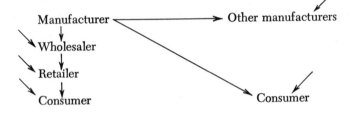

Messages, however, do not follow the pattern shown on the left. If they did, the manufacturer would find himself at the mercy of middlemen. Their interest and competence in passing along his message, not his own ability, would determine his success. Some part of his message would be lost at each step along the way. To keep this from happening, manufacturers communicate directly with each audience, in this fashion.

free point-of-purchase materials. Finally, through "cooperative advertising," he offers to pay part of the cost of the retailer's advertising that mentions his brand.

Perhaps the most difficult task of a purchaser is brand comparison, a time-consuming job that often leaves him feeling frustrated and incompetent. Yet he feels guilty if he does not compare brands as an intelligent, provident householder should. If the conflict becomes great enough, he may

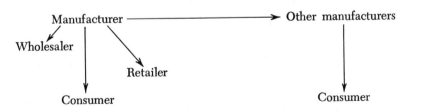

A manufacturer uses different channels and sends different kinds of messages to each of these audiences: engineers solve technical production problems of other

delay buying or refuse any purchase. The salesman who comes to his home frees the prospect from the brand comparison dilemma. Thus the encyclopedia publisher who sends salesmen directly to the consumer frees himself from dependence on a middleman who may be uncooperative or incompetent and insulates himself from competition; both total sales of the product and his share of those sales increase. He pays for these two advantages by using a channel, face-to-face selling, which has a high cost per purchaser.

By selling through franchised outlets, automobile and appliance manufacturers also gain some insulation from competition, since comparison of their brands with their competition is the means by which department store and supermarket attract customers.

Audiences in Industrial Marketing

The audiences of industrial marketing differ in important respects from both consumer and retailer audiences.

There are far fewer of them—about 3,150,000 business firms,[14] as compared with the nation's 210 million consumers; less than 50,000 of these have as many as 50 employees. Services and retailing-wholesaling, with about 1 million firms each, account for most of the separate companies. (Most firms are small; in 1965 less than 50,000 manufacturers had as many as 50 employees; in most industries, 99% of firms had less than 100 employees.) Yet, because most finished consumer products consist of many parts manufactured and assembled in many stages by many different firms, the number of sales that precede consumer purchase may be very large. Moreover, each sales transaction is likely to involve more money and to commit buyer and seller for longer periods of time. Because of this, the sale-purchase transaction is likely to take longer, involve more persons, and be accomplished with greater care. The purchasing agent is often backed up by laboratories which can help him compare competing products, and he is highly-motivated: his rewards, indeed his continued employment, depend on his making the right choices.

Buyer and seller are more nearly equals in industrial marketing than they are in consumer markets; either may enjoy a bargaining advantage or neither, depending on relative size and on the number of competing suppliers or buyers. A purchasing agent ordinarily hesitates to make all his purchases from a single supplier, since this would diminish his bargaining power and make the buyer co-victim should the seller be visited by strike, fire, or bankruptcy. Even when formal bidding procedures are used, the door remains open to nonprice competition; a supplier who excels in research, delivery, or troubleshooting may get a larger and larger share of the buyer's business.

Joint decisions are more common among industrial buyers; one firm has listed no less than 150 persons as influencing the purchase of steel.

Industrial advertising must serve two different kinds of audiences in a given firm, and perform two different functions. It must open doors for the salesman with purchasing agents. It must substitute for the salesman with executives who refuse to see the salesman himself, yet who draw up the specifications he must meet or hold veto power over the purchase. As a member of the buying "team," the purchasing agent may be a more effective advocate for a supplier than the supplier's own salesman would be, were he permitted to talk to these same executives.

Despite the large number of persons who often participate in purchasing decisions, bad decisions can probably be detected more quickly and responsibility for them traced more accurately than in consumer purchasing.

In part, this is because a consumer's desire for a "sweet" lemon is a poorer criterion than an engineer's insistence on tolerances of a thousandth of an inch. The product sold to a manufacturer is subject to two tests: a quality control engineer's measuring instruments and the necessity that parts fit together on an assembly line and perform specified functions when they leave it. A consumer may be ignorant of or indifferent to wide differences in both quality and price, because he visits only a limited number of retail outlets, lacks the ability or instruments needed to detect differences in quality, or perceives potential savings as not being worth the time and energy that search and comparison would require. A firm purchasing thousands of units, however, finds savings of a fraction of a cent per unit worth considerable effort in search, comparison, and bargaining.

The largest number of persons who may influence an industrial purchase-sale decision and their varied positions on its organizational chart present the seller with several different audiences. Industrial publications offer readers at several different levels in a single industry; magazines like *Fortune,* on the other hand, appeal to top executives in all industries. Still other business publications appeal to occupants of a specific role: to design engineers, purchasing agents, or factory superintendents. The seller places his advertising so as to reach the ideal composite audience; the buyer must decide which publications to subscribe to and how best to circulate them within his plant.

Several studies suggest that advertising may be far more effective in producing requests for information than are firms in meeting such requests. One study, for instance, showed that 12% of the firms making inquiry of advertisers in five trade journals got no reply at all, and that a salesman called on only 18% of them.[15] A fork lift firm found that only 39% of the inquiries it received were followed up, although 28% of them produced sales. Follow-up seems particularly important in the case of innovations. One firm, which received 5000 inquiries (at a cost of $10 each) converted 40% of them into sales.

An important difference between industrial purchaser and consumer is the former's wider choice of alternatives. He has three not available to most consumers.

He can decide to make rather than to buy what he needs.

He may employ reciprocity, buying from suppliers who agree, in turn, to buy from him.

He may vary the size of his purchases.

He may increase them to gain quantity discounts from seller or common carrier or reduce paperwork costs (which are more closely geared to number than to size of purchases).

He may reduce them to keep from tying up funds, save storage and insurance costs, avoid physical deterioration, or because he fears innovations will make his present products obsolete.

Thought, Talk, and Action

1. For men and for women and for extremes on the demographic variables of age, income, occupation, and education, suggest two *products* appealing to persons who differ on each. Then suggest how these pairs of persons differ in chances of exposure to messages on a given *medium.* (*Example.* The aged: dentures and Reader's Digest; preschoolers: Kool Aid and Saturday morning cartoons on TV.)
2. You are manufacturing a new puncture-resistant and self-sealing plastic that is ideal for waterbeds. How would you divide your promotional budget between advertising and selling directed to waterbed manufacturers? to retailers? to customers? Write advertising copy directed to each of these audiences.

3. Find, in U.S. census tract data, figures for the neighborhood in which you now live. Now locate another tract (whose number is half or twice the number of the tract in which you live). Which tract—on the basis of census information only—would be more suitable for a gourmet restaurant? a discount store? a baby shop? a Golden Age club?

Notes

Chapter 20

1. J. Walter Thompson, Population and its distribution, 8th ed. (1961).
2. Alfred Politz, Life study of consumer expenditures (New York: Time, 1957).
3. *Ibid.*
4. *Ibid.*
5. Leo Bogart, Strategy in advertising (New York: Harcourt, Brace & World, 1967), p. 198.
6. *Ibid.*
7. *Ibid.*, p. 197.
8. *Ibid.*, p. 203.
9. James F. Engel et al., Consumer behavior (New York: Holt, Rinehart and Winston, 1968), p. 578.
10. Reference No. 5, p. 200.
11. Joseph W. Newman, editor, On knowing the consumer (New York: John Wiley & Sons, 1966), p. 179.
12. *Ibid.*, p. 185.
13. Mason Haire, "Projective techniques in marketing research," Journal of Marketing, 14:X:649–56.
14. Ralph S. Alexander et al., Industrial marketing, 3rd ed. (Homewood, Ill.: Richard D. Irwin, 1967).
15. *Ibid.*, p. 413. This reference covers all studies cited in paragraph.

Job, IQ, and Understanding

Demographic details concerning media audiences may be used to predict their ability to understand one's message, thanks to such intelligence tests as the Stanford-Binet, Wechsler-Bellevue, and Wechsler Adult Intelligence Scale. Intelligence quotients, based on the first of these, show patterns of this kind.

I.Q.	Percent in Population	Related Achievement	
140–169	1.3		
120–139	11.3	130:	mean for Ph.D.'s
		120:	mean for college graduates
110–119	18.1	110:	mean for high school graduates
90–109	46.5	105:	has 50–50 chance of passing high school
		90:	mean for low-income city or rural homes
80–89	14.5		
30–79	8.2	75:	has 50–50 chance of entering high school

Sources

Lewis M. Terman and Maud A. Merrill, *Stanford-Binet Intelligence Scale: Manual for the Third Revision, Form L-M* (New York: Houghton Mifflin, 1960).

Lee J. Cronbach, *Essentials of Psychological Testing* (New York: Harper and Row, 1960, 2nd ed.).

IQ scores also show some relationship to *occupation,* as shown by these figures.

Median	Occupation	Range of Individual Scores
128.1	Accountant	94–157
126.8	Lawyer	96–157
125.8	Engineer	100–151
123.7	Teacher	76–155
121.4	Stenographer	66–151
120.7	Sales manager	90–137
119.2	Purchasing agent	82–153
116.2	Salesman	60–153
116.2	Retail store manager	52–151
113.0	Stock clerk	54–151
111.4	Foreman	60–151
110.4	Sales clerk	42–149
108.1	Sheet metal worker	62–153
105.9	Auto serviceman	30–141
104.8	Plumber	56–139
101.8	Auto mechanic	48–151
100.1	Painter	38–147
97.8	Truck driver	16–149
98.1	Barber	42–141
93.4	Farmer	24–147
90.6	Miner	42–139

Since these results are based on scores for slightly less than 19,000 white men enlisted in the air force in World War II, they have their limitations. First, men in occupations requiring a high IQ, such as atomic physicists, were unlikely to become enlisted men. Second, it's possible that the smartest individuals in most occupations managed to stay out of the military. Third, there is an apparent floor under the topmost occupants, with even the dullest accountant or engineer having an IQ within the average range of 90–109— but elsewhere the range in any occupation is very wide. Every occupation had someone classed as "very superior" (IQ of 140–169) and many had members classed as mentally defective (IQ of 30–69).

Source. Thomas W. Harrell and Margaret S. Harrell, "Army general classification test scores for civilian occupations," *Educational and Psychological Measurement,* 5:229–39.

Reach, Frequency, and Size

There is a good deal of evidence that *increasing the size* of an ad or its *frequency* will bring more persons into the audience. Unfortunately, the really important figures, indicating *how many* more, are not available. Below a certain size or frequency, some persons may not see the ad at all; above a certain size or frequency, spending more money will produce a less than proportionate increase in response. The Weber-Fechner formula provides constants, differing by each sensory dimension, which tell how big a change in the stimulus is needed to be noticed. (Ads appear to be too complex a mixture of stimuli, however, and the responses to them too multidimensional for any such convenient constants, although the threshold and diminishing return principles do apply.)

A rule of thumb in advertising suggests that ad recall increases as the square root of an increase in ad size. This rule, supported by a number of research studies from 1914 to date, seems to hold for both print and broadcast media. Here are some scattered results.

Studies made in 1936 and 1959 indicate that a half-page ad produces only 70% as many coupon returns as a full-page ad.

Recall of a 30-second commercial is about two-thirds that of a 60-second broadcast advertisement. Twenty-second commercials obtain 71% of the sales points and 92% of the brand names recalled by commercials three times as long.

Effects of *repetition* on recall have been shown in such studies as these.

Two days after delivering a copy of the *Saturday Evening Post* to 150 subscribers, interviewers quizzed them about its advertising and left another copy of the same issue. Then 3½ days later, they showed up for a second interview. Four key ads appeared in both issues, and four in only one; by noting which glue spots holding pages together had been broken, interviewers could determine exposure as well as recall. Analysis showed that two exposures doubled familiarity with the brand and its claims and willingness to buy; belief in the claims was tripled.

In a similar study using two sets of six test ads, subjects were given one day to look at a copy of *Reader's Digest* or two one-day exposures separated by a three-day interval. The second day increased brand recall from 12 to 21%, association of brand claims and brand name from 15 to 25%, high-quality ratings for advertised brands from 11 to 17% and would-buy ratings from 15 to 26%.

In both instances, repeated exposure depended on a voluntary act of the reader. The seller had no control—nor did repetition cost him anything.

Source. Leo Bogart, *Strategy in Advertising* (New York: Harcourt, Brace & World, Inc., 1967), pp. 148–9 and 175–6.

Only 20% of an unexposed control group showed awareness of a tire cord brand name (Tyrex) as compared to 65% of those who saw a spot TV commercial and 92% of those who saw at least three commercials.

Only 15% in a control group interviewed before an ad campaign began in a magazine named a brand; this rose to 18% of those exposed once and 21% of those exposed to two ads.

Effects of repetition have also been revealed in studies of the effects of halting an advertising campaign.

Recognition of the Eversharp brand name rose from 15 to 38% after five months of advertising, fell to 29% after a 2-month halt in advertising, climbed back up to 36% after 10 more months of advertising.

Advertising caused recognition of a firm's name to rise from 35% in 1955 to 44% in 1957, when advertising was stopped. By 1960, recognition had dropped to 31%.

Source. James F. Engel et al., *Consumer Behavior* (New York: Holt, Rinehart & Winston, Inc., 1968), p. 210.

Three more-detailed studies showing the effects of size or repetition are the following.

Three researchers made some 12,000 telephone calls in Chicago in 1963, asking housewives whether they had been watching a given channel at the time a commercial was aired and whether they recalled the commercial. Both questions were asked with prompting (aided) and without (unaided recall). Commercials of three different lengths were studied. Here are the percentages reporting exposure and recall.

	Length of Commercial		
	20 Seconds	30 Seconds	60 Seconds
Unaided			
Exposure	21	28	33
Ad recall	6	14	16
Aided			
Exposure	25	33	37
Ad recall	9	18	20

Only about a third of those "exposed" to a 20-second commercial "recalled" it, whether prompted or not, as compared with about half of those exposed to the 30-second commercial, but doubling the length of the half-minute commercial did *not* improve recall.

Source. William D. Barclay, Richard M. Doubt, Lyron T. McMurtrey, "Recall of TV commercials by time and program slot," *Journal of Advertising Research,* 5:2:41–7.

An ad agency employee who mailed housewives a series of 13 advertisements, one each week, found that the first of them was recalled by only 14% of those who had received it. By the 13th week, 63% of them recalled the ad. When he mailed the ads at four-week rather than weekly intervals, he found recall had risen to only 48% at the end of the study. Meanwhile, of course, ad recall in the first group, whose last mailing had occurred 39 weeks earlier, had followed the usual course of memory decay. The 48%, therefore, probably represented considerably greater effectiveness—at least 39 weeks longer effectiveness—than the 63%. A decision as to which kind of ad schedule, massed or spaced, is better would depend, in large part, on whether the 48% were more active prospects than the 63%; it seems not unlikely that they were.

Source. H. A. Zielske, "The remembering and forgetting of advertising," *Journal of Marketing,* 23:X:239–43.

In a study financed by the newspaper industry, the city of Fort Wayne, Ind., was divided into four sections. One got no advertising, another four weeks of ads, the third eight weeks advertising, and the fourth a 1000 line newspaper ad each week for 20 weeks. The ads concerned two new products, frozen Chicken Sara Lee and a bleach called Lestare. Interviews with a total of 6200 residents probed awareness, product information, and attitudes.

Very few housewives in the no-advertising group tried either of the new products. Some of those getting *four* ads bought sooner than they otherwise would have. *Eight* advertisements doubled the number of customers. *Twenty* ads produced the largest number of customers but *15* ads produced the best results per ad dollar: the five additional ads gained less in sales than they cost.

Beyond 6 to 10 appearances of the ads, depending on which of the products was involved, repetition was more effective in preventing responses from decaying than from increasing them. The second four ads were more effective for one product than the first four. For the other product, however, the second four ads were less effective than the first four, suggesting that here a change in copy might have been advisable.

At least four factors other than advertising copy affected results. One of the two products, for example, never managed to get on the shelves of more than about half of available retail outlets. One of the products was closer in price to competing products than the other. One of the products apparently was of higher relative quality than the other, since users seemed more satisfied with it. Variations in the housewives affected results. Of those who were educated and familiar with the brands in the relevant product category, 44% reported awareness of one of the test products, compared with only 7% of their less-educated, less-familiar colleagues. These differences in a carefully designed, expensive, and time-consuming study may explain why "laws" concerning the audience effects of size and repetition are likely to be a long time in coming, and why each seller has to make his own studies to guide marketing decisions.

Source. John B. Stewart, *Repetitive Advertising in Newspapers* (Boston: Harvard University, Graduate School of Business Administration, 1964).

Additional Research Readings

Repetition. Retests of 81 TV commercials showed that recall had declined for poor ones, stayed level for good ones. **Valentine Appel, "On advertising wear out," Journal of Advertising Research, 2:1:11–13.** Phone interviews found recall of ads rose over 13 weekly mailings, but brand preference fell. Repetition affected purchase intentions for convenience but not for shopping goods. **Michael L. Ray et al., "Frequency effects revisited," Journal of Advertising Research, 11:1:14–20.** Package preferences reversed themselves in 3 out of 6 trials when subjects saw and rated actual packages on 4 dimensions and were shown paired packages on film for intervals of 1 to 3 seconds. **Herbert E. Krugman, "The learning of consumer preference," Journal of Marketing, 26:2:31–3.** As proportion of a given digit rose in a series of 20, up to a maximum of 30%, five digits being used as stimuli, choices of that digit rose. Choices increased from 9 to 21% when digits appeared last in the series, rather than first. **William D. Wells and Jack M. Chinsky, "Effects of competing messages, a laboratory simulation," Journal of Marketing Research, 2:141–5.**

Chapter 21 Synopsis

- The symbol is a cue whose relationship to the object it stands for is arbitrary. This fact frees a source from constraints of time, space, and reality. His listener tends to distrust symbols for that reason, knowing that they bear no necessary relationship to the category that they label.

- There are three important kinds of symbols: pictures, numbers, and language. Pictures may appear to be less subject to manipulation than words, as may numbers. Pictures may express mood and emotion, but may also be used to depict relationships in time (process) and in space (structure). Although numbers are often perceived as being highly objective, they too may be manipulated to present varying views of reality.

- Language has two dimensions—vocabulary and syntax— and actually consists of two separate subsystems: speech and the written transcription of speech. Speech, in turn, has several dimensions: some 40 meaningful tones or phonemes; intensity, which provides a cue to distance; and pitch, which provides information about the speaker. Intrasentence variations in stress, pitch, and juncture modify meanings expressed by the phonemic tones. In addition, the vocal qualities of paralanguage and the gestures of kinesics affect meanings.

- These dimensions of speech provide multiple channels for meaning. By transmitting the same meaning on several channels, a source can insure communication in noisy circumstances. By transmitting different meanings, the source can achieve subtle effects. These multiple channels also carry information about the source and his intentions, whether he is aware or desirous that they do so or not.

- Speech and the written word perform different functions in different ways; speech tends to use fewer words and shorter sentences, to be less formal, and to be more affected by feedback.

- English speech uses only about half of the sounds which the voice can produce and the ear can hear, and an even smaller proportion of the possible combinations of words and their combinations. There are wide variations in the frequencies of those it does use.

- Context provides cues to meaning. The most important kind of context is grammar or syntax, which operates through word order, and word-endings. A child who starts with two categories of words develops, as an English-speaking adult, four major types, roughly corresponding to nouns, verbs, adjectives, and adverbs, plus "function words." All children appear to be endowed with basic matrices of meaning; through experience with a given language they develop transformational rules by which basic structures can be expressed in speech appropriate to the language they are learning.

● The surplus cues of syntax and those of vocabulary permit endless variations in selling appeals used to hold the interest of a given prospect and to appeal to different kinds of prospects.

● Through content analysis, the researcher tries to specify causes operating in his messages and effects displayed by the verbal behavior of his audiences. Content analysis requires sampling and the specification of coding units.

● Persuasive devices which go undetected by an audience may succeed in changing attitudes as the source desires; those detected may reveal the nature and intentions of the source himself, conveying an unintended meaning which may defeat his purposes. Canny readers may detect such devices; content analysis may reveal techniques which source as well as audience are unaware of. Three studies are cited which reveal patterns of sounds, of word choice, and of literary style in the round.

Research Articles

Sounds.   Their origin, rules for combining, and meaning of combinations reported (Brown).

Meanings.   Three dimensions of meaning identified: good-bad, hard-soft, active-passive (Osgood).

Word Order.   Sequence of syntax conveys meaning for five types of words (Miller); morphemes and phonemes distinguished (Miller); tree-diagrams of phrase-structure grammar solve ambiguity (Lindzey); 12 kinds of modifiers assigned position in sentence (Brown); three sentence structures vary in ease of producing, receiving (Miller).

Type.   Three dimensions of type produce five factors of meaning (Tannenbaum).

Chapter 21 Cues, Symbols, and Codes

The seller manipulates price, place, and product attributes to persuade prospects to become purchasers and so profit the purveyor. But the prospects' responses depend on their *perceptions* of the marketing mix. If their senses fail to report the cues that the seller has manipulated, no action results. If their memories fail to retain them or their brains distort them, the seller is likely to be disappointed. The seller, that is, must alter perceptions either by manipulating the market mix or directly through sales and advertising messages.

If a survey shows that prospects think the seller's price is "too high," he can lower it, manipulating the mix. But the survey may also find that prospects overestimate the price by 50%. If this is true, messages that make prospects aware of the actual price may achieve the same result as a price cut, but a lot faster and quicker, and with less trouble from costs and competitors.

Or consider this example: Consumers complain that a seller's lemons are sour. A botanist wants a year's time and $50,000 to make lemons *taste* less sour or more sweet. The processor says he'll need six months and at least $10,000 to install coloring equipment which will make the lemons *look* sweeter. A friendly local adman, however, may be able to produce a picture or string together some words which will make prospects *perceive* a different taste—and do it in five minutes, at the cost of a fresh sheet of paper for his typewriter or a search of his picture files. He *may*—aye, there's the rub. Genius is unpredictable and hasn't yet been programmed for the computer; even the best man has his bad days and may eventually run dry. But this possibility highlights an important difference between the kind of cues which the botanist and the adman manipulate.

Symbols: Arbitrary Cues to Meaning

The cues of the botanist are attributes inherent in the product itself, alterable only through the processes of plant breeding and horticulture. The cues of the copywriter bear an arbitrary relationship to the product. Because of this arbitrary relationship, they are given a special name. They are called symbols, labels, or words—language being a vast pool of symbols which can be used in communications.

In Chapter 4, we discovered that meaning resides in a man's categories, and that each category has three parts—attributes, a value, and a label that reflects both the attributes of which the category is constructed and the value placed on it. (We assume that a man has learned a category when he can retrieve a label for it from his memory and use that label in communicating to other persons.)

Much of the time we forget how arbitrary the relationship between label and category is, as when we argue heatedly about what a given word "really" means. In fact, of course, a word may mean whatever we want it to, whatever two of us can agree it means, or nothing at all. A four-legged animal does not change its nature when we call it *pferd* or *cheval* instead of *horse* although if we lack German or French neither term has any meaning for us. Thus different names may have the same "meaning." Another animal will be very differently perceived, however, depending on whether we call it *pet, puppy, dog, St. Bernard,* or *nuisance*—and on whether the animal so designated has four legs or two. Meaning changes with the person perceiving rather than the thing perceived.

The arbitrary nature of link between label and category can be a great advantage to any communicator. It frees him from the constraints of time and space. He can talk about things invisible, like angels and "truth"; things long dead, like Julius Caesar and the dinosaur; and things that never were, like unicorns and universal peace. He can choose labels that will make a given category—an object, event, or person—look good, look bad, or look neutral—depending on how he regards it and how he would like other persons to perceive it. He can do this with adjectives, such as "admirable" and "disgusting"; with verbs, such as "sauntered" and "slunk"; and with nouns, such as "hero" and "villain." He can suit his language to the medium that will transmit it—sober for the printed page, perhaps, or light-hearted for radio—and to the audience that will hear it—down-to-earth for the housewife or stuffily erudite for the college professor. He can suit it to time, place, and circumstance. Indeed, he must, for the same words will not convey the same meanings to different people at different times and places.

At the same time, however, the arbitrary nature of the link between label and category makes language suspect. The listener tends to distrust words for that reason, dismissing them as "just advertising," in a preference for actual experience with the product. Although the lemon's hue may be as imperfect a cue to its sensory rewards as the words used to describe it, buyers bet the probabilities and tend to put more trust in color than in language.

Words are not the only set of arbitrary symbols or "code" available to seller and buyer—they are only the most flexible, most used, and best known. Pictures and numbers are also important.

Pictures and Numbers

Pictures can carry the entire burden of an advertiser's message; since the advent of photography they have carried a large and increasing share of the burden. Although still regarded as bearing a less arbitrary relationship to the men and events they depict than the words used to describe them, even photographs can be used to create a wide range of attitudes in the perceiver.

Pictures, like words, can be highly denotative in content, as in the instructions for assembling a bicycle or in the contour map of a damsite, or they can be highly connotative, as in the typical *New Yorker* perfume advertisement. Some persons argue that advertising is most effective when it avoids words and persuades through pictures.[1] Words, they suggest, should be used only to give the guise of rational behavior to a man who has already been persuaded by a pictorial message. Pictures return high reward for little effort, and so are useful in communicating with the illiterate or with persons who speak a different language. They have been less associated than words with the penalty-fraught classroom of formal schooling.

Although pictures, like the spoken word, predate writing, and although writing itself began with pictures, we know very little of the vocabulary and syntax, the elements and structure, of pictorial communication. Despite this lack of knowledge, pictures are performing these major functions in marketing communication.

Attention. In advertising, pictures, through contrast with a verbal context, attract attention. By presenting objects in unusual settings or contents which contrast with one's expectations and experiences, they attract attention. The contrast between color and black and white attracts attention too.

Mood. Well-composed pictures may, in themselves, be rewarding, aside from any reward implied by the objects that they picture. They create moods, nonverbal feelings of pleasure or displeasure. Since most of us control our environment through the use of words, we may be less aware that we can be influenced by pictures—and less able to resist their influence, even if we are aware of it. (Before one can argue with a picture, he must express its meaning in words. Even if he is willing to go to the effort, the very process tends to influence him.)

Recognition. With the rise of self-service retailing, it is crucial that a customer be able to recognize a brand quickly. A picture of a package can develop this ability more easily than dozens of words.

Structure. If one wants to describe how elements are related to one another in space, a picture is usually the most efficient way of doing so. Maps and organizational charts do this and so does every diagram that accompanies an assemble-it-yourself toy.

Process. Pictures are also useful in relating objects, or events, to one another in time. This can be done with moving pictures, as in the demonstration on a television commercial, or with still pictures, in which relations-in-space are used to symbolize relations-in-time. A flow chart of an industrial process or a sequence of pictures showing how to bake a cake are examples of the advantage over moving pictures because they can be studied in detail, over and over again, at one's own pace.

In business and in science, numbers are steadily increasing in importance as a symbol system, whether they are numbers on a manager's balance sheet, on a computer program that directs an orbiting satellite, or in a table that forms the core of the behavioral scientist's article in a scholarly journal. Salesmen discussing purchase of supplies, materials, or equipment with manufacturers ply their slide rules; industrial advertising often makes its pivotal points with the aid of numbers.

Only in consumer advertising are numbers usually missing. Although we may be told that children have 23% fewer cavities or that Ivory Soap is 99.44% pure, we will find few graphs, few bar charts, few percentages, and few indices in most advertisements directed at consumers.

This may change as the rising level of education and the increasing importance of mathematics in education make consumers feel more at ease with figures. Whether it does or not, the marketing communicator needs to know how to choose the number that best conveys his message, how to combine several numbers in a message, and how to pick the best verbal label for the numbers he decides to use.

Both words and pictures may be used in combination with numbers to extend or modify their meaning. Speaking to a union audience, for instance, a public relations man may report that his firm suffered "a 40% drop in profits as compared with last year" or "a return of only 2% on sales." Working from the same balance sheet, he may then tell stockholders that the firm earned "a 10% return on investment," made "a $15 million profit" or experienced "a rise in profits of 30% over the 10-year average." Same firm, same basic facts, but different selected figures and labels. Similarly, an identical amount of money paid to employees can be described as a fall in pay (a lower rate per hour); no change in pay (if hours worked per day rose enough to offset the drop in hourly rate), or an increase in pay (if eliminating layoffs led to higher *annual* wages). Union officials trying to win a pay increase from the employer would probably emphasize the per-hour figure. The same officials would probably use the annual rate in attempting to persuade their members to accept a management offer.

"Pictures," such as graphs and bar charts, can be used in similar fashion to emphasize whatever aspect of a set of figures a source feels will best move a given audience in the direction of his goal. Altering the scale at the left or base of a chart can steepen a curve or flatten it, for example. Both pictures and words are often employed to show relationships between figures, as are percentages, ratios, index numbers, coefficients, and cross-tabulations. Too many figures can confuse; when one tries to relate too many variables to one another, he may not be understood. A series of simpler tables which show relationships in sequence rather than simultaneously may be useful, since success in communications is measured not by the amount of information built into a message, but the amount that a receiver can extract from it.

Language, however, remains the primary symbol system. Too often taken for granted, it needs closer examination by both buyer and seller. Two of its dimensions—vocabulary and syntax—are of great importance; we need to look at words and at the way words are combined into meaningful sentences and sentences into messages.

Vocabulary of Speech

Our senses, we have seen, ordinarily supply an abundance of cues which preserve perceptual constancies in a world where stimuli are constantly changing. A similar quality exists in language and presumably for the same reason—to enable a message to pass from sender to receiver in a very "noisy" environment.

Every child can produce and apparently does produce any sound used in any language anywhere in the world—some experts recognizing 72 separate consonant sounds and 42 classes of vowel sounds.[2] If these were combined into simple consonant-vowel-consonant syllables, every one of us would have a vocabulary of 217,-728 one-syllable words ($72 \times 42 \times 72$). However, many sounds and many syllables "drop out" of the child's repertoire because, not being accepted in his parents' language, they are not rewarded. Of the vast potential number of sounds or *phones* which the throat and mouth can produce and the ear can detect, only a few are allowed to have meaning; these are called *phonemes*. (The most limited language so far discovered has a phonemic vocabulary of 15 meaningful sounds and the most extensive has 85. English has about 40: 14 or 15 vowels and 24 consonants.)[3]

English-speaking adults have a great deal of difficulty recapturing sounds which they could produce as babies but since have lost. They also have great deal of difficulty, as do speakers of any language, in distinguishing between sounds that their language says belong to the same phonemic category. In some languages, but not in English, a long vowel sound, such as the "o" in *toad*, conveys a different meaning from a short vowel, such as the "o" in *tote*. In some languages, the difference between the initial sounds of *keep* and *cool* or *ski* and *school* has denotative significance. Not in English, however; as a result, only speech experts are likely to hear any difference in sound. Hold your hand before your mouth, and you can feel a puff of air when you say *pill*, one that is lacking when you say *spill*. American voices have learned, without our being aware of it, that a stop consonant (p, b, d, t, g, k) is *aspirated* when it begins a word and unaspirated when combined with other consonants—but American ears have learned to ignore this rule. Not so in other languages where this difference in sound represents a difference in meaning.

The sounds and combinations that a language permits do not occur with equal probability. In fact, nine of the 40 sounds accepted by English account for about 50% of our speech, the "i" of *lip* and "n" being most common and the "z" of *pays* and the "oy" of *boy* being used least often.[4] In written English, "e" is more common than "z" and the word *mother* appears more frequently than *pother*. Alternative choices are not equally likely nor independent of one another. If one sees the letter "q" in English, he does not need to ask what letter comes next: he knows that "u" must follow. Thus context guides selection, under noisy circumstances, among sounds and letters and combinations of either. (If one's ear reports "nef" his brain will hear *net,* if the conversation concerns tennis, or *knife,* if he is talking about food.)

The human ear can distinguish some 1600 different *frequencies* in the range of 15,000 to 20,000 cycles per second, but the human voice, which joins to every frequency its multiples or harmonics (so that 125 cycles per second is accompanied by 250, 375, etc.), can produce only about 80 tones. These 80 tones, which are heard as vowels and consonants, represent only one of sound's three dimensions, however. The other two dimensions carry meaning, not of the object a speaker is talking about but concerning the speaker himself.

Differences in *intensity,* or the size of the puffs of air emitted, are interpreted as indicating how distant the source of the sound is. Humans adjust the loudness of their speech to the distance between speaker and listener and adjust this distance, in turn, to two things: the relationship between source and receiver and the subject-matter of their conversation.

Differences in *frequency,* the rate at which puffs of air are emitted, are interpreted as indicating the sex or age of the speaker, since women and children tend to have higher voices than men.

Three additional variations within speech enable an individual to use the same basic vowels and consonants but attach different meanings to them.

Stress distinguishes the noun *per' mit* from the verb *per mit',* and can alter the meaning of a sentence. The following nine-word question will get seven different answers depending on where stress is placed: *WHY did you drive to the movies last night? Why DID you drive to the movies last night? Why did YOU drive to the movies last night? Why did you DRIVE to the movies last night? Why did you drive to the MOVIES last night? Why did you drive to the movies LAST night? Why did you drive to the movies last NIGHT?*

Pitch distinguishes a white house from the White House.

Pauses (technically known as *juncture*) distinguish the command *mark it* from the noun *market.*

There are at least two other symbol systems associated with speech which appear important, *paralanguage* and *kinesics.*[5] Paralanguage includes vocal qualities which reveal something about the source or modify his effectiveness such as a forceful or a hesitant, a rasping or a resonant voice as well as such substitutes for words as a laugh, yawn, or cough. Kinesics or bodily movement includes two categories. One is the *gesture,* produced deliberately as a substitute for words: smile, wink, military salute, pointing finger. The other consists of the *movements,* apparently produced unconsciously, which accompany speech. Americans, at least, appear to move hand, finger, head, or glance *toward* themselves when using pronouns, such as *I* and *us,* which refer to the speaker, and *away* from the body in using pronouns that refer to others. A sweep of hand or foot seems to mark a plural; verbs like *go* and *come* and prepositions like *over* and *under* are accompanied by distinctive bodily movements. Fingers drumming on a desk indicate impatience; a jiggling foot may indicate indifference. Each culture seems to have its own kinesic code, that used in

Italy being particularly expressive. Within a given individual, kinesic differences provide insights of importance to therapist and to actor.

These several sets of symbols associated with speech perform three functions.

By providing multiple cues for any given meaning, they allow communications to occur under very noisy conditions. A source can send the *same* message on several channels so that interference with one or more of them need not prove fatal.

They provide information about the setting and about the persons exchanging messages: who they are, what they want, and what they are talking about (even if their *words* can't be heard).

They enable a source to make very subtle distinctions, by sending *different* messages on his several channels. His tone of voice or his gestures may add to or take away from whatever meaning his words themselves convey. An angry tone can make words that look friendly in print sound sarcastic in speech. A wink, crossed fingers, or a shrug of the shoulders may indicate that a speaker's words are not to be taken at face value.

Speech Versus the Written Word

We have spoken so far as if language were a single symbol system. It is not one system but two: speech and the transcription of speech into writing or print. Because both systems use words, men often act as if they constituted a single system when in fact they do not. Indeed, the combinations of meaningful sounds (*phonemes*) which constitute the meaning-units (*morphemes*) of speech are very different from the *letters* which constitute the meaning-units (*words*) of the written language. Written language is, at best, a partial and clumsy version which attempts, with the aid of punctuation, capital letters, and italics, to mirror the complex dimensions of the former system.

Speech is the more universal of the two systems, in both time and space. It is the first we learn, although very few of us study it formally. Of the two systems it requires less effort; its range of use, both as a means and as an end in itself, is very wide. On the other hand, it lacks the permanence, cheapness, and prestige of print.

Speech, the original mode of teaching, now serves largely ceremonial and entertainment purposes in mass education. (When we are really serious we turn to printed textbooks, journal articles, and written examinations.) In marketing, on the other hand, when we are serious enough about selling to be willing to forego mass methods for a one-to-one relationship between seller and buyer, we send a salesman to talk-and-listen to the customer.

We tend to use different words in writing than we do in speaking, to use a greater variety of words, and to string them together in longer sentences. One reason is that there tends to be less "noise" present when we are writing or reading than when we are talking or listening. As noise increases, our vocabulary becomes more limited; we use fewer words, shorter words, and shorter sentences. The telephone, for example, is a "noisy" communications channel; of the 800 words used most frequently on the telephone, the top 100 are nearly all monosyllables and very few have as many as three syllables.[6] A pilot in a fighter plane, with the distractions of exploding flak, enemy planes, and his own churning viscera, to say nothing of the static on his radio, uses an even more limited vocabulary and repeats a lot of the little he uses. The writer of a television commercial, knowing it must compete with crying babies, slamming refrigerator doors, and churning dishwashers, tends to use similar techniques.

It takes a vocabulary of only 50 words to make up 60% of what we say—and 45% of what we write.[7] Ordinarily we can go only 10 to 15 words without repeating at least one word. This repetition is so common that it has been expressed in a formula, called Zipf's law, which predicts word frequency over a considerable range of content.[8] (This formula says that if the most frequent word in a message occurs 1000 times, the second most common will appear about 500 times, the third 333, the fourth 250, and so on.) In writing, the most common word is likely to be "the"; in a telephone conversation it is usually "I."

Sentences, too, tend to be shorter in speech than in writing. We have to make them short so that the person we are talking to can get a word in edgewise; if we do not, he will break in on us, or leave. Although formal lecturers escape such pressure, they often adopt some of the characteristics of informal conversation if only because a spoken sentence which becomes too long will cause the audience to forget the first half before the last half can be emitted. Verbs are more common in speech than in writing, and adjectives more common in writing than in speech. The ratio between the two has been found in one study to vary from 9 verbs per adjective in drama, to 5 verbs per adjective in legal statutes, 3 verbs in fiction, 1.5 verbs in master's theses, and 1.1 in Ph.D. dissertations.[9]

Individual Differences

Not only do people tend to write differently than they speak, but they differ in the amount of each. Some persons write or read very little; we would expect their speech to show less resemblance to written language than the speech of professional writers and avid readers.

The words a person uses, both spoken and written, tell us a great deal about the place and times he is writing in, as well as about his age, sex, education, and social class. All of these things, in turn, may be important to an audience which is trying to decipher the source's attitudes and intentions toward them.

Both authors and their editors, of course, adjust their vocabularies and the length of their sentences to their intended audiences. *All-Story* magazine, for example, in one study averaged 13 syllables per sentence compared with 34 syllables for the *Review of Reviews*.[10] Formulas have been developed to measure both reading ease or readability and human interest.[11]

The diversity of vocabulary that a source employs can be indexed by the *type-token ratio*, the percentage of different words (types) in a sample of 100 to 1000 words (tokens).[12] Such indices have revealed that mental patients vary their speech less than normal persons and that mental therapy increases the diversity of their speech.

Syntax: Encoding a Complex World

Language is rich enough to describe a vast, complex and steadily expanding universe of knowledge: new labels can be coined for every advance in physics, biology, or psychology.

A good English dictionary may contain a million words, at most, of which most persons recognize only about 50,000 and use far fewer. Men can get along with a limited vocabulary because of the many ways in which words can be combined. Thus it's estimated, conservatively, that the English language could produce 10^{20} 20-word sentences, and that listening to them would take 1000 times the age of the earth itself.[13] Language reduces this vastness to manageable proportions by excluding some combinations of sounds, letters, and words and by varying the probability of others. If a speaker says *chair*, about one listener in five will respond with *table*, about 16% with *sit* or *sitting*, and 13% with *seat*.[14] Similarly, *dog* tends to evoke *cat* and *knife* to evoke *fork*. Such expectancies are useful in marketing, since they help us to determine product images and to select trade names, a good brand name being one that evokes favorable associations.

The more words one strings together, up to about 32, the easier it becomes to supply one that is missing or garbled.[15] Previous experience explains why we'd have no trouble filling in these blanks: *"Now is the time for all good _____ to come to the aid of their party"* and *"_____'s taste good, like a cigarette should."*

In the sentence, *A whale eats sardines*, the order of words tells us who does the eating, but the "s" on the verb also indicates that the eater is the singular and not the plural noun. In the sentence, *Most men have whiskers*, there are no less than three cues to a plural subject: the word *most*, the use of *men* rather than *man*, and the use of *have* rather than *has*. Multiple cues help overcome noise; errors in using them also suggest something about the user.

But why is there meaning in a sentence like *The nasty little pup next door yarped all night long?* Experience with both words and things next door that are active in the nighttime again may help, to the point that we hear the verb as *barked* or misread it as *yapped*. But how did we know *yarped* was a verb? And what enables us to say that *Is the sif porled* is a question or to guess that *Porl the spif* must be a command? The special kind of context we call *syntax*, the meaning that comes from the way words are combined into sentences, provides an answer.*

If language distinguishes men from

---

* To obtain a label free from any implication of "ought" or "correct" the more common term *grammar* gives way to *syntax*. Linguists also prefer *lexicon* to the more familiar term *vocabulary*. We'll go along with them halfway.

beasts, it must be its syntax that does it, for animals have vocabularies and can communicate with them. Crows have distress calls, that appear to vary from one region or country to another, and bees can report to their fellows how far they must go and in what direction to find food. The dolphin not only has "words" in its own language but can reproduce human nonsense syllables in recognizable fashion, if suitably rewarded for the effort.

English syntax employs two cues: word order and auxiliary words (am, have, will) or syllables (-ed, -s) to suggest tense (present, past, future, etc.), number (singular, plural) and other important variables.

Seller Use of Symbols

Syntax, like vocabulary, provides many "surplus" cues that enable messages to be received despite interference, furnish information about the source himself and the time and place of message transfer, and permit subtle distinctions to be made.

There are, after all, a limited number of basic emotions that advertising can appeal to, and only 20 sensory dimensions that products can stimulate pleasurably. If syntax and vocabulary were not complex, what would the seller do who wants to suggest that his brand should be bought because it's cheaper? Six ads, perhaps, and he'd have to start repeating himself.

The seller must, of course, begin with a product feature that can be plausibly linked to a consumer benefit, one that he hopes no rival can claim. This feature may be air, whipped into a soap to make it float, so that a bather does not have to grope around on the bottom of the tub when the soap slips out of his hand. It may be a decay-preventing toothpaste ingredient which has the endorsement of the nation's dentists. It may be the fact, exploited by Volkswagen, that one year's model cannot be distinguished from another's, or the fact, exploited by other auto manufacturers, that each year's model can be.

Having found such a feature, the communicator seeks symbols to convey his meaning to a receiver, using these symbols in a trademark, slogan, brand name, or advertising campaign. To catch an audience's attention, to be believed, and to be remembered, the communicator must express the same idea in different ways, both to avoid boring audiences and to suit different audiences and different media.

Content Analysis

Readability formulas are one example of *content analysis*, a research tool needed by a copywriter, a student of history or public opinion, an analyst of answers to open-end survey questions, and a scholar watching a committee make decisions.[16] Content analysis is used to study both causes and results—to devise messages and study responses to them. It is used to find what makes advertising copy effective, how much violence there is on TV, and in analyzing psychiatric interviews. It is also used when interviewers can't get access to respondents, because they are too rich, too dead, or too distant, but do have samples of their verbal output. The systematic sampling, classifying, and counting techniques of content analysis also are needed when the volume of material to be studied is so large that one has to employ assistants, study only a sample of it, or do both. (An example in point is the study that examined 19,553 editorials appearing in the "prestige" newspapers of five nations from 1890 to 1949, looking for 416 key geographical and ideological terms!)[17]

In 1961, Daniel Starch and Associates reviewed readership scores for 45,000 advertisements obtained from 400,000 interviews over a 16-year period, in an attempt to compare "good" ads with "bad" ones and find out what causes the difference.[18] In 1969 adman Rosser Reeves began using Starch data to select and reprint the 400 "best" ads of the previous years—that is, those with the highest readership scores in their product categories.[19] The 1961 figures and the 1968 reprints contain valuable clues to the million-dollar question, *What makes a good ad?* To find those clues via content analysis one must make these decisions.

Population. The content-population must be specified. Is it to be ads just in *Life* and *Saturday Evening Post,* as in the 1961 Starch study, in all magazines surveyed by Starch, or in all consumer magazines of 100,000 circulation or over?

Sampling. Within the constraints of time, money, and trained manpower, should one study all 45,000 ads or try to do a more detailed job on a few of them? Should the number of ads selected be proportional to the circulation of the magazines? (Yes, if one wants to draw conclusions about ads in general; no, if one wants to contrast the effects of content characteristics in high- and low-circulation magazines.) Once one has decided which publications to study, how does he decide which *issues* to examine? (The daily newspaper is fat with grocery ads on Thursdays, thin on Saturdays; *New Yorker* magazine is ad-fat during the pre-Christmas weeks of November, slim in January. Are samples to be equal or proportionate samples in fat and lean periods?) Within each issue, is one going to look at all ads, full-page ads, ads in color, or the ads for only certain products? Often the scholar stratifies on hypothesized causes and makes random selections within strata. (He may select a "composite week," drawing separate newspaper samples for each weekday. Fine for some purposes, this sampling method would wreck a study that wanted to examine the day-to-day sequence of effects in either news or advertising columns.) In observing human behavior, as behind a one-way screen in a nursery school or a mirror-window in a small-group laboratory simulating executive decision making, observers may be instructed to record activities at 30-second intervals and only segments of a taped record may be analyzed. (A whole book has been written, for example, on the words and paralanguage exchanged by psychiatrist and patient in the first five minutes of one single session.)[20]

Coding rules: These, again, depend both on the type of material to be analyzed and the kind of conclusions one seeks.

1. Categories must be chosen that are relevant to the cause-effect relationship being studied. The analyst may be concerned with *how* or *what:* with syntax, rhetoric, and style or with substance. The *what* may include values and goals, methods used to attain the goals, persons acting and their personalities, time and place of the action, target audience and the sources, and intensity and outcome of conflict. The set of categories devised must allow every item to be put into one and only one category.

2. Three types of units must be specified. The *recording unit* is the unit put into a category; word, simple sentence, person (real or imaginary), "item" (speech, book, advertisement, magazine article, or TV program), arbitrary unit of time (10 seconds, 5 minutes) or space (column inches of copy, square inches of illustration). The *unit-to-be-counted* may be identical to the recording unit or it may not. In a study of soap operas, roles were recorded in terms of occupation, but in any scene each occupation was tallied only once, regardless of how many persons in that occupation appeared in the scene. The *context unit* specifies how much of a message must be studied before a recording unit can be classified.

Suppose a scholar decides to *count* the pro- and antiadvertising statements in an issue of *Advertising Age.* How is he to *record* the sentence, *Advertising is the most powerful influence on men's behavior in the world today?* If uttered by the head of the J. Walter Thompson agency at a meeting of the Association of National Advertisers presumably it will be classed as *proadvertising* (as well as self-serving). The same sentence is likely to be classed as *anti*advertising if delivered by author Vance Packard to the Consumers Union in a talk entitled "The Huckster Menace." Author, audience, title, and the sentences that precede and follow it all may be part of the *context* necessary to code this sentence as to direction. Choice of units may affect results: a study of editorials found that the *direction* of bias remained unchanged but its *amount* increased as the size of recording and context units increased. The reason: neutral units vanished.

Coding. Content analysis seeks to substitute for the wide variations of individual judgments and endless arguments as to whose judgment is "correct," categories so clear-cut that all will agree on what items go into them. One way to do this is to screen and train coders. A better way is to refine categories: to avoid making them too small since fine distinctions are hard to make and coders are likely to disagree, and to simplify the decisions coders have to make by offering them only two alternatives at a time. Students would find it difficult to classify news items in *Marketing/Communications* as involving trade publications, want ads, TV commercials, foreign publications, and retail advertising in newspapers, unless these five categories were presented as a series of two-valued choices.

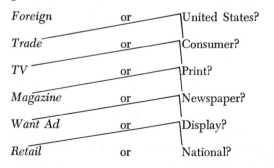

Foreign	or	United States?
Trade	or	Consumer?
TV	or	Print?
Magazine	or	Newspaper?
Want Ad	or	Display?
Retail	or	National?

Note that only the *underlined* kinds of news items on the left need be counted and that any type of news item which has to be counted doesn't have to be subdivided. This system works: its originator found that it boosted interjudge agreement from the 61% obtained with multiple-category judgments to 90%.[21]

What Makes Such Efforts Worthwhile?

As in any survey, content analysis may have trouble distinguishing cause from effect: does a given message represent what its source wants his audience to believe or reflect his opinion of what they want to be told? Movies and TV programs, we assume, are designed to entertain rather than to influence and therefore are likely to reflect (someone's view of) what the audience wants to hear. Grade school textbooks, we would guess, represent what society feels children ought to believe. Source intent thus should be clearest in a content analysis of textbooks, and audience attitudes (as perceived by the source) clearest in analyses of movies. Advertisements probably represent a mixture of the two.

Content analysis may reveal aspects of a message that are missed by the casual reader and are unsuspected by its author. A trained psychologist, for example, failed to discover three themes that content analysis revealed in Richard Wright's autobiography, *Black Boy:* personal safety, lack of interest in social goals, and lack of identification with other Negroes.[22] Here are three examples of content analysis detective work, drawn from three different levels of linguistic analysis—sounds, words, and sentences.

In the first, tape recordings were taken in New York City of members of the upper and lower middle classes and the working class.[23] Four speech situations were recorded: the pronunciation of isolated words, reading of a text, the careful speech of an interview, and the casual speech used

in talking about an emotionally tinged occurrence. The study found New Yorkers using three forms of the "th" sound in *thin, thing,* and *think:* a voiceless fricative called the prestige form; a stop consonant, as in *tin, ting,* and *tinker;* and a mixture of the two. It counted the number of deviations from the prestige form, scoring them on a scale from 0, representing no deviations, to 200, representing no prestige forms at all.

Here are typical results.

Isolated Words	Reading of Text	Responses in Interview	Relating Incident
A. 25	35	75	105
B. 0	5	20	35
C. 0	0	15	19

A. Italian-descent laborer
B. White-collar worker
C. College-graduate professional

Education and other social-class characteristics tended to eliminate the low-prestige sound, but informal and stressful circumstances tended to encourage its reappearance.

The second study looked at *bias* of the media vehicle, which was 10 issues of *Time* during the Truman, Eisenhower, and Kennedy administrations.[24] Summary figures showed that *Time's* picture of Truman was almost totally negative, that of Eisenhower unrelievedly positive, and that of Kennedy somewhere in between.

	Nature of Bias	
	Positive	Negative
Truman	1	92
Kennedy	31	14
Eisenhower	81	1

Five different types of bias were identified and counted.

1. *Attribution.* Truman *snapped,* Eisenhower *smiled.* (The neutral term *said* was not counted in the study.)
2. *Adjectives.* Truman's *flat* voice, Eisenhower's *serene* state of mind.
3. *Adverbs.* Truman barked *sarcastically,* Eisenhower chatted *amiably.*
4. *Outright opinions. The nation read of Truman's reply and fumed* vs. *The strong leadership of President Eisenhower undoubtedly retrieved much of the United States prestige and influence recently lost in Asia.* (Time does not hesitate to project its own editorial feelings onto whole nations and continents.)
5. *Photographs.* Bias here consisted both of the picture itself—dignified or not, calm or nervous—and captions.

Although much journalistic bias consists of prejudicial selection of detail, in this study biased words were used for similar behavior: Eisenhower was *calm and confident,* Truman "*cocky*"; *frankness was the rule* with Eisenhower, but Truman *probed with a blunt finger;* Truman was caught *grinning slyly* but Eisenhower had *a happy grin.* (In contrast to both, Kennedy merely *said, announced, recommended,* and *promised.*)

The third example compares the writing styles of two authors who lived as friends and neighbors in the same small town in Massachusetts, attended the same university, held almost identical opinions, and wrote on the same topics.[25] One was Emerson, whose abstract style of writing appears to have reflected his retiring nature, and Thoreau, whose vivid and concrete style matched the vigor of a man who didn't fear the solitude of a cabin in the woods or a jail cell in town. Thoreau wrote with

the blunt vigor found in good advertising, Emerson in the style of an academic dissertation, whatever the topic.

Both men admired nature.

Emerson. To the body and mind which have been cramped by noxious work or company, nature is medicinal and restores their tone.

Thoreau. We need the tonic of wildness . . . the seacoast with its wrecks, the wilderness with its living and its decaying trees.

Both men deplored the execution of John Brown, following his slave-freeing raid at Harper's Ferry.

Emerson. Nothing can resist the sympathy which all elevated minds must feel with Brown. . . . It is the *reductio ad absurdum* of Slavery when the governor of Virginia is forced to hang a man whom he declares to be a man of the most integrity, truthfulness and courage he has ever met.

Thoreau. Whose safety requires that Captain Brown be hung? . . . If you do not wish it, say so distinctly. . . . A man sent to be the redeemer of those in captivity, and the only use to which you can put him is to hang him at the end of a rope!

Authors of this study note that Thoreau makes greater use of the first-person, of negatives, and of concrete rather than abstract nouns: he seems to regard the reader as an opponent to be argued with. Emerson, in contrast, seems to assume that other men are as enlightened as himself.

Thought, Talk, and Action

1. List your current instructors. Opposite each name note down at least one characteristic gesture and one characteristic phrase. Cut the lists apart and give them to fellow students. See if they can identify the instructors from gesture and phrase, and whether they tend to characterize the instructors in the same way.
2. From a magazine such as *Life* or *Time*, take the first five ads. Note how many square inches of each are devoted to copy and how many to illustration. Is the purpose of illustrations to create an emotion or to present facts? How many separate facts can you identify in the copy? Do your findings appear to differ in terms of the *product* being advertised? (As a check on this, look through the magazine until you find an ad for a similar product and compare content.)
3. Keeping subject matter the same insofar as possible, select passages from widely varying sources such as *True Story* magazine and *Atlantic Monthly*, a radio newscast and the *New York Times*, a criminology textbook and a tabloid crime story. Now begin reading each to a friend, asking him to guess the source as soon as he feels he can. How many words before he (a) was willing to make a guess, (b) was correct? Was the decisive cue vocabulary or syntax?

Notes

Chapter 21

1. Pierre Martineau, Motivation in advertising (New York: McGraw-Hill Book Co., 1957).
2. George A. Miller, Language and communication (New York: McGraw-Hill Book Co., 1951), pp. 19–20.
3. Jerome Kagan and Ernest Havemann, Psychology: An introduction (New York: Harcourt, Brace & World, 1968), p. 198.
4. David Krech et al., Elements of psychology, 2nd ed. (New York: Alfred A. Knopf, 1969), pp. 366–8.
5. Ray L. Birdwhistell, Kinesics and context (Philadelphia: University of Pennsylvania Press, 1970).
6. Reference No. 2, p. 89.
7. *Ibid.*, p. 89.
8. *Ibid.*, p. 91.
9. D. P. Boder, "The adjective-verb quotient: A contribution to the psychology of language," Psychological Record, 3:309–43.
10. Reference No. 2, p. 125.
11. Rudolf Flesch, "A new readability yardstick," Journal of Applied Psychology, 32:221–33.
12. J. W. Chotlos, "Studies in language behavior: IV, a statistical and comparative analysis of individual written language samples," Psychological Monographs, 56:75–111.
13. George A. Miller, "Some preliminaries to psycholinguistics," American Psychologist, 20:15–20.
14. G. H. Kent and A. J. Rosanoff, "A study of association in insanity," American Journal of Insanity, 67:37–96, 317–90.

15. N. G. Burton and J. C. R. Licklider, "Long-range constraints in the statistical structure of printed English," American Journal of Psychology, 68:650–3.
16. A convenient summary of content analysis is: Ole R. Holsti, "Content analysis," in Gardner Lindzey and Elliot Aronson, editors, The Handbook of Social Psychology, 2nd ed. (Reading, Mass.: Addison-Wesley Publishing Co., 1968), Vol. II, pp. 596–692.
17. Harold D. Lasswell et al., The comparative study of symbols (Stanford, Calif.: Stanford University Press, 1952).
18. Daniel Starch and Staff, Measuring product sales made by advertising (Mamaroneck, N.Y.: Starch, 1961).
19. Rosser Reeves, 400 Best Read Ads of 1968 (Mamaroneck, N.Y.: Starch and Associates, 1969).
20. R. E. Pittenger et al., The first five minutes: A sample of microscopic interview analysis (Ithaca, N.Y.: Martineau, 1960).
21. W. C. Schutz, "On categorizing qualitative data in content analysis," Public Opinion Quarterly, 22:503–15.
22. George A. Miller, "Psycholinguistics," in Gardner Lindzey, editor, Handbook of social psychology (Cambridge, Mass.: Addison-Wesley Publishing Co., 1954), Vol. II, p. 602.
23. Ibid., p. 768.
24. J. C. Merrill, "How Time stereotyped three U.S. presidents," Journalism Quarterly, 42:563–70.
25. Reference No. 22, pp. 764–6.

The Sounds of Speech

Language is limited to what the ear can hear and what the throat, mouth, and nose can produce. Perhaps because speech seems to be an afterthought, using bodily equipment originally designed for eating and breathing, the limits that articulation place on language seem more stringent than those resulting from audition.

Formation of vowels and consonants begins in the throat; if the vocal cords are open, the sounds produced are *voiceless;* if the cords are set vibrating as air presses through they are *voiced.*

Alterations in the shape of the oral cavity give the 15 vowels which English accepts (out of a possible 42). These alterations eliminate some frequencies in the complex tones and cause others to "echo" or resonate, making a distinction between *bit, bat,* and *bite.*

The tongue and lips produce the 24 English consonants (out of a possible 72), by altering which movable parts approach one another and how they let the stream of air through.

The two lips produce a voiced "b" and a voiceless "p."

Lower lip and upper teeth produce a voiced "v" and voiceless "f."

Tip of tongue touching gum just behind upper teeth produces a voiced "d" and voiceless "t."

Back of tongue touching soft palate produces "g" and "k."

Now for how the air is permitted to pass through.

Sudden release produces *stops* or explosive sounds like "b," "p," "d," "t," "g," and "k."

Thin stream of air produces *fricatives* like "v," "f," and the two different "th" sounds in *the* and *thin.*

Air jetting against a surface produces *sibilants* like "z" and "s."

Air forced through the nose produces *nasals* like "m," "n," and the final "ng" sound of *sing.*

The 15 vowels and 24 consonants that the English language accepts cannot be put together at random. Certain combinations are found in real words; other combinations (a potential source of new brand names) are permitted; still other combinations are unlawful.

An English word may begin with any single consonant, for example, except the final sound of *sung* and the middle sound of *azure.* If two consonants are used at the beginning, the second is usually "r," "l," "w," or "y." Groups of three consonants are rare and all must begin with an "s." What consonants may begin a word? See list at bottom of page.

Note that these combinations are *not* permitted by these rules: *vrew, tland, fwog, wule, sbap, shpoon, spkay, skbob.* If a source utters them, his receiver is very likely to distort them to fit the rules:

vrew may be heard as *threw,* if the context permits, and *fwog* as *frog.*

(Some languages are more liberal than English: Serbo-Croatian permits about three times as many consonant combinations to begin a word. Other languages are more limited; Polynesian languages allow no combinations at all.)

Similar rules for clusters of consonants at the *ends* of words exist: there are more such combinations but they are different from those which may begin a word. Clusters *inside* an English word are drawn from initial or final combinations or a mixture of the two.

Some sounds resemble one another so closely that they are often confused; "b" and "p," for example, are both *stops* produced by the *two lips;* only the voiced-voiceless difference distinguishes them. (Persons speaking a language which ignores the voiced-voiceless distinction have a hard time hearing or producing an English "b" and "p"; to them *pat* and *bat* sound the same.) On the other hand "d" is very different from "f," which is voiceless, a *fricative* rather than a *stop,* and produced by two lips rather than tongue-tip-to-gums. This three-dimensional figure pictures this relationship among these three qualities. The top of the cube represents *voiced* (vibrating vocal cords) and the bottom *voiceless* sounds; the front those formed with lips and the back those formed with tongue-tip-to-gums; the left face the *stops* and the right face the *fricatives.*

		Possible	Actual
(a)	All except ɓ , z	loo	do
(b)	These plus r: b, d, f, g, k, p, š, t, θ	frew	brew
(c)	These plus l: b, f, g, k, p, s	fland	bland
(d)	These plus w: d, g, h, k, s, t (p, θ, b, š)	dwill	dwarf
(e)	These plus yw: b, f, g, h, k, m, p, v, θ (d, l, n, r, s, t)	bule	few
(f)	s plus these: k, m, n, p, t, w (θ, v)	smig	skill
(g)	š plus these: l, m, n	shloo	shmoo
(h)	sp plus these: r, l, y	splob	spring
(i)	sk plus these: r, l, w, y	sklit	scram
(j)	str	strab	string

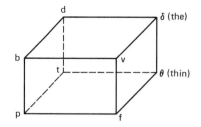

Other languages, of course, permit sounds that English forbids—as well as forbidding sounds that English permits. Rounded lips produce the "u" of a French *lieu;* trills and nasals are also examples.

Some changes in sound cause an arbitrary change in meaning. There is no relationship, for example, between the words *risk* and *brisk* or between *brisk, brick,* and *frisk.* Their similarity in sound is arbitrary. This is not true of other changes: both *risky* and *risked* bear a definite relationship to *risk.*

All major parts of speech in English, except adverbs, can be switched around by appropriate additions. Nouns change to adjectives (*risk* to *risk-y, norm* to *norm-al, boy* to *boy-ish*) and adjectives to nouns (*risky* to *riski-ness, normal* to *normal-ity*). Similarly, verbs can become nouns (*depart-ure, sell-er*) and nouns can become verbs (*saliva-te* and *beauti-fy*). (Businessmen in general and advertising men in particular are notorious for such coinages as *final-ize,* to the horror of more conventional users of the language.) Such changes are called *derivational.*

Another type of change is called *inflectional.* Such changes convey these types of meanings.

Possession: Sears Roebuck's advertisement.

Plurals: Three advertisements.

Past tense: Sears purchased three full pages.

Comparisons: I was happy with my purchase; my wife was even happier and the salesman was happiest of all.

In print, "s" is used to create a plural and "d" to indicate the past tense but each of these letters actually stands for three different *sounds.* In each instance a voiceless consonant follows a voiceless one, as in *cats* and *walked,* and voiced consonant follows voiced consonant, as in *dogs* and *bribed* or a vowel as in *prayed.* If the word ends in the same kind of consonant as that used to make a plural noun or past-tense verb, one first adds a "neutral" vowel, like the "uh" sound of *the* and then the voiced consonant, as in *horses* and *batted.*

When "rules" like these are violated, the violation itself adds a dimension of meaning to what has been said. The man who says "shpeak" is likely to be perceived as drunken or German or both, as is the man who puts the plural "ssss" ending of *cats* on the word *dog* or the "z" ending of *dogs* on the word *cat.* The "surplus" meaning is used to provide information about the source of the message.

Source. Adapted from Roger Brown, *Social Psychology* (New York: The Free Press, 1965).

Words

Words differ in the extent to which they identify a category or express a value for it. Identification implies widespread agreement on the category, and is achieved by words that denote or point to, particularly the labels for physical objects. Value suggests a difference of opinion, expressed by words that connote, whose referents tend to be social, rather than physical reality. (Most of us agree on the attributes of such physical realities as death, and agree that it is likely to follow a ten-story fall to a paved street. We are less likely to agree that winning a majority vote makes a candidate the "best" man for the job.)

Connotative words tend to express the values of the user; they do not necessarily cause the receiver to accept those values.

Perhaps the most thorough study ever made of connotative words and their meanings is that of Charles Osgood, whose semantic differential technique presents a series of concepts, followed by pairs of adjectives of opposite meaning. Respondents make one check between each pair of adjectives, to indicate what the concept means to them.

vary with the concepts studied. Relationship among scales varies with concept: a soft pillow may be good, a soft banana bad. (We like our enemies to be weak and inactive and our friends to be strong and vigorous; the "good" qualities in an enemy are "bad" qualities in a friend!)

Source. Charles E. Osgood, George J. Suci, and Percy H. Tannenbaum, *The Measurement of Meaning* (Urbana, Ill.: University of Illinois Press, 1957).

These ratings indicate that the respondent feels *mother* is very good, somewhat soft, but neither active nor passive.

In a typical Osgood experiment, 18 students in an advertising class in copywriting sorted 289 sets of polar adjectives, drawn from a thesaurus, into 17 categories, on the basis of their similarity (pages 48–9). The 76 scales finally selected were then used by 100 other college students to rate 20 concepts, equally divided among nouns labeling persons, physical objects, such abstract concepts as modern art and sin, events like birth, and institutions such as the United Nations. Factor analysis followed.

A series of such studies showed that a strong *evaluating* factor (represented by good-bad in the scale above) accounts for 50 to 75% of variance in individual ratings (pages 72–4). Second in importance is a *potency* factor (represented by hard-soft), which explains about half as much variance as the first factor. Third is an *activity* factor, about equal to potency in explanatory ability. Additional factors—stability, novelty, aggressiveness, and so on—

Types of Sentences

Sentences, as well as words, differ in the extent to which they point to a category or attach a value to it, and in the extent to which men find it easy or difficult to agree on their meanings.

Judgments, such as *Too much money is spent on advertising in the United States,* tell a good deal about the speaker. We can agree or disagree with the beliefs expressed in them, but we cannot say that the beliefs are either true or false. *Reports,* on the other hand, can be verified. *An average of 3% of national income was spent on advertising during the 20 years preceding World War II* is a statement whose truth or falsity can be determined.

The difference is one of degree, however. There can be a great deal of disagreement on how to define *national income* and *advertising expenditures* in testing the *report* just made. It may be fairly easy, on the other hand, in any specific audience, to reach agreement that the proposition *if 3% of national income is spent on advertising, that is too much* is either acceptable or unacceptable.

Two kinds of reports are particularly hard to verify: predictions and statements of an association between facts. To verify predictions, such as, *Advertising costs will double in the next decade,* we must wait until the facts are available. Verifying a statement of cause and effect relationships is even more difficult. *Advertising expenditures are rising because of increasing competition* is an example. We must define what we mean by advertising expenditures and competition; determine whether each is, in fact, increasing; determine whether the two increases are causally related; and finally, specify in which direction causation operates.

Judgmental statements, like connotative words, are perceived as expressing the values of the user and revealing his goals. This revelation itself may cause a receiver to reject the source's messages whereas he might accept statements that appear to report (on the grounds that their falsity is so easy to determine that no source would dare report what was not true). A receiver may accept statements of causation because he finds it difficult to determine whether they are true or not (or to provide any alternative explanation). Predictions may, like reports, be accepted because they appear easy to check in the future; a source may use them loosely, however, because he is sure that very few people will remember them or bother to check on their truthfulness. In short, we place different degrees of credibility on these sentence types and apply different discount ratios to them.

Source. Derived from David K. Berlo, *The Process of Communication* (New York: Holt, Rinehart and Winston, 1960), pp. 217–77.

Syntax

Students of syntax try to avoid circularity in explanation by developing rules in which one can determine meaning from syntax without having first to determine syntax by meaning. This means that they must find equivalents to what the rest of us call nouns and verbs by classifying words by their *position* in a sentence—not by their meaning. When they do this they come up with five different types.

Class I. Any word that will fit into the following blank: (The) _____ is/are good. (Usually these are nouns.)

Class II. Any word that would follow a Class I word and, in turn, be followed by another Class I word, such as *good* or *here.* (Ordinarily these would be verbs, placing the word in a category, positioning it in space, or attaching a value to it.) The adman _____ clever.
$$\text{Class II}$$
Class III. Any word which can fill *both* blanks in the phrase: (The) _____
$$\text{clever}$$
(Class I word) is/was _____. (As the
$$\text{clever}$$
subscripts indicate, these words tend to be adjectives.)

Class IV. Any word which can fill this blank: "(Class I word) went _____." (Here one uses such adverbs of manner as *slowly* or of position as *there.*)

Class V. Includes about 150 *function* words—such as *not, very, what, of, an*—which make up about a third of our speech and have little meaning in themselves.

English word order alone may show how words are related: *Son hits father* conveys a different meaning than *father hits son.* But given two words, each of which can be either a noun (Class I) or verb (Class II), order alone will not always convey meaning clearly. The ambiguity of *ship sails* then must be resolved by the function word *the* into a simple statement, *The ship sails,* or an order, *Ship the sails.* This ambiguity can also be resolved by an ending—called a morpheme because it conveys meaning although it is not a word—which indicates which word is the verb. *-ed* represents such an ending: *shipped sails* is not the same event as *ship sailed.* (The ending *-s* is not helpful here since it may indicate either a plural of the noun or the present tense of the verb.)

Phonemes and Morphemes

A *phoneme* is a sound that, although itself without meaning, can change the meaning of a word; in English, "b" and "p" are phonemes. *Bail* and *pail* have very different meanings, and there is no way to predict what effect on meaning a change in the initial sound will have.

A *morpheme,* on the other hand, is a sound that does have meaning of its own. It comes in two varieties, those that can stand alone as *free* and independent words, and those that cannot, being *bound.* Here, reading vertically, is a sentence, one word to a line, with the morphemes in it separated by diagonal lines and labeled.

phrase, *The housewife's bags*), a verb (*included*), and an object (the noun phrase, *the finest tripe*).

This order of S (subject), verb (V), and object (O), or SVO, although customary in English, is one of six theoretically possible orders. However, a study of 30 languages, ranging from Basque to Berber and from Hindi and Maori to Maya, has revealed that only three of these orders actually appear in declarative sentences: SVO, SOV, and VSO. (*None* of the languages puts object before subject.) All of the six VS languages studied put adjectives after the noun, instead of the usual English order. Six of the 11 SOV languages let the adjective precede the noun, and five make it follow.

In speech, the slight pause which separates the three parts of a sentence, the S, V, and O, cues meaning for sentences which, in print, are highly ambiguous. In the sentence, *They are winning boats,* a slight pause between *are* and *winning* suggests that the speaker is pointing to boats crossing a finish line, and that *winning* is an

The	Article
house/wife/'s	Two free morphemes and the bound morpheme indicating possession.
bag/s	A free morpheme and the bound morpheme indicating a plural.
in/clude/d	Two bound morphemes plus the bound morpheme indicating past tense.
the	Another article.
fin/est	A free morpheme plus the bound morpheme indicating the superlative degree.
tripe	A free morpheme.

Source. Based on George A. Miller, "Psycholinguistics," in Gardner Lindzey, ed., *Handbook of Social Psychology* (Cambridge, Mass.: Addison-Wesley Publishing Co., Inc., 1954) 2:698–9.

The words in this sentence can be combined into three major constituents of a sentence; a subject (the noun

adjective, part of a noun phrase making up O. If pauses precede *are* and follow *winning,* setting them apart as a compound verb, it becomes apparent that *they* refers to the beneficiaries in a raffle—a very different meaning. On paper, these two meanings can be pictured by tree diagrams used in *phrase-structure* grammar. (Page 418.)

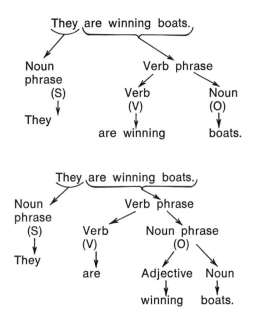

Source. Gardner Lindzey and Elliot Aronson, editors, *The Handbook of Social Psychology* (Reading, Mass.: Addison-Wesley Publishing Co., 1968, 2nd ed.), Vol. III, pp. 743–7 and 672–5.

Modifiers

Each of these three major parts of the sentences, S, V, and O, can be expanded at great length, provided certain rules are followed. One can use 12 different kinds of modifiers for an English noun, for example, if they are attached in this order.

The (particle) *retailer's* (possessive) *last* (ordinal number) *six* (cardinal number) *rare* (characteristic) *large* (size) *fat* (shape) *hot* (temperature) *old* (age) *brown* (color) *Chinese* (origin) *fortune* (noun) *cookies*. . . .

One still has to add a verb phrase (*will have been baking*) and perhaps a noun phrase as well to get a complete sentence!

Fortunately, the dimensions of speech are sufficient to convey meaning even where print sometimes fails. With the proper stresses, even such a horrendous sentence as the following, where *had* shifts from noun (label for a word) to verb and auxiliary verb, can make sense.

Mary, where Jane had had HAD, had HAD had; HAD had had HAD the teacher's approval.

Source. Roger Brown, *Social Psychology* (New York: The Free Press, 1965), pp. 282 and 256.

Deeper Structures

Linguists distinguish between the surface ambiguities, which arise in both writing and speech as we send and receive messages, and a deeper structure of meaning. They suggest that the gap between meanings and messages is bridged by a series of rules, learned without awareness at an early age, so that an infinite number of sentences can be generated from minimal storage in the brain, particularly the short-term storage we employ in extracting meaning from a sentence as it is being spoken.

The distinction between underlying meaning and surface appearance is necessary because sometimes not even a pause or punctuation can indicate which meaning is intended; only rephrasing of a sentence can end the ambiguity. For example, *The shooting of the civilians was inexcusable* could be intended (or interpreted) as criticism of marksmanship or of choice of target. In other instances, very different sentence structures may convey the same meaning.

Possessive. The copywriter's creativity is exceptional.

Preposition. The creativity of the copywriter is exceptional.

Clause. The creativity that the copywriter possesses is exceptional.

Now suppose we want to indicate that the copywriter belongs to our agency. As qualifications pile up we give these names* to our three choices.

Left-branching. The agency's copywriter's creativity is exceptional.

Right-branching. The creativity of the copywriter of the agency is exceptional.

Self-embedded. The creativity that the copywriter that the agency employs possesses is exceptional.

The self-embedded version has become gibberish and the left-branching version is awkward; right-branching sentences are preferred in English and other Indo-European languages.

---

* These names indicate where the parentheses pile up as in this right-branching example: (*The creativity (of the copywriter (of this agency)))* is exceptional. The left-branching version is: (((*The agency's) copywriter's) creativity) is exceptional.*

Source. George A. Miller and David McNeill, "Psycholinguistics" in Gardner Lindzey and Elliot Aronson, editors, *The Handbook of Social Psychology* (Reading, Mass.: Addison-Wesley Publishing Co., 1968, 2nd ed.), Vol. III.

Print: Little Knowledge of Source

Handwriting provides a great many clues to its author's age, sex, education, and even, if analyzed by an expert, to his personality and state of health. Print tells little or nothing about the source but can contribute a good deal to the effect of a message, by overcoming noise and adding connotative dimensions to the message. Type itself has three dimensions.

Size. Within limits, as size increases, so do attention-getting power and legibility. (One gains these advantages at the cost of fitting fewer words into a given space.)

Family. Some type families, whether by use or intrinsic qualities, are interpreted as being masculine, others as feminine. Subtle differences affect legibility and attention-getting power, and suggest connotations suitable to product, medium, or target audience.

Face. Italic, bold, and condensed faces are easier for the layman to distinguish than other type families. Each may provide emphasis; used in quantity, italics tend to suggest feminine qualities.

Still other factors affect responses to a message. *Layout,* involving proportion of white space and arrangement of pictorial and typographical elements on the page, affects attention, legibility, and connotation. A basic problem in all of these dimensions is whether current uses are merely conventions, whose violation may attract attention, or reflect something intrinsic in print itself.

Experts often make finer distinctions in these dimensions than laymen are able to articulate.

Three different audiences were asked to rate alphabets set in 16 different kinds of type on 25 semantic differential scales. Each audience included 25 persons: the expert audience consisted of editors and teachers of typography; a lay audience, of university students; and an intermediate audience, of students who had taken a one-semester course in typography.

The type included 2 "cases" (capital letters and lowercase letters); 2 "inclinations" (italics and regular); and

4 type families (Bodoni, Garamond, Spartan, and Kabel): 16 combinations in all.

Factor analysis showed that 5 factors accounted for at least 60% of the variance in all 3 audiences—the importance of factors varying from one audience to the next.

Both activity and potency scales explained more lay reactions than evaluation; ratings on these scales were more simply determined than the evaluative ratings. Experts were inclined to extreme, favorable judgments; laymen showed least unanimity. Importance of type variables varied with factor.

Percentage of Total Variance Explained by Each Factor

Factors	Experts	Students	Laymen
Evaluation ("pleasant, good, beautiful")	24	17	11
Potency ("rugged, masculine")	15	20	15
Activity ("fast, young")	9	13	21
Complexity ("fancy, complex")	16	14	7
Physical aspects ("large, angular")	6	6	5
Total variance	70	70	59

The best way to indicate strength in a message would be to use regular, Kabel capitals, and the best way to indicate activity would be to use Spartan italics. Evaluative ratings were more complex; meanings of both case and inclination varied with family of type and type of audience.

Source. Percy H. Tannenbaum, Harvey K. Jacobson, and Eleanor L. Norris, "An experimental investigation of typeface connotations," *Journalism Quarterly,* 41:1:65–73.

Pictures: The Search for a Vocabulary

Pictures are so complex that men have searched for a basic vocabulary. Here is one attempt to work with five kinds of eyebrows, four kinds of eyes, three shapes of the mouth!

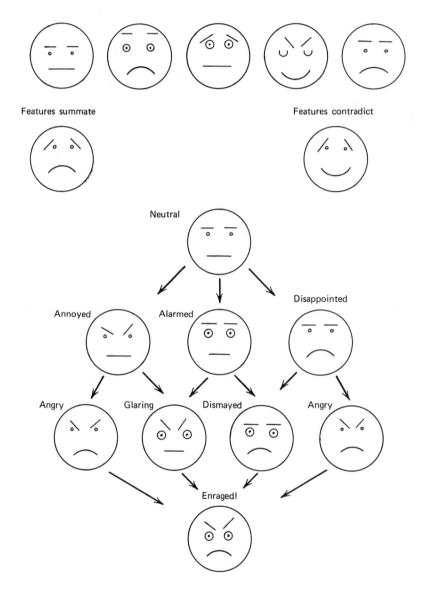

Features summate

Features contradict

Neutral

Annoyed   Alarmed

Disappointed

Angry   Glaring   Dismayed   Angry

Enraged!

Source. Randall P. Harrison, *Pictic Analysis: Toward a Vocabulary and Syntax for the Pictorial Code* (East Lansing, Mich.: Ph.D. Thesis, 1964).

Additional Research Readings

Nonverbal codes. When read stories about happy, sad, angry, and fearful people, New Guinea members of a stone-age culture correctly identified happy and angry photos more than 80% of the time, but tended to interpret fear as surprise. In turn, U.S. collegians correctly judged emotions on New Guinea faces, suggesting a universal relationship between facial expression and emotion. **Paul Ekman and Wallace V. Friesen, "Constants across cultures in the face and emotion," Journal of Personality and Social Psychology, 17:124–9.** But sex differences do exist. Smiling fathers were evaluated favorably in studies of children from 40 families, but smiles of middle-class mothers were unrelated to speech content. (Lower-class mothers didn't smile at all.) **Daphne E. Bugental et al., "Perfidious feminine faces," Journal of Personality and Social Psychology, 17:314–28.**

Chimps. Using plastic symbols as "words," a chimpanzee has labeled objects, constructed sentences, asked questions, and given a multiple-choice quiz to the experimenter. **David Premack, "The education of Sarah," Psychology Today, 4:4:54–8.** In Nevada, another chimp has learned 130 signs of the deaf mute's hand language which she used to ask questions, apologize and talk to herself. *Science News, Nov. 6, 1971, p. 313.*

Distraction. Subjects distracted by having to identify one of four lights flashing at random while listening to a taped speech urging an increase in tuition were more influenced by the speech than undistracted subjects. (The flashes kept them from arguing with the talk.) **Robert A. Osterhouse and Timothy C. Brock, "Distraction increases yielding to propaganda by inhibiting counterarguing," Journal of Personality and Social Psychology, 15:344–58.** Success on a finger-maze induced high self-esteem which, in turn, made students less resistant to distraction by a sound tape and thus more persuaded by an essay, read simultaneously, which advocated TV in the schools, a practice they had earlier opposed. **Brendan Gail Rule and David Rehill, "Distraction and self-esteem effects on attitude change," Journal of Personality and Social Psychology, 15:359–65.**

Syntax. Nouns and verbs (such as *kitten, general, borrowed,* and *hammered*) proved to have high or low potency, when rated separately on three bipolar scales (weak-strong, etc.). When combined in sentences, words influenced one another's ratings. A given word was judged more potent when used as sentence subject rather than object. **David R. Heise, "Potency dynamics in simple sentences," Journal of Personality and Social Psychology, 16:48–54.**

Chapter 22 Synopsis

- Advertising messages pose two dilemmas. The first, of simultaneously attracting attention through novelty and gaining understanding through familiarity, may be resolved by presenting familiar elements in new structures. The second, of using the same message for audiences of great diversity, is largely unresolved.

- The copy platform—product features linked to buyer benefits—represents a prescription for message content. Guidelines to style, which tell how the link between features and benefits may be made most effectively, are largely lacking. In real life, style and content cannot be separated in the mind of the copywriter or the prospect.

- In making competitive claims, advertisers use the persuasive techniques of immunization, category, fusion and fission, attitude imbalance, and use of sensory cues to alter perceptions.

- The "boy finds girl" plot of the slick-fiction potboiler and situation comedy, capable of easy variation, is also useful in the ads which appear alongside fiction and comedy. This plot can also be expressed in terms of the triangle of attitudinal balance theory and the syllogism, other possible models for ad construction, or for the advertiser's entire channel mix.

- From public opinion research, the advertiser may draw guidelines concerning conclusion-drawing, need-arousal, primacy vs. recency, immunizing prospects against competitors' claims, and the desirability of public commitment. He must keep in mind that public opinion involves two-side, zero-sum conditions which are not typical of buying and selling.

- The classic AIDA formula has its limitations: not all of its elements need be present in every instance nor is their order invariant.

Research Articles

Readability. Three formulas reveal reading ease (Flesch, Farr, Danielson).

Word Associations. Frequency of occurrence of different types identified for adults and for children (Woodrow); bad associations kill ad campaign (Lucas).

Message Attributes. Factor analysis and multiple regression relate ad attributes to recognition scores (Twedt, Diamond); two authors compared in six dimensions of writing style (Carroll).

Structure.   Coupon returns, mail sales measure effectiveness of positive and negative appeals (Lucas); forcing receivers to draw own conclusions affects comprehension but not attitudes (Thistlethwaite); timing of presentations and of test determine whether primacy or recency is better (Miller).

Fallacies.   Adman's copy encourages receiver illogic, sells products (Whiteside).

Chapter 22 Messages

Advertising messages must seize the attention of someone who usually is involved in a very different activity such as laughing at a situation comedy on TV, driving down a freeway, or reliving the details, via a newspaper, of the game in which his favorite team got clobbered.

Advertising messages must be understood by audiences of extraordinary diversity in IQ and reading ability, interests and experience, even keenness of vision and hearing.

To be understood, advertising messages must be composed of familiar symbols of words and pictures whose meanings are plain to persons whose decoding skills are poor and whose backgrounds are diverse.

To seize attention, advertising messages must be novel; they must challenge rather than conform to expectations and previous experience.

This is the first dilemma of message construction: a need for messages which are both familiar and novel. How is it resolved? Most often, by presenting familiar elements in new combinations.

A second paradox arises when one contrasts the audiences which the media assemble for the advertiser with the messages he transmits on those media. Magazines, for example, pinpoint the most diverse of audiences, ranging from apiarists to zealots of the xylophone.

In theory, an advertiser would benefit by using a separate message for each media vehicle he employs: one for *Ladies' Home Journal,* another for *Woman's Day,* a third for *Look,* taking account of what is novel and what is familiar to the readers of each. In practice, an advertiser is more likely to drop a vehicle from his schedule, if he feels his message is inappropriate to its audience, than he is to order a new message devised for that audience. (At most, he may order one message for consumers and another for the trade.) When he is forced to use different *symbols* by the difference in sensory modalities employed by radio and magazines, he tries to make the symbols express the same meanings, despite the differences in both symbols and audience. It would be too costly to do otherwise, he argues. Moreover, he says, similarity in messages will increase their cumulative effects.

These two factors—the need to combine the novel and the familiar and the need to use various sets of symbols to reach diverse audiences—thus serve to constrain a seller's messages.

Copywriters need to immerse themselves in what has been done, like the "sedulous ape" of fiction writing, if only to avoid what has been done before. They do need, both first-hand and through books, to study people in the act of buying and using products. They do need to study products: how they are made and used and how they differ from one another, even if the differences are hard to detect and at first glance seem to be of no possible consequence to anyone. Above all, they need to look to content, to style, and to an artful blend of the two.

Copy Platform: Key to Message Content

Message content in advertising is best summed up in the three-part copy platform.

Buyer benefits. What sensory experiences does the consumer want from the seller's product? What operations and functions does the manufacturer or retailer expect the products sold him to perform?

Marketing mix. What values on the several dimensions of product, place, and price do buyers—consumer, trade, and industrial —desire?

Links between mix and benefits. What cues convince buyers that the mix does contain the desired features? What symbols persuade them that these features will produce the desired benefits?

Technology tells us what features can be built into a product, and what combinations of place and price can be offered without going bankrupt. Psychology tells us what benefits buyers want, their theories as to cause-and-effect relationships, and the responses they are likely to make to messages concerning benefits, cues, and causal relationships.

A seller can begin by taking each product feature, by itself or in combination with others, and asking: "Do buyers want it? Does our product have it? If they don't know, can we inform them? If our product lacks the feature, can we add it? If a buyer is beset by two desires, how can we make him feel that the one our product will satisfy is the one that most needs to be satisfied?"

The seller cannot end here, however, but must ask one more question: "Do my competitors have this feature? How long will it take them to get it or to convince buyers that they have it?"

Good messages, then, must begin with a marketing mix whose elements can be perceived by buyers, elements which buyers perceive will produce effects which they strongly desire, and elements which will do so faster, better, cheaper, and more reliably than those offered in competitors' mixes.

Good messages must be expressed in words and sentences, pictures and numbers which are novel enough to attract attention and simple enough to be understood. They must use or build on concepts—categories and their attributes—which receivers already possess. They must induce favorable evaluation of these concepts, creating favorable associations between the seller's brand and things that the prospect already favors. They must induce action now, or facilitate

storage of a brand name and its favorable associations so as to be easily retrieved in preference to competitive brand names at some future time of choosing and purchasing. Message content must be expressed in a style that is suited to the product itself, including all aspects of the marketing mix, and of the particular market-and-audience segment to whom the message is addressed.

Style and Structure

Guidelines to style may be sought in many places. One would hope to find clues, for example, in the hundreds of works that have analyzed and reanalyzed the themes, symbols, and style of most major authors and most major works.

Even if scholars were to consent, there are obvious difficulties facing such studies. One is the brevity of most advertising messages. Another is the mixture of symbols systems in most ads; scholarly techniques for analyzing pictures are far less developed than those for analyzing language. A third difficulty is the specificity of most advertising. Not only is it directed to a particular product but it is aimed at a specific market segment; we need many separate sets of "rules" rather than a single set that ignores differences in products and people. And then there is the factor of novelty; if novelty is a necessity in advertising, the chief use of rules based on past experience may lie in their violation.

Despite these difficulties, men have attempted to determine the features that make an effective ad, usually by classifying ads as good or bad on the basis of recall scores, and comparing content characteristics of the two categories.

Interdependence of Style and Content

One problem in such attempts is that *content* and *style* represent an arbitrary division of a seamless whole. Creative admen do not think first of content and then seek ways to express it but of both together. Word-juggling alone is worthless but content is only as good as the manner in which it is expressed.

Let's illustrate this relationship by talking about *economy*, a fundamental concern in any sale-purchase, and *price*, seemingly an obdurate aspect of the marketing mix.

To suggest that a Volkswagen is economical, an adman reminds us that the *original cost* is low by listing all the other things one can buy with the money saved. Then he points out that Volkswagen doesn't change appearance each year; its *trade-in value* remains high. *Operating costs?* The adman talks about miles per gallon. *Repairs?* Volkswagen doesn't need repairs often; when it does they are simple and cheap.

Every sales argument, like every honest coin, has its flip side; each advantage is accompanied by disadvantages. Since low cost suggests low quality, Volkswagen emphasizes the number of inspections each car gets by a picture of inspectors filling a stadium, or a Volkswagen covered with their initials. Does unchanged appearance suggest failure to progress? Volkswagen ads describe internal, invisible changes.

When Volkswagen vaunts advantages other than economy, each of *them* implies disadvantages. Small size make a VW easy to park—but cramped? Volkswagen admits Wilt Chamberlain won't fit inside. (We smile, knowing we're not Wilt.) Or VW suggests that if the Bug's size bugs you, a VW microbus can carry an elephant. Does a small, cheap car suggest poor performance when the going is tough? Volkswagen shows its air-cooled engine starting in sub-zero temperatures and skipping through drifts.

Manipulating perceptions of price presents a problem in persuasion, for price can be determined to the penny and must be revealed before a sale can be made.

A national advertiser sidesteps the problem. His messages seldom mention price, ostensibly because varying distances between factory and retail outlet require higher prices in some regions or because variations in dealer volume and efficiency necessitate store-to-store variation.

Retailers justify charging more by saying "You get what you pay for," or "It costs a few cents more but it's worth it." They argue that the buyers "deserve the best." They suggest that if the buyer considers *all* costs, the high-priced brand is cheaper in the long run. They minimize price by describing it as "only X cents more per day."

Low-price competitors meanwhile offer brands that are as "just as good for half the price," because they've "done away with the frills you don't want anyway." They boast that they make up in volume what they lose in markup and stress opportunity costs by pointing out all of the things that a canny buyer can purchase with the money he saves.

Four Persuasive Techniques

These two simple illustrations, involving economy and price, employ four fundamental techniques of communications.

The first is *immunization*. How do we anticipate the counterarguments of a prospect or our competitors? When should we ignore such objections and when laugh them off with a Wilt Chamberlain? Or should we steal our competitors' thunder by presenting his strong points in weakened form at a time and place and in a context of our choosing?

The second technique involves the *combining* and the *splitting of categories*. The English language has a short, blunt label for things low in cost: *cheap*. Unfortunately, this label implies low quality as well as low cost. Volkswagen had to create a new category of objects with the *joint attributes* of *high* quality and *low* cost.

Like Yankees and Quakers before them, VW took the sting out of labels originally applied in derision; VW gleefully answers to the names of "bug" and "beetle." It uses such labels to suggest that a car doesn't have to be a chrome-bedecked behemoth to get people places. It has thus suggested using attributes of *function* rather than *form* in categories of cars. (Cadillacs counter that *both* form and function are important and employ *relational* attributes; true cost of a car, they suggest, is reflected by the ratio or difference between original cost and trade-in value.)

The third technique seeks to change buyer attitudes by messages that upset the *balance of attitudinal structure.* VW suggests that a microbus can be small on the outside (easy to park), but large on the inside. (The curious disbelief created by such an argument may cause a prospect to read the VW ad more carefully or send a prospect to a showroom.) Other sellers introduce imbalance by making feelings or actions inconsistent with beliefs. Pierre Martineau,[1] for example, argued that most buying decisions are emotional and that the emotions are best reached via pictures with words used after a decision had been made to provide a "rational" explanation to the buyer and others of the decision. To Martineau, the sequence was feelings—decisions—beliefs. Procter and Gamble, on the other hand, has through the years attempted to change actions first, by delivering samples of new products door-to-door, expecting beliefs and feelings to change so as to become consistent with behavior.

The fourth technique involves two steps. First, a seller builds into his products *sensory cues* to imperceptible qualities. Then he exploits these cues in his messages. Few housewives would be moved by the argument that "If you rub hard enough and long enough, any cleanser will get your sink clean." They prefer a cleanser which promises to do the job all by itself. Since

it's hard to believe that a powder which just lies there, looking pale and wan, is doing anything, sellers added a substance which changed the color when it became wet or foamed furiously, visible evidence that something (presumably dirt and grease removal) is *happening*. Given such excitement in the sink, the memorable jingle, "Ajax—the foaming cleanser," writes itself. In somewhat similar fashion, the very ugliness of the VW made it visible on the highway, high visibility added "It must be good if it's so popular" to the first impression, "Anything that ugly must have some redeeming qualities—wonder what they are?"

These four techniques—and there are more—suggest some of the fundamental themes on which an adman, like a musician, can build variations without number. They illustrate and emphasize the point that an effective ad involves an artful combination of content and style and a strategy based on fundamental principles of category construction, attitude change, and perception of cues.

Changing Labels and Attributes

Sometimes pinning a new label on a product helps move it from a category that people reject to one that they accept: when "pool" was renamed "pocket billiards," it became acceptable in the home. (A boost for bowling, on the other hand, required automatic pinsetters, a change of setting, women's leagues, and baby sitting services.)

Advertisers have been surprised by the attributes that influence choice, surprised to discover people buy lemons not for their flavor but to cure constipation; luggage not for strength but for style; and men's shoes not for style but comfort. One household product advertised that it "worked faster";[2] a survey showed that only 2% of the purchasers bought it for that reason. In contrast, 58% bought it because it was easy on their hands, 20% because it was not messy, and 18% because it was "more effective."

When no existing product appears to fill needs, a seller can produce a new product to meet them, add an ingredient to an existing product, or advertise that his present product already satisfies such needs. People who worried because they could not brush their teeth after every meal or because their dogs did not get enough exercise were relieved of these worries, at least, when a toothpaste claimed it could take care of the first condition and a dog food promised to handle the second. Words can help people discover benefits and brand differences more quickly; they can also suggest benefits and differences that have little counterpart in objective reality, although illusory benefits are vulnerable to user experience and a competitor's counterattack.

The person who knows that one cigarette can't be distinguished from another in blindfold tests nevertheless may pick one brand because the line, "This one tastes good, like a cigarette should," pops into his mind when he confronts a vending machine. A man may seize at straws when forced to choose among brands which are indistinguishable; the straw he seizes may break a Camel's back.

Headlines in print media which provide such memorable cues to brand choice serve two functions: alone or combined with a picture they arouse a reader's interest in ad copy; if the copy fails to hold a reader's interest, if he is too hurried to read copy of any length, the headline should convey a message complete in itself. Headlines that perform well in practice tend to graduate into the status of easily retained, easily retrieved slogans; the best headlines therefore include brand names.

The advertiser's words and pictures may emphasize product, people, or people using product. The people themselves may be famous figures of fact or fiction, or anonymous users of the product with whom a prospect can identify. (Occasionally ads employ nonusers, miserable wretches whom the prospect may use as a negative reference group.) Ads may show benefits from product use, often by contrasting "before" with "after," or they may tell *how* to use the product.

We said earlier that attempts have been made to relate such style variables as these to ad recall scores. In 1946, Starch selected 50 best-read ads, which had been recalled by up to 35% of the audience, and 50 "worst" ads, recalled by only 1 or 2%.[3] About the same time Rudolph summed up Starch scores for 2500 *Saturday Evening Post* ads.[4] Both men classified the ads according to style, and got the following results.

Starch

	Number of Ads (%)	
	Read Most	Read Least
People acting or talking in text and pictures	29	10
How to cook, launder and do other chores	15	2
Startling facts and events	6	2
General claims: X lasts longer, looks better	6	4
Products and packages, but no people	0	32

Rudolph

	Readership Index
Product or firm stressed	100
People using product	100
Dialogue by users	107
Why YOU should use product	109
Why I, *a famous person*, used the product	153

An attempt to determine how much style contributed to the effect of an ad was made asking 120 judges to rank 80 advertisements twice—first on the copy, presented in typewritten form, and then the ads themselves.[5] The two rankings correlated only .40. However, copy seemed more important for one subset of 10 ads, all of which involved testimonials by actors; correlation between ad and typewritten copy for this subset was .86.

It should be noted that the results of such studies depend not only on what message elements one chooses to study, but the measure of their effects that one employs. Starch and Rudolph used recognition scores as a measure of effectiveness; Hepner used judges' ratings. Other decision makers will prefer other measures.

Potboiler Plot and Balance Theory

Such studies as these represent attempts to develop a vocabulary of words and pictorial symbols and rules for combining symbols in ad copywriting. Meanwhile the ad writer may look to other areas for guidance. One that has been suggested is found in fiction, in the potboiler plot.

The simplest, hoariest plot is said to be: *X sees Y, X wants Y, X gets Y.* Substitute *boy* for *X* and *girl* for *Y* and one has the original movie plot. Substitute *housewife* for *X* and *product* for *Y* and one has the script for an advertisement.

Variations on this basic plot multiply

and alter the status or role of elements in the formula and one gets the *poor-but-honest boy* in love with the *rich girl* (or vice versa) and the *older man* in love with the *young girl* (or vice versa). Substitute "dog" for "girl" in the basic formula and one has the plot of a Disney movie. Make subject and object the same sex and one has something more modern and decadent. Adding adjectives to the basic nouns appearing as subject and object or altering the verb gives infinite variety to the basic SVO sentence of English. By repeating the basic plot in space, one obtains the subplots of Shakespearean drama. By repeating it in time, the sequence, *Boy likes $Girl_1$ who likes Boy_2 who likes $Girl_2$ who likes . . . ,* is produced, reflecting plots found both in life and on the stage.

Changing the verb from *like* to *dislike* gives the beginning of the typical dandruff, body odor, or greasy hair commercial: *X has Y, X dislikes Y, X gets rid of Y.* All one needs to do to complete the commercial is add a subordinate clause indicating that *X dislikes Y* (dandruff, B.O.) *because Z* (the girl) *dislikes Y.* The whole plot is easily summed up in the classic triangle of attitude imbalance in which a plus sign indicates possession or liking and a negative sign dislike or lack of, as shown at the left. This necessarily leads to the neatly balanced triangle at right in which Boy likes Product Z which is hostile toward their common enemy, Dandruff.

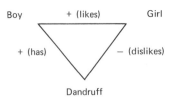

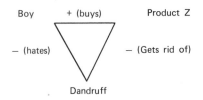

with ease and abandon. Switching X and Y provides an echo of the encyclopedia salesman's pitch: product (X) wants you (Y) for a customer. Mix in a little demography

Take "Boy" out of the picture, give signs to both the points (objects) and sides (relationships) of the triangle, and one gets this picture of the Boy's attitudes.

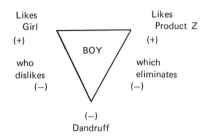

Likes Girl (+) — BOY — Likes Product Z (+)
who dislikes (−) — which eliminates (−)
(−) Dandruff

The ad, of course, goes further by implying that once the dandruff goes, so will the girl's only objection to Boy; in fact, she will be so attracted to Boy that she will be also + (grateful) toward Product Z. The possibility of other Boys and Products is blissfully absent in the advertisement, though not necessarily in life.

Testimonial ads can be plotted in similar fashion, using X-likes-Y formulas, attitudinal triangles or series of syllogisms. The process seems to go something like this.

The kind of girls (boys) I like admire men (women) like Paul Newman (Joanne Woodward). Paul Newman (Joanne Woodward) eats/wears/drinks Product L. If I ate/wore/drank Product L, I would be like Paul Newman (Joanne Woodward), the kind of girls (boys) I like would like me—and then I would be happier (for all time/than I am now).

The logical implausibility of this sequence, which shows up far more clearly in this description than it does in the typical testimonial ad, may be pictured in the overlapping circles of a Venn diagram. Only the shaded area holds much hope for the sequence just described.

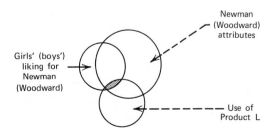

Girls' (boys') liking for Newman (Woodward)

Newman (Woodward) attributes

Use of Product L

A seller's plot may employ several channels, beginning with an ad which induces a state of *curious disbelief:* housewife (X) sees product-brand (Y) and wonders if she'd like it. Then other channels take over: a salesman demonstrates a snowbuggy, or the housewife tries a sample of detergent left on her doorstep or quizzes a neighbor about a new kind of coffee.

Only future research can tell whether syllogism, attitude triangle, or potboiler plot can be deliberately taught a copywriter and produce effective ads. It is not surprising, however, that ads, in their basic organization, may resemble plots found in the soap operas and situation comedies of TV and women's magazines that provide their context.

Studies of Public Opinion

To date, the best research into the structure and organization of effective messages has concerned public opinion and involved issues with two sides, where one must win and one must lose.

These two-person, zero-sum conditions differ from the consumer's problem of choosing among several brands which vary only slightly, and the purchasing agent's practice of dividing his custom among at least two suppliers. Both buyer and seller are presumed to benefit from the purchase-sale; it is not a zero-sum game. Nor does any seller's success depend on driving his competitors out of business, as does victory for a political candidate.

Despite these important differences, insights from research into public opinion may be helpful to the advertiser.

Conclusions. By carefully selecting his evidence, a propagandist can make a given conclusion almost inevitable. If he then states his conclusion, won't his intentions become more obvious and cause the audience to fight back? Isn't it better to let listeners think they've reached the conclusion of their own volition?

Two experiments suggest that if a source fails to draw a conclusion, audiences may miss the point. In the first, college students in psychology were exposed to tape-recorded messages on devaluation of the currency.[6] When the conclusion was stated, 48% changed their opinions in the desired direction. When it was not, only 19% did so. In another experiment, military recruits listened to speeches approving United States entry into the Korean War.[7] Educated subjects were equally affected by the version with conclusions and the version without, but other subjects were more influenced by the version with conclusions.

More advertising texts suggest that every advertisement should end with a specific request for action; some even supply a coupon or a prepaid, ready-to-mail postcard. Insurance salesmen insist on getting seven "no's" before they will let the door close behind them. Are ads and salesmen wrong?

Failure to draw a conclusion *can* aid a source by helping to conceal his intent. This may be useful in some forms of communication, but in advertising and selling intent of the source is clear from the outset. The receiver expects to be asked to buy. If he isn't, the encounter is a waste of time.

Solutions. Advertisers are willing to pay a premium for an audience with a high proportion of prospects—persons who have a problem for which they are seeking a solution. Why waste costly space or time on reminding prospects of a need they are already aware of? This sounds logical, but research studies disagree. When pairs of advertisements for 20 products, one emphasizing the need and the other its solution, were compared,[8] the ads which emphasized need-arousal proved superior. In an experiment with college students on the issue of grading on a curve,[9] a need-arousing message changed more student opinion im-

mediately and retained its superiority over a 3-month period.

On the other hand, some audiences have such a strong need and are so conscious of it, that a message can move directly to a solution. Moreover, it is possible to go too far in need-arousal, as shown by studies of the so-called negative or "fear" appeal. In one experiment, a message threatening serious illness from tooth decay increased worry but did not improve behavior.[10] In another experiment subjects were asked to write down later as much of each message as they could remember.[11] The group that got the high-threat message recalled more of the unfavorable consequences; the low-threat group recalled more of the *causes* of such consequences.

Although these studies derogate high-threat messages, later studies, as so often happens, suggest that they oversimplified in failing to recognize three sources of fear in a communications situation: fear appeals in the message, premessage level of anxiety in the subject himself, and fearsomeness of the action that the message asks him to perform. Degree of fear is determined by summing up the amount of fear in subject, message, and behavior. If subjects are *not* anxious and the behaviors sought are *not* fearsome, a high-fear message may be very effective, as has been shown with messages involving tooth decay, lockjaw, and automobile seat belts.[12] A high-fear message reduced amount of smoking, but it took a low-fear message to persuade subjects to take the more threatening step of getting an X-ray check for lung cancer. Subjects getting high-fear messages said they *intended* to quit smoking and get an anti-tetanus injection, but low-fear messages were as effective in getting persons to actually stop smoking or get injections. High-fear messages, like a 100% reinforcement schedule in learning, were more effective in accomplishing *immediate* attitude change but less resistant to counterpropaganda presented later.

First or Last? The advertiser who first stakes out a claim is usually considered to have gained an advantage over his rivals. Even if they advertise, quite truthfully, that their products have or will do the same thing, it's likely that prospects, in recalling later ads, will attribute them to the original claimant. Thus johnny-come-lately Firm B's ad budget boomerangs by broadcasting ads which memory attributes to Firm A.

Laboratory experiments, however, suggest that the second of two speakers has the advantage, more often than not. Two out of three groups in one experiment and three out of four in another showed "recency" to be superior to "primacy." This is true only if the messages are presented by two different persons, however. When a single person presents a second message that contradicts his first one, students suspect a trick and discount the second view.[13] Much depends on what happens between the first and the second message. If the first message is preceded by a warning that first impressions are often erroneous, its advantage is reduced. Its advantage is reduced even more if the warning follows the first message and is reduced most of all if some unrelated activity intervenes between the first and second message. Such intervening activity, in fact, produces much the effect of having two different speakers give the message: the second message proves most effective.

Immunization. The advertiser who is first on the scene may be able to immunize his audience against subsequent messages from his competitors, by using any of four techniques. First, he may steal their thunder by presenting their strong points in weakened form. Second, he may *anchor* new beliefs by linking them to old beliefs. Third, he may encourage prospects to make a decision, announce it publicly, and act on it, hoping that their desire to appear consistent (to themselves and others) will prevent them from reversing the decision later.

Fourth, he can link the beliefs to reference groups, reminding prospects that they value these groups and that these groups hold the belief that the source advocates.

When should a source present only data that favors his side of an issue and when should he mention both pros and cons in hopes of obtaining an immunization effect?

Following Germany's surrender in World War II, some 400 American GI's were asked how long they thought the war with Japan would continue.[14] Then half the group was exposed to a one-sided 15-minute talk arguing that the war would last at least two more years. The other half got the same message but with some added material, citing Japanese weaknesses, to suggest that there was something to be said on the other side.

The results depended on the original attitudes of the men exposed to the messages. Among men originally opposed to the long-war conclusion, the two-sided message changed 48%, and the one-sided message only 36%. Among men who originally agreed with the long-war thesis, the one-sided message was superior, 52% to 23%. The two-sided message was more effective among men who had graduated from high school than with those who had not, regardless of their original position. In short, two-sided messages appear best with educated audiences and with audiences opposed to the source's point of view.

The two-sided message also is better with audiences likely to hear an opposing view at some time in the future. Several months before Russia set off its first atomic bomb, taped messages arguing that Russia would not be able to produce such bombs in quantity for at least 5 years were played for 197 high school pupils.[15] One-sided messages changed the opinions of 69%. A week later, however, half the pupils heard new messages describing four plants in Russia which were already supposed to be manufacturing bombs. Almost all of the change caused by the original one-sided messages was wiped out; only 2% of the students in this group held to the belief that Russia lagged 5 years behind the United States. In contrast, 61% of the group which originally heard a two-sided message held to the belief that Russia lagged. Even Russia's explosion of its first atomic bomb did not wipe out the effects of the two-sided message received months earlier. Immunization may work directly, by weakening the force of arguments. It may also work indirectly, either by increasing the prestige of the source, by making him appear fair minded, or by getting the audience to make up its mind now, under the impression that it has already considered both sides of the question.

This effect of the two-sided message is usually labeled "immunization." It is argued that exposing audiences to a "weakened dose" of an opponent's arguments immunizes them against those arguments when they are later presented in full force. To this extent the advantage of the second speaker, mentioned earlier, must be modified.

There are dangers in using a two-sided message, however. One danger is that it will make persons aware of a product's disadvantages, disadvantages which they previously did not know existed. Another danger is that failure to mention an important disadvantage that prospects *are* aware of, will cause them to discredit the source.

Commitment. Most salesmen know that a sale is more likely if the prospect can be induced to make a series of minor decisions and commitments along the way. And so they ask: *If you should decide to buy a refrigerator, what color would you prefer?* Or, *Which kind of binding do you think is most practical for an encyclopedia?*

Commitment does appear to immunize against subsequent messages. In one experiment, high school pupils[16] heard two speeches, one arguing that the voting age be lowered and the other that it should be kept where it is. After hearing the first speech, each pupil wrote an essay stating his personal opinion, half being told their essays might be published in the school newspaper. This half, who thought their essays would put them on the record publicly, showed more resistance to the second speech than did pupils who did not expect their opinions to be published. (Other experiments have shown that filling out an *anonymous* questionnaire does not tend to immunize.)[17]

The AIDA Tradition

Still in the realm of untested theory, although it has been regarded as gospel for years, is the idea that the elements of all advertisements should be ordered so as to evoke, in order, a prospect's Attention, Interest, Desire, and Action.[18]

Obviously a message creates interest and desire if prospects are unaware of any need for a product, unaware it exists, or indifferent to its claims. Attracting attention requires far less effort from an advertiser with prospects who are actively seeking what he has to offer. Rather than immediate action, most ads seek to create a favorable attitude which will be stored in memory to be retrieved when a purchase is imminent. Buyers may be influenced by messages which do not seize their attention, as attention is usually measured, and by messages which they do not understand, as understanding is usually measured. A change in attitude may precede a change in behavior, but it may also be a consequence of behavior. We often desire without action and sometimes act without any real desire.

Devices used to get attention may attract the wrong people and repel the right ones: 65% in one test audience recalled the girl in a white bathing suit who appeared in a TV commercial, but only 10% could remember what she was advertising.

Understanding does not necessarily create

a change in attitude. When groups of 500 to 1000 soldiers in World War II were shown a film, *Battle of Britain,* designed to increase their motivation to serve in the armed services, a familiar "funnel effect" was shown.[19] Some 78% of those who saw the film (compared with 21% who did not see it) could tell how the British safeguarded planes on the ground from enemy attack. The film caused an increase of 27 percentage points in agreement that British resistance gave the United States time to build up its own military strength. But the film did not cause GI's to look more favorably on their involvement in the war. Films on prejudice or socioeconomic attitudes have shown similar results: learning of facts but failure to accept the conclusions that the facts imply.

Not everyone who believes a message will act on it: the drugstore may be closed, or the prospect may lack money or transportation. Interestingly enough, dislike of an advertisement need not hurt sales of the brand it advocates. The National Broadcasting Company sponsored 3270 interviews with matched groups of consumers, some of whom owned television sets and some of whom did not. It observed the changes that occurred when people bought sets or a brand began to advertise on television, studying purchases of 12 different products including gasoline, cigarettes, toothpaste, and coffee.[20] Viewers, even those who disliked a commercial, bought more of brands advertised on TV than did nonviewers. On the other hand, a study was done in which matched groups of soldiers were exposed to

several messages which had been rated on a 100-point like-dislike scale urging them to take care of their shoes.[21] A subsequent check of actual shoe care showed it improved most among men exposed to the best-liked messages and least among those who got messages ranked in the middle. An advertising man says that when consumer juries pick advertisements they like, positive appeals win out; coupon tests of the same advertisements show that actual buying behavior favors negative appeals.[22]

Mere repetition of a brand name, however irritating, may fix it so firmly in our minds that when someone says toothpaste we reply "Pepsodent" as automatically as we say "cat" when someone says "dog." Neither awareness nor understanding nor belief seems to be involved. Behavior need not result from attitudes. It may be unrelated to them or it may be cause rather than effect. Living in integrated housing has changed attitudes toward integration.[23] Making speeches saying that college students face three years of military service has changed attitudes toward the draft.[24] Pupils induced to argue in favor of a type of comic book they did not like have changed their comic-book preference.[25]

Even if research were to provide guidelines for designers of both marketing mix and message, we seem to be a long way from programming such guidelines for a computer. Creative individuals are needed to design mix and message; the next chapter discusses how such individuals and the environment needed for their job may be identified.

Thought, Talk, and Action

1. Examine the first 10 ads in a variety of magazines such as *Fortune, Playboy, Harper's, True Romances,* and *Reader's Digest.* For each ad, list all of the product features and buyer benefits that are specifically mentioned. Do number and specificity of each appear to vary with product or with vehicle?

2. Keeping at least a rough count of the number of ads examined, locate one example each of conclusion drawing, need arousal, immunization, category fusion or fission, and request for public commitment. Which was easiest to find—and therefore probably most frequent? Which was hardest to find?

3. Locate five testimonial ads. Is the primary appeal to expertise or trustworthiness? How are product, witness, media vehicle, and presumed target segment related to one another? How common are such ads today? (How many ads did you have to examine to find five testimonials?)

Notes

Chapter 22

1. Pierre Martineau, Motivation in advertising (New York: McGraw-Hill Book Co., 1957).
2. Harry Walker Hepner, Advertising, 3rd ed. (New York: McGraw-Hill Book Co., 1964), pp. 417, 421.
3. Daniel Starch, "Why readership of ads has increased 24%," Advertising & Selling, August 1946, p. 47. Cited in reference No. 2, p. 500.
4. Harold J. Rudolph, "Attention and interest factors in advertising," Printer's ink business bookshelf (New York: Funk & Wagnalls Co., 1947). Cited in reference No. 2, p. 425.
5. Reference No. 2, p. 435.
6. Carl I. Hovland and Wallace Mandell, "An experimental comparison of conclusion-drawing by the communicator and by the audience," Journal of Abnormal and Social Psychology, 47:581–8.
7. Donald L. Thistlethwaite et al., "The effects of 'directive' and 'nondirective' communication procedures on attitudes," Journal of Abnormal and Social Psychology, 51:107–13.
8. Edward K. Strong, Jr. and J. E. Loveless, "Want and 'solution' advertisements," Journal of Applied Psychology, 10: 346–66.
9. Carl I. Hovland et al., The order of presentation in persuasion (New Haven, Conn.: Yale University Press, 1957), pp. 135–6.
10. Irving L. Janis and Seymour Feshbach, "Effects of fear-arousing communications," Journal of Abnormal and Social Psychology, 48:78–92.
11. Irving L. Janis and W. Milholland, "The influence of threat appeals on selective learning of the content of a persuasive communication," Journal of Psychology, 37:75–80.
12. Studies mentioned in this paragraph are reviewed and specific journal citations are available in Gardner Lindzey and Elliot Aronson, Handbook of Social Psychology, 2nd ed. (Reading, Mass.: Addison-Wesley Publishing Co., 1969), pp. 203–5.
13. Reference No. 9, pp. 133–4.

14. C. I. Hovland et al., Experiments on mass communication (Princeton, N.J.: Princeton University Press, 1949).
15. Arthur A. Lumsdaine and Irving L. Janis, "Resistance to 'counterpropaganda' presentations," Public Opinion Quarterly, 17:311–8.
16. Reference No. 9, pp. 131–2.
17. *Ibid.*, pp. 132–3.
18. Kristian S. Palda, "The hypothesis of a hierarchy of effects: a partial evaluation," Journal of Marketing Research, 3:13–24.
19. Reference No. 14.
20. Thomas E. Coffin and Jack B. Landis, How television changes strangers into customers (New York: NBC Television, 1955).
21. *Ibid.*
22. Reference No. 2, p. 430, citing work of Horace Schwerin.
23. Morton Deutsch and M. E. Collins, Interracial housing (Minneapolis, University of Minnesota Press, 1951), condensed in Guy E. Swanson et al., Readings in Social Psychology, 2nd ed. (New York: Henry Holt, 1952), pp. 582–93.
24. Carl I. Hovland et al., Communication and persuasion (New Haven, Conn.: Yale University Press, 1953).
25. Herbert C. Kelman, "Attitude change as a function of response restriction," Human Relations, 6:185–214.

Making Messages More Readable

Simplicity, as measured by readability formulas, serves two functions. It helps insure that the reader will understand what is being said and it helps keep him reading. Here are two reports, the first written by a student and the second by an experienced editor. Both concern the same study—the classic experiment by Asch in how group pressures make an individual conform. Read the reports, then note how they rated on three readability formulas.

Inexperienced Writer

Interpersonal Influence. Chapter 5—READINGS IN SOCIAL PSYCHOLOGY, Effects of Group Pressure upon the Modification and Distortion of Judgments by S. E. Asch.

The immediate object of this study was to ascertain the social and personal conditions that induce individuals to resist or to yield to group pressures when the latter are perceived to be *contrary to fact.* The issues which this problem raises are of obvious consequence for society; it can be of decisive importance whether or not a group will, under certain conditions, submit to existing pressures. Equally direct are the consequences for individuals and our understanding them, since it is a decisive fact about a person whether he possess the freedom to act independently, or whether he characteristically submits to group pressures.

The problem under investigation required the direct observation of certain basic processes in the interaction between individuals, and between individuals and groups. To clarify these seems necessary if we are to make fundamental advances in the understanding of the formation and reorganization of attitudes, of the functioning of public opinion, and of the operation of propaganda. Today we do not possess an adequate theory of these psycho-social processes.

The investigators worked with a group of eight members. With the exception of one member, they met previously with the experimenter and received instructions to respond at certain points with wrong (and unanimous) judgments. The outstanding person (the critical subject) was the object of investigation. He faced, possibly for the first time in his life, a situation in which a group unanimously contradicted the evidence of his sense.

The quantitative results are clear and unambiguous. There was a marked movement toward the majority. Other observations demonstrated the role of social support as a source of power and stability, in contrast to the preceding investigations which stressed the effects of social opposition. Both aspects must be explicitly considered in a unified formulation of the effects of group conditions on the formation and change of judgments.

Experienced Writer

Asch, S. E., "Effects of group pressure upon the modification and distortion of judgments," in *Readings in Social Psychology,* 3rd edition; Eleanor Maccoby et al., editors (New York: Holt, Rinehart, and Winston, Inc., 1958).

Groups of eight college students were shown three unequal lines and asked to state publicly which matched in length a fourth line. Seven in each group were privately instructed to name the most discrepant line in 12 out of 18 trials. Faced with a unanimous but mistaken majority, 32% of the judgments made by 50 uninstructed, naive subjects erred in the majority direction. Three factors affecting error were studied.

1. *The individual:* Wide differences existed here. A fourth of naive subjects never yielded to the majority, a third yielded at least half the time, and some 11 out of 12 times.
2. *The stimulus:* The greater the discrepancy between lines, the fewer errors (and vice versa).
3. *The group structure:* A break in unanimity, by giving naive subjects support of a partner, reduced errors from 32% to 5 to 10%. However, if this partner "deserted" to the majority halfway through errors rose at once from 5 to 25%. Faced with an errant majority of two, subjects erred 13% of the time; faced with a majority of three, they erred 32% of the time. Increasing the majority beyond three did not increase errors.

The difference between the two summaries can be expressed quantitatively by three different readability formulas.

The first summary has 14 sentences, 304 words, 573 syllables, 69 one-syllable words or 1659 characters, 309 spaces, and 15 sentences. The second summary has 12 sentences, 189 words, 330 syllables, 109 one-syllable words or 905 characters, 163 spaces, and 12 sentences.

Here are the formulas used to obtain the ratings.

Flesch: 206.835 — (.846 × No. of syllables per 100 words) — (1.015 × Average sentence length). From Rudolf Flesch, "A new readability yardstick," Journal of Applied Psychology, *32*:221–33.

	Readability Rating of Article by	
	Inexperienced Writer	Experienced Writer
Flesch formula	25.8 (Very difficult)	43.1 (Difficult)
Farr-Jenkins-Patterson	17.3 (Very difficult)	44.7 (Difficult)
Computerized formula	53.96 (Fairly difficult)	110.56 (Very easy)

Farr-Jenkins-Patterson: (1.599 × No. of one-syllable words per 100 words) — (1.015 × average sentence length) — 31.517. From James N. Farr, James J. Jenkins, and Donald G. Paterson, "Simplifications of Flesch reading ease formula," Journal of Applied Psychology, *35:*333–37.

Computerized: 131.059 — 10.364 (No. of characters/No. of spaces) — 1.94 (No. of characters/No. of sentences). From Wayne A. Danielson and Sam Dunn Bryan, "Computer automation of two readability formulas," Journalism Quarterly, *39:*201–6.

Knowledge of Word Associations Is Useful

Through repetition, advertisers often attempt to strengthen verbal habits, so that when a man identifies the cause of his discomfort as a *headache* the word will call up from his memory a product, *aspirin,* and the name of the product, in turn, will call up the name of a brand, *Bayer.*

Such associations also are important in the choice of a brand name, or a campaign slogan.

A brewer planning to emphasize that his beer had been properly aged by referring to it as *lagered* discovered that only 36% of persons questioned knew the word had anything to do with beer, that 38% apparently confused it with *laggard,* and that the rest couldn't associate it with anything.

Source. D. B. Lucas and S. H. Britt, *Measuring Advertising Effectiveness* (New York: McGraw-Hill, 1963), p. 135.

When given a word and asked to give the first association that comes to mind, people sometimes think of a word that is similar or one that is opposite in meaning. Or nearness in time or space may suggest an association. In interpreting the results of any word association test, it helps to know that these eight kinds of association predominate.

Children, who often define words in terms of their function ("A hole is to dig") or drop out verbs ("House [is] big") are more likely than are adults to give the *second* four types of associations listed. Taking the three highest frequencies in each instance, a comparison of responses by adults and by children is shown on page 440. The words children offer tend to be briefer and more specific—the kinds which get high ratings on a readability index, fit into headlines and onto billboards—and may evoke the warm,

Relationship	Examples	Percentage of Adults Giving This Type of Response
Coordinate	Table-chair; deep-low	10.9
Contrast	Dark-light; sickness-health	10.6
Similar	Dark-black; sickness-illness	8.9
Superordinate	Table-furniture	7.6
Adjective-noun	Deep-hole; soft-bed	6.9
Verbs	Table-eat; dark-see	6.4
Contiguity	Table-dish; dark-night	6.0
Noun-adjective	Mountain-high; house-big	4.3

Stimulus Word
- Table
- Man
- House
- Sickness
- Joy

Adult Responses
Chair, wood, furniture
Woman, male, boy
Home, building, barn
Health, death, illness
Happiness, sorrow, pleasure

Children's Responses
- Eat, dishes, legs
- Work, hat, person
- Live, warm, big
- Doctor, bed, ill
- Happy, glad, fun

childlike responses which advertisers seek!

Source. Herbert Woodrow and Frances Lowell, "Children's Association Frequency Tables," *Psychological Monographs,* Vol. 22: No. 5, pp. 81–96, 106.

Some words arouse emotions in us because of our experiences with the things they symbolize—*garbage* and *hypodermic needle,* for example. We may have equally strong feelings toward words that label events of an abstract, impersonal, and general nature, like *communism* or *colonialism,* with which few of us have had personal experience. The word *advertising* covers such a multitude of things and events that it's hard to see how anyone could develop a feeling toward it—and yet people do.

What Are the Ingredients of a Successful Ad?

Among factors influencing readership of an advertisement are interest in product and brand advertised, readability of the prose, and attention-getting qualities of illustration and layout. Several attempts have been made to weigh the importance of these elements. Here are two examples.

Taking 137 advertisements in the February 1950 issue of the 80,000 circulation business paper, *American*

Rotated Factor Loadings

Variable	Picture-Color	Size	Type	Infor-mation	Field	Prevs. Adv.	h^2r
Sq. in. illustration	51	48	25	06	23	04	6111
Pictures of Use	51	23	−18	09	10	−44	5571
Number of colors	49	−07	23	11	−15	01	3326
Size of Ad	18	69	26	45	45	04	9827
No. of Prod. Facts	20	37	−24	28	−12	−35	4498
Brad-Vern Schedules	21	37	−25	−01	07	34	3641
Largest Type	15	45	62	36	12	03	7543
Largest Prod. Ident.	18	34	43	21	−06	04	4277
Number Type Sizes	01	37	47	47	−16	−19	6405
Body Type Size	12	04	46	09	00	25	2982
Headline Size	26	24	34	30	14	27	4233
Number Words	05	46	−10	71	00	−03	7291
Number Copy Blocks	25	27	−13	65	10	−33	6937
Number Prod. Ident.	31	29	−20	64	19	06	6695
No. Prod. Benefits	14	52	−22	57	−06	−17	6658
Surround	−05	−13	61	10	76	17	1.0064
Previous Schedule	42	46	−21	19	14	47	7087
Pica Width	35	−01	34	14	05	43	4452
Number Illust.	36	17	−05	27	25	−40	4564

(Decimals omitted. Italics indicate factor on which each variable has its highest loading.)

Builder, the author counted and measured 15 mechanical variables and 19 content variables. He chose the 19 which showed highest correlation with scores on "recall reading any part of this advertisement," correlated each of them with one another, and subjected the resultant 19 × 19 matrix to centroid factor analysis, graphic rotation for orthogonal factors. This gave him the following factor table; the first 2 factors *picture-color* and *size* account for 53% of observed variance and 4 others for another 15%.

Next he chose three of the original variables to represent the major factors, found they produced a multiple correlation coefficient with readership of .77, and constructed a multiple regression formula.

His formula: Readership = 10.456 + 8.29 (size of advertisement in pages) + 3.87 (number of colors) + .18 (square inches of illustration). This formula predicted readership for advertisements in 6 different publications with correlations of .58 to .80 between predicted and actual, and an average of .71.

Source. Dik Warren Twedt, "A multiple factor analysis of advertising readership," *Journal of Applied Psychology,* 36:207–15.

Using 1070 ads from *Life* magazine, February 7 to July 31, 1964, a researcher measured 12 attributes of each. Seven were characteristics of the ad itself: size, number of colors, "bleed," layout, number of words, and prominence of brand or headline. Three involved the magazine: number of ads in issue, position of ad in magazine, and whether it appeared on a lefthand or righthand page. The remaining two designated which of 16 product classes the ad concerned, and the past advertising budget.

Using multiple regression, he then related these 12 variables to 6 Starch readership scores (noted,

seen-associated, and read-most for men and for women). Products affected readership scores, readership falling as number of ads in an issue rose (especially for noted scores and for men). Readership rose with color and fell as number of words in the text rose above 50.

To test his equations—438 regression coefficients are given in the original article—the researcher predicted scores for 43 ads in the February 26, 1965 issue of *Life.* Here are the coefficients of determination between actual and predicted.

Men		
Noted	Seen-associated	Read Most
.68	.69	.32
Women		
Noted	Seen-associated	Read Most
.74	.74	.56

(Starch "read-most" scores are typically so low in percentage of respondents and the range so restricted that one would expect correlations to be low.)

As the author points out, an advertiser could weight the several scores in terms of his goals—how important women are as compared with men, or whether "read most" is more important than "noted"—and take account of any restraints on his freedom to manipulate the 12 variables. (He might not be able to afford bleed or color, for example, or to buy a full page.) If he wanted women to read the text of an ad, but was content if men remembered his brand name, and wanted to reach 3 men for every woman, and to maximize readers per dollar, his objective function would be: .3 (seen-associated score for men) plus .7 (read-most score for women) divided by ad cost.

Source. Daniel S. Diamond, "A quantitative approach to magazine advertisement format selection," *Journal of Marketing Research,* 5:376–86.

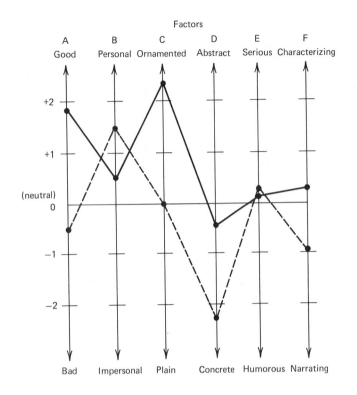

Figure 22.1

Source. John B. Carroll, "Vectors of prose style," in Thomas A. Sebeok, editor, *Style in Language* (New York: John Wiley & Sons).

Factor analysis was also used, this time in a study of a wide-ranging variety of printed matter, involving both ratings by expert judges and objective counts of the sort used in the two studies of advertising.

Eight experts, using 29 polar-adjective scales, rated 150 passages, of about 300 words each, selected from American and British 19th and 20th century novels and from newspaper reports, biographies, texts, speeches, sermons, etc. In addition, 39 objective counts were made, ranging from number of possessive pronouns to percent of copulative verbs. Six factors were extracted to represent independent dimensions of style. They are shown in Figure 22.1, as applied to two very different writers.

When Should an Advertiser Accentuate the Positive?

First create a felt need, we're told, and then offer a product which will meet it. Fortunes have been made by making prospects aware of bad breath, dingy teeth, bald spots, and body odor. But should ads emphasize the unpleasant fate that threatens or the bright future that beckons?

The number of coupons returned for 117 pairs of positive and negative advertisements for the same product, appearing in the same periodical at about the same season, were compared.

Variations within the two types of

Product Advertising	Number of Pairs in Which Best Ad Was:		
	Positive	Negative	No Difference
Toothpaste	17	13	1
Food drink	19	17	1
Breakfast food	4	9	
Sanitation products	3	4	
Extension courses	14	14	1
	57	57	3

appeal appeared more important than differences between them.

Source. D. B. Lucas and C. E. Benson, "The relative values of positive and negative advertising appeals as measured by coupons returned," *Journal of Applied Psychology,* 13:274–300.

Twenty-eight advertisements promoting a book to educate-by-mail were compared on the basis of sales produced. One negative-appeal advertisement was only 36% as effective as a matching positive appeal advertisement while another was 29% more effective. In terms of costs, a negative advertisement was 49% as effective as the positive member of the pair, while another was 325% as effective. Overall, differences favored 16 positive advertisements, and 12 negative advertisements.

Another comparison involved sales of a proprietary drug in 5 groups of 3 test markets each over a 4-month period. A negative appeal here showed an increase of 71% over the same period of the previous year; a positive appeal produced a decrease of 10%.

Source. D. B. Lucas and C. E. Benson, "Some sales results for positive and negative advertisements," *Journal of Applied Psychology,* 14:363–70.

Who Should Draw Conclusions: Source or Audience?

Common sense suggests that if a source lines up his arguments but lets the audience draw a conclusion, he'll be more effective. First, they won't feel he's forcing his views down their throat; second, they have participated, not just been passive listeners. But there's a risk involved: some listeners may not be *able* to draw a conclusion or *willing* to exert effort.

Ten questions on United States policies in Korea were buried in a 62-item questionnaire given to 720 Air Force recruits. A week later, 4 groups were played tape-recorded messages 20 to 24 minutes long, accompanied by slides on the subject; a fifth control group listened to a program on tooth decay. Each experimental group then filled out an 18-item questionnaire, 4 questions of which measured subjects' comprehension of the speaker's overall conclusion. This was followed by a repeat of the opinion questionnaire given earlier.

For two groups, messages ended with a one-minute conclusion by the speaker; for two others no conclusion was drawn. Each pair was further divided, with 1 group getting a "well-organized" message in which two minutes were devoted to 23 statements that introduced and recapitulated issues and subtopics.

All four of the experimental programs changed attitudes toward the Korean war, as compared with the control group, differences being significant at the .05 level. Some of the differences were still significant three weeks later.

Three things influenced recruits' *comprehension* of the messages, as shown in the following table.

Analysis of Variance of Comprehension Scores of 444 Subjects

	F	p Values
A. Conclusion drawing	3.84	.05
B. Good organization of message	3.84	.05
C. Higher IQ	28.61	.001

(None of the interactions—A $\times$ B, A $\times$ C, B $\times$ C, and A $\times$ B $\times$ C—was significant.) Differences favored no conclusion for 110 subjects getting the poorly organized messages and were not significant for the 118 receiving well-organized messages. However, neither of the message variables—conclusion drawing and organization—produced significant differences in *attitude change*.

Source. Donald L. Thistlethwaite et al., "The effects of 'directive' and 'non-directive' communication procedures on attitudes," *Journal of Abnormal and Social Psychology,* 51: 107–13.

In a Controversy, Which Is Better, First or Last?

Where controversy exists, should one try to speak first or last if he wants his side remembered? Which position is better, in terms of changing attitudes?

Testimony of witnesses, cross examinations, and lawyers' statements from a damage suit involving a defective vaporizer were used as messages in a study involving 144 social science students at Northwestern. The messages were recorded on tape, a different voice for each character, and ran 45 minutes.

Variables studied were order of arguments (plaintiff-defendant and defendant-plaintiff), time lapse between arguments (none vs. one week) and time lapse between arguments and testing (following second argument or after one week's delay). This produced eight conditions (2 $\times$ 2 $\times$ 2).

A 28-item multiple choice test showed more recent messages were recalled better. The advantage of recency was greatest when a week elapsed between arguments but there was no delay between final argument and test. The advantage of recency was lowest when there was no delay between arguments but a week's delay between final argument and testing.

Average Recall Scores Condition

	Which Case Was Presented Last?		
	Defendant	Plaintiff	Diff.
Single session, immediate test	−.56[a]	−.89	.33
Single session, delayed test	−.22	−.61	.39
Two sessions, immediate test	2.38	−3.27	5.65
Two sessions, delayed test	1.00	1.89	1.89

[a] Negative scores mean plaintiff superior to defendant, positive scores indicate the reverse.

Mean Attitude Scores

	Which Case Was Presented Last?		
	Defendant	Plaintiff	Diff.
Single session, immediate test	5.94	5.88	.06
Single session, delayed test	4.50	6.61	−2.11
Two sessions, immediate test	6.00	4.33	1.67
Two sessions, delayed test	5.47	5.58	−.11

A 9-point scale measured attitude change, high scores indicating acceptance of the defendant's viewpoint. The first message was most effective when the two were given at the same session, but the test was delayed; the second message was most effective when a week intervened between messages but there was no delay between second message and test.

Source. Norman Miller and Donald P. Campbell, "Recency and primacy in persuasion as a function of the timing of speeches and measurements," *Journal of Abnormal and Social Psychology,* 59:1–9.

Fooling Around With Fallacies

A copy platform, which links product features to consumer benefits, can easily be expressed in the form of a syllogism for either brand or product.

Major premise: All consumers desire these satisfactions.

Minor premise: (Only) these product features can produce these satisfactions.

Conclusion: Therefore, all consumers desire these product features.

Major premise: All consumers desire these product features.

Minor premise: (Only) this brand offers these product features.

Conclusion: Therefore, all consumers desire this brand.

The total message consists of two linked syllogisms, technically called a *sorites* or series. No ad would be written in such plodding and pedestrian prose, however. A copywriter would telescope the sorites into a simpler slogan: *When comfort is your thing, your choice* (of a car) *will be Chevrolet.* By omitting elements in his argument, the copywriter has created an *enthymeme,* or, as in this instance, a sorites made up of enthymemes. His omissions may help him avoid trouble with the Federal Trade Commission, if the syllogisms are fallacious, since the fallacy occurs within the mind of the reader and not on paper. The copywriter runs a risk that readers won't be able or motivated to complete his incomplete argument, that some will complete it in a way that doesn't do him any good, or that they'll complete it in so many different ways that their responses will become unpredictable. However, forcing the reader to complete the argument means such participation improves learning and memory. Moreover, dissonance theory suggests that expenditure of effort makes men value things more.

Sometimes part of the syllogism is expressed in pictures and part in words. When a Pepsodent commercial showed toothpaste removing the yellow stains on enamel caused by a smoke machine, it was the viewer who inferred that machine-caused stains were the same as stains built up on his teeth over time (and that the enameled surface was the same thing as his teeth). (Despite a rule barring ads worded so that a careless or naive reader would be led to believe something false, the FTC vindicated Pepsodent with only two dissenting votes.) Logicians would say the viewer committed a *four-term fallacy* or a *fallacy of equivocation,* since the *stain* which the toothpaste removed was not the same *stain* which appears on viewers' teeth.

Great reputations have been built on use of such fallacies. In the words of Rosser Reeves, master of the hard-sell, as reported in the *New Yorker.*

> Eight out of 10 women wound up with dirty clothes, because they didn't use enough hot water, enough soap or didn't rinse properly. . . . So we showed them the proper way. . . . With this methodology and Supersuds, eight out of 10 got a cleaner, more dazzling wash.

Apparently most women assumed that Supersuds was a *necessary* part of the technique; some may even have assumed that it was a *sufficient* part of the technique. Yet Reeves was in the clear since he didn't *know* that any other soap would accomplish the same results; he had been very careful not to test any other brand. Subsequently he tried the technique again, with Colgate Dental Cream, used after every meal. As he tells the story.

> A very fuzzy-minded man from an advertising trade publication attacked me at lunch. He said, "Your commercial should state that you can keep your teeth clean and healthy with any toothpaste." I told him, "The tests that we talk about were conducted with Colgate Dental Cream. . . . I know only that these findings are true for Colgate Dental Cream. And I am entitled to advertise the fact."

Source. Quotations taken from Thomas Whiteside, "Annals of television: the man from iron city," *New Yorker,* Sept. 27, 1969, pp. 72, 78.

Additional Research Readings

Two-sided messages. When husbands and wives were asked to pick one of seven phonographs, those given a product evaluation like that of *Consumer Reports* took 12 minutes to make a choice, twice as long as those given only a manufacturer's brochure. **David M. Gardner, "Can Bales' interaction process analysis be used to explore consumer behavior," in Robert J. Holloway et al., Consumer Behavior (Boston: Houghton-Mifflin Co., 1971).** Salesmen and *Consumer Reports* were more effective in improving attitudes toward an unfamiliar brand of shirt, Truval, than when they confirmed existing preferences for Van Heusen; *Consumer Reports* was more influential in this than salesmen. **Donald J. Hempel, "An experimental study of the effects of information on consumer product evaluations," Raymond Haas, editor, Science, Technology and Marketing (Chicago: American Marketing Association, 1966).**

Fear appeals. High fear appeals were most effective in changing the dental care practices which students reported, but a no-fear, positive-affect message proved superior in changing actual behavior as revealed by a chemical test. **Richard I. Evans et al., "Fear arousal, persuasion and actual versus implied behavioral change . . . ," Journal of Personality and Social Psychology, 16:220–7.**

Readability. Information gains after reading articles on enzymes written by nine science writers and one biochemist ranged from 1.5 to 19.7%. Correlations between readability and either information gain or "enjoyment" were over .80. **G. Ray Funkhouser and Nathan Maccoby,**

"Communicating specialized science information to a lay audience," Journal of Communication, 21:58–71. Analogies comparing U.S. aid to Brazil to urban renewal or to a snowstorm switched more attitudes to an antiaid position than control messages. James C. McCroskey and Walter H. Combs, "The effects of the use of analogy on attitude change and source credibility," Journal of Communication, 19:333–9.

Public Service Advertising

The ads on these five pages run a gamut from such widely-accepted causes as aid to fatherless children to issues as controversial as gun control. The best-known source of such volunteer campaigns is the Advertising Council—which itself became controversial when one of its causes, Radio Free Europe, was revealed as a front for the CIA, and another of its campaign was accused of exploiting prisoners of war to combat anti-war sentiments. Here are samples of 12 campaigns by an individual ad agency, Frank M. Hutchins. Also shown are two different attempts to get tougher penalties on drunk driving, sponsored by insurance agencies whose rates presumably would fall if drunk driving decreased.

Boarding a Bandwagon

By associating themselves with the ecological movement, advertisers can borrow for themselves some of the public favor it enjoys, *congruity theory* suggests. This motive seems clearest in the case of a maker of men's perfume, which accentuates the positive. In contrast, *Equitable* tries a *negative appeal*—showing the slum environment one's children may grow up in if he dies without adequate insurance, as well as reporting the firm's contributions to urban renewal. A public utility attracts *attention* both to pollution problem, and to its offer of a kids' coloring book by presenting the crude drawing of a 6-year-old.

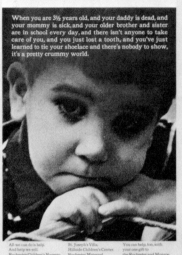

How to help stop the war and start something better.

Consensus or Controversy?

The two ads at the top of the page represent causes to which few can object, as they tug at the heartstrings on behalf of the fatherless child served by Community Chest Agencies and of the child who suffers from muscular dystrophy. Their *goal* is contributions. The two ads at the bottom of the page, in contrast, seek to affect *attitudes* toward controversial issues.

Magazine Publishers use a comic strip to defend advertising against those who say money spent to spur brand-switching is a social waste. Joe Meehan offers an unusual method of registering one's opposition to the war in Vietnam, involving both dollars and "demon-directed" correspondence.

Vietnam.

When the U.S. entered the war,
George Proctor had 2 sons.

Steve was 8. He's now 16.

Larry was 11. He's now dead.

Do you have sons?

What are you doing to keep them alive?

BEM BUSINESS EXECUTIVES MOVE FOR VIETNAM PEACE
An organization of hundreds of Chicago businessmen and thousands
throughout the U.S. who are opposed to the deaths and futility of purpose
of the Vietnam War. We urge you to add your voice to ours. Write or call
BEM, 116 S. Michigan, Chicago 60603. (312) 332-3282.

Vietnam.

Week ending	Americans killed
April 26	163
April 19	216
April 12	204
April 5	222
March 29	312
March 22	266
March 15	351
March 8	336
March 1	453

A dead issue. Unless you do something about it.

BEM BUSINESS EXECUTIVES MOVE FOR VIETNAM PEACE
An organization of hundreds of Chicago businessmen and thousands
throughout the U.S. who are opposed to the deaths and futility of purpose
of the Vietnam War. We urge you to add your voice to ours. Write or call
BEM, 116 S. Michigan, Chicago 60603. (312) 332-3282.

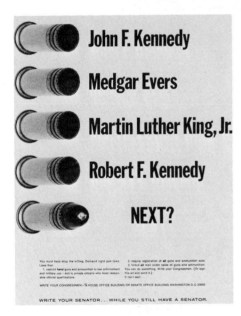

Gun Control at Home and Abroad

Seldom has the advertising world seen harder-hitting ads on controversial issues, ads arousing stronger reactions from both friends and foes, than those on this page. Some say the solutions offered are inadequate to ease the fears aroused; others object that the ads over-simplify complex issues. The two at the top of the page seek to recruit members for an anti-war group made up of business executives; those at the bottom urge one write his congressman demanding stiffer gun-control laws.
NEXT PAGE: Controversy reaches its peak here in an adman's ad attacking advertising!

448d

Chapter 23 Synopsis

● The source, as a cause of change in the receiver, has four attributes: visibility, credibility, power, and attractiveness. The seller is most visibly the source when his messages are transmitted via advertising and selling; his identity tends to be concealed if his messages are transmitted via publicity and word of mouth.

● The effectiveness of a source's power depends on the sanctions at his disposal, his ability to observe compliance, and his desire to enforce it. Power is most often employed within the hierarchical organization but is of little importance in relations between buyer and seller.

● Attractiveness, a powerful influence in voluntary and informal groups, depends on member familiarity and similarity; it has some influence in selling, virtually none when advertising is used for buyer-seller communications.

● Credibility, depending on buyer perceptions of a source's expert knowledge and his trustworthiness, is a critical factor in advertising. Opinions differ as to which of these perceptions is more important. There are reasons to believe that advertising is often perceived as being more credible than selling.

● Messages affect buyer attitudes toward their sources as well as toward their content; Osgood's congruity model tries to predict, given original attitudes toward both, which of the two will be most affected by a given message.

● The source's own attitudes are affected by the audiences he anticipates, by the act of transmission, and by audience responses during transmission. Anticipation is most important in advertising as is audience interaction in personal selling.

● Finding and motivating sources creative enough to prepare messages is a major problem for the seller. Neither the creative individual nor the creative person fit well into a hierarchical organization which depends on regularity of work flow and minimizes individual differences. Attempts to program the creative function and to segregate the creative deviant have failed to solve this basic contradiction. However, division of the advertising task among three different organizations whose relations and members change frequently has given creative people some of the freedom that they seem to require.

● Since creativity tends to peak early in life, efforts to isolate its correlates and to use them in finding creative individuals at an early age are most important. Also important are attempts to determine the working conditions that foster creativity.

Research Articles

Effective Source.   Is it better to be trusted or expert? It all
depends (Pastore, Hovland, Kelman, Bauer); agreement with
audience on one issue enhances effectiveness of publication
on second issue (Weiss).

Effect on Source.   Feedback from listener alters source behavior
(Verplanck); perception of audience's viewpoint alters source
behavior (Zimmerman); source expressing views contrary
to his own finds himself influenced thereby (Scott).

Identity of Source.   Computer word count reveals author of
disputed work (Miller), distinguishes between real and fake
suicide notes (Osgood, Ogilvie), and provides clues to author's
education, class, age (Goldschmidt).

Chapter 23 The Source as Cause and as Effect

The source of a message is always both a cause that one manipulates in communications and an effect that one obtains.

When an advertiser seeks to change his firm's image and buyers' attitudes toward his brand, he designs messages that treat source as an effect. When he uses his firm's image or user testimonials to get prospects to purchase his product, source becomes a causal variable. Audience attitudes toward the source always exert some influence on their response to the message, and attitudes toward both the source and message content are always affected to some degree.

An audience's attitudes toward the source of a message affect its response to the message. This was demonstrated dramatically when 330 high school pupils listened to a taped message urging leniency for juvenile delinquents.[1] For part of the audience, the speaker was identified as a juvenile court judge; for part as a member of the studio audience; and for the remainder as a dope-peddling suspect out on bail. The judge's audience showed most shift toward leniency for delinquents, the suspect's audience least change. Since the arguments were the same, why should it matter who made them? Subsequent investigation showed that the meanings, as received by the audience, were not the same. Just as the word *revolution* spoken by a Jefferson or a Lincoln does not mean the same thing as the same word coming from Lenin or Stalin, so a judge's *leniency* is not the same thing as that of the suspect who would benefit from it. On a list of occupations, *politics* may refer to the job of a president or a ward-heeler, depending on who is using it.[2]

Identifying the Source

Before a buyer's attitudes toward a source can influence his response to the source's message, and before a message can influence his attitudes toward its source, the buyer must be able to identify the source. In the experiments just cited, this identity was manipulated by the experimenter. In marketing communications, the identity and visibility of the source vary with the channel that carries his message. By definition, advertising has an identified source. When controversial issues are involved, however, a source may hide behind "front organizations." At one time, the prestigious Advertising Council used free media time and space to appeal for funds for Radio Free Europe, a facility amply and secretly supported by tax funds provided by the CIA. Laws that require an identified sponsor of ads for political candidates are circumvented by a host of paper organizations; one-man "organizations" have sponsored a fair number of issue-oriented political ads. (In response, groups not bankrolled by a handful of wealthy contributors often make a point of listing all of their donors, however small the type required.)

Unethical salesmen, at the door or on the telephone, may attempt to conceal the role they are playing until well into their pitch, but ordinarily a salesman's identity is as visible as is the source of an advertisement. The problem here is that of a multiple or composite source, of which the salesman is only one element. For a given buyer, how much weight does the salesman as an individual have in contrast to the firm he represents? A canned pitch suggests that the salesman is primarily a channel rather than a source. Cues to the salesman's personal credibility become irrelevant because canned-pitch salesmen are mere puppets for a faceless source. Since puppets presumably lack power to bargain and negotiate, the prospect submits to all of the disadvantages of face-to-face communications (personal pressure, inability to terminate the encounter, lack of a permanent record) without being able to influence the terms of the purchase and sale. Nothing the prospect may say or do can change the pitch; little wonder, then, that the prospect detests it.

The salesmen's importance as an element in the composite source tends to increase with repeated visits to the same buyer. In their first contact, a prospect probably is most influenced by the firm a salesman represents; over time, however, the salesman exerts more and more influence. So long as the salesman puts his firm's interests first, this may work to the employer's advantage, even though he loses a measure of control over the salesman.

Every advertisement, like every salesman's message, has been produced by a composite source, although a prospect may not perceive this fact or be influenced by it. Although the advertiser's name is signed to the ad, it usually has been prepared by an advertising agency; within broad limits, the medium that carries the message stands back of it.

Source identity for messages carried on the other two major channels—word of mouth and publicity—is more varied and often more in doubt. One's neighbor and one's newspaper *may* have picked up the message they transmit from an eyewitness or an actual participant in the event reported. These messages, however sincerely believed by the person who told them to the reporter or one's neighbor, may have originated from a most suspect source or been badly distorted over the days, years, or even generations of retelling. Moreover, although newspapers like to attribute statements of fact or opinion to specific individuals, vague "informed sources" proliferate with only the newspaper to validate their accuracy. A public figure may err or lie without having reporters, who depend on his continued cooperation, or editors, who may share his views, feel compelled

to expose the lie. (The press often seems to feel that this responsibility lies with a politician's opponents. It is a fact, says the press, that the candidate made the statement; whether the statement itself is factual is someone else's responsibility.) Meanwhile, readers may accept a newspaper account as true either because they are naive or because they have no choice. Business firms may benefit from a staged event; even when newspapers know who is staging the play and why, they do not always feel compelled to share this information with their readers. When they fail to do so, the channel also is perceived as the source of the message.

Opinions differ, as we shall see, on whether it is better to attribute one's messages to a clearly identified and obviously self-interested source, the firm, by employing such channels as selling and advertising or to conceal the firm's role as source by using the channels of publicity and word of mouth. Self-interest affects a source's *credibility*—one of three attributes of a source which determine how effective it is as a causal variable.

Three Source Attributes

Theorists suggest that all sources possess varying degrees of three attributes, each of which affects audience response in a different manner.[3]

Power. A powerful source can compel receivers to act, without changing their beliefs and feelings. (Indeed, an act performed under compulsion may cause feelings to move in the opposite direction.) Power depends on receivers' perceptions of a source's *ability* to impose rewards and punishments; of the strength of his *desire* to compel their behavior; and of his facilities for *surveillance*—the extent to which he can detect yielding and resistant acts.

Attractiveness. Receivers are attracted by sources whom they perceive as *similar* or *familiar,* and respond so that they may identify or associate with such sources. The reverse cause-effect relationship also holds: receivers tend to see a source they like as being more similar than he actually is, and they seek to become more familiar with someone they like.

Credibility. A credible source gets an audience to incorporate into their belief structure the views expressed in his message. A source is credible if he is perceived as *able* (expert enough to know what the truth is) and as *willing* (trustworthy enough to tell the truth). Evidence to date suggests that when the two elements conflict, the former is more important.

These three attributes interact with one another. Once a receiver yields to power, his beliefs may change to justify his yielding, particularly if the amount of power employed is minimal. Similarly, attractive sources tend to become credible and credible sources to become attractive.

Although common sense suggests that maximum credibility, which causes an audience to accept a message without question or thought, is desirable, this may not be true in marketing. One theorist[4] suggests that the ideal marketing message engenders sufficient disbelief to challenge the prospect to buy the product, to "see for himself." This theory assumes, of course, that use of the product will validate the extravagant claim made for it.

The relative importance of these three source attributes—power, attractiveness, and credibility—varies with the situation.

Attractiveness is most important in voluntary organization and informal groups, where it creates close bonds among peers and gets them to conform to norms of the group. *Power,* a characteristic of hierarchical organizations, affects relations between the president of a firm and his advertising manager. A sales manager's exercise of power over salesmen is limited by the difficulty of observing their interaction with

customers; sanctions are determined by the outcome of this interaction rather than by its nature. In his relations with the buyer, the salesman may attempt to employ attractiveness as a supplement to credibility. *Credibility,* of course, is the most important source attribute in marketing communications.

If the newspaper has a better image than the seller's firm, publicity will be a more effective medium than advertising for the seller's messages in terms of source identity. If professional athletes are regarded as more expert and trustworthy than actors, commercials will present testimonials from baseball and football stars rather than film stars. (On the other hand, a movie star advertising toupees to the audience of a late late movie may be as effective as a baseball star demonstrating razor blades between innings: credibility, power, and attractiveness tend to be specific to product, market, audience, time, and place.)

Since prospects usually recognize that a seller knows more about his product than they do, the *expert* aspect of credibility seldom is a problem in marketing communications. The seller knows the truth—but can he be trusted to reveal it to a prospect? Knowledge is power and the more knowledgeable and powerful a seller is, the more dangerous an antagonist he is if the buyer can't trust him. Since emphasis on seller expertise is often both unnecessary and unwise, messages can often emphasize trustworthiness and suggest that the seller has the interest of the buyer at heart, or that the seller's self-interest overlaps, at least in part, the self-interest of the prospect. Prospects who expect a seller to stress his product's desirable qualities tend to discount what an advertiser has to say. Since self-interest tends to be accepted as a legitimate part of the businessman's role, its damaging effects are lessened in a degree not always found in other situations. Finally, the consumer knows that society has placed limits on the advertiser's manipulations: external, in the form of law and control by the advertising media and internal, in a seller's desire for repeat sales of a product or a favorable image.

Even in the experimental laboratory, dealing with nonmarketing issues, it has been found that obvious self-interest need not reduce a source's effectiveness. One study[5] found no immediate disadvantage for a disreputable source. Other studies, concerning such varied phenomena as drugs, atomic submarines, steel shortages, and juvenile delinquency,[6] found that the original disadvantage of a disreputable source dissipated after four weeks. In advertising, few sources are actually disreputable, and effects are often observed more than a month following exposure. (Only retail, point-of-purchase, and direct-mail advertising are ordinarily expected to produce immediate rather than delayed results.)

Credibility of the Salesman

After reviewing 10 different experimental approaches to the problem, McGuire[7] concluded that awareness of a source's desire to influence them does not usually cause subjects to resist his efforts more fiercely. Perceptions of a source's *competence* have more effect on audience response than do perceptions of his objectivity. (In marketing, the opposite may be true. Few advertisers are perceived as inexpert or as untrustworthy as the sources used in most of these experiments.)

The salesman as source often lacks the credibility of the advertisement. Individual salesmen, particularly those seen frequently, may be trusted but salesmen in general tend to be suspect. Behind advertising stand not only the advertiser, but the agency and media with reputations of their own to maintain. Moreover, the public, permanent nature of the advertising message, in contrast to the remarks of the salesman, pro-

vides evidence useful in court, with regulatory agencies, and for postal inspectors, and so induces caution in its user. As a result, the buyer seems to have a whole series of discount rates to apply to seller's messages, differing for advertising and sales messages, for retail clerks and door-to-door salesmen, and for such products as new cars and used ones.

Since the salesman is often seen as both powerful and suspect, he may spend considerable time in suggesting commonality of interest with the prospect. A salesman may avoid use of evaluative terms but accomplish the same end with denotative words by careful selection of the facts he reports. (It probably is more effective to describe a prospective blind date as "six foot two, black curly hair, a Gregory Peck type" than it is to describe him as "tall, dark, and handsome.")

Aware that even denotative words can be used to persuade, many prospects prefer to depend on nonverbal cues in assessing a salesman's real intentions, feeling that he is less able to control them than he is the words he uses. Just as a high-pitched voice suggests youth or female, and a quaver indicates age or rage, so may facial expression, stance, and vocal timbre be perceived as indicating sincerity or duplicity in the salesman. (Because of this, salesmen, like actors, are carefully trained to avoid the sarcastic tone which can turn words of praise into an insult or the skeptical tone which indicates disbelief in product claims, and to put on the garb of honesty.) Establishing credibility becomes easier for a salesman, of course, if his messages include such concrete evidence of honest intentions as moneyback guarantees and service warranties.

Changes in the Source's Own Attitudes

In many communications encounters any distinction between source and receiver vanishes: both participants send, both receive, and both are influenced by the messages exchanged. To some extent this is also true of salesman and prospect, although the salesman, having more information to transmit, greater interest in the outcome, and more control over the process than does the prospect, tends to dominate the role of source.

Even before a salesman comes face to face with a prospect, his anticipations of prospect and encounter exert an influence on him. He selects content which he thinks will be well received. He chooses symbols which he thinks the audience will understand and be influenced by, because they are congruent with past experiences and present attitudes. He takes account of an audience's salient roles and reference groups and the context in which the message will be received, including any residue left from prior exposure to competing messages.

These effects of "anticipated audiences" are not restricted to salesmen. Reporters who say they had hostile audiences in mind when writing news stories tend to be more accurate in handling content that they expected such audiences to dislike—whether as a protection against hostile criticism or as a way of getting even with hostile audiences.[8] In contrast, newsmen anticipating friendly audiences were accurate in reporting news such audiences would like, but erred on material such audiences would find unpleasant. Harvard graduate students in business who said they thought an adman should try to keep a client happy remembered more of the selling points used in a Lestoil commercial than did students who said the adman should dare to tell a client unpleasant truths.[9] In short, a source's pictures of his audience affect his accuracy in transmitting messages and his ability to recall such messages even when he has no physical encounter with the audience.

Since admen seldom come face to face with an audience, their behavior is most influenced by their anticipations; in contrast, the salesman is more powerfully influenced by his actual encounter with prospects.

A buyer may influence a salesman without either person being aware that such influence has been exerted. In the laboratory, for example, an experimenter has controlled the content of subjects' conversation, without the subject being aware of what he was doing or why, by a series of approving nods or simple *mmm-hmmm*. Whether the salesman consciously alters his behavior to obtain the informal rewards of a pleasant relationship with the prospect or is unaware that his behavior has been altered by buyers' responses, the consequences for his employer are the same: loss of predictability and loss of control.

Not only is the salesman's behavior affected by the responses of his audience, actual or anticipated; it is also affected by his own message and the act of transmitting it. Such effects have been found in a variety of experiments. Opinions of students who give speeches are more affected than are opinions of students who listen to them,[10] and the more freedom students have in constructing their speeches, the more their opinions change.[11] This is true not only of issues on which students are neutral but on issues where they have strong opinions.[12] However, the *less* extraneous inducement a student is offered for expressing ideas that run counter to his own attitudes, the more effect such expression seems to have. (If rewards are small, the theory of *cognitive dissonance* suggests, speakers justify their behavior by changing their attitudes to agree with their behavior.[13] If rewards or penalties are large, this appears to justify behavior inconsistent with belief, and attitude change is less likely.) Recent studies suggest that attitude change caused by publicly espousing views one does not in fact hold may be limited to situations in which subjects are told that they have *successfully* persuaded others.[14] To this extent the phenomenon resembles that of the anticipated audience: both effects on source attitudes depend on his perception of audience views, either before or after his speech.

Creativity: An Ill Fit for the Firm

As we have seen, selecting the appropriate mix of source attributes and exposing (or concealing) source identity represent two of the major decisions that a seller must make, two problems that he must solve. There is a third major problem: finding and motivating creative individuals who can prepare advertising and sales messages.

Creative individuals and the creative process itself fit poorly into the business firm. Organizations value predictability and a steady flow of work, since idle machines and idled men are costly and so are sudden spurts in sales. The essence of the creative process, on the other hand, seems to be an indefinite period of incubation following input of experiences and data, a period during which there is no visible activity or output but one which is followed by sudden problem-solving insights, which may or may not work and which come after irregular, indeterminate lapses of time. Organizations also seek employees who can be forced into preexisting pigeonholes called *roles*, so that when one man dies, quits, or is fired, he can be replaced with a minimum amount of disturbance and delay. Creativity, on the other hand, thrives on individual differences and would alter organizational charts to fit men, rather than the reverse.

Business firms have tried to resolve this fundamental contradiction between organizational efficiency and creativity in two ways. One is to eliminate the creative individual by programming the creative process. The other is to segregate creative individuals in time and space, so as to minimize the disturbance that they cause. Neither method has been notoriously successful.

Attempts to program creativity and so eliminate the need for the creative personality usually occur in two stages. First, products or messages are analyzed into their constituent attributes, both formal and functional, and then these attributes are systematically and exhaustively recombined in all possible ways, to produce a new kind of hammer, a bathtub that converts into bed or bookcase, or a three-wheeled, electric-powered bicycle-boat-glider. The number of combinations generated by such methods is so large, however, and many of them so outrage common sense, that only the relaxed mind of a very creative person is able to separate the possibles from the incredibles and use the more ridiculous to stimulate his own imagination.

Artists and copywriters can be banished to a back room in the advertising agency, so they will not subvert other employees, confuse clients, or upset the general public. But copywriters need direct contact with the buyer, as a source of input and as a check on output, and even, on occasion, with the client-audience which guards the gate between source and consumer.

Segregating the deviant creative role in *time* has also been attempted. To build morale in the business firm, status barriers may be let down at an annual picnic, a Christmas party, a sensitivity weekend of nude bathing, or a workshop. To foster creativity, Adman Alex Osborn invented *brainstorming*, a group-think session in which critical comments were barred, and kudos went to the men with the wildest ideas and the most ideas and to those best able to build on the ideas of others.

At best, however, such techniques seem merely to overcome the barriers on creativity imposed by the presence of others. Careful studies reveal that the same men spending the same number of man hours by themselves are often more productive than when thrown together in a group-think session, even one which puts a hundred ideas on tape for every hour of brainstorming. Although the presence of others may heighten overt, physical responses, it seems to hamper such creative processes as concept formation, reasoning by analogy, and perception of relationships, and to discourage diversity of ideas.[15]

In an on-going group, norms soon develop as to "proper" thoughts and behaviors and propriety kills creativity. In a new group, members often seek to discover similarities rather than emphasize the differences vital to creativity. They do so because they want acceptance as individuals, believe the purpose of any group is consensus or seek norms that will provide structure and goals for the group.

Since it takes time to organize a group and coordinate its activities, groups tend to move slowly. To the extent that individual thinking in the group is geared to verbal interchange, the inability of everyone to speak at once limits the number of new ideas that can be produced per man-hour. Surprisingly, pressures to conform do not appear to make groups more cautious than individuals. Group participation, instead, seems to cause a *risky shift:*[16] after a group experience individuals are willing to take more chances than before. Reasons suggested include discovery, in discussion, that others are not more conservative than oneself and that venturesomeness is expected of men and managers. Other reasons suggested are that the language has more colorful and effective words favoring risk than urging caution and that more intense emotions, exercising greater influence on listeners, are aroused in go-for-broke speakers than look-before-you-leap types.

Although fitting creative individuals into an organization remains a problem, the division of the advertising function among three separate organizations—advertiser, agency, and advertising medium—tends to

free admen from the command structure by making them subject to the give and take of the marketplace. If any one of the three organizations becomes dissatisfied, the relationship can be broken off. It often is; the average length of a relationship between client and agency is said to be less than six years. (One reason for such frequent changes is the difficulty of determining how much an ad or a campaign is increasing one's sales, if at all; ads may be contributing to a decline in sales. Thus ads are likely to get the blame and the ad agency to get the axe when sales and profits falter.)

Firing an agency, unlike firing an employee, leaves morale and output of the client firm's employees untouched. And a client must be extremely fickle to dissuade new agencies from seeking his account. Shifts of agency are made easier in that all but two of the nation's largest agencies and 37 of the 55 billing more than $25 million a year have their headquarters in New York City.[17]

A world distinguished by frequent shifts of employees among agencies and of agencies among clients tends to increase the freedom of the creative individual. Such shifts are frequent in advertising, a Chicago study showing that admen in their thirties change jobs every 3.3 years, on the average; those in their forties every 4 years, those in their fifties every 5.[18] True, some of these changes are more apparent than real, since a copywriter may tag along with an account when it shifts agencies, but real changes are frequent enough to cause comment.

Locating the Creative Individual

Even more important than fitting creative types into business is the problem of finding creative individuals in the first place. Studies of creativity suggest that the ability itself is rare, being possessed in usable amounts by only about 1% of the population. In today's world, creativity must be built on a certain amount of familiarity with the past which is gained through education which, in turn, requires an IQ in the neighborhood of 120. This means that a search for creative individuals begins with the 11% of the population with such IQ's, and then tries to find the one creative man in 100 in this select sample. Moreover, the search must identify such men early in their careers, when their creativity is at its peak. These are the model age ranges for maximum rate of creative production in different fields.[19]

Before 30	Chemistry, poetry
30 to 34	Mathematics, physics, botany, symphonies
35 to 39	Astronomy, physiology, philosophy, opera
40 and up	Novels, architecture

Advertising is considered a young man's game. In 1960 when white American males lived an average of 67.2 years and physicians 68.9, admen averaged only 61.5. Analyzing 300 obituaries appearing in its pages in 1969, *Advertising Age* reported admen dying at a mean age of 62.9 and a median age of 65.3, compared with a mean of 64.5 for media employees.[20] (The range for the media ran from 59.1 for broadcasters to 66.9 for newspaper executives.)

It often appears that creative potential in copywriting tends to level off or diminish with age and experience. Management skills are learned through experience with people, and a manager may have to spend years working his way up a table or organization before he can show what he can do. An ability to manipulate symbols needs no such experience. Moreover, a copywriter has less far to travel, up the chart, since ad agencies and media tend to have few employees relative to other firms. Visibility is high for the able adman; it's not too hard for a prospective employer to find out what young genius produced the brilliant new detergent commercial. A young man who feels lost in a large agency can start one of his own; of 7500 agencies studied in 1963, more than one-third were one-man concerns.[21] As a result of such factors, able admen may be near the top of their trade's financial ladder early in life; departure of older, less able men for more settled occupations tends to lower the overall average age.

Morale isn't always high in the advertising trade, however; a study reported in 1961 found that only 37% of admen would recommend the career to a nephew in preference to five other occupations.[22] At that, morale was higher than reputation; not one of these admen's neighbors said they would recommend such a career to their nephews! One common complaint, particularly by the creative individual, is the number of barriers between the copywriter's desk and his audience. When an as does appear, it may represent the tinkering of dozens of persons, no one of whom is happy with the result or would want his name associated with it. One estimate is that 40 persons outside the ad agency itself must approve a TV commercial before it is aired.[23] Of course it's possible that any of the 40 may have contributed the slight twist which converts a routine ad into a great one; some admen even concede that a client has on occasion made such a contribution.

Creative people tend to have been raised in permissive families, to accept themselves and others, to be independent and unafraid of authority or convention, and to view life in relative rather than black-and-white terms.[24] They are typically self-confident and free from anxiety. They place a high value on practical matters and avoid unwarranted risks. Their interest in novelty and change and their ability to combine familiar objects in unfamiliar ways are not limited to any single area but tend to be part of their whole life style.

One useful cue to creativity is occupational preference. In one study, out of 28 high school pupils with high IQ's but low creativity scores, 23 chose conventional careers like law and medicine; in contrast, 16 of the 26 with high creative scores and lower IQ's, chose unconventional careers like inventor and writer.[25] Drawings are another tip-off to creativity: 14 out of 26 creative pupils put humor into their pictures, as compared with only 5 out of 28 high IQ-low creativity pupils.[26] Creative people also score higher than "normal adults" (although lower than artists) in a sophisticated preference for art that is complex and asymmetrical.[27]

Normal adults	14
Student engineers	22
Research scientists	24
Mathematicians	27
Writers	32
Artists	40

As suggested by these figures, creativity appears to have several dimensions. Some creative dimensions correlate with IQ and some do not, correlations varying by sex. When subjects were asked to perform five paper-and-pencil tasks—form word associations, devise novel uses for objects like bricks and coat hangers, detect hidden shapes, invent fables, and make up problems—highest correlations among the tests for boys were.[28]

Word association: .42 with making up problems, .38 with IQ
Hidden shapes: .41 with making up problems, .37 with IQ

(However, hidden shapes and word association correlated only .34 with one another.)
Highest correlations for girls were.

Word association: .49 with making up problems, .37 with novel uses and with IQ

Making up problems: .53 with hidden shapes, .39 with IQ

Another test asked fifth-graders what they "saw" in simple drawings. A tangled line which looked like "string" to an ordinary student became "toothpaste squeezed from a tube" to the pupil with high creative potential.[29] Ordinarily people saw a triangle with a circle on each side as three people sitting at a table; the creative fifth-grader saw it as three mice nibbling cheese.

Creative people differ, and so do their work habits. By nature, creative people seem more relaxed; in a permissive atmosphere they become even more relaxed —and more creative. When they relax, familiar associations between ideas, objects, and stimulus and response drift away, allowing less common and salient associations to emerge. New insights may appear, ending the incubation process, when a creative person is strolling in the woods, about to fall asleep, or engaged in a routine activity which can be switched off when a newly hatched insight needs attention. On the other hand, a deliberate attempt to focus attention on a problem and force a solution may strengthen the very common, salient associations which prevent creative novelty. For this reason, attempts to study the creative process introspectively are likely to halt it in its tracks. Denied introspection, scholars tend to avoid study of the incubation process, shifting their attention to the input processes. They find that uncreative men spend too little time in analysis, too much time in attempting and failing to achieve synthesis. Creative men, in contrast, work slowly while analyzing problems and gathering data, but they synthesize rapidly. (Researchers agree that if one spends enough time and effort in asking a question it may answer itself.)

Although the creative man appears to be

playing a deviant role in many firms today, management experts suggest that such roles will become increasingly common in the firm of tomorrow. Gellerman argues that employees who find their work self-fulfilling will produce higher profits, be less resistant to change, place fewer restrictions on output, and exhibit less apathy and anomie than is commonly true now.[30] Work that is self-fulfilling, he predicts, will become common when managers recognize that it is easier for them to change their ideas and behaviors than to change those of their employees. Methods for inducing such recognition in managers, commonly lumped together under the tag of *sensitivity training*, closely resemble methods used to stimulate creativity. Basically they involve a free, permissive, and uncritical exchange of feelings and beliefs among peers and a minimizing of differences of role and status.

Thought, Talk, and Action

1. You have four decisions to make: what candidate for governor to vote for, which store to buy a new suit in, where to go to graduate school, and what CPA firm should make out your income tax return. Which three persons would you consult on each decision?
2. List the following sources: a college instructor, your spouse, the Better Business Bureau, the editor of your daily newspaper, your father, your best friend, and your pastor, or your psychiatrist. Rank them from 1 to 7 on each of the following characteristics. *Power:* sanctions, willingness to use them, ability to use them. *Attractiveness:* similarity, familiarity. *Credibility:* expertise, trustworthiness. Now total scores. Do totals reflect actual frequency with which you consult each of these on purchasing decisions? If not, who do you consult most?
3. Taking these same seven sources, now rerank them in terms of your likelihood of consulting them for each of the four decisions listed under No. 1 above.

Notes

Chapter 23

1. Herbert C. Kelman and Carl I. Hovland, "Reinstatement of the communicator in delayed measurement of opinion change," Journal of Abnormal and Social Psychology, 48: 327–35.
2. Helen Block Lewis, "Studies in the principles of judgments and attitudes: IV. The operation of 'prestige suggestion'," Journal of Social Psychology, 14:229–56.
3. William J. McGuire, "The nature of attitudes and attitude change," in Gardner Lindzey and Elliot Aronson, The handbook of social psychology, 2nd ed. (Menlo Park, Calif.: Addison-Wesley Publishing Co., 1969), Vol. 3, pp. 179–200.
4. John C. Maloney, "Curiosity versus disbelief in advertising," Journal of Advertising Research, 2:2:2–8.
5. Walter Weiss, "The influence of source credibility on communication effectiveness," Public Opinion Quarterly, 15: 635–50.

6. Reference No. 1.

7. Reference No. 3, pp. 183–7.

8. Raymond A. Bauer and Ithiel de Sola Pool, The effects of audiences on communicators (Cambridge: Harvard Graduate School of Business Administration, 1960).

9. *Ibid.*

10. Irving L. Janis and Bert T. King, "The influence of role playing on opinion change," Journal of Abnormal and Social Psychology, 49:211–18.

11. Carl I. Hovland et al., Communication and persuasion (New Haven: Yale University Press, 1953).

12. Herbert C. Kelman, "Attitude change as a function of response restriction," Human Relations, 6:185–214.

13. Leon Festinger, A theory of cognitive dissonance (Stanford, Calif.: Stanford University Press, 1962).

14. William A. Scott, "Attitude change through reward of verbal behavior," Journal of Abnormal and Social Psychology, 55: 72–5.

15. Harold H. Kelley and John W. Thibaut, "Group problem solving," in Handbook of Social Psychology (see Reference No. 3 above), Vol. 4, p. 5.

16. *Ibid.*, pp. 78–84. Also see Roger Brown, Social psychology (New York: The Free Press, 1965), pp. 656–706, for an earlier, more readable account.

17. For current figures, see annual "billings issue" of *Advertising Age* during February of current year.

18. Harry Walker Hepner, Advertising, 4th ed. (New York: McGraw-Hill Book Co., 1964), p. 662. (*Advertising Age* updates figures annually.)

19. Harvey C. Lehman, Age and achievement (Princeton, N.J.: Princeton University Press, 1953), p. 326.

20. Advertising Age, January 12, 1970. (Figures are updated annually.)

21. S. Watson Dunn, Advertising, 2nd ed. (New York: Holt, Rinehart and Winston, 1969), p. 130.

22. Advertising Age, April 3, 1961.

23. Reference No. 18, p. 37.

24. Bernard Berelson and Gary A. Steiner, Human behavior (New York: Harcourt, Brace and World, 1964), pp. 226–35.

25. Jacob W. Getzels and Philip W. Jackson, Creativity and intelligence: Explorations with gifted students (New York: John Wiley & Sons, 1962), pp. 57–8.

26. Same reference as No. 25, pp. 46, 48. Cited in reference No. 24, p. 231.

27. Donald W. McKinnon, "Creativity in architects," Institute of Personality Assessment and Research, The creative person (Berkeley, Calif.: University of California, 1961). Cited in reference No. 24, p. 230.

28. Reference No. 25, p. 228.
29. M. A. Wallach and N. Kogan, Modes of thinking in young children (New York: Holt, Rinehart and Winston, 1965).
30. Saul W. Gellerman, Motivation and productivity (New York: American Management Association, 1963).

Expert and Trustworthy? Yes; Effective? Maybe

Common sense suggests that the most effective source is one perceived as both expert and trustworthy. An early experiment supported this viewpoint.

Ten statements like this one were prepared.

Every artist should attempt to reflect and advance the social and economic aims of society in his work.

Each statement was assigned a "good" author (Ernest Hemingway for the statement above) or a "bad" one (Dmitri Shostakovich). Each author was assigned a "good" motive (*To show an artist can advance desirable aims without sacrificing his ideals*) or a "bad" motive (*To win wider approval for work criticized as inartistic*).

Four source-and-motive combinations are possible: each of 85 student subjects received one combination per statement and indicated, on three 9-point scales, how much he accepted statement, author and motive.

In only 3 of 20 cases did a statement accompanied by a "bad" motive win higher acceptance than did the matching "good" motive version. In 19 of 20 cases, "good"-motive authors were judged more acceptable than those with "bad" motives.

Source. Nicholas Pastore and Milton W. Horowitz, "The influence of attributed motive on the acceptance of statement," *Journal of Abnormal and Social Psychology*, 51: 331–2.

However, a subsequent study showed that although trustworthy authors won favorable ratings, their messages were no more effective.

Identical taped messages urging devaluation of the currency were attributed to a bad-motive importer, who would benefit from devaluation, or a presumably impartial economist from a major university. Here are the results.

	Percentage of Subjects Agreeing	
	Importer	*Economist*
Source was fair and honest	37	53
Yes, the U.S. should devalue its currency	31	36

Source. Carl I. Hovland and Wallace Mandell, "An experimental comparison of conclusion-drawing by the communicator and by the audience," *Journal of Abnormal and Social Psychology*, 47:581–8.

Tape recordings were used with high school pupils in another study, which asked *how long* the effects of a credible source persist.

Pupils completed an eight-item questionnaire concerning treatment of juvenile delinquents, and then listened to messages opposing any form of punishment and urging that delinquents be treated as sick children.

The message was attributed to three different sources, one for each group of subjects: a juvenile court judge, a "neutral" member of the studio audience, and a former delinquent suspected of dope peddling. Ratings of the sources were what one would expect.

Percentage Giving Source a
Favorable Rating

Judge	Neutral	Suspect
Judge	*Neutral*	*Suspect*

Source is "highly qualified"

78	33	9

I would trust the source's judgment

87	66	25

This time opinion change was in line with ratings of the source. On a 16-item scale, with a score of 64 indicating maximum acceptance of source's position, the judge's subjects averaged 46.7, the neutral's subjects 45.7, and the suspect's audience 42.7. However, when half of the subjects checked the scale again three weeks later, source effects had vanished. Average scores on the leniency scale were almost the same for judge (43.5) and dope suspect (43.4). The other half of the subjects were reexposed to the descriptions of the two men, and then completed rating scales—and the original 4-point difference returned: 45.3 for the judge's group, 41.5 for the suspect's audience.

Experimenters concluded that source effects wash out over time because the link between source and message vanishes from memory although message content does not.

Source. Herbert C. Kelman and Carl I. Hovland, "Reinstatement of the communicator in delayed measurement of opinion change," *Journal of Abnormal and Social Psychology*, 48:327–35.

Another study suggests that an untrustworthy source may be *more* effective in producing change which can withstand subsequent attack by a competing point of view. (The argument is that one accepts a trustworthy source's position without bothering to look at the evidence he offers for it. Later, lacking such evidence, one then becomes vulnerable to his opposition. In contrast, one is likely to take a good, hard look at the "facts" presented by an expert but untrustworthy source and to remember them.)

Some 1500 employees of Massachusetts' department of public works were gathered in an auditorium, tested on their attitudes toward civil defense, given a letter to read that opposed civil defense, and then retested.

All 1500 had been sent a message *favoring* civil defense two and a half weeks earlier. Each message was accompanied by a letter describing the source of the message. Four different descriptions were used.

Expert and trustworthy: an engineer known for his objectivity.

Expert but not trustworthy: an engineer fired from the atomic energy commission because he had become a civil defense nut.

Trustworthy but not expert: a lawyer of good character but lacking any technical background.

Neither expert nor trustworthy: a defeated politician appointed to a civil defense office because of political pull.

In the first test in the auditorium, the expert and trustworthy source proved to have been most effective. In the second test, after employees had been exposed to counterpropaganda, he proved *least* effective, and the untrustworthy expert *most* effective.

A second study showed that the delay was crucial; when the counterpropaganda followed immediately upon the original procivil defense message, the persuasive effects of the expert-trustworthy source remained higher than in any other experimental condition. The author suggests that in automobile advertising, with a long delay likely to occur between ad exposure and purchase, giving one's competition an opportunity of filling this time period with counterpropaganda, the untrustworthy expert may be dangerous.

Source. Raymond A. Bauer, "Personality, perception of source and persuasibility," in *On Knowing the Consumer,* Joseph W. Newman, ed. (New York: John Wiley & Sons, Inc., 1966).

What Do You Do When Two Strikes Have Been Called?

A salesman calling on a prospect for the first time often establishes his credibility by finding some viewpoint, experience, or value which he and the prospect share.

Would the same technique work if the salesman were actually disliked by the prospect? Or make the test a really tough one: suppose the salesman, who is disliked, must get a prospect to accept a viewpoint he's already rejected.

In Boston, a survey revealed that student subjects favored academic freedom and fluoridation of water, and felt that the *Daily Worker* was untrustworthy and *The New York Times* trustworthy. Weiss tried to use an article supposedly reprinted from the *Daily Worker* to get students to oppose fluoridation.

Before reading this article, four student groups read another article. The key experimental group read a second *Daily Worker* article, this one echoing the students' favorable attitude toward academic freedom. Control groups 2 and 3 read a descriptive article on Uganda, a subject on which they had no opinion; control group 4 read the article on academic freedom, but attributed to the *New York Times.* Six three-point questions then measured attitudes toward fluoridation. Here are the percentages opposed to fluoridation after reading the messages.

Preliminary Message

1. Academic freedom (*Daily Worker*)	64
2. Uganda (*Daily Worker*)	39
3. Uganda (*Daily Worker*)— No sources quoted	48
4. Academic freedom (*New York Times*)	36

Although balance theories would suggest subjects might adjust to the situation by becoming less favorable to academic freedom when it was favored by the *Daily Worker* this effect did not occur.

Source. Walter Weiss, "Opinion congruence with a negative source on one issue as a factor influencing agreement on another issue," *Journal of Abnormal and Social Psychology,* 54:180–6.

Influence Travels Both Ways in Face-to-Face Encounters

When salesman meets customer, not all of the influence travels from salesman to customer. A good salesman responds quickly to a frown, a shake of the head, a grimace, or a noncommittal grunt. How effective such reactions can be is shown in this experiment.

Seventeen psychology students engaged 24 subjects—13 friends, 7 roommates, one date, one uncle, and one total stranger—in 30-minute conversations in various settings: 17 in student dormitories, 2 in restaurants, 2 in private homes, and 1 each in a hospital ward, a public lounge, and over the telephone. Topics discussed included dates, vacations, Marxism, man's need for religion, Liberace, architecture, and the theory of music.

For the first 10 minutes, psychology students counted the number of statements their subjects made, and the proportion which were opinion statements. For the next 10 minutes, students rewarded every opinion statement by agreeing with it, or paraphrasing and repeating it. Then, for a final 10 minutes, students "extinguished" opinion statements by making no response to them or by disagreeing.

Seventeen subjects received this treatment. The remaining 7, a control group, were rewarded for opinion statements for the first and last 10-minute periods, extinguished or punished for them during the middle period. Frequency of opinion statements nearly doubled under "reward" conditions.

Every subject increased the proportion of opinion statements when rewarded; 21 of the 24 subjects decreased the proportion when rewards were lacking.

Median Percentage of Opinion Statements

Experimental Group (N = 17)	
No audience response	32
Opinions rewarded	56
Opinions extinguished	33

Control Group (N = 7)	
Opinions rewarded	57
Opinions extinguished	30
Opinions rewarded	60

Paraphrasing appeared to be a more effective reward than agreement. When students conducting the experiment began disagreeing or not responding to subjects, 7 subjects stopped talking or left the room. No subject indicated that he realized his behavior was being manipulated and his response recorded.

Source. William S. Verplanck, "The control of the content of conversation: reinforcement of statements of opinion," *Journal of Abnormal and Social Psychology*, 51:668–76.

A salesman's conduct may be influenced even before he encounters an audience by the reactions he anticipates from them. Here's another experiment showing how audiences influence sources.

Subjects came from teachers' colleges and from schools of journalism, half in each group being told they were to write a talk for The National Council of Teachers (who presumably would favor more pay for teachers) and the other half that the talk was intended for the American Taxpayers Economy League (a group that would oppose more pay for teachers). Eighteen journalism students and 18 teachers college

Expected Audience:	Taxpayers		Teachers	
Arguments Heard:	Raise Pay	Do Not Raise Pay	Do Not Raise Pay	Raise Pay
Type of student				
Journalism school	4.9	11.3	6.1	13.7
Teachers college	8.6	11.5	8.8	11.7

students who expected to talk to taxpayers heard a message containing 25 arguments *favoring* higher pay for teachers. Another 18 journalists and 18 education students, also expecting to talk to taxpayers, heard 25 arguments *against* paying teachers more money. (In all, eight groups, representing all possible combinations of audience, arguments, and students—2 × 2 × 2— were used.)

Each set of arguments was read twice, students being given 15 minutes to write down all of the points they could remember. A week later they were again asked to write down all of the points they could remember.

No significant differences showed up until a week had passed. Then subjects who heard arguments consistent with the attitudes of their expected audiences remembered more of them than did subjects who heard arguments opposed to the views of their audiences. Journalism students proved more sensitive to "audience effect" than teachers college students.

Average number of points recalled out of 25 originally presented are shown in table at top of page.

Source. Claire Zimmerman and Raymond A. Bauer, "The effect of an audience upon what is remembered," *Public Opinion Quarterly*, 20:238–48.

Source Is Influenced by His Own Message

Playing a role contrary to one's be- liefs, as when a debater argues for a point of view not his own, may cause a temporary change in attitudes. But unless the debater then affiliates with a group which shares the viewpoint, he is likely to backslide; this is es- pecially true if he rejoins his old asso- ciates who punish him for his change of heart. The effects of reward and penalty on "freezing" attitude change were looked at in this study.

Opinions were obtained in 29 psychology classes on three issues: a proposal that all men 18 to 25 be subject to two years' service in the peacetime army; a lifting of curfew for all coeds, even freshmen; and a condemnation of overemphasis on football and favoritism toward football players.

Outside of class, students with definite views both pro and con were persuaded to take a side, in a subsequent debate, contrary to the opinions they had just given. Each class was then asked to ballot as to the "winner," the count so manipulated that half the time the pro side won and half the time their opponents. Results were announced, and then everybody retook the original opinion inventory.

The reward of "winning" proved far more effective than the much longer time debaters had spent preparing and giving their talks. (Each had three minutes, plus a two-minute rebuttal.) It made no difference which issue was involved or whether the debater had originally been "pro" or "con." Each group numbered 36 persons.

	Winners	Losers	Control
Number changing away from original position (toward position taken in debate)	21	7	11
Number becoming more extreme in original position (opposite viewpoint taken in debate)	3	9	7
Mean change on opinion scale (+ is in direction taken in debate)	+1.25	−.17	+.31

Source. William Abbott Scott, "Attitude change through reward of verbal behavior," *Journal of Abnormal and Social Psychology,* 55:72–5.

Using Message Style and Content to Identify an Unknown Source

Careful word-counts by a computer may reveal patterns, not always visible to the casual reader, which enable one to tell which of two possible authors actually wrote a given message or, if the author is completely unknown, to tell something of his background.

1. *Size of vocabulary.* On his first birthday, a child has about three words in his vocabulary; on his second, 270; and on his sixth, about 2500. College students can recognize 112,000 to 193,000 words, the average being about 156,000. As he grows older, a child strings these words into longer and longer sentences; a five year old averages sentences five words long.

2. *Variation in word use.* A person with a small vocabulary must repeat words more often than a man with a large vocabulary. Repetition is also more likely to occur in speech than in writing. An *index of diversification* reflects the number of words appearing between repetitions of the most frequent word in a message. Written material averages ten to fifteen words between two appearances of the word "the." We can also determine the ratio of different words (*types*) to total words (*tokens*).

3. *Length of sentences.* Authors differ, one using 60-word sentences and another using sentences a third as long. Even when averages are similar, one author may vary length from one sentence to the next more than another.

Source. George A. Miller, *Language and Communication* (New York: McGraw-Hill Book Co., 1961).

Two studies have uncovered distinctive language patterns which would enable one to predict, by glancing at output tables from a computer, which messages were produced by people likely to or on the verge of committing suicide.

Osgood found that genuine suicide notes used less-varied vocabularies than ordinary letters, were less discriminating in the words they used, tended to qualify verbs but, except for verbs, used unqualified terms. In another study, nonsuicidal white, Protestant males aged 25 to 59 were asked to write as realistic suicide notes as they were capable of doing. These were then matched against 33 genuine notes taken from police files in Los Angeles. Content of both sets was then tagged by a computer which spotted things (roles and objects) and processes (emotional states and actions), plus institutions, statuses, qualities, and symbolic referents. Genuine notes were found to be more likely to contain names of specific places, people, and things, to mention women, and to give instructions detailed enough to be carried out. Fake notes were more likely to suggest that the writer was thinking about suicide.

Sources

C. E. Osgood, "Some effects of motivation on style of encoding," in T. A. Sebeok, ed., *Style in Language* (Cambridge: M.I.T. Press, 1960).

Daniel M. Ogilvie et al., "Some characteristics of genuine versus simulated suicide notes," in Philip J. Stone et al., *The General Inquirer* (Cambridge: M.I.T. Press, 1966).

Knowing a source, we can often predict what kinds of messages he will produce. In similar fashion, we can often identify a source by the style and content of his messages. The words a man uses, his vocabulary, tell a good deal about the man himself, the place and times in which he speaks or writes, even his age, sex, education, and social class.

Language reveals *nationality:* An American rides a streetcar and walks on a sidewalk; an Englishman rides a tram and walks on the pavement. Language reveals *region:* In some parts of the United States men fish with earthworms or eat hotcakes; in others they fish with angledogs or eat pancakes. Language reveals *age and sex:* When we see the line, "I don't want to be catty, but, my deah, it was simply too terrible," we know the speaker was a woman, even if we cannot hear her voice.

We do not expect to see the sentence, *Innovations in demography are determined by the impingement of historical events,* in a child's primer, or the sentence, *See Dick and Jane run,* in a book intended for adults. Words change over time: we no longer pray, as did the Anglo-Saxons in 1000 A.D., *Faeder ure thu the eart on heofonum; si thin name gehalgod.* Words change and so do their referents, and the words we use reflect the spirit of the *times.* Shakespeare's time produced many new words dealing with feeling and occupations; the new words we produce concern material objects.

When Englishmen depended on the hunt for their food, they had extensive vocabularies for groups of animals— flock, herd, covey, brood, swarm, pack, skulk, and gaggle. When Americans rode horses, our language was full of names for horses, harness, and carriages; today we distinguish between hardtop and convertible, station wagon and pickup.

Every trade has its jargon: the criminal his badger game, gunmoll, and stool pigeon; the printer his cold type, pages that bleed, and stories that are killed. Words and the way they are combined can reveal how much education a man has had, where he got it, and even provide clues as to the neighborhood he grew up in and the origins of his parents.

Source. Drawn from Walter Goldschmidt, ed., *Ways of Mankind* (Boston: The Beacon Press, 1954), containing scripts of 14 radio programs, also available on LP records from the National Association of Educational Broadcasters.

Additional Research Readings

Creativity. It's not the formal authority structure of the business firm but the men in it who inhibit creativity, concludes the experimenter. When he asked students to suggest unusual uses for paper clips and toothpicks and to check items revealing tolerance for complexity and ambiguity, business majors proved inferior to English majors on both tasks. **Russell Eisenman, "Creativity and academic major," Journal of Applied Psychology, 53:392–5.**

Sleeper effect. Over a 26-day period, the enhancing effects of prestigious sources (judges, doctors) and the inhibiting effects of derogated sources (addicts, hippies) on message-induced attitude change dissipated, as the sources were forgotten. Thus recall of the source both increased and decreased effects. **Gary I. Schulman and Chrysoula Worrall, "Salience patterns, source credibility and the sleeper effect," Public Opinion Quarterly, 34:371–82.**

Experts. Reports of majority opinion reversed subjects' original choices among pairs of grammatical expressions (62%) and character traits (50%) more readily than for musical notes; subsequently, "expert" opinion caused least choice switching for grammar. **Henry T. Moore, "The comparative influence of majority and expert opinion," American Journal of Psychology, 3:215–20.**

Volkswagen's Victory

Perhaps no *product* better illustrates a key concept of successful marketing—that one must listen to one's prospects before starting up one's production lines—than Volkswagen. While Detroit thrust power, speed and chrome down the public's throat, VW captured a major market segment by answering demands for small-car economy. Few *ad campaigns* can match VW in consistently demonstrating, year after year, an ability to catch the attention of both prospect and non-prospect. Shown on this page are four ads in which VW speaks to persons sick and tired of the psychological obsolescence caused by auto makers' insistence on annual model changes.

It never touches a drop.

Dealer Name

It takes you to extremes.

Dealer's Name

Q. How many beans are in the box?

A. About twice as many beans as you'd find in a normal station wagon.

Dealer Name

Live below your means.

Dependable, Roomy, Cheap

The two ads at the top of this page show how a *product feature*—the fact that the VW engine is cooled by air not water—can be linked to a *consumer benefit*—dependability in extremes of climate and weather. Thus does VW emphasize that it is a nation-wide, year-around product. Recognizing that emphasis on its small size may cost it large-family sales, VW emphasizes the roominess of its microbus by filling it with beans, an example of self-deprecatory humor characteristic of men who boast of their "bug" or "beetle." Finally VW emphasizes economy from original cost to trade-in value, from gas mileage to repairs.

It can uphold the Supreme Court.

It will feed a family of 900 for a day.

You never know when you'll have to take an elephant someplace.

Dealer Name

One Idea—Three Ads

By stuffing unlikely objects into its microbus, VW manages simultaneously to attract *attention* via incongruity, to *overcome objections* that the VW is too small for a large family, and to *reward* the reader with a joke at its own expense. (Many of us tend to feel that a firm which can laugh at itself must be self-confident and assume it has good reason for such confidence.) Thus Volkswagen gains *credibility* for itself and its message by showing that it can stuff an elephant, nine Supreme Court justices or 2700 meals into a single microbus.

470c

It takes this many men to inspect this many Volkswagens.

Every new one comes slightly used.

Every now and then a VW runs into a little trouble at the factory.

Resolving Paradoxes

Most sales arguments contain built-in counter-arguments. If a small car is easy to park and save on gasoline—it's likely to be cramped inside. When one calls a car "cheap" he implies that it's low in quality as well as cost. Volkswagen has been able to resolve these paradoxes in ads that point out that it is simultaneously low in original cost, yet high in trade-in value and that its microbus is small on the outside, yet roomy on the inside. While not giving ground on its low price, VW here emphasizes quality by dramatizing number of inspections and rigor of road-testing given each VW—and the fate of any car that doesn't pass such tests.

Bibliography

Chapter numbers following a reference indicate use in a footnote; numbers in bold refer to a citation of research by this author.

Abelson, R., and J. C. Miller, "Negative persuasion via personal insult," *Journal of Experimental Social Psychology*, 3:321–33. Ch. 12.

———, and M. J. Rosenberg, "Symbolic psycho-logic: a model of attitudinal cognition," *Behavioral Science*, 3:1–13. Ch. 4.

Abrams, Jack, "A new method for testing pricing decisions," *Journal of Marketing*, 28:3:6–9. **32.**

Advertising Age, Annual ad spending by industry, firm, medium, ad agency. **380–2.**

Albaum, Gerald, "Horizontal information flow . . ." *Journal of the Academy of Management*, 7:1:21–33. **290.**

Alexander, Ralph S., et al., *Industrial marketing* (Homewood, Ill.: Richard D. Irwin, 1967) 3rd ed. Ch. 17, 20.

Allison, Ralph I., and Kenneth P. Uhl, "Influence of beer brand identification on taste perception," *Journal of Marketing Research*, 1:3:36–9. **93.**

Allport, Gordon W., and Leo J. Postman, "The basic psychology of rumors," in Guy E. Swanson et al., eds., *Readings in social psychology*, rev. ed. (New York: Henry Holt, 1952). Ch. 18.

———, Pattern and growth in personality (New York: Holt, Rinehart and Winston, 1961). Ch. 6.

Anderson, Lynn R., and Martin Fishbein, "Prediction of attitude from the number, strength and evaluation aspect of beliefs about the attitude object," *Journal of Personality and Social Psychology*, 3:437–43. **92.**

Anderson, N. H., "Averaging versus adding as a stimulus combination rule in impression formation," *Journal of Experimental Psychology*, 70:394–400. **92.**

Arndt, Johan, *Word of mouth advertising* (New York: Advertising Research Foundation, 1967). Ch. 18. **362.**

Aronson, Elliot, et al., "Communicator credibility and communication discrepancy as determinants of opinion change," *Journal of Abnormal and Social Psychology*, 67:31–6. **171.**

Aronson, E., and D. Linder, "Gain and loss of esteem as determinants of interpersonal attractiveness," *Journal of Experimental Social Psychology*, 1:156–71. Ch. 12.

———, and J. Mills, "The effect of severity of initiation on liking

for a group," *Journal of Abnormal and Social Psychology,*
59:177–81. Ch. 12.

Asch, S. E., "Effects of group pressure . . ." in Eleanor E. Maccoby et al., *Readings in social psychology,* 3rd ed. (New
York: Holt, Rinehart and Winston, 1958). Ch. 14. **437,8.**

———, "Forming impressions of personality," *Journal of Abnormal and Social Psychology,* 41:258–90. Ch. 4.

Atkin, K. L., "Advertising and store patronage," *Journal of Advertising Research,* 2:4:18–23. Ch. 18. **362.**

Attneave, F., "Some informational aspects of visual perception,"
Psychological Review, 61:183–93. Ch. 10.

Axelrod, Joel N., "Induced moods and attitudes toward products," *Journal of Advertising Research,* 3:3:19–24. **378.**

Bales, Robert F., "Task roles and social roles in problem solving
groups," in Eleanor Maccoby et al., *Readings in social psychology,* 3rd ed. (New York: Holt, Rinehart and Winston,
1958). **285.**

Banks, Seymour, "The measurement of the effect of a new packaging material upon preference and sales," *Journal of Business,* 23:71–80. **214.**

———, "The relationships between preference and purchase of
brands," *Journal of Marketing,* 15:2:145–7. **91.**

Barclay, William D., et al., "Recall of TV commercials by time
and program slot," *Journal of Advertising Research,* 5:2:41–7.
395.

Bauer, Raymond A., et al., "The marketing dilemma of Negroes,"
Journal of Marketing, 29:3:1–6. Ch. 7.

———, "Personality, perception of source and persuasibility," in
Joseph W. Newman, ed., *On knowing the consumer* (New
York: Wiley, 1966). **464.**

———, and Robert D. Buzzell, "Mating behavioral science and
simulation," *Harvard Business Review,* 42:5:116–24. **38.**

———, and Ithiel de Sola Pool, *The effects of audiences on communicators* (Cambridge: Harvard Graduate School of Business Administration, 1960). Ch. 23.

Becknell, James C., Jr., "Comment on Webb's case for the effectiveness index," *Journal of Advertising Research,* 2:4:42–3.
Ch. 11.

———, and Robert W. McIsaac, "Test marketing cookware
coated with Teflon," *Journal of Advertising Research,* 3:3:
2–8. **69.**

Bendix, Richard, and Seymour M. Lipset, Class, status and power
. . . (Glencoe, Ill.: The Free Press, 1953). Ch. 16. **329.**

Benedict, Ruth, "Continuities and discontinuities in cultural conditioning," *Psychiatry,* 1:161–7. Ch. 6.

Bennett, E. B., "Discussion, decision, commitment and consensus
in group decision," *Human Relations,* 8:251–74. **302.**

Berelson, Bernard, and Gary A. Steiner, *Human behavior* (New York: Harcourt, Brace & World, 1964). Ch. 0, 9, 23.

Berkowitz, Leonard, "Personality and group position," *Sociometry*, 19:210–22. **144.**

Berlo, David K., *The process of communication* (New York: Holt, Rinehart & Winston, 1960). **416.**

Berry, Leonard L., "The components of department store image," *Journal of Retailing*, 45:3–20. **31.**

Bettelheim, Bruno, and Morris Janowitz, *The dynamics of prejudice* (New York: Harper and Brothers, 1950). Ch. 16.

Birdwhistell, Ray L., *Kinesics and context* (Philadelphia: University of Pennsylvania Press, 1970). Ch. 21.

Blau, Peter M., and W. Richard Scott, *Formal organizations* (San Francisco: Chandler Publishing Co., 1962). Ch. 14.

Blodgett, H. C., "The effect of the introduction of reward . . ." *University of California Publications in Psychology*, 4:113–4. **197.**

Blood, Robert O., Jr., and Donald M. Wolfe, *Husbands and wives* (New York: The Free Press, 1960). **282.**

Blum, Milton L., and Valentine Appel, "Consumer versus management reaction in new package development," *Journal of Applied Psychology*, 45:222–4. **73.**

Boder, D. P., "The adjective-verb quotient . . ." *Psychological Record*, 3:309–43. Ch. 21.

Bogardus, E. S., "Measuring social distance," *Journal of Applied Sociology*, 9:299–308. Ch. 5.

Bogart, Leo, Strategy in advertising (New York: Harcourt, Brace & World, Inc., 1967). Ch. 5, 19, 20. **53, 379, 394.**

Bordua, David J., and Albert J. Reiss, Jr., "Law enforcement" in Paul F. Lazarsfeld et al., *The uses of sociology* (New York: Basic Books, Inc., 1967). Ch. 7.

Bott, Elizabeth, "The concept of class as a reference group," *Human Relations*, 7:259–85. Ch. 16.

Breed, Warren, "Social control in the newsroom . . ." *Social Forces*, 33:326–35. Ch. 6.

Brink, E. L., and W. T. Kelley, *The management of promotion* (Englewood Cliffs, N.J.: Prentice-Hall, 1963). Ch. 10.

Brock, Timothy C., "Communicator-recipient similarity and decision change," *Journal of Personality and Social Psychology*, 1:650–4. **345.**

Bronfenbrenner, "Socialization and social class through time and space," in Eleanor E. Maccoby et al., *Readings in social psychology*, 3rd ed. (New York: Holt, Rinehart and Winston, 1958). Ch. 16.

Brown, F. E., "Price image versus price reality," *Journal of Marketing Research*, 6:185–91. Ch. 1. **33.**

Brown, Robert L., "Wrapper influence on the perception of freshness in bread," *Journal of Applied Psychology*, 42:257–60. **214.**

Brown, Roger, *Social psychology* (New York: The Free Press, 1965). Ch. 14, 23. **96, 414, 418.**

Bruner, Jerome S., "Expectation and the perception of color," *American Journal of Psychology*, 64:216–27. Ch. 4, 10.

———, A study of thinking (New York: Wiley, 1956). Ch. 4.

———, and Cecile C. Goodman, "Value and need as organizing factors in perception," *Journal of Abnormal and Social Psychology*, 42:33–44. **217.**

Bucklin, Louis P., "The informative role of advertising," *Journal of Advertising Research*, 5:3:11–5. **166.**

Buckner, H. Taylor, "A theory of rumor transmission," *Public Opinion Quarterly*, 29:54–70. **365.**

Burton, N. G., and J. C. R. Licklider, "Long-range constraints in the statistical structure of printed English," *American Journal of Psychology*, 68:650–3. Ch. 21.

Cannell, C. F., et al., "Reporting of hospitalization in the health interview survey," *Vital and Health Statistics*, Series 2, No. 6. Ch. 12.

———, and James C. MacDonald, "The impact of health news on attitudes and behavior," *Journalism Quarterly*, 33:315–23. Ch. 10.

Caplovitz, David, *The poor pay more* (New York: The Free Press, 1963). Ch. 7.

Carey, Alex, "The Hawthorne studies: a radical criticism," *American Sociological Review*, 32:403–16. Ch. 0.

Carlsmith, J. M., et al., "Studies in forced compliance . . ." *Journal of Personality and Social Psychology*, 4:1–3. Ch. 12.

Carlson, Earl R., "Attitude change through modification of attitude structure," *Journal of Abnormal and Social Psychology*, 52:256–61. **118.**

Carmichael, L., et al., "An experimental study of the effect of language on the reproduction of visually perceived form," *Journal of Experimental Psychology*, 15:73–86. **95.**

Carroll, John B., "Vectors of prose style," in Thomas A. Sebeok, ed., *Style in language* (New York: Wiley, 1960). **442.**

———, and Joseph B. Casagrande, "The function of language classifications in behavior," Eleanor Maccoby et al., *Readings in social psychology* (New York: Holt, Rinehart and Winston, 1958). **95.**

Carroll, Ronald, "Selecting motion pictures for the foreign market," *Journal of Marketing*, 17:2:162–71. **31.**

Charters, W. W., Jr., and Theodore M. Newcomb, "Some attitudinal effects of experimentally increased salience of a membership group," in Guy E. Swanson et al., *Readings in social psychology* (New York: Henry Holt & Co., 1952). Ch. 15. **304.**

Chotlos, J. W., "Studies in language behavior . . ." *Psychological Monographs,* 56:75–111. Ch. 21.

Clover, Vernon T., "Relative importance of impulse buying in retail stores," *Journal of Marketing,* 15:66–70. **52.**

Coch, Lester, and John R. P. French, Jr., "Overcoming resistance to change," *Human Relations,* 1:512–32. Ch. 14. **302.**

Coffin, Thomas E., and Jack B. Landis, *How television changes strangers into customers . . .* (New York: NBC Television, 1955). Ch. 22.

Colley, Russell H., *Defining advertising goals for measured advertising results* (New York: Association of National Advertisers, 1961). Ch. 3. **37.**

Copp, James H., et al., "The function of information sources in the farm practice adoption process," *Rural Sociology,* 23: 146–57. **54, 168.**

Corey, Lawrence G., "How to isolate product attributes," *Journal of Advertising Research,* 10:4:41–4. **92.**

Cornsweet, T. N., "The staircase method in psychophysics," *American Journal of Psychology,* 75:485–91. **215.**

Cox, Donald F., *Risk taking and information handling in consumer behavior* (Boston: Graduate School of Business Administration, Harvard University, 1967). Ch. 2.

Cronbach, Lee J., *Essentials of psychological testing,* 2nd ed. (New York: Harper and Row, 1960). Ch. 20. **393.**

Cunningham, Ross M., "Brand loyalty: what, where, how much," *Harvard Business Review,* 34:1:116–28. **191.**

Cunningham, Scott M., "Perceived risk as a factor in informal consumer communication," in D. F. Cox, ed., *Risk taking and information handling in consumer behavior* (Boston: Graduate School of Business Administration, Harvard University, 1967). **363.**

Cyert, Richard M., and James G. March, *A behavioral theory of the firm* (Englewood Cliffs, N.J.: Prentice-Hall, 1963). Ch. 14. **283.**

Dahl, Robert A., et al., *Social science research on business . . .* (New York: Columbia University Press, 1959). Ch. 16.

Dahrendorf, Ralf, "Integration and values versus coercion and interests" in Jack L. Roach et al., *Social stratification in the United States* (Englewood Cliffs, N.J.: Prentice-Hall, 1969). Ch. 16.

Dalrymple, Douglas J., and Donald L. Thompson, *Retailing . . .* (New York: The Free Press, 1969). Ch. 17.

Danielson, Wayne A., and Sam Dunn Bryan, "Computer automation of two readability formulas," *Journalism Quarterly,* 39:201–6. **439.**

Dean, Joel, "Does advertising belong in the capital budget?" *Journal of Marketing*, 30:4:15–21. Ch. 3.

Delgado, Jose M. R., *Physical control of the mind* (New York: Harper & Row, 1969). **145.**

Dennis, Wayne, "Uses of common objects as indicators of cultural orientations," *Journal of Abnormal and Social Psychology*, 55:21–8. **72.**

DeSoto, Clinton B., et al., "Social reasoning and spatial paralogic," *Journal of Personality and Social Psychology*, 2:513–21. **100.**

Deutsch, J. A., "The physiological basis of memory," in *Annual Review of Psychology*, Vol. 20 (Palo Alto, Calif.: Annual Reviews, Inc., 1969). Ch. 9.

Deutsch, Morton, and M. E. Collins, *Interracial housing* (Minneapolis: University of Minnesota Press, 1951). Ch. 22.

Diamond, Daniel S., "A quantitative approach to magazine advertisement format selection," *Journal of Marketing Research*, 5:376–86. **441.**

Dollard, John, "Under what conditions do opinions predict behavior?" *Public Opinion Quarterly*, 12:623–32. **119.**

Donnermuth, William P., "The shopping matrix and marketing strategy," *Journal of Marketing Research*, 2:128–32.

Douvan, Elizabeth, "Social status and success strivings," *Journal of Abnormal and Social Psychology*, 52:219–23. **73.**

Dudycha, G. J., "An objective study of punctuality in relation to personality and achievement," *Archives of Psychology*, 1936, No. 204. Ch. 6.

Dunn, S. Watson, *Advertising*, 2nd ed. (New York: Holt, Rinehart and Winston, 1969). Ch. 23.

Dunnette, Marvin D., and Wayne K. Kirchner, "Psychological test differences between industrial salesmen and retail salesmen," *Journal of Applied Psychology*, 44:121–5. **377.**

Edwards, Alba M., "A social economic grouping of the gainful workers in the United States," *Journal of the American Statistical Association*, 28:377–87. **32.**

Engel, James F., et al., *Consumer behavior* (New York: Holt, Rinehart, and Winston, 1968). Ch. 2, 7, 16, 17, 19, 20. **394.**

Evans, Franklin B., "Psychological and objective factors in the prediction of brand choice: Ford versus Chevrolet," *Journal of Business*, 32:340–69. **139.**

Farr, James N., et al., "Simplifications of Flesch reading ease formula," *Journal of Applied Psychology*, 35:333–7. **439.**

Faust, G. W., and R. C. Anderson, *The role of incidental material in programmed instruction* (Urbana: University of Illinois Press, 1966). Ch. 8.

Feldman, Sidney P., "Some dyadic relationships associated with consumer choice," in R. M. Haas, *Science, technology and marketing* (Chicago: American Marketing Association, 1966). **167**.

Ferber, R., and H. Wales, "Detection and correction of interviewer bias," *Public Opinion Quarterly*, 16:107–27. Ch. 12.

Festinger, Leon, *A theory of cognitive dissonance* (Evanston, Ill.: Row and Peterson, 1957); rev. ed. (Stanford, Calif., Stanford University Press, 1962). Ch. 5, 23.

Festinger, Leon, and James M. Carlsmith, "Cognitive consequences of forced compliance," *Journal of Abnormal and Social Psychology*, 58:203–10. **116**.

Fink, Raymond, "The retrospective question," *Public Opinion Quarterly*, 24:143–8. **262**.

Fleishman, Edwin A., and C. J. Bartlett, "Human abilities," *Annual Review of Psychology*, Vol. 20 (Palo Alto, Calif.: Annual Reviews, Inc., 1969). Ch. 9.

Flesch, Rudolf, "A new readability yardstick," *Journal of Applied Psychology*, 32:221–33. Ch. 21. **438**.

Freedman, Jonathan L., and Scott C. Fraser, "Compliance without pressure . . ." *Journal of Personality and Social Psychology*, 4:195–202. **343**.

Gellerman, Saul W., *Motivation and productivity* (New York: American Management Association, Inc., 1963). Ch. 18, 23.

Getzels, J. W., "The question-answer process . . ." *Public Opinion Quarterly*, 18:80–91. Ch. 12.

——, and Philip W. Jackson, *Creativity and intelligence . . .* (New York: Wiley, 1962). Ch. 23.

Gibson, J. J., *The perception of the visual world* (Boston: Houghton-Mifflin, 1950). Ch. 10.

Goldschmidt, Walter R., "Class denominationalism in rural California churches," *American Journal of Sociology*, 49:348–55. Ch. 16.

——, ed., *Ways of mankind* (Boston: The Beacon Press, 1954). Ch. 23. **468**.

Graham, Saxon, "Class and conservatism in the adoption of innovations," *Human Relations*, 9:91–100. **327**.

Greenberg, Bradley S., and Percy H. Tannenbaum, "Communicator performance under cognitive stress," *Journalism Quarterly* 39:169–78. **39**.

Greenblum, Joseph, and Leonard I. Pearlin, "Vertical mobility and prejudice . . ." in Richard Bendix and Martin Seymour Lipset, eds., *Class, status and power . . .* (Glencoe, Ill.: The Free Press, 1953). Ch. 16.

Gross, N., et al., *Explorations in role analysis* (New York: Wiley, 1958). Ch. 6.

Guilford, J. P., *An inventory of factors STDCR* (Beverly Hills, Calif.: Sheridan Supply Co., 1940). Ch. 6.

————, *The nature of human intelligence* (New York: McGraw-Hill, 1967). Ch. 9.

Guest, Lester, "Brand loyalty—twelve years later," *Journal of Applied Psychology*, 39:405–8. **192**.

Gusfield, Joseph R., and Michael Schwartz, "The meanings of occupational prestige," *American Sociological Review*, 28: 265–71. **322**.

Guttman, L., "A basis for scaling qualitative data," *American Sociological Review*, 9:139–50. Ch. 5.

Haer, John L., "Predictive utility of five indices of social stratification," *American Sociological Review*, 22:541–6. Ch. 16.

Haire, Mason, "Projective techniques in marketing research," *Journal of Marketing*, 14:5:649–56. Ch. 20. **146**.

Hall, Edward T., *The silent language* (Garden City, N.Y.: Doubleday, 1959). Ch. 7.

Hall, Max, "Case report: the great cabbage hoax," *Journal of Personality and Social Psychology*, 2:563–9. **376**.

Hamblin, Robert L., et al., "Changing the game from get the teacher to learn," *Trans-Action*, January 1969, 20–31. **195**.

Hammond, K. R., "Measuring attitude for error-choice . . ." *Journal of Abnormal and Social Psychology*, 43:38–48. Ch. 12.

Harrell, Thomas W., and Margaret S. Harrell, "Army general classification test scores for civilian occupations," *Educational and Psychological Measurement*, 5:229–39. **393**.

Harrison, Randall P., *Pictic analysis . . .* (East Lansing, Mich.: Ph.D. thesis, 1964). **420**.

Hastorf, Albert H., and Hadley Cantril, "They saw a game: a case study," *Journal of Abnormal and Social Psychology*, 49: 129–34. **118**.

Hatt, Paul K., "Occupation and social stratification," *American Journal of Sociology*, 55:533–43. Ch. 16.

Heidbreder, E., "The attainment of concepts . . ." *Journal of General Psychology*, 35:2:173–89. Ch. 4. **100**.

Heider, F., *The psychology of interpersonal relations* (New York: Wiley, 1958). Ch. 5.

Henle, M., "An experimental investigation of past experience as a determinant of visual form perception," *Journal of Experimental Psychology*, 36:1–21. Ch. 10.

Hepner, Harry Walker, *Advertising*, 4th ed. (New York: McGraw-Hill, 1964). Ch. 22–3. **71**.

Heron, W., et al., "Visual disturbances after prolonged perceptual isolation," *Canadian Journal of Psychology*, 10:13–8. Ch. 10.

Hilgard, Ernest R., *Theories of learning*, 2nd ed. (New York: Appleton-Century-Crofts, 1956). Ch. 9.

Hockberg, J. E., and E. McAlister, "A quantitative approach to figural goodness," *Journal of Experimental Psychology*, 46: 361–4. Ch. 10.

Hodge, Robert W., et al., "Occupational prestige in the United States, 1925-63," *American Journal of Sociology,* 70:286–302. **322**.

Hollingshead, August B., and Frederick C. Redlich, *Social class and mental illness* (New York: Wiley, 1958). Ch. 16. **323**.

Homans, George Caspar, "Group factors in worker productivity," in Eleanor E. Maccoby et al., *Readings in social psychology* (New York: Holt, Rinehart and Winston, 1958). **259**.

Horney, Karen, *Our inner conflicts* (New York: Norton, 1945). Ch. 6.

Hovland, Carl I., "Reconciling conflicting results derived from experimental and survey studies of attitude change," *American Psychologist,* 14:8–17. **258**.

———, et al., "Assimilation and contrast effects in reactions to communication and attitude change," *Journal of Abnormal and Social Psychology,* 55:244–52. **170**.

———, et al., *Communication and persuasion* (New Haven: Yale University Press, 1953). Ch. 11, 22, 23.

———, et al., *Experiments on mass communication* (Princeton: N.J.: Princeton University Press, 1949). Ch. 22.

———, et al., *The order of presentation in persuasion* (New Haven, Conn.: Yale University Press, 1957). Ch. 22.

———, and Wallace Mandell, "An experimental comparison of conclusion-drawing by the communicator and by the audience," *Journal of Abnormal and Social Psychology,* 47:581–8. Ch. 22. **462**.

———, and Henry A. Pritzker, "Extent of opinion change as a function of amount of change advocated," *Journal of Abnormal and Social Psychology,* 54:257–61. **169**.

———, and Robert R. Sears, "Experiments on motor conflict . . ." *Journal of Experimental Psychology,* 23:477–93. Ch. 6.

Hunter, Ian M. L., *Memory* (Baltimore, Md.: Penguin Books, 1964). Ch. 9. **196**.

Jacobson, D. J., *The affairs of dame rumor* (New York: Rinehart, 1948). Ch. 18.

Jackson, Jay M., "Reference group processes in a formal organization," *Sociometry,* 22:307–27. **303**.

Janis, Irvin, et al., *Personality and persuasibility* (New Haven, Conn.: Yale University Press, 1959). Ch. 6.

———, and Seymour Feshbach, "Effects of fear-arousing communications," *Journal of Abnormal and Social Psychology,* 48:78–92. Ch. 22. **140**.

———, and Bert T. King, "The influence of role playing on opinion change," *Journal of Abnormal and Social Psychology,* 49:211–8. Ch. 23.

———, and W. Milholland, "The influence of threat appeals on

selective learning . . ." *Journal of Psychology,* 37:75–80. Ch. 22.

Jones, Austin, et al., "Information deprivation as a motivational variable," *Journal of Experimental Psychology,* 62:126–37. **120**.

Judson, A. J., and C. N. Cofer, "Reasoning as an associative process . . ." *Psychological Reports,* 2:469–76. Ch. 4.

Jung, Allen F., "Price variations among automobile dealers in Chicago, Illinois," *Journal of Business,* 32:315–26. **343**.

Kagan, Jerome, and Ernest Havemann, *Psychology: an introduction* (New York: Harcourt, Brace and World, 1968). Ch. 4, 8, 10, 21.

Kahl, Joseph A., *The American class structure* (New York: Holt, Rinehart and Winston, 1961). Ch. 16. **323**.

———, and James A. Davis, "A comparison of indexes of socio-economic status," *American Sociological Review,* 20:317–25. Ch. 16.

Kamen, Joseph M., and Robert J. Toman, "Psychophysics of prices," *Journal of Marketing Research,* 7:27–35. **34**.

Katona, George, *The powerful consumer* (New York: McGraw-Hill Book Co., 1960). Ch. 2, 5. **56**.

Katz, Elihu, and Paul Lazarsfeld, *Personal influence* (Glencoe, Ill.: The Free Press, 1955). Ch. 18.

Kelley, Harold H., "The warm-cold variable in first impressions of persons," *Journal of Personality,* 18:431–9. Ch. 4.

———, and K. Ring, "Some effects of suspicious versus trusting training schedules," *Journal of Abnormal and Social Psychology,* 63:294–301. **194**.

———, and John W. Thibaut, "Experimental studies of group problem solving and process," in Gardner Lindzey, ed., *Handbook of social psychology,* Vol. 2 (Cambridge: Addison-Wesley, 1954). Ch. 14.

———, and John W. Thibaut, "Group problem solving," in Gardner Lindzey and Elliot Aronson, eds., *Handbook of social psychology,* 2nd ed. (Reading, Mass.: Addison-Wesley, 1969). Ch. 14, 23.

Kelly, E. L., "Consistency of the adult personality," *American Psychologist,* 10:659–81. Ch. 6.

Kelman, Herbert C., "Attitude change as a function of response restriction," *Human Relations,* 6:185–214. Ch. 22, 23.

———, and Carl I. Hovland, "Reinstatement of the communicator . . ." *Journal of Abnormal and Social Psychology,* 48:327–35. Ch. 23. **463**.

Kenkel, William F., "Husband-wife interaction in decision choices," *Journal of Social Psychology,* 54:255–62. **70**.

Kent, G. H., and A. J. Rosanoff, "A study of association in insanity," *American Journal of Insanity,* 67:37–96, 317–90. Ch. 21.

Kilbourne, William E., "But do they believe it?" Unpublished manuscript, University of Houston, 1971. **97.**

Klapper, Joseph T., "The comparative effects of the various media," in Wilbur Schramm, *The process and effects of mass communication* (Urbana: University of Illinois Press, 1960). Ch. 19.

Kotler, Philip, *Marketing management* (New York: Prentice-Hall, 1967). Ch. 2, 7, 18.

Krech, David, et al., *Elements of psychology* (New York: Alfred A. Knopf, 1969). Ch. 9, 10, 21.

——, et al., *Individual in society* (New York: McGraw-Hill, 1962). Ch. 6.

Krugman, Herbert E., "The draw a supermarket technique," *Public Opinion Quarterly,* 24:148–9. **269.**

Kuhn, Alfred, *The study of society* (Homewood, Ill.: Richard D. Irwin, 1963). Ch. 10.

Laird, Donald A., "How the consumer estimates quality by subconscious sensory impressions," *Journal of Applied Psychology,* 16:241–6. Ch. 10. **285.**

Lambert, W. W., et al., "Reinforcement and extinction as factors in size estimation," *Journal of Experimental Psychology,* 39: 637–41. **217.**

Lansing, J. G., and L. Kish, "Family life cycle as an independent variable," *American Sociological Review,* 22:512–19. Ch. 2.

LaPiere, R. T., "Attitudes vs. actions," *Social Forces,* 13:230–7. Ch. 11.

Lasswell, Harold D., et al., *The comparative study of symbols* (Stanford, Calif.: Stanford University Press, 1952). Ch. 21.

Lazarus, R. S., and R. A. McCleary, "Autonomic discrimination without awareness," *Psychological Review,* 58:113–22. **216.**

Lefkowitz, Monroe, et al., "Status factors in pedestrian violation of traffic signals," *Journal of Abnormal and Social Psychology,* 51:704–6. **324.**

Lehman, Harvey C., *Age and achievement* (Princeton, N.J.: Princeton University Press, 1953). Ch. 23.

Lenski, Gerhard, *Power and privilege* . . . (New York: McGraw-Hill, 1966). Ch. 16.

Leventhal, Howard, et al., "Effects of fear and specificity of recommendation upon attitudes and behavior," *Journal of Personality and Social Psychology,* 2:20–9. **141.**

——, and Jean C. Watts, "Sources of resistance to fear-arousing communications on smoking and lung cancer," *Journal of Personality,* 34:155–75. **142.**

Levine, Jerome M., and Gardner Murphy, "The learning and forgetting of controversial material," *Journal of Abnormal and Social Psychology*, 38:507–17. **168.**

Lewin, Kurt, "Group decision and social change," in Eleanor Maccoby et al., *Readings in social psychology* (New York: Holt, Rinehart and Winston, 1958). **301.**

Lewis, Helen Block, "Studies in the principles of judgments and attitudes . . ." *Journal of Social Psychology*, 14:229–56. Ch. 23.

Likert, Rensis, "A technique for the measurement of attitudes," *Archives of Psychology*, 1932, No. 140. Ch. 5.

Lindzey, Gardner, and Elliot Aronson, eds., *The handbook of social psychology*, 2nd ed. (Reading, Mass.: Addison-Wesley, 1969). Ch. 3, 4, 12, 21, 22. **418.**

Lionberger, Herbert F., *Adoption of new ideas and practices* (Ames, Iowa: Iowa State University Press, 1960). Ch. 2, 16.

———, "Some characteristics of farm operators sought as sources of farm information in a Missouri community," *Rural Sociology*, 18:327–38. **325.**

Littell, R., and J. J. McCarthy, "Whispers for sale," *Harpers*, 172: 364–72. Ch. 18.

Lockard, Robert B., "Reflections on the fall of comparative psychology," *American Psychologist*, 27:168–79. Ch. 0, 9.

Longenecker, *Principles of management and organizational behavior* (Columbus, Ohio: Charles E. Merrill, 1964). Ch. 14.

Longman, Kenneth A., *Advertising* (New York: Harcourt Brace Jovanovich, 1971). Ch. 17.

Lucas, D. B., and C. E. Benson, "Some sales results for positive and negative advertisements," *Journal of Applied Psychology*, 14:363–70 and "The relative values of positive and negative advertising appeals as measured by coupons returned," *Journal of Applied Psychology*, 13:274–300. **443.**

———, and S. H. Britt, *Measuring advertising effectiveness* (New York: McGraw-Hill, 1963). **439.**

Lumsdaine, Arthur A., and Irving L. Janis, "Resistance to 'counterpropaganda' presentations," *Public Opinion Quarterly*, 17: 311–8. Ch. 22.

McCarthy, E. J., *Basic marketing* (Homewood, Ill.: Richard D. Irwin, 1964). **35.**

McClelland, D. C., and J. W. Atkinson, "The projective expression of needs . . ." *Journal of Psychology*, 25:205–22. Ch. 10.

McGinnies, Elliott, "Emotionality and perceptual defense," *Psychological Review*, 56:244–51. **216.**

McGeoch, John A., and Arthur L. Irion, *The psychology of human learning*, 2nd ed. (New York: Longmans, Green, 1958). Ch. 9.

McGraw-Hill Laboratory of Advertising Performance (New York: McGraw-Hill). Ch. 18.

McGuire, William J., "Cognitive consistency and attitude change," *Journal of Abnormal and Social Psychology*, 60: 345–53. **99**.

———, "The nature of attitudes and attitude change," in Gardner Lindzey and Elliot Aronson, eds., *The handbook of social psychology*, 2nd ed. (Reading, Mass.: Addison-Wesley, 1969). Ch. 23.

McKenna, Mary L., "The influence of in-store advertising," in Joseph Newman, ed., *On knowing the consumer* (New York: Wiley, 1966). Ch. 17.

McKinnon, Donald W., "Creativity in architects," in Institute of Personality Assessment and Research, *The creative person* (Berkeley, Calif.: University of California, 1961). Chapter 23.

McMurry, Robert, N., "The mystique of super-salesmanship," *Harvard Business Review*, 39:118. **143**.

McNeal, James U., ed., *Dimensions of consumer behavior*, 2nd ed. (New York: Appleton-Century-Crofts, 1969). Ch. 6.

McNemar, Quinn, *Psychological statistics*, 3rd ed. (New York: Wiley, 1962). Ch. 11.

Maccoby, Eleanor E., et al., *Readings in social psychology*, 3rd ed. (New York: Holt, Rinehart and Winston, 1958). Ch. 14.

Magazine Advertising Bureau, *Split run and regional advertising in magazines* (New York: Magazine Publishers Association). Ch. 19.

Maloney, John C., "Curiosity versus disbelief in advertising," *Journal of Advertising Research*, 2:2:2–8. Ch. 23.

Martineau, Pierre, "Social classes and spending behavior," *Journal of Marketing*, 23:121–30. Ch. 16, 21.

Maslow, A. H., *Motivation and personality* (New York: Harper & Brothers, 1954). Ch. 6.

Massy, William F., "Statistical analysis of relations between variables," in Ronald E. Frank et al., *Quantitative techniques in marketing analysis* (Homewood, Ill.: Richard D. Irwin, 1962). **271**.

Mayer, David, and Herbert M. Greenberg, "What makes a good salesman," *Harvard Business Review*, 42:119–25. **143**.

Mayer, Albert J., and Philip M. Hauser, "Class differences in expectation of life at birth," in Reinhard Bendix and Seymour M. Lipset, eds., *Class status and power* . . . (Glencoe, Ill.: The Free Press, 1953). Ch. 16.

Mednick, Sarnoff A., *Learning* (Englewood Cliffs, N.J.: Prentice-Hall, 1964). Ch. 19.

Mehling, Reuben, "A study of non-logical factors of reasoning in the communication process," *Journal of Communication*, 9:118–26. **98**.

Menzel, Herbert, and Elihu Katz, "Social relations and innovation in the medical profession: the epidemiology of a new drug," *Public Opinion Quarterly*, 19:337–52. Ch. 2.

Merrill, J. C., "How Time stereotyped three U.S. presidents," *Journalism Quarterly*, 42:563–70. Ch. 21.

Merton, Robert K., et al., *Sociology today* (New York: Basic Books, 1959). Ch. 7.

———, and Paul F. Lazarsfeld, eds., *Continuities in social research* (New York: The Free Press, 1950). **291**.

Mickwitz, Gosta, *Marketing and competition* (Helsingfors, Finland: Centraltrycheriet, 1959). Ch. 2.

Milgram, S., "Behavioral study of obedience," *Journal of Abnormal and Social Psychology*, 67:371–8. Ch. 12.

———, "The lost-letter technique," *Psychology Today*, 3:1:30–3. .Ch. 12.

———, "The small world problem," *Psychology Today*, 1:1:60–7. **365**.

Miller, George A., *Language and communication* (New York: McGraw-Hill, 1951). Ch. 21. **467**.

———, "The magical number 7 plus or minus 2 . . ." *Psychological Review*, 60:81–97. Ch. 10.

———, "Psycholinguistics," in Gardner Lindzey, ed., *Handbook of social psychology* (Cambridge: Addison-Wesley, Inc., 1954). Ch. 21. **417**.

———, "Some preliminaries to psycholinguistics," *American Psychologist*, 20:15–20. Ch. 21.

———, and David McNeill, "Psycholinguistics" in Gardner Lindzey and Elliot Aronson, eds., *Handbook of social psychology*, 2nd ed. (Reading, Mass.: Addison-Wesley, 1968). **419**.

Miller, N. E., "Experiments on motivation," *Science*, 126:127–1–8. Ch. 12.

Miller, Norman, and Donald P. Campbell, "Recency and primacy in persuasion as a function of the timing of speeches and measurements," *Journal of Abnormal and Social Psychology*, 59:1–9. **445**.

Munroe, Ruth L., *Schools of psychoanalytic thought* (New York: The Dryden Press, 1955). Ch. 6.

Myers, James H., and William H. Reynolds, *Consumer behavior and marketing management* (Boston: Houghton-Mifflin, 1967). Ch. 7, 16.

National Opinion Research Center, "Jobs and occupations . . ." *Opinion News*, 9:3–13. Ch. 16.

Naylor, James C., "Deceptive packaging: are the deceivers being deceived?" *Journal of Applied Psychology*, 46:393–8. Ch. 10. **286**.

———, and C. H. Lawshe, "An analytical review of the experimental basis of subception," *Journal of Psychology*, 46:75–96. **216**.

Newman, Joseph ed., *On knowing the consumer* (New York: Wiley, 1966). Ch. 17, 20.

Nunnally, Jum C., and Howard M. Bobren, "Variables governing the willingness to receive communications on mental health," *Journal of Personality,* 27:38–46. **142.**

Ogilvie, Daniel M., et al., "Some characteristics of genuine versus simulated suicide notes," in Philip J. Stone et al., *The general inquirer* (Cambridge, MIT Press, 1966). **468.**

Orne, M., "On the social psychology of the psychological experiment," *American Psychologist,* 17:776–83. Ch. 12.

O'Rourke, John F., "Field and laboratory . . ." *Sociometry,* 26: 422–35. **261.**

Osgood, Charles E., "Dimensionality of the semantic space for communications via facial expressions," *Scandinavian Journal of Psychology,* 7:1–30. Ch. 4.

———, et al., *The measurement of meaning* (Urbana, University of Illinois Press, 1957). Ch. 4, 5. **240, 415.**

———, *Method and theory in experimental psychology* (New York: Oxford University Press, 1953). Ch. 10.

———, "On the whys and wherefores of E, P, and A," *Journal of Personality and Social Psychology,* 12:194–9. Ch. 4.

———, "Some effects of motivation on style in encoding," in T. A. Sebeok, ed., *Style in language* (New York: Wiley, 1960). **468.**

Palda, Kristian S., "The hypothesis of a hierarchy of effects . . ." *Journal of Marketing Research,* 3:13–24. Ch. 22.

Parry, Hugh J., and Helen Crossley, "Validity of responses to survey questions," *Public Opinion Quarterly,* 14:61–80. Ch. 12.

Pastore, Nicholas, and Milton W. Horowitz, "The influence of attributed motive on the acceptance of statement," *Journal of Abnormal and Social Psychology,* 51:331–2. **462.**

Pavlov, I. P., *Conditioned reflexes* (London: Oxford University Press, 1927). Ch. 9.

Payne, Stanley L., *The art of asking questions* (Princeton, N.J.: Princeton University Press, 1951). Ch. 12.

Penfield, W., and T. Rasmussen, *The cerebral cortex of man* (New York: MacMillan, 1950). Ch. 9.

Pennington, Allan L., "Customer-salesman bargaining behavior in retail transactions," *Journal of Marketing Research,* 5:255–61. **344.**

Pessemier, Edgar A., "A new way to determine buying decisions," *Journal of Marketing,* 24:2:41–6. **32.**

Pittenger, R. E., et al., *The first five minutes . . .* (Ithaca, N.Y.: Martineau, 1960). Ch. 21.

Politz, Alfred, *Life study of consumer expenditures* (New York: Time, 1957). Ch. 20.

Postman, L., and R. S. Crutchfield, "The interaction of need, set and stimulus—structure in a cognitive task," *American Journal of Psychology*, 65:196–217. **218**.

———, et al., "Personal values as selective factors in perception," *Journal of Abnormal and Social Psychology*, 43:142–54. **217**.

Premack, David, "The education of Sarah," *Psychology Today*, 4:4:54–8. Ch. 0.

Preston, Ivan L., "Logic and illogic in the advertising process," *Journalism Quarterly*, 44:231–9. **97**.

Quenon, E. L., "A method of pre-evaluating merchandise offerings," *Journal of Marketing*, 16:158–71. Ch. 5. **171**.

Rainwater, Lee, et al., *Workingman's wife* (New York: Oceana Press, 1959). Ch. 16.

Reeves, Rosser, *The 400 best advertisements of 19—* (Mamaroneck, N.Y.: Starch and Associates). Ch. 21.

Rhine, Ramon J., and Betsy A. Silun, "Acquisition and change of a concept attitude as a function of consistency of reinforcement," *Journal of Experimental Psychology*, 55:524–9. **193**.

Rice, S. A., "Contagious bias in the interview, . . ." *American Journal of Sociology*, 35:420–3. Ch. 12.

Ring, Kenneth, and Harold H. Kelley, "A comparison of augmentation and reduction as modes of influence," *Journal of Abnormal and Social Psychology*, 66:95–102. **194**.

Roach, Jack L., et al., *Social stratification in the United States* (Englewood Cliffs, N.J.: Prentice-Hall, 1969). Ch. 16.

Rogers, Everett, *Diffusion of innovations* (New York: The Free Press, 1962). Ch. 2.

Rose, Arnold, "The social scientist as an expert witness in court cases," in Paul F. Lazarsfeld et al., *The uses of sociology* (New York: Basic Books, 1967). Ch. 7.

Rosen, Bernard C., "The achievement syndrome . . ." *American Sociological Review*, 21:203–11. **324**.

Rosenberg, Milton J., "Cognitive reorganization in response to the hypnotic reversal of attitudinal effect," *Journal of Personality*, 28:39–63. **117**.

———, "Cognitive structure and attitudinal effect," *Journal of Abnormal and Social Psychology*, 53:367–72. **117**.

Rosenthal, R., and K. L. Fode, "The effect of experimenter bias on the performance of the albino rat," *Behavioral Science*, 8:183–9. Ch. 12.

———, and K. L. Fode, "Psychology of the scientist . . ." *Psychological Reports*, 12:491–511. Ch. 12.

———, and Ralph L. Rosnow, *Artifact in behavioral research* (New York: Academic Press, 1969). Ch. 0.

Rotter, Julian B., "External control and internal control," *Psychology Today*, June 1971. **193**.

Ruch, Floyd L., and William W. Ruch, "The K factor as a (validity) suppressor variable in predicting success in selling," *Journal of Applied Psychology*, 51:201–4. **143**.

Rudolph, Harold J., "Attention and interest factors in advertising," *Printer's Ink Business Bookshelf* (New York: Funk & Wagnalls Co., 1947). Ch. 22.

Runkel, P. J., "Cognitive similarity in facilitating communication," *Sociometry*, 19:178–91. Ch. 4.

Sandage, C. H., and Vernon Fryburger, *Advertising theory and practice* (Homewood, Ill.: Irwin, 1936 etc.). Ch. 0.

Schachter, Stanley, and Harvey Burdick, "A field experiment of rumor transmission and distortion," *Journal of Abnormal and Social Psychology*, 50:363–71. **364.**

Schramm, Wilbur, ed., *The process and effects of mass communication* (Urbana: University of Illinois Press, 1960). Ch. 16, 19.

Schutz, W. C., "On categorizing qualitative data in content analysis," *Public Opinion Quarterly*, 22:503–15. Ch. 21.

Scott, William A., "Attitude change through reward of verbal behavior," *Journal of Abnormal and Social Psychology*, 55:72–5. Ch. 23. **467.**

Sebeok, Thomas A., *Style in language* (New York: Wiley, 1960).

Selltiz, Claire, et al., *Research methods in group relations,* rev. ed. (New York: Holt, Rinehart and Winston, 1961). **260.**

Selznick, Philip, "The sociology of law," in Robert K. Merton et al., *Sociology today* (New York: Basic Books, 1959). Ch. 7.

Sherif, Muzafer, and Carl I. Hovland, *Social judgment* (New Haven, Conn.: Yale University Press, 1961). Ch. 5.

Shomer, Robert W., and Richard Centers, "Differences in attitudinal responses under conditions of implicitly manipulated group salience," *Journal of Personality and Social Psychology*, 15:125–32. **305.**

Shuttleworth, Frank K., "The nature versus nurture problem . . ." *Journal of Educational Psychology*, 26:655–81. Ch. 9.

Siegel, Alberta Engvall, and Sidney Siegel, "Reference groups, membership groups and attitude change," *Journal of Abnormal and Social Psychology*, 55:360–4. **303.**

Siipola, E. M., "A study of some effects of preparatory set," *Psychological Monographs*, No. 210. **217.**

Simon, Herbert A., "Theories of decision-making in economics and behavioral science," *American Economic Review*, 49:253–83. Ch. 3.

Skinner, B. F., *The behavior of organisms* (New York: Appleton, 1938). Ch. 9.

Smelser, William T., "Dominance as a factor in achievement and perception in cooperative problem solving interactions," *Journal of Abnormal and Social Psychology*, 62:535–42. **145.**

Smith, George Horsley, *Motivation research in advertising and marketing* (New York: McGraw-Hill, 1954). Ch. 5.

Staats, Arthur W., and Carolyn K. Staats, "Attitudes established by classical conditioning," *Journal of Abnormal and Social Psychology*, 57:37–40. **192**.

Star, Shirley A., and Helen MacGill Hughes, "Report on an educational campaign . . ." *American Journal of Sociology*, 55: 389–40. **376**.

Starch, Daniel, and Staff, *Measuring product sales made by advertising* (Mamaroneck, N.Y.: Starch, 1961). Ch. 21. **238**.

——, "Why readership of ads has increased 24%," *Advertising and Selling*, August 1946. Ch. 22.

Stevens, S. S., *Handbook of experimental psychology* (New York: Wiley, 1951). Ch. 5, 9, 10.

——, "The surprising simplicity of sensory metrics," *American Psychologist*, 17:29–39. Ch. 10.

Stewart, John B., *Repetitive advertising in newspapers* (Boston: Graduate School of Business Administration, Harvard University, 1964). **396**.

Stouffer, Samuel A., "An analysis of conflicting social norms," *American Sociological Review*, 14:707–17. Ch. 6. **304**.

——, et al., The American Soldier (Princeton, N.J.: Princeton University Press, 1949). **291**.

Strodtbeck, Fred L., "Husband-wife interaction over revealed differences," *American Sociological Review*, 16:468–73. **69**.

——, and L. Harmon Hook, "The social dimensions of a twelve-man jury table," *Sociometry*, 24:397–415. **329**.

Strong, Edward K., Jr., and J. E. Loveless, "Want and solution advertisements," *Journal of Applied Psychology*, 10:346–66. Ch. 22.

Sturdivant, Frederick D., and Walter T. Wilhelm, "Poverty, minorities and consumer exploitation," *Social Science Quarterly*, 50:1064–71. **344**.

Swanson, Guy E., et al., eds., *Readings in social psychology*, rev. ed. (New York: Henry Holt, 1952). Ch. 18, 22.

Tannenbaum, P. H., "Initial attitudes toward source and concept as factors in attitude change through communication," *Public Opinion Quarterly*, 20:412–25. Ch. 5.

——, et al., "An experimental investigation of typeface connotations," *Journalism Quarterly*, 41:65–73. **420**.

Tapp, June L., "Psychology and the law: the dilemma," *Psychology Today*, 2:9:16–22. Ch. 7.

Terman, Lewis M., and Maud A. Merrill, *Stanford-Binet intelligence scale* . . . (New York: Houghton-Mifflin, 1960). **393**.

Thistlethwaite, et al., "The effects of 'directive' and 'nondirective' communication procedures on attitudes," *Journal of Abnormal and Social Psychology*, 51:107–13. Ch. 22. **444**.

Thorndike, E. L., "Animal intelligence," *Psychological Monographs*, Vol. 1, No. 8, 1898. Ch. 9.

Thurstone, L. L., and E. J. Chave, *The measurement of attitude* (Chicago: University of Chicago Press, 1929). Ch. 5.

————, and T. G. Thurstone, *Factorial studies of intelligence* (Chicago: University of Chicago Press, 1941). Ch. 9.

Triandis, Harry, "Cultural influences upon cognitive processes," in Leonard Berkowitz, ed., *Advances in experimental social psychology* (New York: Academic Press, 1964), Vol. 1. **72.**

————, and Martin Fishbein, "Cognitive interaction in person perception," *Journal of Abnormal and Social Psychology,* 67:446–53. **93.**

Tucker, W. T., "The development of brand loyalty," *Journal of Marketing Research,* 1:3:32–5. **94.**

————, and John J. Painter, "Personality and product use," *Journal of Applied Psychology,* 45:325–9. **138.**

————, *The social context of economic behavior* (New York: Holt, Rinehart and Winston, 1964). Ch. 14, 16, 17, 18.

Twedt, Dik Warren, "A multiple factor analysis of advertising readership," *Journal of Applied Psychology,* 36:207–15. **441.**

Udell, Jon G., "Prepurchase behavior of buyers of small electrical appliances," *Journal of Marketing,* 30:4:50–2. **167.**

Verplanck, William S., "The control of the content of conversation . . ." *Journal of Abnormal and Social Psychology,* 51:668–76. **465.**

Wales, Max, et al., "Message exaggeration by the receiver," *Journalism Quarterly* 40:339–42. **39.**

Wallach, M. A., and N. Kogan, *Models of thinking in young children* (New York: Holt, Rinehart, and Winston, 1965). Ch. 23.

Warner, W. Lloyd, et al., *Democracy in Jonesville* (New York: Harper and Brothers, 1949). Ch. 16.

————, et al., *Social class in America* (Chicago: Science Research Associates, 1949). Ch. 16.

————, and James C. Abegglen, *Occupational mobility in American business and industry* (Minneapolis: University of Minnesota Press, 1955). Ch. 16.

Warren, J. M., "The comparative psychology of learning," *Annual Review of Psychology,* Vol 16 (Palo Alto, Calif.: Annual Reviews, Inc., 1965). Ch. 9.

Weiss, Walter, 'The influence of source credibility on communication effectiveness," *Public Opinion Quarterly,* 15:635–50. Ch. 23.

Weiss, Walter, "Opinion congruence with a negative source on one issue as a factor influencing agreement on another issue," *Journal of Abnormal and Social Psychology,* 54:180–6. **464.**

————, "The relationship between judgments of a communicator's position and extent of opinion change," *Journal of Abnormal and Social Psychology,* 56:380–4. **170.**

Westfall, Ralph, "Psychological factors in predicting product choice," *Journal of Marketing,* 26:2:34–40. **139.**

Whiteside, Thomas, "Annals of television: the man from iron city," *New Yorker*, Sept. 27, 1969, 72. **446**.

Whyte, William Foote, *Human relations in the restaurant industry* (New York: McGraw-Hill, 1948). **328**.

Whyte, William H., Jr., "The web of word of mouth," *Fortune*, 50:5. **54**.

Willett, Ronald P., and Allan L. Pennington, "Customer and salesman . . ." in R. M. Haas, ed., *Science, technology and marketing* (Chicago: American Marketing Association, 1966). **344**.

Wilson, Allan R., "Qualitative market research," *Harvard Business Review*, 30:1:75–86. **287**.

Witkin, Arthur A., "Differential patterns in salesmen," *Journal of Applied Psychology*, 40:338–40. **377**.

Wolfe, Harry Deane, et al., *Measuring advertising results* (New York: National Industrial Conference Board, Inc., 1969). Ch. 3.

Wolgast, Elizabeth H., "Do husbands or wives make the purchasing decisions?" *Journal of Marketing*, 23:151–8. Ch. 3, 5. **283**.

Woman's Day, *Reports on toiletries*, Vol. 2 (New York: Fawcett Publications, Inc., 1963). **55**.

Woodrow, Herbert, and Frances Lowell, "Children's association frequency tables," *Psychological Monographs*, Vol. 22, No. 5, pp. 81–96, 106. **440**.

Woodworth, Robert S., and Harold Schlosberg, *Experimental psychology*, rev. ed. (New York: Holt, Rinehart and Winston, 1964). Ch. 4, 10.

Wright, Charles R., and Muriel Cantor, "The opinion seeker and avoider . . ." *Pacific Sociological Review*, 10:2:33–43. **166**.

Zaleznik, Abraham, and Anne Jardim, "Management" in Paul F. Lazarsfeld, et al., eds., *The uses of sociology* (New York: Basic Books, 1967). Ch. 14.

Zeisel, Hans, "The law," in Paul F. Lazarsfeld, et al., eds., *The uses of sociology* (New York: Basic Books, 1967). Ch. 7.

————, *Say it with figures* (New York: Harper and Brothers, 1947). Ch. 11. **237**.

Zielske, H. A., "The remembering and forgetting of advertising," *Journal of Marketing*, 23:3:239–43. Ch. 9. **395**.

Zimmerman, Claire, and Raymond A. Bauer, "The effect of an audience upon what is remembered," *Public Opinion Quarterly*, 20:238–48. **466**.

Subject Index

Operational definitions, 79, 264
Organizations, 276-277
Orientation, family of, 299
Osgood attitude theory, 239
  semantic differential, 108
Overlap of audience, market, 28
Overlearning aids recall, 188
Overt versus covert responses, 245

Panel study, 191, 234
Paralanguage, 403
Part versus whole in learning, 186
Partial correlation, 270
Partial reinforcement, 193
Participant observation, 246
Participation in group, 279
Pass-along rate for magazines, 374
Passers versus buyers in store, 336
Pavlov's dog, 179
Percentage of sales spent on ads, 381
Perceptions change over time, 261-262
Perceptual defense, 113, 206-207, 215-217
Perceptual-motor skill, 175
Perceptual vigilance, 216-217
Perceptual versus objective reality, 148, 399
Perfect information, Bayesian value of, 266-267
Permanence and media choice, 369
Personal influence on purchases, 354
Personality, Allport's 7 developmental stages of, 128
  in the firm, 64
  measurement of, 125-127
  in purchasing, 139
  traits, 127-128
  versus role, 144
Persuasibility, 128
Persuasion, stages of, 36, 45
  techniques of, 427-428
Phonemes, meaningful sounds, 402
Phrase-structure grammar, 417-418
Phrasing of questions, 251-253
Physiology affects role eligibility, 130
  detects lying, 253
  reveals attitudes, 107
Pictures, five functions of, 400
Picture Frustration Test, 253
Place, element in marketing mix, 20, 31
Placement of ad, 374
Point-of-purchase ads, 336
Potboiler plot for ad, 430
Potency, factor of meaning, 415
Power, causes of, 133
  creates tension, 279
  in family, 282-283
  in firm, 64
  in society, 151
  in source, 452
Practice affects learning, 184
Precedent in legal system, 152

Predictions, how verified, 416
Precision versus probability, 231
Prejudice and mobility, 308-309
Presentation of data, 226-230
Prestige of occupations in 1947, 1963, 321-322
Price, 20, 31-33
  affects buyer-seller interaction, 332-333
  flow-chart in firm, 284
  interacts with rest of Four P's, 155
  objective versus perceptual change in, 399
  use in advertising, 427
Primacy versus recency, 433-444
Print, three dimensions of, 419
Priority affects groups' power, 299
Probability, of sounds in speech, 402-403
  use of subjective in Bayesian study, 266-269
Problem-solving salesmen, 358
Process, 19, 401
Procreation, family of, 299
Product, 20
  affects ad repetition goal, 395-396
Product feature and copy platform, 29, 425
Product image, 108
Product life cycle, 44-46, 164
Productivity, aids to, 277, 298, 302
Profit centers, 278
Projective questions, 106, 253
Prospects, 20, 34
Proximity versus similarity, closure, 208
Publicity, 349, 359-360
Public opinion as source of insights, 432
Psycho-logic, 89
Psychological obsolescence, 43
Psychological set, 206, 217-218, 364
Psychophysics, 201
Punishment versus reward, 193-195
Purchase-sale, 17, 332, 358
Push versus pull in ad strategy, 389

Qualifying prospects, 355
Qualitative research, 287
Question, types of, 244, 249-254
Questionnaire construction, 254
Quota sampling, why discarded, 255

Ranges of acceptance, rejection, 113
Rapid eye movements in sleep, 187
Rate of use of brand, product, 387
Reach versus frequency, 372, 393
Readability, 405, 437-439
Readership scores, 229, 237
  affected, by class, 311
    by content, style, 429, 440-441
Recall, 181, 394-396
Recency versus primacy in persuasion, 433, 444
Reciprocity in industrial buying, 391
Recognition, 181, 401, 429
Reconstruction measures memory, 181

Reference group effects, 295, 303-305
Regulatory agencies: a legal subsystem, 150
Regression equation, 68, 109, 270-271, 441
Reinforcement, partial or fixed interval, 180
Rejection, range of, 113
Relational attributes in ads, 428
Relative advantage, 48
Relative deprivation, 226, 279
Relearning, measure of memory, 181
Relevance, dimension of channel choice, 350-352
Reminiscence, spontaneous rise in memory, 184
Repetition, 38, 288, 373, 394-396
Reports, a sentence type, 415-416
Reproductive mobility, 317
Reputation of admen, 458
Research, estimating value of, 266-269
Respondent bias, 251-253, 261-262, 283
Response differences, 72-73
Results, 5 techniques to report, 269-271
Retailing, 266, 340-342
Retail versus industrial salesmen, 377
Retrospective questions, 261-262
Rewards, six ways to define, 182-183
    audience use of, 455
    of experimenter, subject, 279
    induce group conformity, 298
    interim ones needed, 177
    provided by senses, 200
    in sale-purchase, 337-338
Reward versus punishment in learning, 193-195
Risk stimulates word of mouth, 49, 362-363
Risky shift, controversy over, 457
Rite of passage signalizes role change, 130
Roles, four interest marketing communicator, affect
        purchases, 145
    media use, 388
    ascribed or achieved? 134
    buyer versus seller, 18
    extend life of organization, 279
    influence goals, power within firm, 60, 64
    versus personality, 144
Role conflict, four basic types, 132
    methods of study, 254
Role continuity decreasing, 130
Role prescriptions, 297
Role set affects behavior, 129
Rules of thumb in phrasing questions, 252
Rumor in field and laboratory, 353

Sales, measurement of, 243
Salesmen, one of four channels, 349, 355-356
    credibility of, 454
    definitions of, 77
    functions and traits of, 143, 377
    identifying, 451
    induce brand-switching in study, 345
    poor channel for input to employer, 290
    problems of status with buyer, 339

Salience of memory, 188
Sampling of behaviors, 222
    of causal variables, 224
    of content, 407-408
    quota method criticized, 255
    of respondents, 222
Satisficing as goal of firm, 61
Savings decisions and social class, 311
Scholar versus businessman, 265
Screening questions, 249-250
Search, internal versus external, 159-160, 163-164
Sears Roebuck, how goals change, 281
Secondary data in research, 245
Segments in marketing, 30, 34
Select versus mass audience, 368-369, 372
Selective exposure, 112-113
    recruitment to group, 298
Self-censorship by respondent, 245
Self-concept, 177, 188
Self-interest, 453-454
Seller goals and decisions, 63, 275
Semantic differential, 85, 108, 415, 419
Senses, taste, smell, touch, hearing, vision, 202
Sensitivity, diminishes over time, 210
    in Bayesian studies, 266
Sensory cues to hidden qualities, 428
Sensory deprivation, 119
Sensory receptors, 161
Sequence of questions and bias, 250
Set, persistence of psychological, 185
Setting of study and bias, 260-261
Sex, and creativity, 459
    and intelligence, 187
    and media use, purchasing, 386
Shape of audience for media, 371
Shelf-space and turnover rates, 335-336
Shopping goods, 83
Shopping within or between stores, 337
Show or tell, choice in experiments, 247
Similarity, of group members, 279, 298
    of source and receiver, 452
    versus proximity in categorizing, 208
Skinner's pigeon, 179
Sleeper effect in memory, 224
Small-world problem, 364
Smell, sense of, 202
Smoking and cancer, 432
Social class, two theories of, 318-319
    six dimensions of, 313-314
    affects purchases, 295
    affects values and motives, 323-324
    ascribed or achieved? 316
    cued by language differences, 312
    goals affected by, 308
    in kitchen, courtroom, 327-329
    prestige versus occupation, 329
    response to rewards, 72
    similar in United States, Japan, Russia, 315